Communications in Computer and Information Science 2878

Series Editors

Rationale
The CCIS series is devoted to the publication of proceedings of computer science conferences. Its aim is to efficiently disseminate original research results in informatics in printed and electronic form. While the focus is on publication of peer-reviewed full papers presenting mature work, inclusion of reviewed short papers reporting on work in progress is welcome, too. Besides globally relevant meetings with internationally representative program committees guaranteeing a strict peer-reviewing and paper selection process, conferences run by societies or of high regional or national relevance are also considered for publication.

Topics
The topical scope of CCIS spans the entire spectrum of informatics ranging from foundational topics in the theory of computing to information and communications science and technology and a broad variety of interdisciplinary application fields.

Information for Volume Editors and Authors
Publication in CCIS is free of charge. No royalties are paid, however, we offer registered conference participants temporary free access to the online version of the conference proceedings on SpringerLink (http://link.springer.com) by means of an http referrer from the conference website and/or a number of complimentary printed copies, as specified in the official acceptance email of the event.

CCIS proceedings can be published in time for distribution at conferences or as post-proceedings, and delivered in the form of printed books and/or electronically as USBs and/or e-content licenses for accessing proceedings at SpringerLink. Furthermore, CCIS proceedings are included in the CCIS electronic book series hosted in the SpringerLink digital library at http://link.springer.com/bookseries/7899. Conferences publishing in CCIS are allowed to use our online conference service (Meteor) for managing the whole proceedings lifecycle (from submission and reviewing to preparing for publication) free of charge.

Publication process
The language of publication is exclusively English. Authors publishing in CCIS have to sign the Springer CCIS copyright transfer form, however, they are free to use their material published in CCIS for substantially changed, more elaborate subsequent publications elsewhere. For the preparation of the camera-ready papers/files, authors have to strictly adhere to the Springer CCIS Authors' Instructions and are strongly encouraged to use the CCIS LaTeX style files or templates.

Abstracting/Indexing
CCIS is abstracted/indexed in DBLP, Google Scholar, EI-Compendex, Mathematical Reviews, SCImago, Scopus. CCIS volumes are also submitted for the inclusion in ISI Proceedings.

How to start

To start the evaluation of your proposal for inclusion in the CCIS series, please send an e-mail to ccis@springer.com

Shihui Guo · Ye Tao · Zhu Wang
Editors

Harmonious Human-Machine Environment

21st National Joint Conference, HHME 2025
Dalian, China, August 21–25, 2025
Proceedings, Part I

Springer

Editors
Shihui Guo
Xiamen University
Xiamen, China

Ye Tao
Hangzhou City University
Hangzhou, China

Zhu Wang
Northwestern Polytechnical University
Xi'an, China

ISSN 1865-0929 ISSN 1865-0937 (electronic)
Communications in Computer and Information Science
ISBN 978-981-92-3990-0 ISBN 978-981-92-3991-7 (eBook)
https://doi.org/10.1007/978-981-92-3991-7

This Springer imprint is published by the registered company Springer Nature Singapore Pte Ltd.
The registered company address is: 152 Beach Road, #21-01/04 Gateway East, Singapore 189721, Singapore

Preface

HHME (Harmonious Human-Machine Environment) is an annual conference organized by the China Computer Federation (CCF). As one of China's premier computer science events, HHME serves as the flagship forum for researchers and practitioners from academia, industry, and government to share groundbreaking ideas, research results, and professional experiences. The mission of this conference is to foster synergy between humans and machines, promoting a future where technology integrates seamlessly and harmoniously into our daily lives. The papers contained in these proceedings address a wide array of challenging issues, including multimodal interaction, intelligent sensing, wearable computing, smart environments, social robotics, and the ethical considerations of human-centered AI. By bridging the gap between hardware systems and human experience, these works contribute significantly to the technical and theoretical foundations of harmonious environments both domestically and internationally.

This year, HHME comprised two major constituent conferences: the 21st China Conference on Human–Computer Interaction (CHCI) and the 21st Pervasive Computing Conference (PCC). CHCI 2025 received 119 submissions, including 48 regular papers, 57 exchange papers representing high-quality research from top-tier venues, and 14 technical demonstrations presented through live demos. Following a rigorous single-blind peer-review process in which submissions received three reviews each on average, 24 papers were selected for publication from the regular submissions, reflecting an acceptance rate of 50%. PCC 2025 received 160 submissions, including 101 regular papers, 11 extended abstracts, and 48 exchange papers. Among the regular submissions, 31 papers were selected for publication, reflecting an acceptance rate of 30.69%. Collectively, these contributions represent the high caliber of research and innovation presented at the conference.

The realization of this high-quality program would not have been possible without the authors who chose HHME 2025 as the venue for their publications. We are also deeply grateful to the Program Committee members and Organizing Committee members, who dedicated a tremendous amount of effort to soliciting and selecting research papers that balance academic excellence with innovative applications.

We hope that you enjoy reading and benefit from the proceedings of HHME 2025.

April 2026

Shihui Guo
Ye Tao
Zhu Wang

Organization

Organizing Committee

Advisory Committee

Dongyi Chen	University of Electronic Science and Technology of China, China
Guozhong Dai	Institute of Software, Chinese Academy of Sciences, China
Hai Jin	Huazhong University of Science and Technology, China
Yuanchun Shi	Tsinghua University, Qinghai University, China
Yongtian Wang	Beijing Institute of Technology, China
Guoping Wang	Peking University, China
Daqing Zhang	Peking University, China
Xingshe Zhou	Northwestern Polytechnical University, China

Honorary Chair

Xingshe Zhou	Northwestern Polytechnical University, China

Conference Chairs

Zhongxuan Ro	Dalian University of Technology, China
Zhiwen Yu	Harbin Engineering University, China

Executive Advisory Committee

Ximing Sun	Dalian University of Technology, China
Zhenming Tang	Chinasoft International, China
Xiaopeng Wei	Dalian University of Technology, China
Zumin Wang	Dalian University, China
Qiang Zhang	Dalian University of Technology, China

Executive Chairs

Liming Chen	Dalian University of Technology, China
Xuejun Li	China Unicom (Dalian Branch), China
Bin Guo	Northwestern Polytechnical University, China
Haiwen Liu	Dalian University, China
Yuntao Wang	Tsinghua University, China

Organizing Committee Chairs

Chi Lin	Dalian University of Technology, China
Yin Zhang	University of Electronic Science and Technology of China, China

Organizing Committee Vice Chairs

Heng Qi	Dalian University of Technology, China
Jia Liu	Nanjing University, China

Special Events Chairs

Feng Tian	Institute of Software, Chinese Academy of Sciences, China
Gang Pan	Zhejiang University, China

Conference Forum Chairs

Lei Xie	Nanjing University, China
Yuntao Wang	Tsinghua University, China
Jun Lu	Fudan University, China
Lingling Fang	Liaoning Normal University, China

Program Committee Chairs

Xin Yang	Dalian University of Technology, China
Ye Tao	Hangzhou City University, China
Zhu Wang	Northwestern Polytechnical University, China
Xuan Liu	Hunan University, China

Co-chairs of Technical Demonstrations of CHCI

Yulong Bian	Shandong University, China
Qi Wang	Tongji University, China

Chair of Special Events of CHCI

Wei Sun	Institute of Software, Chinese Academy of Sciences, China

Corporate Activities Chair

Xiaofan Zhang	OPPO, China

Sponsorship Chairs

Xing Xie	Microsoft Research Asia, China
Chun Yu	Tsinghua University, China
Changqi Yao	China Unicom (Dalian Branch), China
Yikun Tang	Dalian University of Technology, China

Publications Chairs

Lei Xie	Nanjing University, China
Zhiyong Yu	Fuzhou University, China
Shihui Guo	Xiamen University, China

Tutorial Chairs

Longbiao Chen	Xiamen University, China
Boyu Gao	Jinan University, China
Sha Zhao	Zhejiang University, China
Xin Tong	Hong Kong University of Science and Technology (Guangzhou), China

Publicity Chairs

Pengfei Wang	Dalian University of Technology, China
Yang Tian	Guangxi University, China
Yan Liu	Northwestern Polytechnical University, China
Yimeng Liu	East China Normal University, China

Tong Wang	Harbin Engineering University, China

Website Chairs

Yuqi Han	Dalian University of Technology, China
Meng Xu	University of International Business and Economics, China

On-Site Chairs

Ling Ro	Dalian University of Technology, China
Mingyan He	Dalian University, China
Shuo Yu	Dalian University of Technology, China

Affairs Chairs

Yuxin Wang	Dalian University of Technology, China
Jing Zhang	Liaoning Normal University, China
Jinghao Sun	Dalian University of Technology, China
Qi Xu	Dalian University of Technology, China

Registration Chairs

Xuefeng Li	Liaoning Normal University, China
Jing Qin	Dalian University, China

Finance Chair

Jiyu Tian	Dalian University of Technology, China

Secretaries

Hanbo Bi	Dalian University of Technology, China
Qiongyu Zhang	Dalian University of Technology, China

Program Committee

Bin Zhu	Hangzhou City University, China
Boyu Gao	Jinan University, China
Guanyun Wang	Zhejiang University, China

Jian He	Beijing University of Technology, China
Jiangtao Gong	Shanghai Jiao Tong University, China
Mingming Fan	Hong Kong University of Science and Technology (Guangzhou), China
Nan Gao	Nankai University, China
Qi Wang	Tongji University, China
Teng Han	Institute of Software, Chinese Academy of Sciences, China
Wei Sun	Institute of Software, Chinese Academy of Sciences, China
Wei Xiang	Zhejiang University, China
Weinan Shi	Tsinghua University, China
Xin Tong	Hong Kong University of Science and Technology (Guangzhou), China
Xin Yang	Dalian University of Technology, China
Yanan Wang	Donghua University, China
Yang Tian	Guangxi University, China
Ye Tao	Hangzhou City University, China
Yimeng Liu	East China Normal University, China
Yue Li	Xi'an Jiaotong-Liverpool University, China
Yulong Bian	Shandong University, China
Zhan Zhang	Harbin Institute of Technology, China
Yanling Bu	Nanjing University of Aeronautics and Astronautics, China
Hui Cai	Nanjing University of Posts and Telecommunications, China
Xiangmao Chang	Nanjing University of Aeronautics and Astronautics, China
Xiaoping Che	Beijing Jiaotong University, China
Chao Chen	Chongqing University, China
Huihui Chen	Foshan University, China
Yaxing Chen	Northwestern Polytechnical University, China
Hongju Cheng	Fuzhou University, China
Shiwei Cheng	Zhejiang University of Technology, China
Helei Cui	Northwestern Polytechnical University, China
Xiaoheng Deng	Central South University, China
Yasan Ding	Northwestern Polytechnical University, China
Jinlong E	Renmin University of China, China
Guangsheng Feng	Harbin Engineering University, China
Zhenguo Gao	Huaqiao University, China
Yang Gu	Institute of Computing Technology, Chinese Academy of Sciences, China
Suiming Guo	Jinan University, China

Zhanjun Hao	Northwest Normal University, China
Fangwan Huang	Fuzhou University, China
Zhenge Jia	Shandong University, China
Weijin Jiang	Hunan University of Technology and Business, China
Xianlong Jiao	Chongqing University, China
Zhanpeng Jin	South China University of Technology, China
Xiangjie Kong	Zhejiang University of Technology, China
Nuo Li	Fudan University, China
Qingyang Li	Xidian University, China
Shijian Li	Zhejiang University, China
Wei Li	Harbin Engineering University, China
Zhijun Li	Harbin Institute of Technology, China
Yunji Liang	Northwestern Polytechnical University, China
Feng Lin	Zhejiang University, China
Chao Liu	Ocean University of China, China
Jia Liu	Nanjing University, China
Sicong Liu	Northwestern Polytechnical University, China
Wenbin Liu	Jilin University, China
Xuan Liu	Hunan University, China
Zhidan Liu	Hong Kong University of Science and Technology (Guangzhou), China
Li Lu	Zhejiang University, China
Jianfeng Lu	Wuhan University of Science and Technology, China
Haiyong Luo	Institute of Computing Technology, Chinese Academy of Sciences, China
Hongbo Ni	Northwestern Polytechnical University, China
Jianquan Ouyang	Xiangtan University, China
Jiefan Qiu	Zhejiang University of Technology, China
Jiaxing Shang	Chongqing University, China
Guangzhong Sun	University of Science and Technology of China, China
Wen Sun	Northwestern Polytechnical University, China
Chuyu Wang	Nanjing University, China
En Wang	Jinan University, China
Feng Wang	Hubei University of Arts and Science, China
Jiliang Wang	Tsinghua University, China
Leye Wang	Peking University, China
Lu Wang	Shenzhen University, China
Pengfei Wang	Dalian University of Technology, China
Qianru Wang	Xidian University, China

Organizers

Organized by

China Computer Federation

Hosted by

Dalian University of Technology

Dalian University

In Cooperation with

Technical Committee on Pervasive Computing
Technical Committee on Human-Computer Interaction
Technical Committee on Cooperative Computing

Dalian Computer Society

Contents

Multichannel and Novel Human–Computer Interaction

Research on the Dynamic Innovation Design of Traditional Embroidery Using Flexible Electroluminescent Threads 3
Yao Lu, Xuezhu Wang, Beituo Liu, Zhihao Yao, Xiwen Yao, Ziqi Liu, Mingzhen Xie, Yijie Guo, Tianyu Yu, Guanhong Liu, and Haipeng Mi

Assessment and Analysis of Tactile Perception in Older Adults 13
Wenyu Wang, Zhelin Li, Shiyu Dong, Lijun Jiang, Shuo Hou, and Qin Wang

Dynamic Human Action Recognition Method Based on Recursive Graphs and LeNet-5 25
Yizhong Xin, Xuzhu Jin, Dongliang Li, and Lijun Zhang

Efficient Two-Stream Fusion Network for Skeleton-Based Hand Gesture Recognition 40
Hongming Shao, Juan Li, Xiaoyi Wang, and Xuri Li

FlexiStiff-Fabric: A Programmable Stiffness 3D-Printed Fabric Technology Based on Dual-Material Interlocking Weaving 54
Jiacheng Cao, Runjun Liu, Yicheng Wang, Jiarong Zhang, Zhaojia Yang, Yulu Chen, Tianshu Dong, Jiaji Li, Preben Hansen, Yijun Zhao, and Guanyun Wang

ScentEcho: Exploring Adsorbent Materials for Accurate Odor Collection and Playback 68
Chih-Hung Lee, Yuchi Sun, Rui Zhang, Suhang Wei, and Qi Lu

PosturePet: Glanceable, Emotion-Driven Biofeedback for Correcting Neck Posture 81
Grace Yi, Ziyad Fawzy, Lily Sheng, Hanyu Zhou, and Yuntao Wang

A Study on Immersive Experience Design for Ancient Paintings from the Perspective of Interactive Digital Narrative 98
Hui-Zhu Han, Xiao-Na Ma, Huang-Yi-Ming Wu, Dong Ye, Xin-Yu Wang, and Yu-Chen Li

Human–Computer Interaction Theory, Methods, and Interface Design

Building Bridges of Communication: A Card-Based Approach to Cross-Disciplinary Design Collaboration ... 113
Xuezhu Wang, Yao Lu, Tianyu Yu, Yishan Duan, Jialu Ni, Yijie Guo, Xiwen Yao, Kejin Yu, Wenjing Deng, Xueqing Li, Zhiyu Li, Guanhong Liu, Haipeng Mi, and Yuan Yao

Human-Computer Interaction Design of Manned Lunar Rover Based on Fear Dual-Pathway Theory: Neurocognitive Mechanisms and Engineering Mitigation Strategies ... 128
Cen Chunhao, Lin Xinyue, and Liu Gang

Multisensory Integrated Haptic Interaction Design for Smartphones ... 139
Rui Zhang, Ziyao Zhang, and Yang Jiao

EmoChatBot: Integrating Fine-Grained Emotional Talking-Head Generation Into Face-to-Face Dialogue ... 156
Hanlin Yan, Fang Liu, and Cuixia Ma

Exploring the Impact of Human-Machine Identity Labels on Patients' Emotional Experiences in Dialogue ... 169
Yu Qiao, Yan Gao, Yiyi Zhang, and Shuyuan Zou

Pingjiang Mystery: A Map-Based Board Game for Navigating the Ancient City of Suzhou ... 188
Yanli Jiang, Jiachen Liang, Yingpin Zhang, and Yue Li

LibreVibPen: Enhancing Stylus Interaction with Real-Time Haptic Feedback on Large Touch Screens ... 210
Shengsheng Jiang, Jian He, Rongqi Cao, Yifan Zhen, and Yiheng Pan

VR/AR and Natural Human–Computer Interaction

My-Meetings: LLM-Based Multi-agent Conference Scene Designer ... 229
Xi Cheng and Guihuan Feng

Applicability Analysis and Interaction Optimization of Pen Pressure Input for Fitts and Steering's Tasks ... 257
Yizhong Xin, Liang Sun, and Lijun Zhang

Gesture Recognition Based on Improved VanillaNet for sEMG-Driven Prosthetic Hand Control ... 270
Yazhou Li and Kairu Li

NanyinVR: Gesture-Based Immersive Virtual Reality Game for Enhancing Learning of Ancient Chinese Music and Instruments 283
Yiping Wu, Kai Chen, and Yue Li

StringWave VR—An Immersive Interactive System for Traditional Music Intangible Cultural Heritage 302
Wei Hui, Huancheng Jiang, and Zichun Guo

A Study on Construction and Classification of Multi-condition EEG Datasets for Chinese Mandarin Speech Decoding 313
Haoming Wang, Gaoyuan Zhang, Xurong Xie, Ying Qin, Chao Zhou, Hui Chen, and Feng Tian

Roughness Rendering in XR Via Pseudo-Haptics and Auditory Feedback 325
Ming Ye, Yang Tian, Zhao Su, and Zhenrong Zhang

Transcendent Vehicles: Augmented Reality-Based Transportation Experiences for Cultural Heritage 340
Ji Yaru, Shen Ruohan, Sun Xueyang, Chen Ziyi, Ren Yuetong, and Yao Yuan

Assisted Driver System Based on Augmented Reality 352
Peifeng Zhang, Pan Jiang, Kaifan Sun, Xiaoxu Sun, Hao Wen, Dejian Zhang, and Hao Zhang

Author Index 371

Multichannel and Novel Human–Computer Interaction

Research on the Dynamic Innovation Design of Traditional Embroidery Using Flexible Electroluminescent Threads

Yao Lu[1], Xuezhu Wang[1], Beituo Liu[1], Zhihao Yao[1], Xiwen Yao[1], Ziqi Liu[1], Mingzhen Xie[1], Yijie Guo[1], Tianyu Yu[2], Guanhong Liu[3](✉), and Haipeng Mi[1](✉)

[1] Tsinghua University, Beijing, China
mhp@tsinghua.edu.cn
[2] University of California, Berkeley, Berkeley, CA, USA
[3] Tongji University, Shanghai, China
liugh23@tongji.edu.cn

Abstract. Traditional embroidery serves as a vital medium for intangible cultural heritage, reflecting unique aesthetic and cultural values. Nevertheless, it struggles with dynamic expression and interactivity in modern contexts. This study employs Electroluminescent (EL) threads and introduces a "Core Dimension-Innovation Dimension" framework to explore ways to modernize traditional embroidery. The core dimension focuses on preserving craftsmanship, technique, and cultural importance, while the innovation dimension emphasizes dynamic lighting effects, interactivity, and broader applications. Experimental validation in automotive interiors shows that EL threads enhance the expressiveness and interaction of traditional embroidery while maintaining craftsmanship continuity. This research presents a novel approach to merging traditional arts with modern technology, paving the way for cultural preservation and sustainable innovation.

Keywords: Traditional Embroidery · Electroluminescent Threads · Craft Inheritance · Intangible Cultural Heritage · Dynamic Expression · Modern Transformation

1 Introduction

Traditional embroidery, a key aspect of intangible cultural heritage, has unique aesthetic and cultural significance, but faces numerous challenges in modern development [1–3]. Current practices rely on static threads, limiting dynamic visuals and interactive experiences, with functionality primarily for decoration[1]. Furthermore, the lack of integration between traditional craftsmanship and modern design hampers innovative progress [3]. While new technologies present

Y. Lu and X. Wang—contributed equally to this work.

[1] https://www.averyverylongexamplewebsite.com/some/path/to/page.

S. Guo et al. (Eds.): HHME 2025, CCIS 2878, pp. 3–12, 2027.
https://doi.org/10.1007/978-981-92-3991-7_1

opportunities for innovation [3,4] balancing tradition with modernity is essential for sustainable development.

Recent advancements in embroidery focus on three areas: material innovation, dynamic expression, and interactive experience. Innovations such as conductive threads and biomaterials have broadened embroidery's functional scope [5–7], particularly in electronic textiles [8–11]. However, these materials often struggle with mechanical performance and compatibility with traditional techniques, necessitating significant adjustments [9,12]. In dynamic expression, shape memory alloys and motion-driven technologies enable dynamic effects[2], yet their integration with traditional methods remains limited. Interactive projects like "Soft Speakers" showcase embroidery's potential for smart interaction [1,12,13], but technology-driven innovations can elevate the skill requirements for creators [1,11,14], potentially disrupting traditional processes and undermining craft inheritance [2,3].

This study investigates the integration of electroluminescent threads with traditional embroidery. These threads, similar in structure and operation to conventional threads, offer luminous and interactive properties, making them an ideal choice. The research is organized around two dimensions: the "Core Dimension", which emphasizes craftsmanship, technique preservation, and cultural significance, and the "Innovation Dimension", which focuses on dynamic effects, interactive functionality, and expanded applications. By merging these dimensions, the study explores pathways for modernizing traditional embroidery.

The study contributes in three key ways: it proposes a "Core-Innovation Dimension" framework to provide new perspectives on transforming traditional crafts; it demonstrates the integration of dynamic visuals and interactive experiences using electroluminescent threads; and it validates this approach through applications in automotive interiors, offering a model for incorporating traditional crafts into modern design.

2 Methodology

This study examines the cultural preservation and innovative craftsmanship of traditional embroidery through a framework grounded in two dimensions: the Core Dimension and the Innovation Dimension (Fig. 1).

Core Dimension: This encompasses the embroidery process, traditional techniques, and artisans' cognitive patterns—key elements that remain stable. These factors contribute to the continuity of cultural heritage amid material innovation. "Artisans' cognitive patterns" refers to the unique understanding craftspeople develop over years of practice, including their grasp of processes, material properties, design logic, and intuitive decision-making. These patterns extend beyond technique mastery; they embody the philosophical thinking and cultural essence inherent in traditional craftsmanship, representing a crucial aspect of its heritage.

[2] https://www.milab.design/p-mulan,https://www.milab.design/p-orchid-butterfly.

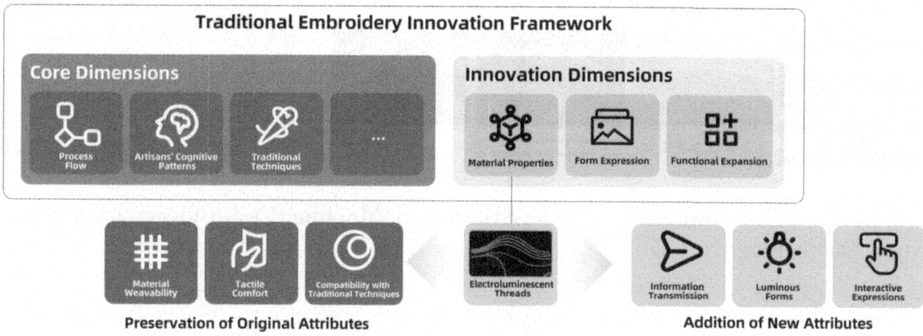

Fig. 1. The Core Dimension and the Innovation Dimension

Innovation Dimension: This highlights the properties of materials, form expression, and functional expansion. Electroluminescent (EL) threads, known for their unique luminous and conductive qualities, add dynamics and interactivity to embroidery, enabling new design possibilities.

The experiment seeks to integrate both dimensions, preserving the traditional Core (processes and foundational techniques) while enhancing the Innovation Dimension (dynamic lighting effects and functional expressions) to infuse embroidery with new cultural value. The focus of the study is on the significance of EL threads as a medium for cultural and functional innovation, rather than the technical development of thread preparation.

The research utilized commercially available EL threads that emit blue or green light when powered, operating based on an EL light unit mechanism. While thicker (0.3 mm to 0.5 mm in diameter), stiffer, and less elastic than traditional threads, EL threads' dynamic conductivity and luminous properties create exciting possibilities for expanding the temporal and interactive dimensions of embroidery.

3 Embroidery Experiment and Craft Exploration

This section examines the characteristics of electroluminescent (EL) threads through experiments in both hand and machine embroidery. Various stitching techniques, patterns, and dynamic lighting effects are tested to assess the material's adaptability and its capacity to convey cultural narratives.

1. Hand Embroidery Experiments: Hand embroidery offers advantages when working with EL threads due to its flexibility, effectively addressing their rigidity and unique lighting needs. Basic stitching tests—such as straight, chain, and couching stitches—showed that EL threads maintained good luminosity (Fig. 2a). Couching stitches, which secure EL threads with traditional threads, helped mitigate challenges from their rigidity. However, this coverage reduced the luminous effect. To optimize light performance while ensuring stitch stability, adjustments to the coverage area are necessary.

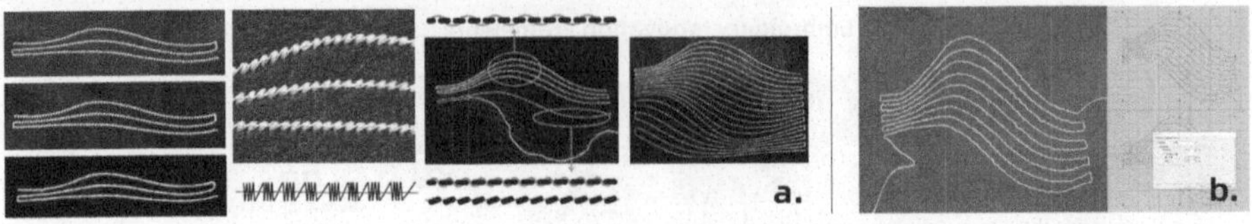

Fig. 2. a. Hand Embroidery: Couching Stitches, b. Machine Embroidery: 2.5mm as the Optimal Stitch Length

2. Machine Embroidery Experiments: Machine embroidery tests assessed the compatibility of EL threads with automated processes and identified areas for technical improvements. Issues like breakage under high tension and speed arose due to the rigidity of EL threads. In straight stitch evaluations with varying lengths (1.5 mm, 2.5 mm, 3 mm), a 2.5 mm stitch length proved optimal, protecting the EL threads while maintaining both uniformity and luminosity (Fig. 2b). Additionally, lowering bobbin thread tension and operating the machine at 500–700 stitches per minute improved overall quality.

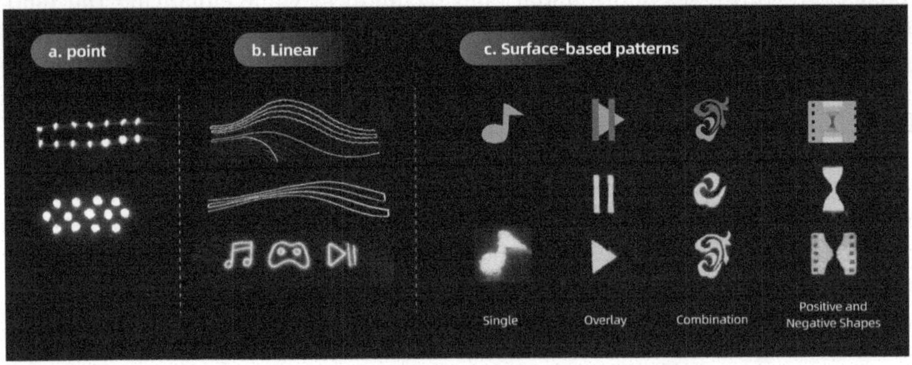

Fig. 3. Pattern Design Experiments

3. Pattern Design Experiments: Pattern design experiments evaluated EL threads in creating dot, line, and surface patterns (Fig. 3), demonstrating the material's versatility in producing diverse visual effects and its potential for creative applications.

4. Lighting Effect Design Experiments: Leveraging the luminous properties of EL threads, experiments explored dynamic lighting effects in embroidery designs (Fig. 4):

- Breathing Effect: Gradual brightening and dimming cycle for a soft, rhythmic visual.

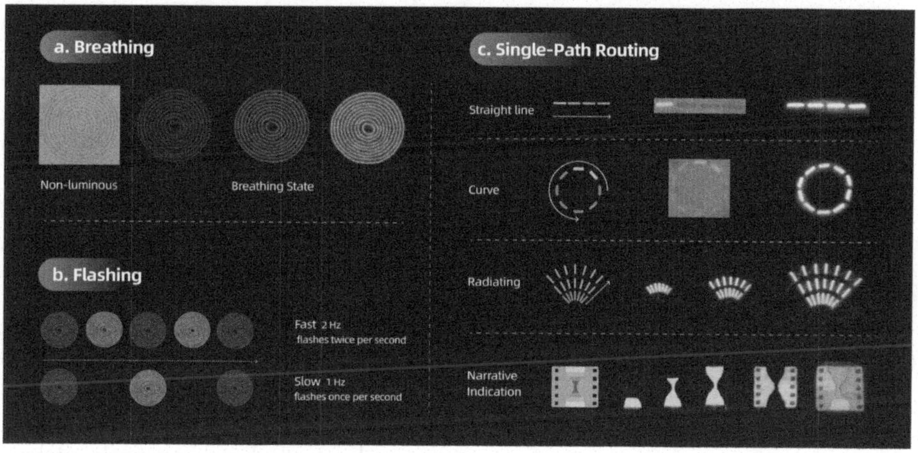

Fig. 4. Lighting Effect Design Experiments

- Flashing Effect: Flickering at varying frequencies enhances visual rhythm while guiding attention.
- Path Effect: Dynamic light flow along predefined paths creates intricate patterns with a sense of temporality, well-suited for modern design.

These experiments collectively highlight the potential of EL threads to enrich traditional embroidery with dynamic and interactive features while addressing the material's technical challenges.

4 Summary of Core and Innovation Dimensions

This section summarizes the experimental results from the perspectives of the Core Dimension and Innovation Dimension, supporting future design practices.

Core Dimension: Stability in Craft Processes, Technique Adaptability, and Cultural Value Preservation The Core Dimension emphasizes traditional embroidery's stability, focusing on craft processes, technique compatibility, and cultural value. Key findings include:

- Craft Processes: EL threads were integrated into traditional embroidery through stitch optimization and circuit planning, maintaining process continuity.
- Technique Adaptability: Single and couching stitches showed compatibility with EL threads, increasing flexibility in working with complex materials.
- Cultural Value: The combination of traditional patterns and modern lighting effects achieved a harmonious balance, preserving cultural symbols.

Innovation Dimension: Expanding Technology and Design Language The Innovation Dimension focuses on the expansion of technical capabilities and modern design languages. Key findings include:

- Dynamic Lighting Effects: Effects such as breathing light and path light introduced temporality and interactivity to embroidery, overcoming the limitations of traditional static designs.
- Design Language Expansion: The integration of lighting effects with traditional symbols, expressed through point, line, and surface designs, revealed the potential of symbol reinterpretation in a modern context.
- Technical Challenges: The rigidity of EL threads and the complexity of lighting effect planning posed challenges for large-scale patterns, tension control, and uniformity of light effects.

The Core Dimension's stability ensures the feasibility of integrating EL threads into traditional embroidery, while the Innovation Dimension reveals new opportunities for merging embroidery with modern technologies. Despite challenges like material rigidity and process complexity, the potential of EL threads for cultural preservation and contemporary applications has been preliminarily validated.

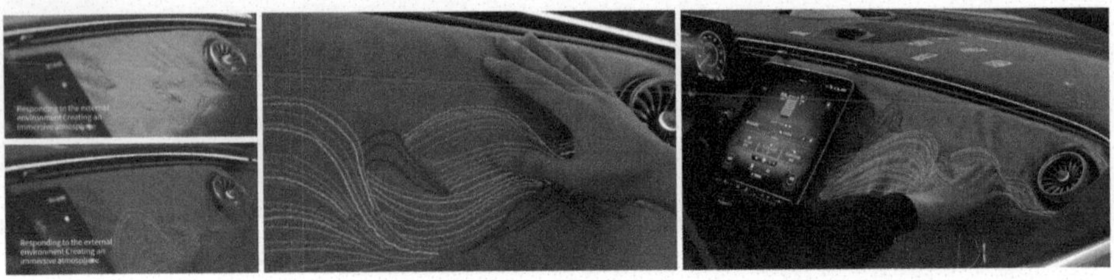

Fig. 5. Dynamic Interactive Dashboard Decorations

5 Design Practice in Automotive Interiors

The choice of automotive interiors as a practical application is influenced by several key factors. The complex lighting conditions in cars, from day to night and tunnel transitions, create an ideal environment for testing the dynamic effects of electroluminescent (EL) embroidery. The decorative areas in vehicles are well-suited for embroidery craftsmanship, and the enclosed space ensures a reliable power supply, essential for the stable performance of EL threads. Additionally, automotive interiors require visual designs that reflect refinement and technological sophistication while balancing clear information display and safety. The high standards for automotive-grade products also provide a rigorous testing ground for assessing the stability and durability of embroidery techniques. However, current automotive embroidery is mainly static and decorative, lacking dynamic interaction. This study seeks to overcome this limitation by integrating dynamic information display and interactive functionality using EL threads, exploring the innovative potential of traditional embroidery in modern automotive interior design.

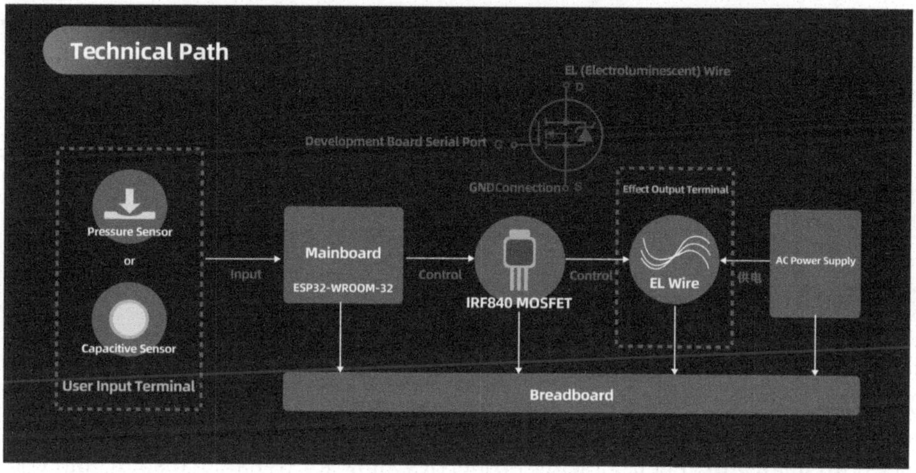

Fig. 6. Technical Path

6 Dynamic Interactive Dashboard Decorations

Inspired by traditional Chinese landscape painting, this study designs a dynamic embroidery artwork for car dashboards (Fig. 5), merging static and dynamic elements to create a multi-layered visual effect. Traditional embroidery threads depict the static "mountains and rocks", while electroluminescent (EL) threads simulate the dynamic "river", harmonizing stillness and motion.

The landscape patterns are modernized using parametric design techniques, ensuring they complement the fluidity of the car's interior. During the day, the embroidery appears static, but under varying light or touch interaction, the EL threads illuminate, creating a dynamic effect of "coexisting mountains and rivers". Localized illumination simulates interactive water flow, enhancing the immersive experience.

Technically, the system employs pressure and capacitive sensors as inputs, with an ESP32 microcontroller processing the signals (Fig. 6). These components work in tandem with driver modules and a stable power supply to control the dynamic lighting effects, mimicking the river's flow. By blending traditional cultural themes with modern technology, this design offers a unique and artistic experience within car interiors.

6.1 Innovation and Functional Exploration

Electroluminescent (EL) threads introduce dynamic displays and interactive features into automotive interiors, transforming embroidery from a decorative element into a blend of functionality and aesthetics. These threads create lighting effects that respond to environmental changes and facilitate touch-based interactions, enhancing the emotional experience within the car.

Integrating traditional embroidery threads with EL threads maintains the tactile quality of craftsmanship while aligning embroidery with contemporary needs. The dynamic lighting not only enhances the vehicle's interior ambiance but also modernizes traditional cultural elements.

This design showcases the innovative potential of EL-embedded embroidery, paving the way for the modernization and functional expansion of traditional craftsmanship.

7 Finding and Discussion

7.1 Medium Innovation in Traditional Craftsmanship

Electroluminescent (EL) threads represent an innovative medium that enhances material, functionality, and expression while maintaining the essence of embroidery craftsmanship. Their glowing properties allow for dynamic display and concealment, expanding material applications and ensuring compatibility with both hand and machine embroidery techniques. By incorporating dynamic lighting effects and sensing technologies, EL threads elevate embroidery from a static decorative element to an interactive medium, introducing features like interactivity and real-time responsiveness. They also enrich visual storytelling, enabling dynamic narratives through "positive-negative shape interaction", where forms are revealed and concealed (Fig. 4c), or patterns that alternate between "play" and "pause" modes (Fig. 3c). Future research is needed to assess the performance of EL threads across various applications and production processes, facilitating a deeper integration of traditional craftsmanship with modern technology.

7.2 Design Exploration of Dynamic Interaction

1. Dual-State Design Strategy for Patterns and Light Effects The brightness and darkness of electroluminescent (EL) threads add a new expressive layer to pattern design. By carefully planning illuminated and non-illuminated states, designers can create patterns with multiple meanings. Traditional landscape images are transformed into streamlined motifs that retain their decorative quality when unlit while offering dynamic storytelling when illuminated. Notably, alternating lighting units simulate the rhythm of flowing water, overcoming the limitations of single-thread gradients.
2. Innovative Exploration of Interactive Modes in Traditional Craft Incorporating environmental sensing and human-machine interactions allows embroidery artworks to adapt to their surroundings, creating emotional connections between users and the art. This multi-dimensional interaction design broadens the functional potential of traditional embroidery, providing fresh insights into innovation in a contemporary context.
3. Design Considerations for Technology Integration Integrating technology necessitates a balance between system complexity and practicality. Overly complex solutions can impede product development, making it essential to consider visual effects, energy efficiency, and system stability. Technology

should enhance the design's intent rather than dictate it, offering insights for optimizing future research and development.

7.3 Innovation Pathways Based on Design Thinking

Through the design practice of electroluminescent (EL) threads, a "core dimension-innovation dimension" analytical framework was established to support the innovation of traditional embroidery. In the innovation process, the introduction of EL threads merely altered the material properties without departing from the traditional medium, allowing artisans to seamlessly translate their expertise into new knowledge. This approach enables innovation while preserving the core logic of the craft.

The study provides an innovative pathway for other non-productive handicrafts, including material integration, design optimization, and process improvement. It explores the boundaries between tradition and modernity, highlighting the critical role of design in cross-disciplinary coordination and multidimensional integration. By injecting new momentum into the modernization of traditional crafts, this work offers valuable insights and serves as an important reference for future endeavors.

7.4 Limitations and Challenges

The durability and stability of electroluminescent (EL) threads in dynamic environments need further optimization for long-term use in automotive interiors. Additionally, the intricate electrical properties and craftsmanship pose challenges in integrating with in-car electrical systems and optimizing light effect distribution, which may hinder commercialization. Achieving dynamic lighting effects requires extra hardware, raising costs and production time, which could restrict scalability and widespread adoption of this technology.

8 Conclusion

This study incorporates electroluminescent (EL) threads into traditional embroidery and introduces a "core dimension-innovation dimension" framework. By merging craftsmanship heritage with material innovation, it expands functionality and demonstrates practicality through experiments in automotive interiors. Results show that EL threads enhance the expressiveness and interactivity of embroidery while preserving traditional techniques, facilitating the integration of old skills with new technologies. Future research could explore the use of smart materials in traditional crafts across various contexts, supporting the preservation of cultural heritage alongside sustainable innovation.

Acknowledgments. This study was supported and funded by the Tsinghua University-Daimler China Sustainable Transportation Joint Research Center (Project No.: 20223910001) under the management of the Overseas Division. We sincerely appreciate the valuable guidance and assistance provided by the relevant teams.

References

1. Zhang, L., Li, M., Zhang, L., Liu, X., Tang, Z., Wang, Y.: Mastersu: the sustainable development of Su embroidery based on digital technology. Sustainability **14**(12), 7094 (2022)
2. Zhong, X., Chudasri, D.: A review of traditional embroidery from China in relation to knowledge management and design. In: 2019 Joint International Conference on Digital Arts, Media and Technology with ECTI Northern Section Conference on Electrical, Electronics, pp. 276–281. IEEE (2019)
3. Yusof, S., Aris, A., Sajar, N.: Recreating the Malay traditional Tekat embroidery for its preservation and continuity as a cultural heritage. In: Proceedings of the Art and Design International Conference (AnDIC 2016), pp. 421–429. Springer (2018)
4. Jones, L., Nabil, S.: Goldwork embroidery: interviews with practitioners on working with metal threads and opportunities for e-textile hybrid crafts. In: Proceedings of the 14th Conference on Creativity and Cognition, pp. 364–379 (2022)
5. Marterer, V., Radouchová, M., Soukup, R., Hipp, S., Blecha, T.: Wearable textile antennas: investigation on material variants, fabrication methods, design and application. Fashion Text. **11**(1), 9 (2024)
6. Glazko, K., Portnova-Fahreeva, A., Mankoff-Dey, A., Psarra, A., Mankoff, J.: Shaping lace: machine embroidered metamaterials. In: Proceedings of the 9th ACM Symposium on Computational Fabrication, pp. 1–12 (2024)
7. Zhu, J., Winagle, L., Kao, H.-L.: EcoThreads: prototyping biodegradable e-textiles through thread-based fabrication. In: Proceedings of the CHI Conference on Human Factors in Computing Systems, pp. 1–17 (2024)
8. Salvado, R., Loss, C., Gonçalves, R., Pinho, P.: Textile materials for the design of wearable antennas: a survey. Sensors **12**(11), 15841–15857 (2012)
9. Stoppa, M., Chiolerio, A.: Wearable electronics and smart textiles: a critical review. Sensors **14**(7), 11957–11992 (2014)
10. Posch, I., Stark, L., Fitzpatrick, G.: eTextiles: reviewing a practice through its tool/kits. In: Proceedings of the 2019 ACM International Symposium on Wearable Computers, pp. 195–205 (2019)
11. Ali, S.M., Sovuthy, C., Imran, M.A., Socheatra, S., Abbasi, Q.H., Abidin, Z.Z.: Recent advances of wearable antennas in materials, fabrication methods, designs, and their applications: State-of-the-art. Micromachines **11**(10), 888 (2020)
12. Nabil, S., Jones, L., Girouard, A.: Soft speakers: digital embroidering of DIY customizable fabric actuators. In: Proceedings of the Fifteenth International Conference on Tangible, Embedded, and Embodied Interaction, pp. 1–12 (2021)
13. Hamdan, N.A.-H., Voelker, S., Borchers, J.: Sketch&Stitch: interactive embroidery for e-textiles. In: Proceedings of the 2018 CHI Conference on Human Factors in Computing Systems, pp. 1–13 (2018)
14. Tsolis, A., Whittow, W.G., Alexandridis, A.A., Vardaxoglou, J.C.: Embroidery and related manufacturing techniques for wearable antennas: challenges and opportunities. Electronics **3**(2), 314–338 (2014)

Assessment and Analysis of Tactile Perception in Older Adults

Wenyu Wang[1], Zhelin Li[1,2], Shiyu Dong[1], Lijun Jiang[1,2], Shuo Hou[3], and Qin Wang[1](✉)

[1] South China University of Technology, Guangzhou 510006, China
wqin@scut.edu.cn

[2] Guangdong Provincial Engineering Technology Research Center for Human-Computer Interaction Design, Guangzhou 510006, China

[3] China Academy of Building Research, Beijing 100013, China

Abstract. Tactile perception ability in the elderly is closely associated with high-quality healthy living. To quantitatively reveal age-related trends and primary influencing factors of fingertip tactile perception among older adults in China, Pattern recognition experiments were conducted to assess tactile recognition ability, while roughness discrimination experiments evaluated fine texture perception capability. Data collection spanned five communities across three Chinese cities (Guangzhou, Chengdu, and Beijing), yielding Pattern recognition data from 551 older adults and roughness discrimination data from 226 older adults. Key findings revealed that the tactile pattern recognition threshold significantly increased with age. The thresholds for the 60–69, 70–79, 80–89, and 90–99 age groups were 6.75 mm, 7.23 mm, 7.56 mm, and 10.57 mm, respectively. Notably, the threshold in the 90–99 age group was 56.6% significantly higher than that in the 60–69 age group. Females demonstrated lower accuracy in roughness discrimination (45.0%) compared to males (53.2%, $U = 4836.500$, $Z = -2.068$, $p = 0.039$). The findings provide data support for the design of age-friendly products and the development of intelligent tactile interaction technologies, and also offer methodological references for research on the physiological mechanisms of tactile perception in older adults.

Keywords: Ergonomics · Chinese Older Adults · Tactile Perception · Texture Discrimination

1 Introduction

China is experiencing rapid population ageing, with 264 million adults aged 60 and above in 2020, projected to exceed 400 million by 2035 [1]. As a fundamental sensory modality, tactile perception significantly influences cognition, motor function, and social participation in older adults. Tactile decline is associated with increased fall risk, daily activity limitations, social withdrawal, and depression, making it a critical target for healthy ageing interventions [[2–4]].

S. Guo et al. (Eds.): HHME 2025, CCIS 2878, pp. 13–24, 2027.
https://doi.org/10.1007/978-981-92-3991-7_2

In light of these health risks, optimizing the tactile design of industrial products for older adults has emerged as a key intervention strategy. Contemporary industrial products are predominantly characterized by geometric forms, with operational components such as switches, buttons, knobs, and indicator markings frequently employing geometric shapes. Studies indicate that such pattern elements effectively assist older adults in information comprehension [5]. Optimizing tactile design of industrial products has emerged as a key intervention strategy. While product design has traditionally emphasized visual appearance, age-related visual decline limits this approach [6]. However, older adults retain effective tactile judgment of surface contours [7], and cross-modal integration regions remain structurally intact with age [8]. Therefore, enhancing tactile design is vital for age-friendly products, where surface texture serves as a key channel for users to perceive functionality and is closely tied to safety and comfort—for instance, through tactile feedback on assistive device handgrips that conveys functional information and aids operation.

Although considerable research has elucidated tactile physiological mechanisms, large-scale data on Chinese older adults remain scarce. Global tactile research has focused on affective touch, sensory substitution, perceptual mechanisms, feedback, and marketing [9]. Tactile perception involves complex physical attributes—roughness, hardness, elasticity [10], softness, thermal perception, friction [11] - modulated by skin condition, scanning velocity, material properties, interactive behaviour, and emotional context [12]. Existing studies report elevated thresholds and material preferences in older adults [[13, 14]]. However, they often overlook skin biomechanics, neural conduction, and multimodal influences from psychological, cognitive, and cultural domains.

Western studies indicate age-related tactile decline correlates with degraded skin biomechanics and reduced receptor density [15], manifesting as elevated thresholds and diminished discrimination [16], and linking to frailty indicators [4]. However, these patterns may not fully apply to Chinese populations due to somatic and cultural differences. Research suggests notable East–West differences in tactile thresholds [[17, 18]], and cultural practices like Tai Chi enhance tactile resolution [19]. Although the China National Institute of Standardization has established a fingertip tactile database for ages 18-75 [20], data on the tactile capacities of the oldest-old remain limited.

Owing to the lack of empirical data based on large-scale samples, systematic research on the tactile perception abilities of China's elderly population remains underdeveloped. Based on the large-scale data of the elderly aged 60 and above in many cities, the study deeply explores their physiological characteristics and tactile perceptual capacities through a quantitative analysis of tactile pattern recognition and roughness discrimination, in order to improve the tactile interaction experience of age-friendly products.

2 Pattern Recognition Experiment

2.1 Pattern Recognition Experimental Procedure

This study was approved by the Ethics Committee of Beijing Hospital (Review Number: 2023BJYYEC-143-02). From August 2023 to July 2024, pattern recognition tests were carried out with the elderly in three urban communities in Guangzhou, Chengdu, and Beijing.

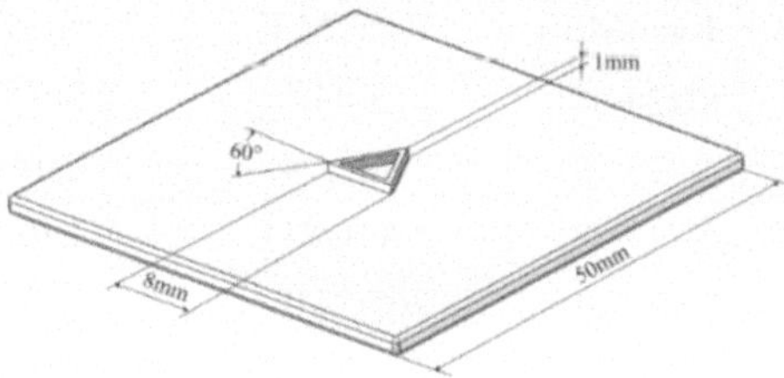

Fig. 1. A representative example (triangle, △) of the 3D-printed character plates used for tactile pattern recognition. All characters (△, □, ○, →, —) were produced in five size gradients (4, 8, 12, 16, and 24 mm) with a constant relief height of 1 mm

Participants for the Pattern recognition experiment were recruited using a stratified sampling strategy. Eligible individuals were community-dwelling adults aged 60 years and above, capable of independent living, and with no history of finger skin lesions or neurological damage. The test was carried out in indoor community settings (temperature: 22 ± 3°C; humidity: 51 ± 11%) to minimize perceptual interference. The volar surface of the dominant index finger served as the test site. Standardized hand hygiene protocols were implemented prior to testing, and ambient temperature was maintained throughout the session.

The stimuli consisted of 3D-printed character plates (△, □, ○, →, —) produced in five size gradients (4, 8, 12, 16, and 24 mm; constant relief height: 1 mm). During testing, participants inserted their hand into a dark box to tactually identify each character. A visual reference depicting the possible characters was available for consultation. The smallest character size correctly identified was recorded as the threshold [21], as illustrated in **Fig. 1**. Each trial allowed up to 30 s of tactile exploration, followed by a 4-s rest interval. The final individual mean discrimination threshold (mm) was calculated as the average of three valid measurements.

Concurrently, the following ergonomic data were collected at the measurement site: cognitive ability, assessed using the Mini-Mental State Examination (MMSE), and grip strength, measured with a Jamar Smart dynamometer.

2.2 Pattern Recognition Experimental Data Analysis

The pattern recognition measurement initially included 596 participants. Among these, 45 individuals exhibited recognition thresholds exceeding the maximum tested value of 24 mm and were excluded from subsequent analysis. The final valid sample thus included 551 participants, Guangzhou 271 individuals (49.2%), Chengdu 98(17.8%), and Beijing182 (33.0%). Participants were categorized into four age groups: 202 individuals aged 60–69 years (36.7%), 205 aged 70–79 years (37.2%), 130 aged 80–89 years (23.6%), and 14 aged90–99 years (2.5%), as summarized in Table 1.

Table 1. Pattern recognition experiment sample demographic data

Region	Total Sample	60-69 years	70-79 years	80-89 years	90-99 years
		Total(M/F)	Total(M/F)	Total(M/F)	Total(M/F)
Guangzhou	271	87(23/64)	113(44/69)	67(34/33)	4(2/2)
Chengdu	98	48(25/23)	35(11/24)	15(2/13)	0(0/0)
Beijing	182	67(19/48)	57(16/41)	48(23/25)	10(5/5)
Total	551	202(67/135)	205(71/134)	130(59/71)	14(7/7)

Descriptive analysis of the pattern recognition thresholds revealed a range from 4.00 mm to 21.33 mm, with a mean of 7.22 mm (SD = 2.99mm). Analysis of individual symbols showed distinct recognition thresholds: the horizontal line "—" was identified most easily (M = 6.10 mm, SD = 2.93), followed by the triangle "△" (M = 6.34 mm, SD = 3.02), the circle "○" (M = 6.77 mm, SD = 3.08), the square "□" (M = 7.39 mm, SD = 4.32), and the right arrow "→", which proved most difficult to recognize (M = 9.96 mm, SD = 4.42), as illustrated in **Fig. 2** A.

Intergroup Comparison. Comparing the average pattern recognition thresholds across different genders and age groups, statistical findings revealed a general increase in recognition thresholds with age, with a pronounced acceleration observed in the 90–99 age group. The mean threshold for males over 90 years reached 11.81 mm (SD = 4.38), increased by 71.0% compared with the 60–69 years baseline, and the individual variability was significantly. Gender differences exhibited age-dependent patterns: in the 60–69 group, males (M = 6.90 mm) showed slightly higher thresholds than females (M = 6.68 mm); this pattern reversed in the 70–79 group, where females (M = 7.46 mm) exceeded males (M = 6.78 mm); the smallest gender difference was observed in the 80–89 group (males: 7.75 mm, females: 7.40 mm; difference = 4.7%); the most substantial divergence occurred in the 90–99 group, with males (11.81 mm) exceeding females (9.33 mm) by 26.5%, as shown in **Fig. 2** B.

As the threshold data violated normality assumptions, non-parametric tests were employed for statistical comparisons. The Mann-Whitney U test revealed no significant difference in threshold distributions between male and female groups (U = 35110.000, Z = -0.159, p = 0.874), indicating statistically equivalent recognition performance across genders (**Fig. 2** C). Conversely, the Kruskal-Wallis test identified significant differences among age groups ($\chi^2 = 25.196$, df = 3, $p<0.001$). Post-hoc pairwise comparisons with Bonferroni correction showed significant differences between the 60–69 and 80–89 groups (p=0.050), 60–69 and 90–99 groups (p = 0.002), 70–79 and 90–99 groups (p=0.013), and 80–89 and 90–99 groups (p = 0.001), confirming that the pattern

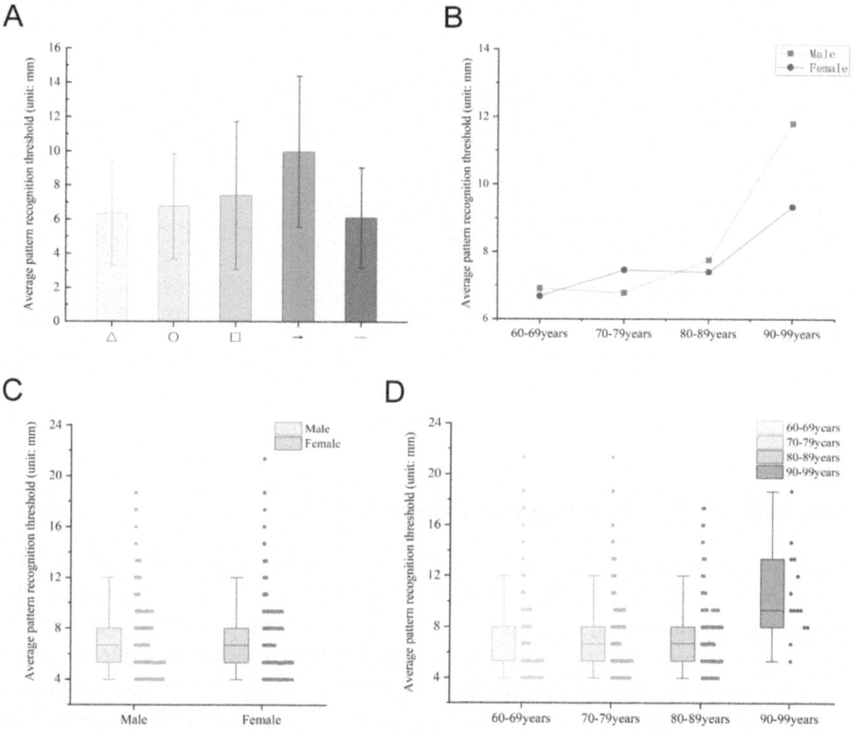

Fig. 2. Pattern recognition ability in older adults. (A) Recognition thresholds for the five 3D-printed character plates. (B) Comparison of pattern recognition thresholds across genders and age groups. (C) Comparison of pattern recognition thresholds between sex groups. (D) Comparison of pattern recognition thresholds between age groups

recognition threshold increases with age, particularly in the highest age group (**Fig. 2** D).

Correlation Analysis. Spearman's correlation analysis was conducted to examine the relationships of age, cognitive ability (MMSE), and dominant hand grip strength with pattern recognition thresholds. Results indicated a significant positive correlation between age and recognition threshold ($r_s = 0.200$, $p < 0.001$), confirming that older age is associated with elevated thresholds. A weak negative correlation was observed between dominant hand grip strength and recognition threshold ($r_s = -0.123$, $p = 0.049$), suggesting that greater grip strength is marginally associated with better tactile resolution. No significant association was found between cognitive ability and recognition threshold ($r_s = -0.111$, $p = 0.130$), as illustrated in **Fig. 3**.

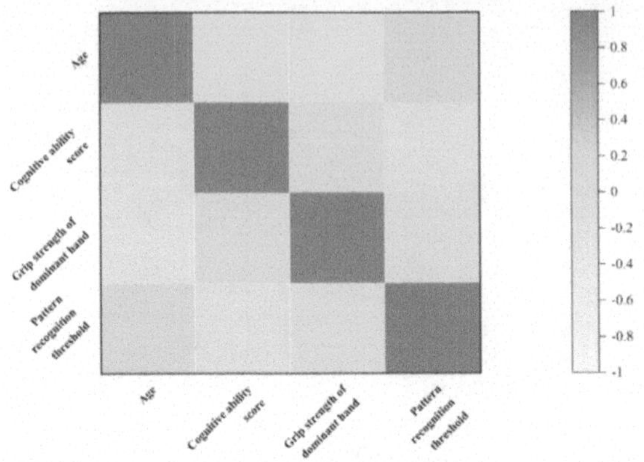

Fig. 3. Pattern recognition threshold correlation heatmap

2.3 Percentile of Pattern Recognition Threshold

Percentile values were calculated from the individual mean discrimination thresholds of 551 participants using the Weighted Percentile Method (Table 2). The threshold distribution showed significant right-skewness (skewness = 1.599, kurtosis = 3.437). Age-stratified analysis revealed the most concentrated distribution in the 60–69 age group (P5–P25 = 4.00–5.30 mm), where the minimum stimulus size (4.00 mm) comprised the lower decile (P5 = P10 = 4.00 mm). With increasing age, the distribution shifted rightward and dispersion increased: the median (P50) rose to 6.67 mm in the 70–79 group, while P95 reached 13.93 mm in the 80–89 group. Although P95 for the 90–99 group could not be reliably estimated due to limited sample size, its P75 (13.33 mm) exceeded the corresponding value for the 80–89 group (8.00 mm) by 66.6%. The kurtosis value of 3.437 (>3) confirms a leptokurtic distribution, characterized by a sharp peak—particularly evident in the younger age group. The interquartile range (P25–P75) was only 2.67 mm (5.33→8.00 mm) in the 60–69 group, but expanded to 5.33 mm (8.00→13.33 mm) in the 90–99 group, demonstrating a non-linear widening with age.

Table 2. Pattern recognition threshold percentile (mm)

Age Group	P5	P10	P25	P50	P75	P90	P95
60-69years	4.00	4.00	5.30	5.33	8.00	10.27	12.00
70-79 years	4.00	4.00	5.33	6.67	8.00	10.68	13.33
80-89 years	4.00	4.00	5.33	6.70	8.00	10.70	13.93
90-99 years	5.33	6.00	8.00	9.33	13.33	16.67	/
Total	4.00	4.00	5.33	6.67	8.00	10.67	13.33

2.4 Discussion on the Pattern Recognition Experiment

Age-related decline in hand tactile function, marked by higher thresholds and reduced pattern recognition, varies greatly among individuals [[4, 21]]. This study used 3D-printed characters to assess this ability in Chinese adults aged 60+, finding an average recognition threshold of 6.99 mm that increased significantly with age—particularly in the 90-99 cohort—while gender showed no significant effect. To explore factors influencing this decline, we examined its associations with cognitive function and grip strength. Although tactile decline is often linked to cognitive impairment [22], our study found no significant association, possibly due to the limited scope of our cognitive data or assessment tool. However, supporting prior research [23], we found that better tactile recognition correlated with greater dominant-hand grip strength, suggesting that greater muscular capacity and neuromuscular coordination may contribute to superior tactile performance.

3 Roughness Discrimination Experiment

3.1 Roughness Discrimination Experiment Procedure

This study was approved by the Ethics Committee of Beijing Hospital (Review Number: 2023BJYYEC-143-02). Roughness discrimination measurements were conducted between August 2023 and July 2024 among older adults across four communities—three in Guangzhou and one in Chengdu.

All sessions were held indoors under controlled environmental conditions (temperature: 22 ± 3°C; humidity: 51 ± 11%). Five grades of sandpaper (P180, P400, P600, P800, P1000) served as stimulus materials. These were cut into 5 cm × 5 cm squares and clearly labelled with their respective grit numbers, as illustrated in **Fig. 4 A**. The P600 grade was designated as the standard stimulus. A dark box with bilateral openings was used to present the samples, thereby eliminating visual cues.

The procedure of experiment is as follows. (1) Preparation: The standard stimulus (P600 sandpaper) was placed on a horizontal table outside the dark box, fully visible and accessible to the participants. Participants ensured the fingertip of their dominant index finger was clean and free of debris. (2) Adaptation: A one-minute training was conducted prior to formal testing (with 4 -second intervals between trials) to familiarize participants with the task and the tactile sensations. (3) Testing: Participants inserted the dominant index finger into the dark box to tactually explore five sandpaper samples presented in random order. Their task was to identify which sample matched the roughness of the visible standard stim-ulus (P600) located outside the box. (4) Recording: The experimenter documented the grit number of the selected sandpaper.

The same suite of ergonomic data was collected concurrently: cognitive ability (MMSE) and grip strength (Jamar Smart dynamometer).

3.2 Roughness Discrimination Data Analysis

The roughness discrimination measurement included 226 participants, comprising 114 from Guangzhou (50.4%) and 112 from Chengdu (49.6%). The sample was divided into four age groups: 60–69 years (n = 80, 35.4%), 70–79 years (n = 96, 42.5%), 80–89 years (n = 49, 21.7%), and 90–99 years (n = 1, 0.4%), as detailed in Table 3.

Table 3. Roughness discrimination experiment sample demographic data

Region	Total Sample	60-69 years	70-79 years	80-89 years	90-99 years
		Total(M/F)	Total(M/F)	Total(M/F)	Total(M/F)
Guangzhou	114	30(12/18)	56(17/39)	27(8/19)	1(0/1)
Chengdu	112	50(26/24)	40(12/28)	22(2/20)	0(0/0)
Total	226	80(38/42)	96(29/67)	49(10/39)	1(0/1)

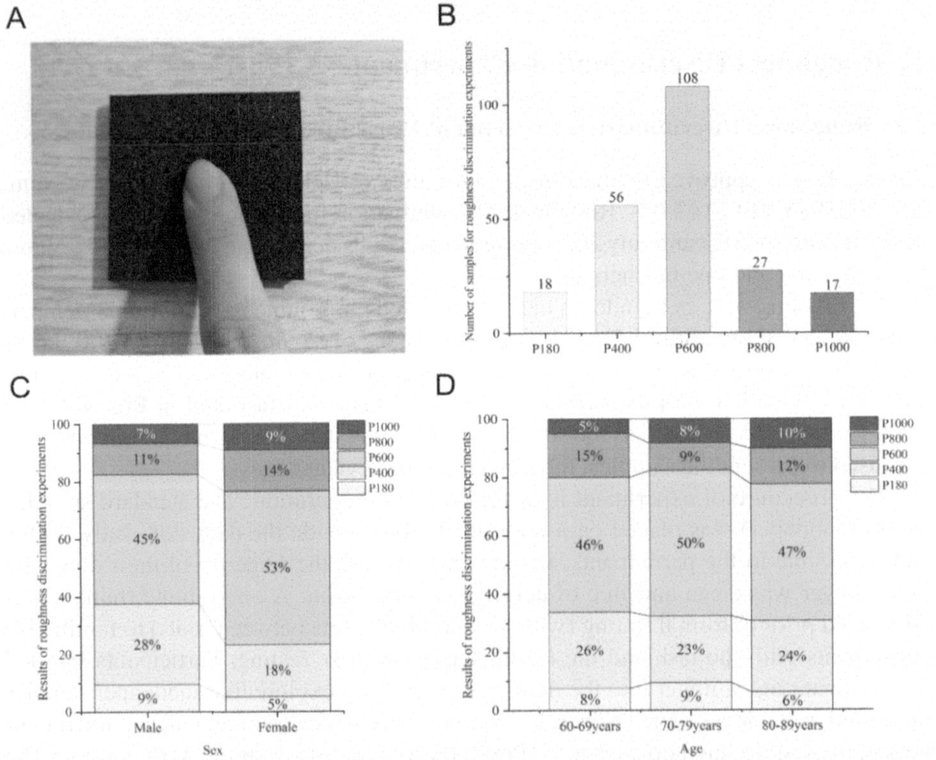

Fig. 4. Roughness discrimination ability in older adults. (A) Schematic representation of the sandboard of the P180 touched by the index finger of the dominant hand. (B) Frequency of discrimination results for the five roughness types. (C) Comparison of the percentage of roughness discrimination results between sex groups. (D) Comparison of the percentage of roughness discrimination results between age groups.

Frequency analysis of roughness matching responses revealed that 108 participants (47.8%) identified P600 as closest to the standard stimulus; 56 (24.8%) selected P400;

27 (11.9%) chose P800; 18 (8.0%) selected P180; and 17 (7.5%) chose P1000(**Fig. 4** B).

Intergroup Comparison. Mann-Whitney U test showed that there was a significant gender difference in roughness discrimination performance ($U = 4836.500$, $Z = -2.068$, $p = 0.039$), as illustrated in **Fig. 4** C. However, the Kruskal-Wallis test showed no significant differences in roughness discrimination ability among the different age cohorts ($H = 1.585$, $df = 3$, $p = 0.663$), suggesting minimal impact of increasing age on roughness discrimination ability within the 60-89 year age range. Tactile perception across different age groups demonstrated consistent performance in this task, as illustrated in **Fig. 4** D.

3.3 Discussion on the Roughness Discrimination Experiment

Age-related tactile decline is most pronounced in spatial discrimination, followed by detection thresholds, with texture discrimination being least affected [24]. Consistent with this, our study of adults aged 60-99 found no significant age-related differences in roughness discrimination, confirming its relative stability in later life. This dissociation likely stems from distinct neural mechanisms: spatial discrimination relies on afferent spatial organization, whereas roughness perception depends more on intensity-based coding [25].

However, we did observe significant gender differences, with females showing poorer roughness discrimination accuracy despite no difference in perception time. This contrasts with previous reports of gender-independent roughness discrimination thresholds [25], suggesting potential influences from sample characteristics or methodological variations that warrant further investigation.

Overall, roughness perception, while following the general pattern of tactile function, appears less vulnerable to aging than spatial discrimination and is subject to multifactorial modulation by factors including age and gender.

4 Discussion

4.1 Analysis of the Relationship between Pattern Discrimination Ability and Roughness Discrimination Ability

A total of 196 participants took part in both the pattern recognition and roughness discrimination measurements. The sample was evenly split between Guangzhou ($n = 98$, 50.0%) and Chengdu ($n = 98$, 50.0%), and distributed across age groups as follows: 60–69 years ($n = 77$, 39.3%), 70–79 years ($n = 83$, 42.3%), 80–89 years ($n = 35$, 17.9%), and 90–99 years ($n = 1$, 0.5%), as detailed in Table 4.

Spearman's correlation analysis indicated no significant association between roughness discrimination ability and pattern recognition thresholds ($p > 0.840$). This suggests that roughness discrimination and Pattern recognition engage distinct neural perceptual mechanisms: the former likely depends more on local signal processing by skin mechanoreceptors, whereas the latter necessitates spatial integration and higher-level pattern recognition.

Table 4. Sample demographic data for both measures of participation

Region	Total Sample	60-69 years	70-79 years	80-89 years	90-99 years
		Total(M/F)	Total(M/F)	Total(M/F)	Total(M/F)
Guangzhou	98	30(12/18)	47(11/36)	20(7/13)	1(0/1)
Chengdu	98	47(25/22)	36(11/25)	15(2/13)	0(0/0)
Total	196	77(37/40)	83(22/61)	35(9/26)	1(0/1)

4.2 Future Applications

The tactile perception data obtained in this study—including a 14 mm pattern recognition threshold for the 80–89 cohort, a 47.8% correct identification rate for P600 sandpaper, and an 18.3% gender-related decline in tactile matching accuracy—provide empirical benchmarks for advancing haptic interface design tailored to older adults.

In the domain of bioelectric stimulation, these thresholds can inform the optimization of electrovibration signals, particularly by prioritizing low-frequency protocols that accommodate age-related declines in high-frequency sensitivity [[26, 27]]. For VR-based rehabilitation, roughness discrimination data can calibrate haptic rendering algorithms, enabling more accurate simulation of textured surfaces in virtual environments designed for geriatric training [[28, 29]]. Furthermore, integrating such feedback into service robot interfaces could enhance elderly users' ability to perform delicate tasks by compensating for visual impairments through tactile encoding of object properties [30].

Collectively, these findings establish key design constraints for developing personalized, home-based VR rehabilitation systems and human-centred multimodal interfaces that support ageing-friendly robotics.

4.3 Limitations

This study has several limitations. Data collection was restricted to Guangzhou, Beijing, and Chengdu, excluding elderly populations from other regions of China and potentially limiting the representativeness and generalizability of the findings. Additionally, the sample size for roughness discrimination was relatively small, particularly for the 90–99 age group, which may reduce the robustness of conclusions for this cohort. While these findings offer preliminary guidance for age-friendly product design, more comprehensive, multi-dimensional data are needed to inform detailed design specifications. Future research should expand regional coverage, increase sample sizes, and incorporate additional objective metrics for a more comprehensive assessment of tactile perception in older adults.

5 Conclusion

The present study systematically evaluated tactile perception capabilities in older adults across mainland China through assessments of pattern recognition and roughness discrimination. Our findings yield several key observations:

(1) The threshold for pattern recognition progressively increases with age and exhibits a significant negative correlation with declining grip strength; differences in thresholds between age groups are statistically significant.
(2) The ability to distinguish roughness is less affected by age, with significant differences observed between males and females in roughness discrimination.
(3) Tactile function decline exhibits multidimensional complexity: pattern recognition and roughness discrimination demonstrate distinct ageing patterns and influencing factors, with no significant correlation between the two.

These results reveal patterns of tactile aging in the Chinese population that underscore the need for multidimensional assessments and targeted interventions. The dissociation between spatial and intensive tactile processing offers valuable insights for informing the development of age-friendly interfaces and rehabilitation strategies.

Acknowledgments. This study was funded by the National Key Research and Development Programme project 'Research and Application of Key Technical Standards for Community-Based Age-Friendly Ergonomics' (Project No. 2022YFF0607000).

Disclosure of Interests The authors have no competing interests to declare that are relevant to the content of this article.

References

1. Leading Group Office of the State Council Seventh National Population Census. 2020 China Seventh National Population Census Data. National Bureau of Statistics, Beijing (2021)
2. Hafstrom, A.: Perceived and functional balance control is negatively affected by diminished touch and vibration sensitivity in relatively healthy older adults and elderly. Gerontol. Geriatr. Med. **4**, 2333721418775551 (2018)
3. Vanbellingen, T., Ottiger, B., Pflugshaupt, T., et al.: Spatial neglect predicts upper limb use in the activities of daily living. Cerebrovasc. Dis. **44**(3-4), 122–127 (2017)
4. Vieira, A.I., Nogueira, D., Reis, E.A., et al.: Hand tactile discrimination, social touch and frailty criteria in elderly people: A cross sectional observational study. Arch. Gerontol. Geriatr. **66**, 73–81 (2016)
5. Huang, H., Yang, M., Yang, C., et al.: User performance effects with graphical icons and training for elderly novice users: A case study on automatic teller machines. Appl. Ergon. **78**, 62–69 (2019)
6. Song, W.Q., Song, W.M., Du, J.B., et al.: Event-related potential study on aging of visuospatial attention under cued conditions. Chin. J. Geriatr. **25**(5), 346–349 (2006)
7. Norman, J.F., Kappers, A.M.L., Beers, A.M., et al.: Aging and the haptic perception of 3D surface shape. Atten. Percept. Psychophys. **73**(3), 908–918 (2011)
8. Ballesteros, S., Mayas, J.: Preserved cross-modal priming and aging: A summary of current thoughts. Acta Psychol. Sin. **41**(11), 1063–1074 (2009)
9. Xu, Z.X., Chen, Y.S.: Research hotspots and development trends of tactile design. Packag. Eng. **45**(12), 77–90 (2024)
10. Bolton, D.A., Staines, W.R.: Age-related loss in attention-based modulation of tactile stimuli at early stages of somatosensory processing. Neuropsychologia. **50**(7), 1502–1513 (2012)
11. Tiest, W.M.B.: Tactual perception of material properties. Vision Res. **50**(24), 2775–2782 (2010)

12. Etzi, R., Spence, C., Zampini, M., et al.: When sandpaper is 'Kiki' and satin is 'Bouba': an exploration of the associations between words, emotional states, and the tactile attributes of everyday materials. Multisens. Res. **29**(1-3), 133–155 (2016)
13. Yang, A.P., Cheng, G., Fu, W.Y., et al.: Experimental study on discrimination thresholds for haptic perception of size in manual operation. In: Duffy, V.G. (ed.) DHM 2016 LNCS, vol. 9745, pp. 1–12. Springer, Cham (2016)
14. Men, Y.L.: A research on the correlation between tactile perception characteristics and aging-suitable design in the elderly based on a testing tools development. In: Stephanidis, C., Harris, D. (eds.) HCII 2021 LNCS, vol. 13094, pp. 277–294. Springer, Cham (2021)
15. Skedung, L., El Rawadi, C., Arvidsson, M., et al.: Mechanisms of tactile sensory deterioration amongst the elderly. Sci. Rep. **8**(1), 1502 (2018)
16. Kenshalo Sr., D.R.: Somesthetic sensitivity in young and elderly humans. J. Gerontol. **41**(6), 732–742 (1986)
17. Hwu, C.M., Chang, H.Y., Chen, J.Y., et al.: Quantitative vibration perception thresholds in normal and diabetic subjects: influence of age, height and body mass index. Neuroepidemiology. **21**(6), 271–278 (2002)
18. Deshpande, N., Metter, E.J., Ling, S., et al.: Physiological correlates of age-related decline in vibrotactile sensitivity. Neurobiol. Aging. **29**(5), 765–773 (2008)
19. Kerr, C.E., Shaw, J.R., Wasserman, R.H., et al.: Tactile acuity in experienced Tai Chi practitioners: evidence for use dependent plasticity as an effect of sensory-attentional training. Exp. Brain Res. **188**, 317–322 (2008)
20. China National Institute of Standardization. The latest survey of Chinese adults ergonomics basic parameters has been completed (2020).
21. Manning, H., Tremblay, F.: Age differences in tactile pattern recognition at the fingertip. Somatosens. Mot. Res. **23**(3-4), 147–155 (2006)
22. Kalisch, T., Kattenstroht, J.C., Kowalewski, R., et al.: Cognitive and tactile factors affecting human haptic performance in later life. PLoS ONE. **7**(1), e30420 (2012)
23. Melchior, H., Vating, J.J., Weiss, P.L.: Is there a relationship between light touch-pressure sensation and functional hand ability? Disabil. Rehabil. **29**(7), 567–575 (2007)
24. Godde, B., Bruns, P., Wendel, V., et al.: Effects of age and individual experiences on tactile perception over the life span in women. Acta Psychol. **190**, 135–141 (2018)
25. Libouton, X., Barbier, O., Plaghki, L., et al.: Tactile roughness discrimination threshold is unrelated to tactile spatial acuity. Behav. Brain Res. **208**(2), 473–478 (2010)
26. Zhao, L., Liu, Y., Song, W.: Tactile perceptual thresholds of electrovibration in VR. IEEE Trans. Vis. Comput. Graph. **27**(6), 2618–2626 (2021)
27. Basdogan, C., Giraud, F., Levesque, V., et al.: A review of surface haptics: enabling tactile effects on touch surfaces. IEEE Trans. Haptics. **13**(3), 450–470 (2020)
28. Zhang, J., Huang, M., Chen, Y., et al.: TouchMark: partial tactile feedback design for upper limb rehabilitation in virtual reality. IEEE Trans. Vis. Comput. Graph. **30**(11), 7430–7440 (2024)
29. Sadihov, D., Migge, B., Gassert, R., et al.: Prototype of a VR upper-limb rehabilitation system enhanced with motion-based tactile feedback. In: 2013 World Haptics Conference (WHC), pp. 449–454. IEEE, Piscataway (2013)
30. Shi, Y., Shen, G.: Haptic sensing and feedback techniques toward virtual reality. ACM Comput. Surv. **55**(5), 1–35 (2022)

Dynamic Human Action Recognition Method Based on Recursive Graphs and LeNet-5

Yizhong Xin[1(✉)], Xuzhu Jin[1], Dongliang Li[1], and Lijun Zhang[2]

[1] Shenyang University of Technology, Shenyang, China
xyz@sut.edu.cn, jxz@smail.sut.edu.cn
[2] Liaoyang Hongyu Crystal Co., Ltd., Liaoyang, China

Abstract. In recent years, human action recognition technology has received widespread attention from researchers and has potential application value in many fields, such as medical health monitoring, interactive somatosensory games, and military affairs. Existing human action recognition methods based on machine vision are subject to interference from environmental factors such as light effects, object occlusion, and may infringe on users' personal privacy. Based on a mobile device such as a smartphone, this thesis collects three-axis acceleration data during motion, and then analyzes and studies human action recognition methods. The specific work is as follows. At the source of the experimental data, a data acquisition and preprocessing system based on acceleration sensors has been designed. The manual feature extraction process in human action recognition tasks is complex and difficult to extract nonlinear features from temporal signals, a human action recognition method based on recurrence plot and convolutional neural network is proposed. Firstly, the original one-dimensional acceleration signal is reconstructed and preprocessed to obtain an RGB color image. Then, it is fed into a convolutional neural network to complete feature extraction and recognition of human actions. The experimental results indicate that this method is more suitable for human motion recognition tasks compared to existing studies, specifically compared to other studies that use triaxial acceleration and triaxial angular velocity data, this method still has the best classification performance under the condition of only using triaxial acceleration data from the UCI HAR dataset, with a classification accuracy of 98.37%.

Keywords: Human action recognition · Acceleration sensor · Recurrence plot · Convolutional neural network

1 Introduction

Human actions encompass a wide range of movements such as walking, running, jumping, and climbing. Through these actions, humans express emotions, convey information, and demonstrate aesthetics. Human action recognition (HAR)

S. Guo et al. (Eds.): HHME 2025, CCIS 2878, pp. 25–39, 2027.
https://doi.org/10.1007/978-981-92-3991-7_3

technology has broad application value in areas such as smart healthcare, smart homes, and interactive somatosensory games [1–3]. Research in HAR can be broadly divided into two directions: vision-based methods using visual sensors and sensor-based methods using various motion sensors. Although machine vision–based approaches have achieved remarkable results in motion analysis [4–6], they are easily affected by environmental factors such as lighting conditions and occlusions, which limits their practical applications [7]. In contrast, wearable sensor–based methods can be applied in somatosensory interaction, smart home systems, and sports training assistance. These approaches can capture a variety of signals, such as acceleration, angular velocity, blood oxygen saturation, and heart rate, while being relatively low-cost; users only need a smartphone or other mobile device to perform daily action recognition, which facilitates real-world deployment.

Among these approaches, accelerometer-based methods have long been a popular research direction because of the similarity between the temporal properties of accelerometer signals and those of speech signals in speech recognition. Consequently, early accelerometer-based HAR methods were inspired by speech recognition techniques [8]. Inman et al. [9] conducted the first exploration of this topic in 1953, but due to the large size and high cost of the early accelerometers, their study did not attract sufficient attention. Ghasemzadeh et al. [10] applied accelerometer-based recognition to golf training by attaching sensor devices to the athletes' arms, recording motion data throughout the swing, and using statistical analysis to compute detailed motion parameters such as wrist rotation angles, thus providing targeted guidance.

Current research on accelerometer-based HAR can be classified into handcrafted features-based methods [11] and deep learning–based methods. Liu et al. [12] analyzed different gesture signals in gesture interaction and developed a gesture recognition system based on accelerometers. They collected accelerometer data from the dominant wrist for various gestures, extracted discriminative features, and used a discrete hidden Markov model for classification, achieving an average accuracy of 99.4% for 11 gesture types. Mekruksavanich et al. [13] developed a system based on ensemble learning models, achieving an accuracy of 98. 53% to recognize three daily activities: walking, climbing up and down stairs. Ahmed et al. [14] addressed the high-dimensional nature of feature vectors in HAR by proposing a hybrid feature selection method using sequential floating forward search to obtain an optimal feature subset, followed by classification using an SVM, achieving an accuracy of 98.13% on six daily actions.

With the rapid development of deep learning, models can automatically learn abstract representations from data without manual feature engineering and are applicable to a variety of data modalities. Zhao et al. [15] proposed a gesture recognition method that reconstructs images from triaxial accelerometer signals collected by smart devices. This method normalizes and compresses triaxial sequences into grayscale images, which are then classified using a Softmax regression model, achieving an average precision of 99. 23% for 26 alphabet gestures with an average recognition time of 15 ms. Challa et al. [16] integrated convolutional neural networks and bidirectional long- and short-term memory networks into a multibranch CNN-BiLSTM architecture that captures both local temporal characteristics and long-term dependencies, achieving a classification accuracy of 96. 37% in the HCI HAR dataset.

Despite these achievements, different feature extraction strategies have their own applicability and limitations for different data types and application scenarios, and their recognition performance often degrades in complex environments for dynamic human actions. To address these issues, this study proposes a human action recognition method based on recurrence plots and the LeNet-5 convolutional neural network. The main contributions are summarized as follows: (1) recurrence plots are introduced into HAR for the first time, providing a new approach for analyzing motion data; (2) reconstructing and fusing triaxial accelerometer data into images embeds prior knowledge such as signal periodicity and intrinsic similarity, enriching the information content of the images and improving data quality; and (3) the proposed reconstruction and fusion algorithm directly converts triaxial accelerometer data into RGB images, making the data more expressive and better suited for convolutional neural network feature extraction.

2 Accelerometer-Based Data Acquisition and Preprocessing System

2.1 Data Acquisition

In this study, the smartphone model used for data collection was the iPhone 13 Pro, whose built-in accelerometer can capture acceleration signals in real time during movement. The Phyphox mobile application was used to collect sensor data from the device. After data collection, the recorded data was transferred to a personal computer via Bluetooth for subsequent processing.

Before data collection, the types of human actions to be recorded in this study were determined through a user questionnaire. The selected actions included five common daily activities: walking, running, jumping, ascending stairs, and descending stairs.

To objectively capture the characteristics of the acceleration signal of different individuals performing these actions, eight volunteers were recruited as subjects, including four men and four women between the ages of 21 and 35 years. Before the experiment, the volunteers were informed about the purpose of the study, the experimental procedure, the placement of the device, and the relevant precautions. The smartphone was fixed to the upper arm of each participant using a sports armband.

During the data collection process, each volunteer performed the designated actions without interference or restrictions, except for assistance in wearing the equipment. They were asked to perform the actions naturally, as in their daily routines. The sampling frequency was set at 50 Hz, which has been shown to be a commonly used value in studies based on accelerometers for recognizing human action [17]. Each action lasted 10 s, resulting in 500 triaxial acceleration samples per action. Each sample was saved in CSV format on the phone and later transferred via Bluetooth to a computer for analysis.

2.2 Data Preprocessing

The preprocessing of the collected data involved two steps: filtering and window segmentation. In this study, a Butterworth filter [18] was applied to remove noise from the data. For illustration, Fig. 1 shows the waveform of the acceleration signal on the y axis during a walking action before and after filtering. It can be observed that the solid line after filtering is smoother than the dashed line before filtering, reducing sharp peaks in the raw signal while preserving the overall trend of the motion data.

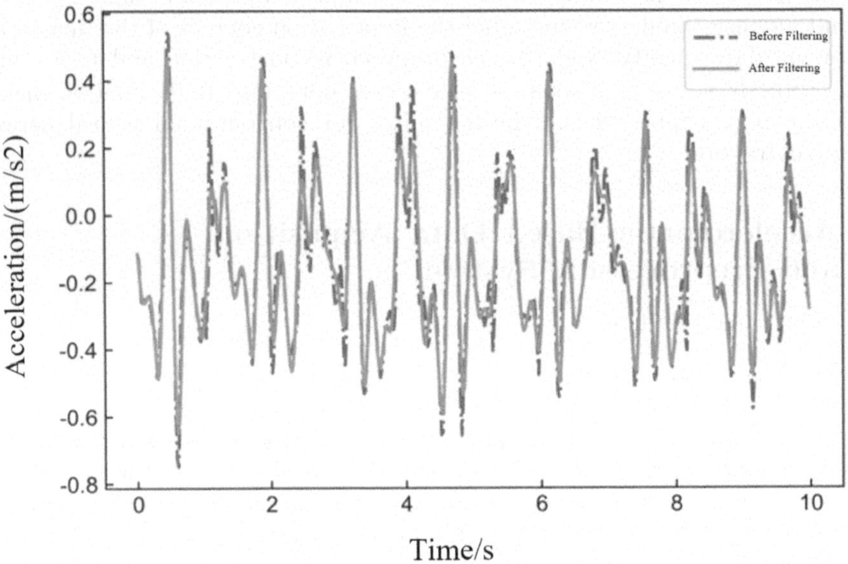

Fig. 1. Visualization of acceleration signal waveforms before and after filtering

During the windowing process, each window should contain at least one complete motion cycle and the window size should not be too large or too small. Otherwise, it may directly affect the training efficiency and accuracy of subsequent models. An excessively high overlap ratio may lead to overfitting of the model to the experimental data. Based on an analysis of the collected data and a review of the literature on human action recognition [19], this study set the window length to 2.56 s, with a 50% overlap between adjacent windows to ensure a certain correlation between neighboring samples. The visualization of the windowing process is shown in Fig. 2.

The list of data from the experimental sample after preprocessing is shown in Table 1. The final generated dataset is referred to as the HHAR database in this paper.

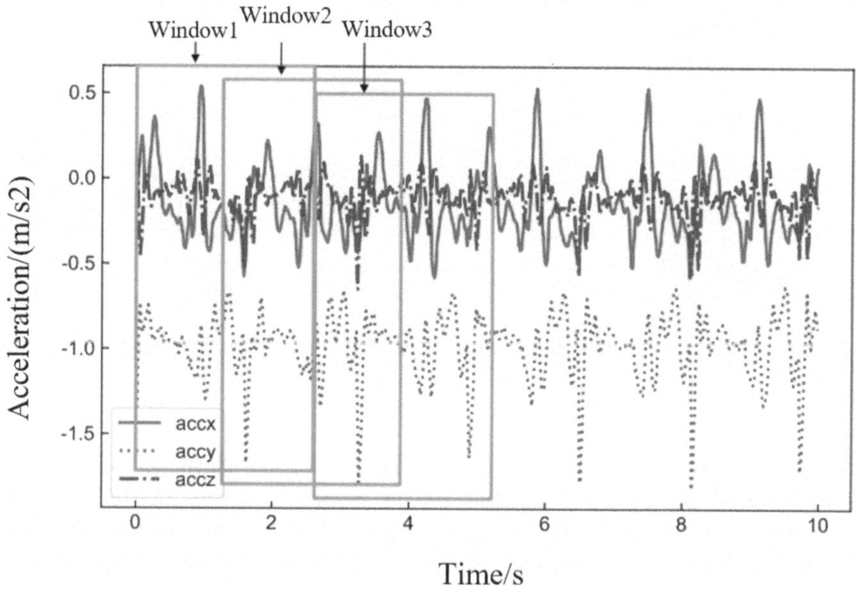

Fig. 2. Visualization of the data windowing process

Table 1. Number of samples before and after windowing for each action category.

Action Category	Pre-window	Post-window
Walking	250	1500
Running	200	1200
Jumping	220	1320
Ascending Stairs	200	1200
Descending Stairs	200	1200

3 Dynamic Human Action Recognition Network Architecture Based on Recurrence Plots and LeNet-5

In this study, we propose a network model that integrates recurrence plots with LeNet-5. By analyzing the characteristics of triaxial acceleration data from human actions, we observed that representing the hierarchical and recurrent properties of motion using recurrence plots is highly effective. Based on this observation, we designed a network model that combines recurrence plots with LeNet-5. The overall network architecture is illustrated in Fig. 3.

3.1 Data Reconstruction and Fusion Algorithm

First, the triaxial acceleration data within each window are separated into three individual acceleration sequences. Next, for each sequence, a recurrence plot with

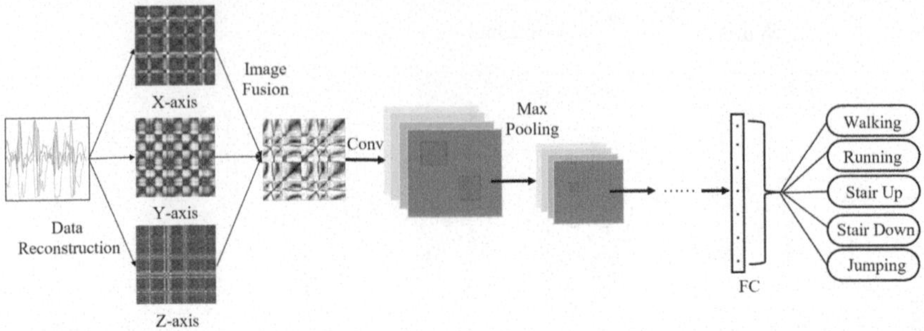

Fig. 3. Overall architecture of the proposed dynamic human action recognition network based on recurrence plots and LeNet-5

or without thresholding is computed to reconstruct the data. Finally, multiple two-dimensional images generated from the triaxial signals at the same time step are fused to produce the final experimental data required by the model. The structure of the data reconstruction and fusion algorithm is illustrated in Fig. 4.

In the data pre-processing stage, the window length is set to 2.56 seconds, which means that each experimental sample contains three acceleration sequences of length 128. A recurrence plot is computed separately for each sequence, and the resulting image consists of 128×128 pixels, that is, the size of each recurrence plot is 128×128. These images are then fused.

Note that in addition to image height and width, the number of channels is an important parameter in image storage formats. For example, a grayscale image has a single channel, whereas an RGB color image has three channels. For each window, data reconstruction generates three single-channel images corresponding to the x-, y-, and z-axis recurrence plots. These can be mapped to the R, G, and B channels of a color image. After the image fusion operation, the result is stored as a RGB image, which serves as input data for the deep learning model.

3.2 Feature Extraction from Fused Images

Taking into account the computational limitations and energy constraints of mobile devices for potential real-world deployment, this study uses an improved lightweight convolutional neural network, LeNet-5, to perform feature extraction on fused images.

The general framework of the convolutional neural network is shown in Fig. 5. The network consists of multiple hierarchical layers, each layer contains several two-dimensional feature maps. The architecture consists mainly of an input layer, convolutional layers, pooling layers, and fully connected layers. In this network, the initial input layer is responsible for receiving the experimental data fed into the model. The subsequent series of convolution and pooling operations extract

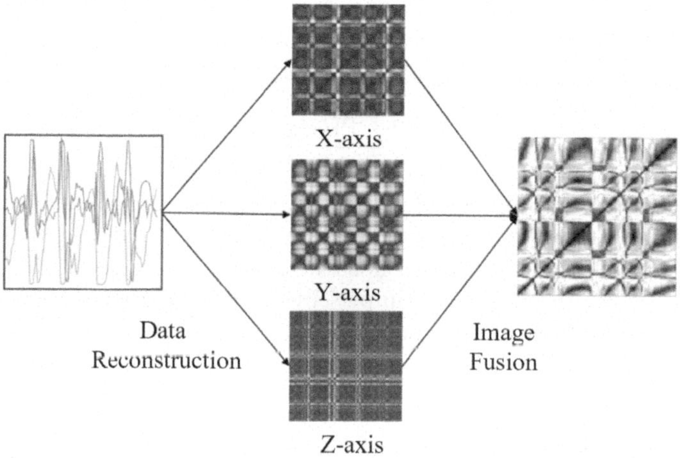

Fig. 4. Structure of the proposed data reconstruction and fusion algorithm

features from the input samples, while the final fully connected layers, which include multiple hidden layers, carry out the final classification task.

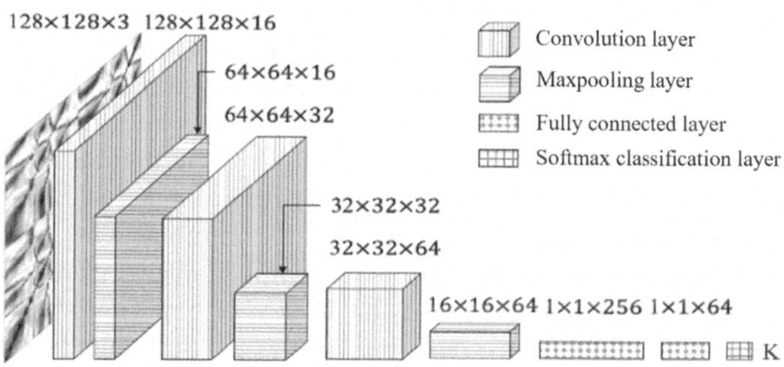

Fig. 5. Overall framework of the convolutional neural network for feature extraction

4 Experiments and Results Analysis

In the experimental evaluation stage, four commonly used metrics in the field of machine learning were selected to evaluate the network model: accuracy (A), precision (P), recall (R), and F1-score. They are defined as follows:

$$\text{Accuracy} = \frac{TP + TN}{TP + TN + FP + FN} \tag{1}$$

$$\text{Precision} = \frac{TP}{TP + FP} \tag{2}$$

$$\text{Recall} = \frac{TP}{TP + FN} \tag{3}$$

$$F1\text{-score} = \frac{2 \times \text{Precision} \times \text{Recall}}{\text{Precision} + \text{Recall}} \tag{4}$$

where TP denotes the number of true positives, i.e., the positive samples correctly predicted as positive; TN denotes the number of true negatives, i.e., the negative samples correctly predicted as negative; FP denotes the number of false positives, i.e., the negative samples incorrectly predicted as positive; and FN denotes the number of false negatives, i.e., the positive samples incorrectly predicted as negative.

4.1 Impact of Different Data Reconstruction Algorithms on Recognition Results

To investigate the effect of images generated by different data reconstruction algorithms on recognition performance, we conducted a comparative experiment between the thresholded and threshold-free recurrence plot methods proposed earlier. For the selection of the threshold parameter in the formula of the recurrence plot, we followed the "empirical rule" suggested in the related literature [20], where the threshold was set at 10% of the maximum diameter of the phase space. Considering that the choice of thresholds in other domains may differ from that in human action recognition, we additionally set the thresholds to 5%, 15%, and 20%, resulting in a total of 12 experimental groups.

The human action data collected were fed into 12 human action recognition networks that integrate recurrence plots (with different threshold values) and convolutional neural networks as input for model training. The initial parameters of the convolutional neural networks were kept identical in all experiments. Finally, the mean and median values of the 12 sets of experimental results were calculated. The box plot of the recognition results for different data reconstruction algorithms is shown in Fig. 6.

In Fig. 6, the horizontal axis represents different types of recurrence plots, including the threshold-free recurrence plot and thresholded recurrence plots with various threshold parameters, while the vertical axis represents the classification accuracy of the model. The horizontal line in each box indicates the median of multiple repeated experiments, and the triangle denotes the mean value. It can be clearly seen that the model using threshold-free recurrence plots achieves higher median and mean classification accuracy (0.978 and 0.976, respectively) than those using thresholded recurrence plots with various threshold parameters. These results indicate that employing threshold-free recurrence plots combined with LeNet-5 for feature extraction and classification yields better performance. In addition, the classification results of the threshold-free group are more concentrated compared to other combinations, which demonstrates that the final model exhibits stable performance in different test sets. Since the training and test sets were identical across all groups, this stability also indicates that the model possesses a certain degree of robustness, making it better suited for handling different test scenarios in practical applications. Therefore, threshold-free recurrence plots are used as the data reconstruction method for all subsequent experiments.

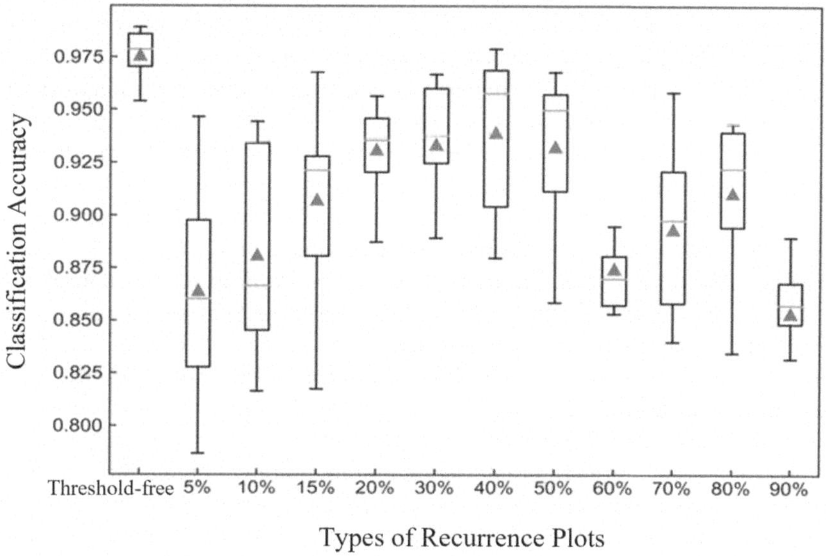

Fig. 6. Boxplot of classification results under different data reconstruction algorithms

4.2 Comprehensive Performance Comparison of Models Under Different Network Architectures

Considering that the human action recognition algorithm studied in this paper may be deployed in real-world applications in the future, a model with high classification accuracy but very high computational complexity would be difficult to apply widely on mobile devices of users. Therefore, we conduct a comprehensive performance comparison of models under different network architectures. The results are shown in Fig. 7. Figure 7 presents the comprehensive results of the performance comparison of models with different network architectures. The horizontal axis represents computational complexity, measured in millions of floating point operations (MFLOPs), which reflects the number of floating point operations required for a single forward pass of the algorithm. This metric is independent of whether a GPU is used and depends only on the complexity of the network, thereby eliminating the impact of different hardware on runtime and providing a more objective measure of model complexity. The vertical axis represents the classification accuracy corresponding to different network architectures. Each small circle in the figure corresponds to an experimental group with a specific network structure, and the text near each data point denotes the detailed network parameters. The label consists of three parts: (1) the first digit indicates the number of convolutional layers; (2) the second digit indicates the number of kernels in the first convolutional layer, and the number of kernels doubles in each subsequent layer. For example, if the first convolutional layer has 16 kernels, the second and third layers will have 32 and 64 kernels, respectively; (3) the third digit denotes the kernel size, where the digit "2" indicates a kernel size of 2 × 2.From Fig. 7, it can be seen that models with network structures (3.16.7), (3.32.5) and (3.32.7) achieve similar classification precision, all exceeding 98%. These three groups share a three-layer network structure with relatively large kernel sizes, indicating that deeper network architectures and larger kernels lead to better classification performance in deep learning-based human action recognition. Although the classification accuracy of (3.32.7) is not significantly higher than that of (3.16.7), the computational complexity of (3.32.7) is approximately four times higher. We infer that when using a 7 × 7 kernel, a smaller number of kernels is sufficient to extract discriminative features from the threshold-free recurrence plots of human action data. Blindly increasing the number of kernels does not help improve classification performance, but dramatically increases computational complexity.

In addition, the network structure (3.16.5) achieves a classification accuracy of 98%. Compared to (3.16.7), the classification accuracy decreases only by about 0. 3%, but the computational complexity is reduced by nearly 50%. This

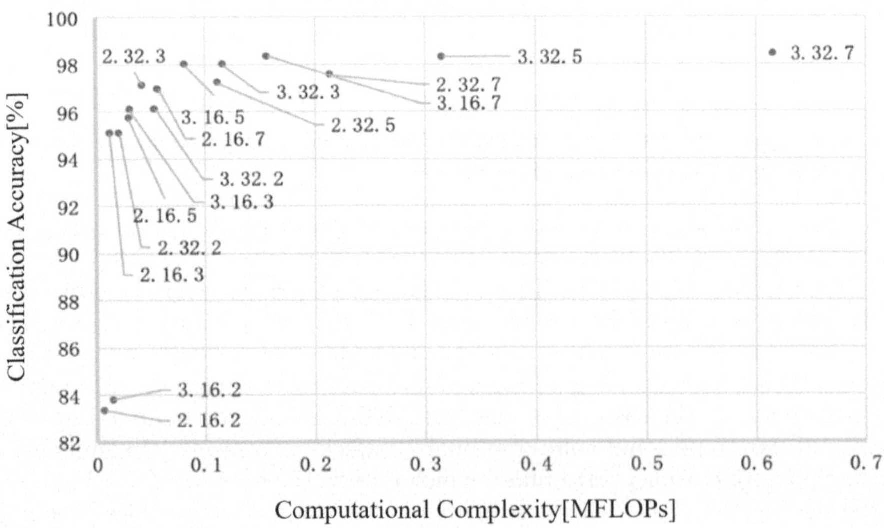

Fig. 7. Comprehensive performance comparison of models under different network architectures

result is particularly valuable for mobile devices, such as smart wristbands and smartwatches, where energy efficiency and battery life are critical.

4.3 Network Parameter Settings and Performance Analysis

During network training, the variations of the loss values in the training and validation sets, as well as the classification accuracy with respect to the number of training iterations, are shown in Fig. 8 and Fig. 9.

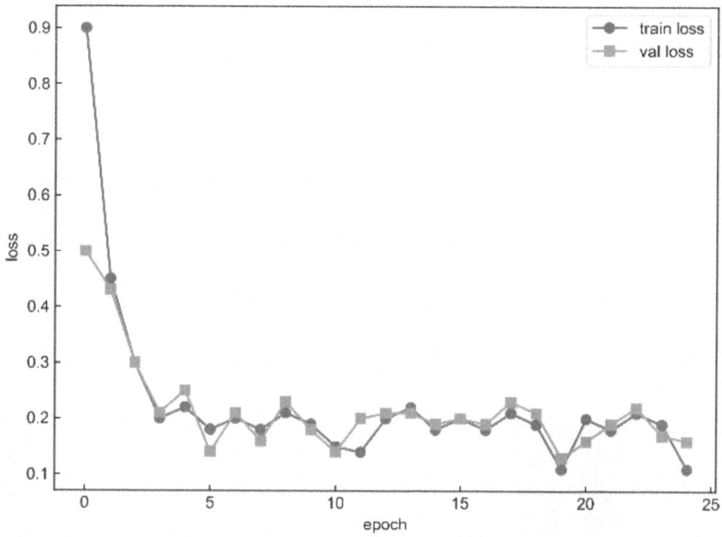

Fig. 8. Loss values on training and validation sets versus the number of iterations

In these figures, the horizontal axis corresponds to different epochs. In deep learning, an epoch refers to one complete pass through the entire training dataset. After each epoch, the model parameters are updated to achieve better performance. It can be observed that around the 10th epoch, both the network loss and classification accuracy begin to stabilize, indicating that the model starts to converge. The experiments show that when the dataset contains relatively low-complexity images, the model can quickly learn the discriminative features and achieve its best performance after only a few epochs. By examining the trends of various evaluation metrics on both the training and validation sets, we find that their overall trends are very similar. This indicates that the model performs similarly on the training and validation sets and there is no sign of overfitting or underfitting. Therefore, the model exhibits good generalizability and can adapt to new experimental data with reliable predictive performance.

The confusion matrix of the classification results on the HHAR database test set, obtained from the model with the highest classification accuracy during training, is shown in Fig. 10.

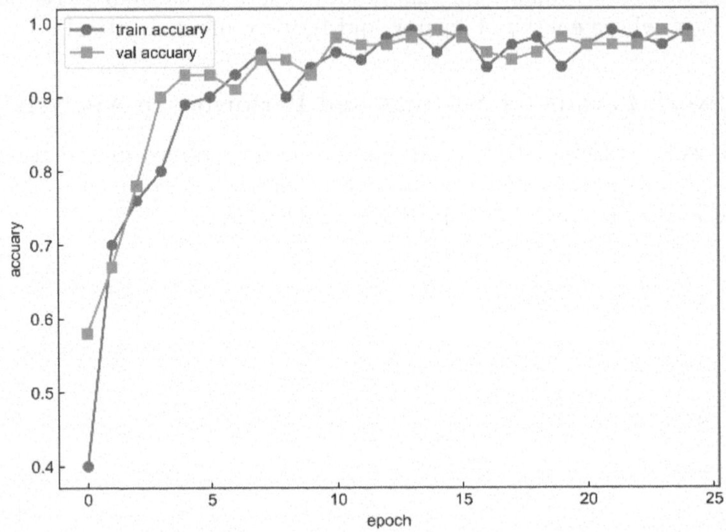

Fig. 9. Classification accuracy on training and validation sets versus the number of iterations

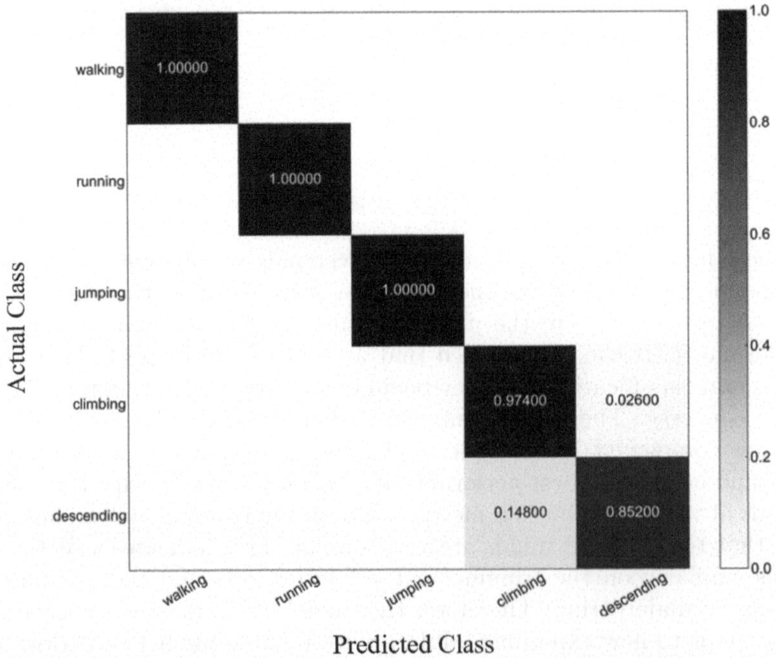

Fig. 10. Confusion matrix of classification results on the HHAR database test set

From the confusion matrix of classification, it can be observed that the three actions –walking, running, and jumping – achieve the accuracy of 100% classification, while most misclassifications occur between stairs. ascending and descending. A possible reason for these misclassifications is that, in order to make the collected data closer to daily life scenarios, no strict constraints were imposed on the volunteers' movements during data collection. This inevitably introduces a certain degree of misclassification.In this chapter, we analyze the influence of different convolutional neural network architectures on the accuracy of model classification. Considering the computational cost for potential deployment on mobile devices, we further compared the comprehensive performance of the models under different network architectures. Finally, the optimal network parameters were selected and the model was trained and tested on multiple public datasets. Based on these results, we analyzed the application scenarios of the proposed human action recognition approach, which combines recurrence plots and convolutional neural networks, and compared it with models from related research, demonstrating the advantages and feasibility of the proposed method.

5 Conclusion

Human action recognition technology based on inertial sensors has been widely applied in areas such as medical monitoring, virtual reality, and sports training. In recent years, extensive research efforts have been conducted worldwide on topics including daily human activity recognition, abnormal behavior detection, and gait analysis. Building upon previous studies, this work focuses on human action recognition methods using data collected from built-in sensors in mobile devices. The main contributions of this paper are summarized as follows:

1. A data acquisition and pre-processing system based on an accelerometer was designed. Before data collection, an action category library was established. Data from the built-in accelerometer of a smartphone during different actions were collected and transmitted to a host computer via Bluetooth. The collected data samples were then preprocessed, including label encoding, missing value handling, filtering and denoising, and window segmentation, resulting in data sets for subsequent model training and testing.
2. A human action recognition method based on support vector machines (SVM) was developed. The features were extracted from both the time and frequency domains and the principal component analysis (PCA) was used for the selection of the features. Comparative experiments with different kernel functions were conducted. The experimental results demonstrate that the SVM model with the RBF kernel is the most suitable, achieving effective recognition of common daily human actions.
3. A human action recognition method based on recurrence plots and convolutional neural networks (CNNs) was proposed. The triaxial acceleration signals produced by human movements were transformed into a single RGB color image using recurrence plots, a nonlinear analysis method, for data

reconstruction and fusion. The CNN was then used to automatically extract discriminative features from the images and perform the final action classification. Comparative experiments with different data reconstruction methods show that CNN models trained on datasets generated by threshold-free recurrence plots achieve better classification accuracy and outperform the SVM-based method proposed in Chap. 3.

In summary, the proposed human action recognition method based on recurrence plots and CNNs demonstrates significant advantages over existing research, particularly in recognizing dynamic human actions in complex scenarios. Future work may focus on designing a branched network structure for distinguishing between static and dynamic actions, first classifying the type (static/dynamic) and then performing recognition using separate specialized models, thus further enhancing the effectiveness of the proposed approach. Finally, comparative experiments with related work confirm the effectiveness of the proposed recurrence plot and the CNN-based human action recognition method.

Acknowledgments. This work was partially supported by the Liaoning Provincial Department of Science and Technology's "Unveiled and Leading" Science and Technology Project (2023JH1/10400081), the "Transplantation with Soil" Innovation Team Project of the "Liaoyang Talent Plan" (LYYC220501), the National Natural Science Foundation of China (No. 61100091), the Program for Liaoning Excellent Talents in University (LJQ2012007), and the SRF for ROCS, SEM ([2013]693).

Disclosure of Interests. The authors declare that they have no competing interests relevant to the content of this article.

References

1. Lemoyne, R., Mastroianni, T., Cozza, M., Coroian, C., Grundfest, W.: Implementation of an iPhone for characterizing Parkinson's disease tremor through a wireless accelerometer application. In: Engineering in Medicine & Biology Society, pp. 4954–4958 (2010). https://doi.org/10.1109/IEMBS.2010.5627240
2. Kinnunen, H., Tanskanen, M., Kyröläinen, H., Westerterp, K.R.: Wrist-worn accelerometers in assessment of energy expenditure during intensive training. Physiol. Meas. **33**(11), 1841 (2012). https://doi.org/10.1088/0967-3334/33/11/1841
3. Nordstrøm, M., Hansen, B.H., Paus, B., Kolset, S.O.: Accelerometer-determined physical activity and walking capacity in persons with down syndrome, Williams syndrome and Prader-Willi syndrome. Res. Dev. Disabil. **34**(12), 4395–4403 (2013). https://doi.org/10.1016/j.ridd.2013.09.021
4. Moeslund, T.B., Hilton, A., Krüger, V.: A survey of advances in vision-based human motion capture and analysis. IEEE Trans. Med. Imaging **104**(2–3), 90–126 (2006)
5. Najafi, B., Aminian, K., Paraschiv-Ionescu, A., Loew, F., Bula, C.J., Robert, P.: Ambulatory system for human motion analysis using a kinematic sensor: monitoring of daily physical activity in the elderly. IEEE Trans. Biomed. Eng. **50**(6), 711–723 (2003)

6. Jiang, M.: Research on human action monitoring and recognition based on somatosensory network. Ph.D. thesis, Liaoning (2012)
7. Wang, H.B.: Research on human behavior recognition based on tri-axial accelerometers. Ph.D. thesis, Jiangnan University (2014)
8. Saunders, J.B.D.M., Inman, V.T., Eberhart, H.D.: Major determinants in normal and pathological gait. J. Bone Joint Surg. **35-A**(3), 543–558 (1953)
9. Ghasemzadeh, H., Loseu, V., Guenterberg, E., Jafari, R.: Sport training using body sensor networks: a statistical approach to measure wrist rotation for golf swing. In: ICST Conference on Body Area Networks (BODYNETS) (2009). https://doi.org/10.4108/ICST.BODYNETS2009.6035
10. Thakur, D., Biswas, S.: An integration of feature extraction and guided regularized random forest feature selection for smartphone-based human activity recognition. J. Netw. Comput. Appl. **204**, 103417 (2022). https://doi.org/10.1016/j.jnca.2022.103417
11. Wang, C.X., Yang, X.J., Xu, Q.: Upper limb action recognition system based on three-dimensional accelerometer. J. Sens. Technol. **6**, 816–819 (2010). https://doi.org/10.3969/j.issn.1004-1699.2010.06.014
12. Liu, R., Liu, M.: Gesture recognition based on three-axis accelerometer. Comput. Eng. **37**(24), 141–143 (2011). https://doi.org/10.3969/j.issn.1000-3428.2011.24.047
13. Mekruksavanich, S., Jitpattanakul, A.: Classification of gait pattern with wearable sensing data. In: 2019 Joint International Conference on Digital Arts, Media and Technology (ECTI DAMT-NCON) (2019). https://doi.org/10.1109/ECTI-NCON.2019.8692229
14. Ahmed, N., Rafiq, J.I., Islam, M.R.: Enhanced human activity recognition based on smartphone sensor data using hybrid feature selection model. Sens. (Basel) **20**(1) (2020). https://doi.org/10.3390/s20010317
15. Zhao, Y., Jiang, T., Zou, W.: Gesture recognition system using reconstructed image from the acceleration sensor signal. In: IEEE International Symposium on Communications and Information Technologies (ISCIT) (2017). https://doi.org/10.1109/ISCIT.2017.8261169
16. Challa, S.K., Kumar, A., Semwal, V.B.: A multibranch CNN-BiLSTM model for human activity recognition using wearable sensor data. Vis. Comput. 1–15 (2021). https://doi.org/10.1007/s00371-021-02283-3
17. Bersch, S., Azzi, D., Khusainov, R., Achumba, I., Ries, J.: Sensor data acquisition and processing parameters for human activity classification. Sens. (Basel) **14**(3), 4239 (2014). https://doi.org/10.3390/s140304239
18. Anguita, D., Ghio, A., Oneto, L., Parra, X., Reyes-Ortiz, J.L.: A public domain dataset for human activity recognition using smartphones. In: Proceedings of the 21st European Symposium on Artificial Neural Networks (ESANN) (2013)
19. De Marsico, M., Mecca, A.: A survey on gait recognition via wearable sensors. ACM Comput. Surv. (CSUR) (2019). https://doi.org/10.1145/3340293
20. Marwan, N., Romano, M.C., Thiel, M., Kurths, J.: Recurrence plots for the analysis of complex systems. Phys. Rep. **438**(5–6), 237–329 (2007). https://doi.org/10.1016/j.physrep.2006.11.001

Efficient Two-Stream Fusion Network for Skeleton-Based Hand Gesture Recognition

Hongming Shao[1], Juan Li[1], Xiaoyi Wang[2(✉)], and Xuri Li[1]

[1] Beijing University of Technology, Beijing, China
{hongmingshao,juanli,xurili}@emails.bjut.edu.cn
[2] Qiyuan Lab, Beijing, China
xiaoyi.wang@email.qiyuanlab.com

Abstract. Research in the field of gesture recognition has made remarkable advancements. However, previous work often focused excessively on improving accuracy, resulting in complex network architectures, an enormous number of parameters, and high computational resource demands, making them difficult to apply in real-time scenarios. On the other hand, some approaches have concentrated on efficiency, but have struggled to achieve high model accuracy. Therefore, developing gesture recognition methods with fewer parameter and higher accuracy remains challenging. In this paper, we propose an efficient two-stream network with enhanced fusion for skeleton-based hand gestures recognition (ETNet),which assists the position feature stream (global information) with the orientation feature stream (dynamic information) while utilizing efficient feature extraction modules to maintain network lightweight. We further introduce an attention-based fusion to enhance the weight of key features from both streams, and use a classic classification head structure at the network's output layer to perform classification on the fused features. Eventually, through experiments compared with several state-of-the-art approaches, we demonstrate that our method achieves comparable results with fewer parameters on SHREC'17 Track and DHG-14/28 datasets, balancing both accuracy and efficiency.

Keywords: Hand Gesture Recognition · Gesture-based Interaction · Two-Stream Network · Real-time Interaction

1 Introduction

Real-time gesture recognition is crucial for intelligent interaction applications, yet existing algorithms often struggle with a trade-off: requiring substantial GPU power for accuracy or sacrificing accuracy for speed. Addressing this efficiency-accuracy balance is a key goal.

S. Guo et al. (Eds.): HHME 2025, CCIS 2878, pp. 40–53, 2027.
https://doi.org/10.1007/978-981-92-3991-7_4

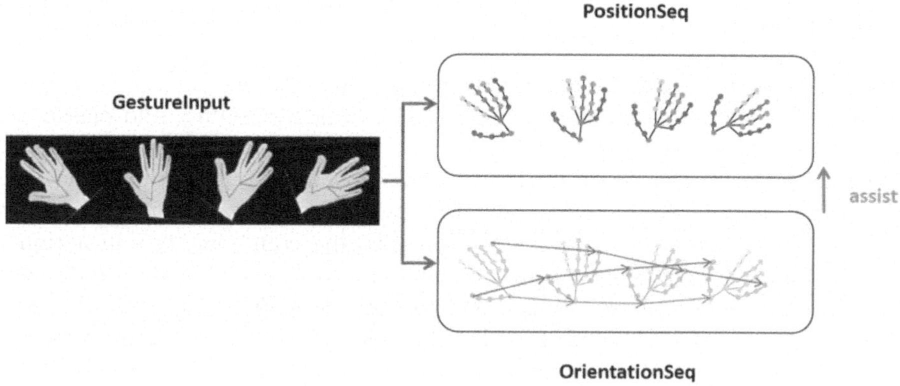

Fig. 1. Employ orientation sequence to assist position sequence as a supplementary dynamic information source.

Gesture recognition inputs are typically images or skeletons. Skeletons, being sparse yet feature-rich, are preferred for lightweight designs over noise-prone images. Mainstream deep learning methods predominantly use skeleton sequences. Inspired by [1], Graph Convolutional Networks (GCNs) [2–4] leverage graph topology to enhance skeleton relationships but face transferability issues and high training costs (memory, speed). Two-stream networks [5–7] can improve accuracy with more input features, but their fusion modules are demanding, simple concatenation can be detrimental, and network complexity often doubles, degrading performance.

As illustrated in Fig 1, global skeleton coordinate sequences lack non-temporal dynamic features, which orientation vectors can provide. Effective fusion can amplify these two-stream benefits, while lightweight feature extraction can mitigate performance overhead. Based on this, we propose an efficient two-stream network with enhanced fusion. It uses skeleton position sequences (global stream) assisted by computed skeleton orientation sequences (dynamic stream). Inspired by EfficientNetV2 [8], efficient MBConv/FusedMBConv blocks process both streams. An attention-based fusion module then integrates these streams, enhancing key features without letting the auxiliary stream weaken the main one, before a classification head predicts gestures.

- We propose an efficient two-stream network with enhanced fusion(ETNet) for skeleton-based hand gestures recognition, which represents gestures as both position and orientational information, employing a effective two-stream structure and an attention-based enhanced fusion mechanism that balances accuracy and efficiency.
- Experiments on benchmarks demonstrate that ETNet achieves state-of-the-art accuracy on the SHREC'17 Track dataset and delivers comparable results with fewer parameters when compared to several state-of-the-art approaches.

2 Related Work

Skeleton-Based Hand Gesture Recognition extracts information from hand skeleton sequences for gesture recognition, understanding, and classification, without strictly differentiating from dynamic action recognition. Skeletons are crucial for action recognition due to their close relation to human motion. As a sparse, lightweight modality, skeleton data processing is computationally inexpensive. This abstract representation, capturing commonalities in actions, generally affords strong generalization capabilities to these recognition methods.

Traditional skeleton-based action recognition methods [9,10] utilized handcrafted features. While computationally efficient and robust to small datasets, these features are sensitive to data variations and prone to information loss, leading to poor generalization. Deep learning has since become prominent, with various approaches applied to this task. CNN-based methods [11–13] transform skeleton data into formats like matrices or images for network input. RNN-based methods, including LSTM and GRU [14–16], capture the temporal nature of action sequences. Hybrid approaches [17–20] combine CNNs for spatial feature extraction and LSTMs for temporal evolution. Transformer-based methods [21,22] use skeleton position encoding/decoding for long-term dependencies and accuracy.

GCN-based methods [2–4,23] have gained success by modeling the topological structure and spatiotemporal features of skeletons. Some two-stream network methods [9,10] process original and second-order features independently before fusion, emphasizing richer spatiotemporal information from second-order features for improved accuracy. Departing from deeper networks, [24] introduced the lightweight Semantic Guidance Network (SGN) for gesture recognition, significantly reducing model size. Furthermore, approaches like [1,25] employ 1D-CNN frameworks, focusing on input feature research for excellent performance.While existing methods have explored both high-accuracy models, such as GCNs, and various lightweight networks, bridging the performance gap to achieve both recognition accuracy and computational efficiency has become a core challenge that urgently needs to be addressed in the field.

3 Method

This section details our proposed efficient two-stream network for skeleton-based hand gesture recognition, which separately extracts and subsequently fuses position and orientation features for prediction. The network's feature extraction components adapt EfficientNetV2 [8] concepts, for which we manually configured FusedMBConv and MBConv blocks for skeleton data, avoiding Neural Architecture Search (NAS) for transferability. A specialized enhanced fusion mechanism is incorporated for effective two-stream feature integration. The overall architecture is depicted in Fig 2.

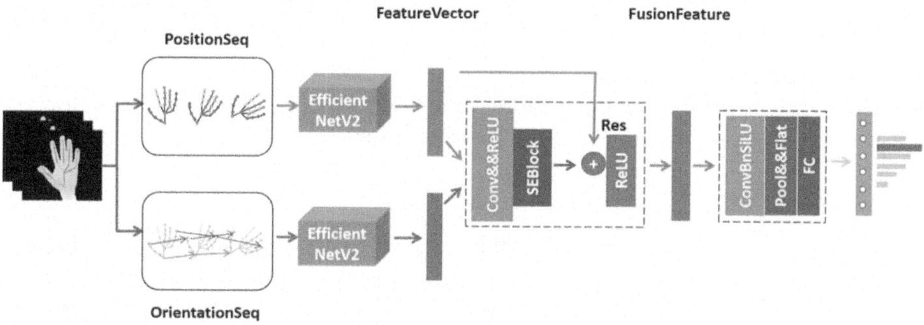

Fig. 2. The framework architecture of our ETNet. Gestures are represented as position sequences and orientation sequences, with the orientation sequence serving as a supplementary dynamic information source. The concept of EfficientNetV2 is adopted, utilizing FusedMBConv and MBConv as our backbone to implement efficient feature extraction. Attention mechanisms (via the SE Block) and residual connections are employed to enhance the fusion of position and orientation features. A classical classification head structure is employed for result prediction.

3.1 Position and Orientation as Input

The classic input used in skeleton-based gesture recognition is typically the position sequence of skeletons, which provides global information that aids the network in understanding the structural information of the skeletons on every frame. However, the sequence does not directly capture dynamic features such as the orientation and velocity of movement. Consequently, some detailed information may be lost during the convolution process along the non-temporal dimensions, on the other hand, the orientation sequence serves as a typical dynamic feature, offering a more effective representation of the movement trends of the skeletons. As a natural dynamic feature, it complements the lack of dynamic information during the convolution of position data along non-temporal dimensions. Moreover, the relative motion information embedded in the orientation sequence is less sensitive to the deviation of absolute positions, thus better mitigating the interference caused by global position noise. Therefore, adopting both position and orientation sequences as inputs enables the network to more effectively learn the detailed features of gesture data.

In this work, we propose a two-stream network architecture, with each stream processing a different type of input sequence. The two input types are: the position sequence and the orientation sequence, both of which are represented in a 4-dimensional tensor format. The input data for each stream are structured as $[B, C, J, T]$, where:B is the batch size,C is the number of channels, representing the spatial dimensions (XYZ coordinates for the position sequence) or the three components of the relative motion vector (for the orientation sequence),J is the number of joints or keypoints, T is the number of time frames in the sequence. Let $P_b \in \mathbb{R}^{C \times J \times T}$ represent the position sequence for the b-th sample in the batch, and let $O_b \in \mathbb{R}^{C\times J\times T}$ represent the orientation sequence for the same sample.

Position Sequence. The position sequence $P_b = [P_{b,1}, P_{b,2}, \ldots, P_{b,T}]$ for the b-th sample is given by 3D coordinates of J joints over T frames, where:

$$P_{b,t} = [x_{b,t,j}, y_{b,t,j}, z_{b,t,j}]^T \quad \text{for } t = 1, 2, \ldots, T,\ j = 1, 2, \ldots, J$$

Each element of the tensor P_b a 3D position vector for joint j at time step t. The position sequence simply represents the absolute spatial coordinates of the joints.

Orientation Sequence. The orientation sequence $O_b = [O_{b,1}, O_{b,2}, \ldots, O_{b,T}]$ is derived from the temporal differences in the position sequence. Specifically, the relative motion vector (orientation vector) at time t is computed as the difference between the position at time t and the position at time $t-1$:

$$O_{b,t} = P_{b,t} - P_{b,t-1} = (x_{b,t,j} - x_{b,t-1,j}, y_{b,t,j} - y_{b,t-1,j}, z_{b,t,j} - z_{b,t-1,j})$$

Thus, the orientation sequence $O_b$is a tensor of shape $[C, J, T-1]$,where $C = 3$ for the three components of the motion vector, and $T-1$ denotes the time steps after the first. for the first frame, we use a zero vector to keep the tensor of shape $[C, J, T]$.Since the orientation data can be directly computed from the position input, we allow the outer network to accept only the position sequence, while placing the computation of the orientation vector sequence on the device at the very beginning of the model's forward pass. Subsequently, the features of the two-stream network are fed into the model. When the target device is a GPU, this approach helps accelerate the inference process of the network.

3.2 Features Extract

EfficientNetV2 introduces FusedMBConv and a progressive learning strategy, significantly accelerating the training speed of the network while maintaining a low parameter count compared to EfficientNet [26]. We aim to adopt its core architecture for feature extraction to alleviate the pressure of trainable parameters brought by the two-stream network structure. The position sequence and orientation sequence, obtained in the previous section, are passed into two structurally identical blocks for feature extraction. Benefiting from the efficient implementation of EfficientNetV2, the structure of our feature extraction layer is shown in Fig3.

Given that our skeleton data sequences are sparse, and the initial channels in the network are relatively few, shallow feature extraction does not require highly separated convolution operations. Therefore, the FusedMBConv operation with a single step is more efficient, helping prevent the premature filtering of inter-channel relationships in the skeletons while accelerating the early feature dimensionality expansion. Depthwise separable convolutions and expansion factors are more suitable for capturing sparse global spatiotemporal features in

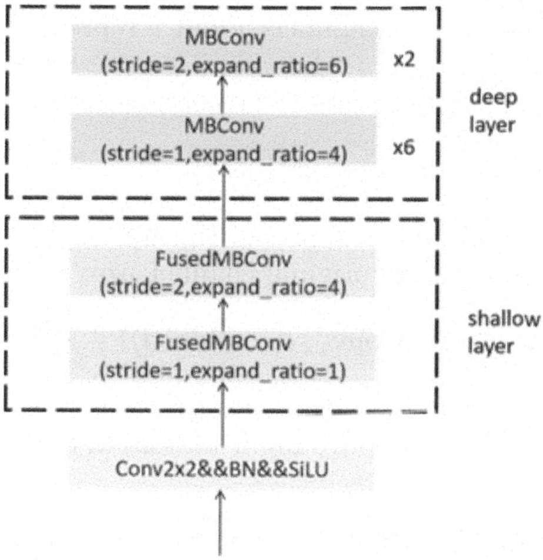

Fig. 3. The structure of the backbone module. By adopting the concept of EfficientNetV2, In the shallow layers, FusedMBConv is employed, while in the deeper layers, MBConv blocks are stacked, thereby achieving efficient feature extraction.

higher layers, while simultaneously controlling the parameter count by reducing attention to inter-channel relationships. As a result, at the later stages of the network, high-dimensional global dynamic features of the skeletons can be effectively captured through multiple MBConv blocks in the deeper layers.

Based on the above analysis, the shallow layers of our network for each input stream employ a FusedMBConv block (`stride=1, expand_ratio=1`) followed by a second FusedMBConv block (`stride=2, expand_ratio=4`). In the subsequent deeper layers, where feature channels are processed in a higher-dimensional space, we sequentially stack six MBConv blocks (`stride=1, expand_ratio=4`) and two MBConv blocks (`stride=2, expand_ratio=6`). These modules form the core of the feature extraction stage. This architecture allows each of the two input sequences to yield high-quality features for subsequent fusion and classification. Furthermore, this design ensures an efficient feature extraction process and an optimized number of trainable parameters.

3.3 Enhanced Fusion

The Fusion module is designed to combine and enhance features from two separate sources. It takes as input two feature tensors, processes them through a series of operations, and outputs a fused feature representation. This module leverages both channel-wise feature fusion and selective enhancement to ensure that the resulting features retain important information from both input streams.

Preliminary Fusion. We first perform preliminary fusion on the input features to obtain a unified representation for subsequent processing. Let the input feature tensors be feature1 $\in \mathbb{R}^{B\times C\times J\times T}$ and feature2 $\in \mathbb{R}^{B\times C\times J\times T}$. Where B is the batch size,C is the number of channels,J and T represent the dimensions generated by the feature extraction module. The feature tensors are concatenated along the channel dimension, yielding the combined tensor:

$$\text{combined} = \text{concat}(\text{feature1}, \text{feature2}) \in \mathbb{R}^{B \times 2C \times J \times T}$$

Next, the concatenated tensor is passed through a 1×1 convolution, which projects the features back to the original channel size:

$$\text{pre}_{\text{fused}} = \text{ReLU}(\text{Conv}_{1\times 1}(\text{combined})) \in \mathbb{R}^{B \times C \times J \times T}$$

The 1×1 convolution reduces the number of channels from 2C to C,thus integrating the information from both input tensors to form a preliminary fusion result.

Recalibrate Channel Weights. We aim for the preliminary fusion results to filter out some unimportant feature channels while enhancing the proportion of effective features. The focus is on ensuring that each important channel can attend to global information. The fused features are then passed through a Squeeze-and-Excitation (SE) block [27], which adaptively recalibrates the importance of each channel. First Global average pooling computes the channel-wise mean across the dimensions J and T of the feature map. For each channel c, the global average pooling operation is defined as:

$$y_c = \frac{1}{J \times T} \sum_{j=1}^{J} \sum_{t=1}^{T} (\text{pre}_{\text{fused}})_{b,c,j,t}$$

The result is a tensor $y \in \mathbb{R}^{B \times C}$ where each element represents the average value of a channel across the dimensions J and T.Then the pooled tensor y is passed through two fully connected (FC) layers to learn channel dependencies:

$$z = \text{FC}_2(\text{ReLU}(\text{FC}_1(y)))$$

Then a *Sigmoid* activation is applied to produce channel-wise attention weights:

$$y = \frac{1}{1 + \exp(-z)} \in \mathbb{R}^{B \times C}$$

Finally, the output y is reshaped to $\mathbb{R}^{B \times C \times 1 \times 1}$ and used to rescale the fused feature tensor $fused_{pre}$ element-wise, enhancing important channels while suppressing less relevant ones:

$$\text{fused} = \text{fused}_{\text{pre}} \times y$$

Final Optimization. To prevent the loss of critical information from the original global input, a residual connection is employed.

$$\text{output} = \text{ReLU}(\text{fused} + \text{feature1})$$

This ensures that the dynamic auxiliary information is fused, and the features of certain channels are enhanced, such that the original global features are at least not lost. This design enables the model to effectively combine and enhance features, leveraging the complementary information from the input streams.

3.4 Final Output

At the model's end, a classic classification head efficiently transforms features into class predictions using a sequential design. It begins with a 1×1 convolutional layer, followed by batch normalization for stable training and better generalization, and a SiLU activation function for non-linearity. Global average pooling then aggregates spatial information into a compact representation, reducing complexity while retaining global characteristics. The features are subsequently flattened. A dropout layer is applied to prevent overfitting, and finally, a fully connected layer maps these processed features to the class outputs. This architecture systematically refines features for computational efficiency and high predictive accuracy.

4 Experiments

4.1 Datasets

We evaluate our model on two classical benchmarks (SHREC'17 Track [28],DHG-14/28 [10]).

SHREC'17 Track. The dataset consists of 14 gesture sequences, performed in two ways: using a single finger and the entire hand. Each gesture is performed 1 to 10 times by 28 participants, resulting in a total of 2800 sequences. The dataset consists of depth images and hand skeletons, and we solely use the 3D skeletons data.

DHG-14/28. The DHG-14/28 dataset adopts a similar collection method to the SHREC'17 Track dataset, producing 2800 sequences performed 5 times by 20 participants. As such, we only use the 3D skeletons data.

4.2 Train Details

All experiments were conducted using Pytorch on NVIDIA RTX 3060 mobile graphics card. The training was conducted using a batch size of 32 for 100 epochs, with an Adam optimizer (learning rate = 0.001, weight decay = 5e-4) and a cross-entropy loss function. A learning rate scheduler was applied with a factor of 0.1, a patience of 10 epochs, and a minimum learning rate of 1e-8.

Table 1. Recognition accuracy (%) of our method for different input structure on SHREC'17 Track dataset and DHG-14/28 dataset.

Method	SHREC 14G	SHREC 28G	DHG 14G	DHG 28G
Single Stream	95.18	92.32	91.61	89.11
Two-Stream	95.89	93.57	92.14	89.64
Two-Stream+Enhanced Fusion	97.32	94.82	93.57	90.36

4.3 Ablation Study

To investigate the impact of various components in our model, we conduct all ablation experiments on both the SHREC'17 Track and DHG-14/28 datasets.

Different Input Structure. To assess the impact of assisting position features with gesture orientation features in a two-stream architecture, we first established a baseline single-stream network (EfficientNetV2-like) using only position sequences. We then implemented a two-stream structure with a simple fusion mechanism (concatenation plus a convolution layer). As shown in Table 1, this simple two-stream approach outperformed the baseline by 0.71% (SHREC'17-14) and 1.25% (SHREC'17-28), and approximately 0.5% on DHG-14/28 datasets. We attribute the modest gains to simple fusion equally weighting auxiliary orientation features with primary position features, which is suboptimal for relative dynamic orientation data. In our complete model, we apply an attention-based enhanced fusion mechanism. Compared to the simple fusion two-stream structure, this full model achieved additional improvements of 1.43% (SHREC'17-14), 1.25% (SHREC'17-28), 1.43% (DHG-14/28-14), and 0.72% (DHG-14/28-28). This clearly indicates that the fusion layer's recalibration of feature weights significantly boosts recognition accuracy.

Different Backbone Layers. To explore the influence of different MBConv layers on the performance, we configured the deep modules of the backbone network differently and conducted experiments on the SHREC'17 Track dataset with 14 gestures protocol. Results are shown in Fig. 4. The examined settings include: a single MBConv layer with a stride of 2(Layer1); a sequence of three MBConv layers with a stride of 1 followed by one with a stride of 2(Layer4); and a deeper sequence consisting of six MBConv layers with a stride of 1 followed by two with a stride of 2(Layer8). As observed from the results, the model with the minimal layer configuration achieves the lowest parameter count and the fastest inference speed, but also yields the lowest accuracy at 95.71%. While the Layer4 configuration shows only a marginal improvement in accuracy, its inference time increases by 2.95 ms, indicating a noticeable upward trend. The full version of ETNet (Layer8) achieves the highest accuracy, but this comes at the cost of further increased inference time.

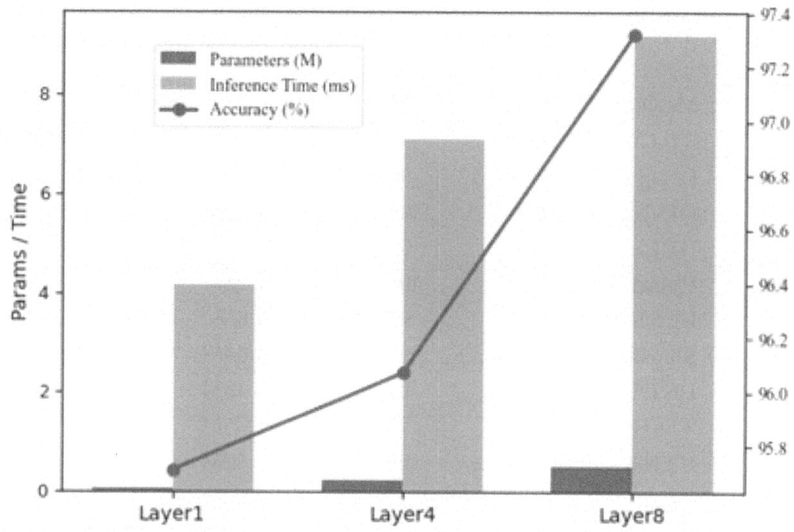

Fig. 4. Influence of different MBConv layers on the performance on the SHREC'17 Track dataset with 14 gestures protocol.

4.4 Comparison with the State-of-the-Art

To validate the performance of ETNet, we conducted experimental comparisons with several state-of-the-art methods on both the SHREC'17 Track and DHG-14/28 datasets, respectively.

SHREC'17 Track Dataset. To provide a more comprehensive comparison in terms of both accuracy and efficiency, we selected multiple categories of SOTA methods from the field: Graph Convolutional Network (GCN)-based approaches [2,23], Transformer-based methods [22,29], Long Short-Term Memory (LSTM)-based methods [15,16], and 1D-CNN-based methods including [1,25], as well as two-stream feature-based approaches [7].

Table 2 presents the recognition accuracy and corresponding parameter counts for all methods, with most data sourced from the respective papers. Notably, some papers [23,29]did not disclose the model parameter counts, so we ran the source code of these papers on the SHREC'17 Track dataset to obtain the parameter counts. Due to memory overflow issues, the method in [22] could not run on our GPU, and [7] did not release the source code. Therefore, we only report their accuracy data from the respective papers.

Our method achieved an accuracy of 97.32% and 94.82% on the 14 gestures and 28 gestures protocol, respectively. Notably, our method achieved state-of-the-art performance on the 14 gestures protocol, with the fewest parameters (0.52M). For the 28 gestures protocol, the best performance was still maintained by [2], with our method falling short by 0.54%.

Table 2. Recognition accuracy and comparison with the state-of-the-art approaches on SHREC'17 Track dataset.14G and 28G represent 14 and 28 gestures protocol settings.

Method	SHREC 14G	SHREC 28G	parameters
ST-GCN	92.7	87.7	3.08M
DG-STA	94.4	90.7	–
DD-Net	94.6	91.9	1.82M
HPEV	94.9	92.3	–
PointLSTM	95.9	94.7	1.2M
FPPR-PCD	96.1	95.2	4.6M
Sharing-Net	96.55	95.26	3.64M
DSTA-Net	97.0	93.9	3.43M
TD-GCN	97.02	95.36	1.35M
ETNet(ours)	97.32	94.82	0.52M

Table 3. Recognition accuracy and comparison with the state-of-the-art approaches on DHG dataset.14G and 28G represent 14 and 28 gestures protocol settings.

Method	DHG 14G	DHG 28G	parameters
ST-GCN	91.2	87.1	3.08M
DG-STA	91.90	88.0	–
HPEV	92.54	88.86	–
FPPR-PCD	92.0	91.7	4.6M
DSTA-Net	93.8	90.9	3.43M
TD-GCN	93.9	91.4	1.35M
ETNet(ours)	93.57	90.36	0.52M

DHG-14/28 Dataset. In the previous benchmark comparison, several methods, such as [1,15,25], did not disclose their training results on the DHG-14/28 dataset, so these methods were excluded from the comparison.

The results are shown in Table 3. On the DHG-14/28 dataset, the state-of-the-art performance on the 14-gesture protocol and 28-gesture protocol was maintained by [2] and [16], respectively. Although our method has the fewest parameters (0.52M), its performance fell short of the best results by 0.33% and 1.34% on the two protocols. Upon analysis, we believe that the configuration of the feature extraction blocks may be one contributing factor. Due to the leave-one-subject-out experimental protocol [10], the DHG-14/28 dataset is relatively more challenging. Furthermore, we did not employ the Neural Architecture Search (NAS) technique proposed by EfficientNetV2 to determine the optimal block configuration for this benchmark, but rather reused the block configuration from SHREC'17 Track to ensure network transferability for gesture recognition tasks.

5 Conclusion

We present an efficient two-stream network with enhanced fusion for skeleton-based hand gesture recognition, representing gestures as position and orientation sequences. Through the efficient two-stream architecture and an attention-based enhanced fusion module, our method strikes a balance between accuracy and efficiency. Experimental results demonstrate that our approach achieves comparable performance on two benchmarks with fewer parameters with several state-of-the-art methods. However, there remains room for improvement in the design of the feature extraction module, which will be a primary focus in future work. Additionally, due to its lightweight design, our method holds great potential for real-time applications.

References

1. Zhao, Y., Gao, Q., Ju, Z., Zhou, J., Guo, Y.: Sharing-net: Lightweight feedforward network for skeleton-based action recognition based on information sharing mechanism. Pattern Recogn. **146**, 110050 (2024)
2. Liu, J., Wang, X., Wang, C., Gao, Y., Liu, M.: Temporal decoupling graph convolutional network for skeleton-based gesture recognition. IEEE Trans. Multimedia **26**, 811–823 (2023)
3. Liu, Z., Zhang, H., Chen, Z., Wang, Z., Ouyang, W.: Disentangling and unifying graph convolutions for skeleton-based action recognition. In: Proceedings of the IEEE/CVF Conference on Computer Vision and Pattern Recognition, pp. 143–152 (2020)
4. Peng, W., Hong, X., Chen, H., Zhao, G.: Learning graph convolutional network for skeleton-based human action recognition by neural searching. In: Proceedings of the AAAI Conference on Artificial Intelligence, vol. 34, pp. 2669–2676 (2020)
5. Zhang, J.-K., Li, Q., Lyu, X.-Q., Liang, Y.: Two-stream spatial-temporal fusion graph convolutional network for dynamic gesture recognition. In: 2022 8th International Conference on Virtual Reality (ICVR), pp. 444–453. IEEE (2022)
6. Shi, L., Zhang, Y., Cheng, J., Lu, H.: Two-stream adaptive graph convolutional networks for skeleton-based action recognition. In: Proceedings of the IEEE/CVF Conference on Computer Vision and Pattern Recognition, pp. 12026–12035 (2019)
7. Liu, J., Liu, Y., Wang, Y., Prinet, V., Xiang, S., Pan, C.: Decoupled representation learning for skeleton-based gesture recognition. In: Proceedings of the IEEE/CVF Conference on Computer Vision and Pattern Recognition, pp. 5751–5760 (2020)
8. Tan, M., Le, Q.: EfficientNetv2: smaller models and faster training. In: International Conference on Machine Learning, pp. 10096–10106. PMLR (2021)
9. Vemulapalli, R., Arrate, F., Chellappa, R.: Human action recognition by representing 3D skeletons as points in a lie group. In: Proceedings of the IEEE Conference on Computer Vision and Pattern Recognition, pp. 588–595 (2014)
10. De Smedt, Q., Wannous, H., Vandeborre, J.-P.: Skeleton-based dynamic hand gesture recognition. In: Proceedings of the IEEE Conference on Computer Vision and Pattern Recognition Workshops, pp. 1–9 (2016)
11. Du, Y., Fu, Y., Wang, L.: Skeleton based action recognition with convolutional neural network. In: 2015 3rd IAPR Asian Conference on Pattern Recognition (ACPR), pp. 579–583. IEEE (2015)

12. Choutas, V., Weinzaepfel, P., Revaud, J., Schmid, C.: Potion: pose motion representation for action recognition. In: Proceedings of the IEEE Conference on Computer Vision and Pattern Recognition, pp. 7024–7033 (2018)
13. Devineau, G., Moutarde, F., Xi, W., Yang, J.: Deep learning for hand gesture recognition on skeletal data. In: 2018 13th IEEE International Conference on Automatic Face & Gesture Recognition (FG 2018), pp. 106–113. IEEE (2018)
14. Sharma, A., Singh, R.: ConvST-LSTM-net: convolutional spatiotemporal LSTM networks for skeleton-based human action recognition. Int. J. Multimedia Inf. Retrieval **12**(2), 34 (2023)
15. Min, Y., Zhang, Y., Chai, X., Chen, Y.: An efficient pointLSTM for point clouds based gesture recognition. In: Proceedings of the IEEE/CVF Conference on Computer Vision and Pattern Recognition, pp. 5761–5770 (2020)
16. Bigalke, A., Heinrich, M.P.: Fusing posture and position representations for point cloud-based hand gesture recognition. In: 2021 International Conference on 3D Vision (3DV), pp. 617–626. IEEE (2021)
17. Lai, K., Yanushkevich, S.N.: CNN+ RNN depth and skeleton based dynamic hand gesture recognition. In: 2018 24th International Conference on Pattern Recognition (ICPR), pp. 3451–3456. IEEE (2018)
18. Nunez, J.C., Cabido, R., Pantrigo, J.J., Montemayor, A.S., Velez, J.F.: Convolutional neural networks and long short-term memory for skeleton-based human activity and hand gesture recognition. Pattern Recogn. **76**, 80–94 (2018)
19. Si, C., Chen, W., Wang, W., Wang, L., Tan, T.: An attention enhanced graph convolutional LSTM network for skeleton-based action recognition. In: Proceedings of the IEEE/CVF Conference on Computer Vision and Pattern Recognition, pp. 1227–1236 (2019)
20. Zhang, P., Lan, C., Xing, J., Zeng, W., Xue, J., Zheng, N.: View adaptive neural networks for high performance skeleton-based human action recognition. IEEE Trans. Pattern Anal. Mach. Intell. **41**(8), 1963–1978 (2019)
21. Hou, J., Wang, G., Chen, X., Xue, J.-H., Zhu, R., Yang, H.: Spatial-temporal attention Res-TCN for skeleton-based dynamic hand gesture recognition. In: Proceedings of the European conference on computer vision (ECCV) workshops (2018)
22. Chen, Y., Zhao, L., Peng, X., Yuan, J., Metaxas, D.N.: Construct dynamic graphs for hand gesture recognition via spatial-temporal attention. arXiv preprint arXiv:1907.08871 (2019)
23. Yan, S., Xiong, Y., Lin, D.: Spatial temporal graph convolutional networks for skeleton-based action recognition. In: Proceedings of the AAAI Conference on Artificial Intelligence, vol. 32 (2018)
24. Zhang, P., Lan, C., Zeng, W., Xing, J., Xue, J., Zheng, N.: Semantics-guided neural networks for efficient skeleton-based human action recognition. In: Proceedings of the IEEE/CVF Conference on Computer Vision and Pattern Recognition, pp. 1112–1121 (2020)
25. Yang, F., Wu, Y., Sakti, S., Nakamura, S.: Make skeleton-based action recognition model smaller, faster and better. In: Proceedings of the 1st ACM International Conference on Multimedia in Asia, pp. 1–6 (2019)
26. Tan, M., Le, Q.: EfficientNet: rethinking model scaling for convolutional neural networks. In: International Conference on Machine Learning, pp. 6105–6114. PMLR (2019)
27. Hu, J., Shen, L., Sun, G.: Squeeze-and-excitation networks. In: Proceedings of the IEEE Conference on Computer Vision and Pattern Recognition, pp. 7132–7141 (2018)

28. De Smedt, Q., Wannous, H., Vandeborre, J.-P., Guerry, J., Le Saux, B., Filliat, D.: Shrec'17 track: 3D hand gesture recognition using a depth and skeletal dataset. In: 3DOR-10th Eurographics Workshop on 3D Object Retrieval, pp. 1–6 (2017)
29. Shi, L., Zhang, Y., Cheng, J., Lu, H.: Decoupled spatial-temporal attention network for skeleton-based action-gesture recognition. In: Proceedings of the Asian Conference on Computer Vision (2020)

FlexiStiff-Fabric: A Programmable Stiffness 3D-Printed Fabric Technology Based on Dual-Material Interlocking Weaving

Jiacheng Cao[1], Runjun Liu[2], Yicheng Wang[1], Jiarong Zhang[1], Zhaojia Yang[1], Yulu Chen[1], Tianshu Dong[1], Jiaji Li[1], Preben Hansen[3], Yijun Zhao[1](✉), and Guanyun Wang[1](✉)

[1] Zhejiang University, Hangzhou 310058, Zhejiang, China
{zhaoyj,guanyun}@zju.edu.cn
[2] Zhejiang Haers Vacuum Containers Co., Ltd., Yongkang 321300, Zhejiang, China
[3] Stockholm University, 164 55 Kista, Sweden

Abstract. This research introduces FlexiStiff-Fabric, a programmable 3D printed fabric stiffness technology. Addressing the limited stiffness tunability and structural integrity issues of existing 3D printed fabrics, our technology leverages a dual-material interlocking weaving method. This geometric design mechanically locks flexible and rigid material units, effectively maintaining overall structural integrity and resolving delamination challenges often caused by material incompatibility in FDM printing. Unlike single-material 3D printing, which is inherently limited in achieving extreme stiffness variations through geometric adjustments (e.g., infill density, wall thickness, or lattice design), and traditional fabric stiffening processes (e.g., embroidery) with insufficient stiffness control, FlexiStiff-Fabric integrates two materials with intrinsically distinct properties. Combined with its unique interlocking design, this achieves a more refined and locally controllable range of stiffness. We developed a software-assisted design platform. Mechanical tests, supported by multi-sample analysis and statistical validation, quantitatively demonstrate the programmable stiffness and structural robustness. Diverse application cases showcase the novel potential of technology in wearables and smart textiles.

Keywords: Softness and Stiffness · 3D Printed Fabric · Multi-material Printing

1 Introduction and Related Work

The texture and stiffness of fabrics offer diverse tactile experiences and functionalities for clothing. The application of additive manufacturing in fabric production has given rise to the emerging field of 3D-printed fabrics, attracting

R. Cao and R. Liu—These authors contributed equally to this work.

S. Guo et al. (Eds.): HHME 2025, CCIS 2878, pp. 54–67, 2027.
https://doi.org/10.1007/978-981-92-3991-7_5

widespread attention from both academia and industry [10,11]. This technology revolutionizes the design and production methods of traditional textiles, providing innovative solutions for wearables, interactive surfaces, and educational tools [13,17,26]. Through Fused Deposition Modeling (FDM) technology, researchers can simulate traditional fabric weaving structures, creating novel materials that combine softness with customizability, and exploring the possibility of achieving programmable mechanical properties.

In the field of Human-Computer Interaction (HCI), 3D-printed fabrics can seamlessly integrate sensing and interactive functionalities into apparel and other textiles, expanding their utility and user experience [12]. For instance, the IrOn-Tex and FabriClick projects demonstrate how electronic components can be embedded into fabrics, enhancing their adaptability in ubiquitous computing environments [5,28]; Flexmock offers a rapid prototyping workflow that supports the quick creation of complex fabric patterns [20]. In digital manufacturing, research on softness and stiffness involves multidisciplinary applications across materials science, mechanical engineering, and computer-aided design [5,28]. However, existing research still faces challenges in leveraging multi-materials to achieve complex fabric functionalities, particularly the inherent limitations of single-material 3D printing in transitioning between extreme softness and stiffness, and the difficulty in maintaining structural integrity between dissimilar materials in multi-material FDM printing. FDM technology forms flexible, lightweight, and customizable fabric materials by controlling the extrusion process of thermoplastic materials. For example, the DefeXtiles project developed thin, flexible fabrics with woven-like structures [4,21]; Ma Hua et al. combined 3D printing with traditional techniques to create interactive fabrics [9,24].

Despite these advancements, 3D-printed fabric technology still faces challenges such as high material costs and reliance on specialized equipment (affecting accessibility for general users) [20,21]. Furthermore, there are shortcomings in fabric morphology monotony, texture, stiffness, and environmental sustainability [4,22]. In digital manufacturing, creating materials with variable softness and stiffness through 3D printing has become a research focus [18]. Researchers have developed various methods to control the elastic properties of 3D-printed objects, such as utilizing microstructures [18] or internal tethers to enhance the stiffness and stability of inflatable devices [6]. However, in the realm of fabrics and wearable technology, achieving a broad range of precise and robust programmable stiffness remains challenging, especially in overcoming the inherent performance limitations of single materials and structural integrity issues in multi-material integration. Some scholars have explored hybrid manufacturing strategies, combining 3D printing with traditional handcrafted techniques to create diverse and high-performance fabrics [1]. Simultaneously, teams have also developed new tools and technical platforms to assist designers in adjusting material properties [3].

In the field of additive manufacturing, the combination of multiple materials aims to integrate materials with different properties to achieve more complex functionalities and design flexibility [2,7,19,27]. For example, Foundry is an interactive authoring system for designing multi-material 3D-printed objects and materials [25]; Julian Panetta et al. designed textured structures with predetermined elasticity through additive manufacturing [14]. However, effectively combining materials with significantly different mechanical properties remains a significant challenge [23]. Traditional 3D printing technologies face adhesion problems in both vertical and horizontal directions when processing multiple materials, easily leading to interlayer delamination and compromised structural integrity [8]. To overcome these difficulties, researchers have proposed various strategies and techniques, such as introducing special geometric structures to enhance adhesion in FDM 3D printing through Multi-Attach technology [8]. Nevertheless, these existing solutions typically focus on addressing adhesion issues between components, rather than achieving precise, periodic mechanical interlocking of flexible and rigid materials within continuous fabric units to construct programmable stiffness fabrics with overall structural robustness.

This study proposes a dual-material interlocking weaving method to address the common problem of insufficient structural integrity in multi-material 3D-printed fabrics, particularly delamination caused by material incompatibility. By alternately using flexible and rigid materials (e.g., PLA, TPU) during the 3D printing process, and combining changes in the printing direction of adjacent layers and adjusting the material distribution ratio, we achieve precise control over fabric stiffness. This method does not rely on chemical adhesion between materials; instead, through a specific geometric interlocking design, it ensures that flexible and rigid material units can mechanically interlock when subjected to force, thereby effectively maintaining the overall structural robustness.

2 Overview of Flexistiff-Fabric

2.1 Dual-Material Interlocking Weaving Method in 3D Printing

In 3D printing, adhesion between two different materials is often poor, which limits the performance and application range of multi-material printed parts. In this section, we selected two of the most common soft and hard 3D printing filaments on the market—PLA (polylactic acid) and TPU (thermoplastic polyurethane)—for verification and demonstration. PLA is a rigid material with high stiffness and strength, while TPU is a soft material with good elasticity and flexibility. However, the significant thermal and mechanical property differences between PLA and TPU lead to poor interfacial bonding quality in traditional dual-material printing processes, thereby causing problems like interlayer delamination that affect the overall performance and reliability of printed parts.

To address this issue, this study proposes an innovative dual-material interlocking weaving method. This method draws inspiration from multi-layer weaving techniques in textiles [15,16] and staggered layer printing methods in 3D printing [29]. By changing the printing direction between adjacent layers and alternately using flexible and rigid materials, we construct a composite material structure with specific programmable mechanical properties and structural robustness. Specifically, during the printing process of each layer, the extruded

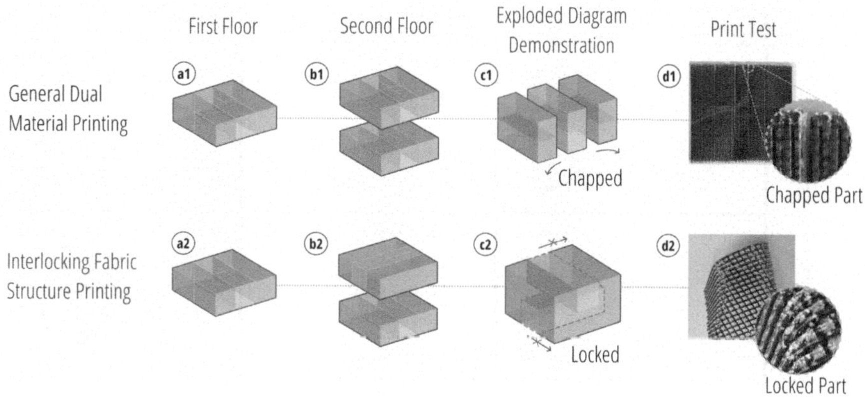

Fig. 1. Demonstration of the Dual-material Interlocking Weaving Method

lines of flexible and rigid materials are arranged in a specific sequential combination. For example, n rigid material strands (represented by the number 1) and x flexible material strands (represented by the number 0) can be printed horizontally, forming specific arrangement sequences such as 010101 or 011011011 (Fig. 3). As shown in Fig. 1(a2), the first layer is printed horizontally in the 0° direction; as shown in Fig. 1(b2), the second layer is horizontally rotated by 90° for printing, with the sequence combination of both layers remaining consistent. This design not only enhances the mechanical interlocking between layers but also makes the fabric structure more uniform and stable. Because each material layer is arranged alternately in different directions, the mechanical properties of the fabric are more balanced in all directions, avoiding the anisotropy problems that single-direction printing might cause. We employed two printing methods—general dual-material printing and interlocking fabric structure printing (as shown in Fig. 1(d1, d2))—to verify the stability of the interlocking structure.

2.2 Software-Aided Design and Fabrication

This section will detail the complete workflow of FlexiStiff-Fabric, from software design to print production, using a cubic example composed of six different stiffness levels. Additionally, we will demonstrate the bonding strength of these cubes with varying stiffness grades.

We developed an auxiliary design tool for FlexiStiff-Fabric in Grasshopper, a plugin for Rhinoceros 3D. It automatically generates an interlocking weaving structure by inputting the designed line drawings. Users can control the line properties through a simple GUI to meet their desired stiffness, and after the design is completed, the model can be exported to Rhino for further adjustments or directly generated in a file format supported by slicing software, such as STL. Below, we will use a cube composed of six different stiffness levels to illustrate

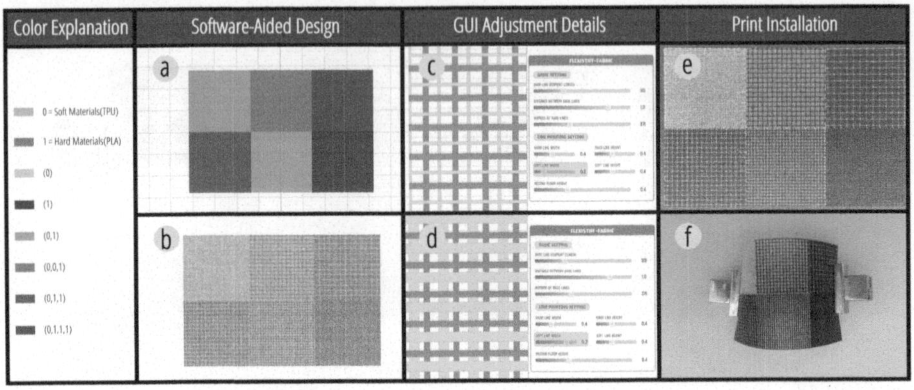

Fig. 2. Overall Design Process Flowchart

the process from line drawing design to parametric modeling to print production, with specific operational steps as follows:

Line Drawing Input: Users import their line drawings designed in familiar software (such as AI, Figma, etc.) into Rhino, open the provided GH file, and input the line drawings into the "Curve" component. Our programmed script will automatically generate the interlocking weaving structure. If users need to adjust the curves, they only need to control the points on the line to the desired position, and the generation range of the structure will adjust in real-time based on the line drawing. In Fig. 2(a), we input the line drawing of the cube, and by inputting the required lines into the Curve component, the interlocking weaving structure as shown in Fig. 2(b) is automatically generated.

Adjusting Stiffness: In the GUI we provide, there are adjustments for the length, width, and height of both soft and hard lines, with the smallest unit being 0.2 mm, but we recommend 0.4mm based on the success rate of 3D printing. We also provide options for the spacing between the two types of lines to achieve more variations in stiffness. The key to adjusting stiffness is the combination ratio of the two materials, which users can achieve by changing the sequence order in our software. Figures 2(c, d) demonstrate how to adjust the width of the hard lines through the GUI.

Generating and Exporting Files: We provide two methods for file export. One is to export the separate combined models of the two materials, which users can customize and modify in Rhino, and then export in a format supported by slicing software through Rhino. The other is to directly generate files in formats such as STL through the software. Afterward, users only need to import the file into slicing software, select the corresponding nozzles for the two material models, and proceed with printing, referring to the recommended parameters for the printer and printing materials.

Printing and Assembling Fabric: We recommend using a 3D printer with dual nozzles, as the structure of FlexiStiff-Fabric frequently switches materials between layers. Using a single nozzle with manual addition would be inefficient.

Our structure supports adjusting the spacing between each line, facilitating subsequent processing such as sewing or adding rivets. Figure 2(e) shows a cube composed of six different stiffness levels printed using the E2 printer from Raise3D.

Connecting Different Stiffness Levels: Since FlexiStiff-Fabric, except for the stiffness levels composed of individual materials 0 and 1, prints two materials in each layer for other stiffness levels. Therefore, the same material in adjacent layers of different stiffness levels is connected, thereby enhancing stability. Figure 2(f) demonstrates the stable effect of connecting cubes of different stiffness levels.

3 Design Space

3.1 Quantifying the Stiffness Range

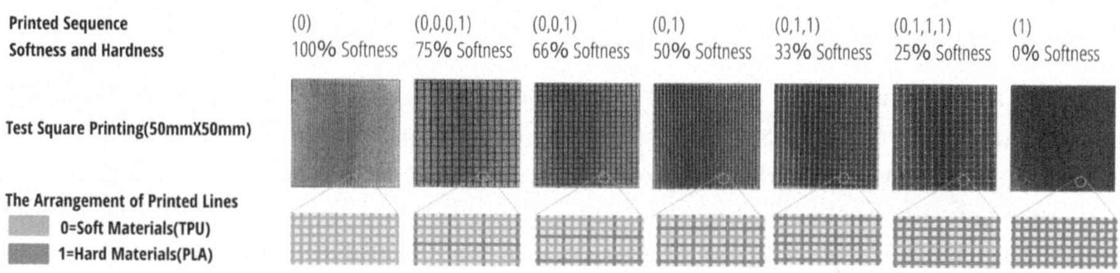

Fig. 3. Illustrations of Print Line Distribution for Seven Stiffness Levels

This section aims to quantify the stiffness range achievable with FlexiStiff-Fabric through systematic three-point bending tests, and to verify the robustness of structures constructed using the dual-material interlocking weaving method across various stiffness levels.

Sample Preparation and Testing Methods. To systematically quantify the mechanical properties of fabrics with different stiffness levels, we prepared seven distinct stiffness gradient test samples. These samples were 3D-printed using flexible materials (e.g., TPU) and rigid materials (e.g., PLA) via the dual-material interlocking weaving method proposed in this study. For each stiffness gradient, N = 5 rectangular beam-shaped samples were prepared to ensure the rigor of statistical analysis.

All test samples had uniform geometric dimensions: a length (L) of 80 mm and a width (w) of 10 mm. The sample thickness (h) was 3.2 mm, formed by four stacked printed layers, with each layer having a thickness of 0.8 mm. By adjusting the distribution ratio and arrangement pattern of flexible and rigid material print lines within each layer, as shown in Fig. 3, we systematically constructed seven stiffness levels ranging from soft to hard.

We subjected these samples to a Three-Point Bending Test to evaluate their bending stiffness. The tests were conducted on a universal testing machine equipped with fixtures suitable for three-point bending tests. The support span (Lsupport) of the testing setup was set to 60 mm. The temperature and humidity of the testing environment were kept constant. Load was applied at the center of the sample, pressing downward at a constant rate until the sample reached a preset deflection (Table 1).

Table 1. Average results from three-point bending tests

Parameter	Rigidity Wiring Arrangement						
	0	0001	001	01	011	0111	1
F (N)	4	8	13	17	20	23	25
E_f (MPa)	65.92	131.84	214.23	280.15	329.59	379.03	411.99

Results and Analysis. By analyzing the data from the three-point bending tests, we quantified the flexural modulus (Ef) of samples at different stiffness levels as a quantitative indicator of their macroscopic stiffness. The flexural modulus is an intrinsic property of the resistance of a material to bending deformation. For a beam with a rectangular cross-section, its calculation formula is:

$$E_f = \frac{FL_{\text{support}}^3}{4wh^3\delta}$$

Here, F is the load at a specific point on the load-deflection curve, Lsupport is the support span (60 mm), w is the sample width (10 mm), h is the sample thickness (3.2 mm), and δ is the deflection corresponding to load F, which we set to 10 mm in our experiments.

The test results clearly show a significant linear increase in the flexural modulus of the samples as the proportion of PLA within the interlocking structure increases (Fig. 4a). This directly reflects an enhanced resistance to bending deformation.

These quantitative results confirm that FlexiStiff-Fabric, by precisely adjusting the distribution ratio of flexible and rigid materials, can achieve stiffness control within a broad range from a minimum flexural modulus of 66 MPa to a maximum of 412 MPa. This covers a continuous transition from highly flexible to rigid support.

Structural Robustness Validation. Throughout all three-point bending tests, we closely monitored the physical integrity of the samples. The results showed no observation of any interlayer delamination, interlayer peeling, or overall structural disintegration due to interfacial bonding failure in any of the samples. Even in samples with higher stiffness levels, where rigid PLA strands experienced local fracture at their material strength limit, the flexible TPU material

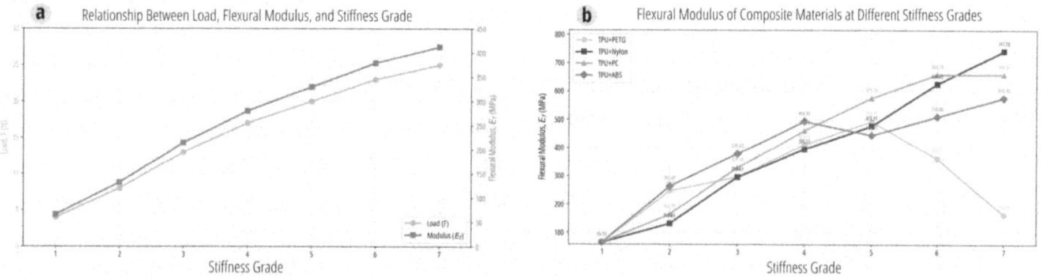

Fig. 4. Relationship between flexural modulus and material ratio

and the interlocking geometric structure effectively maintained the geometric connection between different material layers and the overall structural integrity, thus avoiding the common interfacial failure problems seen in traditional multi-material FDM printing.

3.2 Exploring Material Combinations

Section 3.1 validated the feasibility of FlexiStiff-Fabric in achieving a broad stiffness range and structural robustness using the PLA and TPU combination. This section will further explore the applicability of the dual-material interlocking weaving method to different combinations of flexible and rigid materials. By testing multiple material pairs, we aim to demonstrate the versatility and universality of this method, thereby expanding the design space of FlexiStiff-Fabric to meet more diverse functional fabric application requirements.

To evaluate the universality of this interlocking weaving structure, we consistently selected TPU 95A as the flexible material and systematically tested its compatibility with various commonly used FDM rigid materials. Based on comprehensive considerations such as durability, hardness, and versatility, we chose the following rigid materials for testing: PETG, Nylon, PC (Polycarbonate), and ABS (Acrylonitrile Butadiene Styrene). For each new material combination, we prepared test samples using the same interlocking weaving strategy and geometric parameters (length 80 mm, width 10 mm, thickness 3.2 mm, 4 layers) as described in Sect. 3.1. To explore the stiffness range achievable by each combination, we also prepared a series of samples with different distribution ratios of flexible and rigid materials. For each stiffness gradient within each combination, N = 5 samples were prepared.

We subjected these new material combination samples to the same three-point bending test as detailed in Sect. 3.1. The testing equipment, support span (60 mm), loading rate, and environmental conditions were kept consistent with Sect. 3.1 to ensure the comparability of test results. We calculated their flexural modulus (Ef) as the primary indicator for quantifying stiffness(Fig. 4b). The test results show that the dual-material interlocking weaving method remains effective with these new material combinations, successfully constructing fabric structures with varying stiffness levels (Table 2).

Table 2. Average bending modulus of TPU 95A combined with different hard materials

Material Combination	Rigidity Wiring Arrangement						
	0	0001	001	01	011	0111	1
TPU+PETG	65.92	247.19	296.63	411.99	494.38	362.55	164.79
TPU+Nylon	65.92	131.84	296.63	395.51	477.91	626.22	741.58
TPU+PC	65.92	164.79	329.59	461.43	576.78	659.18	659.18
TPU+ABS	65.92	263.67	379.03	494.38	444.95	510.86	576.78

These exploratory test results strongly demonstrate the excellent material versatility of the dual-material interlocking weaving method proposed by FlexiStiff-Fabric. Although TPU 95A and different rigid materials may exhibit variations in print compatibility and the achievable range of mechanical properties (e.g., the PC combination achieved higher maximum stiffness, while the Nylon combination might show a haptic feel and abrasion resistance closer to traditional textiles), the core geometric interlocking mechanism effectively prevented interlayer delamination in all tested cases, ensuring structural robustness. This indicates that the method is not limited to specific PLA and TPU combinations but can be applied to a wider range of FDM printing material pairs, thereby greatly expanding the design space for functional fabrics.

3.3 Applications

FlexiStiff-Fabric, with its unique dual-material interlocking weaving method, achieves precise and localized control over the macroscopic stiffness of fabrics while solving the bonding challenges between dissimilar materials in multi-material FDM printing. These characteristics give it immense application potential across various fields. This section will illustrate some application scenarios of FlexiStiff-Fabric through specific design examples.

Assistive Touch Watch Strap. Group One designed a watch strap with three distinct stiffness zones (Fig. 5 a1): a 100% TPU-filled strap head limit zone, a 50% stiffness adhesive zone, and a 25% stiffness commonly deformed zone. This strap requires no post-production processing. Users can locate the appropriate adhesive position by touch without shifting their gaze. The TPU material in the limit zone prevents the strap from falling off, and due to TPU's elastic recovery properties, users can still adjust the force and angle to remove the restriction area.

Printed mask. Figure 5(d1, d2) shows an integrated mask that supports custom textures, consisting of five different stiffness zones: a 100% softness cord area; a 75% softness zone for the fixed cord; a 50% softness main mask area; a 75% softness nose bridge support area; and a 0% softness texture area. This mask eliminates the traditional step of installing a metal strip and provides more design flexibility.

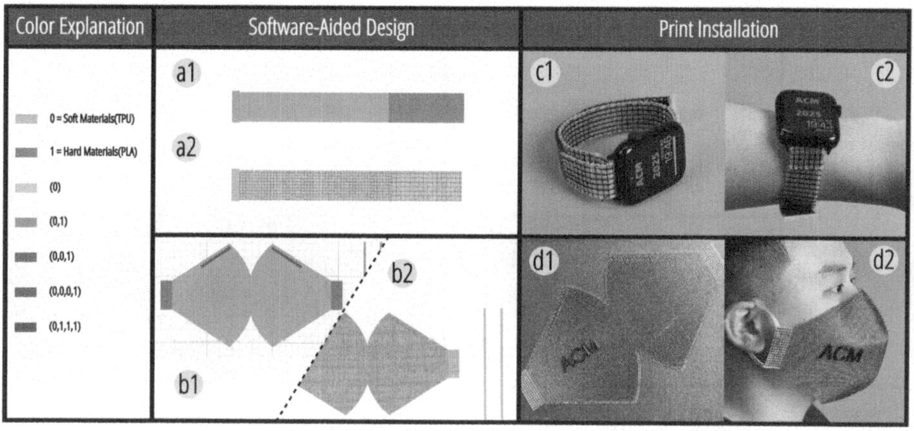

Fig. 5. Design Process Flowchart for Assistive Touch Watch Strap and Printed mask

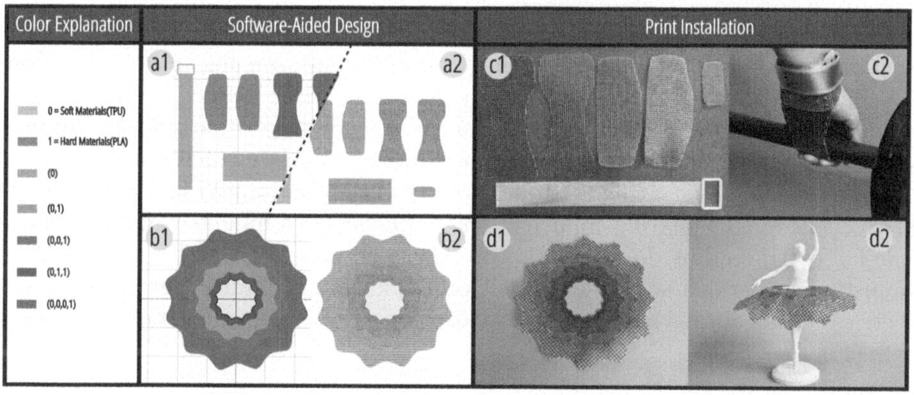

Fig. 6. Design Process Flowchart for Assist Strap and Customized evening dress

Assist Strap. Figure 6(a1, a2) shows an assist strap designed to provide support and protect the wrist during physical activities. This strap consists of four zones with different levels of stiffness: a 100% softness buckle and wristband area; a 66% softness wrist pad area; a 50% softness thickened layer area; and a 33% softness grip area. After printing is completed, rivets and Velcro need to be added for assembly, as shown in Fig. 6(c1, c2). Traditional assist straps require different materials for each area with varying stiffness levels, whereas this strap only needs two materials, reducing the number of processing steps.

Customized evening dress. Figure 6(b1,b2) shows an evening dress with customized stiffness levels in different areas from the bodice to the hem. The hem of the dress is divided into two levels of softness, 75% and 66%, which create a more layered effect when it swings. The bodice is divided into two levels of softness, 50% and 33%, which provide stability while also creating a better transition with the hem. Figure 6(d1,d2) is an example of printing.

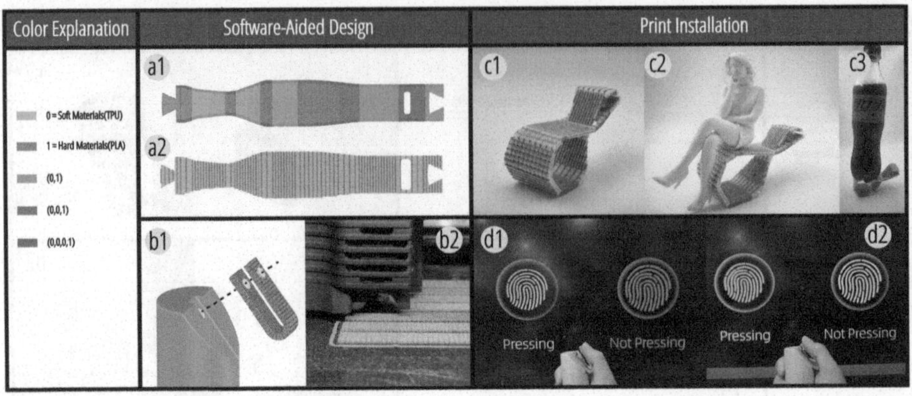

Fig. 7. Integrated Softness/Stiffness Customizable Chair and Quick-Release Soft/Hard Button Handle

Beyond traditional fabric applications, we also explored FlexiStiff-Fabric technology in furniture manufacturing and electronic sensing. Figures 7a1 and 7a2 illustrate the design process for an integrated chair based on mortise and tenon joints. As seen in Fig. 7c1, the chair is divided into three distinct stiffness zones for support, deformation, and adjustment. Figure 7c2 shows a 3D printed female model demonstrating the functionality of the chair, and Fig. 7c3 highlights its excellent weight-bearing capacity. The tactile feel of a handle comes from multiple factors, including damping, texture, and stiffness. We used FlexiStiff-Fabric to customize various soft-to-hard buttons, allowing for quick detachment and electrical connection via magnetic adsorption (Fig. 7b1), and conducted press tests (Fig. 7d).

4 Conclusion and Future Work

Current multi-material 3D printing in functional fabrics primarily faces significant challenges with interfacial bonding between heterogeneous materials, which limits printed component performance and application. To address this, we introduce FlexiStiff-Fabric, an innovative dual-material interlocking weaving method. This approach uses a unique geometric design to achieve mechanical locking between materials, rather than relying on chemical adhesion, thus significantly enhancing interlayer bonding strength and overall structural robustness. Through systematic three-point bending tests, we quantified and validated a broad and precisely controllable stiffness range and demonstrated its universality across various flexible and rigid material combinations. Our findings confirm that FlexiStiff-Fabric effectively prevents delamination and constructs stable structures with diverse material pairings, greatly expanding the design space for functional fabrics.

FlexiStiff-Fabric provides a robust and efficient solution, overcoming the inherent drawbacks of traditional multi-material FDM printing. This opens new design and manufacturing possibilities for smart textiles, wearables, and human-computer interaction interfaces. Our research not only enhances the performance and reliability of 3D-printed functional fabrics but also streamlines manufacturing and reduces costs. For future work, we will focus on optimizing the printing process for efficiency, expanding the material library, and simplifying post-processing steps to minimize manual intervention. We also plan to explore more complex interlocking geometries and investigate its applicability to other 3D printing processes, alongside in-depth application case development and user studies, to promote its broader adoption towards truly intelligent programmable fabrics.

Acknowledgments. This project was supported by the Fundamental Research Funds for the Central Universities (No. 226-2025-00086) and ZJU-Cornell Joint Seed Fund. The authors have no competing interests to declare that are relevant to the content of this article.

References

1. Albaugh, L., Gonzalez, J.T., Hudson, S.E.: Tensions and resolutions in hybrid basketry: joining 3D printing and handweaving. In: Proceedings of the Eighteenth International Conference on Tangible, Embedded, and Embodied Interaction (2024). https://api.semanticscholar.org/CorpusID:267212399
2. Eguchi, S., Takamori, R., Yuasa, R., Tanaka, H.: Morphing design for socially interactive autonomous car by multi-material 3D-printing. In: Extended Abstracts of the 2019 CHI Conference on Human Factors in Computing Systems (2019). https://api.semanticscholar.org/CorpusID:144207813
3. Fabian, K., Wittchen, D., Strohmeier, P.: 3D-printed cells for creating variable softness. In: Proceedings of the Eighteenth International Conference on Tangible, Embedded, and Embodied Interaction (2024). https://api.semanticscholar.org/CorpusID:267212548
4. Forman, J., Dogan, M.D., Forsythe, H., Ishii, H.: DefeXtiles: 3D printing quasi-woven fabric via under-extrusion. In: Proceedings of the 33rd Annual ACM Symposium on User Interface Software and Technology (2020). https://api.semanticscholar.org/CorpusID:222805119
5. Goudswaard, M., Abraham, A., da Rocha, B.G., Andersen, K., Liang, R.H.: FabriClick: interweaving pushbuttons into fabrics using 3D printing and digital embroidery. In: Proceedings of the 2020 ACM Designing Interactive Systems Conference (2020). https://api.semanticscholar.org/CorpusID:220323512
6. Han, C., Takahashi, R., Yahagi, Y., Naemura, T.: 3D printing firm inflatables with internal tethers. In: Extended Abstracts of the 2021 CHI Conference on Human Factors in Computing Systems (2021). https://api.semanticscholar.org/CorpusID:233987387
7. Hanton, O., Fraser, M., Roudaut, A.: DisplayFab: the state of the art and a roadmap in the personal fabrication of free-form displays using active materials and additive manufacturing. In: Proceedings of the CHI Conference on Human Factors in Computing Systems (2024). https://api.semanticscholar.org/CorpusID:269745346

8. Kwon, N., Deshpande, H., Hasan, M.K., Darnal, A., Kim, J.: Multi-ttach: techniques to enhance multi-material attachments in low-cost FDM 3D printing. In: Proceedings of the 6th Annual ACM Symposium on Computational Fabrication (2021). https://api.semanticscholar.org/CorpusID:238638783
9. Ma, H., Yamaoka, J.: Smart textile using 3D printed conductive sequins. In: Proceedings of the Sixteenth International Conference on Tangible, Embedded, and Embodied Interaction (2022). https://api.semanticscholar.org/CorpusID: 246653075
10. Masuda, R., Noma, Y., Narumi, K.: Computational design and fabrication of 3D printed zippers connecting 3D textile structures. In: ACM Symposium on User Interface Software and Technology (2024). https://api.semanticscholar.org/CorpusID:273311948
11. Moustafa, S., Sultan, J., Wang, S., Nabil, S.: Fabric-Lego: 3D-printing fabric-based Lego-compatible designs for assistive wearables, personalization, and self-expression. In: Companion Publication of the 2024 ACM Designing Interactive Systems Conference (2024). https://api.semanticscholar.org/CorpusID:270846183
12. Nicolae, M., Roussel, V., Koelle, M., Huron, S., Steimle, J., Teyssier, M.: Biohybrid devices: prototyping interactive devices with growable materials. In: Proceedings of the 36th Annual ACM Symposium on User Interface Software and Technology (2023). https://api.semanticscholar.org/CorpusID:262057849
13. Nylin, M., Lundberg, J., Bång, M., Kucher, K.: Glyph design for communication initiation in real-time human-automation collaboration. Vis. Inf. **8**(4), 23–35 (2024). https://doi.org/10.1016/j.visinf.2024.09.006. https://www.sciencedirect.com/science/article/pii/S2468502X24000470
14. Panetta, J., Zhou, Q., Malomo, L., Pietroni, N., Cignoni, P., Zorin, D.: Elastic textures for additive fabrication. ACM Trans. Graph. (TOG) **34**, 1 – 12 (2015). https://api.semanticscholar.org/CorpusID:14541159
15. Pouta, E., Mikkonen, J.V.: Woven eTextiles in HCI — a literature review. In: Proceedings of the 2022 ACM Designing Interactive Systems Conference, DIS 2022, pp. 1099–1118. Association for Computing Machinery, New York, NY, USA (2022). https://doi.org/10.1145/3532106.3533566
16. Pouta, E., Mikkonen, J.V., Salovaara, A.: Opportunities with multi-layer weave structures in woven e-textile design. ACM Trans. Comput.-Hum. Interact. **31**(5) (2024). https://doi.org/10.1145/3689039
17. Rivera, M.L., Hudson, S.E.: Desktop electrospinning: a single extruder 3D printer for producing rigid plastic and electrospun textiles. In: Proceedings of the 2019 CHI Conference on Human Factors in Computing Systems (2019). https://api.semanticscholar.org/CorpusID:140220640
18. Schumacher, C., Bickel, B., Rys, J., Marschner, S., Daraio, C., Gross, M.H.: Microstructures to control elasticity in 3D printing. ACM Trans. Graph. (TOG) **34**, 1–13 (2015). https://api.semanticscholar.org/CorpusID:5096860
19. Sitthi-Amorn, P., et al.: MultiFab: a machine vision assisted platform for multi-material 3D printing. Acm Trans. Graph. (TOG) **34**(4), 1–11 (2015)
20. Takahashi, A., Soma, Y., Sato, H., Tomonaga, K.: Flexmock: fast, easy, stock-able smocking method using 3D printed self-shrinkable pattern sheet. In: ACM Symposium on User Interface Software and Technology (2024). https://api.semanticscholar.org/CorpusID:273294040
21. Takahashi, H., Kim, J.: 3D printed fabric: techniques for design and 3D weaving programmable textiles. In: Proceedings of the 32nd Annual ACM Symposium on User Interface Software and Technology (2019). https://api.semanticscholar.org/CorpusID:204812116

22. Te, S.A., Ben-Alon, L.: 3D printed earth-fiber textiles. In: Proceedings of the 8th ACM Symposium on Computational Fabrication (2023). https://api.semanticscholar.org/CorpusID:265364593
23. Valkeneers, T., Leen, D., Ashbrook, D., Ramakers, R.: StackMold: rapid prototyping of functional multi-material objects with selective levels of surface details. In: Proceedings of the 32nd Annual ACM Symposium on User Interface Software and Technology (2019). https://api.semanticscholar.org/CorpusID:203703986
24. Valle, A.D., Toka, M., Aponte, A., Jacobs, J.: PunchPrint: creating composite fiber-filament craft artifacts by integrating punch needle embroidery and 3D printing. In: Proceedings of the 2023 CHI Conference on Human Factors in Computing Systems (2023). https://api.semanticscholar.org/CorpusID:258218088
25. Vidimce, K., Kaspar, A., Wang, Y., Matusik, W.: Foundry: hierarchical material design for multi-material fabrication. In: Proceedings of the 29th Annual Symposium on User Interface Software and Technology (2016). https://api.semanticscholar.org/CorpusID:207242786
26. Wang, G., et al.: PneuFab: designing low-cost 3D-printed inflatable structures for blow molding artifacts. In: Proceedings of the 2023 CHI Conference on Human Factors in Computing Systems (2023). https://api.semanticscholar.org/CorpusID:258217232
27. Yang, M., Yamaoka, J.: MultiJam: fabricating jamming user interface using multi-material 3D printing. In: Proceedings of the Sixteenth International Conference on Tangible, Embedded, and Embodied Interaction (2022). https://api.semanticscholar.org/CorpusID:246653053
28. Yu, J., et al.: IrOnTex: using ironable 3D printed objects to fabricate and prototype customizable interactive textiles. Proc. ACM Interact. Mob. Wearable Ubiquitous Technol. **8**, 138:1–138:26 (2024). https://api.semanticscholar.org/CorpusID:272585649
29. Zhang, P., Heyne, M.A., To, A.C.: Biomimetic staggered composites with highly enhanced energy dissipation: modeling, 3D printing, and testing. J. Mech. Phys. Solids **83**, 285–300 (2015). https://doi.org/10.1016/j.jmps.2015.06.015. https://www.sciencedirect.com/science/article/pii/S0022509615300053

ScentEcho: Exploring Adsorbent Materials for Accurate Odor Collection and Playback

Chih-Hung Lee[1,2], Yuchi Sun[1,2], Rui Zhang[2], Suhang Wei[1], and Qi Lu[2(✉)]

[1] Academy of Arts and Design, Tsinghua University, Beijing, China
[2] The Future Laboratory, Tsinghua University, Beijing, China
luq@mail.tsinghua.edu.cn

Abstract. Delivering odors that feel realistic and recognizable remains a core challenge for olfactory interaction systems, particularly in applications that demand precise scent delivery. A key limitation lies in the difficulty of capturing, preserving, and playing back real-world scent sources in a reliable and scalable manner. This study explores the potential of adsorbent materials for supporting realistic scent playback. We present ScentEcho, a portable system that enables modular scent collection and release. Through user evaluations, we identify which adsorbent materials tend to perform better for specific odors, and observe that perceived intensity strongly influences similarity ratings. In addition, odor recognition follows a graded pattern, with users moving from broad category identification to more specific source recognition as similarity increases. These findings offer practical insights for designing olfactory interfaces that are both expressive and perceptually aligned with user expectations.

Keywords: Olfactory interaction · Scent collection · Adsorbent materials · Odor similarity · User evaluation

1 Introduction

In daily life, vision and hearing account for about 90% of our sensory input [1]. While the sense of smell occupies a smaller proportion, it has a unique ability to evoke emotions and memories [2]. Leveraging this characteristic, HCI (Human-Computer Interaction) research explores how integrating smell can create more immersive experiences and enhance user engagement [3–6].

However, current systems often rely on pre-defined odors [7,8], such as preset fragrances like the smell of roses, which may not align with individual perceptions and memories. While some studies enable users to customize mixtures by adjusting proportions of base compounds [9,10], these approaches remain constrained by a fixed set of source materials. As a result, they hinder the personalization and contextual adaptability of olfactory interaction, making it difficult for users to engage with scents that authentically reflect their experiences, surroundings, or emotional states.

S. Guo et al. (Eds.): HHME 2025, CCIS 2878, pp. 68–80, 2027.
https://doi.org/10.1007/978-981-92-3991-7_6

To address these challenges, one potential direction is to allow users to obtain scents directly from their surroundings, giving them the ability to collect and preserve odors they find personally meaningful or interesting. Prior work by designers and companies has proposed various scent collection concepts [11–13], but many remain exploratory or artistic in nature without validating the technical performance of materials or systems. Notably, the "smell camera" [14], presents a creative approach to scent capture and playback, yet issues such as bulkiness, limited reusability, and the inability to store or switch between multiple scents still hinder practical deployment. These gaps highlight the importance of systematically investigating materials and methods for achieving reliable and realistic odor capture in real-world contexts.

We therefore developed ScentEcho, a compact and portable device designed to support personalized scent collection and playback. Its modular structure and simple pneumatic system allow for the storage and release of multiple odors in a lightweight format. In this study, we employed ScentEcho to evaluate the performance of different adsorbent materials in capturing and reproducing commonly studied odors in HCI, such as lemon, coffee bean, mint, and lavender [15–19]. Participants assessed the similarity and intensity of the replayed scents. In addition to evaluating material performance, our study also revealed a notable correlation between perceived intensity and odor similarity, as observed through participant ratings and interviews. This insight offers a deeper understanding of how users perceive olfactory realism and the factors that influence their interpretation of scent fidelity.

2 Related Work

2.1 Scent Sources in Olfactory Interaction

Olfaction has gained significant attention in HCI, with research focusing on its integration with other sensory modalities to create immersive and emotionally engaging user experiences [20–23]. However, most existing studies rely on commercially available sources such as perfumes or synthetic fragrance compounds [4,5,9,24,25]. While these sources are convenient, their labels or descriptors often fail to accurately reflect olfactory perception. Prior studies have indicated that verbal scent descriptors do not always align with individual olfactory perception, suggesting that even familiar terms may be interpreted differently across users. While these findings emerge primarily from linguistic and cognitive research, they point to the challenge of relying on predefined scent labels in olfactory interface design [26,27].

Although not all studies explicitly emphasize realism or semantic alignment, these aspects are especially valuable when olfactory cues are used to evoke emotion, trigger memory, or support interpersonal communication. To better align with users' lived experiences and olfactory memories, systems should move beyond predefined commercial fragrances and support more diverse, personalized scent inputs that reflect real-life contexts and meaningful interactions.

2.2 Scent Collection and Playback

To support more authentic olfactory interaction, researchers and designers have proposed various scent collection and playback systems. Traditional methods such as solvent extraction or hydrodistillation can chemically capture real-world odors with high accuracy [28–30], but they are typically time-consuming, equipment-intensive, and require large quantities of raw materials to produce even small amounts of extract. This limits their feasibility in interactive systems, particularly those aimed at supporting personal, context-aware, or real-time scent experiences.

In response, designers and companies have explored alternative approaches, proposing physical devices for capturing and re-releasing target odors [11–13]. While such designs introduce creative interaction concepts, many remain exploratory or artistic in nature and lack rigorous evaluation of technical performance. Among prior work, the "smell camera" [14] offers an illustrative example of a novel HCI interface exploring user expectations for scent collection—such as duration, convenience, and intended use. While offering valuable insights, its practical deployment remains limited due to bulkiness, one-time usability, and the inability to store or switch between multiple scents. Crucially, most existing systems do not assess whether the released scent retains perceptual similarity to its source, leaving a fundamental gap in understanding the fidelity of olfactory reproduction.

3 Design and Implementation

ScentEcho is composed of two separate compartments: the upper compartment, which houses the electronic components and serves as the control unit, and the lower compartment, which contains four independent odor storage units, forming the device's core functional component. Figure 1 illustrates the overall structure and operation of ScentEcho.

The upper compartment includes four self-locking buttons, a three-position toggle switch, and a power connection. It houses two air pumps (5 V, 1.1 L/min) for odor collection and playback. To ensure pump longevity and odor delivery stability, a toggle switch ensures only one pump operates at a time. Four two-way solenoid valves (5 V) are individually controlled by self-locking buttons. For ease of maintenance, the lower compartment features only the odor storage units and support structures. Magnets connect the upper and lower compartments, facilitating easy inspection and replacement. Figure 1(b) details the internal structure of the compartments.

The pneumatic system is depicted in Fig. 1(c), with red lines indicating airflow. Air pumps provide the driving force, and solenoid valves control specific pathways. Two pumps connect to four solenoid valves via three-way and four-way connectors, and these valves are linked to the odor storage units in the lower compartment through air hoses. Users operate the device by pressing one or more self-locking buttons to activate the corresponding solenoid valves, followed by toggling the switch to start the aspirator or blowing pump for odor collection

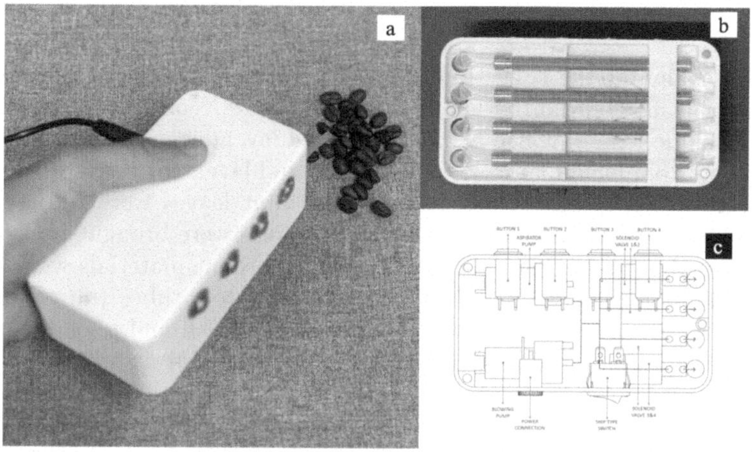

Fig. 1. Illustrations of the Device Structure and Operation. a) Schematic of the odor collection process, b) Internal view of the upper compartment, c) Schematic of the upper compartment structure and pneumatic pathways.

or playback. Backlit buttons provide visual feedback, indicating the active odor storage unit, as shown in Fig. 1(a).

ScentEcho offers several key advantages: 1. Odor Collection and Playback, it can manage four different odors simultaneously, with reserved space in the lower compartment for additional storage units, enabling expansion; 2. Compact Design and Maintenance, the device's small size (127 × 68 × 47 mm), light weight (248 g), and simple structure make it easy to operate and maintain with one hand. 3. Simple Controls, no programming or integrated circuits are required, as functionality is managed by four buttons and a toggle switch, ensuring user-friendliness. 4. Portability and Power Supply, although it lacks a built-in battery, the device is designed to connect to a power bank via a simple adapter, with all components running on a 5 V power supply.

After implementation, ScentEcho was employed to evaluate and select suitable adsorption materials for its odor storage units. The device's efficient and user-friendly design proved highly effective for testing the performance of different materials in capturing and replaying various odors.

4 Scent Playback Performance Evaluation

This study evaluates the performance of different adsorbent materials in capturing odorants, primarily through user experiments focusing on the similarity and intensity of reproduced odors. In addition to quantitative ratings, we conducted qualitative interviews to understand how people experience odor fidelity and form expectations about the reproduction of everyday scents.

4.1 Experiment Setup

This study evaluates the collection and playback performance of various adsorbent materials for odorants. The selected odorants, commonly used in HCI research, include lemon, coffee beans, mint, and lavender, as shown in Fig. 2(a), all purchased from local markets. Coffee beans and lavender were stored at room temperature (25 °C), while fresh lemons and mint leaves were refrigerated at −4 °C. Before the experiments, refrigerated samples were brought to room temperature for adsorption. The specifications of adsorbent materials were listed in Table 1. The materials were packed into stainless steel tubes (outer diameter: 6 mm, length: 90 mm) with a particle size of 60–80 mesh and a loading amount of 200 mg. Before use, the adsorption tubes were purged at 250 °C for 30 min and cooled to room temperature.

All experiments were conducted under controlled conditions of 25 ± 2°C and $50 \pm 10\%$ relative humidity. Prior to the experiment, all participants signed an informed consent form, indicating their understanding of the experiment's procedure and their right to withdraw at any time.

Table 1. Specifications of adsorbent materials used in this study.

Code	Type	Supplier's Note
A	Tenax TA	C7–C26[a]
B	Carbopack X	C3–C6
C	AC	–
D	T-CXmix	Tenax TA + Carbopack X

[a] Carbon number range of substances suitable for adsorption.

4.2 User Evaluation Procedure

Both odor collection and playback were conducted using the ScentEcho device. During odor collection, the target odors (lemon, coffee beans, mint, and lavender) were adsorbed onto the selected adsorbent materials (A-D). The collection time was set to 1 min, with minor adjustments based on a study by Lu et al. [14] investigating acceptable durations for odor collection. Then, participants were exposed to the reproduced odors (playback) and asked to rate their similarity and intensity relative to the target odors using a Likert scale [31,32], where the target odor was defined as 7 points (1 = completely dissimilar or no odor; 7 = identical to the target). To evaluate the relationship between odor similarity and intensity ratings, the Pearson Correlation Coefficient was used to assess the relationship between odor similarity and intensity, calculated as Eq. 1, where, X and Y represent similarity and intensity ratings, while $\bar{X}$ and $\bar{Y}$ are their means.

$$\gamma = \frac{\sum(X - \bar{X})(Y - \bar{Y})}{\sqrt{\sum(X - \bar{X})^2 \sum(Y - \bar{Y})^2}} \tag{1}$$

Participants were instructed to rate the reproduced odors within 10 s and were allowed to re-smell the target odor as needed—see Fig. 2(b). The rating form (Appendix A) collected personal information and scoring data, as well as responses to questions such as: "Do you regularly use perfumes or fragrance-related products?" and "Do you consider yourself to have a keen sense of smell?" Additionally, exploratory questions were posed during the experiment to further investigate participants' perceptions. These included: "Can you independently evaluate the similarity and intensity of an odor?" and "At what similarity score do you feel confident in identifying the odor source without needing to see the actual object?" The experiment consisted of two main stages. Odor preparation, including collection and playback setup, required approximately 40 min. And participant evaluations took an additional 30 min. To minimize fatigue and ensure accuracy, a 3-min rest period was provided between exposure to different target odors.

Fig. 2. Evaluation and analysis. a) Odor materials used in the experiment, from left to right: coffee beans, fresh lemon, mint leaves, and dried lavender, b) A participant using ScentEcho to evaluate odor similarity and intensity.

5 Results

This study recruited 12 participants (6 males and 6 females) aged between 22 and 49 years, with an average age of 31.2 years (standard deviation: 7.3). Regarding the question, "Do you regularly use perfumes or fragrance-related products?", 2 participants reported frequent use, 9 reported occasional use, and 1 reported no use. For self-assessed olfactory sensitivity, 1 participant strongly agreed they were sensitive, 5 agreed, 4 were neutral, and 2 disagreed. Overall, most participants had experience using perfumes or fragrances, but their self-perception of olfactory sensitivity varied widely. These background characteristics help contextualize participants' olfactory evaluations in the subsequent analyses.

5.1 Ratings of Odor Playback Fidelity

The similarity and intensity rating results are shown in Fig. 3. For similarity, different adsorbent materials showed varying performance across odor types. For example, material A performed well with mint, receiving an average similarity score of 4.5, while material D achieved a relatively high score of 5.3 for lavender. The similarity scores for coffee and lemon odors showed relatively small differences across the four adsorbent materials (coffee: 4.2–4.3; lemon: 3.9–4.1). In terms of intensity, material D stood out for lavender (5), whereas materials A, B, and C all achieved relatively high intensity scores for coffee (above 4). Overall, the findings suggest that different adsorbent materials are better suited for different types of odors, with their effectiveness varying across both similarity and intensity dimensions.

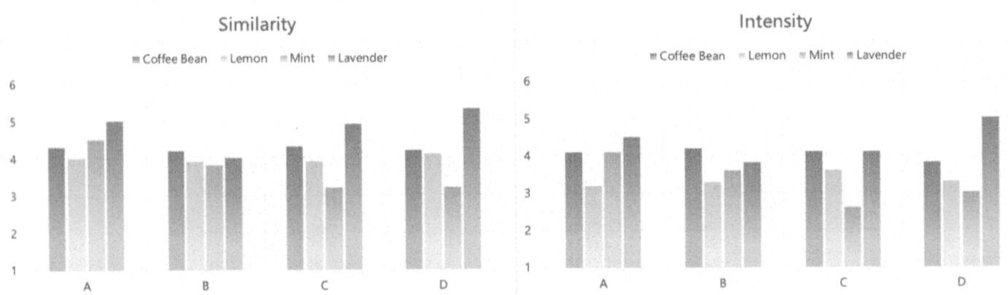

Fig. 3. The score of odor similarity (left) and intensity (right).

5.2 User Perceptions of Odor Similarity and Intensity

Analysis of user ratings revealed a strong positive correlation between perceived similarity and intensity, with a Pearson correlation coefficient of 0.8295 (Fig. 4). This indicates that similarity ratings tended to increase with perceived odor strength.

During the experiment, participants were asked whether they could evaluate similarity and intensity independently. Among the 12 participants, 7 reported difficulty in distinguishing the two dimensions, particularly when the reproduced scent was weak. The remaining 5 participants indicated that they could evaluate them separately when intensity was sufficiently strong.

Participants were also asked how similarity ratings related to odor recognition. At similarity scores of 3–4, users tended to associate the scent with general categories (e.g., mint with toothpaste or mint candy). At scores of 5–6, they were able to identify more specific odor sources, such as "fresh mint leaves."

In this study, several adsorbent materials achieved playback that received user-rated similarity scores above 5 for specific target odors. This indicates that the system was capable of reproducing scents with a high degree of perceptual fidelity, where the released odors closely matched the original odor sources as experienced by users.

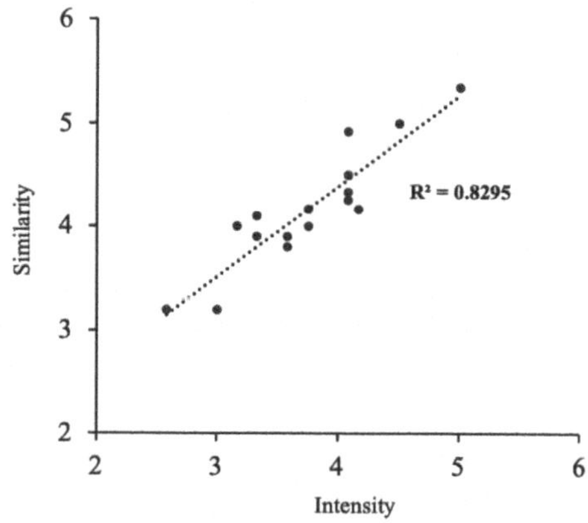

Fig. 4. Correlation between scores of odor similarity and intensity (across all odors and participants).

6 Discussion

This section examines how odor similarity and intensity influence perception, and how different adsorbent materials impact recognition. We discuss key design challenges in olfactory interaction based on user feedback and perceptual evaluation results.

6.1 The Interdependence of Similarity and Intensity in Odor Perception

A strong correlation was found between perceived intensity and similarity ($r = 0.8295$), suggesting that users often conflate these two dimensions when evaluating odors. During the experiment, 7 out of 12 participants reported being unable to distinguish similarity from intensity, especially when the reproduced scent was weak. However, 5 participants noted that once the scent reached a certain intensity threshold, they could evaluate similarity more independently. This reveals a key challenge in olfactory perception—where reduced intensity can obscure odor characteristics and impair recognition.

Interestingly, when asked about auditory perception as a comparison, most participants (8 out of 12) indicated they could distinguish between timbre (analogous to odor similarity) and volume (analogous to odor intensity). This contrast suggests that olfactory perception may involve more entangled perceptual dimensions than auditory ones, potentially due to its chemical basis and less practiced use in discrimination tasks.

These findings imply that odor playback systems must ensure not only that the scent composition reflects the original odor profile, but also that the intensity is sufficient for users to perceive the intended similarity. Therefore, intensity should be considered a foundational design parameter, especially in use cases that demand precise recognition.

6.2 Hierarchies of Odor Recognition and Design Implications

User feedback also revealed a perceptual hierarchy in odor identification. At similarity scores of 3–4, participants could identify general categories (e.g., associating mint with toothpaste or mint candy), while at scores of 5–6, they could pinpoint specific odor sources such as "fresh mint leaves." This observation suggests that olfactory recognition occurs along a graded spectrum, and system designers may leverage this knowledge to define fidelity goals based on context.

For instance, in ambient experience design, evoking general odor categories may suffice to create emotional or atmospheric effects. In contrast, applications requiring precision (e.g., culinary training or fragrance reproduction) may demand more accurate scent reconstruction. Thus, the level of perceptual resolution achievable through a given system should be aligned with its intended purpose.

6.3 Practical Considerations and Future Directions

This study identified several practical considerations that may inform future refinement of the ScentEcho system. First, the sample size was limited to 12 participants aged 23–35, whose olfactory sensitivity may not reflect broader user populations. Second, the intensity of the reproduced odors was generally weaker than the original, as reported by multiple participants. While longer adsorption times might enhance scent strength, this would also increase preparation time and reduce responsiveness in real-time applications. Third, some participants noticed faint metallic smells when testing weaker odor samples, likely due to the use of stainless steel adsorption tubes. Additionally, the current design activates the air pump even when all solenoid valves are off, potentially affecting the pump's lifespan and compromising airtightness.

To address these issues, several improvements are planned. These include refining the circuit to ensure the air pump activates only when an airflow pathway is open, and incorporating a heating element to enhance control over release intensity. Additionally, inert alternatives such as fluoropolymers will be investigated to minimize material-related interference. Future experiments will also include a wider range of scent compounds, from light to heavy odors, to better reflect the diversity of smells encountered in real-world settings. To improve odor reproduction fidelity, we plan to evaluate modified or composite adsorbent materials and consider integrating electronic nose systems for continuous monitoring.

Despite these limitations, ScentEcho demonstrates strong potential as a modular scent playback platform for HCI. Its flexible configuration and compatibility with multiple adsorbent materials make it a promising tool for applications in personalized scent experiences, scent-triggered memory recall, multisensory storytelling, and sensory training.

7 Conclusion

This study presents ScentEcho, a portable system for personalized scent collection and playback. By integrating modular hardware and adsorbent material evaluation, it enables realistic odor reproduction beyond predefined fragrances. User studies revealed how scent similarity and intensity interact in perception, underscoring the importance of human-centered evaluation in material selection. ScentEcho bridges a key gap in HCI by supporting more contextual and emotionally resonant olfactory interactions. Although the current prototype supports four odor channels, its modular structure is designed to accommodate future expansion through additional units and improved component integration. Its flexible design opens new possibilities in applications such as targeted scent delivery, memory recall, and multisensory storytelling.

Acknowledgments. This work was supported by the Foundation of the National Key Laboratory of Human Factors Engineering (Grant No. HFNKL2023J08) and the National Natural Science Foundation of China (Grant Nos. 62441219 and 62172252).

Disclosure of Interests. The authors have no competing interests to declare that are relevant to the content of this article.

Appendix A: Odor Similarity and Intensity Rating Form (For User Experimentation)

I. Personal Information

Name: ________________ Gender: ___________ Age: ___________

1. Do you usually have the habit of using perfumes or fragrance-related products?

☐ Never ☐ Occasionally ☐ Sometimes ☐ Often ☐ Daily

2. Do you consider yourself a person with a keen sense of smell?

☐ Strongly Disagree ☐ Disagree ☐ Neutral ☐ Agree ☐ Strongly Agree

II. Odor Similarity and Intensity Evaluation

Instructions for Scoring: The similarity and intensity of the standard sample are defined as 7 points. Please use this as a reference to evaluate the scores for samples A–H.

(1 = Completely dissimilar or no odor at all; 7 = Identical to the standard sample)

Code	Target Odor 1		Target Odor 2	
	Similarity (1–7)	Intensity (1–7)	Similarity (1–7)	Intensity (1–7)
A				
B				
C				
D				

Code	Target Odor 3		Target Odor 4	
	Similarity (1–7)	Intensity (1–7)	Similarity (1–7)	Intensity (1–7)
A				
B				
C				
D				

References

1. Iseki, M., Prasetyawan, D., Yokoshiki, Y., Nakamoto, T.: A study of odor reproduction using multi-component olfactory display. Electric. Eng. Japan **215**(3), e23392 (2022)
2. Krusemark, E.A., Novak, L.R., Gitelman, D.R., Li, W.: When the sense of smell meets emotion: anxiety-state-dependent olfactory processing and neural circuitry adaptation. J. Neurosci. **33**(39), 15324–15332 (2013)
3. Amores, J., Maes, P.: Essence: olfactory interfaces for unconscious influence of mood and cognitive performance. In: Proceedings of the 2017 CHI Conference on Human Factors in Computing Systems, pp. 28–34 (2017)
4. Brooks, J., Lopes, P.: Smell & paste: low-fidelity prototyping for olfactory experiences. In: Proceedings of the 2023 CHI Conference on Human Factors in Computing Systems, pp. 1–16 (2023)
5. Lu, Q., et al.: Atmospheror: towards an olfactory interactive system for enhancing social presence and interaction in synchronous online classes. In: Extended Abstracts of the 2023 CHI Conference on Human Factors in Computing Systems, pp. 1–8 (2023)
6. Obrist, M., Tuch, A.N., Hornbaek, K.: Opportunities for odor: experiences with smell and implications for technology. In: Proceedings of the SIGCHI Conference on Human Factors in Computing Systems, pp. 2843–2852 (2014)
7. Covington, J.A., Agbroko, S.O., Tiele, A.: Development of a portable, multichannel olfactory display transducer. IEEE Sens. J. **18**(12), 4969–4974 (2018)
8. Zhang, Y., et al.: OdorAgent: generate odor sequences for movies based on large language model. In: 2024 IEEE Conference Virtual Reality and 3D User Interfaces (VR), pp. 105–114. IEEE (2024)

9. Fu, S., Chen, J., Cai, Y., Fan, M.: AromaBlendz: an olfactory system for crafting personalized scents. In: Extended Abstracts of the CHI Conference on Human Factors in Computing Systems, pp. 1–5 (2024)
10. Prasetyawan, D., Nakamoto, T.: Odor reproduction technology using a small set of odor components. IEEJ Trans. Electr. Electron. Eng. **19**(1), 4–14 (2024)
11. Mohan, M.: Smell camera: record, play, rewind (2017). https://www.media.mit.edu/projects/smell-camera2/overview/
12. Murins, S.: Can you imagine finally being able to capture scent of the moments? (2021). https://www.scentcamera.com
13. Radcliffe, A.: Madeleine "smell camera" records odors for the future (2013). https://newatlas.com/smell-camera-madeleine/28126/
14. Lu, Q., Liang, W., Wu, H., Wong, H., Mi, H., Xu, Y.: Exploring potential scenarios and design implications through a camera-like physical odor capture prototype. In: Proceedings of the 2020 ACM Designing Interactive Systems Conference, pp. 2021–2033 (2020)
15. Brianza, G., Tajadura-Jiménez, A., Maggioni, E., Pittera, D., Bianchi-Berthouze, N., Obrist, M.: As light as your scent: effects of smell and sound on body image perception. In: Lamas, D., Loizides, F., Nacke, L., Petrie, H., Winckler, M., Zaphiris, P. (eds.) INTERACT 2019. LNCS, vol. 11749, pp. 179–202. Springer, Cham (2019). https://doi.org/10.1007/978-3-030-29390-1_10
16. Fraune, M., Derflinger, A., Grosofsky, A.: A scent to impress: the smell of lavender enhances trust of robots. In: Proceedings of the 10th International Conference on Human-Agent Interaction, pp. 245–246 (2022)
17. Garcia-Ruiz, M., El-Seoud, S.A., Edwards, A., Aljaam, J.M., Aquino-Santos, R.: Integrating the sense of smell in an educational human-computer interface. Interact. Comput. Aided Learn. (2008)
18. Herz, R.S., Beland, S.L., Hellerstein, M.: Changing odor hedonic perception through emotional associations in humans. Int. J. Comp. Psychol. **17**(4) (2004)
19. Madzharov, A., Ye, N., Morrin, M., Block, L.: The impact of coffee-like scent on expectations and performance. J. Environ. Psychol. **57**, 83–86 (2018)
20. Gao, P., et al.: Mul-O: encouraging olfactory innovation in various scenarios through a task-oriented development platform. In: Proceedings of the 37th Annual ACM Symposium on User Interface Software and Technology, pp. 1–17 (2024)
21. Lei, Y., Lu, Q., Xu, Y.: O&O: a DIY toolkit for designing and rapid prototyping olfactory interfaces. In: Proceedings of the 2022 CHI Conference on Human Factors in Computing Systems, pp. 1–21 (2022)
22. Wang, Y., Cui, Z., Gong, H., Chen, T.: OlfacKit: a toolkit for integrating atomization-based olfactory interfaces into daily scenarios. Int. J. Hum.-Comput. Interact. **40**(16), 4392–4411 (2024)
23. Yan, Y., Yuan, M., Wang, Y., Wang, Q., Liao, X., Li, X.: ScentCarving: fabricating thin, multi-layered and paper-based scent release through laser printing. In: Adjunct Proceedings of the 36th Annual ACM Symposium on User Interface Software and Technology, pp. 1–3 (2023)
24. Fei, X., Tian, Y., Wang, Y.: Laseroma: a small-sized, light-weight, and low-cost olfactory display releasing multiple odors through pointed heating. In: Adjunct Proceedings of the 36th Annual ACM Symposium on User Interface Software and Technology, pp. 1–3 (2023)
25. You, J., Chen, Y., Wang, X.: Fragrance in sight: personalized perfume production based on style recognition. In: Proceedings of the 30th ACM International Conference on Multimedia, pp. 7239–7240 (2022)

26. Kaeppler, K., Mueller, F.: Odor classification: a review of factors influencing perception-based odor arrangements. Chem. Senses **38**(3), 189–209 (2013)
27. Iatropoulos, G., Herman, P., Lansner, A., Karlgren, J., Larsson, M., Olofsson, J.K.: The language of smell: connecting linguistic and psychophysical properties of odor descriptors. Cognition **178**, 37–49 (2018)
28. Azmir, J., et al.: Techniques for extraction of bioactive compounds from plant materials: a review. J. Food Eng. **117**(4), 426–436 (2013)
29. Gallagher, M., Wysocki, C.J., Leyden, J.J., Spielman, A., Sun, X., Preti, G.: Analyses of volatile organic compounds from human skin. Br. J. Dermatol. **159**(4), 780–791 (2008)
30. Lucchesi, M.E., Chemat, F., Smadja, J.: Solvent-free microwave extraction of essential oil from aromatic herbs: comparison with conventional hydro-distillation. J. Chromatogr. A **1043**(2), 323–327 (2004)
31. Stoklasa, J., Talášek, T., Luukka, P.: Fuzzified Likert scales in group multiple-criteria evaluation. In: Soft Computing Applications for Group Decision-Making and Consensus Modeling, pp. 165–185. Springer (2017)
32. Torriani, G., Torresin, S., Lara-Ibeas, I., Albatici, R., Babich, F.: Perceived air quality (PAQ) assessment methods in office buildings: a systematic review towards an indoor smellscape approach. Build. Environ., 111645 (2024)

PosturePet: Glanceable, Emotion-Driven Biofeedback for Correcting Neck Posture

Grace Yi, Ziyad Fawzy, Lily Sheng, Hanyu Zhou, and Yuntao Wang(✉)

Tsinghua University, Beijing, China
{yixy24,fjz24,cqr24,zhouhany24}@mails.tsinghua.edu.cn,
yuntaowang@tsinghua.edu.cn

Abstract. "Tech neck" is a growing health concern driven by prolonged use of mobile devices. Many posture correction applications employ intrusive notifications, which leads to notification fatigue and eventual user disengagement. This paper introduces PosturePet, a novel iOS application that provides persistent, glanceable, and emotionally resonant biofeedback to encourage healthy neck posture. Leveraging the built-in inertial measurement unit (IMU) of Apple AirPods, PosturePet monitors the user's head position in real-time. Feedback is delivered ambiently through Apple's Dynamic Island and Lock Screen Live Activities, featuring an animated virtual pet. The pet's emotional state—happy, sad, or sick—directly mirrors the user's posture, creating a continuous, low-friction channel of communication. This design aims to transform posture correction from a clinical chore into an empathetic interaction. We conducted a user study comparing our animated pet with two different visual feedback icons (a static Dot and an Emoji) to evaluate its impact on user experience, engagement, adoption intent, and real-world corrective behavior. Our findings suggest that while all glanceable interfaces were equally effective at prompting timely posture correction, the use of an affective agent like the pet significantly improved the overall user experience, making the interaction more attractive, stimulating, and enjoyable.

Keywords: Neck Posture Detection · mHealth · Biofeedback · Glanceable Interfaces · User Engagement

1 Introduction

The ubiquity of digital devices has given rise to a modern ailment commonly known as 'tech neck'—the musculoskeletal discomfort and postural strain caused by prolonged smartphone and laptop use [8]. This issue is a direct consequence of an increasingly sedentary lifestyle [24] and is associated with significant negative health side effects [20]. While many mobile health (mHealth) systems have been developed to address this, they often struggle with long-term user retention and engagement [2] (Fig. 1).

G. Yi, Z. Fawzy, L. Sheng and H. Zhou—Authors contributed equally to this research.

S. Guo et al. (Eds.): HHME 2025, CCIS 2878, pp. 81–97, 2027.
https://doi.org/10.1007/978-981-92-3991-7_7

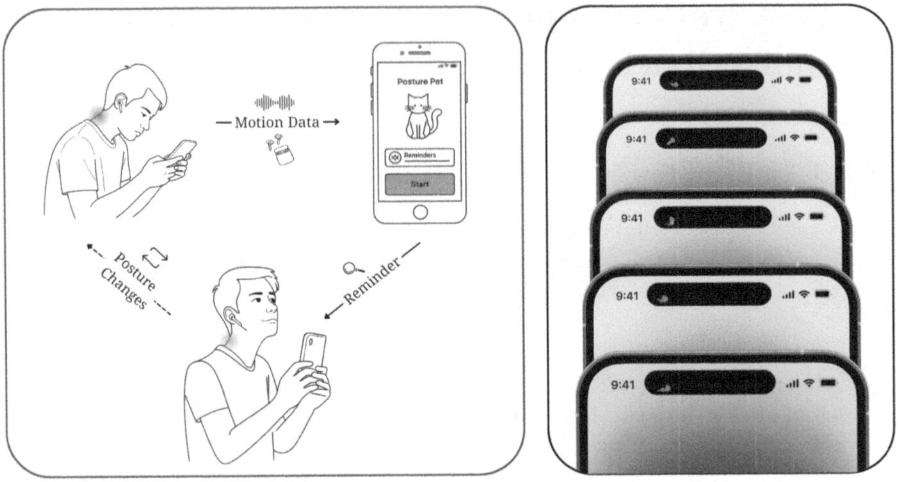

Fig. 1. The mobile app PosturePet reminds the user to adjust their neck posture.

A growing body of research demonstrates the efficacy of employing digital companions (or virtual pets) as a means of boosting user engagement and adherence in various health-related contexts, including healthy diet, physical activity, and mental health. Byrne et al. [4] conducted a field experiment showing that adolescents who received feedback from a virtual pet were twice as likely to eat breakfast compared to those who did not. Ahn et al. [1] demonstrated a sustained increase in physical activity among 6- to 11-year-olds who received support from a virtual dog. Demiris et al. [7] utilized digital companions for daily conversations and reminders, showing a reduction in depressive symptoms over a three-month period among community-dwelling older adults with mild cognitive impairment. Similarly, Chi et al. [6] reported an alleviation of feelings of social isolation among older adults who used their conversational digital pet. These outcomes echo long-standing observations of the "Tamagotchi effect," where sustained emotional bonds with digital companions drive repeated, attentive interaction [13].

The need for a more engaging and less intrusive approach is evident even in the current market. For instance, while commercial products such as the Samsung Galaxy Buds2 Pro offer posture detection, they employ a delayed, all-or-nothing notification model: the system provides no intermediate cues and delivers only a single, interruptive alert after a ten-minute threshold is met. This lack of real-time awareness, combined with usability challenges, motivated our work. Drawing inspiration from the "Tamagotchi effect," we designed PosturePet to transform posture biofeedback into an engaging, empathetic interaction. The system leverages the built-in inertial measurement unit (IMU) in Apple AirPods to unobtrusively monitor neck posture. Instead of traditional notifications, feedback is delivered through a virtual pet that resides in the iPhone's Dynamic Island—a persistent, glanceable display area. The pet's emotional state, from happy to sick, directly mirrors the user's posture quality, creating a continuous, low-friction feedback loop intended to encourage users to maintain a healthy posture not simply to dismiss an alert, but to care for their digital companion.

By combining emotion-driven design with glanceable biofeedback, PosturePet offers a novel approach to posture correction. In a controlled comparative study, we evaluated our virtual pet against two simpler, functionally similar baselines. Our results demonstrate that while all glanceable interfaces were equally effective at prompting timely posture correction, the affective pet significantly improved the overall user experience, engagement, and adoption intent. These findings suggest that fostering an affective bond is a key strategy for addressing the challenge of long term adherence in mHealth interventions.

2 Related Work

2.1 Digital Biofeedback for Behavioral Change in mHealth

Mobile health applications (mHealth apps) have emerged as effective tools for managing and enhancing health-related behaviors by facilitating patient engagement, improving communication with healthcare providers, and promoting healthy habits. These applications empower patients to track health metrics, manage chronic conditions, and access personalized health resources, thereby improving overall health outcomes and reducing healthcare costs [18]. A critical component of successful mHealth interventions is the integration of timely feedback and reminders, as well as the provision of social and clinical support within the app ecosystem [2]. One powerful form of such feedback is biofeedback, a process in which systems capture data about a user's physiological state and "feed it back" through a perceptible cue, enabling the user to learn self-regulation.

Feedback systems embedded in digital applications effectively disrupt and alter habitual behaviors by enhancing self-monitoring capabilities. Hermsen et al. [9] highlighted that digital feedback interventions demonstrate efficacy in habit disruption across various behaviors and contexts. However, the durability of habit change and the precise conditions under which digital feedback is most effective remain areas requiring further exploration.

2.2 Posture Monitoring and Detection

Persistent neck- and back-related musculoskeletal disorders have motivated a steady evolution of digital posture-support systems, moving from laboratory hardware toward everyday wearables [20,23]. Early prototypes depended on external sensing rigs—for example depth-camera setups or chairs outfitted with pressure matrices—to estimate joint angles and prompt users on a workstation display [11,22]. Subsequent work placed the sensing directly on the body, embedding multiple inertial-measurement units (IMUs) in rigid braces, compression shirts, or smart vests so that posture could be tracked continuously during naturalistic activity [16,19].

Table 1. Mapping of posture states to the corresponding visual feedback for each of the three experimental conditions.

System State	PosturePet	PostureEmoji	PostureDot	Posture State
Neutral				Good Posture
Sad			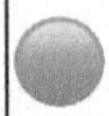	Bad Posture
Sick			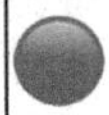	Sustained Bad Posture
Dancing				Corrected Posture
Happy				Sustained Corrected Posture

To lighten the device burden, recent studies have repurposed commodity electronics with built-in IMUs, including smartphones, smartwatches, and wireless earbuds to infer head or trunk orientation with little extra hardware [14,17,21]. Across these platforms, feedback is typically utilitarian: coloured dots, brief vibrations, or warning tones delivered as soon as the wearer's posture strays beyond a threshold, occasionally augmented by simple scoreboards or points to reinforce compliance [16,19]. While such cues produce timely corrections, their largely non-affective nature limits long-term engagement.

On the algorithmic front, posture-classification accuracy has benefited from hybrid and deep-learning pipelines that fuse traditional machine-learning features with convolutional or adversarial networks, enabling robust pose estimation even under occlusion or noisy sensor readings [5,15]. Yet, despite these technical gains, sustaining healthy posture habits over weeks or months remains challenging, underscoring the need for solutions that pair reliable sensing with feedback able to foster durable user commitment.

2.3 Enhancing Engagement Through Emotional Cues

Emotional engagement has increasingly become recognized as pivotal in user interface and experience design, particularly within health-related mobile applications. The incorporation of emotional cues, such as personalized avatars or narrative storytelling, helps establish an affective bond, thereby significantly enhancing user engagement and promoting sustained behavioral change [3]. Additionally, gamification strategies incorporated into mobile health apps effectively drive user engagement and promote sustained behavioral changes. By leveraging intrinsic motivation through mechanisms like feedback loops, rewards, and social interactions, gamification has shown positive impacts on health-related behaviors such as increased physical activity and adherence to health routines [3,10]. Crucially, the effectiveness of gamification depends heavily on user-centered design, ensuring that the elements resonate personally with users [2].

3 Design and Implementation

PosturePet is implemented as an iOS application that monitors a user's head posture using motion data from connected AirPods. The system processes a real-time stream of sensor data, maps posture to different states, and uses the iOS Live Activities framework to provide a persistent, ambient display of feedback. This allows feedback without requiring the main application to be in the foreground. To investigate the role of affective engagement, we designed three interfaces with progressively richer emotional cues (see Table 1).

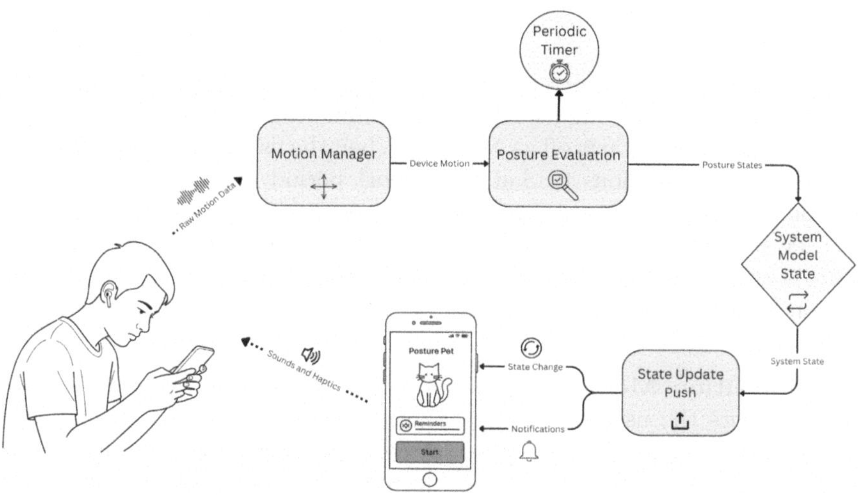

Fig. 2. General system architecture of the application for the three experimental conditions.

3.1 System Architecture

The system consists of a native iOS application with a Widget Extension. The main application handles the main user interface, including an onboarding tutorial that teaches the user the mappings of the posture to the different states, user controls for starting and stopping the tracking, and status views of the posture (Fig. 2).

The Widget Extension creates the Live Activity and is a separate process that receives state updates from the main applications. A Live Activity is a dynamic, real-time display of information from an app that appears prominently on an iPhone's Lock Screen and within the Dynamic Island (on compatible models). The Dynamic Island is an interactive, adaptive area at the top of certain iPhone screens. Unlike traditional notifications that are static or disappear, Live Activities provide continuous, glanceable updates about ongoing events or tasks, allowing users to stay informed without unlocking their phone or opening the main application.

A feature unique to PosturePet is the ability to name the pet when the user first enters the application, a key component of the gamification strategy. The chosen pet name is consistently used throughout the app, reinforcing user attachment.

For real-time posture detection, the system implements a rule-based mapping between raw motion data to posture state.

Input Data. The system registers a delegate to receive a continuous stream of motion data objects when monitoring is active.

State Model. There are five possible states (Sick, Sad, Neutral, Happy, Dancing). Each state is associated with distinct animation frames for different baselines. The user's state starts off as Neutral. When the user's neck posture becomes poor, the state transitions to Sad for a short period of time and then to Sick when the poor posture is sustained for a long period of time. When the user corrects their posture, the state transitions from Sick to Dancing. When the correct posture is sustained for a long period of time, the Dancing transitions to Happy and then back to Neutral.

State Transition Model. A periodic timer triggers an evaluation method, which considers the user's current posture based on the head's pitch angle. A value of below $-20.0°$ is considered as "bad posture". The system maintains timers to track both the continuous duration of good posture and bad posture respectively. State transitions are determined by comparing these durations against predefined time thresholds.

Content and Alert Updates. The system pushes state updates to the Live Activity (Dynamic Island and Lock Screen Widget). This allows for silent UI refreshes for animation frames. It also triggers a system-level notification with sound and haptics, that the user can turn on by choice, providing another modality of gaining the user's attention when posture correction is needed.

4 User Study

To evaluate the user experience and behavioral impact of our three glanceable feedback interfaces, we conducted a within-subjects laboratory experiment with 12 participants recruited from a university campus.

4.1 Participants and Apparatus

Participants (7 M, 5 F) reported using their phones frequently during the day, with screen time averaging a few hours a day. The study was conducted using an iPhone 16 and a pair of Apple AirPods Pro (2nd generation). Each of the three experimental conditions had their own customized app and data logging system.

4.2 Design and Hypotheses

The study used a 3×1 within-subjects design where the independent variable was the feedback interface style with three levels: PostureDot, PostureEmoji, and PosturePet. Based on our design rationale, we formulated the following hypotheses:

H1: The affective interfaces (Emoji and Pet) will yield a higher subjective user experience (as measured by the UEQ) and higher ratings for enjoyment and emotional connection compared to the non-emotional Dot baseline.
H2: The anthropomorphic Pet interface will score significantly higher on hedonic qualities (Attractiveness, Novelty, Stimulation) and emotional connection than the simpler Emoji interface.
H3: All three glanceable interfaces will be equally effective at prompting timely posture correction (i.e., there will be no significant difference in correction latency).

4.3 Experimental Conditions

We designed and evaluated three feedback styles with progressively richer visual and emotional cues (see Table 1).

- **PostureDot**: An instrumental baseline using simple color changes (green, yellow, red) based on established warning-signal semantics.
- **PostureEmoji**: An interface introducing a layer of affect using universally understood emojis to map posture quality to facial expression.
- **PosturePet**: Our core experimental condition featuring a small animated avatar[1] whose movements and expressions dynamically respond to the user's posture, designed to foster an emotional connection.

[1] The avatar we used in our app was taken from: https://bowpixel.itch.io/cat-50-animations.

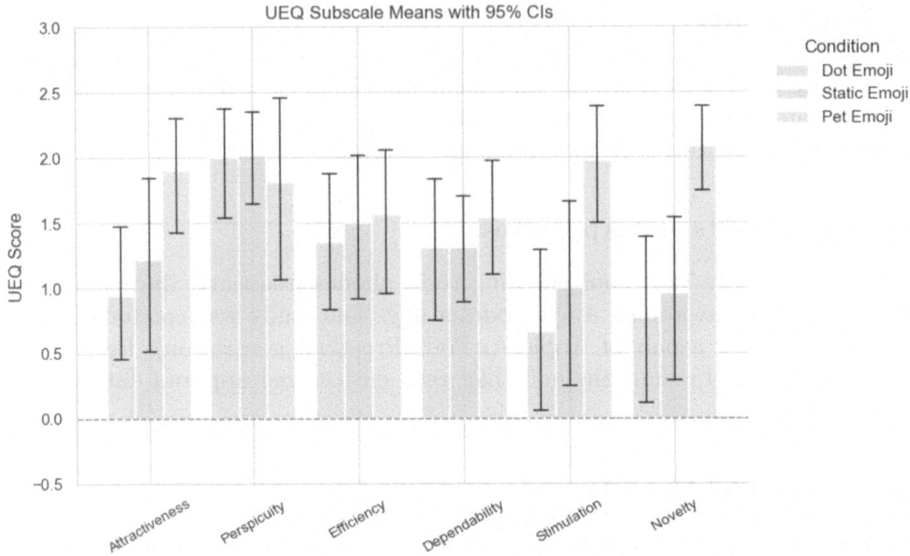

Fig. 3. Mean UEQ scores on the standard -3 to +3 scale for the six subscales across the three feedback conditions (Dot, Emoji, Pet). Error bars represent 95% bootstrapped confidence intervals. The Pet condition consistently outperforms the other two, with particularly large advantages in Stimulation and Novelty.

4.4 Procedure

Using a counterbalanced design, each participant completed three 10-minute blocks of a passive task (video watching). During each block, one of the three feedback styles was active on the Dynamic Island. After each block, participants completed the User Experience Questionnaire (UEQ) and our custom Likert-scale questions. Blocks were separated by a short break to prevent fatigue. At the end of the entire session, participants answered the final adoption intent questions.

4.5 Metrics

To capture both experiential and behavioral outcomes, we designed our metrics to investigate three complementary dimensions: User Experience & Engagement, Adoption Intent, and Correction Latency.

User Experience and Engagement. After each feedback block, participants completed two questionnaires to rate their experience:

User Experience Questionnaire (UEQ). The User Experience Questionnaire (UEQ) [12] is a validated, multi-dimensional instrument specifically designed for rapid, comprehensive assessment of interactive products. It comprises 26 bipolar adjective pairs, empirically reduced via exploratory factor analysis to six scales—Attractiveness, Perspicuity, Efficiency, Dependability, Stimulation, and Novelty.

Custom Likert Items. Three statements probing participants' emotional bond with the feedback icon their motivation to correct posture, and the enjoyment of the interaction. Participants were asked to rank their opinions on a scale of 1 to 7, with 1 representing strong disagreement and 7 representing strong agreement with the statement.

1. I felt an emotional connection to the feedback icon.
2. The feedback icon made me want to correct my posture.
3. I found interacting with the feedback icon enjoyable.

Adoption Intent. At the end of the session, we asked two global questions (1–7 scale) to evaluate real-world applicability:

1. "Compared to your phone's standard notifications (e.g. vibration or banners), how likely would you be to use one of these Dynamic Island feedback interfaces, and which of the three interfaces (Dot, Emoji, Pet) did you prefer the most?"
2. "Overall, compared to how you normally correct your posture (without any app), how much did these feedback interfaces help?"

Correction Latency. Throughout each block we logged objective posture-correction latency (time from "poor posture" alert to when the user corrects their posture). These timestamps allowed us to quantify real-time responsiveness for each feedback style.

By triangulating *UEQ & Likert* (subjective experience), *adoption intent* (stated preference), and *correction latency* (observable behavior), we comprehensively evaluated how Dot, Emoji, and Pet feedback–delivered via a glanceable Dynamic Island overlay–impact engagement, perceived utility, and actual posture improvement.

5 Results

5.1 User Experience and Engagement

Our analysis of the User Experience Questionnaire (UEQ) reveals a clear and statistically significant preference for the **Pet** feedback condition, particularly on the hedonic quality scales. As shown in Fig. 3, the Pet condition received higher mean scores in five out of six dimensions.

To test for statistical significance, we conducted a Friedman test for each of the six UEQ subscales (see Table 2). The analysis revealed a significant difference in perceived **Novelty** across the three conditions ($\chi^2(2) = 17.333$, $p < .001$). Post-hoc analysis with Wilcoxon signed-rank tests with a Bonferroni correction showed that the Pet condition was rated as significantly more novel than both the Dot condition ($T = 0.0$, $p = .003$) and the Emoji condition ($T = 0.0$, $p = .001$).

Similarly, a significant effect was found for **Stimulation** ($\chi^2(2) = 11.619$, $p = .003$). Post-hoc tests confirmed the Pet condition was significantly more stimulating than both the Dot ($T = 3.5$, $p = .015$) and the Emoji ($T = 5.0$, $p = .015$) conditions. For **Attractiveness**, the overall difference was also highly significant ($\chi^2(2) = 8.844$, $p = .012$), with post-hoc tests revealing that the Pet was significantly more attractive than both the Dot ($T = 4.0$, $p = .015$) and the Emoji ($T = 9.0$, $p = .048$).

In contrast, there were no statistically significant differences across conditions for the pragmatic quality scales: **Perspicuity** ($\chi^2(2) = 0.045$, $p = .978$), **Efficiency** ($\chi^2(2) = 0.545$, $p = .761$), and **Dependability** ($\chi^2(2) = 0.533$, $p = .766$). This indicates that while all three interfaces were perceived as equally usable, the Pet interface provided a demonstrably superior user experience.

To assess engagement directly, we analyzed responses to our three custom Likert-scale questions. The mean ratings, shown in Fig. 4, indicate that while all three conditions were similarly motivating, the Pet condition was perceived as more emotionally engaging and enjoyable.

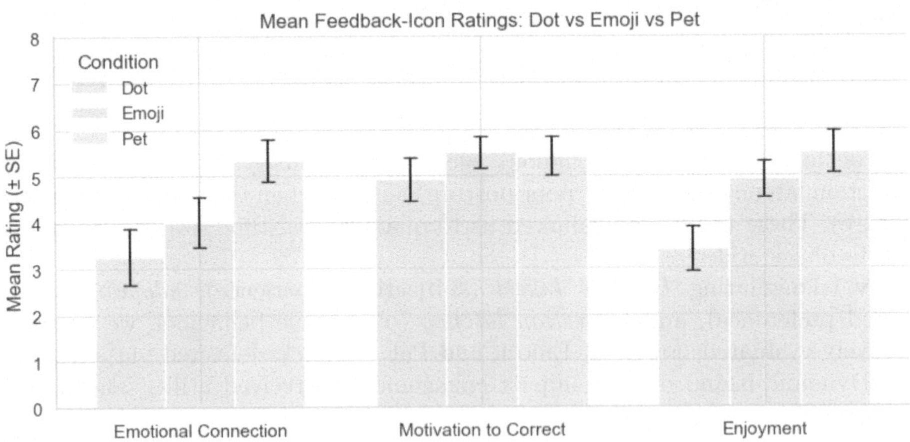

Fig. 4. Mean ratings for the custom Likert-scale questions (1–7 scale). Error bars represent standard error of the mean.

As shown in Table 3, a Friedman test was conducted for each of the three questions. For the statement, *"I found interacting with the feedback icon enjoyable,"* the analysis revealed a highly significant difference, $\chi^2(2) = 15.12$, $p = .001$. Post-hoc tests with a Bonferroni correction confirmed that both the **Pet** ($T = 3.0$, $p = .009$) and the **Emoji** ($T = 0.0$, $p = .006$) were rated as significantly more enjoyable than the Dot.

For *"I felt an emotional connection to the feedback icon,"* the overall difference was also significant ($\chi^2(2) = 9.38$, $p = .009$). While post-hoc tests did not reach the significance threshold after Bonferroni correction, there was a strong trend indicating a stronger emotional connection to the Pet compared to the Dot ($p = .059$).

Crucially, for the statement, *"The feedback icon made me want to correct my posture,"* we found no statistically significant difference among the conditions ($\chi^2(2) = 2.24$, $p = .326$). This important finding suggests that while more expressive interfaces improve the experience, all three glanceable feedback styles were perceived as equally effective at motivating the core corrective action.

Table 2. Results of the Friedman tests for each UEQ subscale across the three conditions. Significant results ($p < .05$) are shown in bold. Pairwise comparisons were conducted using Wilcoxon signed-rank tests with a Bonferroni correction.

Subscale	Statistic (χ^2)	p-value	Significant Pairwise Comparisons ($p < .05$)
Novelty	17.333	$<$ **.001**	Pet > Emoji, Pet > Dot
Stimulation	11.619	$=$ **.003**	Pet > Emoji, Pet > Dot
Attractiveness	8.844	$=$ **.012**	Pet > Emoji, Pet > Dot
Perspicuity	0.045	$=$ .978	None
Efficiency	0.545	$=$ .761	None
Dependability	0.533	$=$ .766	None

Table 3. Friedman test results for custom Likert-scale questions. Significant overall results are in bold. Pairwise comparisons used Wilcoxon signed-rank tests with Bonferroni correction.

Question	Statistic (χ^2)	p-value	Significant Pairwise Comparisons ($p < .05$)
Enjoyment	15.12	$=$ **.001**	Pet > Dot, Emoji > Dot
Emotional Connection	9.38	$=$ **.009**	None after Bonferroni correction
Motivation to Correct	2.24	$=$ .326	None

5.2 Adoption Intent

At the end of the study, we asked participants two global questions to gauge the overall utility and adoption intent of glanceable feedback. Participants reported a high likelihood of using a glanceable feedback interface over standard notifications (M = 5.75, Median = 6, SD = 1.05). A one-sample Wilcoxon signed-rank test confirmed this was a statistically significant positive sentiment compared to the neutral midpoint of 4 ($T = 0.0$, $p = .002$).

Similarly, participants found the feedback interfaces helpful for posture correction compared to no app at all (M = 6.08, Median = 6, SD = 0.90). This sentiment was also highly statistically significant ($T = 1.5$, $p = .0015$). These results confirm that the overall approach was perceived as both desirable and useful.

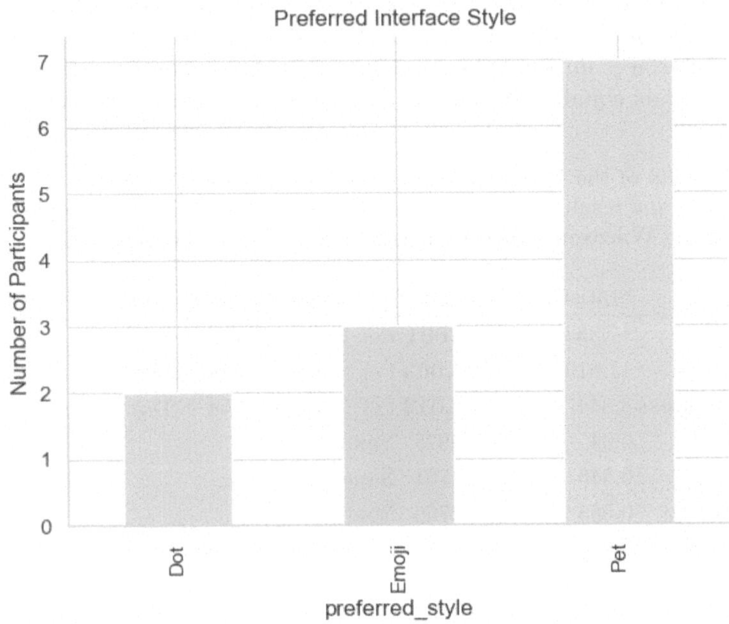

Fig. 5. Count of participants who selected each feedback style as their overall preference at the end of the study.

When asked to choose their preferred feedback style (Fig. 5), a majority of participants (7 of 12, or 58%) selected the **Pet**, followed by the Emoji (3 participants, 25%) and the Dot (2 participants, 17%). While this indicates a strong numerical preference for the Pet interface, a Chi-Squared Goodness-of-Fit test showed that this distribution was not statistically significant ($\chi^2(2) = 3.5$, $p = .174$), likely due to the limited sample size.

5.3 Correction Latency

To complement our analysis of subjective experience, we analyzed the objective posture-correction latency data to determine if feedback style influenced behavioral response time. The data was found to have high variance, which is common for response time measurements.

First, to validate our counterbalanced design, we checked for ordering effects. A Friedman test found no significant difference in response times based on block order ($\chi^2(2) = 0.60$, $p = .739$). This confirms that no significant learning or fatigue effects were present.

Our primary analysis compared the correction latency across the three feedback types (Fig. 6). The median response time was similar across the three conditions: PosturePet (Mdn = 11.0 s), PostureDot (Mdn = 10.0 s), and PostureEmoji (Mdn = 14.0 s). Given the high variance common in response time data, we found no statistically significant difference in latency among the Dot, Emoji, and Pet conditions ($\chi^2(2) = 1.72$, $p = .423$). This important null result suggests that while the hedonic and emotional experience of the interfaces differed significantly, all three glanceable feedback styles were equally effective at prompting a timely behavioral correction.

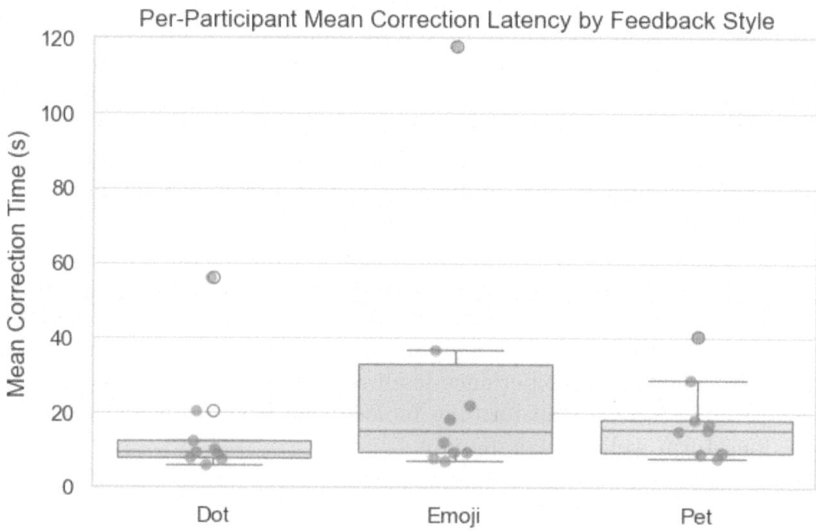

Fig. 6. Box plot of per-participant mean posture correction latency across the three feedback conditions. Note: The Y-axis is clipped at 120 s for readability; three outlier data points with higher values are not shown.

6 Discussion

Our results present a nuanced and important distinction between user experience and behavioral efficacy for glanceable biofeedback. The central finding of our study is that while all three glanceable interfaces were equally effective at prompting posture correction, the use of an affective agent in the Pet condition provided a demonstrably superior user experience.

The most compelling evidence for this distinction lies in the contrast between our subjective and objective measures. Participants rated the Pet as significantly more attractive, stimulating, and novel. They found the interaction more enjoyable and reported a stronger trend towards an emotional connection. Yet, this enhanced experience did not translate into a lower correction latency or a higher self-reported motivation to correct their posture. This null result is a critical finding: for a simple, binary corrective action, the presence of a persistent, non-intrusive cue appears to be the primary driver of behavior, regardless of the cue's emotional valence.

This suggests that the core value of PosturePet's affective design may not be in improving the immediate performance of the corrective task, but in enhancing the user's long-term relationship with the system. Health and wellness applications often suffer from poor long-term adherence. By making the interaction significantly more enjoyable and emotionally resonant, the Pet interface may foster the sustained engagement necessary for habit formation. Users are more likely to continue using a system they enjoy, even if its immediate behavioral prompts are no more effective than a simpler alternative. This aligns with findings from Amagai et al. [2], who identify poor engagement as a primary challenge for mHealth apps, and suggests that focusing on hedonic qualities may be a direct solution to this problem. The high ratings for adoption intent for glanceable feedback in general further support this, indicating a user preference for non-intrusive systems over traditional, disruptive notifications.

Our findings offer a clear design implication for ambient wellness systems: when the goal is to prompt a simple, discrete action, designers may have two equally effective paths. A minimalist, instrumental interface can achieve the behavioral goal, but an affective, hedonic-focused design can achieve the same goal while also making the experience itself a rewarding part of the interaction. This could be the key to transforming biofeedback from a clinical chore into a welcome, long-term wellness companion.

7 Limitations and Future Work

Our study has several limitations which, in turn, motivate clear avenues for future research.

7.1 Controlled Tasks and Notifications

This study was conducted in a controlled setting with standardized tasks and competing system notifications enabled. This setup introduces confounding variables and does not fully capture real-world usage, where tasks like full-screen video viewing are common. Future work should directly compare our glanceable interface against traditional banner alerts in a controlled setting that isolates notification styles. A follow-up study could then systematically investigate the parameters of the pet's animation (e.g., speed, expressiveness) to quantify the trade-off between its attention-grabbing properties and its potential for distraction during varied mobile tasks.

7.2 Statistical Power and Design Questions

With a sample size of N = 12, our statistical power was limited, which is the likely reason the strong numerical preference for the Pet did not reach statistical significance. A future, larger-scale study is needed to confirm this preference and to investigate more nuanced design questions. For example, our results show a strong trend towards a greater emotional connection with the pet, but a future study should compare this affective feedback against a more literal, instrumental avatar that directly mirrors the user's neck angle. This would help disentangle the motivational effects of empathetic connection from those of direct biofeedback.

7.3 Longitudinal Study and Feature Enhancements

One notable limitation is the single-session, lab-based nature of the study, which cannot account for long-term use or ecological validity. Therefore, our primary future work is a long-term, "in-the-wild" deployment of PosturePet. Such a study would allow us to investigate the novelty effect on engagement over time and to measure lasting behavioral change in users' default posture. This deployment would be supported by new features designed to deepen the user experience, including prescriptive guided stretches, seamless gamification (e.g., unlocking pet animations, pet costumes, and custom interactions), personalized AI-driven feedback, and integration with other holistic health data.

8 Conclusion

We presented PosturePet, a system that uses an affective, glanceable interface to provide posture biofeedback. Our user study compared a virtual pet against more traditional emoji and dot interfaces, finding that the Pet provided a significantly more attractive, stimulating, and enjoyable user experience. While all three glanceable interfaces were equally effective at prompting timely posture correction, our results highlight the value of affective design in making health interventions more engaging. This work contributes to the design of ambient wellness technologies, suggesting that focusing on hedonic qualities can be a powerful tool for fostering long-term user adherence, even when not directly improving short-term task performance.

Acknowledgments. We thank the Pervasive Human-Computer Interaction Lab at Tsinghua University for providing the hardware and funding for this work. We also extend our sincere gratitude to all the participants for their time and valuable feedback.

Disclosure of Interests. The authors have no competing interests to declare that are relevant to the content of this article.

References

1. Ahn, S.J., et al.: Virtual fitness buddy ecosystem: a mixed reality precision health physical activity intervention for children. NPJ Digit. Med. **7**(1), 134 (2024)
2. Amagai, S., Pila, S., Kaat, A.J., Nowinski, C.J., Gershon, R.C.: Challenges in participant engagement and retention using mobile health apps: literature review. J. Med. Internet Res. **24**(4), e35120 (2022)
3. Bitrián, P., Buil, I., Catalán, S.: Enhancing user engagement: the role of gamification in mobile apps. J. Bus. Res. **132**, 170–185 (2021)
4. Byrne, S., et al.: Caring for mobile phone-based virtual pets can influence youth eating behaviors. J. Child. Media **6**(1), 83–99 (2012)
5. Chen, Y., Shen, C., Wei, X.S., Liu, L., Yang, J.: Adversarial PoseNet: a structure-aware convolutional network for human pose estimation. In: Proceedings of the IEEE International Conference on Computer Vision, pp. 1212–1221 (2017)
6. Chi, N.C., Sparks, O., Lin, S.Y., Lazar, A., Thompson, H.J., Demiris, G.: Pilot testing a digital pet avatar for older adults. Geriatr. Nurs. **38**(6), 542–547 (2017)
7. Demiris, G., Thompson, H.J., Lazar, A., Lin, S.Y.: Evaluation of a digital companion for older adults with mild cognitive impairment. In: AMIA Annual Symposium Proceedings, vol. 2016, p. 496 (2017)
8. Hansraj, K.K.: Assessment of stresses in the cervical spine caused by posture and position of the head. Surg. Technol. Int. **25**(25), 277–9 (2014)
9. Hermsen, S., Frost, J., Renes, R.J., Kerkhof, P.: Using feedback through digital technology to disrupt and change habitual behavior: a critical review of current literature. Comput. Hum. Behav. **57**, 61–74 (2016)
10. Johnson, D., Deterding, S., Kuhn, K.A., Staneva, A., Stoyanov, S., Hides, L.: Gamification for health and wellbeing: a systematic review of the literature. Internet Interv. **6**, 89–106 (2016)
11. Kim, J., Lee, N.H., Bae, B.C., Cho, J.D.: A feedback system for the prevention of forward head posture in sedentary work environments. In: Proceedings of the 2016 ACM Conference Companion Publication on Designing Interactive Systems, pp. 161–164 (2016)
12. Laugwitz, B., Held, T., Schrepp, M.: Construction and evaluation of a user experience questionnaire. In: Holzinger, A. (ed.) HCI and Usability for Education and Work, pp. 63–76. Springer, Heidelberg (2008). https://doi.org/10.1007/978-3-540-89350-9_6
13. Lawton, L.: Taken by the Tamagotchi: how a toy changed the perspective on mobile technology. iJournal Stud. J. Fac. Inf. **2**(2) (2017)
14. Lee, H., Choi, Y.S., Lee, S., Shim, E.: Smart pose: mobile posture-aware system for lowering physical health risk of smartphone users. In: CHI'13 Extended Abstracts on Human Factors in Computing Systems, pp. 2257–2266 (2013)
15. Liaqat, S., Dashtipour, K., Arshad, K., Assaleh, K., Ramzan, N.: A hybrid posture detection framework: integrating machine learning and deep neural networks. IEEE Sens. J. **21**(7), 9515–9522 (2021)
16. Lind, C.M.: A rapid review on the effectiveness and use of wearable biofeedback motion capture systems in ergonomics to mitigate adverse postures and movements of the upper body. Sensors **24**(11), 3345 (2024)
17. Mollyn, V., Arakawa, R., Goel, M., Harrison, C., Ahuja, K.: IMUPoser: full-body pose estimation using IMUS in phones, watches, and earbuds. In: Proceedings of the 2023 CHI Conference on Human Factors in Computing Systems, pp. 1–12 (2023)

18. Okolo, C.A., Babawarun, O., Arowoogun, J.O., Adeniyi, A.O., Chidi, R.: The role of mobile health applications in improving patient engagement and health outcomes: a critical review. Int. J. Sci. Res. Arch. **11**(1), 2566–2574 (2024)
19. Pereira, A.P., Neto, O.J.M., Elui, V.M.C., Pimentel, M.D.G.C.: Wearable smartphone-based multisensory feedback system for torso posture correction: iterative design and within-subjects study. JMIR Aging **8**(1), e55455 (2025)
20. Simpson, L., Maharaj, M.M., Mobbs, R.J.: The role of wearables in spinal posture analysis: a systematic review. BMC Musculoskelet. Disord. **20**, 1–14 (2019)
21. Takayama, Y., Ishii, S., Yokokubo, A., Lopez, G.: Detecting forward leaning posture using eSense and developing a posture improvement promoting system. In: Adjunct Proceedings of the 2021 ACM International Joint Conference on Pervasive and Ubiquitous Computing and Proceedings of the 2021 ACM International Symposium on Wearable Computers, pp. 178–179 (2021)
22. Taylor, B., Birk, M., Mandryk, R.L., Ivkovic, Z.: Posture training with real-time visual feedback. In: CHI'13 Extended Abstracts on Human Factors in Computing Systems, pp. 3135–3138 (2013)
23. Tlili, F., Haddad, R., Bouallegue, R., Mezghani, N.: A real-time posture monitoring system towards bad posture detection. Wireless Pers. Commun. **120**(2), 1207–1227 (2021)
24. Woessner, M.N., Tacey, A., Levinger-Limor, A., Parker, A.G., Levinger, P., Levinger, I.: The evolution of technology and physical inactivity: the good, the bad, and the way forward. Front. Public Health **9**, 655491 (2021)

A Study on Immersive Experience Design for Ancient Paintings from the Perspective of Interactive Digital Narrative

Hui-Zhu Han, Xiao-Na Ma(✉), Huang-Yi-Ming Wu, Dong Ye, Xin-Yu Wang, and Yu-Chen Li

Beihang University, Beijing, China
373547114@qq.com

Abstract. Immersive digital exhibitions have become an important medium for cultural heritage display, showing great potential in enhancing audience engagement. To overcome the limitations of traditional static displays in conveying cultural narratives, this study proposes an immersive experience design method based on interactive digital narrative theory. Using Zhang Xuan's Tang Dynasty painting "Court Ladies Preparing Newly Woven Silk" as a case study, we created a digital exhibition integrating theatrical scenarios, dual-path narratives, and an intelligent director system. Through multimodal interaction, visitors transition from viewers to active participants, exploring Tang Dynasty social life through pattern discovery and craft experience. Exhibited at the 798 Art Center, user studies confirmed its effectiveness in cultural cognition and emotional immersion. This research provides new approaches for narrative reconstruction and digital transmission of traditional paintings.

Keywords: Immersive Experience · Interactive Digital Narrative · Digitalization of Ancient Paintings · Court Ladies Preparing Newly Woven Silk

1 Introduction

Chinese painting has profoundly influenced global art, yet its preservation faces challenges due to material fragility and aging. Many works have suffered irreversible damage—stains, mold, or loss—before being discovered [1,2]. Traditional exhibitions, often static and planar, further limit engagement, rendering the historical and cultural layers of these works "visible yet hardly comprehensible." Digital replica displays offer an alternative. Current research follows two paths: one focuses on technical restoration, such as Liu Huiyuan's use of the ACP-LaMa algorithm for high-definition reconstruction of ancient paintings [3]; the other explores interactive experiences, such as Wei Ma et al.'s virtual candlelight interface for detail exploration [4], and Yi Zhang et al.'s Ink-Restorer for simulating restoration [5].

S. Guo et al. (Eds.): HHME 2025, CCIS 2878, pp. 98–109, 2027.
https://doi.org/10.1007/978-981-92-3991-7_8

While these approaches improve public access, most remain at the level of viewing or operation, lacking narrative depth and contextual immersion. This limits meaningful audience connection.

To bridge this gap, this paper employs Koenitz's interactive narrative framework to redesign the display of Zhang Xuan's Court Ladies Preparing Newly Woven Silk—an important visual record of Tang dynasty life and culture [6]. Through multimodal interaction involving visual, auditory, and spatial elements, we construct an immersive environment where visitors can "enter" the painting, deconstruct character actions and patterns, and reconstruct their understanding of Tang social life through participatory experience.

The main contributions of this paper are:

Introducing interactive digital narrative theory into ancient painting display design, constructing a narrative-type experience framework for traditional painting;

Through the method of multi-sensory interaction and scene reconstruction, exploring the transformation path of ancient paintings from "objects of viewing" to "spaces of experience";

Providing new design ideas for the reinterpretation and dissemination of traditional paintings in digital media environments.

2 Related Work

This section will focus on the related work of interactive works for ancient paintings and interactive digital theory, understanding the development status of related fields by reviewing previous work, and identifying research gaps.

2.1 Interactive Works for Ancient Paintings

Digital ancient painting projects serve two primary purposes: "restoration" and "interaction." Restoration-focused tools like CAnnotator facilitate color annotation through multi-view interfaces [7], while PColorizor combines cultural semantics with deep learning for accurate color restoration [8]. In interaction, RestoreVR offers virtual conservation experiences for Dunhuang murals [9], and VR animations have reconstructed ancient polo scenes from Yulin Caves [10]. MuralAgent further enables culturally consistent content generation through RAG-based outpainting [11].

Despite these advances, narrative depth remains limited. We thus propose an interactive platform for "Court Ladies Preparing Newly Woven Silk" that promotes embodied engagement with the painting's historical context through direct element interaction.

2.2 Theoretical Research on Interactive Digital Narrative

The theoretical basis of interactive digital narrative lies at the intersection of computer science, narratology, and dramatic aesthetics. Three scholars have laid the foundational framework for this field.

Brenda Laurel, in Computers as Theatre, conceptualizes human-computer interaction as theatrical performance. She views the interface as a “stage” where users become both audience and participant, emphasizing emotional and experiential completeness over mere functionality [6].

Marie-Laure Ryan’s “possible worlds” theory frames user choices as explorations of multiple narrative universes predefined by the system [12]. Janet Murray addresses the “narrative paradox” between user freedom and story structure, proposing “transformative narrative” and “director AI” to maintain dramatic coherence while allowing agency [13].

Building on these works, we propose an Emotion-oriented Intelligent Narrative Framework with three dimensions: - Theatrical Experience Architecture: transforming user actions into meaningful dramatic performances - Possibility Narrative Network: creating multi-path narrative structures - Intelligent Narrative Director: using AI to balance user agency and narrative drama

This integrated approach provides theoretical and practical support for developing interactive narrative systems.

2.3 Interactive Digital Narrative Works

Interactive Digital Narrative (IDN) utilizes multimodal systems and user participation to shape narrative outcomes across various fields. In education, projects like AdLer employ 3D story environments to enhance learning [14], while personalized narratives adapt content to improve engagement [15]. Technologies including voice interaction and AIGC continue to expand IDN’s capabilities [16–18].

In cultural heritage, IDN serves as an important medium for dissemination [9]. The “Revealing the Layers of History” project, for example, uses a 4D model to present architectural evolution through both exploratory and guided narratives [19].

However, existing research focuses primarily on visual reconstruction, leaving traditional craft narratives underdeveloped. We therefore integrate IDN with ancient paintings and pounding craft, creating an interactive framework for narrative reconstruction and cultural transmission through user participation (Fig. 1).

3 Design

3.1 Cultural Investigation of Court Ladies Preparing Newly Woven Silk

“Court Ladies Preparing Newly Woven Silk,” as a silk-based elaborate color painting by Zhang Xuan of the Tang Dynasty, constructs three continuous groups of scenes in the form of a long scroll: pounding silk, weaving and repairing, and ironing. Four women on the right hold pestles pounding silk, three in the middle thread needles and sew clothes, and four on the left cooperate in ironing supplemented by child details, forming a rhythmic visual narrative through scattered perspective, creating an immersive aesthetic experience [20].

Fig. 1. "Court Ladies Preparing Newly Woven Silk" by Zhang Xuan.

The patterns in the painting contain profound cultural connotations, [5] we selected the scrolling lotus pattern, round ke persimmon calyx pattern, tortoise-back auspicious flower pattern, and round ke auspicious flower pattern as the core design elements, symbolizing life force, auspicious meaning, aesthetic of order, and meaning of fulfillment respectively. On the basis of retaining original characteristics, modernization transformation was carried out by increasing color saturation and refining details, making them more suitable for contemporary aesthetics and enhancing visual expression (Fig. 2).

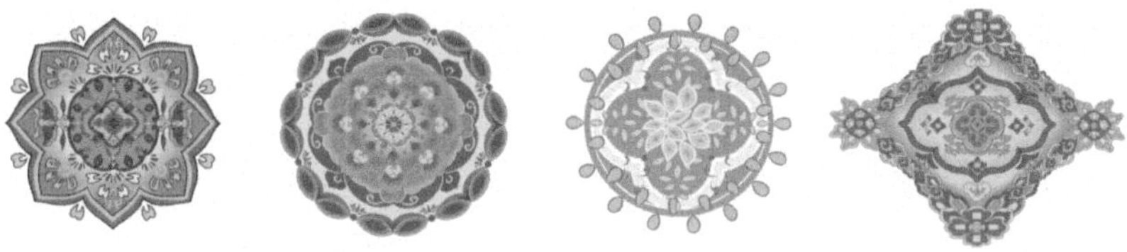

Fig. 2. Designs of Four Representative Patterns in the Picture of Women Pounding Silk.

3.2 Experience Flow Design and Narrative

(1) Theatrical Scenario Foundation: Role Transition from Viewer to Participant

The entrance follows Laurel's theatrical metaphor, constructing a narrative stage with Tang Dynasty court aesthetics. The central dynamic court lady serves as the "narrative guide," whose voice guidance is not simply directional, but an invitation to transform the audience from viewers into the "protagonist" of the story, laying the dramatic foundation for the subsequent experience through spatial and lighting design.

(2) Possibility Narrative Network: Cultural Exploration and Emotional Resonance under the Dual Paths

Based on Ryan's "possible worlds" theory, the visitor's choice opens two parallel narrative universes, each with its own unique narrative logic and emotional trajectory:

Pattern Universe: Narrative of Patterns and Sublimation of Emotion

In the pattern exhibition hall, visitors trigger interaction through the gesture of opening and closing their palms, causing classic patterns like the scrolling lotus pattern to dynamically unfold and present explanations; finally, all patterns diffuse towards the surroundings, creating an immersive experience environment.

Craft Universe: Narrative of Action and Resonance of the Body

In the pounding exhibition hall, visitors can follow the screen prompts and sequentially touch the action nodes of the court ladies pounding silk in the picture——such as "ironing," "folding," "pounding," etc. Each completed touch triggers the system to play the animation demonstration and craft description of that step, constructing a complete cognitive understanding of the textile process. Visitors establish an emotional connection with the Tang Dynasty female labor scene through simulated participation.

(3) Intelligent Narrative Director: Dynamic Generation of Personalized Emotional Paths

To realize Murray's vision of the "digital Aristotle," the system has a built-in intelligent regulation mechanism that can perceive audience behavior in real time and dynamically adjust the narrative experience: extending pattern interpretation for contemplative audiences, strengthening craft feedback for interactive audiences, and introducing unexpected narrative nodes such as poetic lines or special effects when perceiving a decline in emotional investment, to reactivate narrative tension.

4 Implementation

4.1 Scene Construction

In the scene construction for this exhibition, we fully utilized the rectangular screen modules of the Hecoos system to construct two independent yet harmonious display spaces, providing sufficient venue for the two areas of pattern re-creation and pounding process display. Three vertical screens were deployed in each space, including one main front screen sized 9.5 m long and 4 m high, and two side screens each 9 m long and 4 m high, collectively enclosing an immersive visual environment. Furthermore, each space was equipped with a floor screen 9.5 m long and 9 m wide, seamlessly connecting with the vertical screens to form a complete three-dimensional display interface. The pattern re-creation and pounding process display spaces are interconnected, allowing users to choose the area they wish to experience, leveraging users' subjective initiative. This structure not only provides a multi-dimensional visual carrier for the presentation of the patterns and the pounding process of "Court Ladies Preparing Newly Woven Silk" but also becomes a medium for conveying design philosophy and emotional connection, ensuring that the moment the audience enters the space, they can obtain a good immersive experience in both the pattern display and pounding process spaces.

4.2 Technical Realization

(1) The pounding part uses radar and TouchDesigner to build a contactless interaction system. Two-dimensional point cloud data is collected by radar and transmitted to TouchDesigner in real time via the TCP/IP protocol. Geometry COMP and Python scripts are used for cluster analysis to identify hand spatial coordinates and map them to standard screen coordinates. The interface presets 3D virtual hot zones. When the hand stays continuously in a hot zone for a set duration, a click event is triggered, converted into OSC/MIDI signals through the DAT module or Python scripts, controlling the Container COMP to achieve interface switching, and simultaneously triggering audio and animation feedback, forming a complete interaction loop.

(2) The pattern part integrates Kinect and MediaPipe to achieve gesture recognition. Kinect collects depth images, MediaPipe extracts 21 hand key point coordinates, and recognizes the open hand and clenched fist states by analyzing the spatial relationships of the key points. The gesture state is converted into Boolean signals through the CHOP channel, driving the Container COMP to switch interfaces, and cooperating with audio feedback to enhance immersion. This solution utilizes depth vision and neural network models to achieve natural and accurate contactless interaction.

(3) The system architecture is divided into three layers: The perception layer tracks audience trajectory and posture through OpenPose and RGBD cameras, combined with Kinect Azure API for facial expression analysis; the decision layer uses the K-means algorithm to classify audiences into "contemplative," "interactive," and "wandering" types, and dynamically adjusts the narrative tension value based on behavioral data, triggering unexpected nodes; the execution layer controls content presentation through Unity Timeline, adjusting animation speed, knowledge content, and visual feedback for different types of audiences, and calls Tang Dynasty poetic lines and special effects from a preset database to achieve unexpected narratives. The system implements module communication based on the ROS framework, constructing an intelligent narrative environment capable of dynamically responding to audience status.

5 User Study

5.1 Exhibition Site Record

In 2024, this immersive exhibition hall was exhibited at the 798 Art Center, displayed within two semi-open spaces of 9.5×9 m each. The spatial configuration design reflected the core theme of the project, dividing the entire exhibition into two zones, creating an interactive space for non-linear narrative that visitors could choose autonomously. A court lady as a guide was projected at the entrance, reminding visitors of the content and creative background of the two halls through voice, helping users choose their preferred branch. Compared with other digital exhibition halls focused mainly on visual presentation, as an interactive work, it not only combines guidance with autonomous choice but also constructs a relatively reasonable narrative sequence while providing users with freedom of choice. Therefore, the entire exhibition hall occupies a large area, providing sufficient space for users to explore freely (Fig. 3).

Fig. 3. User interaction with patterns (left image) User interaction with the pounding cloth illustration (right image).

5.2 Procedure

The experiment was divided into two parts: questionnaire survey and semi-structured interview.

We randomly selected participants in the immersive exhibition hall, inviting them to fill out the questionnaire and participate in the interview. The questionnaire survey took 3–5 min, and the semi-structured interview took 5–10 min.

Due to time constraints, some participants only completed the questionnaire survey and did not participate in the further interview. Participants scanned the QR code for the online questionnaire and filled out the Likert scale on their mobile devices.

The questions are as follows: Q1-Q4 involve basic information, while Q5-Q10 involve the experience of the immersive exhibition hall. The survey evaluated their preferences and experience feelings. The semi-structured interview mainly included personal basic information and questions related to the immersive exhibition hall experience.

Personal information inquired about age range, purpose for visiting the immersive exhibition hall, and frequency of visiting immersive exhibition halls, etc. Questions mainly raised about the immersive exhibition hall experience included: "First impression of the exhibition hall", "Feelings about the story and plot during the experience", "Whether the interaction felt natural" and "Willingness to recommend this exhibition hall" (Fig. 4, Table 1).

Table 1. Questionnaire on the Immersive Exhibition Hall of Dantianu Painting

Q1	Age
Q2	Gender
Q3	Did this experience pique your interest?
Q4	Do you feel the response is sensitive when interacting with the pattern/daolian?
Q5	Do you think this way of understanding ancient paintings is novel?
Q6	During the experience, did you forget the passage of time?
Q7	Do you feel you can master the interaction process proficiently?
Q8	During operation, do you know what to do next and perform actions naturally?
Q9	Can you clearly tell from the screen or system whether your operation was successful?
Q10	Do you think the process of learning about Tang Dynasty patterns and craftsmanship itself is a pleasure?

5.3 Results

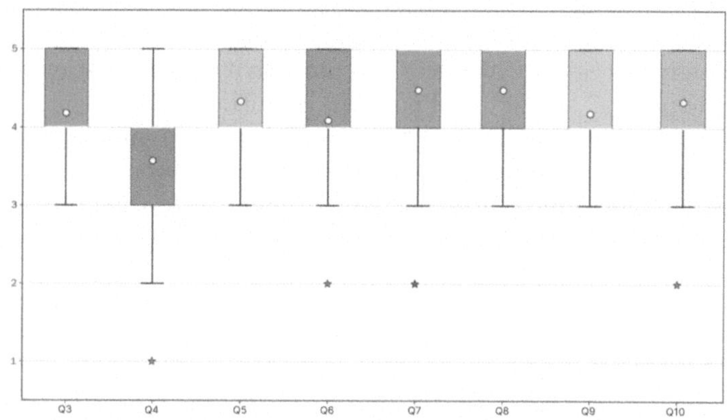

Fig. 4. Quantitative Results.

5.3.1 Quantitative Results

Analysis based on the Likert scale of valid questionnaires shows: the vast majority of participants held a positive and approving attitude towards the digital experience of "interactive technology + traditional culture". The median of core dimensions (interest, novelty, operational feedback, etc.) was approximately 4 (representing "relatively agree" on the 5-point system), and the overall evaluation was good (M = 4.35, SD = 0.58).

Specifically, experiencers gave positive evaluations to the "integration method of pattern interaction with 'Court Ladies Preparing Newly Woven Silk"'. Most respondents believed that this form could effectively convey the cultural connotations of Tang Dynasty patterns (M = 4.20, SD = 0.72), indicating that digital interaction has a prominent function in carrying the dissemination of traditional culture.

However, there were obvious shortcomings in the experience: the evaluation of "interaction response sensitivity" was the lowest among all dimensions (median $\approx$3.6), and there were extremely low negative feedback scores; at the same time, a few participants had poor experiences in "immersion" and "sense of operational control," with individual negative outliers. Overall, users hold an open and accepting attitude towards "digital presentation + traditional cultural inheritance," but the fluency of interaction response is the direction that needs key optimization in the current experience.

5.3.2 Qualitative Results

Audience feedback showed that most audiences could clearly perceive the narrative clues of the exhibition. A mother described it as "like experiencing an afternoon in the painting"; an art student thought "the transition of the three scenes was very dramatic"; a middle-aged audience member said "understood the Tang Dynasty textile process through interaction". This proves that the dual-path design successfully achieved the narrative transformation from "viewing" to "participating". In terms of cultural cognition, art students "recognized the symbolic system of Tang Dynasty patterns through dynamic pattern deconstruction"; middle-aged audiences felt "the pounding process was like an elegant labor ritual"; foreign tourists could also "understand the process of making cloth through interaction". This indicates that multi-modal interaction effectively transmitted cultural knowledge.

In terms of interactive experience, young audiences felt "gesture recognition was intuitive," but art students pointed out that "opening and closing the palm required repeated adjustments"; middle-aged and elderly audiences hoped to "provide a touch screen solution"; foreign tourists thought "there was a lack of operational guidance"; children mastered it quickly while parents were concerned about recognition stability. This reflects that gesture interaction needs optimization in guidance, accuracy, and alternative schemes.

Regarding system response, digital native users noticed that "staying longer would display more detailed content"; audiences with rich cultural background discovered that "content depth changed with the exploration path"; but most ordinary audiences "did not noticeably perceive system adjustments"; parents with children reported that "children could maintain interest all the time". This indicates that the explicit perception of intelligent regulation still needs improvement.

Improvement suggestions included: in terms of content, hoping to "increase interpretation of the ancient painting" and "supplement historical details"; in terms of interaction, expecting "multi-person collaboration" and "haptic feedback"; in terms of the system, needing "more explicit guidance" and "generating user deliverables"; technical experience suggestions included "optimizing recognition accuracy," "adding teaching segments," and "multi-language support".

These suggestions point towards building a more complete, intelligent, and social digital cultural experience ecosystem.

6 Discussion and Future Work

Based on user observation, we found that audiences from different backgrounds present rich and diverse perceptual dimensions in interactive behavior and narrative understanding, mainly reflected in the ways of capturing narrative clues, perspectives for interpreting cultural connotations, and sensitivity to interactive feedback. These differences reflect both the diversity of audience art literacy and media usage habits, and the influence of traditional cultural cognitive foundation on the depth of experience.

When the system transmits complex cultural information through multi-modal methods such as dynamic pattern deconstruction and process restoration, the audience's interpretation of cultural symbols and emotional resonance show significant personal characteristics. Exploring how to maintain the accuracy of cultural expression through intelligent interactive design while supporting personalized meaning construction has become an issue worthy of in-depth discussion.

In the future, we will continue to explore in the following aspects: First, improve the narrative guidance mechanism and enhance the system's ability to dynamically adapt to users' cognitive trajectories; for the interactive experience, we will optimize the accuracy and feedback immediacy of gesture recognition, introduce progressive teaching and multi-modal alternative schemes, and strengthen the system's implicit guidance for users' exploratory behavior. At the same time, integrate environmental lighting and spatial sound more organically into the interactive context, deepening the immersion of the cultural atmosphere.

7 Conclusion

This paper discussed the design path of interactive digital narrative theory in the immersive experience of traditional ancient paintings, taking Zhang Xuan's Tang Dynasty "Court Ladies Preparing Newly Woven Silk" as an example, constructed and implemented a digital exhibition hall integrating theatrical scenarios, dual-path narratives, and an intelligent director system. The exhibition used two narrative lines to show the pounding craft and the patterns of "Court Ladies Preparing Newly Woven Silk" to the audience respectively. The exhibition attracted many people, and the audience generally showed great interest.

References

1. Zhang, Y., et al.: Ink restorer: virtual restoration of ancient Chinese paintings inheriting traditional restoration processes. In: Proceedings of the 2025 CHI Conference on Human Factors in Computing Systems, pp. 1–16 (2025)

2. Wei, S.: Research on hierarchical image restoration of chinese painting. In: 2014 9th International Conference on Computer Science & Education, pp. 663–666 (2014)
3. Liu, H.: Research and practice of ai-based restoration methods for ancient Chinese paintings. Art Stud. Res. **02**, 144–152 (2024)
4. Ma, W., et al.: Walking into ancient paintings with virtual candles. In: Proceedings of the 24th ACM Symposium on Virtual Reality Software and Technology, pp. 1–2 (2018)
5. Li, H.: Viewing tang dynasty women's clothing from zhang xuan's "court ladies preparing newly woven silk". Western Leather **47**(17), 143–145 (2025). https://doi.org/10.20143/j.1671-1602.2025.17.143
6. Laurel, B.: Computers as Theatre, pp. 7–17. Addison-Wesley (2013)
7. Tang, T., et al.: Cannotator: photo-guided color annotation for degraded ancient paintings. In: Proceedings of the 38th Annual ACM Symposium on User Interface Software and Technology, pp. 1–14 (2025)
8. Tang, T., Wu, Y., Xia, P., Wu, W., Wang, X., Wu, Y.: Pcolorizor: re-coloring ancient Chinese paintings with ideorealm-congruent poems. In: Proceedings of the 36th Annual ACM Symposium on User Interface Software and Technology, pp. 1–15 (2023)
9. Fu, X., Zhu, Y., Xiao, Z., Xu, Y., Ma, X.: Restorevr: generating embodied knowledge and situated experience of dunhuang mural conservation via interactive virtual reality. In: Proceedings of the 2020 CHI Conference on Human Factors in Computing Systems, pp. 1–13 (2020)
10. Yan, C.X., Yang, C.: Display of ancient sports games in dunhuang frescoes based on virtual reality animation technology: Take the "boy's batting" on the south wall of cave 15 of the fifth generation in the yulin grottoes as an example. In: Proceedings of the 2023 8th International Conference on Information and Education Innovations, pp. 62–67 (2023)
11. Xu, Z., et al.: Muralagent: enhancing ancient mural outpainting with rag-based texts and multimodal integration. ACM Trans. Multimed. Comput. Commun. Appl. **21**(9), 1–17 (2025)
12. Ryan, M.-L.: Possible Worlds, Artificial Intelligence, and Narrative Theory, pp. 109–158. Indiana University Press, Bloomington, IN (1991)
13. Higgins, J.: Janet h. murray, hamlet on the holodeck: The future of narrative in cyberspace (new york: The free press, 1997), 324 pp. isbn 0-684-82723-9. Convergence 4(4), 128–130 (1998)
14. Dörringer, A., Klopp, M., Rossmann, R.: Digital storytelling in serious games: Empirical research on the impact of narrative in 3d learning worlds, pp. 96–105. (2025). Proceedings of the 6th European Conference on Software Engineering Education
15. Auer, C., Lankes, M.: Enhancing player satisfaction through personality-based narrative adaptation in digital games. In: Proceedings of the 20th International Conference on the Foundations of Digital Games, pp. 1–11. (2025)
16. Chatzifoti, O.: Voice-based interactions in immersive interactive digital narratives. In: Proceedings of the 3rd International Conference of the ACM Greek SIGCHI Chapter, pp. 238–241 (2025)
17. Miao, J., Zhou, Z., Meng, F.: Exploring eco-narrative interaction through aigc: the creative journey of "plast-ocean". In: Companion Publication of the 2025 ACM Designing Interactive Systems Conference, pp. 242–245 (2025)
18. Kong, B., Liang, R.-H.: From sci-fi imagination to everyday interaction: a narrative framework for the self-awakening journey of a smart lamp. In: Proceedings of the 2025 ACM Designing Interactive Systems Conference, pp. 1417–1429 (2025)

19. Andújar, C., Cayuela, B., Lorés, I., Bosch, C., Guardia, M., Munoz-Pandiella, I.: Revealing the layers of history: enriching medieval cultural heritage 4d models with interactive narratives. IEEE Comput. Graphics Appl. **45**, 90–99 (2025)
20. Liu, Q.: Narrative turn and new changes in figure painting: An investigation centered on zhang xuan's "court ladies preparing newly woven silk". Art Observation (06), 100–103 (2025)

Human–Computer Interaction Theory, Methods, and Interface Design

Building Bridges of Communication: A Card-Based Approach to Cross-Disciplinary Design Collaboration

Xuezhu Wang[1], Yao Lu[1], Tianyu Yu[2], Yishan Duan[1], Jialu Ni[1], Yijie Guo[1], Xiwen Yao[1], Kejin Yu[1], Wenjing Deng[1], Xueqing Li[1], Zhiyu Li[5], Guanhong Liu[3], Haipeng Mi[1(✉)], and Yuan Yao[4(✉)]

[1] Tsinghua University, Beijing, China
mhp@tsinghua.edu.cn
[2] University of California, Berkeley, Berkeley, CA, USA
[3] Tongji University, Shanghai, China
[4] Beijing Jiaotong University, Beijing, China
yuanyao@bjtu.edu.cn
[5] Beijing Institute of Technology, Beijing, China

Abstract. With the increasing prevalence of cross-domain innovation practices, design teams face communication challenges from stakeholders with diverse disciplinary backgrounds. While existing research has focused on developing design methods and tools, there has been limited exploration of how to facilitate effective multi-stakeholder dialogue in real design scenarios. This study aims to address communication barriers in cross-disciplinary design collaboration through developing a card-based discussion toolkit. Taking the application of smart materials in automotive interior design as a case study, we organized a workshop involving technical researchers (on smart material), interaction designers, and specific industrial teams (on automotive interior design) for validation. The results demonstrate that this toolkit effectively balanced different perspectives and improved collaboration efficiency through structured knowledge transfer and gamified interaction. This research provides new methodological references for cross-disciplinary multi-stakeholder design collaboration while revealing key elements in facilitating cross-domain dialogue in practical design settings.

Keywords: Cross-disciplinary collaboration · co-design · Card-based tools · Design communication · design complexity · human-centered design

1 Introduction and Related Work

As design tasks become increasingly complex and emerging technologies rapidly develop, design work has evolved from single-domain practices to cross-

X. Wang and Y. Lu—contributed equally to this work.

S. Guo et al. (Eds.): HHME 2025, CCIS 2878, pp. 113–127, 2027.
https://doi.org/10.1007/978-981-92-3991-7_9

disciplinary multi-stakeholder collaboration [1–4][1], with the core objective of integrating multi-stakeholder knowledge and resources, solving complex problems, and facilitating practical innovation. However, communication barriers exist among team members with different backgrounds, skills, and interests [5–8]. The communication challenges in cross-disciplinary design collaboration involve complex collaborative environments and multi-stakeholder relationships. These challenges mainly manifest in several aspects: knowledge gaps hinder team members from understanding each other's terminology and concepts, impeding accurate information transfer [7,9–11]; divergent stakeholder interests lead to conflicting objectives, making it difficult for teams to establish unified direction [1,6,8]; while ambiguity in information transmission further reduces communication efficiency, causing delays in decision-making and deviations in execution [6,12,13].

To address coordination and communication issues in design collaboration, existing approaches include participatory design and collaborative design tools and methods. While these tools have certain advantages in identifying user needs and supporting internal team collaboration, they show limitations when dealing with multiple stakeholders. For example, although participatory and collaborative design methods contribute to needs identification and internal collaboration [14,15][2], they fail to effectively address conflicts in stakeholder perspectives or knowledge asymmetry when balancing multi-stakeholder needs [2,14,16]. These limitations result in inefficient multi-stakeholder collaboration, hindering the achievement of design objectives [12,17]. Regarding design tools, card-based tools show potential in improving communication efficiency and collaboration flexibility during the collaborative process due to their structured framework and intuitive presentation [9,18]. However, specialized tools that effectively reduce knowledge gaps and promote efficient multi-stakeholder collaboration remain scarce, increasing the challenge of addressing multi-stakeholder communication barriers [6,7,19,20].

In multi-stakeholder collaboration, establishing a platform that ensures equal voice while effectively guiding all parties in discussion becomes crucial due to differences in knowledge backgrounds and professional perspectives [6,13,21,22]. Ideal communication tools should be based on design process logic, balancing speaking rights through structured approaches, inspiring creativity, and reducing communication burden to provide flexible and efficient solutions for complex collaboration [9,18,23,24].

This research addresses the inefficient communication and consensus-building challenges in cross-disciplinary design collaboration by developing a card-based discussion toolkit. The toolkit balances speaking rights, improves communication efficiency, and stimulates creativity through gamification while supporting outcome documentation and optimization. Its effectiveness in mitigating perspective conflicts and bridging knowledge gaps was validated through workshops

[1] https://www.mindtheproduct.com/managing-misaligned-stakeholders-by-rich-mironov/.

[2] https://www.figma.com/blog/the-future-of-design-systems-is-semantic/.

in complex design scenarios, providing practical reference for cross-disciplinary design methodologies.

2 Methodology

2.1 Design Objectives

Our objective is to design a card-based communication toolkit that enhances multi-stakeholder collaboration efficiency through building a shared information platform and standardized discussion framework. The toolkit should present information in a structured manner, lower understanding barriers, support flexible discussion, and incorporate documentation capabilities. It aims to balance speaking rights among team members, reduce communication barriers, and facilitate efficient multi-stakeholder collaboration.

2.2 Card Toolkit Structure Design

Our card toolkit comprises four core modules, each fulfilling distinct roles in the collaboration process.

- **Knowledge Card:** Facilitates team consensus on professional knowledge and terminology, eliminating misunderstandings caused by information asymmetry.
- **Objective Card:** Promotes unified understanding of problem requirements through user, emotion, and scenario information, inspiring scenario-based thinking in communication.
- **Interaction Card:** Simulates user-system interactions and data to clarify operational pathways.
- **Expression Card:** Provides team members with opportunities for open expression and equal participation in output.

Cards should have a cohesive visual style that integrates graphics and text, with color coding to differentiate categories, ensuring clarity and ease of use.

2.3 Workshop Setup

We validated the card toolkit's effectiveness through workshops, utilizing their strengths in strong interaction and immediate feedback [4,18,23]. The validation focused on smart materials in automotive interior design, addressing functionality, aesthetics, and user experience while balancing technical feasibility, user needs, and market value. During the pilot study's focus group discussions, we identified three main participant groups: technical researchers in smart materials, interaction designers, and specific industrial teams in automotive interior design, which guided the creation of a cross-disciplinary discussion framework.

Card Design in Specific Context. We adapted the toolkit for smart material applications in automotive interior design based on the proposed card structure, as illustrated in Fig. 1a.

- **Knowledge Card (Material Card):** Includes 17 smart material and hardware cards featuring functions like shape-changing, light-emitting, color-changing, and temperature-changing. Barriers for non-technical audiences are reduced through categorized tables and application examples, as illustrated in Table 4.
- **Objective Card:** Subdivided into User Card, Emotion Card, and Scenario Card, each containing 12–17 common entries with icons and designated note areas, as detailed in Table 1.
- **Interaction Card:** We created 18 Input Card entries detailing user behaviors and sensor data to illustrate user-vehicle system interactions, aiding teams in understanding interaction pathways, as presented in Table 2.
- **Expression Card:** Divided into technical, design, and business perspectives, each containing evaluation factor keywords specific to their respective domains, as shown in Table 3. We encourage participants to express from different perspectives, enabling more comprehensive solution assessment and richer cross-domain dialogue.
- **Interior Layout Board:** To aid in visualizing and discussing solutions more intuitively, we offer a top-view floor plan of the automotive interior design as a layout reference, as illustrated in Fig. 1b.

Blank cards are included in each category to promote openness and interactivity, allowing participants to freely contribute content and fostering more equitable discussions.

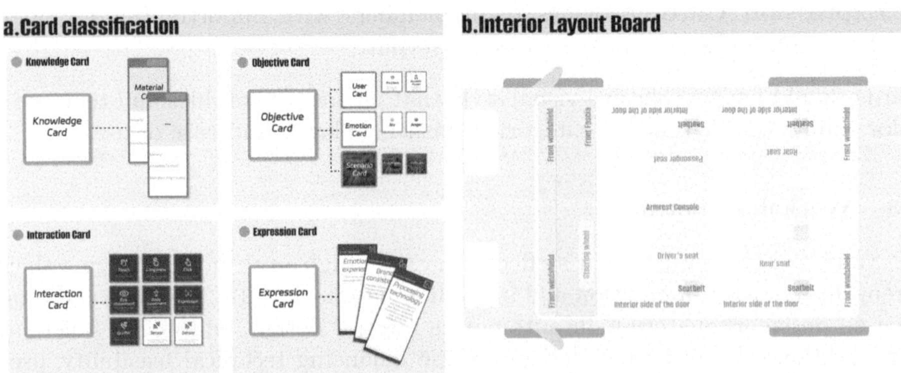

Fig. 1. a. Card classification. b. Interior Layout Board.

Participants. Following the multi-stakeholder framework, we recruited 26 participants (as shown in Table 5), including 5 technical researchers, 11 interaction designers, and 10 industry practitioners. The participants were organized into five groups, each consisting of one technical researcher, at least two designers, and one industry representative to maintain a balance in expertise and gender distribution. Although some groups could not cover all roles due to limited industry member availability, the overall representativeness of data analysis was ensured through the integration of all members' perspectives.

Workshop Process. The workshop, structured into four phases: Explanation, design, evaluation, and summary, systematically guided participants in exploring smart material applications for automotive interiors, ensuring coherent discussions and practical design outcomes (Fig. 3).

- **Explanation Phase (30 min).** This phase introduces workshop objectives, procedures, grouping methods, and tool usage guidelines to help participants understand the stakeholder collaboration model. After announcing group assignments and distributing card tools, each group conducts ice-breaking self-introductions and familiarizes themselves with the card contents, as shown in Fig. 2a.
- **Design Phase (120 min).** This phase employs card tools to facilitate group brainstorming on smart material applications in automotive interiors, encouraging diverse perspectives. Participants follow specific steps, and groups may revisit this phase to explore various design solutions. Each group is expected to produce at least 5 design concepts with varying levels of detail, as shown in Fig. 2b.
- **Evaluation Phase (60 min).** This critical phase involves assessing the previously generated design proposals and soliciting feedback from various stakeholders to gain practical insights. Participants utilize expression cards to provide specific suggestions or comments on each proposal, while documenting the evaluation results, as shown in Fig. 2c.
- **Summary Phase.** The final phase aims to organize and summarize the design proposals explored during the workshop. Participants structure the card contents used in each design proposal and prepare formal written descriptions, as shown in Fig. 2d. Each group is expected to summarize at least 3 design proposals as their final workshop output.

2.4 Data Collection and Analysis

The 18 design concepts from the workshops were refined into 16 structured solutions, categorized by functionality, interior components, and materials (see the Fig. 4), which support the validation of the card toolkit's effectiveness.

We conducted semi-structured interviews to gather feedback on the toolkit's impact on communication efficiency, knowledge sharing, and perspective balance. Through thematic analysis [25], we assessed its effectiveness in fostering

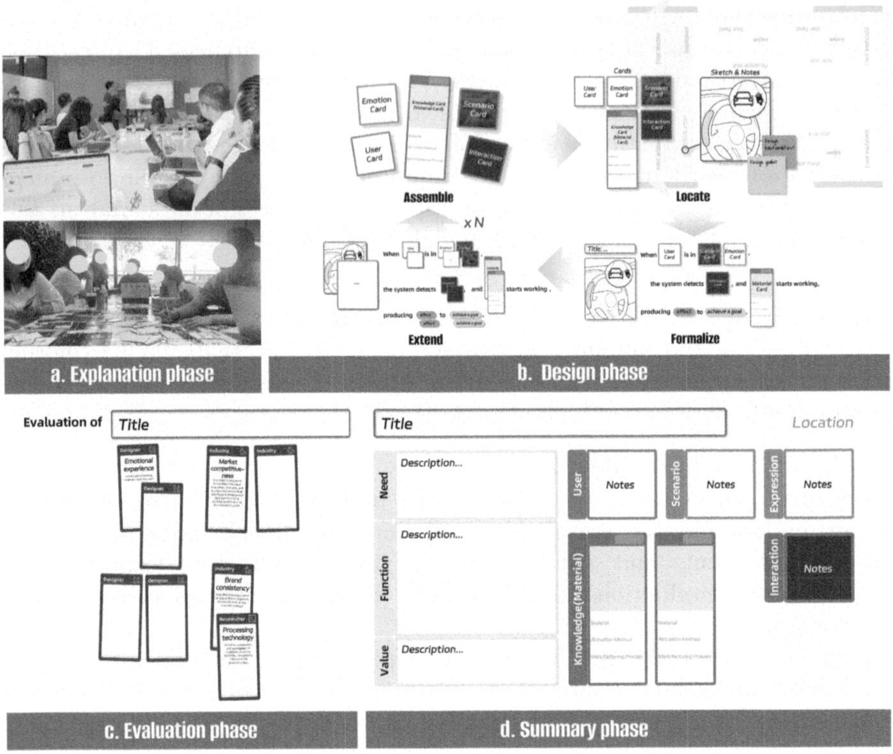

Fig. 2. a. Explanation phase, b. Design phase, c. Evaluation phase, d. Summary phase.

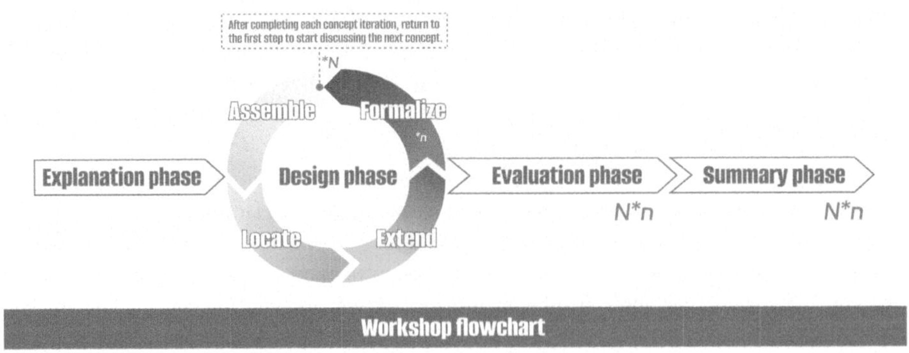

Fig. 3. Workshop flowchart.

collaboration and enhancing efficiency, while also collecting improvement suggestions.

3 Qualitative Analysis

3.1 Providing Unified Language and Mitigating Knowledge Asymmetry

The card toolkit used gamification and a structured framework to bridge communication gaps in cross-disciplinary teams caused by differing knowledge backgrounds.

Interaction designers found the card toolkit effective in clearly conveying user needs and experiences, especially when collaborating with technical researchers and industrial teams. Designer D8 noted, *"The toolkit enabled us to initiate design discussions based on user needs more naturally, avoiding the constraints of professional jargon."*

Technical researchers indicated that the card toolkit enabled them to answer technology-related questions more efficiently while helping teams quickly identify convergence points between technical capabilities and design requirements. Researcher T3 shared, *"With the card toolkit, we could directly focus on the alignment between technology and design, without getting bogged down by irrelevant technical details."*

Certain industrial team members believed the card toolkit enabled a more intuitive expression of market demands and practical constraints, minimizing information distortion from terminology or background differences. Industry representative I6 noted, *"The card toolkit facilitated translating market requirements into design language, allowing the team to reach consensus quickly."*

3.2 Advancing Balanced Perspectives and Equitable Multi-stakeholder Contributions

The card toolkit's fair discussion rules and structured process enhanced power balance in multi-stakeholder collaboration, fostering a more equitable environment.

Interaction designers guided team discussions through cards from user needs and aesthetic perspectives, while avoiding unilateral dominance. Designer D2 stated, *"The card toolkit allowed us to share views more equally, rather than depending on one party's expertise."*

Technical researchers, traditionally seen as providers of technical support, were encouraged by the card toolkit to actively engage in design discussions. Technical researcher T5 stated, *"The card toolkit helped me act like an AI assistant, allowing us to share views more equally, rather than depending on one party's expertise."*

Industrial team members incorporated market demands and brand traits into discussions using the card toolkit, steering clear of idealized design solutions. Designer D5 noted, *"The industry representatives offered numerous practical suggestions that helped align our designs with market needs."*

3.3 Lowering Learning Costs and Enhancing Collaborative Efficiency

The gamified design of the card toolkit simplified the learning process, allowing teams to quickly break the ice and collaborate efficiently while fostering creativity. Participants noted that the gamification enhanced engagement and interactivity in discussions, leading to faster productivity. Interaction designer D10 stated, *"The card toolkit functioned like a board game, creating a relaxed atmosphere that naturally improved efficiency."*

The toolkit's structured process enabled team members to quickly identify key issues and avoid unproductive discussions. Industry representative I5 stated, *"We generated many valuable ideas in a short time; the card toolkit significantly improved our discussion efficiency."*

4 Discussion

4.1 Design Potential of Card Toolkit in Multi-stakeholder Collaboration

Unified Language and Knowledge Sharing. Research shows that the card toolkit creates a common language for multi-stakeholder collaboration by standardizing design variables. This approach reduces communication barriers stemming from knowledge asymmetry, allowing stakeholders from various backgrounds to engage in discussions within a shared framework. The cards function as both a communication tool and a medium for knowledge sharing, simplifying complex tasks to help participants quickly understand essential concepts and propose innovative design solutions.

Structured Dialogue and Creative Stimulation. The card toolkit stimulates creativity in multi-stakeholder collaboration through the "Design Chain" dialogue pattern [30, 31]. This pattern encourages participants to engage in-depth discussions drawing from their diverse backgrounds, integrating multiple perspectives, and driving the iteration and optimization of design objectives. Research demonstrates that the toolkit's structured process provides a dynamic mechanism for creative generation, allowing design goals and solutions to be continuously refined through iterations, achieving innovation outcomes that exceed expectations.

4.2 Implications for Design Practice

This study's card toolkit offers an innovative design methodology that fosters multi-stakeholder collaboration through structured processes and gamified experiences. It effectively lowers communication costs and enhances collaborative efficiency. Design practice can utilize the toolkit's structured approach to simplify complex design tasks into manageable, comprehensible modules, thereby improving communication and collaboration. The research shows that active industry participation enhances design by aligning solutions with market demands.

In product-oriented design, involving industry professionals is crucial, as their expertise and market insights are vital for effective goal setting and optimizing solutions.

5 Limitations and Future Work

While the card toolkit offers significant advantages, it does have some limitations. First, an excessive number of cards can clutter the workspace and hinder user experience. Second, the toolkit's fixed variable definitions limit its responsiveness to dynamic design needs, especially in complex and evolving tasks. Additionally, although this study created a collaborative framework among technical, design, and industry stakeholders, real-world applications may involve a broader range of participants, such as manufacturers and end-users, requiring further validation of the toolkit's effectiveness in diverse cooperative contexts. Future efforts could focus on implementing digital formats for dynamic variable adjustment to enhance interactivity and practicality, utilizing artificial intelligence and data analytics to create data-driven collaboration models for better problem analysis and categorization, and strengthening the integration of industry perspectives alongside standardized evaluation frameworks to promote the "Design Chain" pattern in emerging areas like artificial intelligence and sustainable design, thereby improving interdisciplinary design task collaboration.

A Contents of the Card-Based Tool

Table 1. Items of *Objective Card*

Card Types	Items
User Card	Elderly, Businessperson, Children, Pets, Family, Friends, Couples, Long-distance Travelers, Commuters, Disabled Individuals, High-end Clients, Music Lovers, Disabled Individuals, Travelers, Emergency Personnel, Environmentalists, Infants, Fitness Enthusiasts, {Blank Card}
Emotion Card	Joy, Anger, Boredom, Relaxation, Anxiety, Drowsiness, Focus, Surprise, Nostalgia, Disappointment, Curiosity, Guilt, {Blank Card}
Scenario Card	Smooth Ride, Traffic Jam, Sharp Turn, Night Driving, Emergency Braking, Driving in the Rain, Narrow Road, Tunnel Driving, Emergency Evasion, Speed Limit Zones, Crosswalk, Overtaking Lane, {Blank Card}

Table 2. Items of *Interaction Card*

Card Types	Items
Interaction Card	Long Press, Touch, Tap, Double Tap, Swipe, Drag, Pinch, Rotate, Light Tap, Voice, Air Gestures, Press, Eye Movement, Body Movement, Facial Expression, Writing/Drawing, Sensor, {Blank Card}

B Participants

Table 3. Items of *Expression Card*

Expression Card Types	Items	Explanation
Technical researchers (on smart material)	Materials	Material selection, substitution, and optimization, involving multiple performance evaluations such as mechanical performance, thermal performance, bio-compatibility, etc.
	Driving Method	Driving method, control method, power supply, involving energy consumption, controllability, response speed, etc.
	Processing Technique	Selection, substitution, and optimization of processes, involving the feasibility of production processes, compatibility, cost, etc.
	Design Application Method	Customization and design of various structures and functions to meet different needs.
	Input Method	Triggering and response methods of system functions to form a complete interaction loop and meet various needs.
	{Blank Card}	{Custom Content}
Interaction designers	Aesthetics	Visual effects, color coordination, consistency in style, etc.
	Creativity	Is the design innovative and able to spark curiosity and exploration?
	Sustainability	Has sustainability been considered in materials and production processes?
	Usability	Does it meet the functional needs of users? Is the product clear and easy to use?
	Emotional Experience	Can it evoke an emotional connection with the user?
	{Blank Card}	{Custom Content}
Specific industry teams (on automotive interior design)	Customer Benefit	Does it meet the user's needs? How strong is the demand and how much benefit does it bring to the user?
	Brand Identity	How luxurious does it feel? Does it align with the company's brand identity, values, and core strategy?
	Market Competitiveness	How does it compare with competitors in terms of innovation, advantages, and disadvantages? Is it aligned with future market trends? What is its potential contribution to the company's profits?
	Production Process	What changes does it bring to the existing production process? Is the supply chain supportive, stable, and feasible? How long would it take to bring it to market?
	Engineering Feasibility	How does it perform in terms of durability, heat resistance, safety, environmental impact, power consumption, etc.?
	{Blank Card}	{Custom Content}

Table 4. The 2-dimensional material palette of *Knowledge Card (Material Cards)*

	Fiber	Membrane	Surface	3D structure
Shape-changing	OmniFiber [26], Patch-O [27]	Aeromorph [28]	Flat Panel Haptics [29]	xSlate (shape- & stiffness-changing) [30], SnapInflatables [31], HERMITS [32]
Light-emitting	Textiles display research [33]	PrintScreen [34]	ProtoSpray [35]	Illumination Aesthetics [36]
Color-changing	Ebb [37]	TransPrint [38]	Photo-Chromeleon [39]	Fluidic fiber research [40]
Temperature-changing	–	ThermalBracelet [41]	Thermotion (temperature- & color-changing) [42]	–

C Concept Design Outcomes

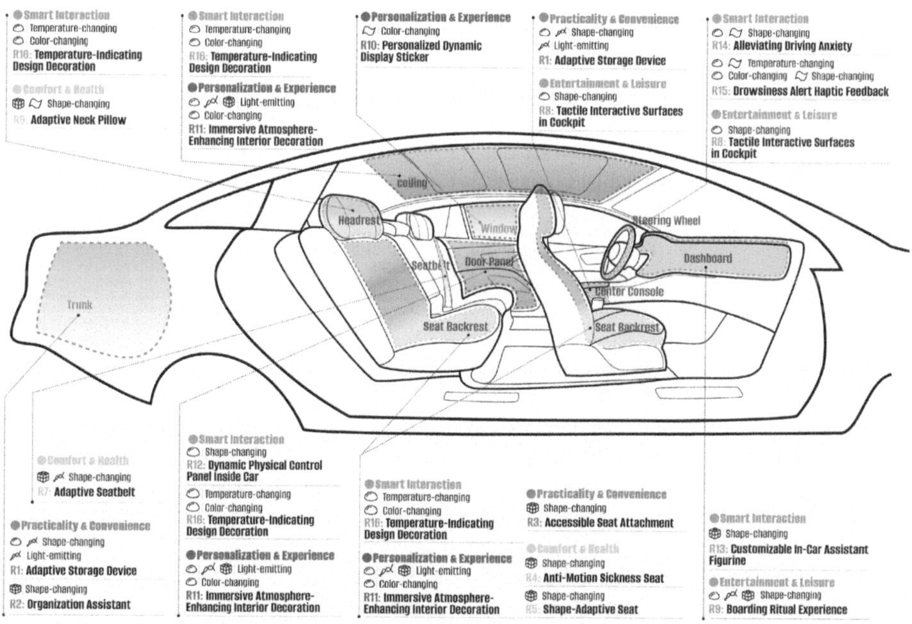

Fig. 4. Workshop Output: 16 Design Solutions.

Table 5. Demographic information of participants and group assignments

Group No.	Participant No.	Professional or Major Background	Title
Group 1	T1	Human-computer interaction	Ph.D. researcher
	D1	Interaction design	Master designer
	D2	Product design	Undergraduate designer
	I1	Innovation Management & Tech Scouting	Manager
	I2*	Business Marketing & Customer Insights	Senior manager
Group 2	T2	Mechanical engineering	Ph.D. researcher
	D3	Interaction design	Undergraduate designer
	D4*	Interaction design	Master designer
	I3*	Research & Development (Body in White), Innovation Management	Manager
	I4*	Research & Development (Interior Seating)	Engineer
Group 3	T3	Human-robot interaction	Ph.D. researcher
	D5	Product and interaction design	Master designer
	D6	Service and interaction design	Ph.D. researcher
	D7	Product design	Master designer
	I5	Innovation Management & Tech Scouting	Manager
Group 4	T4	Computer science	Master researcher
	D8	Product design	Master designer
	D9	New media art	Undergraduate designer
	I6	Business Marketing & Customer Insights	Manager
	I7	Research & Development (Electrical/Electronic Systems)	Engineer
Group 5	T5	Electronic Engineering and Computer Science	Undergraduate researcher
	D10	Interaction design	Master designer
	D11	New media art	Undergraduate designer
	I8*	Research & Development (Body in White), Innovation Management	Senior manager
	I9	Research & Development (Body in White), Innovation Management	Intern
	I10*	Research & Development (Infotainment & Connectivity), Research & Development (UXUI)	Manager

T# - Technical researchers; D#- Designers; I# - Specific industry team;
* - Participants who did not participate in the post-workshop interview

References

1. Shukla, P., Naik, S., Obi, I., Bui, P., Parsons, P.: Communication challenges reported by UX designers on social media: an analysis of subreddit discussions. In: Extended Abstracts of the CHI Conference on Human Factors in Computing Systems, pp. 1–6 (2024)
2. Heo, J., Lee, U.: Form to flow: exploring challenges and roles of conversational UX designers in real-world, multi-channel service environments. Proc. ACM Hum.-Comput. Interact **7**(CSCW2), 1–24 (2023)
3. Miller, T.R., Baird, T.D., Littlefield, C.M., Kofinas, G., Chapin III, F.S., Redman, C.L.: Epistemological pluralism: reorganizing interdisciplinary research. Ecol. Soc. **13**(2) (2008)
4. Ribéreau-Gayon, A., d'Avray, D.: Interdisciplinary research-based teaching: Advocacy for a change in the higher education paradigm. In: Tong, V.C.H., Standen, A., Sotiriou, M. (eds.) Shaping Higher Education with Students: Ways to Connect Research and Teaching, pp. 139–149. UCL Press (2018). https://doi.org/10.2307/j.ctt21c4tcm.23
5. Feng, K.K., Coppock, M.J., McDonald, D.W.: How do UX practitioners communicate AI as a design material? Artifacts, conceptions, and propositions. In: Proceedings of the 2023 ACM Designing Interactive Systems Conference, pp. 2263–2280 (2023)
6. MacDonald, C.M., Rose, E.J., Putnam, C.: How, why, and with whom do user experience (UX) practitioners communicate? Implications for HCI education. Int. J. Hum.-Comput. Interact. **38**(15), 1422–1439 (2022)
7. Maudet, N., Leiva, G., Beaudouin-Lafon, M., Mackay, W.: Design breakdowns: designer-developer gaps in representing and interpreting interactive systems. In: Proceedings of the 2017 ACM Conference on Computer Supported Cooperative Work and Social Computing, pp. 630–641 (2017)
8. Edmond, J.: Collaboration and infrastructure. In: Schreibman, S., Siemens, R., Unsworth, J. (eds.) A New Companion to Digital Humanities, pp. 54–65. Wiley Blackwell (2015). https://doi.org/10.1002/9781118680605.ch4
9. Brandt, E., Messeter, J.: Facilitating collaboration through design games. In: Proceedings of the Eighth Conference on Participatory Design: Artful Integration: Interweaving Media, Materials and Practices, vol. 1, pp. 121–131 (2004)
10. Brewer, E.C., Holmes, T.L.: Better communication = better teams: a communication exercise to improve team performance. IEEE Trans. Prof. Commun. **59**(3), 288–298 (2016)
11. Lefroy, E.C.: Interdisciplinary research is about people as well as concepts and methods. In: Bammer, G. (ed.) Disciplining Interdisciplinarity: Integration and Implementation Sciences for Researching Complex Real-World Problems, pp. 365–374. ANU Press (2013)
12. Janicki, K.: A hindrance to communication: the use of difficult and incomprehensible language. Int. J. Appl. Linguist. **12**(2), 194–217 (2002)
13. Do, H.J., Kong, H.-K., Lee, J., Bailey, B.P.: How should the agent communicate to the group? Communication strategies of a conversational agent in group chat discussions. Proc. ACM Hum.-Comput. Interact **6**(CSCW2), 1–23 (2022)
14. Bertran, F.A., Pometko, A., Gupta, M., Wilcox, L., Banerjee, R., Isbister, K.: Designerly tele-experiences: a new approach to remote yet still situated co-design. ACM Trans. Comput.-Hum. Interact **29**(5), 1–30 (2022)

15. Harrington, C., Erete, S., Piper, A.M.: Deconstructing community-based collaborative design: towards more equitable participatory design engagements. Proc. ACM Hum.-Comput. Interact **3**, 1–25 (2019)
16. Wilson, A.: Being Interdisciplinary: Adventures in Urban Science and Beyond. UCL Press (2022)
17. Alzoubi, Y., Gill, A.: The critical communication challenges between geographically distributed agile development teams: empirical findings. IEEE Trans. Prof. Commun. **64**(4), 322–337 (2021)
18. Halskov, K., Dalsgård, P.: Inspiration card workshops. In: Proceedings of the 6th Conference on Designing Interactive Systems, pp. 2–11 (2006)
19. Koch, J., Taffin, N., Beaudouin-Lafon, M., Laine, M., Lucero, A., Mackay, W.E.: Imagesense: an intelligent collaborative ideation tool to support diverse human-computer partnerships. Proc. ACM Hum.-Comput. Interact. **4**(CSCW1), 1–27 (2020)
20. Wang, Q., Schneider, J.W.: Consistency and validity of interdisciplinarity measures. Quant. Sci. Stud. **1**(1), 239–263 (2020)
21. Sutton, S.E., Kemp, S.P.: Integrating social science and design inquiry through interdisciplinary design charrettes: an approach to participatory community problem solving. Am. J. Community Psychol. **38**(1–2), 51–62 (2006)
22. Morss, R.E., Lazrus, H., Demuth, J.L.: The "inter" within interdisciplinary research: strategies for building integration across fields. Risk Anal. **41**(7), 1152–1161 (2021)
23. Lucero, A., Vaajakallio, K., Dalsgaard, P.: The dialogue-labs method: process, space and materials as structuring elements to spark dialogue in co-design events. CoDesign **8**(1), 1–23 (2012)
24. Nae, H.-J.: An interdisciplinary design education framework. Des. J. **20**(sup1), S835–S847 (2017)
25. Braun, V., Clarke, V.: Thematic analysis. In: Cooper, H., Camic, P.M., Long, D.L., Panter, A.T., Rindskopf, D., Sher, K.J. (eds.) APA Handbook of Research Methods in Psychology, Vol. 2: Research Designs: Quantitative, Qualitative, Neuropsychological, and Biological, pp. 57–71. APA (2012). https://doi.org/10.1037/13620-004
26. Kilic Afsar, O., et al.: OmniFiber: integrated fluidic fiber actuators for weaving movement based interactions into the 'fabric of everyday life'. In: The 34th Annual ACM Symposium on User Interface Software and Technology, UIST 2021, pp. 1010–1026. ACM, New York, NY, USA (2021). https://doi.org/10.1145/3472749.3474802
27. Ku, P.-S., Huang, K., Kao, C.H.-L.: Patch-O: deformable woven patches for on-body actuation. In: Proceedings of the 2022 CHI Conference on Human Factors in Computing Systems, CHI 2022, pp. 1–12. ACM, New York, NY, USA (2022). https://doi.org/10.1145/3491102.3517633
28. Ou, J., Skouras, M., Vlavianos, N., Heibeck, F., Cheng, C.-Y., Peters, J., Ishii, H.: aeroMorph - heat-sealing inflatable shape-change materials for interaction design. In: Proceedings of the 29th Annual Symposium on User Interface Software and Technology, UIST 2016, pp. 121–132. ACM, New York, NY, USA (2016). https://doi.org/10.1145/2984511.2984520
29. Shultz, C., Harrison, C.: Flat panel haptics: Embedded electroosmotic pumps for scalable shape displays. In: Proceedings of the 2023 CHI Conference on Human Factors in Computing Systems, CHI 2023, pp. 1–16. ACM, New York, NY, USA (2023). https://doi.org/10.1145/3544548.3581547

30. Hirai, T., Nakamaru, S., Kawahara, Y., Kakehi, Y.: xSlate: A stiffness-controlled surface for shape-changing interfaces. In: Extended Abstracts of the 2018 CHI Conference on Human Factors in Computing Systems, CHI EA 2018, pp. 1–4. ACM, New York, NY, USA (2018). https://doi.org/10.1145/3170427.3186496
31. Yang, Y., et al.: SnapInflatables: designing inflatables with snap-through instability for responsive interaction. In: Proceedings of the CHI Conference on Human Factors in Computing Systems, CHI 2024, pp. 1–15. ACM, New York, NY, USA (2024). https://doi.org/10.1145/3613904.3642933
32. Nakagaki, K., Leong, J., Tappa, J.L., Wilbert, J., Ishii, H.: HERMITS: dynamically reconfiguring the interactivity of self-propelled TUIs with mechanical shell add-ons. In: Proceedings of the 33rd Annual ACM Symposium on User Interface Software and Technology, UIST 2020, pp. 882–896. ACM, New York, NY, USA (2020). https://doi.org/10.1145/3379337.3415831
33. Shi, X., et al.: Large-area display textiles integrated with functional systems. Nature **591**, 240–245 (2021)
34. Olberding, S., Wessely, M., Steimle, J.: PrintScreen: fabricating highly customizable thin-film touch-displays. In: Proceedings of the 27th Annual ACM Symposium on User Interface Software and Technology, UIST 2014, pp. 281–290. ACM, New York, NY, USA (2014). https://doi.org/10.1145/2642918.2647413
35. Hanton, O., Wessely, M., Mueller, S., Fraser, M., Roudaut, A.: ProtoSpray: combining 3d printing and spraying to create interactive displays with arbitrary shapes. In: Proceedings of the 2020 CHI Conference on Human Factors in Computing Systems, CHI 2020, pp. 1–13. ACM, New York, NY, USA (2020). https://doi.org/10.1145/3313831.3376543
36. Torres, C., O'Leary, J., Nicholas, M., Paulos, E.: Illumination aesthetics: light as a creative material within computational design. In: Proceedings of the 2017 CHI Conference on Human Factors in Computing Systems, pp. 6111–6122. ACM, Denver, Colorado, USA (2017). https://doi.org/10.1145/3025453.3025466
37. Devendorf, L., et al.: I don't want to wear a screen: Probing perceptions of and possibilities for dynamic displays on clothing. In: Proceedings of the 2016 CHI Conference on Human Factors in Computing Systems, CHI 2016, pp. 6028–6039. ACM, New York, NY, USA (2016). https://doi.org/10.1145/2858036.2858192
38. Jensen, W., Colley, A., Häkkilä, J., Pinheiro, C., Löchtefeld, M.: TransPrint: a method for fabricating flexible transparent free-form displays. Adv. Hum.-Comput. Interact. **2019**(1), 1340182 (2019). https://doi.org/10.1155/2019/1340182
39. Jin, Y., et al.: Photo-chromeleon: re-programmable multi-color textures using photochromic dyes. In: Proceedings of the 32nd Annual ACM Symposium on User Interface Software and Technology, pp. 701–712. ACM, New Orleans, LA, USA (2019). https://doi.org/10.1145/3332165.3347905
40. Liu, G., et al.: It puts life into my creations: understanding fluid fiber as a media for expressive display. In: Proceedings of the 2022 CHI Conference on Human Factors in Computing Systems, CHI 2022. ACM, New York, NY, USA (2022). https://doi.org/10.1145/3491102.3501990
41. Peiris, R.L., Feng, Y.-L., Chan, L., Minamizawa, K.: ThermalBracelet: exploring thermal haptic feedback around the wrist. In: Proceedings of the 2019 CHI Conference on Human Factors in Computing Systems, pp. 1–11. ACM, Glasgow, Scotland, UK (2019). https://doi.org/10.1145/3290605.3300400
42. Yu, T., et al.: Thermotion: design and fabrication of thermofluidic composites for animation effects on object surfaces. In: Proceedings of the 2023 CHI Conference on Human Factors in Computing Systems, CHI 2023, pp. 1–19. ACM, New York, NY, USA (2023). https://doi.org/10.1145/3544548.3580743

Human-Computer Interaction Design of Manned Lunar Rover Based on Fear Dual-Pathway Theory: Neurocognitive Mechanisms and Engineering Mitigation Strategies

Cen Chunhao, Lin Xinyue, and Liu Gang(✉)

School of Design, Shanghai Jiao Tong University, Shanghai, China
seuliujigang@sjtu.edu.cn

Abstract. Aiming at China's ongoing manned lunar landing and permanent lunar scientific research station construction plan, and addressing the problem of astronauts' survival fear caused by the extreme lunar environment, this study proposes strategies to alleviate astronauts' fear and anxiety through human-computer interaction design of manned lunar rovers. By integrating the Fear Dual-Pathway Theory and the Terror Management Theory (TMT), a novel anti-fear lunar rover interaction design framework is put forward. Through constructing a multi-dimensional fear assessment model of "physiology-behavior-environment", hierarchical control strategies based on the neuro-mechanism of amygdala-prefrontal cortex are developed: 1) The fast pathway realizes emergency response to high-dynamic threats; 2) The slow pathway combines with TMT's distal defense mechanism to achieve efficient psychological management. Experiments show that this design reduces fear-related operational error rates in simulated lunar tasks and improves NASA-TLX cognitive load scores. The research provides neuropsychological basis and engineering solutions for the human factors engineering design of deep space exploration equipment.

Keywords: Manned Lunar Rover · Human-Computer Interaction · Fear Management · Terror Management Theory (TMT) · Cognitive Load Optimization

1 Introduction

In the harsh extreme environment of the moon, the psychological threats faced by astronauts cannot be ignored. Radiation, vacuum, and rugged terrain collectively pose enormous challenges to human survival, easily triggering deep-seated survival fear and a sense of loss of control [1]. Such persistent psychological pressure may affect astronauts' judgment and even lead to errors in critical mission decisions. In high-risk environments, how to effectively alleviate these psychological threats and propose engineering design methods using theories such as Terror Management Theory (TMT) has become an important task in manned lunar exploration missions.

S. Guo et al. (Eds.): HHME 2025, CCIS 2878, pp. 128–138, 2027.
https://doi.org/10.1007/978-981-92-3991-7_10

Lunar rovers have two technical routes: light open-type lunar rovers and heavy pressurized manned lunar rovers. The Apollo lunar landing program adopted light open-type lunar rovers. With the advancement of technology, future lunar rovers may adopt pressurized ones. Open-type lunar rover designs have significant limitations in addressing astronauts' psychological threats. For example, the lunar rovers used in the Apollo missions focused mainly on realizing basic functions, with an open driving structure to provide a broad field of vision and direct operability. Although this design concept achieved engineering success, it lacked targeted measures to mitigate lunar fear sources. Astronauts are directly exposed to the open environment, further amplifying their psychological vulnerability. In addition, the human-computer interaction interfaces of open-type lunar rovers generally do not integrate cognitive load theory and emotional feedback mechanisms [2]. In high-pressure environments, complex cognitive loads and interaction methods lacking emotional support may further increase astronauts' psychological burden, thereby affecting operational efficiency and mission execution quality. Therefore, future lunar rover designs urgently need to provide more comprehensive and humanized protection solutions from psychological and cognitive perspectives, adopting pressurized lunar rovers and improving vehicle usability from psychological and physiological aspects.

2 Optimization Methods for Human-Machine Interaction of Lunar Rovers

Focusing on high fear-arousal scenarios on the moon, this section examines the behavioral characteristics, physiological basis of fear in lunar rover design, and explores ways to cope with fear.

2.1 Behavioral Characteristics and Response Patterns of High-Dynamic Fear on the Moon

Fear is an instinctive emotion in response to threats, which is particularly prominent under extreme lunar conditions such as radiation and vacuum. Its core behavior is the "Fight-or-Flight" response, where the autonomic nervous system quickly mobilizes resources to deal with threats, manifested as accelerated heart rate, rapid breathing, etc. This provides immediate protection but may also lead to decision-making errors or operational rigidity. In addition, fear may cause freezing, or in the long term, lead to increased alertness and sleep disorders.

The physiological basis of fear is complex and multi-layered, involving multiple brain regions and neural pathways. The "dual-pathway" theory, proposed by Joseph LeDoux, describes two main pathways through which the brain processes threat information and triggers fear responses: the "fast low road" and the "slow high road".

In the lunar environment, these two pathways work synergistically. The fast low road provides immediate protection in crisis situations; for example, when an astronaut suddenly sees a huge crater while walking on the moon, the body will instinctively take evasive actions. The slow high road, on the other hand, allows astronauts to respond more rationally and effectively. However, under continuous pressure and uncertainty, the fast low road may be frequently activated, causing astronauts to remain in a state of high alert for a long time, consuming a lot of energy, and possibly inhibiting the function of the high road, making it difficult for them to make calm judgments and decisions (Fig. 1).

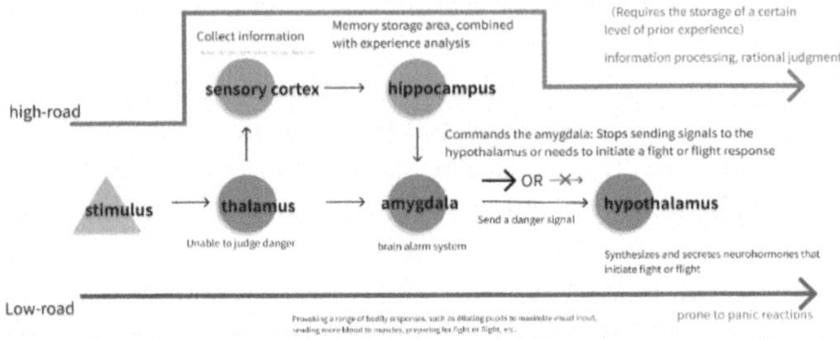

Fig. 1 Basic dual-pathway physiological model of fear

2.2 Theories for Coping with Fear Arousal on the Moon

There are various strategies to cope with fear. "Terror Management Theory (TMT)" provides a unique perspective to explain how humans cope with the fear of death and lays a theoretical foundation for psychological support in lunar missions. The core view of this theory is that humans, as self-aware creatures, can realize the fact that their lives are limited and death is inevitable [3]. This fear of death is a deep-seated and persistent psychological threat to humans. To cope with this "fear of death", individuals have developed two main psychological defense mechanisms:

Pathway Type	Characteristics	Strategies	Role
Proximal Defenses	Conscious, immediate, directly respond to the threat of death	Denial of vulnerability (e.g., "I'm still young"), distraction (e.g., excessive shopping), rationalization (e.g., "The probability of death is low")	Temporarily suppress the fear of death, but cannot fundamentally solve the problem
Distal Defenses	Unconscious, long-term, symbolically respond to the fear of death	Cultural worldviews (e.g., religious beliefs), self-esteem enhancement (e.g., achievement building), establishment of intimate relationships like family bonds (e.g., family ties)	Alleviate the fear of death through symbolic means, continuously buffer existential threats, and provide deep psychological protection

TMT holds that when mortality salience is heightened (e.g., in a high-risk arousal environment like the moon), individuals' adherence to cultural worldviews and pursuit of self-esteem become stronger [4]. In the lunar environment, astronauts can effectively alleviate their fear for personal safety by strongly identifying with mission goals, team collaboration, and the spirit of human exploration. Therefore, providing astronauts with clear mission goals, enhancing team cohesion, setting clear success criteria, and offering positive feedback can all effectively use TMT principles to manage and alleviate fear (Fig. 2).

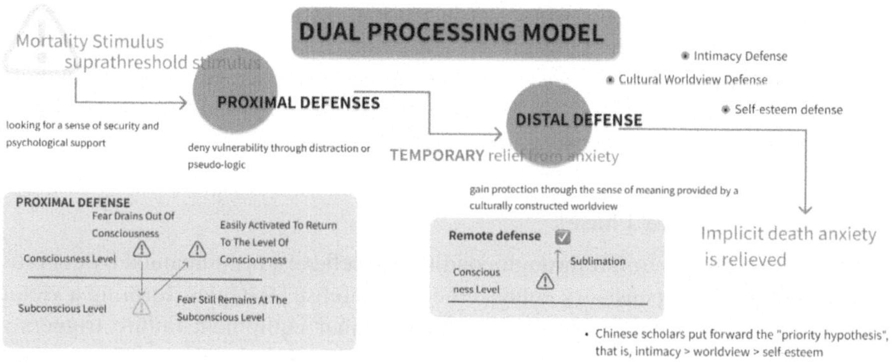

Fig. 2 Construction of the Defense Mechanism Model in Lunar High-Risk Arousal Scenarios

In addition, cognitive behavioral therapy, relaxation techniques, social support, and exposure therapy are also important coping methods. A comprehensive psychological support system for astronauts can be built by integrating these methods (Fig. 3).

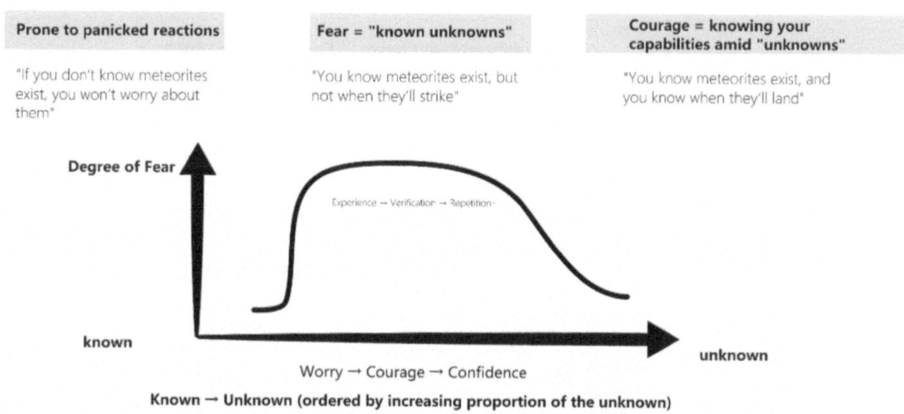

Fig. 3 Construction of the relationship model between fear and the unknown

2.3 Coping Strategies for Fear Arousal on the Moon

Interpretation of the Three Stages of Fear in Lunar Scenarios:

2.3.1 Stage 1: Naïve Phase

When individuals are first exposed to a threat, they lack a cognitive framework and coping experience, relying on instinctive reactions, and the scope of fear is limited to the original stimulus. For example, when astronauts first set foot on the moon and face an unfamiliar environment such as low gravity and strange landforms, they lack a cognitive framework and experience to cope with unknown lunar threats (such as radiation and lunar dust effects), so they can only feel nervous instinctively, and their fear is limited to these direct and primitive sensory impacts in front of them.

2.3.2 Generalized Fear Phase

Fear spreads to similar stimuli through conditioned reflexes, accompanied by cognitive loss of control and compensatory enhancement of defense strategies, forming a vicious circle of a "fear network". For example, after a lunar equipment failure triggers an in-cabin alarm, astronauts will subsequently feel fear when hearing any mechanical noise (such as the normal operation sound of the ventilation system) and even develop avoidance behaviors towards similar warning lights on the operation panel, falling into a generalized association of "all mechanical sounds = danger" cognitively.

2.3.3 Stage 3: Extinction Phase

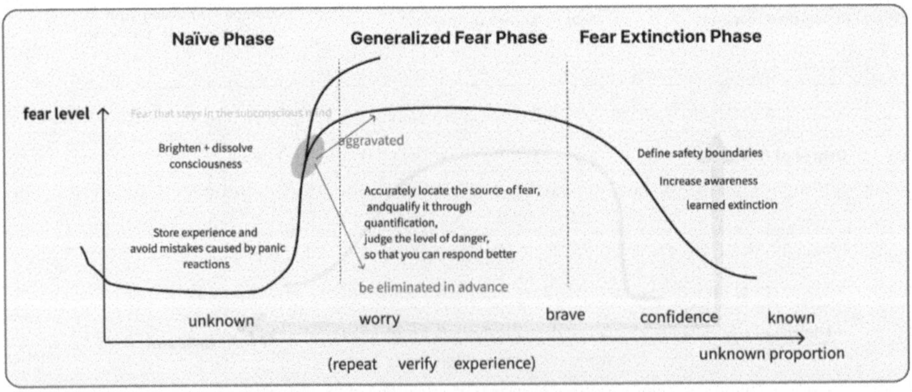

Fig. 4 Refinement of the three stages of fear

Through cognitive reshaping and neuroplasticity, fear responses gradually diminish, and individuals regain adaptive control over threats. After astronauts undergo multiple safe experiences of the "lunar equipment failure - correct disposal" process through virtual reality (VR) simulation training, their fear of mechanical noise gradually fades.

When hearing real equipment noise later, they can rationally judge the risk level (e.g., distinguishing between normal operation sounds and fault alarms), and their defensive behavior changes from "instinctive escape" to "calm investigation" (Fig. 4).

Operational Mechanism and Intervention Model of Fear:

From this, we can summarize the operational mechanism and intervention model of fear that can be applied in lunar scenarios (Fig. 5).

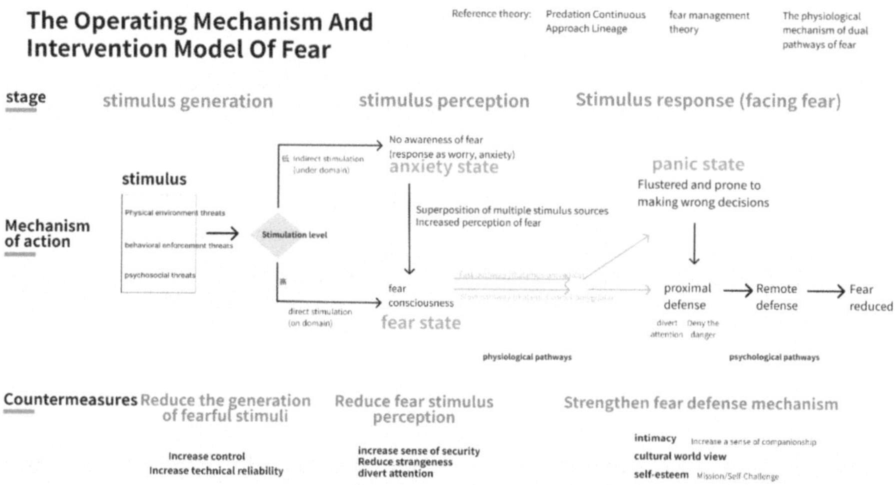

Fig. 5 Operational mechanism and intervention mechanism of fear

3 Interaction Methods for Optimizing the Dual Pathways of Fear

3.1 Mapping Between Lunar Fear Factors and Vehicle Functions

Physical environment threats: microgravity, ionizing radiation, weak magnetic field, cosmic dust collision, open and unfamiliar terrain, day-night cycle, environmental parameter fluctuations, acceleration, vibration, temperature, pressure changes, environmental noise, lighting, air quality.

Task execution threats: movement restrictions, visual restrictions, equipment failure, operational errors, task uncertainty, material scarcity, narrow and enclosed space, workload.

Psychosocial threats: isolation and monotony, information occlusion, megalophobia, fear of the unknown, crew relationships, cultural and gender effects, family concerns, reward and punishment pressure [5].

Fear Trigger	Stress Source	Design of Countermeasure Relationships
Visual Exploration	Extreme risks such as unknown terrain traversal directions, lunar dust interference, etc.	From satellite remote sensing full-scene ground simulation, robotic arm visual inspection, training in optimal lunar traversal scenarios
Sample Collection	Operational failures (tool jamming), robotic arm operation malfunctions, etc.	Robotic arm force control, multi-functional robotic arm and end - effector
In - situ Processing	Payload loss, equipment operation emergencies (power failure)	AI remote medical guidance
Long - term Confinement	Closed - space environment, information overload, etc.	Public welfare task companions, group living quarters, personalized settings

3.2 Specific Heavy Pressurized Vehicle Design Strategies for Lunar Fear Sources

3.2.1 Reducing the Generation of Lunar Fear Stimuli:

The moon, as a typical scenario in extreme environments, has a large number of stimuli that pose great challenges to astronauts. Some fear sources are unavoidable, but others can be avoided through design, such as information occlusion, isolation and monotony, and dim working environment.

1. Adopting separation of public and private screens

The public interaction screen (high-road cognitive regulation) displays global mission progress (e.g., "60% of today's detection goals completed"), team members' physiological indicators (heart rate, blood oxygen, etc.), and environmental risk heat maps (red = dangerous location, blue = safe zone). The fear mitigation logic is to strengthen self-esteem defense (TMT theory) through visualizing "task completion", reducing anxiety caused by "a sense of task loss of control"; sharing team physiological data activates belonging defense, reducing loneliness [6]. (Fig. 6)

Fig. 6 Central public large screen

The private interaction screen (high-road personalized regulation) displays astronauts' personal health reports in real-time, allows viewing of task records, and shows private messages separately. The fear mitigation logic is that the private interaction screen supports uploading photos of family on Earth as wallpapers, combined with regular care from AI voice (e.g., "Your daughter was praised at school today"), strengthening cultural worldview identification (TMT theory), reducing anxiety while increasing a sense of belonging. The personalized interface enhances operational control, filtering a large amount of complex information in lunar work and reducing the working memory load of the dorsolateral prefrontal cortex [7]. (Fig. 7)

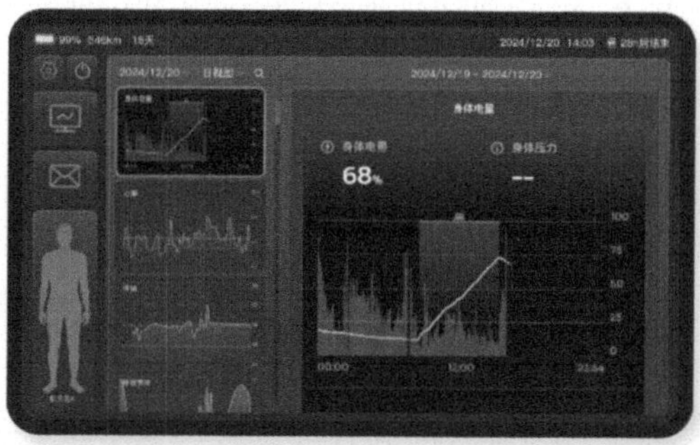

Fig. 7 Private Screen

2. Designing extravehicular activity paths and processes, for example, robots scan the travel route 30 min in advance, display "safety corridors" (marked in green) on the interaction screen, and astronauts moving according to the marked routes can reduce navigation errors;
3. Mechanical arm auxiliary function: the mechanical arm is stored on one side of the roof, and automatically rotates to the front of the astronaut during operation, which can perform functions such as lighting to assist astronauts in fine work, optimizing the working environment and reducing anxiety.

3.2.2 Reducing the Perception of Lunar Fear Stimuli:

For some unavoidable fear sources on the moon, we can adopt design strategies to reduce astronauts' perception of fear, such as increasing a sense of security, reducing strangeness, and diverting attention [8]. (Fig. 8)

1. In terms of cabin space design, the buffer cabin between the pressure chamber and the daily cabin section should ensure that lunar dust can be completely cleaned, and be equipped with workflow voice reminders and first-aid devices. The working space is separated from the personal space, and the personal space has privacy protection; social distance is maintained to enhance a sense of belonging [9]. The living and sports space is equipped with an interaction screen to facilitate astronauts to watch news broadcasts while eating, video chat with family while exercising, and other belonging-linking activities (Fig. 9).

Fig. 8 Appearance of heavy pressurized vehicle

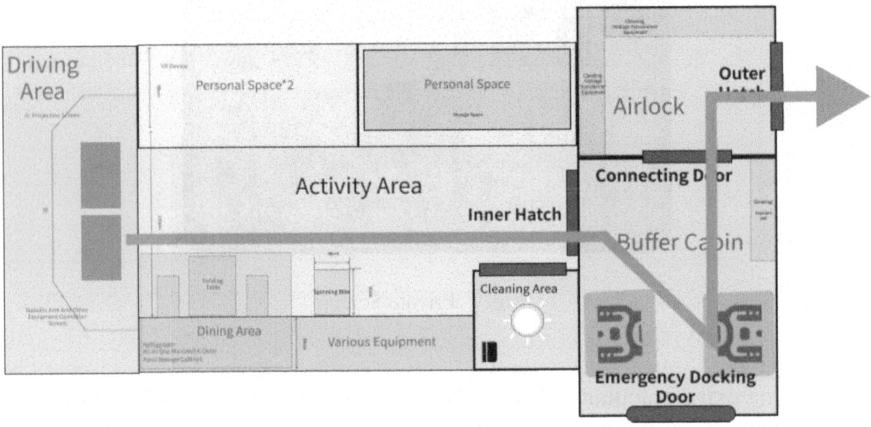

(1)

Fig. 9 Workflow of Extravehicular

2. ActivityEmergency docking port (low-road rapid avoidance): fluorescent guide strips are set on the inner side of the cabin door, guiding the escape direction through peripheral vision (dominated by the low road) when lighting fails. The fear mitigation logic is that the immediate visibility of the physical avoidance path directly stimulates the amygdala to inhibit fear responses, conforming to the "unconscious rapid response" characteristic of the low road [10].

3.2.3 Strengthening Defense Mechanisms against Lunar Fear:

The intimate relationship defense in the distal defense can be strengthened through modular auxiliary robots, intelligent voice conversations, etc. [11]

1. Modular auxiliary robots (low-road emotional anchor + high-road social cognition): the risk early warning signals of detection robots directly act on the low road, guiding active avoidance behaviors; the anthropomorphic interaction of companion robots activates the prefrontal social cognitive area, reducing loneliness (TMT belonging defense mechanism) (Fig. 10)

Fig. 10 Three-Field coupling system of manned lunar rover, astronauts and robots

2. Intelligent voice conversations in the vehicle (high-road cognitive regulation) support multi-language switching, and voice intonation can be customized (e.g., "relative recording mode"); initiate conversations actively during task intervals (e.g., "Remember to move your fingers every hour to prevent muscle stiffness") and record astronauts' preferences (e.g., "Users pay more attention to energy data"). The fear mitigation logic is that personalized voice enhances self-identification (TMT self-esteem defense), reducing the loss of control caused by information occlusion (Fig. 11).

Fig. 11 Three-field coupling system of manned lunar rover, astronauts and robots

4 Conclusion

This study addresses the problem of astronauts' survival fear in the extreme lunar environment and proposes a lunar rover human-computer interaction design framework based on reducing fear. By integrating the Fear Dual-Pathway Theory and Terror Management Theory (TMT), a new anti-fear lunar rover interaction system is designed, which adopts a "physiology-behavior-environment" multi-dimensional fear assessment model and develops hierarchical control strategies based on the amygdala-prefrontal neuro-mechanism.

1. The application of the fear dual-pathway aims at the synergistic effect of the fast low road and slow high road in the lunar environment, proposing hierarchical control strategies to optimize astronauts' psychological responses.
2. Using TMT theory, strategies such as strengthening cultural worldviews and establishing intimate relationships are adopted to alleviate astronauts' fear of high risks and enhance psychological resilience.
3. The functional layout of the pressurized vehicle is designed and its usability is evaluated. The three types of lunar fear sources (physical, task execution, and psychosocial) are classified, and vehicle function mapping strategies are proposed. Specific strategies for reducing fear stimuli, reducing perception of fear stimuli, and strengthening defense mechanisms are put forward.

This research provides a reference for the human factors engineering design of future manned lunar rovers and manned spacecraft, helping to improve astronauts' psychological adaptability and mission execution efficiency in extreme environments.

References

1. Zhang, Q.J., Bai, Y.Q.: Psychological issues in manned spaceflight. J. Aerosp. Med. Med. Eng. **02**, 69–73 (1999)
2. Zhou, Y., Wang, Z.K., Dang, F.: Current status and prospects of space station scientific experiments for lunar surface construction. J. Huazhong Univ. Sci. Technol. (Nat. Sci. Ed.). **52**(08), 121–129 (2024)
3. Meng, X.H., Li, Q., Zhou, Y.B., Wang, J.: Controversies of terror management theory and its implications for the study of death psychology. Adv. Psychol. Sci. **29**(03), 492–504 (2021)
4. Huang, C.L., Hu, C.: Terror management and grief management of death awareness. Acta Psychol. Sin. **55**(02), 318–337 (2023)
5. Wu, R.L., Wang, Y.: Psychological research based on simulated spaceflight missions: tasks, contents and methods. J. Aerosp. Med. Med. Eng. **29**(03), 217–223 (2016). https://doi.org/10.16289/j.cnki.1002-0837.2016.03.012
6. Peng, Q.B., Wang, P., Xing, L.: Perspectives on China's manned lunar scientific research and Test Station. Adv. Astronaut. Sci. Technol. **7**, 51–64 (2024)
7. Moreno, M.R.A., Paige, C.A., Stober, J., Rupasinghe, D., Wood, D., Newman, D.: Capturing the moon: 3D mapping and regolith collection for low-cost lunar rover missions. In: ASCEND 2022. American Institute of Aeronautics and Astronautics, Reston (2022)
8. Melgar, A.C., Puri, N., Robertson, B.E., Mavris, D.N.: Creation of a structural model to facilitate an OpenMDAO-based lunar rover parametric sizing tool. In: AIAA SCITECH 2024 Forum. American Institute of Aeronautics and Astronautics, Reston (2024)
9. Kim, Y., Ahn, J.: Multi-disciplinary and multi-objective design optimization of a lunar rover system with operational considerations. Int. J. Aeronaut. Space Sci. **23**(1), 192–206 (2022)
10. Sutoh, M.: Development and evaluation of mobility and excavation rover toward Lunar Base construction. J. Robot. Mechatron. **36**(2), 334–342 (2024)
11. Barth, A.L., Bisig, C., Ma, O., Dong, J.J., Abdallah, S.: Prototype Design of the Cable cat Lunar Rover. In: ASCEND 2020. American Institute of Aeronautics and Astronautics, Reston (2020)

Multisensory Integrated Haptic Interaction Design for Smartphones

Rui Zhang, Ziyao Zhang, and Yang Jiao(✉)

The Future Laboratory, Tsinghua University, Beijing 100084, China
jiaoyang7@tsinghua.edu.cn

Abstract. Haptic feedback on smartphones often works together with visual and auditory channels to enhance immersion and immediacy. However, current designs rely largely on experience based parameter tuning and lack a systematic perceptual mechanism, which leaves notable room for improvement. This study presents a multisensory haptic design framework that integrates user intention, vibration features and perceptual experience. It establishes a mapping from interaction scenarios to perceptual feedback to improve the structure, transferability and user adaptation of haptic design. Experiments were conducted across ten common scenarios on three smartphones. Twenty four users participated, resulting in 348 samples that included vibration parameters, satisfaction ratings and interview data. The results show that the framework explains 67% of the variance in user satisfaction. Vibration parameters and device differences are the main influencing factors. The framework provides theoretical and methodological support for haptic interaction design on smartphones and other mobile devices.

Keywords: Haptic interaction · Multisensory integration · Smartphone · Interaction design · User experience

1 Introduction

As mobile devices are used more frequently and for increasingly complex scenarios, haptic feedback has become an important channel for enhancing interaction awareness and operational efficiency. It is now widely adopted in smartphones, wearables, and other mobile devices [1,2]. Compared with visual and auditory cues, haptic feedback offers advantages such as privacy, immediacy, and independence from the user's line of sight, making it suitable for fast-paced and multitasking scenarios. However, current haptic design still heavily relies on experience-based adjustments and built-in presets. It lacks a structured approach grounded in user perception, which results in significant experiential differences across devices and real scenarios. This makes it difficult to maintain consistency and support design transferability.

Most studies primarily explore how physical parameters such as vibration frequency, amplitude, and duration affect perceived intensity, or they focus on

S. Guo et al. (Eds.): HHME 2025, CCIS 2878, pp. 139–155, 2027.
https://doi.org/10.1007/978-981-92-3991-7_11

modeling basic physiological mechanisms and psychophysical thresholds [3,4]. However, such studies are mostly conducted under controlled conditions, making it difficult to cover multidimensional factors in real interaction scenarios, including user goals, multimodal collaboration, and device implementation. There is still no theoretical framework that starts from the user's interaction intention and explains differences in haptic perception across devices.

To fill this gap, this study proposes a multisensory haptic feedback design framework for smartphones. The framework divides the user experience process into three modules: the user interaction layer, the explicit perception layer, and the implicit perception layer. These layers relate to user goals, feedback rhythms and structures, and perceptual interpretation. The framework aims to build a clear mapping among scenarios, rhythm, and perception. It integrates user preferences, system feedback patterns, and device implementation, and provides a structured foundation for haptic feedback that is interpretable, adjustable, and transferable.

We conducted a cross-device user study that covered ten typical interaction scenarios. Three mainstream smartphones were tested, and 24 participants took part in haptic experience sessions, satisfaction ratings, and short interviews. Vibration waveform parameters were collected for each scenario, and both quantitative modeling and qualitative analysis were used for validation. The results show that the framework explains 67% of the variance in user satisfaction. Physical parameters, device characteristics, and feedback structure all have significant effects. Users generally prefer short, clear, and rhythmically consistent feedback, showing higher satisfaction, especially in scenarios with well-defined operational rhythms. These findings verify the feasibility of constructing multisensory feedback structures based on user behavior and provide theoretical support and practical basis for the systematic implementation of rhythmic haptic design in smart terminals.

2 Related Work

2.1 Physiological Mechanisms and Psychophysical Foundations of Haptic Perception

Touch, as an important sensory channel besides sight and hearing, has gradually been regarded as the fifth dimension for enhancing the interactive experience of smartphones in recent years. Effective tactile design in human-computer interfaces must simultaneously satisfy physiological perceptibility and psychological distinguishability. That is, vibration stimulation needs to fall within the optimal response range of the skin's mechanoreceptors and deliver coherent and meaningful feedback through parameter differentiation. In haptic research, Verrillo and colleagues identified banded frequency sensitivity in cutaneous receptors, with Pacinian corpuscles showing minimal thresholds around 250 to 300 Hz and Meissner corpuscles responding more strongly to lower ranges near 10 to 50 Hz [5]. Brewster and Brown further quantified how frequency, amplitude, and temporal rhythm jointly influence perceived tactile intensity and can shift the urgency assigned to identical events [6]. Chang and collaborators extended this work by modeling temporal delay and showed that latencies above 40 ms reduce targeting accuracy and increase erroneous activations [7].

Despite establishing key physiological and psychophysical foundations for vibration design, these studies remain two shortcomings. Most experiments were run under ideal laboratory conditions with limited validation on actual smartphone hardware. Moreover, the modulatory effect of user intent, for example tapping and swiping, on perceptual thresholds has not been systematically quantified. To address these gaps, the present study proposes a framework that couples behavioral context with physiological sensitivity and empirically evaluates it in real smartphone interaction environments.

2.2 Theoretical Basis and Design Strategies for Multisensory Integration

In multimodal interaction, Wickens' Multiple Resource Theory indicates that sensory channels can process information in parallel with relatively independent resource pools, and that tactile cues can offload visual and auditory load when appropriately assigned [8]. Oviatt's modality appropriateness principle further suggests that each information type should be assigned to the channel with the greatest processing advantage. Rhythmic alerts are therefore more suited to tactile or auditory delivery, whereas spatial localization is best conveyed visually [9]. Spence and Driver introduced the principle of cross-sensory consistency, emphasizing that temporal and semantic alignment across channels is critical for reducing perceptual conflict [10]. Although these studies provide a foundation for tactile–visual–auditory coordination, two limitations remain. Most models are validated through two-channel experiments and lack systematic examination of three-channel collaboration in smartphone contexts. In addition, how users shift channel weighting during dynamic task switching remains unclear. Addressing these gaps, this study develops a multisensory framework centered on users' real-time scenarios, specifies when tactile cues should take priority, and validates these conditions through multitask smartphone interaction experiments.

2.3 Interaction Framework and Haptic Symbol Models

Brewster's Tactons encode vibration frequency, amplitude, and duration into discrete tactile icons, demonstrating that touch can distinguish information without visual input [6]. Later work by MacLean and Enriquez expanded these icons into multidimensional haptic symbols capable of conveying compound semantics and hierarchical cues [11,13]. Experience-oriented approaches, such as Kim's Haptic Experience Framework, further evaluate perception through sensory, contextual, and affective dimensions [14–19]. Despite these advances, current work largely focuses on encoding isolated vibration events and their subjective evaluation. A longitudinal causal chain linking user behavior, haptic parameters, multimodal semantics, and device constraints has not been fully articulated. Moreover, most evaluations occur in controlled settings and rarely consider the variability of real smartphone use and hardware diversity [20,21]. To bridge this gap, the present research proposes a multi-layered framework for designing and evaluating haptic feedback, providing systematic benchmarks for smartphone haptic interaction in real-world use.

3 Multisensory Framework for Smartphone Haptic Feedback

Grounded in observations, analysis, and synthesis across diverse real scenarios, this study proposes the multisensory smartphone haptic feedback framework illustrated in Fig. 1. With a focus on user experience, the framework describes a causal chain that links operations to perceptions through three layers: user interaction, explicit perception, and implicit perception.

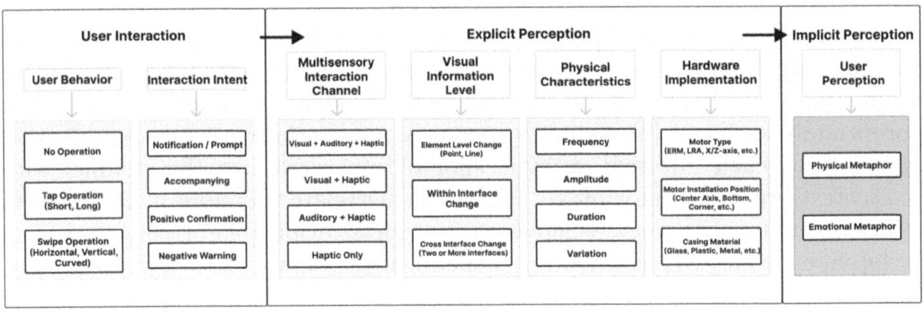

Fig. 1. Multisensory Haptic Feedback Framework for Smartphones

3.1 User Interaction Layer

Haptic feedback on smartphones is often driven by user interaction behaviors and the functional intentions behind them. These behaviors can be divided into passive reception and active operation. Passive reception includes situations such as incoming calls or system notifications that do not require user actions. Active operation includes Tap Operation, which may be short or long, and Swipe Operation, which can follow horizontal, vertical, or curved paths.

Aligned with functional goals and use contexts, smartphone haptics can be grouped into four types. Notification feedback occurs without active input, as in app alerts or reminders, using vibration to increase event perceptibility. Companion feedback is embedded within ongoing interaction, such as swiping, adding smoothness and a sense of engagement rather than conveying explicit information. Positive confirmation feedback verifies that an action has been successfully completed, for example in password entry or fingerprint authentication, and helps establish a clear interaction loop. Negative feedback highlights error or risk, such as authentication failure or restricted access, strengthening sensitivity to system warnings.

3.2 Explicit Perception Layer

The explicit perception layer describes how multisensory feedback produces immediate and consciously accessible effects. A first key dimension is modality combination. Different sensory channels can complement or reinforce each other. The integration of visual and tactile enhances confirmation of actions, while the pairing of tactile and auditory is more effective for alerts and warnings. Three-channel coordination remains more stable in highly demanding or noisy environments. Choosing the appropriate modality combination improves recognizability and allows the system to control the perceptual priority of feedback.

Another important dimension is the level at which visual information changes within the interface. This dimension describes whether the change occurs at the level of a single visual element, within the current interface, or across two or more interfaces. Different levels of change reflect how the system guides user attention. Changes that span across interfaces are more likely to be paired with noticeable haptic or multimodal feedback, which strengthens the user's perception of system state transitions.

The physical characteristics dimension of smartphone vibration is defined by four parameters shown in Fig. 2 and Fig. 3, which are frequency, amplitude, duration, and variation. These parameters describe differences in intensity, density, and rhythmic structure. Proper setting of these parameters helps improve the clarity and distinctiveness of system feedback and forms a structural foundation for later rhythm modeling and mechanism analysis.

The hardware implementation dimension also plays an important role in shaping how explicit feedback is perceived. Even with identical waveform parameters, the actual tactile sensation can differ across devices because of variations in motor type(such as X-axis or Z-axis linear motors, the Taptic Engine, etc.), motor installation position, and device materials. Vibrations produced in metal enclosures often feel crisp and compact, while those in glass enclosures tend to feel softer. These differences may influence how users perceive rhythmic clarity or interpret the intention of the feedback. Therefore, strategies to maintain perceptual consistency need to be considered when designing haptic feedback across devices.

3.3 Implicit Perception Layer

After users experience multimodal haptic feedback, they often form interpretations of system states and emotional responses beyond conscious awareness. The implicit perception layer focuses on the deeper associative mechanism that emerges from sensory experience. Users rely on cues such as rhythm, intensity, and modality coordination to construct judgments about system behavior and to shape their emotional attitudes. This perception layer not only influences how users recognize interaction intentions but also plays a major role in defining the subjective quality and overall character of haptic feedback.

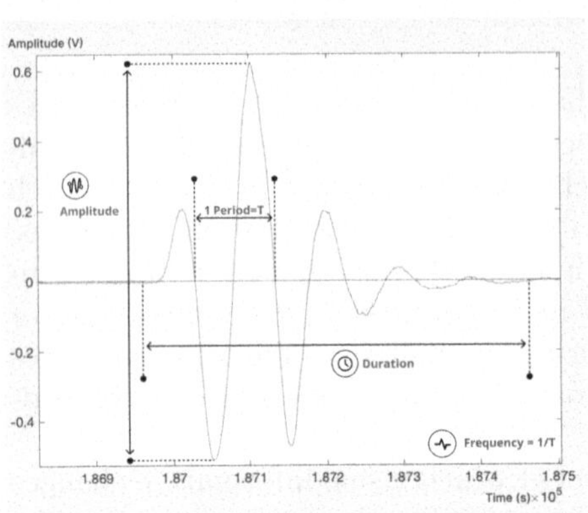

Fig. 2. Vibration Parameter Diagram

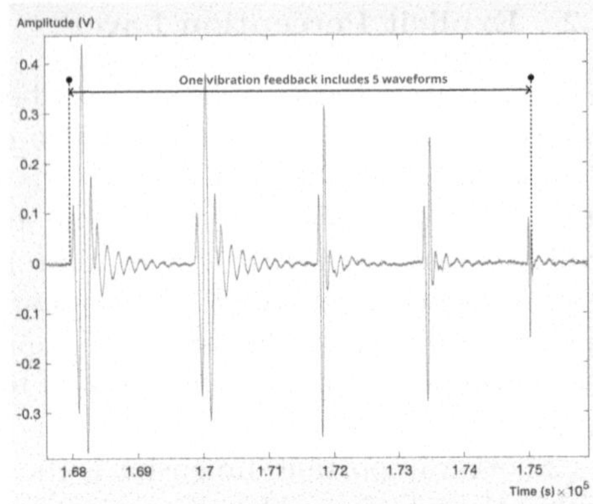

Fig. 3. Vibration Variation Diagram

These associations often appear in the form of metaphors, which this study categorizes into physical metaphors and emotional metaphors. Physical metaphors refer to cases where users map haptic features to familiar physical experiences. For example, the clicking sensation of adjusting an alarm wheel can evoke the rotation of mechanical gears, and the textured feeling at the edge of a swiping gesture can map a damping structure. Such haptic design enhances the sense of physicality in system behavior and makes the interaction feel more natural to users.

Emotional metaphors reflect users' affective interpretations of feedback rhythm and intensity. Feedback that is steady in rhythm and gentle in intensity is often perceived as warm and friendly, making it suitable for accompanying interactions or positive confirmations. In contrast, feedback that is short and strong more easily conveys tension or a warning. This layered emotional perception improves the informational efficiency of haptic feedback and enriches the user's emotional experience.

4 Method

4.1 Devices and Scenarios Selection

To select devices for the study, we considered brand influence, user usage, and the technology of haptic motor. Three smartphones was chosen, including iPhone 14 Pro Max (Apple Taptic Engine), OnePlus 11 (AAC Technologies CSA0916) and Xiaomi 13 Pro (AAC Technologies ESA1016). These devices differ in structural design, motor types, and material configuration.

For the scenarios, the study focused on typical high-frequency and highly interactive operations in daily use. Ten scenarios were selected, as shown in Table 1, covering functions such as input, swiping, editing, photography, and state feedback. All scenarios were triggered through active user operations rather than passive system notifications. These scenarios also provide clear distinctions in interaction behavior, modality structure, and semantic intention.

Table 1. Smartphone Haptic Feedback Scenarios

No.	Scenario	Behavior	Interaction Intention
1	Keyboard Typing	Tap	Positive Confirmation
2	Alarm Setting	Swipe	Accompanying
3	Contacts Alphabet Index	Swipe	Accompanying
4	Camera Zoom Adjustment	Swipe	Accompanying
5	Camera Shutter	Tap	Positive Confirmation
6	Album Long Press Editing	Tap	Positive Confirmation
7	Apps Long Press Editing	Tap	Positive Confirmation
8	Settings Horizontal Toggle	Swipe	Positive Confirmation
9	Swiping Up to Access Recent Tasks	Swipe	Accompanying
10	Fingerprint Unlock Failure	Tap	Negative Warning

4.2 Scenario Feature Identification

After selecting the scenarios and devices, the study analyzed the ten scenarios using the multisensory haptic feedback framework to identify their key features. This step clarifies the factors that shape user perception and provides the foundation for later variable encoding and model construction.

In terms of behavior, the ten scenarios include short tap confirmation operations as well as continuous navigation that relies on swipe operations, reflecting differences in interaction rhythm and feedback needs. Regarding interaction intention, some scenarios convey the result of a completed action, such as Camera Shutter or Settings Horizontal Toggle. Others emphasize accompanying feedback during the operation, such as Alarm Setting or Camera Zoom Adjustment. The Fingerprint Unlock Failure scenario represents a warning and failure condition.

At the multisensory interaction channel dimension, all scenarios involve both visual and haptic feedback, and some scenarios further incorporate auditory cues to form multimodal coordination. The presentation of visual feedback also varies across scenarios. Some scenarios provide immediate responses within the same interface, while others involve interface transitions at the system level. These differences reflect the varying requirements for feedback salience and attention management.

4.3 Physical Data Collection and Parameter Extraction

Data Collection System. The study built a hardware system based on acceleration measurement, as shown in Fig. 4, to collect vibration feedback data from the three smartphones across the typical interaction scenarios. The system uses an ADXL354BZ three axis accelerometer, with sampling focused on the X axis to match the vibration direction of the X-axis linear motors used in all three devices. A Teensy 4.1 serves as the control core to drive the sensor and manage data transmission. The vibration signals are sampled by a Pico 5444D MSO oscilloscope at a sampling rate of 24 kS per second and are then transmitted through a serial connection to a ThinkPad laptop for storage and data analysis.

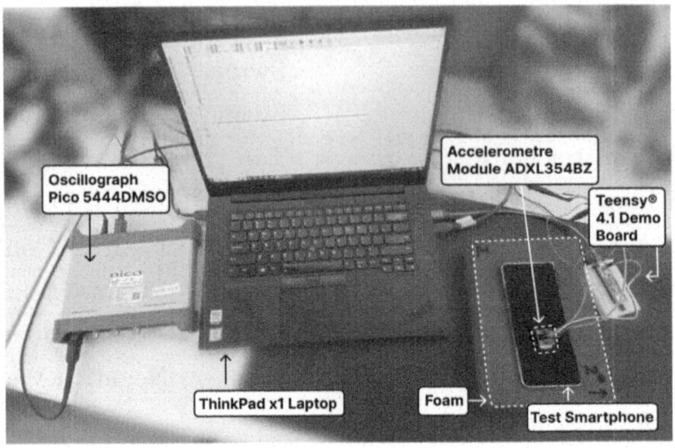

Fig. 4. Vibration Waveform Data Acquisition System

Vibration Parameter Extraction. After collecting the waveforms, key physical parameters were extracted. These parameters include peak amplitude, duration, frequency, and variation. Using the Camera Shutter scenario on the Xiaomi 13 Pro as an example, the time-domain plot in Fig. 5 shows a peak to peak voltage of 0.14 V and a vibration duration of approximately 0.0083 s. Figure 6 shows the frequency-domain plot obtained through a Fourier transform, which has a fundamental frequency of 270 Hz. Because this waveform contains only one complete vibration cycle, its variation value is 1.

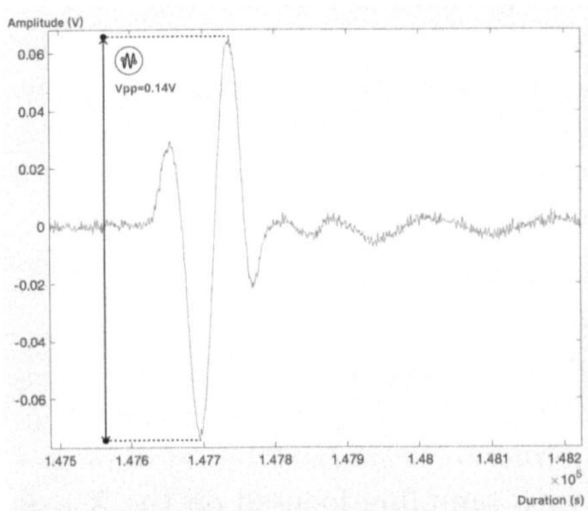

Fig. 5. Time-Domain Plot of the "Camera Shutter" on Xiaomi 13 Pro

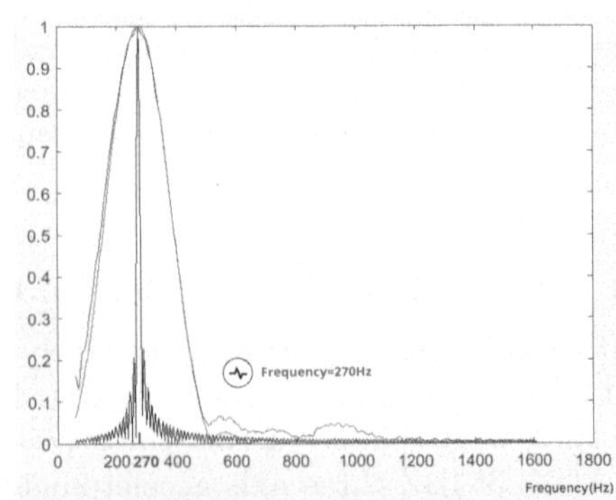

Fig. 6. Frequency-Domain Plot of the "Camera Shutter" on Xiaomi 13 Pro

To further quantify perceived amplitude, the measured voltage values were normalized using a perceptual intensity conversion formula. Based on the Weber Fechner law [22], a constant term and base 10 were introduced to obtain the following equation.

$$S = 10 \times \log_{10}\left(\frac{U}{U_{\mathrm{th}}}\right) \tag{1}$$

In this equation, S represents perceptual intensity in dB SL, U is the measured voltage amplitude, and U_{th} is the minimum detectable voltage for the human hand, which was measured as 0.001 V in this study. The calculated perceptual amplitude for the Xiaomi device in this scenario is 21.46 dB SL. Table 2 lists the four vibration parameters for all three phones in the Camera Shutter scenario.

Table 2. Vibration Parameters in the Camera Shutter Scenario

Smartphones	Frequency (Hz)	Amplitude (dB SL)	Duration (s)	Variation
1	295	19.78	0.0136	2
2	250	21.82	0.0080	2
3	270	21.46	0.0083	1

4.4 User Study and Data Collection

Participants. The experiment included ten representative interaction scenarios. To obtain subjective ratings from twelve participants for each scenario, a total of 120 ratings were required. Since each participant evaluated five different scenarios, 24 participants were recruited for the study, including 10 men and 14 women, aged between 20 and 55 years old (M = 28.17, SD = 8.28). Each participant completed five scenarios, resulting in 120 samples across the ten scenarios. All participants were right handed, physically healthy, and reported no tactile perception impairments. They provided informed consent voluntarily and received monetary compensation corresponding to the duration of the study.

Procedure. To ensure continuous attention and perceptual sensitivity during the study, each participant completed five scenarios, with each scenario involving two to three smartphones. The total duration for each participant was controlled between 60 and 85 min. The experimental procedure is shown in Fig. 7.

Questionnaire. Participants completed a basic information form that included demographic variables such as gender and age.

Instructions. The experimenter briefly introduced the overall procedure, scenario objectives, and rating mechanism, ensuring that participants fully understood the process before starting the trials.

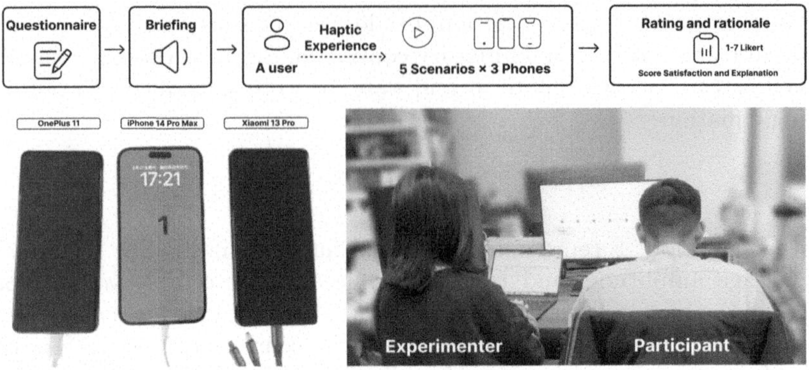

Fig. 7. User Study Procedure, Smartphones, and Environment

Haptic Experience. Participants experienced the vibration feedback of each scenario on different smartphones. To strengthen perceptual contrast, the order of devices was randomized. Participants were encouraged to repeat the experience when needed to form a clear impression.

Rating and Explanation. After each experience, participants rated the feedback of each device in that scenario on a seven point satisfaction scale and provided a brief explanation of the reason for their rating. These explanations supported deeper interpretation of their preferences.

4.5 Data Preprocessing and Coding

The study standardized and encoded the collected data based on the proposed multisensory haptic feedback framework. Two types of variables were included. The first type was continuous variables that describe the physical features of haptic feedback. The second type was categorical dummy variables that represent interaction behavior and device implementation characteristics.

Frequency, amplitude, duration, and variation were treated as continuous variables. They reflect the density, intensity, temporal length, and structural complexity of the vibration, and their raw measured values were directly used for modeling. User ratings were collected on a seven point Likert scale and were used as the dependent variable in the regression model.

Other variables related to modality features, interface structure, behavior type, interaction intention, and device type were encoded as categorical dummy variables. For the multisensory interaction channel, the value was set to 1 if auditory information was present and 0 otherwise. For the visual information level, scenarios involving interface transitions were coded as 1, while scenarios within a single interface were coded as 0. For user behavior, tap operations served as the reference group, and swipe operations were coded as 1. For interaction intention, confirmation scenarios served as the baseline, while accompanying and warning scenarios were coded as 1. At the device level, Apple served as the reference group, and OnePlus and Xiaomi were represented by two variables named Dev_ONE and Dev_MI. Table 3 shows the variable coding for Keyboard Typing (Scenario 1) and Fingerprint Unlock Failure (Scenario 10). Because the iPhone system does not support Fingerprint Unlock Failure, it was not included in data collection for that scenario.

Table 3. Variable Coding for Scenario 1 and Scenario 10

	Freq (Hz)	Amp (dB)	Dur(s)	Varation	Mod_AVT	UI_Cross	Dev_ONE	Dev_MI	Act_Cross	Int_Comp	Int_Alert	Sat
1	270	23.80	0.0104	1	1	0	0	0	0	0	0	5.42
1	292	28.81	0.0068	1	1	0	1	0	0	0	0	4.61
1	160	28.57	0.0125	1	1	0	0	1	0	0	0	4.33
10	255	28.51	0.0450	3	1	1	1	0	0	0	1	4.50
10	531	29.08	0.0700	5	0	0	0	1	0	0	1	3.75

5 Results and Findings

5.1 Descriptive Statistics

Satisfaction Comparison. A descriptive analysis was conducted on the users' subjective ratings. Figure 8 presents the mean satisfaction scores of the three devices across the ten scenarios. Overall, the iPhone 14 Pro Max consistently achieved the highest ratings in all scenarios, with means above 5.0. The OnePlus 11 and Xiaomi 13 Pro received lower scores, with several scenarios falling below 4.0, indicating notable differences between smartphones. Scenario level differences were also evident. Alarm Setting (Scenario 2) received particularly high ratings, whereas Swiping Up to Access Recent Tasks (Scenario 9) and Fingerprint Unlock Failure (Scenario 10) showed consistently lower evaluations.

Parameter Correlations. To explore how physical parameters influence user satisfaction, Pearson correlation coefficients between the four vibration parameters and satisfaction were calculated, as shown in Fig. 9. The results indicate that except for frequency, amplitude, duration, and variation all show negative correlations with satisfaction. Duration ($r = -0.32$) and variation ($r = -0.23$) exhibit similar trends, suggesting that users may prefer vibration patterns that are shorter, simpler, and clearer. This tendency aligns with the emphasis of the Explicit Perception Layer which highlights the role of temporal structure in enhancing perceptual clarity. The findings imply that rhythm optimization may be valuable for improving user experience.

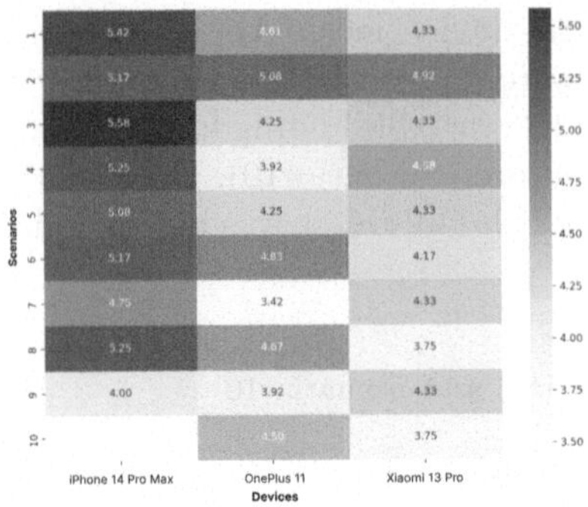

Fig. 8. Satisfaction Distribution of Three Devices Across Ten Scenarios

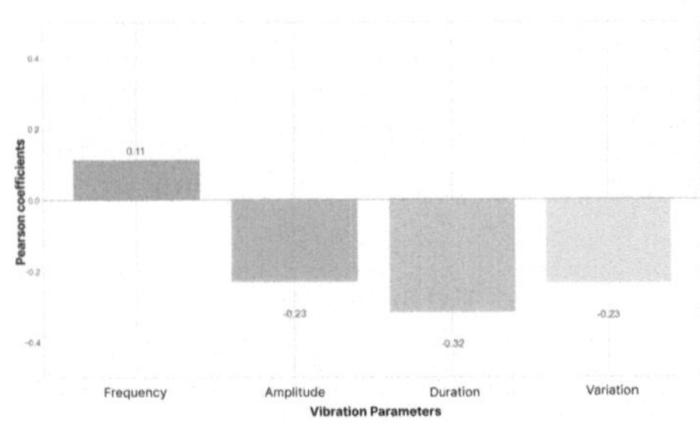

Fig. 9. Pearson Correlation Coefficients Between Vibration Parameters and User Satisfaction

5.2 Hierarchical Regression Model Analysis

Layered Logic. To compute how different dimensions influence user satisfaction with haptic feedback, a four layer regression model was built based on the proposed perceptual framework. Physical parameters of vibration constitute the first layer. The second layer adds explicit perception design factors, namely modality combination and interface level changes. Device type forms the third layer and reflects differences in hardware implementation. Behavior type and interaction intention make up the fourth layer and describe user interaction factors. Variables were entered stepwise, and model contribution was examined through changes in ΔR^2 squared and F statistics.

Table 4. Hierarchical Regression Model Results

Predictor	Model 1		Model 2		Model 3		Model 4	
	β	t	β	t	β	t	β	t
Frequency	0.604	1.868	0.487	1.588	0.289	1.078	0.165	0.531
Amplitude	−0.281	−1.527	−0.300	−1.683	−0.008	−0.046	0.095	0.441
Duration	0.192	0.412	0.437	0.937	−0.069	−0.158	−0.697	−1.171
Variation	−0.765	−1.300	−0.931	−1.641	−0.306	−0.581	−0.102	−0.160
Mod_AVT			0.295	1.698	0.148	0.961	0.067	0.382
UI_Cross			−0.253	−1.247	−0.171	−0.991	−0.098	−0.459
Dev_ONE					−0.569	−2.730**	−0.765	−3.120**
Dev_MI					−0.624	−3.270*	−0.734	−3.562**
Act_Slide							0.281	0.899
Int_Comp							−0.108	−0.349
Int_Alert							0.553	1.179
R^2	0.251		0.398		0.615		0.666	
ΔR^2	0.251		0.148		0.217		0.051	
F	2.008		2.427		3.993**		3.078*	

Note: $^{***}p < 0.001$, $^{**}p < 0.01$, $^{*}p < 0.05$.

Results. The results of the hierarchical regression model are shown in Table 4. The basic physical parameters of vibration, including frequency, amplitude, duration, and variation, explained about 25% of the variance in user satisfaction ($\Delta R^2 = 0.251$). After adding perceptual design factors, including modality combination and interface level, the explanatory power increased to 40% ($\Delta R^2 = 0.15$, $p = 0.090$), indicating that design level variables may influence subjective perception. When device type was further included to represent hardware implementation, the model fit rose to 62% ($\Delta R^2 = 0.22$, $p = 0.006$). Satisfaction for the OnePlus 11 and Xiaomi 13 Pro was significantly lower than for the iPhone 14 Pro Max ($\beta = -0.57$ and -0.62, $p < 0.01$), suggesting a strong impact of hardware implementation on the overall experience.

Although behavior type and interaction intention did not produce a significant improvement in model fit ($\Delta R^2 = 0.05$, $p = 0.480$), they still offer structural value by helping organize contextual differences across scenarios. The final four layer model reached an R^2 of 0.666. This shows that the proposed perceptual framework can explain nearly two-thirds of the satisfaction differences, with most contributions coming from the physical, perceptual design, and hardware layers. These results provide supporting evidence for the framework and offer useful guidance for future haptic design in smart devices.

5.3 Qualitative Data Analysis

We analyzed users' tactile perception in representative interaction scenarios through open coding and thematic induction. Interviews with 24 participants across 10 scenarios were coded and grouped based on interaction intent. Three categories emerged: fine adjustment, rapid tapping, and functional switching. For each category, we identified perceptual keywords and common preference patterns.

For fine adjustment scenarios such as Alarm Setting, Contact Alphabet Index, and Camera Zoom Adjustment, users were highly sensitive to the clarity of the tactile granularity and the stability of the rhythm. Participant P10 described the Alarm Setting feedback as "a tight, condensed drop of water," which helped precisely locate the desired point. In Camera Zoom Adjustment, P19 noted that the vibration "gradually intensifies with the zoom level," creating a "natural and perceivable progression." Some users also reported that overly heavy and sticky textures disrupted smooth movement, especially during fast swiping, leading to a sense of interruption.

Rapid tapping scenarios, including Keyboard Typing and Apps Long Press Editing, emphasized crispness, immediacy, and consistency. In the Keyboard Typing, P5 stated that even slight latency "breaks the entire rhythm of writing." Frequent negative descriptions such as "dragged," "mushy," and "too spaced out" from participants P2, P8, and P11 indicated that any delay undermines input fluency. In Apps Long Press Editing, P2 described an ideal feedback as "like a check mark being completed," delivering a clear and decisive completion cue.

Functional switching scenarios such as Settings Horizontal Toggle, Camera Shutter, and Fingerprint Unlock Failure focused on synchronization between feedback and on-screen actions. Settings Horizontal Toggle were often described as similar to "pulling a zipper," and P19 highlighted that the feeling creates "a sense of ceremony," reinforcing the logic of change. For Camera Shutter, P11 depicted the vibration as "a fax swipe," offering immediate confirmation. In contrast, many users found the feedback for Fingerprint Unlock Failure to be confusing, reporting unclear pacing and abrupt segments that made it difficult to infer the system's intent.

6 Discussion

6.1 Synergy Between Parameter Design and Hardware Differences

The hierarchical regression shows that vibration frequency, amplitude, duration and rhythmic variability explain 25.1% of the variance in user satisfaction, confirming these parameters as the physical substrate of haptic experience. Adding device type increases R^2 by a further 21.7%, indicating that an identical parameter set can feel completely different across handsets. The cause is not simply motor quality; rather, it is the whole hardware–software stack. Motor specification, mounting location and housing material jointly determine how vibration energy propagates and decays, while drive-layer shaping and latency suppression magnify those disparities.

Among the three tested phones, iPhone 14 Pro Max performs best. Its custom Taptic Engine, rigid mid-frame and glass back produce short, crisp and consistent feedback. When the motor sits far from the grip point, the shell absorbs vibration, or the trigger signal is delayed, users describe the sensation as "muffled" or "trailing", even at comparable amplitudes. High-quality haptics therefore require meticulous parameter tuning and implementation optimisation. Cross-device or multi-terminal design must calibrate hardware capability and scheduling in parallel to preserve rhythm and recognisability.

6.2 Rhythm–Intent Mapping

Scenarios with high satisfaction typically feature concise vibrations tightly synchronized with the gesture, whereas low-scoring warning feedbacks tend to be overly long or rhythmically fragmented. The negative correlations between satisfaction and both duration and variability confirm that users are more sensitive to temporal structure than to intensity or frequency in isolation.

Different interaction intents prefer distinct rhythmic patterns. A single short pulse works for confirmation, evenly spaced weak pulses suit continuous accompaniment, and dense high-contrast rhythms communicate warnings or errors. These patterns constitute a basic rhythm–intent map. Designers should start from interaction semantics, specify the temporal characteristics of the target action, and then derive pulse count and spacing that balance discriminability with comfort while preserving rhythmic coherence.

6.3 Layered Features of User Perception

Interviews reveal three jointly acting factors. Timeliness and rhythm coherence dominate. When vibration is synchronous and beat-stable users describe it as "immediate" and "seamless"; any delay beyond the perceptual threshold is judged "sluggish", decoupling action and feedback. Spatial focus and structural simplicity come next: feedback that stays near the touch point and has clear pulses is "neat", whereas device-wide or multi-segment feedback feels "abrupt" or "fragmented". Finally, a balance between force and granularity matters. Medium strength with distinct grains is likened to a "heartbeat", reinforcing confirmation; excessive force induces discomfort, whereas weak or blurry pulses erode recognisability.

Mechanistically, timeliness aligns with the explicit layer's need for rhythmic synchrony, spatial focus reduces attentional load, and force granularity tuning addresses the implicit layer's comfort threshold and affective tone. Haptic design should first ensure trigger latency and rhythm precision, then control propagation range and waveform simplicity, and finally fine-tune strength and granularity to achieve both recognisability and pleasure across scenes and devices.

6.4 Design Applications and Cross-Device Prospects

The proposed Use Interaction – Explicit Perception – Implicit Perception Framework offers a systematic route for haptic design. Practitioners can begin with user behaviour and intent, locate the target semantics, map them onto perceptual channels, visual hierarchy, parameter bounds and then verify hardware feasibility. The final sensation remains subject to physical and affective metaphors in the implicit layer. The framework thus supports causal design from behavioural origin to perceptual outcome, enabling rapid classification and generation of haptic strategies in everyday scenarios.

Its extensibility is high. By adapting motor type and materials, designers can transplant feedback to tablets, wearables or VR devices without altering interaction logic. The same structure also informs channel coordination, feedback priority and perceptual consistency in multimodal work, laying a theoretical foundation for cross-platform haptics.

6.5 Limitations and Future Work

This study presents scope and methodology limitations that require validation in broader interaction contexts. While the study examined ten scenarios and three mainstream devices, the results may not represent the diversity of system configurations or technologies. Future work will extend the framework to more devices, vibration systems, and multiple scenarios to assess its applicability. Current modeling focused on four core physical features. Further research will incorporate finer features such as onset/offset ramps, directionality and propagation, jointly modeled with device structural attributes to better align physical signals with perceptual layers and behavioral intent.

Qualitative analysis has not yet established systematic links between subjective language and physical parameters. Future work will integrate semantic modeling with physiological data to support multimodal evaluation and will explore adaptive tactile generation that responds to scenario demands, user states, and device properties.

Overall, this work verifies the feasibility of a multisensory haptic framework for smartphones. Future research will prioritize multi-device generalization, finer parameter modeling, and cross-modal adaptive feedback to build a scalable foundation for mobile haptic interaction.

7 Conclusion

This study proposes and validates a multisensory haptic design framework for structured vibration feedback on smartphones. The framework integrates user intention, rhythmic structure and perceptual features to build a mapping path. It provides systematic support for improving the adaptability and expressive accuracy of feedback. Through cross device experiments on ten representative scenarios and three mainstream smartphones, combined with vibration measurements, satisfaction ratings and interview data, the study demonstrates that the framework explains user experience differences well. Compared with traditional approaches that rely on intuition or focus only on vibration parameters, this work highlights the importance of grounding feedback design in task context, functional goals and multisensory integration. Future research can expand perceptual dimensions and device adaptation strategies to enhance the role of haptic design in multimodal and multi device experiences.

Acknowledgments. We gratefully acknowledge all research team members, study participants and the anonymous reviewers for their invaluable support and contributions to this work. This study was funded by the Foundation of the Ministry of Education of China (Grant No. 23YJCZH092) and the Assistive-Technology Special Project of the China Disabled Persons' Federation (Grant No. 2024CDPFAT-04).

References

1. Saket, B., Prasojo, C., Huang, Y., Zhao, S.: Designing an effective vibration-based notification interface for mobile phones. In: Proceedings of the 2013 Conference on Computer Supported Cooperative Work, pp. 149–1504. ACM, New York (2013)
2. Yao, H.-Y., Grant, D., Cruz, M.: Perceived vibration strength in mobile devices: the effect of weight and frequency. IEEE Trans. Haptics **3**(1), 56–62 (2009)
3. Zhang, R., Li, Y., Wu, Z., Zhang, Y., Zhao, J., Jiao, Y.: SemanticTap: a haptic toolkit for vibration semantic design of smartphone. In: Proceedings of the 26th International Conference on Multimodal Interaction, pp. 264–273. ACM, New York (2024)
4. Li, Y., Zhang, R., He, L., Jiao, Y.: HapticMetric: a smartphone haptic experience computing system. In: Proceedings of the Twelfth International Symposium of Chinese CHI, pp. 561–570. ACM, New York (2024)

5. Verrillo, R.T., Fraioli, A.J., Smith, R.L.: Sensation magnitude of vibrotactile stimuli. Percept. Psychophys. **6**(6), 366–372 (1969)
6. Brewster, S.A., Brown, L.M.: Tactons: structured tactile messages for non-visual information display. In: Proceedings of EuroHaptics (2004)
7. Chang, A., O'Modhrain, S., Jacob, R., Gunther, E., Ishii, H.: ComTouch: design of a vibrotactile communication device. In: Proceedings of the 4th Conference on Designing Interactive Systems: Processes, Practices, Methods, and Techniques, pp. 312–320. ACM, New York (2002)
8. Wickens, C.D.: Multiple resources and performance prediction. Theor. Issues Ergon. Sci. **3**(2), 159–177 (2002)
9. Oviatt, S.: Ten myths of multimodal interaction. Commun. ACM **42**(11), 74–81 (1999)
10. Spence, C., Driver, J.: Crossmodal Space and Crossmodal Attention. Oxford University Press, Oxford (2004)
11. MacLean, K., Enriquez, M.: Perceptual design of haptic icons. In: Proceedings of EuroHaptics, pp. 351–363 (2003)
12. Ternes, D., MacLean, K.E.: Designing Large sets of haptic icons with rhythm. In: Ferre, M. (ed.) EuroHaptics 2008. LNCS, vol. 5024, pp. 199–208. Springer, Heidelberg (2008). https://doi.org/10.1007/978-3-540-69057-3_24
13. Hoggan, E., Brewster, S.A., Johnston, J.: Investigating the effectiveness of tactile feedback for mobile touchscreens. In: Proceedings of the SIGCHI Conference on Human Factors in Computing Systems, pp. 1573–1582. ACM, New York (2008)
14. Obrist, M., Seah, S.A., Subramanian, S.: Talking about tactile experiences. In: Proceedings of the SIGCHI Conference on Human Factors in Computing Systems, pp. 1659–1668. ACM, New York (2013)
15. Seifi, H., MacLean, K.E.: A first look at individuals' affective ratings of vibrations. In: 2013 World Haptics Conference (WHC), pp. 605–610. IEEE, Daejeon (2013)
16. Tan, J., Ge, Y., Sun, X., Zhang, Y., Liu, Y.: User experience of tactile feedback on a smartphone: effects of vibration intensity, times and interval. In: Cross-Cultural Design, CCD 2019, HCII 2019, pp. 397–406. Springer, Orlando (2019)
17. Ju, Y., Zheng, D., Hynds, D., Chernyshov, G., Kunze, K., Minamizawa, K.: Haptic empathy: conveying emotional meaning through vibrotactile feedback. In: Extended Abstracts of the 2021 CHI Conference on Human Factors in Computing Systems, pp. 1–7. ACM, New York (2021)
18. Anwar, A., Shi, T., Schneider, O.: Factors of haptic experience across multiple haptic modalities. In: Proceedings of the 2023 CHI Conference on Human Factors in Computing Systems, pp. 1–12. ACM, New York (2023)
19. Kim, E., Schneider, O.: Defining haptic experience: foundations for understanding, communicating, and evaluating HX. In: Proceedings of the 2020 CHI Conference on Human Factors in Computing Systems, pp. 1–13. ACM, New York (2020)
20. Shiraga, S., Kinoshita, Y., Totsuka, T., Go, K.: Construction of impression estimation models for the design of smartphone vibration feedback. In: KEER 2018: 7th International Conference on Kansei Engineering and Emotion Research, pp. 350–359. Springer, Kuching (2018)
21. Hwang, J., Hwang, W.: Vibration perception and excitatory direction for haptic devices. J. Intell. Manuf. **22**, 17–27 (2011)
22. Ekman, G.: Weber's law and related functions. J. Psychol. **47**(2), 343–352 (1959)

EmoChatBot: Integrating Fine-Grained Emotional Talking-Head Generation Into Face-to-Face Dialogue

Hanlin Yan[1], Fang Liu[1](✉), and Cuixia Ma[2]

[1] The State Key Laboratory of Media Convergence and Communication, Communication University of China, Beijing 100024, China
yhl_cuc@mails.cuc.edu.cn, fangliu@cuc.edu.cn

[2] Institute of Software, Chinese Academy of Sciences, University of the Chinese Academy of Sciences, Beijing 100190, China
cuixia@iscas.ac.cn

Abstract. Talking-head generation plays a key role in modern communication, but limited emotional expression hinders natural and credible human-computer interaction. In this paper, we introduce *EmoChatBot*, a face-to-face dialogue system designed to leverage both explicit and implicit emotional cues from users' audio-visual inputs, enabling the generation of more natural and emotionally responsive talking-head interactions. Our EmoChatBot is capable of generating emotionally consistent speech and facial response videos based on user input. It accepts user video or text as input, generates response text using a large language model, and performs multimodal emotional analysis by focusing on both the emotional content of the text and the emotional cues in the user's speech and facial expressions. The system then produces fine-grained talking-head response videos that feature emotionally expressive speech and facial expressions. This is achieved by introducing an Action Unit (AU)-based facial expression control mechanism for the talking-head, which aligns multimodal emotional input cues with fine-grained facial expression features. This alignment enables natural and controllable emotional feedback in the generated responses. Extensive experiments validate the effectiveness of our model in enabling face-to-face conversations that achieve both dialogue coherence and emotional consistency.

Keywords: Talking-Head Generation · Expression Control · Multimodal · Action Units

1 Introduction

With the rapid development of large language models and virtual avatars modeling technologies, digital human systems have been widely used in human-computer interaction. Talking-head generation is applied in both personal and

S. Guo et al. (Eds.): HHME 2025, CCIS 2878, pp. 156–168, 2027.
https://doi.org/10.1007/978-981-92-3991-7_12

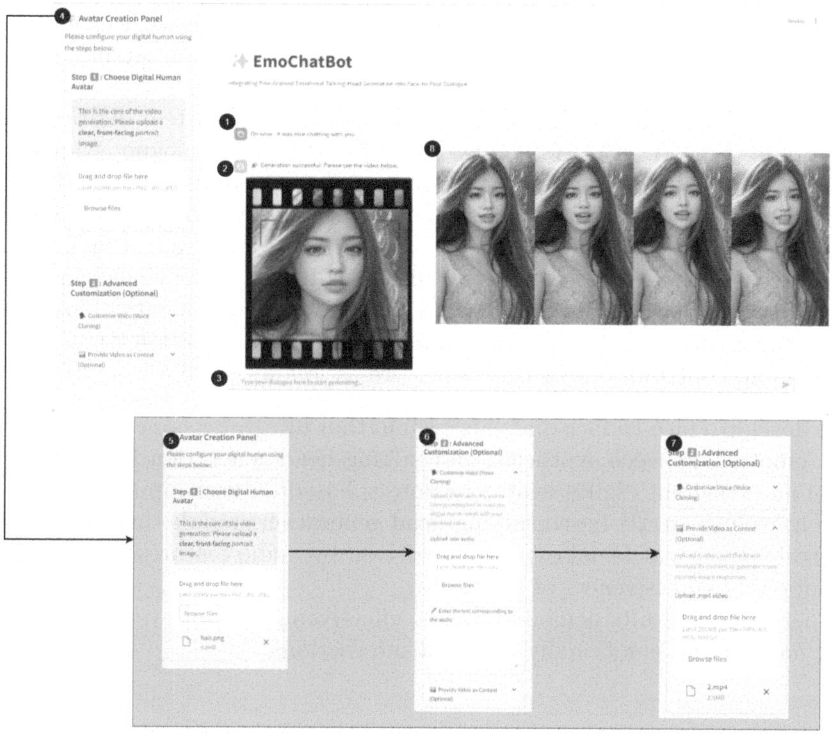

Fig. 1. User interface and workflow of our proposed EmoChatBot system. ❶ The user inputs a dialogue text. ❷ The model generates a response video and displays a synthesized talking-head video below. ❸ The user inputs the next dialogue turn. ❹ The customization panel is divided into three parts: ❺ Avatar creation using the uploaded image, ❻ advanced customization with optional cloned audio, and ❼ contextual customization using background/environmental video for natural interaction. ❽ Example frames from the response video.

professional communication scenarios, such as video conferencing systems [17] and intelligent agent dialogues [12]. However, the lack of natural emotional expression and multimodal coordination still presents significant challenges for achieving natural and engaging human-computer interactions. This is largely due to the absence of fine-grained emotional responses in virtual avatars, which limits both the naturalness of speech and the credibility of human-computer communication.

Although significant progress has been made in areas such as multimodal dialogue models (e.g., LLaVA [11]), emotional speech synthesis [7], and speech-driven talking-head generation [5,10], effectively integrating these components to build a digital avatar chatbot that maintains both semantic accuracy and emotional consistency remains a significant challenge. Specifically, the key challenges lie in generating emotionally appropriate responses based on user input.

This includes accurate emotion recognition, aligning speech with facial expressions in the talking-head module, and maintaining low system latency and high stability.

To address the challenge of generating emotionally consistent digital avatars, we propose EmoChatBot (see Fig. 1), a face-to-face dialogue system that leverages both explicit and implicit emotional cues from users' audio-visual inputs. EmoChatBot integrates emotion recognition, large language model-based response generation, emotional speech synthesis, and fine-grained facial expression control. Specifically, an Action Unit (AU)-based control mechanism uses audio features to drive expressive, controllable facial movements. This enables more natural, emotionally coherent human-computer interaction.

The main contributions of this paper are as follows:

1. We develop a face-to-face dialogue system that integrates large language models, emotional speech synthesis, and talking-head generation to produce natural and coherent digital avatar responses based on user input.
2. We introduce an AU-based talking-head generation module that enables emotionally consistent facial expressions driven by audio features, enhancing the emotional expressiveness of the avatar.
3. Experimental results demonstrate the effectiveness of our system in generating natural and emotionally coherent interactions.

2 Related Work

2.1 Interactive Dialogue Agent Systems

Interactive dialogue agents are becoming a key focus in human-computer interaction, requiring not only accurate understanding and semantically appropriate responses, but also contextual consistency, emotional coherence, and timely feedback across multi-turn conversations.

Earlier dialogue systems such as DialoGPT [26], BlenderBot [19] and LaMDA [20] are based on large-scale pre-trained language models and have achieved significant improvements in context modeling, maintaining personalized styles, and emotion regulation.

In the multimodal domain, LLaVA [11] integrates image and language features, advancing visually-assisted dialogue systems. Visual ChatGPT [23] supports mixed text-image dialogues.

Furthermore, recent studies have integrated speech, emotion, and physiological signals into dialogue systems. For example, the EmpatheticDialogues dataset [18] has advanced empathetic agents that generate warmer responses via emotion recognition and imitation. ERICA [8], a multimodal dialogue prototype, combines voice tone, language, and visual cues to deliver more realistic interactions.

Although significant progress has been made in interactive dialogue agent systems, they often remain limited to text or speech output, lacking natural and emotionally aware responses. In this paper, we propose an end-to-end system that integrates large language model-based dialogue understanding with fine-grained, expression-aware talking-head generation to achieve semantically and emotionally consistent multimodal interactions.

2.2 Multimodal Emotional Analysis via Large Language Models

Early emotion analysis methods relied on keywords and sentiment dictionaries, limiting their ability to handle complex contexts. The advent of pre-trained models like BERT [3] and RoBERTa [13] has greatly enhanced emotion recognition robustness. Moreover, multi-turn emotion reasoning models such as DialogueCRN [6] capture emotional evolution by modeling contextual dependencies throughout conversations.

Large language models like ChatGPT enable emotion-guided responses based on context. Multimodal models such as LLaVA [11] combine images and language, advancing visually-assisted and emotion-aware dialogues. However, these approaches mainly address emotional consistency in text, lacking integration of non-verbal cues like speech and facial expressions, which limit their expressiveness in real interactions.

2.3 Emotional Talking-Head Generation

Talking-head generation methods can be mainly divided into audio-driven and video-driven approaches. Audio-driven methods extract speech features to predict lip movements and facial expression parameters [15,25]. However, audio signals alone often inadequately capture complex emotions, resulting in oversimplified and less vivid expressions. Furthermore, these methods lack precise control of specific facial actions, limiting fine-grained expression modulation during interactions. Video-driven methods generate continuous natural facial animations by transferring dynamic information from reference videos [5]. However, these methods offer limited controllability for interactive applications, lacking explicit adjustment of specific emotions or fine-grained facial actions (e.g., AUs).

To enhance expression control, some studies employ expression parameters (e.g., 3DMM) as intermediate representations for facial image generation [4,22]. However, these approaches lack mechanisms to synchronize expressions with speech rhythm and emotion during natural dialogue interactions. To enable fine-grained expression control in talking-head generation, researchers have introduced Facial Action Units (AUs) as control signals [16,21]. However, video-level generation still struggles with low naturalness and temporal incoherence, particularly in capturing emotional transitions during interactions.

Building on the above, this paper presents an emotional talking-head synthesis method integrated into the proposed interactive dialogue system, enabling natural agent responses with appropriate expressions and emotions.

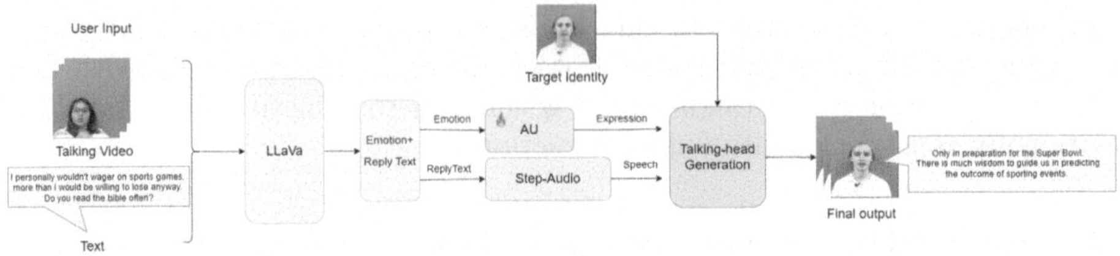

Fig. 2. Our EmoChatBot takes a user-input video and text message as input. The LLaVA model generates a textual response along with emotional attributes. These attributes guide emotional speech synthesis, which is processed by the AU prediction module to produce AU labels. Finally, the talking-head generation module uses these labels to synthesize a response video of the target identity.

3 EmoChatBot

3.1 System Overview

As shown in Fig. 2, our system comprises three main modules: emotion analysis and response generation (Sect. 3.2), emotional speech synthesis (Sect. 3.3), and fine-grained emotion-aware talking-head generation (Sect. 3.4). In the interactive workflow, the user first inputs a text message. The system identifies the emotional category and intensity, then generates an appropriate response. This response is converted into emotionally expressive speech by the emotional speech synthesis module. Audio features are then extracted for AU prediction, which guides the talking-head generation module to produce a facial video response with natural expressions and synchronized lip movements.

Our EmoChatBot system has the following key features:

- **Emotional Consistency Control:** Emotional style consistency is maintained throughout the entire process from text to speech to expression, enhancing the naturalness and appeal of dialogue.
- **Controllable Expression Adjustment:** The introduction of an AU-driven mechanism allows for greater flexibility facial expression generation.
- **Multimodal Coordinated Generation:** It integrates information from language, audio, and image modalities to achieve coordinated unity of speech, expression, and visual dynamics.

3.2 Emotion Analysis and Response Generation

We employ LLaVA [11] to perform four key tasks: 1) emotion recognition, which identifies the user's emotion expressed in text (e.g., happy, sad, anxious, angry); 2) context recognition, which infers the communication context (e.g., formal, casual, tense); 3) response generation, which produces a natural language reply consistent with the detected emotion and context; and 4) emotion target annotation, which assigns a target emotion (e.g., happy, sad) to guide downstream generation. LLaVA is a vision-language model built upon the Transformer's attention mechanism, enabling effective integration of cross-modal information. The attention mechanism is defined as:

$$\text{Attention}(Q, K, V) = \text{softmax}\left(\frac{QK^\top}{\sqrt{d_k}}\right)V,$$

where Q, K, and V represent the query, key, and value matrices, respectively, and d_k is the dimension of the key vectors.

3.3 Emotional Speech Synthesis

To achieve emotionally consistent speech output, we adopt the Step-Audio [7] model. This model takes the response text and target emotion label from the previous stage to generate speech with the specified emotional style. By explicitly modeling emotional features, it enables highly natural speech synthesis while preserving emotional alignment with the text. Step-Audio [7] enhances speech quality by extracting fine-grained audio features. A key step involves computing the Mel-frequency spectrogram (Mel), formulated as:

$$S_{\text{mel}}(m) = \sum_{k=0}^{N-1} |X(k)|^2 \cdot H_m(k)$$

Here, $S_{\text{mel}}(m)$ denotes the energy of the m-th Mel filter, $X(k)$ is the Discrete Fourier Transform (DFT) of the input audio frame, and $H_m(k)$ represents the frequency response of the m-th Mel filter. This computation captures perceptually relevant spectral features essential for emotional speech generation.

3.4 Fine-Grained Emotion-Aware Talking-Head Generation

Audio-Based AU Prediction. We propose a Transformer-based model for frame-level, audio-driven AU prediction to enable precise control of facial expressions (see Fig. 3).

Initially, temporal audio features, i.e., Zero-Crossing Rate (ZCR) and Root Mean Square Energy (RMS), are extracted from the input speech, along with mel-spectrograms and Mel-Frequency Cepstral Coefficients (MFCCs).

Next, emotion labels are extracted from the text corresponding to the speech. These categorical labels are one-hot encoded and concatenated with each frame's input. The combined features are then projected into a high-dimensional space via a linear transformation layer and passed to a Transformer encoder for temporal modeling.

To further integrate the original audio features with the encoded representations, we design a residual fusion mechanism. Specifically, the raw audio features are concatenated with the linearly transformed ZCR and RMS features and passed through an auxiliary linear layer. A residual weighted sum is then applied with the main encoder input, enhancing the model's ability to capture dynamic energy variations. The Transformer output is processed by a two-layer feed-forward network with ReLU to generate 12-dimensional AU vectors, which drive the AU fusion module for expressive and consistent facial sequences.

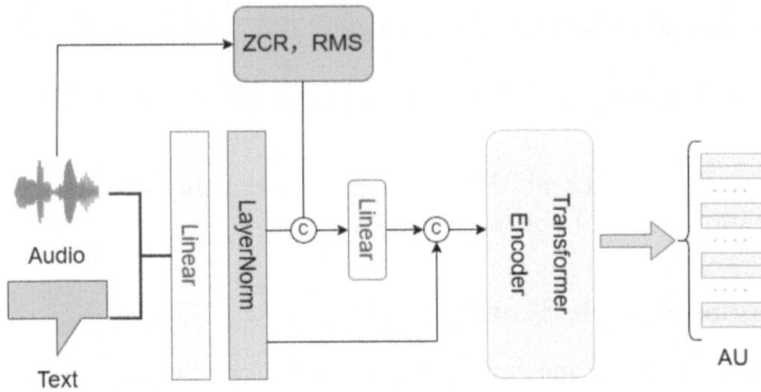

Fig. 3. The AU prediction module takes audio and text as input, extracting ZCR and RMS features to capture temporal dependencies in the audio. The output is a sequence of AU labels that represent the emotional dynamics of the input speech.

We design a multi-loss joint optimization strategy, including Smooth L1 loss and MSE loss, defined as follows:

$$L_{\text{SmoothL1}} = \begin{cases} 0.5(\hat{y} - y)^2 & \text{if } |\hat{y} - y| < 1 \\ |\hat{y} - y| - 0.5 & \text{otherwise} \end{cases} \tag{1}$$

$$\mathcal{L}_{\text{MSE}} = \frac{1}{N} \sum_{i=1}^{N} (\hat{y}_i - y_i)^2 \tag{2}$$

where $\hat{y}$ is the predicted AU value and y is the ground truth label.

The total loss function is as follows:

$$\mathcal{L}_{\text{total}} = \mathcal{L}_{\text{SmoothL1}} + \beta \cdot \mathcal{L}_{\text{MSE}} \tag{3}$$

where β is a balancing coefficient, set to 0.5 in our experiments.

AU-Based Expression Parameter Generation. We develop a GRU-based sequence-to-sequence regression model to generate 63-dimensional expression parameters from 12-dimensional AU sequences. The AUs are Z-score normalized and enhanced with first-order differences, forming a 24-dimensional input per frame. To improve dynamic modeling, we use 12 standard AUs (AU1, AU2, AU4, AU5, AU6, AU9, AU12, AU17, AU20, AU25, AU26, AU43) and apply a temporal mask to retain valid frames during training (see Fig. 4).

The total loss function $\mathcal{L}_{\text{total}}$ consists of two components:

$$\mathcal{L}_{\text{total}} = \mathcal{L}_{\text{fit}} + \lambda_{\text{smooth}} \cdot \mathcal{L}_{\text{smooth}} \tag{4}$$

where $\mathcal{L}_{\text{fit}}$ is the Smooth L1 loss that measures the difference between the predicted and ground-truth expression parameters. $\mathcal{L}_{\text{smooth}}$ enforces temporal

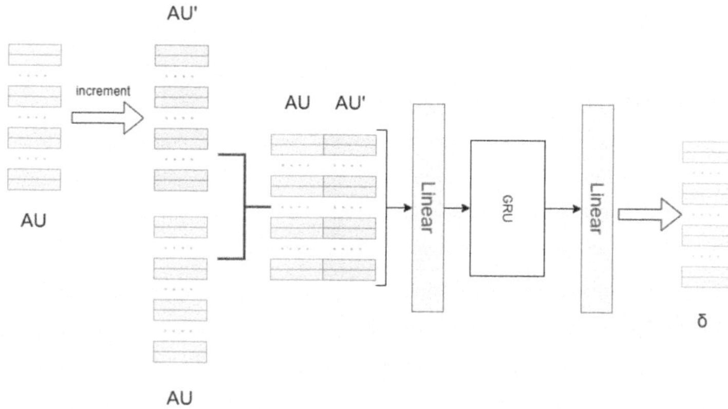

Fig. 4. Our AU-to-Expression module refines the predicted AUs and generates facial expression parameters to synthesize fine-grained, emotionally-aware facial animations.

smoothness by penalizing inconsistencies in the first-order differences of predicted and true expression sequences, and is defined as:

$$\mathcal{L}_{\text{smooth}} = \frac{1}{T-1} \sum_{t=1}^{T-1} \left\| (\hat{\Delta} e_{t+1} - \hat{\Delta} e_t) - (\Delta e_{t+1} - \Delta e_t) \right\|_2^2 \tag{5}$$

Talking-Head Generation. This module builds upon the Ditto framework [10] and incorporates a controllable AU expression fusion module to enhance facial expression adjustability. The process consists of four stages:

- Reference Image Encoding: extracts a static identity code from the user-uploaded image to preserve the digital human's consistent appearance.
- Audio-driven Feature Extraction: extracts low-level audio features closely correlated with expression changes from emotional speech.
- AU Control Fusion: predicts an AU control vector for each frame based on input AU labels, which is then fed into the expression fusion module.
- Video Generation: synthesizes the final emotionally expressive video by inputting the fused dynamic facial encoding vector into the video generator.

4 Experiments of Emotional Talking-Head Generation

4.1 Implementations Details

AU Prediction Module Training. To train the speech-based AU prediction model, we used the MultiDialog dataset, which contains diverse emotional expressions [14]. We processed it to provide frame-by-frame annotated AU labels and corresponding audio emotion labels. The model was trained using the Adam

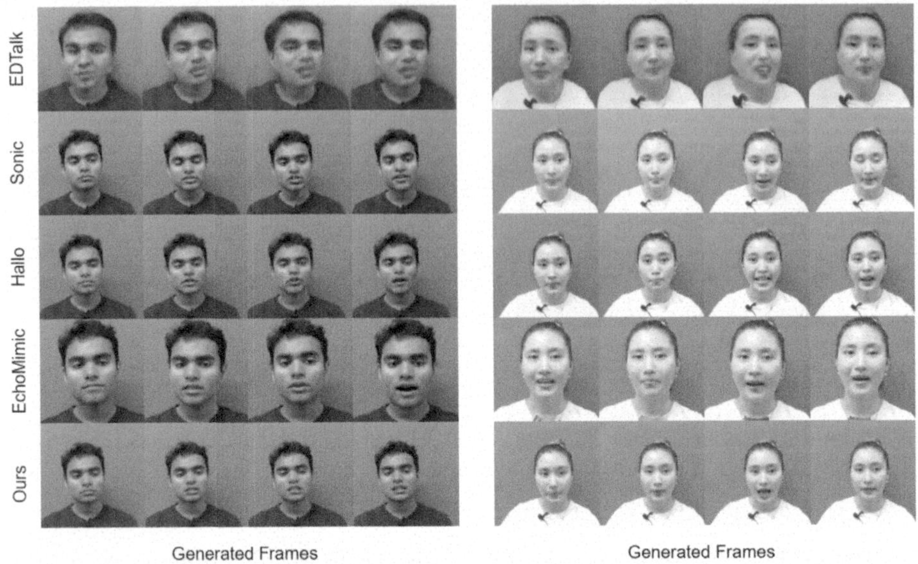

Fig. 5. Comparison of generated frames from our EmoChatBot and baseline methods.

optimizer with an initial learning rate of $1e^{-4}$ and weight decay of $1e^{-5}$. We trained for a total of 150 epochs on the first three training sets of MultiDialog [14].

AU Control Fusion Module Training. We used a subset of the MultiDialog dataset [14] to build a dataset mapping AU labels to expression parameters. AdamW optimizer with a weight decay of 1×10^{-3} and an initial learning rate of 5×10^{-5} is adopted. The batch size was set to 16, and training was conducted for up to 200 epochs with early stopping to prevent overfitting. Input sequences were padded to their true lengths, and a mask was applied to restrict loss calculations to valid frames only.

4.2 Evaluation Metrics and Baseline Methods

Benchmarks. We adopt a set of well-established metrics, including Peak Signal-to-Noise Ratio (PSNR) and Structural Similarity Index Measure (SSIM). These metrics assess the visual fidelity and structural consistency of our results. Evaluations are conducted on the training set of the **MultiDialog** [14] dataset, and compared against strong baseline methods: **Sonic** [9], **EchoMimic** [1], **EDTalk** [2], and **Hallo** [24].

4.3 Qualitative Results

Figure 5 shows a qualitative comparison of facial expressions generated by our proposed model and baseline methods. Baseline models display noticeable artifacts and inconsistencies in facial movements and emotional intensity. In contrast, our model captures subtle emotional nuances, producing more accurate, vivid, and realistic facial animations.

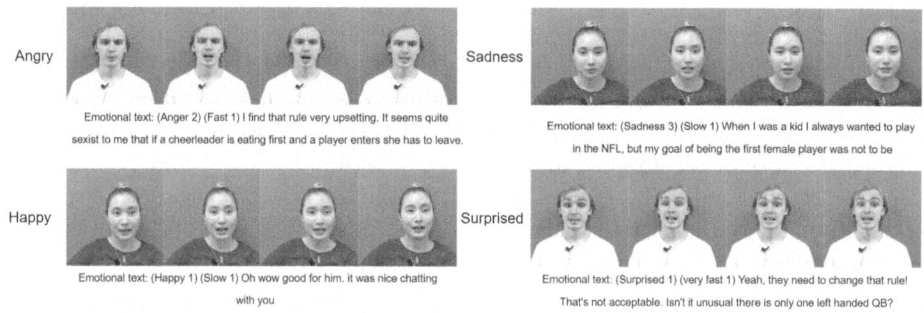

Fig. 6. Qualitative results with different emotional facial expressions.

Figure 6 illustrates the model's ability to generate facial expressions corresponding to various emotions: angry, happy, sad, and surprised. For each emotion, the model synthesizes expressions for both male and female subjects based on text inputs annotated with specific emotional tones and speech rates. The results demonstrate that our model effectively produces realistic and emotionally consistent facial dynamics aligned with the multimodal inputs.

4.4 Quantitative Results

Table 1. Quantitative comparison between our EmoChatBot and the baseline methods.

Method	Sonic	Hallo	EDtalk	EchoMimic	Ours
SSIM ↑	0.8533	0.8598	0.7621	0.6820	**0.8605**
PSNR ↑	22.3618	23.2775	14.8135	12.4050	**23.5865**

Table 1 presents a quantitative comparison between our method and existing audio-driven lip-sync approaches. Our method achieves the best performance across both metrics, demonstrating its superiority in structural preservation and image restoration accuracy.

5 Conclusion

In this paper, we present EmoChatBot, a novel talking-head dialogue system that effectively integrates multimodal emotional cues from users to generate natural and emotionally responsive talking-head interactions. The proposed AU-based facial expression control mechanism enables fine-grained emotional alignment between speech and facial expressions, resulting in realistic and coherent interactions. Experimental results demonstrate the system's effectiveness in enhancing the naturalness and emotional expressiveness of face-to-face dialogue. Our proposed system highlights the potential of digital human generation technologies in advancing human-computer interaction.

While EmoChatBot demonstrates promising emotional expressiveness, its capabilities remain limited and warrant further improvement. We plan to enhance the model to support more precise emotional control and to generate richer, more nuanced facial expressions. Additionally, we will conduct extensive user studies to evaluate perceived naturalness, emotional appropriateness, and user engagement.

Acknowledgements. This work was supported by the Beijing Natural Science Foundation (4262069), the Fundamental Research Funds for the Central Universities (CUC26TD07), and the National Radio and Television Administration Medium- and Long-Term Science and Technology Plan for Broadcasting and Online Audiovisual Services (2024AA0200).

Disclosure of Interests. The authors have no competing interests to declare.

References

1. Chen, Z., Cao, J., Chen, Z., Li, Y., Ma, C.: EchoMimic: lifelike audio-driven portrait animations through editable landmark conditions. arXiv preprint arXiv:2407.08136 (2024). https://doi.org/10.48550/arXiv.2407.08136
2. Cheng, R., Wang, J.: EDTalk: a controllable emotional talking head generation model. arXiv preprint arXiv:2405.18844 (2024). https://doi.org/10.48550/arXiv.2405.18844
3. Devlin, J., Chang, M.W., Lee, K., Toutanova, K.: BERT: pre-training of deep bidirectional transformers for language understanding. arXiv preprint arXiv:1810.04805 (2018). https://doi.org/10.48550/arXiv.1810.04805
4. Feng, Y., Feng, H., Black, M.J., Bolkart, T.: Learning an animatable detailed 3D face model from in-the-wild images. In: Proceedings of the IEEE/CVF International Conference on Computer Vision, pp. 6715–6725 (2021). https://doi.org/10.1109/ICCV48922.2021.00666
5. Guo, J., et al.: LivePortrait: efficient portrait animation with stitching and retargeting control. arXiv preprint arXiv:2407.03168 (2024). https://doi.org/10.48550/arXiv.2407.03168
6. Hu, D., Wei, L., Yang, L.: DialogueCRN: contextual and relational network for multi-turn emotion recognition. In: Proceedings of the AAAI Conference on Artificial Intelligence, vol. 35, pp. 12735–12743 (2021). https://doi.org/10.1609/aaai.v35i14.17508
7. Huang, A., et al.: Step-audio: unified understanding and generation in intelligent speech interaction. arXiv preprint arXiv:2502.11946 (2025). https://doi.org/10.48550/arXiv.2502.11946

8. Ishii, E., Winata, G.I., Cahyawijaya, S., Lala, D., Kawahara, T., Fung, P.: ERICA: an empathetic android companion for COVID-19 quarantine. In: Proceedings of the 22nd Annual Meeting of the Special Interest Group on Discourse and Dialogue, pp. 1–10 (2021)
9. Ji, X., et al.: Sonic: shifting focus to global audio perception in portrait animation. arXiv preprint arXiv:2411.16331 (2024). https://doi.org/10.48550/arXiv.2411.16331
10. Li, T., Zheng, R., Yang, M., Chen, J., Yang, M.: Ditto: motion-space diffusion for controllable realtime talking head synthesis. arXiv preprint arXiv:2411.19509 (2024). https://doi.org/10.48550/arXiv.2411.19509
11. Liu, H., Li, C., Wu, Q., Lee, Y.J.: Visual instruction tuning. Adv. Neural. Inf. Process. Syst. **36**, (2023)
12. Liu, S.: Audio-driven talking face generation: a review. J. Audio Eng. Soc. **71**(7/8), 408–419 (2023). https://doi.org/10.17743/jaes.2023.0031
13. Liu, Y., et al.: RoBERTa: a robustly optimized bert pretraining approach. arXiv preprint arXiv:1907.11692 (2019). https://doi.org/10.48550/arXiv.1907.11692
14. Park, S.J., et al.: Let's go real talk: spoken dialogue model for face-to-face conversation. arXiv preprint arXiv:2406.07867 (2024). https://doi.org/10.48550/arXiv.2406.07867, accepted to ACL 2024 (Oral)
15. Prajwal, K.R., Mukhopadhyay, R., Namboodiri, V.P., Jawahar, C.V.: A lip sync expert is all you need for speech to lip generation in the wild. In: Proceedings of the 28th ACM International Conference on Multimedia, pp. 484–492 (2020). https://doi.org/10.1145/3394171.3413531
16. Pumarola, A., Agudo, A., Sanfeliu, A., Moreno-Noguer, F.: GANimation: anatomically-aware facial animation from a single image. In: Proceedings of the European Conference on Computer Vision (ECCV), pp. 818–833 (2018). https://doi.org/10.1007/978-3-030-01249-6_50
17. Qian, X., et al.: ChatDirector: enhancing video conferencing with space-aware scene rendering and speech-driven layout transition. In: Proceedings of the 2024 CHI Conference on Human Factors in Computing Systems. ACM (2024). https://doi.org/10.1145/3613904.3642110
18. Rashkin, H., Smith, E.M., Li, M., Boureau, Y.L.: Towards empathetic open-domain conversation models: a new benchmark and dataset. arXiv preprint arXiv:1811.00207 (2018). https://doi.org/10.48550/arXiv.1811.00207
19. Roller, S., et al.: Recipes for building an open-domain chatbot. arXiv preprint arXiv:2004.13637 (2020). https://doi.org/10.48550/arXiv.2004.13637
20. Thoppilan, R., et al.: LaMDA: language models for dialog applications. arXiv preprint arXiv:2201.08239 (2022). https://doi.org/10.48550/arXiv.2201.08239
21. Tripathy, S., Kannala, J., Rahtu, E.: ICface: interpretable and controllable face reenactment using GANs. arXiv preprint arXiv:1904.01909 (2019). https://doi.org/10.48550/arXiv.1904.01909, accepted in WACV 2020
22. Wang, T.C., Mallya, A., Liu, M.Y.: One-shot free-view neural talking-head synthesis for video conferencing. In: Proceedings of the IEEE/CVF Conference on Computer Vision and Pattern Recognition (CVPR), pp. 10039–10049 (2021). https://doi.org/10.1109/CVPR46437.2021.00990
23. Wu, C., Yin, S., Qi, W., Wang, X., Tang, Z., Duan, N.: Visual ChatGPT: talking, drawing and editing with visual foundation models. arXiv preprint arXiv:2303.04671 (2023). https://doi.org/10.48550/arXiv.2303.04671
24. Xu, M., et al.: Hallo: hierarchical audio-driven visual synthesis for portrait image animation. arXiv preprint arXiv:2406.08801 (2024). https://doi.org/10.48550/arXiv.2406.08801

25. Zhang, W., et al.: SadTalker: learning realistic 3d motion coefficients for stylized audio-driven single image talking face animation. In: Proceedings of the IEEE/CVF Conference on Computer Vision and Pattern Recognition (CVPR), pp. 8652–8661 (2023). https://doi.org/10.1109/CVPR52729.2023.00836
26. Zhang, Y., et al.: DialoGPT: large-scale generative pre-training for conversational response generation. In: Proceedings of the 58th Annual Meeting of the Association for Computational Linguistics: System Demonstrations, pp. 270–278 (2020). https://doi.org/10.18653/v1/2020.acl-demos.30

Exploring the Impact of Human-Machine Identity Labels on Patients' Emotional Experiences in Dialogue

Yu Qiao, Yan Gao(✉), Yiyi Zhang, and Shuyuan Zou

Department of Design, School of Architecture and Art, Central South University, Changsha 410083, China
231312119@csu.edu.cn

Abstract. The user's perception of the identity of conversational agents is a significant factor influencing emotional experiences. This study investigates the role of identity labels in human-computer dialogue on patients' emotional experiences through a 2 × 2 between-subjects experiment. The experiment manipulated two independent variables: "identity label of the conversational respondent" (human/AI) and "actual respondent in the conversation" (human/AI). Utilizing the Wizard-of-Oz method to simulate dialogue scenarios, data were collected from 96 participants. The results indicate that, at the level of expected emotional experience, participants in the AI identity label group reported higher levels of pleasure and dominance compared to those in the human identity label group. Furthermore, within actual dialogue experiences, participants in the AI identity label group exhibited greater emotional dominance. This research reveals cognitive effects associated with identity labels during conversational experiences in medical contexts and provides empirical evidence for interactive design aimed at enhancing emotional support through AI in healthcare settings. Future studies should aim to expand sample sizes and validate findings within naturalistic settings to enhance the generalizability of these conclusions.

Keywords: AI dialogue agent · Emotional experience · Patient emotional support · User experience · Human-computer interaction

1 Introduction

The patient experience is one of the critical indicators for assessing the quality of healthcare services. Currently, the medical system is undergoing a transition from a traditional biomedical model to a biopsychosocial model, necessitating increased attention to patients' multidimensional needs. However, in existing medical practices, non-clinical demands such as psychological health and well-being are often overlooked [1]. Nursing professionals often face limitations in their specialized knowledge, time constraints, and the burdens of emotional labor, which hinder their ability to provide adequate emotional support to patients.

S. Guo et al. (Eds.): HHME 2025, CCIS 2878, pp. 169–187, 2027.
https://doi.org/10.1007/978-981-92-3991-7_13

In this context, the introduction of AI conversational agents presents new possibilities for enhancing patient medical experiences. Conversational agents (CAs) are software systems that allow users to interact through natural language. They utilize deep learning and natural language processing (NLP) techniques to recognize user emotions, simulate human-like conversations, and deliver immediate, accessible, and personalized responses for emotional support [2, 3]. Users can utilize conversational applications to establish anonymous, streamlined, and continuous communication flows, thereby enhancing the accessibility of mental health services [4]. The platforms such as ChatGPT, Replika, Anima, Kajiwoto, and Character AI provide instant and private emotional support to millions of users, thereby alleviating the labor burden on healthcare professionals. These services have gained widespread popularity [5].

However, the effectiveness of CAs in providing emotional support remains a subject of debate. On one hand, AI can leverage algorithmic advantages to generate more accurate and consistent responses; on the other hand, algorithm aversion [6] suggests that users tend to prefer human support in emotional contexts. The emotional experience of dialogue is determined not only by the quality of the actual responses but also by the perceptions that the recipient holds towards the responder [7].

The original text discusses the potential sources of controversy surrounding users' perceptions of AI identities, particularly in the context of emotional support. Even if AI possesses capabilities for providing emotional assistance, users may still experience distrust due to the identity label associated with "AI." Furthermore, existing research on AI conversational agents predominantly emphasizes the technical implementation of emotional dialogues while neglecting the actual experiences of users as dialogue recipients. There is a scarcity of studies that evaluate dialogue support effectiveness from a user experience perspective.

From this user-centric viewpoint, we aim to validate the impact of AI identity recognition on emotional experiences by focusing on two key elements: "the identity label of dialogue responders" and "the source of dialogue responses." We conducted an embedded Wizard-of-Oz experiment using a 2 (actual responder identity: human vs. AI) $\times$ 2 (identity label: human vs. AI) between-subjects design to explore the following research questions (RQs):

RQ1: Do different identity labels for dialogue responders (human vs. AI) result in differences in patients' emotional experiences during conversations?

RQ2: Is there a difference in patients' emotional experiences based on two types of actual dialogue responders (human vs. AI)?

RQ3: Do different identity labels for dialogue responders (human vs. AI) affect patients' anticipated emotional experiences prior to conversations?

This study contributes in several ways. First, it isolates and quantifies the independent effects of "identity labels" and "actual response sources" on patients' emotional experiences within medical conversation contexts, revealing cognitive effects related to identity labeling during dialogues; second, it provides empirical support for interaction design principles concerning AI conversational agents; finally, it enriches existing research on these agents by further expanding our understanding of how user perception influences interactive experiences.

2 Related Work

2.1 A Study on Emotional Support for Patients Utilizing AI Conversational Agents

In recent years, the application of AI dialogue agents in the field of healthcare has become increasingly widespread. These agents can interact with patients through natural language conversations, positioning themselves as one of the most promising technologies for providing emotional support [8]. Research indicates that patients may experience varying degrees of emotional issues, such as anxiety, tension, or depression, influenced by factors including their medical condition, knowledge about treatment options, and the costs associated with treatment [9]. These emotional disturbances can negatively impact patients' attitudes and behaviors towards treatment, potentially hindering the normal progression of medical interventions. Timely emotional support can assist patients in reconstructing a positive attitude toward treatment, thereby facilitating their recovery [10] . The purpose of emotional support dialogue is to convey understanding, empathy, care, and support through conversation. This approach aims to assist individuals in comprehending and coping with emotional distress, stress, or challenges they may face [11, 12] . In the context of healthcare, AI dialogue agents play a significant role in providing psychological education and enhancing treatment adherence within a short timeframe [13]. They contribute to promoting mental health by improving overall well-being and alleviating stress [14], as well as enhancing individual emotional health [15] through various forms of emotional support. The emotional support function is also integrated with cognitive behavioral therapy [16, 17], Mindfulness-Based Stress Reduction [18] and intervention measures involving the utilization of various therapeutic approaches [17].

The realization of emotional support by dialogue agents is not solely dependent on technological performance; rather, it critically hinges on users' attitudes and perceptions. Although AI dialogue agents have demonstrated their utility in providing emotional support to patients, current research still exhibits notable limitations. Existing studies predominantly focus on the technical implementation of AI dialogue agents, such as the development of conversational systems [19, 20], the construction of emotion recognition and emotional support datasets [21], and the generation of responses for emotional support [22, 23] . There is a significant neglect regarding user experience evaluation in practical usage scenarios, particularly within medical contexts where assessments of AI dialogue agents' effectiveness in delivering emotional support and studies on user attitudes remain scarce. Furthermore, research indicates that compared to human-provided emotional support, AI's limitations are still pronounced. Users generally perceive that AI lacks depth in understanding emotions and that its responses often lack genuine empathy. Additionally, there are concerns regarding privacy protection and data security which contribute to a general mistrust towards these technologies [24]. Despite advancements made by artificial intelligence in emotion analysis techniques—capable of recognizing and simulating expressions of emotion—the core remains constrained by technological logic due to its deficiency in profound emotional understanding and establishing connections with individuals through necessary human empathy and intuition [25]. Future research must seek a balance between optimizing technological performance and addressing user experience concerns, particularly emphasizing enhancing the recipient experience when interacting with AI dialogue agents.

2.2 Comparison Between AI Dialogue Agents and Humans as Respondents in Conversations

In dialogue interactions, the identity attributes of information sources may influence the psychological outcomes experienced by users. Individuals exhibit different responses to computers and humans during conversations; when the source of interaction is a machine, people tend to automatically form stereotypes about computers, perceiving them as mechanical and lacking emotional depth. Furthermore, conversational agents (CAs) often require users to actively disclose personal information [26], which can raise privacy concerns [27] and contribute to negative impressions that affect interaction outcomes. In contrast, human responders are perceived as empathetic, with their emotional support reflecting genuine understanding and care [28].

However, some empirical studies have found that AI dialogue agents exhibit advantages in providing emotional support. For instance, the anonymity of AI agents has been shown to enhance patients' self-disclosure by 42%, particularly when discussing sensitive topics; users are more inclined to confide in non-human entities [29]. Several studies have compared the effectiveness of AI and human responders in dialogue contexts. For example, research comparing AI-assisted emotional venting with traditional venting methods indicated that AI-assisted venting effectively reduced negative impacts associated with high and moderate arousal emotions such as anger, frustration, and fear. However, participants did not report a significant increase in perceived social support or a decrease in feelings of loneliness, suggesting that they did not regard the effective assistance provided by AI as equivalent to social support [30]. Additionally, comparisons between the authenticity, professionalism, and practicality of psychological issue management by both AI and humans revealed that AI outperformed human practitioners across these three dimensions [31]. Furthermore, other studies have examined the effects of human-AI collaboration versus solely using artificial intelligence for dialogue. The findings suggest that cooperation between humans and AIs can facilitate a more empathetic conversational experience within mental health support contexts [32]. In summary, both AI dialogue agents and humans possess unique strengths in delivering emotional support. Further research is needed to explore their respective advantages across different aspects of emotional assistance and how best to integrate these strengths into practical applications for providing emotional support.

3 Methodology

3.1 Study Variables

The purpose of this study is to investigate the impact of identity recognition involving different types of AI on patients' emotional experiences during dialogues. A 2 × 2 between-subjects experimental design was employed, with "identity label of the dialogue responder" and "actual identity of the dialogue responder" as independent variables, each having two levels: human and AI. By manipulating the cross-combinations of these two independent variables, four experimental conditions were formed: (1) human actual response + human identity label; (2) human actual response + AI identity label; (3) AI actual response + human identity label; and (4) AI actual response + AI identity label. A between-subjects design was adopted to avoid retest effects, ensuring that each group of participants received only one type of experimental condition intervention.

The dependent variables include both emotional experience and dialogue experience. Emotional experience is measured through anticipated emotional experience and actual emotional experience, while dialogue experience is assessed across five dimensions: dialogue satisfaction, perceived partner responsiveness, perceived understanding, perceived trustworthiness, and perceived connection. The "identity label of the dialogue responder" and "actual source of responses in dialogues" serve as between-group variables in this experiment.

This study comprises a series of identical dialogue tasks along with corresponding questionnaires for each experimental procedure.

The purpose of this study is to investigate the impact of identity recognition involving different types of AI on patients' emotional experiences during dialogues. A 2 × 2 between-subjects experimental design was employed, with "identity label of the dialogue responder" and "actual identity of the dialogue responder" as independent variables, each having two levels: human and AI. By manipulating the cross-combinations of these two independent variables, four experimental conditions were formed: (1) human actual response + human identity label; (2) human actual response + AI identity label; (3) AI actual response + human identity label; and (4) AI actual response + AI identity label. A between-subjects design was adopted to avoid retest effects, ensuring that each group of participants received only one type of experimental condition intervention.

The dependent variables include both emotional experience and dialogue experience. Emotional experience is measured through anticipated emotional experience and actual emotional experience, while dialogue experience is assessed across five dimensions: dialogue satisfaction, perceived partner responsiveness, perceived understanding, perceived trustworthiness, and perceived connection. The "identity label of the dialogue responder" and "actual source of responses in dialogues" serve as between-group variables in this experiment. The study consists of a series of identical dialogue tasks along with corresponding questionnaires for each experimental procedure.

3.2 Experimental Design

In the manipulation of dialogue agents, an experimental design employing the Wizard of Oz method is utilized. The Wizard of Oz method is a regulated research approach that requires one experimenter to act as a host, introducing the general process of the experiment to participants, while two other researchers operate behind the scenes as "Wizards" (Fig. 1). During the experiment, users interact with an interface that appears fully autonomous but is actually controlled (either wholly or partially) by human operators. Participants are led to believe they are conversing with either an AI dialogue agent or a human expert; however, in reality, the responses during these conversations are managed by the two researchers.

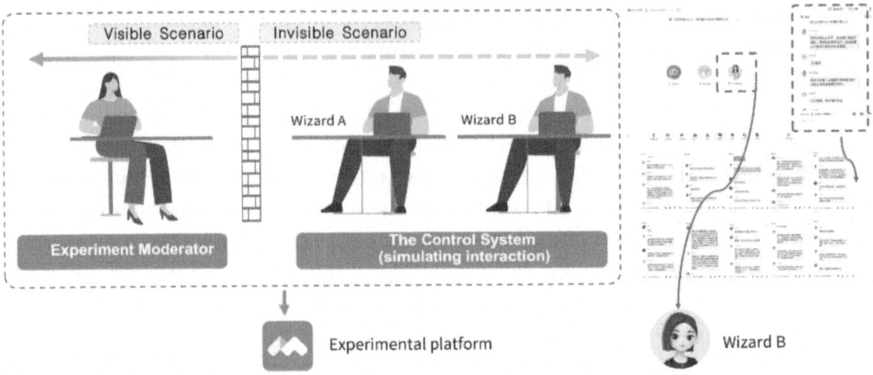

Fig. 1. The Wizard-of-Oz platform and experimental environment

3.3 Participants

Our study received approval from the Ethics Review Committee of the affiliated hospital of our institution (approval number LYG20250041). Participants were recruited through social media and offline channels. We employed a snowball sampling method, encouraging enrolled participants to recommend additional candidates. All individuals who contacted us underwent a rigorous screening process based on standardized criteria; only those confirmed to meet these criteria were formally included in the study. Prior to the official experiment, researchers conducted comprehensive background investigations on each participant. This investigation involved completing a background information questionnaire and conducting one-on-one interviews with each volunteer for the experiment. During these interviews, participants were asked to provide documentation and share their experiences to confirm their eligibility for the study.

Inclusion criteria included: (1) age $\geq$ 18 years; (2) ability to communicate fluently in spoken Chinese; (3) having had clear medical contact records within the past three months, such as outpatient visits, emergency consultations, follow-up appointments, or hospitalization, along with supporting documents like registration slips or examination reports; (4) experience using AI chat tools. During interviews, we requested that participants name specific AI emotional dialogue tools they had used and describe a particular usage scenario and process.

At the time of recruitment, we verbally explained certain aspects of our research objectives (the online chat emotional support experience study), procedures, voluntary participation rights, and confidentiality issues to all potential participants. All individuals included in this study provided written informed consent prior to participating in any experiments, agreeing that their personal information could be utilized for this research.

3.4 Sample Size

Our objective is to investigate whether there are differences in the chat experience based on the identity of the actual respondents (human vs. AI) and their corresponding identity labels (human vs. AI). Given that our study involves two independent variables, and considering the high subjectivity associated with chat behavior and emotional experiences, an within-subjects design is highly susceptible to carryover effects. Therefore, we opted for a between-subjects design requiring four independent groups. Utilizing G*Power for a priori power analysis, we referenced effect size estimates suggested in previous literature [33, 34], resulting in an effect size value of $f = 0.253$ (medium effect size). With a significance level set at $\alpha = 0.05$ and a power level of $1 - \beta = 0.8$, we calculated that a total sample size of 125 participants would be necessary (approximately 31 per group). However, during the recruitment process, challenges such as privacy concerns, participant time burdens, and dropout rates ultimately led to the inclusion of only 96 participants who were randomly assigned to four experimental conditions ($n = 24$ per group). We acknowledge that this final sample size falls short of our initial target.

Although some literature suggests that for studies aimed at providing preliminary evidence using random parallel group designs one might consider employing slightly higher α levels and lower test powers to expand sample sizes [35], we did not adopt this strategy due to considerations regarding our experimental procedures and objectives. Consequently, it is possible that the observed effect sizes in this study may overestimate the 'true' effect magnitude; however, we hope that our findings will enhance understanding of AI identity recognition in interactions with conversational agents or lay groundwork for future larger-scale research endeavors.

3.5 Emotional Dialogue Agent

We adhere to the following principles when selecting tools: (1) availability of a Chinese version; (2) capability for emotional communication through text input; and (3) provision of free products or sufficient free trial features. Additionally, to mitigate biases stemming from prior usage experiences, all candidate tools underwent preliminary screening to ensure that all selected participants had not previously used the tool.

Based on these criteria, this study ultimately selected Doubao (Ver. 10.0) as the conversational agent tool employed in the experiment. "Doubao" is a conversational AI assistant developed by ByteDance in China, boasting a substantial user base among Chinese speakers and demonstrating significant market representation. Although it possesses general functionality, we categorize it within the realm of "emotional dialogue agents" for several reasons:

Guidability of Functionality. As an open-domain system, users can transform Doubao into a tool for emotional interaction through prompts.

Applicability for Emotional Interaction and Content Generation. Doubao integrates fundamental components for emotional capabilities and has an emotional language generation framework that can identify emotional cues in user inputs and respond accordingly.

Emotional Contextualization of Research Situations and Behavioral Intentions. In the context established by this research, where interactions explicitly require emotional support, the participants' usage behaviors and psychological expectations will lead them to perceive Doubao as an emotional agent. Therefore, from both functional implementation and user experience perspectives, under these circumstances, Doubao transcends its generic attributes to effectively assume the role of an emotional dialogue agent.

3.6 Procedure

As an AI dialogue agent in the experiment, the study was conducted through one-on-one Tencent Meetings (as shown in Fig. 2). Prior to the experiment, all participants were randomly assigned to one of four experimental conditions. Before the formal commencement of the experiment, the host introduced the purpose of the study to participants, which aimed to explore how dialogue processes influence emotional expression during medical consultations. After confirming that participants understood this information, demographic data for all subjects were collected.

The experimental procedure is illustrated in Fig. 3. Once the experiment began, participants were first guided to recall and describe three emotional events from their most recent medical visit. This step was intended to help reconstruct scenarios and enhance both realism and immersion (b1 and b2). The descriptions provided by participants were transcribed into text in real-time by research assistants using voice transcription software. Subsequently, the host presented each participant with details about their upcoming dialogue task and informed them of their conversation partner's identity label ("human expert" or "dialogue agent"). To control for confounding variables, a single-blind design was employed; neither participants nor hosts would be made aware of the true identity of their actual conversation partner until after completion of the experiment. Upon learning their identity labels, participants completed a pre-dialogue experience questionnaire designed to measure expectations regarding various dimensions including satisfaction, perceived listening level, perceived understanding, as well as perceived trust and connection. Additionally, in order to regulate response times between human replies and AI responses effectively, hosts needed to provide texts describing emotional experiences from each participant ahead of time to designated Wizards (c1 and c2).

After submitting their questionnaires, participants proceeded into a communication phase with manipulated dialogue roles. Prior to this interaction stage, hosts displayed examples of dialogues along with previously described emotional texts (b1 and b2) so as to facilitate better engagement within chat contexts for participants. Once "Dr. Wang," representing a manipulated dialogue role entered the chat room, conversations commenced on-screen where responses corresponding with each participant's randomly assigned actual responder identity were executed by respective Wizards responsible for replying tasks. All researchers acting as Wizards possessed backgrounds in psychology or user research.

In the context of "human actual responses, " Wizard A strictly adheres to a pre-reviewed guideline and examples for human replies, crafting and sending responses (e1) for participants in the human actual response group. This guideline is developed based on emotional communication techniques and strategies found in nursing literature [36–38]. The following three themes are identified as core characteristics of the responses:

(1) A human-centered communication approach; (2) active listening, restraint, and waiting for responses; (3) empathetic language expression that includes emotional validation and non-directive supportive suggestions. To ensure the professionalism, appropriateness, and safety of the content, we invited two experts in medicine and nursing with extensive clinical experience to review the guidelines. Based on their feedback, multiple rounds of revisions were made until the content received expert approval. Prior to the formal experiment, Wizard A underwent training based on these guidelines and

was subsequently evaluated by both experts during a pre-experimental phase to confirm compliance with established standards.

Wizard B is responsible for presenting messages sent by participants to the AI dialogue agent (d). Following our established guidelines, Wizard B instructs the AI to generate responses while controlling their length to be comparable to the median response length from human interactions observed in pre-experiments. After generating a response, Wizard B forwards this content to participants in the AI response group (e2).

Participants are required to engage in approximately 15 min of conversation within a meeting chatroom (a1 and a2). Upon completion of the dialogue, they must fill out an experience questionnaire assessing various dimensions such as satisfaction with the conversation, perceived level of being listened to, perceived understanding, perceived trustworthiness, and perceived connection. Before formally collecting data, research personnel rehearsed the entire process multiple times to ensure operational consistency.

Fig. 2. Experimental platform

3.7 Data Collection

The study utilized a questionnaire that included indicators such as emotional experience, dialogue satisfaction, perceived partner responsiveness, perceived understanding, perceived trust, and perceived connection to collect data. With the exception of emotional experience, the measurement metrics for all other variables were adapted from existing literature to ensure content validity [7, 39–42].

The present study employs the Forward-backward method to ensure the accuracy of the scale and its cross-cultural consistency, while also making adjustments to these indicators based on the research context. Subsequently, a pilot survey was conducted with five participants to assess the clarity, comprehensibility, and time required for completing

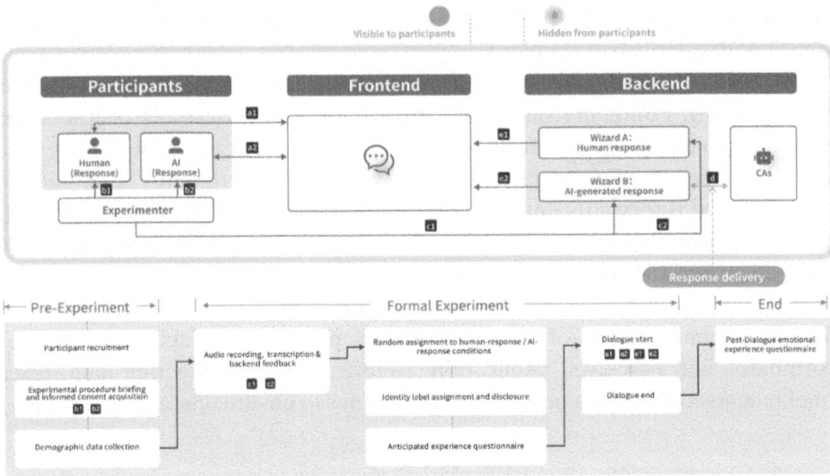

Fig. 3. Experimental procedure

the questionnaire. Based on feedback from this pilot survey and expert consultations, specific items were added or removed to ensure that the structure of the questionnaire is effective and aligned with the research context. The aforementioned indicators are measured using a seven-point Likert scale.

This study utilizes the PAD emotional scale to collect data on participants' emotional experiences. The PAD model categorizes user emotions into three dimensions: pleasure, arousal, and dominance; nearly all emotions can be classified within these three dimensions. It has been widely recognized for assessing emotional responses across various domains. In this experiment, we employed a Chinese version of the PAD emotional scale to gather data on participants' emotional experiences due to its established reliability and validity [43].

4 Results

A total of 96 valid data entries were collected from participants in the experiment. Table 1 provides an overview of the demographic characteristics of these 96 research participants.

We conducted reliability and validity analyses on the scales used for data collection. The results indicated that all scales demonstrated acceptable reliability, and the KMO values confirmed the adequacy of data extraction.

Descriptive statistics for the four independent groups are summarized in Table 2. The Shapiro-Wilk test was employed to assess the distribution of the data. Results showed that both arousal and dominance of emotional experiences, as well as arousal and dominance of anticipated emotional experiences, conformed to a normal distribution ($p > 0.05$). For other variables, corresponding p-values from normality tests were all less than 0.05. Based on the distribution characteristics of each variable, appropriate statistical inference methods will be applied.

Table 1. The demographic data of the research sample (n = 96)

Measure	Item	Frequency	Percentage
Gender	Male	36	38%
	Female	60	63%
Age	18–25	65	68%
	26–35	25	26%
	36 and above	6	6%
Treatment type	Initial consultation	5	5%
	Emergency treatment	62	65%
	Follow-up visit	8	8%
	Rehabilitation therapy	21	22%

Firstly, two-way ANOVA results indicated no significant interaction effect between identity labels and actual response sources ($p > 0.05$), suggesting that we did not find an interaction between labels and actual sources regarding emotional improvement. Therefore, our primary focus is on the main effects of each factor.

Mann-Whitney test results revealed that neither identity labels nor actual conversational identities exhibited significance concerning pleasure level, conversation satisfaction, perceived partner responsiveness, perceived understanding, perceived trustworthiness, or perceived connection ($p > 0.05$). Additionally, different identity labels did not show significant differences in anticipated conversation satisfaction, anticipated perceived partner responsiveness, anticipated perceived understanding, anticipated perceived trustworthiness or anticipated perceived connection ($p > 0.05$). However, different identity labels presented a significant difference in expected pleasure levels ($p = 0.008$; $p < 0.05$). Independent samples t-test results indicate (see Table 3) that identity labels displayed significant differences in expected dominance ($p < 0.01$) and actual dominance ($p = 0.016$; $p < 0.05$). Identity labels and actual conversational identities did not exhibit any significant differences with respect to other variables ($p > 0.05$).

Subsequently, we calculated the correlation coefficients between two groupings of identity labels, two groupings of actual conversational identities, and various variables. The results indicated that different identity labels were negatively correlated with expected pleasure ($r = -0.277$, $p < 0.05$), expected dominance ($r = -0.356$, $p < 0.05$), and actual dominance ($r = -0.247$, $p < 0.05$).

Ultimately, in conjunction with the descriptive statistics results, we found a significant effect of identity labels on participants' expectations and perceptions during chat interactions. Specifically, when users were informed that their interaction partner was an "AI, "they anticipated higher emotional dominance and pleasure compared to when interacting with a human identity prior to the interaction. Furthermore, following the actual interaction, their experience of emotional dominance may also have been heightened. This suggests that the "AI" label itself could confer a positive psychological advantage. Correlation analysis further supports this finding; compared to AI identity labels, human identity labels diminished users' expected pleasure and expected dominance in conversation as well as their perceived dominance during interactions.

Table 2. Descriptive statistical results

Actual response							Identity label						
	Human (n = 48)			AI (n = 48)			Human (n = 48)			AI (n = 48)			
Item	Range	Mean	SD	Range	Mean	SD	Range	Mean	SD	Range	Mean	SD	
AP	−2.25-3.75	1.927	1.158	−0.25-4	2.104	0.996	−2.25-4	1.719	1.168	0.25–4	2.313	0.897	
AA	−2-4	0.167	1.374	−2.75-3.5	−0.125	1.253	−1.75-4	−0.063	1.486	−2.75-3	0.104	1.131	
AD	−2.75 − 4	0.719	1.476	−4-3.5	0.755	1.378	-4-4	0.234	1.473	−1.25-4	1.24	1.18	
ADS	4.5–7	5.958	0.667	4–7	5.854	0.863	4–7	5.984	0.783	4–7	5.828	0.755	
APR	3.5–7	5.854	0.787	2.875–7	5.792	0.882	2.875–7	5.854	0.914	3.5–6.875	5.792	0.75	
APU	3–7	5.667	0.953	2.5–7	5.823	1.064	2.5–7	5.667	1.168	3.5–7	5.823	0.822	
APT	3.667–7	5.756	0.796	3.667–7	5.846	0.83	3.667–7	5.852	0.877	3.667–7	5.75	0.742	
APC	2.333–7	5.264	1.132	2.667–7	5.097	1.083	2.333–7	5.118	1.3	3–6.667	5.243	0.877	
Pleasure	−4.063-3.5	0.374	2.078	−3.25-4	0.555	1.981	−4.063-4	0.25	2.194	−2.875-4	0.678	1.831	
Arousal	−1.75-1.875	0.209	1.008	−2.5-2.219	0.203	1.204	−2.5-2	0.23	1.148	−2.25 − 2.219	0.182	1.071	
Dominance	-2-4	0.43	1.155	−1.5-4	0.309	0.931	−2-2	0.113	0.76	−1.5-4	0.626	1.223	
DS	1.25–7	5.604	1.287	2.75–7	5.974	1.019	1.25–7	5.714	1.343	2.75–7	5.865	0.974	
PR	1.375–7	5.695	1.265	2.875–7	5.641	1.064	1.375–7	5.51	1.352	3.25–6.875	5.826	0.925	
PU	1.313–7	5.612	1.319	2.5–7	5.814	1.155	1.313–7	5.51	1.488	3.5–7	5.915	0.893	
PT	1.667–7	5.639	1.241	3.333–7	5.833	0.996	1.667–7	5.618	1.323	3.667–7	5.854	0.88	
PC	1.451–7	5.472	1.274	2.667–7	5.525	1.118	1.451–7	5.342	1.44	3–6.701	5.655	0.868	
	AI (Response) × AI (Label) (n = 24)			Human (Response) × AI (Label) (n = 24)			Human (Response) ×Human (Label) (n = 24)			AI (Response) ×Human (Label) (n = 24)			
Item	Range	Average	SD	Range	Average	SD	Range	Average	SD	Range	Average	SD	
AP	0.25–4	2.385	0.878	0.25–3.5	2.24	0.928	−2.25-3.75	1.615	1.294	−0.250-4.000	1.823	1.044	
AA	−2.75-2.5	−0.01	1.09	−2-3	0.219	1.183	−1.75-4	0.115	1.567	−1.750-3.500	−0.24	1.411	
AD	−0.25-3.5	1.354	1.021	−1.25-4	1.125	1.333	−2.75-4	0.313	1.526	−4.000-2.250	0.156	1.446	
ADS	4–7	5.813	0.851	4.5–7	5.844	0.663	4.75–7	6.073	0.665	4.000–7.000	5.896	0.891	
APR	4.75–6.875	5.797	0.704	3.5–6.875	5.786	0.808	4–7	5.922	0.777	2.875–7.000	5.786	1.045	
APU	4.5–7	5.896	0.807	3.5–7	5.75	0.847	3–7	5.583	1.06	2.500–7.000	5.75	1.285	
APT	4.667–7	5.88	0.688	3.667–6.667	5.62	0.786	4–7	5.892	0.799	3.667–7.000	5.812	0.965	
APC	3–6.667	5.306	0.873	3–6.667	5.181	0.895	2.333–7	5.347	1.342	2.667–7.000	4.889	1.242	
Pleasure	−2.875-4	0.747	1.857	−2.563-3.5	0.609	1.842	−4.063-3.5	0.138	2.305	−3.250-4.000	0.362	2.12	
Arousal	−2.25-2.219	0.232	1.15	−1.5-1.5	0.132	1.009	−1.75-1.875	0.286	1.024	−2.500-2.000	0.174	1.281	
Dominance	−1.5-4	0.366	1.117	−1.5-4	0.887	1.291	−2-1.75	−0.026	0.79	−1.500-2.000	0.253	0.719	
DS	4–7	6.146	0.844	2.75–6.75	5.583	1.031	1.25–7	5.625	1.523	2.750–7.000	5.802	1.161	
PR	3.25–6.875	5.792	0.938	3.5–6.875	5.859	0.93	1.375–7	5.531	1.532	2.875–7.000	5.49	1.178	
PU	3.625–7	5.99	0.835	3.5–7	5.841	0.96	1.313–7	5.383	1.589	2.500–7.000	5.638	1.402	
PT	3.667–7	5.958	0.897	3.667–6.667	5.75	0.87	1.667–7	5.528	1.538	3.333–7.000	5.708	1.092	
PC	3.625–6.701	5.756	0.818	3–6.667	5.554	0.921	1.451–7	5.39	1.567	2.667–7.000	5.294	1.332	

Notes: PPR, Perceived partner responsiveness; AP, Anticipated pleasure; AA, Anticipated arousal; AD, Anticipated dominance; ADS, Anticipated dialogue satisfaction; APR, Anticipated perceived partner responsivenes; APU, Anticipated perceived understanding; APT, Anticipated perceived trust; APC, Anticipated perceived connection; DS, Dialogue satisfaction; PR, perceived partner responsiveness; PU, Perceived understanding;

PT, perceived trust; PC, perceived connection.

Table 3. T-test analysis results

	t	p
Arousal	−0.213	0.832
Dominance	2.469	0.016*
Anticipated arousal	0.618	0.538
Anticipated dominance	3.690	0.000**

Notes: *$p < 0.05$; **$p < 0.01$.

5 Discussion

5.1 Identity Labels and Anticipated Emotional Experiences

The concept of pleasure reflects the positive and negative characteristics of an individual's emotional state, while dominance indicates the degree to which a person can control their emotional condition. Our findings reveal that prior to interaction, participants held higher expectations for both pleasure and emotional dominance in AI chat interactions. Although this finding diverges from some previous research consensus—where individuals typically have lower expectations for dialogues with artificial intelligence compared to those with humans [44, 45], we hypothesize that this result may stem from two primary reasons based on the dialogue context, participant perceptions, and the nature of AI tools. First, this phenomenon may be attributed to the context of the dialogue. In medical emotional support scenarios, the conversational role of Dr. Wang that we manipulated is portrayed as a psychological counseling expert with many years of clinical experience (whether human or AI). Patients typically regard doctors and similar experts as authorities [46]. When participants are informed that the respondent in the conversation is a human expert, they may automatically categorize them as possessing specialized knowledge based on their social cognitive experiences. This categorization activates cognitive schemas related to interactions with medical authority, such as expectations of a serious atmosphere, professional distance, and fear of negative judgment. Consequently, this can lead to a reduction in anticipated pleasure and sense of control.

In contrast, the non-human identity of AI has the potential to weaken participants' psychological defenses; it may be perceived as a more neutral interaction partner, resulting in relaxed expectations regarding emotional feedback. This finding aligns with existing research indicating that users tend to confide in non-human entities when discussing highly sensitive topics [30]. It is noteworthy that all our participants have prior experience with AI chat tools. The positive mental models regarding AI that participants may have formed during previous interactions could be transferred to the medical dialogue context. Previous research on anthropomorphism and self-disclosure also indirectly supports this hypothesis, suggesting that the relationship between anthropomorphism and self-disclosure is moderated by users' affection for AI chatbots and their cognitive perceptions [47]. When users have a positive impression of chatbots, their expectations for the interaction become more favorable. Therefore, we hypothesize that participants' experiences with AI effectively reinforce their optimistic anticipations regarding conversations.

Secondly, this phenomenon may be influenced by the immediate, accessible, and personalized characteristics of AI agents themselves. From the perspective of social interaction theory, dialogue serves as an example of social engagement; conversational agents can act as social proxies that are often more appealing, simpler, and more predictable than human interactions. Consequently, individuals may experience reduced pressure in social interactions through their engagements with AI [48]. Polished Version: "Particularly for participants with emotional needs, this approach mitigates the potential feelings of shame that may arise from interacting with real humans [3]. In genuine interpersonal emotional support, users often need to balance their emotional expressions with the perceived emotions of others. This dual concern can significantly diminish the anticipated pleasure of interaction; conversely, the simpler supportive attributes of an AI agent relieve users from bearing the social costs associated with emotional empathy, potentially enhancing both their enjoyment and expectations regarding the interaction experience. Furthermore, based on prior experiences reported by researchers, participants may perceive AI as human-like partners, a notion supported by the CASA paradigm [49, 50], leading users to subconsciously engage with AI agents in a manner akin to human interactions. Consequently, participants' emotional expectations for these interactions unconsciously align more closely with positive levels typical of interpersonal engagement. Thus, as indicated by our results, we hypothesize that the effect of an AI identity label on expected emotional experiences is positively influenced by both conversational contexts and the interactive advantages offered by AI agents. It is important to note that participants' previous experiences using AI may serve as antecedent factors contributing to elevated baseline expectations regarding their emotional responses.

5.2 Identity Labels and Emotional Experiences in Dialogue

The results of this study indicate that, following actual interactions, participants in the AI identity label group exhibited a higher sense of emotional dominance compared to those in the human identity label group. This phenomenon may be attributed to the fact that when faced with interlocutors labeled as human experts, participants often perceive a lower sense of control due to disparities in professional knowledge or social role differences [51], which inhibits the formation of a sense of agency during conversations. In contrast, interactions with AI tend to impose less conversational pressure on participants because AI lacks human emotions, biases, and social status. This allows individuals to express their genuine thoughts and needs more freely, thereby enhancing their perceived dominance within the dialogue. These findings align with previous research conclusions; for instance, introverted users are able to articulate their experiences and needs more deeply when interacting with an AI interviewer [52].

In summary, we find that identity labels themselves can influence patients' anticipated emotional experiences (such as pleasure and dominance) as well as their actual sense of control during dialogues. We further hypothesize that AI identity labels may help reduce conversational pressure and fears associated with negative criticism—thus lowering barriers for emotional communication—and encourage patients to actively engage and disclose more information. This also highlights the potential of AI dialogue agents in providing accessible and stigma-free emotional support.

Additionally, anthropomorphism plays a significant role in interactions with AI chatbots [53]. Given that professional identities such as "doctor" or "expert" may increase conversational pressure, caution should be exercised in employing these potentially stress-inducing labels within the design of medical dialogue AIs. Future explorations could consider developing more approachable anthropomorphic character designs. This insight is also relevant for primary providers of emotional support such as caregivers; they may need to proactively establish rapport to mitigate psychological distance stemming from professional images.

6 Conclusion

The present study employs a 2 × 2 between-subjects experimental design to compare the impact of human and AI identity labels on patients' emotional experiences during dialogue. The research yields several key conclusions:

In terms of anticipated emotional experience, AI identity labels may elicit higher levels of emotional dominance and pleasure compared to human identity labels.

During actual conversational interactions, participants under the AI identity label exhibit potentially greater emotional dominance.

This research validates the role of AI's identity perception in shaping both expected and actual emotional experiences from the perspective of user perception. It extends existing studies on AI conversational agents by providing empirical evidence for the interaction design of medical dialogue AIs, thereby contributing to optimizing the efficiency of emotional support interactions in healthcare settings and enhancing user acceptance. These findings also offer design implications; for instance, caution should be exercised when using labels such as "doctor" or "expert, "which may induce pressure in patient dialogues, while visual designs within conversation interfaces should aim to mitigate mechanical perceptions.

7 Limitations and Future Works

This study has several limitations that need to be addressed and expanded upon in future work. First, we selected a single model for experimentation without conducting a comparative analysis with other models. As a result, the findings may lack representativeness; thus, it is essential to incorporate additional AI models for horizontal comparison in order to explore the differential impacts among various models. Second, although we guided participants to recall emotional events within medical contexts during the experiment, there exists a gap between the interactions in the experimental environment and those in real medical scenarios. Consequently, participant responses may not fully reflect their emotional experiences under natural conditions. The dialogue process was conducted under an "observed" state, which could introduce confounding variables. Future research should focus on further validation through replication studies and conduct naturalistic field experiments. Additionally, as noted in Sect. 3.4, more experiments with higher statistical power are needed to establish better estimates of true effects.

Disclosure of Interests. The authors have no competing interests to declare that are relevant to the content of this article.

References

1. Adikari, A., et al.: Empathic conversational agents for real-time monitoring and co-facilitation of patient-centered healthcare. Futur. Gener. Comput. Syst. **126**, 318–329 (2022). https://doi.org/10.1016/j.future.2021.08.015
2. Parimala, M.: Soul support : AI driven emotional assistance ChatBot. Int. J. Sci. Res. Eng. Manag. **9**, 1–9 (2025). https://doi.org/10.55041/IJSREM50039
3. Vijayalakshmi, S., Disney Sandhya, A., Nimala Deve, P.: AI-powered holistic mental health monitoring: integrating facial emotion recognition, chatbot, and voicebot for personalized support. In: 2025 International Conference on Data Science, Agents &Amp; Artificial Intelligence (ICDSAAI), pp. 1–6. IEEE, Chennai, India (2025). https://doi.org/10.1109/ICDSAAI65575.2025.11011757
4. Inkster, B., Sarda, S., Subramanian, V.: An empathy-driven, conversational artificial intelligence agent (wysa) for digital mental Well-being: real-world data evaluation mixed-methods study. JMIR Mhealth Uhealth. **6**, e12106 (2018). https://doi.org/10.2196/12106
5. Ma, Z., Mei, Y., Long, Y., Su, Z., Gajos, K.Z.: Evaluating the experience of LGBTQ+ people using large language model based chatbots for mental health support. In: Proceedings of the CHI Conference on Human Factors in Computing Systems, pp. 1–15. ACM, Honolulu HI USA (2024). https://doi.org/10.1145/3613904.3642482
6. Burton, J.W., Stein, M., Jensen, T.B.: A systematic review of algorithm aversion in augmented decision making. J. Behav. Decis. Mak. **33**, 220–239 (2020). https://doi.org/10.1002/bdm.2155
7. Yin, Y., Jia, N., Wakslak, C.J.: AI can help people feel heard, but an AI label diminishes this impact. Proc. Natl. Acad. Sci. **121**, e2319112121 (2024). https://doi.org/10.1073/pnas.2319112121
8. Wang, Q. et al.: Enhancing the conversational agent with an emotional support system for mental health digital therapeutics. Front. Psych. **14**, 1148534 (2023). https://doi.org/10.3389/fpsyt.2023.1148534
9. Bartova, L.: Typical clinical manifestations of anxiety and depression in patients with medical illness and general notions about their treatment. Eur. Psychiatry. **68**, S50–S50 (2025). https://doi.org/10.1192/j.eurpsy.2025.174
10. Wang, S., Huang, H., Wang, L., Wang, X.: A psychological nursing intervention for patients with thyroid cancer on psychological distress and quality of life: a randomized clinical trial. J. Nerv. Ment. Dis. **208**, 533–539 (2020). https://doi.org/10.1097/NMD.0000000000001157
11. Liu, S. et al.https://arxiv.org/abs/2106.01144, (2021). https://doi.org/10.48550/ARXIV.2106.01144.
12. Bai, X., Chen, G., He, T., Zhou, C., Guo, C.: A holistic comparative study of large language models as emotional support dialogue systems. Cogn. Comput. **17**, 71 (2025). https://doi.org/10.1007/s12559-025-10429-x
13. Vaidyam, A.N., Wisniewski, H., Halamka, J.D., Kashavan, M.S., Torous, J.B.: Chatbots and conversational agents in mental health: a review of the psychiatric landscape. Can. J. Psychiatr. **64**, 456–464 (2019). https://doi.org/10.1177/0706743719828977
14. Ly, K.H., Ly, A.-M., Andersson, G.: A fully automated conversational agent for promoting mental Well-being: a pilot RCT using mixed methods. Internet Interv. **10**, 39–46 (2017). https://doi.org/10.1016/j.invent.2017.10.002
15. Hu, M., Chua, X.C.W., Diong, S.F., Kasturiratna, K.T.A.S., Majeed, N.M., Hartanto, A.: AI as your ally: the effects of AI-assisted venting on negative affect and perceived social support. Appl. Psychol.: Health Well-being. **17**, e12621 (2025). https://doi.org/10.1111/aphw.12621
16. Fitzpatrick, K.K., Darcy, A., Vierhile, M.: Delivering cognitive behavior therapy to young adults with symptoms of depression and anxiety using a fully automated conversational agent

(woebot): a randomized controlled trial. JMIR Ment. Health. **4**, e19 (2017). https://doi.org/10.2196/mental.7785
17. Suganuma, S., Sakamoto, D., Shimoyama, H.: An embodied conversational agent for unguided internet-based cognitive behavior therapy in preventative mental health: feasibility and acceptability pilot trial. JMIR Ment. Health. **5**, e10454 (2018). https://doi.org/10.2196/10454
18. Gardiner, P.M., et al.: Engaging women with an embodied conversational agent to deliver mindfulness and lifestyle recommendations: a feasibility randomized control trial. Patient Educ. Couns. **100**, 1720–1729 (2017). https://doi.org/10.1016/j.pec.2017.04.015
19. Kampman, O.P., et al.: A multi-agent dual dialogue system to support mental health care providers, https://arxiv.org/abs/2411.18429, (2024). https://doi.org/10.48550/ARXIV.2411.18429.
20. Empathy in AI: developing a sentiment-sensitive chatbot through advanced natural language processing. Int. J. Adv. Trends Comput. Sci. Eng. **13**, 140–147 (2024). https://doi.org/10.30534/ijatcse/2024/071332024
21. Chu, Y., Liao, L., Zhou, Z., Ngo, C.-W., Hong, R.: Towards multimodal emotional support conversation systems, https://arxiv.org/abs/2408.03650, (2024). https://doi.org/10.48550/ARXIV.2408.03650.
22. Zhang, T., Zhang, X., Zhao, J., Zhou, L., Jin, Q.: ESCoT: towards interpretable emotional support dialogue systems. In: Proceedings of the 62nd Annual Meeting of the Association for Computational Linguistics (Volume 1: Long Papers), pp. 13395–13412. Association for Computational Linguistics, Bangkok, Thailand (2024). https://doi.org/10.18653/v1/2024.acl-long.723
23. Chu, Y., Liao, L., Zhou, Z., Ngo, C.-W., Hong, R.: Towards multimodal emotional support conversation systems, https://arxiv.org/abs/2408.03650, (2024). https://doi.org/10.48550/ARXIV.2408.03650.
24. Zhou, H., Huang, M., Zhang, T., Zhu, X., Liu, B.: Emotional chatting machine: emotional conversation generation with internal and external memory. In: Proceedings of the AAAI Conference on Artificial Intelligence, vol. 32, (2018). https://doi.org/10.1609/aaai.v32i1.11325
25. Haltaufderheide, J., Ranisch, R.: The ethics of ChatGPT in medicine and healthcare: a systematic review on large language models (LLMs). npj Digit. Med. **7**, 183 (2024). https://doi.org/10.1038/s41746-024-01157-x
26. Kim, H., Wang, Y.: (Mia): unveiling the human touch: how AI chatbots' emotional support and human-like profiles reduce psychological reactance to promote user self-disclosure in mental health services. Int. J. Advert., 1–25 (2025). https://doi.org/10.1080/02650487.2025.2558479
27. Hennekeuser, D., Vaziri, D., Golchinfar, D., Stevens, G.: What I don't like about you?: a systematic review of impeding aspects for the usage of conversational agents. Interact. Comput. **36**, 293–312 (2024). https://doi.org/10.1093/iwc/iwae018
28. Kim, H., McGill, A.L.: AI-induced dehumanization. J. Consum. Psychol. **35**, 363–381 (2025). https://doi.org/10.1002/jcpy.1441
29. Meng, J., Dai, Y.: (Nancy): emotional support from AI chatbots: should a supportive partner self-disclose or not? J. Comput.-Mediat. Commun. **26**, 207–222 (2021). https://doi.org/10.1093/jcmc/zmab005
30. Zou, W., Liu, Z., Lin, C.: The influence of individuals' emotional involvement and perceived roles of AI chatbots on emotional self-efficacy. Inf. Commun. Soc., 1–21 (2025). https://doi.org/10.1080/1369118X.2025.2508394
31. Lopes, E., Jain, G., Carlbring, P., Pareek, S.: Talking mental health: a battle of wits between humans and AI. J. Technol. Behav. Sci. **9**, 628–638 (2023). https://doi.org/10.1007/s41347-023-00359-6

32. Sharma, A., Lin, I.W., Miner, A.S., Atkins, D.C., Althoff, T.: Human–AI collaboration enables more empathic conversations in text-based peer-to-peer mental health support. Nat. Mach. Intell. **5**, 46–57 (2023). https://doi.org/10.1038/s42256-022-00593-2
33. Correll, J., Mellinger, C., McClelland, G.H., Judd, C.M.: Avoid cohen's 'small','medium', and 'large'for power analysis. Trends Cogn. Sci. **24**, 200–207 (2020)
34. Bartlett, M.E., Edmunds, C.E.R., Belpaeme, T., Thill, S.: Have I got the power? Analysing and reporting statistical power in HRI. ACM Trans. Hum.-Rob. Interact. **11**, 1–16 (2022). https://doi.org/10.1145/3495246
35. Khan, I., Sarker, S.-J., Hackshaw, A.: Smaller sample sizes for phase II trials based on exact tests with actual error rates by trading-off their nominal levels of significance and power. Br. J. Cancer. **107**, 1801–1809 (2012). https://doi.org/10.1038/bjc.2012.444
36. Reifarth, E., Böll, B., Kochanek, M., Garcia Borrega, J.: Communication strategies for expressing empathy during family-clinician conversations in the intensive care unit: a mixed methods study. Intensive Crit. Care Nurs. **81**, 103601 (2024). https://doi.org/10.1016/j.iccn.2023.103601
37. Gregory, J.: Understanding the communication skills that support nurses to provide person-centred care. Nurs. Stand. **39**, 61–66 (2024). https://doi.org/10.7748/ns.2024.e12132
38. Laustsen, C.E., Larsson, H., Sjöberg, M., Blomqvist, K., Beck, I.: Awareness of how I am and how I want to be when communicating with people in need of care – nursing students' experiences of theoretical and practical training in person-centred communication. Nurse Educ. Pract. **89**, 104588 (2025). https://doi.org/10.1016/j.nepr.2025.104588
39. Flavián, C., Guinalíu, M., Gurrea, R.: The role played by perceived usability, satisfaction and consumer trust on website loyalty. Inf. Manag. **43**, 1–14 (2006). https://doi.org/10.1016/j.im.2005.01.002
40. Reis, H.T., Crasta, D., Rogge, R.D., Maniaci, M.R., Carmichael, C.L.: Perceived partner responsiveness scale (PPRS): (reis & carmichael, 2006). In: Worthington, D.L., Bodie, G.D. (eds.) The Sourcebook of Listening Research, pp. 516–521. Wiley (2017). https://doi.org/10.1002/9781119102991.ch57
41. Gordon, A.M., Chen, S.: Do you get where I'm coming from?: perceived understanding buffers against the negative impact of conflict on relationship satisfaction. J. Pers. Soc. Psychol. **110**, 239–260 (2016). https://doi.org/10.1037/pspi0000039
42. Rheu, M., Meng, J., Dai, Y., Nancy, Meng, J., Peng, W.: When a chatbot disappoints you: expectancy violation in human-chatbot interaction in a social support context. Commun. Res. **51**, 782–814 (2024). https://doi.org/10.1177/00936502231221669
43. Zhang, S., Wu, Z., Meng, H.M., Cai, L.: Facial expression synthesis using PAD emotional parameters for a chinese expressive avatar. In: Paiva, A.C.R., Prada, R., Picard, R.W. (eds.) Affective Computing and Intelligent Interaction, pp. 24–35. Springer, Berlin Heidelberg, Berlin, Heidelberg (2007). https://doi.org/10.1007/978-3-540-74889-2_3
44. Grimes, G.M., Schuetzler, R.M., Giboney, J.S.: Mental models and expectation violations in conversational AI interactions. Decis. Support. Syst. **144**, 113515 (2021). https://doi.org/10.1016/j.dss.2021.113515
45. Burgoon, J.K. et al.: Application of expectancy violations theory to communication with and judgments about embodied agents during a decision-making task. Int. J. Hum.-Comput. Stud. **91**, 24–36 (2016). https://doi.org/10.1016/j.ijhcs.2016.02.002
46. Larsen, L.T., Cecchini, M.: Connective and tactfully tactical: connective tactics and professional authority in doctor-patient relationships. Soc. Sci. Med. **326**, 115924 (2023). https://doi.org/10.1016/j.socscimed.2023.115924
47. Lee, J., Lee, D.: User perception and self-disclosure towards an AI psychotherapy chatbot according to the anthropomorphism of its profile picture. Telemat. Inform. **85**, 102052 (2023). https://doi.org/10.1016/j.tele.2023.102052

48. Dubois-Sage, M., Jacquet, B., Jamet, F., Baratgin, J.: People with autism spectrum disorder could interact more easily with a robot than with a human: reasons and limits. Behav. Sci. **14**, 131 (2024). https://doi.org/10.3390/bs14020131
49. Xu, K., Chen, X., Huang, L.: Deep mind in social responses to technologies: a new approach to explaining the computers are social actors phenomena. Comput. Hum. Behav. **134**, 107321 (2022). https://doi.org/10.1016/j.chb.2022.107321
50. Gambino, A., Fox, J., Ratan, R.: Building a stronger CASA: extending the computers are social actors paradigm. Hum.-mach. Commun. **1**, 71–86 (2020) https://doi.org/10.30658/hmc.1.5
51. Street, R.L., Krupat, E., Bell, R.A., Kravitz, R.L., Haidet, P.: Beliefs about control in the physician-patient relationship: effect on communication in medical encounters. J. Gen. Intern. Med. **18**, 609–616 (2003). https://doi.org/10.1046/j.1525-1497.2003.20749.x
52. Kim, J.H., Kim, K.H., Choi, R.J.: UX empathy strategy for introverted users through an AI interviewer : exploring the needs and wants of introverted users. Inst. Art Des. Res. **27**, 103–113 (2024). https://doi.org/10.59386/jadr.2024.27.2.103

Pingjiang Mystery: A Map-Based Board Game for Navigating the Ancient City of Suzhou

Yanli Jiang[1], Jiachen Liang[2,3], Yingpin Zhang[1], and Yue Li[2,3](✉)

[1] Suzhou Polytechnic University, Suzhou, China
[2] Xi'an Jiaotong-Liverpool University, Suzhou, China
[3] University of Liverpool, Liverpool, UK
yue.li@xjtlu.edu.cn

Abstract. Globalization and multicultural influences pose significant challenges to the preservation and dissemination of intangible cultural heritage (ICH). Suzhou, a renowned historical city in China, is rich in historical and cultural artifacts. This study employs an interaction design approach, focusing on the *ancient map of Pingjiang* (平江图), to explore solutions for enhancing the learning and dissemination of Suzhou's ICH. Through three participatory design workshops involving target users and design experts, we identified essential cultural content, developed relevant game mechanics, and designed an intuitive gameplay interface. The resulting board game, *Pingjiang Mystery*, effectively supports ICH learning, as evidenced by the positive user experiences, engagement, and educational outcomes observed in evaluation studies. This research contributes to the field of human-computer interaction by presenting a comprehensive case study of a board game design aiming at preserving ICH.

Keywords: Interaction Design · Board Game Design · Cultural Heritage · Serious Games

1 Introduction

The rapid development of media and technologies has significantly transformed how people interact with and experience information. In addition, global cultural convergence poses unique challenges to preserving and disseminating traditional intangible cultural heritage (ICH), particularly among the younger, digitally-oriented generations [19].

Suzhou, located in the Jiangnan region of China, is internationally recognized for its profound cultural legacy spanning over 2,500 years, and it boasts a unique combination of architectural, artistic, and social traditions that continue to influence its contemporary urban life. The city is renowned for its classical gardens [15], which embody traditional Chinese landscape aesthetics and have been

S. Guo et al. (Eds.): HHME 2025, CCIS 2878, pp. 188–209, 2027.
https://doi.org/10.1007/978-981-92-3991-7_14

Fig. 1. The demonstration of *Pingjiang Mystery* setup and components. (a) Four-player experimental setup with the game board and distributed cards. (b) Overview of all game components. (c) Close-up of the customized game map used in the gameplay. (d) Game props used in the gameplay, including character tokens with introduction cards, game cards, coins and paper taels, garden tiles with bamboo and rockery, tile bases, firecracker miniatures, and dice.

meticulously preserved for centuries. Local crafts such as Suzhou embroidery [23], Kesi silk tapestry, and Taohuawu woodblock New Year paintings exemplify both artistic sophistication and deep cultural symbolism. Despite that Suzhou's ICH thrives in its seasonal culinary customs, distinctive festivals, and folklore, the contemporary dissemination of ICH faces challenges. Many young generations have only heard about the iconic landmarks, such as the Suzhou Gardens[1] and the Pingjiang Road[2], while lacking deeper engagement with the underlying stories, customs, and values. As a result, there is an urgent need for innovative approaches that foster meaningful and interactive connections with Suzhou's living traditions.

In this study, we utilize Suzhou's distinctive cultural assets as both inspiration and key content for an interactive board game design. By embedding authentic local narratives, visual motifs, and traditional practices into the mechanics and aesthetics of the game, we aim to facilitate deeper cultural understanding and engagement for a wider range of audiences. In the initial phase of this research, we investigated Suzhou's traditional culture and board game mechanics through comprehensive literature reviews, field visits, and targeted user interviews. This exploratory phase revealed three key challenges: **First**, ICH in the local region struggles to engage younger generations due to monotonous dissemination methods and limited appeal, threatening its continuity [11]. **Second**, traditional board games frequently adopt cultural elements superficially as mere decorations without embedding meaningful cultural experiences into the gameplay, thus failing to resonate with younger audiences. **Third**, tourists' perceptions of Suzhou's ICH tend to focus only on specific landmarks that are widely recognized, such as Pingjiang Road and Suzhou Gardens, lacking an overview of the historical context and a deeper cultural understanding.

Recognizing the popularity of gameplay among the young generations (such as Generation Y and Z [1]), and its potential to disseminate cultural content,

[1] https://whc.unesco.org/en/list/813/.

[2] https://www.chinadiscovery.com/jiangsu/suzhou/pingjiang-road.html.

we aim to address these challenges by designing a board game. We introduce *Pingjiang Mystery*, an interactive board game developed through participatory design workshops involving diverse stakeholders, including target users and cultural experts. Guided by serious game theory, we derived visual symbols from Suzhou's Pingjiang Historical and Cultural District, including architectural styles, traditional clothing craftsmanship, and folk traditions, and integrated them into concrete game mechanics, blending education and entertainment seamlessly.

Our evaluation results highlight that the interactive experiences provided by the serious game successfully transformed abstract cultural symbols into the gameplay, activating players' cultural memories through contextual narratives. Participants reported high satisfaction with the game's immersive experience and replayability, demonstrating significant improvements in their depth of perception and cognitive understanding of Suzhou's traditional culture. This research expands the dialogue on the role of interaction design in cultural preservation and offers practical guidelines for future cultural heritage projects within the HCI community.

This study makes three key contributions to the field of HCI and cultural heritage: (1) We demonstrate a novel approach to embedding intangible cultural heritage meaningfully within game mechanics; (2) We provide empirical insights from participatory design processes tailored to cultural heritage contexts; (3) We present evaluation findings on the effectiveness of interactive board games in enhancing cultural understanding and engagement.

2 Related Work

2.1 Serious Games for Cultural Heritage

Recent advances in human-computer interaction (HCI) and educational technology have fueled the development of serious games as effective tools for cultural heritage education [12,13]. Unlike traditional video games, which are designed solely for entertainment, serious games incorporate educational objectives aimed at facilitating knowledge acquisition [5,22], fostering a sense of participation [10,21], and increasing cultural awareness [8,20].

Cultural heritage serious games utilize constructivist learning principles to allow players to interactively explore and reconstruct historical and cultural knowledge. DaCosta and Kinsell [2] emphasized that such games not only stimulate learning-by-doing but also provide an immersive experience that transcends the limitations of traditional educational methods. These games are increasingly being used in museums, heritage sites, and classroom environments, providing learners with access to tangible and intangible aspects of culture. Ye et al. [22] specifically investigated the impact of a digital puzzle game on learning Chinese cultural heritage motifs and found that students who used the game were superior in terms of knowledge retention and motivation to learn compared to those who learned through traditional video instruction. The study concluded that well-designed serious games, especially those that incorporate scaffolding and interactive elements, can significantly improve students' ability to recognize, understand, and remember complex artifacts. These cases demonstrate a growing consensus that serious games, when thoughtfully designed, are powerful tools for CH learning and engagement. These insights inform the present study's approach to designing and evaluating a Suzhou-themed board game for cultural heritage dissemination.

2.2 Board Game Design Based on History and Culture

Board game design is an integrative discipline that combines creativity, game mechanics, narrative, and user interaction to create engaging play experiences. Board games use components such as boards, cards, tokens, and dice to facilitate interactive gameplay. Engelstein et al. [4] provide a comprehensive analysis of game frameworks, including competitive, cooperative, and team-based structures, demonstrating how distinct architectures shape player interaction and define victory conditions. For example, cooperative games promote collaborative problem-solving, while competitive games foster strategic rivalry. Many classic board games focus primarily on economic strategy and resource management. For example, *Monopoly* introduces players to real estate trading and financial decision-making within a generic urban setting [7]. However, these games are not specifically designed to convey historical or cultural content.

In contrast, history- and culture-themed board games deliberately integrate authentic cultural elements and narratives into their mechanics and design. A successful commercial example is the Chinese board game *A Dream of Splendor in Song Dynasty*[3], which immerses players in the commercial environment of Song Dynasty China. Players expand business empires, develop new dishes, and attract customers, all within a setting that incorporates accurate architectural and mercantile practices of the era. This deep thematic integration not only enhances educational value but also demonstrates how board games can facilitate cultural understanding and engagement. *Ancient Knowledge*[4], a strategy card game, is another example. Players construct monuments and create artifacts to preserve knowledge across generations. This game's mechanic revolves around the impermanence of human achievement: buildings and wonders, ranging from the pyramids of Mexico and the Great Sphinx of Giza to the ancient cities of Tiwanaku and Babylon, inevitably decay over time. Players must optimize synergies among cards to pass down knowledge before their monuments fade into history. By combining real-world landmarks with engaging gameplay and the theme of cultural memory, *Ancient Knowledge* illustrates how board games can simulate the challenges of cultural preservation and highlight the ephemeral nature of civilization's greatest achievements. These examples highlight the potential for well-crafted board games to serve as effective platforms for both entertainment and cultural education, offering valuable insights for future design.

[3] https://boardgamegeek.com/boardgame/404286/a-dream-of-splendor-in-song-dynasty.

[4] https://boardgamegeek.com/boardgame/338093/ancient-knowledge.

3 Methodology

Based on preliminary research, this study aims to effectively facilitate the dissemination of Suzhou's traditional culture through four design goals (DGs):

DG1 Familiarizing players with Suzhou's ancient urban layout.
DG2 Introducing Suzhou's historic architecture and cultural traditions.
DG3 Simulating an authentic Suzhou-style lifestyle experience.
DG4 Cultivating players' affection for Suzhou to inspire visits.

3.1 Double Diamond Model

We adopted the Double Diamond model [3] to structure our serious game design process. This framework, established by the UK Design Council, organizes design into four phases: Discover, Define, Develop, and Deliver, across two iterative spaces: problem and solution. In the **Discover** phase, we performed market research and user interviews to understand needs and context. The **Define** phase involved synthesizing findings and refining design challenges through workshops. In **Develop**, we prototyped gameplay mechanics and validated them via participatory design sessions. The **Deliver** phase focused on iterative user testing and incorporating feedback to finalize the product.

3.2 Participatory Design Workshop

Participatory design emphasizes active collaboration between users and designers, advocating for a "democratization" of design that transforms end-users from passive recipients into active co-creators [18]. By involving users directly in the process, the final product can more accurately reflect their needs and expectations.

In this study, we conducted three participatory design workshops, each co-facilitated by two principal researchers and one moderator. The **first** workshop validated initial cultural research, deepening our understanding of players' cognitive needs regarding Suzhou's traditional culture. Participants discussed key topics related to cultural heritage and urban preservation, analyzed relevant precedents, and helped translate cultural demands into concrete design objectives. The **second** workshop focused on creative ideation and the integration of cultural elements. Participants collaborated with the design team in brainstorming sessions, using the Northern Song "Pingjiang Map (平江图)" as a conceptual board template. They contributed to character and component design and evaluated various approaches to balancing entertainment with cultural dissemination. A low-fidelity prototype reflecting Suzhou's street network was tested for cultural resonance, with participants voting on the most authentic design. The **third** workshop centered on transforming these concepts into a functional game through playtesting and iterative refinement. Participants evaluated cultural accuracy and gameplay, informing the final adjustments. Collectively, these workshops resulted in a Suzhou-themed board game that harmonizes cultural depth with engaging play.

4 Design of the *Pingjiang Mystery*

Suzhou, with a history spanning over 2,500 years, is renowned for its rich intangible cultural heritage (ICH). Historical records, such as the Southern Song Dynasty's "Pingjiang Map (平江图)" (see Fig. 2a-b), illustrate the city's enduring urban layout of parallel waterways and adjacent streets—a structure that is largely preserved today.

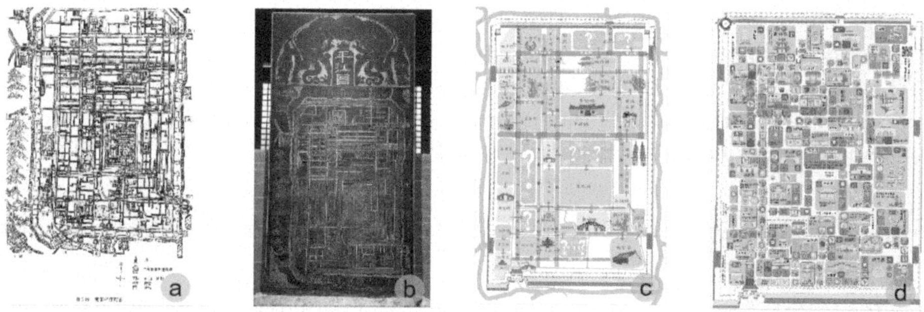

Fig. 2. Design process of the board game map based on the Pingjiang historical district of Suzhou. (a) Map of ancient Suzhou city from the Song Dynasty. (b) The stone carving, *Pingjiang Map* (平江图), records a map of the Song Dynasty as the Song Dynasty capital city of Pingjiang (now in Pingjiang road, Suzhou, China). (c) Low fidelity prototype map integrating key streets and landmarks as gameplay elements. (d) Final version of the board game map, featuring detailed visual representations and refined layout for enhanced gameplay and cultural immersion.

The city's favorable Jiangnan climate fostered flourishing textile and handicraft industries, exemplified by nationally recognized crafts such as Suzhou embroidery, Kesi silk tapestries, Song brocade weaving, and the distinctive Taohuawu woodblock New Year paintings. Suzhou's gardens, celebrated worldwide, epitomize its architectural legacy. Landmarks like the Master of Nets Garden have even inspired international replicas, such as the "Astor Court" at the Metropolitan Museum of Art in New York. The city's urban design, particularly its dual network of canals and roads, also shaped the distinctive combined water-and-land city gates. Although many ancient gates have been lost, Panmen Gate remains a well-preserved example, with restoration efforts reviving Suzhou's historical memory. In addition, Suzhou's folk customs are deeply intertwined with seasonal changes and traditional festivals. Culinary practices follow the rhythms of nature—loquats in May, bayberries in June, and hairy crabs in October. Festival traditions are distinct, such as honoring Wu Zixu during the Dragon Boat Festival and celebrating the Winter Solstice with family feasts, reflecting the city's unique cultural identity.

In this section, we detail the Suzhou-themed serious game design process through three structured participatory workshops, documented with comprehensive meeting minutes outlining research objectives, participant demographics, methods, and key findings.

4.1 First Design Workshop: Discover and Define

Research Design and Participants. Based on the focus group methodology [9], the first workshop aimed to gain deeper insights into players' perceptions regarding Suzhou's traditional culture. We prepared cultural materials from field investigations in advance, such as the history Map of ancient Suzhou city from the Song Dynasty (see Fig. 2a), then recruited participants from the social platform based on target user characteristics.

The study's primary target group consisted of the younger generation who enjoy check-in tourism. Three participants joined in the first workshop, including two females and one male, aged between 23 to 36 ($M = 29.33, SD = 6.51$).

Procedure. The first workshop, lasting 60 min, was structured into four distinct sessions:

(1) Introduction and Warm-up (5 min): Participants introduced themselves, followed by an overview of the project's aims and agenda presented by the researchers.

(2) Data Organization (25 min): Researchers and participants collaboratively categorized the preliminary research findings on Suzhou's culture. Three primary categories were established: (a) representative intangible cultural heritage items (e.g., Kunqu Opera, Suzhou embroidery), (b) classical gardens and architecture (e.g., the Humble Administrator's Garden), and (c) local folk traditions (e.g., seasonal food and fruits). In addition, the team also analyzed the board game *A Dream of Splendor in Song Dynasty* as a typical case study, reviewing its core mechanisms, component design, and victory conditions to inform the development process.

(3) Brainstorming Session (25 min): Researchers posed three open-ended questions to prompt discussion about participants' prior board gaming experiences and their perceptions of Suzhou culture.

- Q1 Based on your previous board game experience, what are the most engaging game mechanics or components? Why?
- Q2 If the Pingjiang map and Suzhou gardens are incorporated as game elements of a board game, what kind of game mechanics or challenges would you like to have?
- Q3 Can you think of any real-world cultural practices that can be effectively translated into engaging game mechanics?

These questions were presented on a whiteboard to foster engagement. Participants contributed ideas freely, with key concepts and preferences recorded and thematically organized into a preliminary framework linking game mechanics with cultural elements.

(4) Debriefing (5 min): The session concluded with a summary of key findings and next steps.

Summary and Discussion. All participants had substantial experience with board games, providing detailed feedback on gameplay mechanics, character development, and component design. However, their knowledge of Suzhou's cultural heritage was notably limited, even among long-term residents. Their awareness of local traditions and history was also superficial to the well-known ones. This gap highlighted both the need and opportunity for cultural discovery, inspiring the eventual naming of the serious game as *Pingjiang Mysteries* to reflect the spirit of exploration and learning at the heart of the design.

4.2 Second Design Workshop: Develop

Research Design and Participants. This workshop focused on the design phase of a board serious game. In addition to the two researchers and the moderator, we invited two board game players and two professionals working in Suzhou's cultural tourism sector, all aged between 20 and 37 years old ($M = 31.50, SD = 7.77$). Building upon the outcomes of the first workshop, we collaboratively developed the game concept and some initial design.

Procedure. The workshop lasted approximately 100 min and comprised four main stages:

(1) Introduction and Warm-Up (10 min): The session began with participant introductions, a review of the first workshop's outcomes by the facilitator, and a presentation of the meeting objectives and agenda.

(2) Serious Game Map Design (30 min): Leveraging insights from the first workshop, participants identified the Pingjiang Map (平江图) (see Fig. 2b), a detailed map of Suzhou's ancient city from the Song Dynasty, as a design foundation. Cultural tourism experts highlighted its significance as a bridge between Suzhou's past and present. Participants selected historically preserved landmarks from the map and proposed a route that connects these sites, creating a cohesive gameplay experience.

(3) Game Mechanics Discussion (50 min): Participants and researchers collaboratively explored two game mechanics options: (1) a cooperative mode based on task-oriented clues, and (2) a competitive mode inspired by Monopoly, emphasizing territorial expansion and financial investment. Participants then simulated gameplay on the drafted map (as shown in Fig. 3), identifying issues and sharing historical anecdotes about the featured attractions. To further enhance gameplay variety and unpredictability, participants contributed design ideas for Opportunity Cards and Knowledge Cards.

(4) Summary and Discussion (10 min): The workshop concluded with a summary of progress and next steps.

Fig. 3. Researchers and participants in workshop 2, simulating the gameplay on the drafted map.

Summary and Discussion. Feedback from participants indicated a clear preference for competitive mechanics in board games as opposed to cooperative play. As a result, the competitive model was adopted as the core design direction. The workshop concluded with (1) the completion of an initial game map (refer to Fig. 2c) featuring Suzhou-specific elements (some elements are shown in Fig. 4), (2) an enriched list of attractions and task points informed by participant input, (3) the design of Opportunity Cards and Knowledge Cards, and (4) a low-fidelity prototype of the board game. This was created to visualize and iteratively test the evolving game concept.

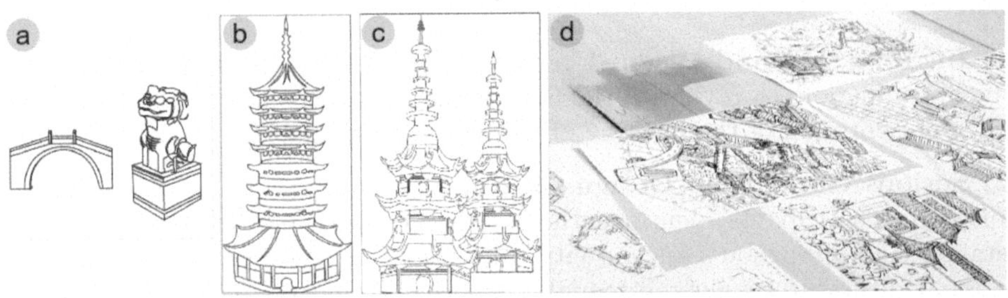

Fig. 4. Line drawings created during the *Pingjiang Mysteries* design process. (a) Initial sketches of architectural elements, including bridges and stone lions. (b) Detailed line drawing of the Bao'En Temple (报恩寺). (c) Line art depicting the Twin Pagodas (双塔). (d) Hand-drawn landscape and architectural scene illustrations are used for various game components, such as cards and map tiles.

4.3 Third Design Workshop: Deliver

Research Design and Participants. The third workshop focused on testing, evaluating, and refining the board game based on insights from the previous workshops. This session aimed to identify usability issues, gather user feedback, and guide iterative improvements through structured playtesting with target users. Four participants (one female, three male, aged 28–32, $M = 29.75, SD = 1.71$) participated in the prototype evaluation guided by the two researchers.

Procedure. This workshop lasted approximately 100 min and comprised three main stages:

(1) Introduction and Warm-Up (10 min): The workshop began with participant introductions. The facilitator outlined the objectives and structure for the current session, setting clear expectations for the prototype evaluation.

(2) Prototype Evaluation (60 min): Participants interacted with the low-fidelity game prototype (as shown in Fig. 5) and provided detailed feedback.

(3) Discussion (30 min): This session concluded with a summary of findings and suggestions.

Fig. 5. Researchers and participants in workshop 3, evaluating the board game prototype.

4.4 Board Game Components and Setup

Figure 1 illustrates the board game set, includes a game board, a dice, 4 character tokens, 12 building bases, 16 Opportunity Cards, 24 Solar Term Cards, 29 Knowledge Cards, 10 Event Cards, 12 Item Cards, and 30 game currency notes.

Summary and Discussion. Overall, participants responded positively to the game's narrative background and character design. However, they noted that the initial board game map lacked immersion and was confusing to navigate because it was too reminiscent of a standard city map. The integration of cultural elements was perceived unnatural, leading to decreased interest and difficulty maintaining focus after approximately thirty minutes. This feedback highlighted areas of improvement in the spatial layout and aesthetic design. Key improvement needs include (1) modularizing the map to clarify routes, (2) improving the chance cards to better reflect the local culture, and (3) streamlining gameplay to improve pacing. Addressing the workshop feedback, the team developed a high-fidelity prototype tested with a comprehensive user study.

5 Design Outcome: *Pingjiang Mysteries*

The final board game is thematically centered on "historical exploration and urban life in Suzhou". Its visual presentation combines traditional ink wash aesthetics with light colors and modern flat illustration techniques, creating a unique and engaging artistic style. Players take on distinct roles and immerse themselves in Suzhou's historical development and cultural richness by completing various tasks and challenges integrated into the gameplay.

Players. The game supports 2 to 4 players. Each participant selects a character and receives a corresponding role card, which records unique attributes and skills, as well as 5 item cards. Optionally, one player may serve as a host to facilitate gameplay and provide guidance.

Game Setup. To setup the gameplay, players place the board on a flat surface and sort cards into their respective categories. Each player places their token at the ancient city gate (marked with a red frame). Players enter the ancient city from the gate and move their tokens according to dice rolls.

5.1 Gameplay Rules

Objective. The game victory can be achieved in two ways: (1) constructing three gardens, with at least one being their exclusive garden. An exclusive garden is indicated by a unique symbol on the map matching their character. Alternatively, (2) accumulating 50 taels[5] while owning at least one exclusive garden. Allowing different victory strategies increases the game's replayability and adds to its strategic complexity. At the start of each turn, the active player rolls the dice and moves their character token.

Game Elements on the Pingjiang Map. The game board features a total of 177 spots divided between two routes: a land route with 93 spots and a water route with 78 spots. Additionally, there are six city gates that connect the two routes, allowing players to choose whether to switch routes upon reaching a gate. Among the spots on the two routes, there are 65 action spots and 78 event spots, with the remaining spots being empty. Detailed explanations of the game elements can be found in Table 1. The *action* spots require players to perform a specific action when they pass by or land on them during their movement. The *activity* spots prompt players to engage in activities associated with a specific icon, such as answering a question in a knowledge quiz or drawing a card and following its instructions.

[5] Liang (两), a traditional Chinese unit of weight and currency.

Table 1. Detailed game elements and icons on the game map.

	Icons		Quantity	Effect
Action Spots		Coin tael	27	Receive **x** taels, **x** = the number of coins on the icon, ranging from 1 to 3.
		Bamboo tile	13	Whether or not to purchase a bamboo tile with 2 taels. A must-have for garden construction.
		Rockery tile	9	Whether or not to purchase a rockery tile with 2 taels. A must-have for garden construction.
		Garden architecture	16	Whether or not to construct a garden, costing 2-8 taels depending on the construction progress.
Activity Spots		Firecracker /Bomb	10/6	Injured, the player pause 1 round and pay 3 taels for medical treatment.
		Character-based assets	24	If landed on others' assets, answer knowledge test questions. 2 taels penalty if incorrect.
		Event	11	Draw an event card. E.g., typhoon arrives, all players rotate positions on the map closewise.
		Opportunity	12	Draw an opportunity card. E.g., exchange a card or the map position with another player.
		Seasonal	15	Draw a seasonal event card. E.g., pay 1 tael for the Qingtuan during the Qingming Festival.

6 Evaluation

6.1 Procedure

The experiments took place in an open public area, and participants were randomly assigned to groups of four, guided through the three phases of the experiment (see Fig. 6 for details). Ethics approval has been obtained from our institution's ethics committee prior to any data collection.

1) **Pre-experiment Phase**. First, we introduced our research to participants and obtained their informed consent. Participants were asked to fill out a pre-experiment questionnaire (see Appendix A).
2) **Experiment Phase**. At this stage, a trained experimenter would guide participants to play the *Pingjiang Mysteries*, observe the entire experiment, and provide assistance and explanations when necessary.

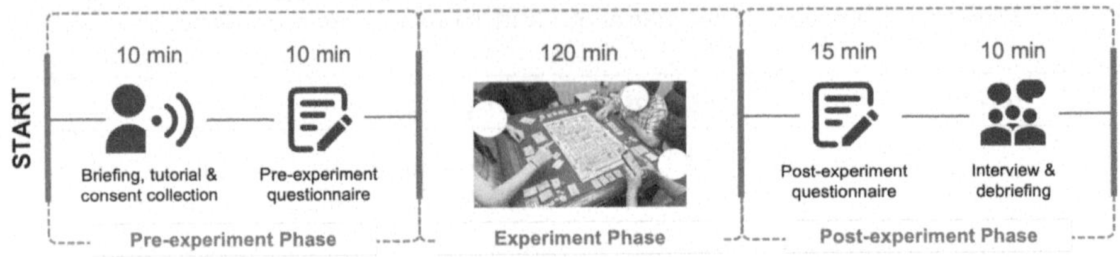

Fig. 6. A flow chart showing the experimental procedure.

3) **Post-experiment Phase**. Following the completion of gameplay, participants were asked to complete a post-experiment questionnaire assessing their experience and learning effectiveness. After that, participants were invited to join an interview to provide further insights into their assessments of the experience.

6.2 Measurement

This study collected both quantitative and qualitative data to assess the user experience. Specifically, we adopted validated questionnaires to understand the user experience, user engagement, and learning outcomes. The detailed items can be found in Appendix B.

System Usability. To evaluate the usability of *Pingjiang Mystery*, we measured three key dimensions. **Cultural Experience (CE)**: Perceived understanding and increased interest in Suzhou's traditional culture (2 items). **Rules Comprehension (RC)**: Clarity of game rules and ease of rule execution (2 items). **Visual Design (VD)**: Satisfaction with the game's visual style and cultural element recognition (3 items). Each item was rated on a 5-point Likert scale (1 = Strongly Disagree, 5 = Strongly Agree). For each dimension, a composite score was calculated as the mean of its corresponding items.

User Experience. User experience was measured by the short version of the User Experience Questionnaire (UEQ-S) [17]. It comprised two sub-scales, namely pragmatic and hedonic quality, along with a total score that reflects users' holistic impression of the system.

User Engagement. User engagement was assessed using the User Engagement Scale Short Form (UES-SF) [16], focusing on four subscales: Focused Attention (FA), Perceived Usability (PU), Aesthetic Appeal (AE), and Reward Factor (RW).

Learning Outcomes. We prepared six specific multiple-choice questions related to Suzhou ICH knowledge involved in the board game to assess the learning outcomes (see the detailed items in Appendix A.2). Each question includes four options plus an *"I don't know"* option. A correct answer receives 1 score, and the total learning outcome score is computed as $\sum_{i=1}^{6} \text{LO}_i$.

6.3 Participants

Participants voluntarily signed up for the board game via social media. We collected 26 sets of evaluation data (16 females, 10 males), aged between 19 and 38 ($M = 25.46, SD = 6.00$). More than half were students ($N = 14$), followed by professionals ($N = 6$) and office staff ($N = 3$). Participants' self-evaluations were recorded on a five-point Likert scale, ranging from 1 (not at all familiar) to 5 (extremely familiar). They showed a moderate familiarity with board games ($M = 3.54, SD = 1.03$. In terms of frequency, 30.8% of participants ($N = 8$) almost do not play board games.

7 Analysis and Results

We used IBM SPSS Statistics (version 29) to conduct the data analysis. The qualitative data were analyzed using the theme-based content analysis [14].

7.1 Quantitative Results

System Usability. Participants rated the Cultural Experience dimension highest ($M = 4.08, SD = 0.58$), suggesting the board game effectively enhanced their understanding and interest in Suzhou's traditional culture. Visual Design also received positive ratings ($M = 3.90, SD = 0.67$), while Rules Comprehension ($M = 3.75, SD = 0.84$) indicated generally clear but potentially improvable rule presentation. The most frequently cited issues for rules comprehension were: chain store and knowledge quiz rules ($N = 10$), movement rules (dice and movement pathways) ($N = 10$), item card usage ($N = 8$), and building rules ($N = 7$).

User Experience. The UEQ-S results also showed positive ratings (see Fig. 7). The pragmatic quality, hedonic quality, and overall experience had mean scores of 0.90 ($SD = 1.38$), 1.62 ($SD = 1.10$), and 1.26 ($SD = 1.23$), respectively, exceeding the threshold value of 0.8 [6]. The results indicate that users had a positive experience with *Pingjiang Mysteries.* Compared to the UEQ benchmark dataset [6], the pragmatic quality of user experience was *Below average* (top 75% to 50%), the hedonic quality was *Excellent* (top 10%), and the overall experience was *Above average* (top 50% to 25%).

User Engagement. Participants rated the Reward Factor (RW) highly ($M = 4.13, SD = 0.77$), indicating that the game effectively engaged them through rewarding experiences. The relatively high Focused Attention (FA) ($M = 3.90, SD = 1.04$) and Aesthetic Appeal (AE) ($M = 3.86, SD = 0.71$) scores suggest participants were immersed and visually pleased during gameplay. Perceived Usability (PU) received a moderate score ($M = 3.56$, $SD = 1.04$), indicating that the usability was generally acceptable, and there is still room for further improvement to enhance the overall user experience. The results can be found in Fig. 8.

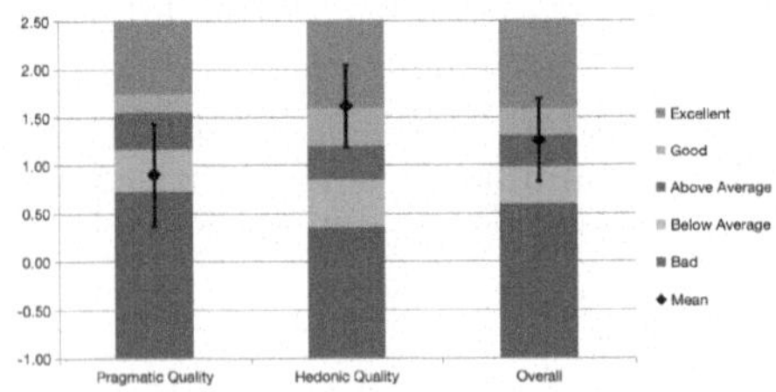

Fig. 7. The results of the user experience questionnaire: pragmatic quality, hedonic quality, and overall user experience.

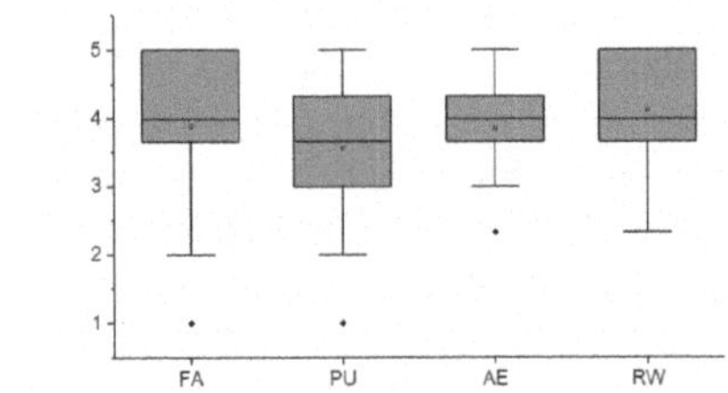

Fig. 8. The results of user engagement scale: Focused Attention (FA), Perceived Usability (PU), Aesthetic Appeal (AE), and Reward Factor (RW).

Learning Outcomes. Shapiro-Wilk tests were conducted to examine the data distributions. As the data did not conform to a normal distribution ($p < 0.05$), we conducted the Wilcoxon Signed Ranks Test. The results (as shown in Fig. 9) indicated that the learning outcomes of the post-test ($M = 4.38, SD = 1.55$) were significantly higher than the pre-test ($M = 3.38, SD = 1.58$), $Z = -3.250, p = 0.001$.

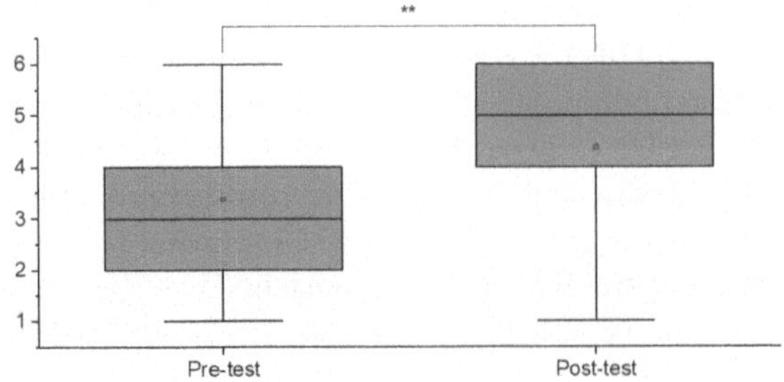

Fig. 9. The results of the knowledge test before and after the game.

7.2 Qualitative Results

Throughout the design and testing of the *Pingjiang Mystery*, participants demonstrated increased knowledge of Suzhou's ancient city layout, local customs, architecture, and landmarks. Several expressed interest in visiting these locations after gameplay, suggesting strong cultural engagement. For example, P3 noted that *"I plan to visit Fengmen Gate to try the local delicacies I purchased in-game with silver taels"*. Participants reported that through quiz elements integrated into gameplay, they were immersed in the game, enjoying tasks such as constructing Suzhou-style gardens and learning historical facts. As P1 remarked, *"While playing, I gradually became immersed and truly enjoyed the process of constructing a Suzhou-style garden."* The cultural integration was described as organic and enjoyable, with many noting that the game's appeal and immersion grew over time.

Participants consistently demonstrated positive emotions and sustained engagement during gameplay, even when encountering penalties or temporary financial strain. The garden-building mechanic was highlighted as particularly enjoyable, providing an intuitive way to learn about Suzhou garden architecture. Participants also highlighted that the inclusion of historically significant landmarks on the map could evoke personal memories, particularly those of places they have visited before (P25, male, 29 years old). Knowledge quizzes were also highly commended as they motivate players to figure out the correct answers. Some players wished to continue seeking answers even after the session ended. We observed that participants discussed strategies and expressed interest in acquiring the game for future social and family gatherings, indicating a broad appeal and the potential market in the cultural and creative product design.

8 Discussion

8.1 Summary of Key Findings

This study demonstrates the effectiveness of culturally embedded game mechanics in facilitating user engagement and learning outcomes in a serious board game context. Specifically, our quantitative results indicate that *Pingjiang Mysteries* effectively increased players' knowledge about Suzhou's urban layout (**DG1**), architecture (**DG2**), and intangible cultural heritage. The board game provided participants with an authentic simulation of the Suzhou lifestyle (**DG3**), effectively cultivating players' affection for the city and inspiring interest in real-world visits (**DG4**).

However, we found that the pragmatic quality score was below average when compared to the benchmark datasets. One notable reason is that in order to maintain multiplayer playability, board games often feature complex game rules, which could have resulted in the low ratings in the dimensions of 'complicated – easy', 'inefficient – efficient', as well as 'confusing – clear'. Another possible reason, as identified by participants, is related to its utility. Participants explained that the utility of board games is comparatively lower when evaluated against more practical, utilitarian cultural products, such as bookmarks or keychains. As one participant commented, *"Compared with items like bookmarks, a board game naturally seems less practical in daily life."* This perception may impact ratings, even though participants acknowledged the game's experiential and educational value. The interview comments also indicated room for improvement in game mechanics, particularly regarding the balance between different character abilities. Participants expressed a desire for more equitable skill design across roles to ensure a fair and engaging experience for all players. Some also suggested increasing the number of knowledge-based quiz questions to further enhance ICH learning within the gameplay.

8.2 Research Implications

Our findings extend the literature on serious games for ICH learning, demonstrating that board games can bridge the gap between entertainment and education when grounded in participatory co-design and authentic cultural narratives. By involving target users and cultural experts throughout the design process, the final product achieved both cultural depth and playability. The results validate the double diamond model and participatory design as effective frameworks for heritage-centered game development in HCI. Furthermore, this study suggests that hedonic qualities (enjoyment and immersion) were perceived to be more important than pragmatic qualities (utilitarian) for the acceptance and success of serious games in cultural contexts.

The methodology employed in this study holds significant potential for broader application across various cities, institutions, educational establishments, and organizational groups. Cities in China possess distinctive cultural characteristics, and many are actively seeking innovative approaches to showcase these cultural tourism assets, as evidenced by the current popularity of cultural creative products and study tour programs. Our study demonstrates the effectiveness of serious board games in achieving such goals. These games leverage tangible assets (i.e., the board game set) for interactive social activities. They offer participants immersive experiences of local cultural heritage and have been found effective in engaging the younger generations. With the support of game facilitators, it can also engage teenagers and children, as well as parent-children social activities. Such interactive gameplay not only captures user interest but also serves as an effective medium for fostering a deeper understanding and appreciation of urban cultural traditions.

8.3 Limitations and Future Work

This study has certain limitations. First, the workshops mainly invited students and young faculty members from educational institutions, with selection criteria focused on the target demographic's age and profession. Despite its potential in engaging children and parents, this demographic group was not included in the co-design process. Furthermore, the designers of this serious board game come from a 2D visual design background. However, some participants found it challenging to locate a specific spot or directions on the game map, despite the use of icons and color-coding. They suggested incorporating three-dimensional icons to improve visual recognition. Lastly, our evaluation results showed a pressing need for a future digital version of the game, such as novel experiences with augmented reality (AR) and virtual reality (VR). Digital implementation would break temporal and spatial constraints while significantly enhancing interactivity. For instance, playing on an AR/VR-enabled map would allow users to see the transitions between Suzhou's historical and modern landscapes and to complete game missions. It could also enable immersive experiences such as creating Suzhou embroidery or Taohuawu woodblock prints, substantially increasing the product's entertainment value and appeal.

9 Conclusion

In this paper, we present the development and evaluation process of "*Pingjiang Mysteries*," a serious board game designed to promote Suzhou's cultural heritage. The game aims to help people understand Suzhou's historical and urban city planning, architecture and gardens, cultural assets, and folk traditions beyond its scenic beauty. Guided by the Double Diamond model, we structured our design process with participatory design at its core. Target users collaborated with researchers throughout the game's design, prototyping, evaluation, and iteration processes. We assessed the game's effectiveness through pre- and post-test questionnaires, conducting both quantitative and qualitative analyses. The results demonstrate that the game significantly enhances players' understanding of Suzhou's culture and effectively motivates them to explore these cultural elements in person. This project contributes to Suzhou's cultural tourism industry while offering unique insights for the cultural creative sector. We anticipate further iterations of *Pingjiang Mystery*, particularly through digital transformation that bridges board gameplay with real-world exploration, ultimately sharing Suzhou's stories with the broader international community (Table 2).

A Pre-experiment Questionnaire

A.1 Demographic Information

1. Participant ID:
2. Age:
3. Gender:
   ◯ Female ◯ Male ◯ Prefer not to say
4. Occupation:
   ◯ Student ◯ Office Staff ◯ Professional (e.g., teacher, lawyer) ◯ Business-related ◯ Freelancer ◯ Other:
5. How familiar are you with board games (e.g., Monopoly, Mahjong)?
   ◯ Very unfamiliar ◯ Unfamiliar ◯ Neutral ◯ Familiar ◯ Very familiar
6. How often do you play board games?
   ◯ Almost never ◯ Once every 3 years ◯ Once a year ◯ Monthly ◯ Weekly

A.2 Knowledge Test

1. Which gate of Suzhou Ancient City is known as "The First Wu Gate"?
   ◯ Pan Gate ◯ Xu Gate ◯ Chang Gate ◯ Qi Gate ◯ I don't know
2. Which street is known for ancient stone roads and traditional residences?
   ◯ Shantang Street ◯ Pingjiang Road ◯ Guanqian Street ◯ Shiquan Street ◯ I don't know
3. What does the Pingjiang Map depict?
   ◯ All street layouts ◯ Major streets ◯ Gates and canals ◯ No street layout ◯ I don't know
4. Who led the constrction of Shantang Street?
   ◯ Li Bai ◯ Bai Juyi ◯ Liu Yuxi ◯ Su Shi ◯ I don't know
5. Which dynasty does the Humble Administrator's Garden belong to?
   ◯ Song ◯ Yuan ◯ Ming ◯ Qing ◯ I don't know
6. Which historical figure is Taohuawu associated with?
   ◯ Fan Zhongyan ◯ Wen Zhengming ◯ Tang Bohu ◯ Wu Zixu ◯ I don't know

B Post-experiment Questionnaire

Table 2. Measure Items

Measure	Factor	Item	Question
System Usability	Culture Experience	CE1	I gained new understanding of Suzhou's traditional culture.
		CE2	This game increased my interest in Suzhou culture.
	Rules Comprehension	RC1	Game rules were clear and easy to understand.
		RC2	Rules were effectively implemented during the play.
	Visual Design	VD1	I liked the overall visual style (e.g., ink wash + flat illustrations).
		VD2	Color usage helped me understand the game (e.g., land/water paths, factions).
		VD3	Visual elements (e.g., characters, props, maps) were highly recognizable.
User Experience	Pragmatic Quality	PQ1	Obstructive–Supportive
		PQ2	Complicated–Easy
		PQ3	Inefficient–Efficient
		PQ4	Confusing–Clear
	Hedonic Quality	HQ1	Boring–Exciting
		HQ2	Not interesting–Interesting
		HQ3	Conventional–Inventive
		HQ4	Usual–Leading edge
User Engagement	Focused Attention	FA1	I was immersed and forgot the surroundings.
		FA2	Time flew by while playing.
		FA3	I was fully focused on the game.
	Perceived Usability	PU1	I felt frustrated while playing.
		PU2	The rules were complex and hard to understand.
		PU3	The game was demanding.
	Aesthetic Appeal	AE1	The game's visual design attracted me.
		AE2	The aesthetics were appealing.
		AE3	Visual elements (illustrations, layout) were enjoyable.
	Reward Factor	RW1	Playing this game was worthwhile.
		RW2	I learned something meaningful.
		RW3	I'm interested in this game.

References

1. Ball, B.L.: Marketing video games to aging demographics: a generational profile analysis. Thesis (2024)
2. DaCosta, B., Kinsell, C.: Serious games in cultural heritage: a review of practices and considerations in the design of location-based games. Educ. Sci. **13**(1), 47 (2022)
3. Design council: the double diamond: 15 years on. design council archive (2019), https://www.designcouncil.org.uk/our-resources/archive/articles/double-diamond-15-years. Accessed 10 Jun 2025
4. Engelstein, G., Shalev, I.: Building Blocks of Tabletop Game Design: an Encyclopedia of Mechanisms. Crc Press (2022)
5. Huang, H., Ng, K.H., Bedwell, B., Benford, S.: A card-based internet of things game ideation tool for museum context. J. Ambient. Intell. Humaniz. Comput. **12**(10), 9229–9240 (2021)
6. Laugwitz, B., Held, T., Schrepp, M.: Construction and evaluation of a user experience questionnaire. In: HCI and Usability for Education and Work (2008)
7. Lew, C., Saville, A.: Game-based learning: teaching principles of economics and investment finance through monopoly. Int. J. Manage. Educ. **19**(3), 100567 (2021)
8. Li, Q., Wang, P., Liu, Z., Zhang, H., Song, Y., Zhang, Y.: Using scaffolding theory in serious games to enhance traditional chinese murals culture learning. Comput. Animation Virt. Worlds **35**(1), e2213 (2024)
9. Li, Y., Li, Y., Liang, J., Liang, H.N.: Easy induction: a serious game using participatory design. In: International Conference on Computer-Human Interaction Research and Applications, pp. 192–211. Springer (2023)
10. Liu, Z., Chen, D., Zhang, C., Yao, J.: Design of a virtual reality serious game for experiencing the colors of dunhuang frescoes. Heritage Sci. **12**(1), (2024)
11. Lu, Z., Tan, P., Ji, Y., Ma, X.: The crafts+ fabrication workshop: Engaging students with intangible cultural heritage-oriented creative design. In: Proceedings of the 2022 ACM Designing Interactive Systems Conference, pp. 1071–1084 (2022)
12. Malegiannaki, I., Daradoumis, T., Retalis, S.: Using a story-driven board game to engage students and adults with cultural heritage. Int. J. Game-Based Learn. (IJGBL) **11**(2), 1–19 (2021)
13. Mortara, M., Catalano, C.E., Bellotti, F., Fiucci, G., Houry-Panchetti, M., Petridis, P.: Learning cultural heritage by serious games. J. Cult. Herit. **15**(3), 318–325 (2014)
14. Neale, H., Nichols, S.: Theme-based content analysis: a flexible method for virtual environment evaluation. Int. J. Hum Comput Stud. **55**(2), 167–189 (2001)
15. Orlenko, M., et al.: The specificity of the restoration and monument protective measures for the preservation of historical chinese gardens. Int. J. Conserv. Sci. **12**(3), 1003–1026 (2021)
16. O'Brien, H.L., Cairns, P., Hall, M.: A practical approach to measuring user engagement with the refined user engagement scale (ues) and new ues short form. Int. J. Hum Comput Stud. **112**, 28–39 (2018)
17. Schrepp, M., Hinderks, A., Thomaschewski, J.: Design and evaluation of a short version of the user experience questionnaire (UEQ-S). Int. J. Interact. Multimedia Artif. Intell. **4**(6), 103–108 (2017)
18. Van der Velden, M., Mörtberg, C., Van den Hoven, J., Vermaas, P.E., Van de Poel, I.: Participatory design and design for values. Development **11**(3), 215–236 (2014)

19. Wu, Y., Liu, C., Liang, H., Cui, R.: Sustaining traditional clothing styles and cultural heritage: a multiple case analysis approach. Fashion Pract. 1–31 (2025)
20. Xu, N., et al.: Heritagesite ar: design and evaluation of a mobile augmented reality exploration game for a chinese heritage site. ACM J. Comput. Cult. Heritage **17**(4), 1–29 (2024)
21. Xu, N., Liang, J., Shuai, K., Li, Y., Yan, J.: Heritagesite ar: an exploration game for quality education and sustainable cultural heritage. In: Extended Abstracts of the 2023 CHI Conference on Human Factors in Computing Systems, pp. 1–8 (2023)
22. Ye, L., Wang, R., Zhao, J.: Enhancing learning performance and motivation of cultural heritage using serious games. J. Educ. Comput. Res. **59**(2), 287–317 (2021)
23. Zhou, Y., Liu, J.: The predicament of suzhou embroidery: implications of intangible cultural heritage in china. TEXTILE **22**(2), 400–417 (2024)

LibreVibPen: Enhancing Stylus Interaction with Real-Time Haptic Feedback on Large Touch Screens

Shengsheng Jiang, Jian He(✉), Rongqi Cao, Yifan Zhen, and Yiheng Pan

Beijing University of Technology, 100 Pingleyuan, Chaoyang, Beijing, China
jianhee@bjut.edu.cn

Abstract. To address the suboptimal user experience in large-screen stylus interaction caused by the lack of haptic feedback, we introduce LibreVibPen, a fully integrated hardware–software system designed to enhance the writing experience in large-screen handwriting scenarios through vibrotactile feedback. The system comprises a wireless stylus embedded with thin-film force-sensitive resistors (FSRs), a six-degree-of-freedom (6-DOF) inertial measurement unit (IMU), linear resonant actuators (LRAs), and a neural network for real-time vibrotactile feedback synthesis. The vibration waveform generation is based on an enhanced Differentiable Digital Signal Processing (DDSP) framework tailored for haptic rendering. The wireless stylus can collect the user's writing parameters (normal force, velocity, acceleration) in real time, generate the corresponding vibration waveform, and provide virtual texture haptic feedback through the linear resonant actuators. The objective indicators, including MSE loss, waveform and spectrum similarity, together with subjective user experiments where 11 participants rated their user experience with 6 tasks, verify that the system can accurately collect the user's touch interaction state in real-time, and improve the user's sense of touch operation position, reality and immersion through virtual haptic vibration waveform rendering.

Keywords: Virtual haptics · Vibrotactile · Pen-based interaction · Human-computer interaction

1 Introduction

Touch screens represent one of the most intuitive and accessible modalities for human-computer interaction (HCI). During user interaction, the system captures touch-related parameters such as contact position, movement trajectory, and velocity, which are then transmitted to the computing system to enable responsive, real-time interaction. In recent years, large-format touch displays have seen widespread adoption across domains such as public information systems, collaborative workspaces, and interactive exhibitions. Consequently, the functional expectations and performance demands placed on these systems have grown significantly.

S. Guo et al. (Eds.): HHME 2025, CCIS 2878, pp. 210–225, 2027.
https://doi.org/10.1007/978-981-92-3991-7_15

The stylus is a widely adopted input modality for interacting with large-format touch screens, particularly in applications such as electronic whiteboards and collaborative work environments. With ongoing technological advancements, modern styluses have incorporated features such as pressure sensitivity and tilt detection to enhance user experience. However, in real-world usage scenarios, persistent issues — such as lack of feedback during writing or drawing — continue to degrade interaction quality. These limitations stem from multiple factors, one of the most prominent being the absence of haptic feedback. The inherently smooth surface of touch screens provides very limited tactile cues, resulting in a diminished sense of control and realism during stylus-based input. Previous studies have shown that haptic feedback can provide diverse feedback information during interaction [1] and can significantly improve user interaction experience and task execution efficiency [2]. Integrating haptic feedback into the stylus writing process has the potential to enhance spatial precision and improve the overall quality of user interaction on touch screens. By delivering tactile cues, users can better perceive contact location and movement dynamics, resulting in a more natural and immersive writing experience.

Recently, researchers worldwide have proposed a wide range of technical approaches for reproducing haptic sensations in digital environments. For instance, mechanical vibrotactile [3], pneumatic tactile [4], and electrotactile [5] feedback mechanisms. When individuals perceive vibrations, they are sensing the mechanical motion or vibrational state of external objects, rather than directly experiencing the intrinsic sensation of touch itself. Consequently, compared to other tactile modalities—such as electrotactile feedback—mechanically driven vibrotactile stimulation is often considered a more natural and perceptually realistic method of conveying tactile information. This approach is widely employed to simulate physical properties such as surface texture, material hardness, and contact dynamics in interactive systems [3].

To address the suboptimal user experience in large-screen stylus interaction caused by the lack of haptic feedback, the present study proposes LibreVibPen. Its core concept is as follows: a stylus embedding thin-film force sensors and a six-degrees-of-freedom (6-DOF) inertial sensor captures the user's normal force, velocity, and acceleration parameters in real time when writing on a large touchscreen; these parameters are transmitted to a PC via low-energy Bluetooth. Based on the received writing parameters and the touchscreen contact coordinates, the PC generates vibration waveforms using an enhanced DDSP algorithm [6], then transmits the waveform data back to the wireless stylus via stereo FM modules. The stylus drives its voice-coil actuators according to the received waveform data to deliver high-resolution vibrotactile feedback to the user.

The main contributions of this work are as follows:

1) **Hardware design of LibreVibPen.** We developed a wireless stylus integrating 5 force-sensitive resistors (FSRs), a 6-DOF inertial sensor, Bluetooth Low Energy (BLE) peripheral, Frequency modulation (FM) radio receiver modules, and linear resonant actuators (LRAs). Through optimized mechanical design, the stylus maintains form factors comparable to a standard whiteboard marker. Sensor data are transmitted via BLE, vibrotactile waveforms are received and amplified via FM, and the absence of physical wiring to the touchscreen enables unencumbered, freehand writing—even during experimental trials.

2) **Novel DDSP-based haptic rendering.** We introduce a modified DDSP architecture [6] into the haptic rendering pipeline, designing an end-to-end neural algorithm that synthesizes vibrotactile waveforms. The model takes the stylus's normal force, velocity, and acceleration vectors as inputs and, combining deep learning with time-frequency domain joint encoding–decoding, generates tactile feedback signals in real time.
3) **Prototype implementation and evaluation.** Through hardware–software co-design, we implemented a vibrotactile feedback prototype system and conducted experiments. Results show that LibreVibPen's simulated vibration waveforms for whiteboard, wood, and paper textures closely match the corresponding waveforms and spectra in the HaTT haptic database (MSE < 0.08). Additionally, tests with eleven participants across six whiteboard writing scenarios demonstrate that the device's vibrotactile feedback significantly enhances user satisfaction during large-screen interactions.

2 Related Work

Styluses provide an intuitive, efficient, and effortless interaction interface for touchscreens—especially large-format touchscreens—and are therefore widely adopted. However, existing stylus devices generally exhibit weak active haptic feedback capabilities, which degrade the overall touch interaction experience. To address this, researchers have attempted to enhance interaction by actively delivering haptic feedback through the stylus during touchscreen use. For example, Bence and Yasemin et al. designed a haptic stylus capable of rendering multimodal textures on a touchscreen by modulating the amplitude and frequency components of the voltage applied to the screen's conductive layer to convey surface roughness and friction, while simultaneously controlling the voice-coil actuator within the stylus to simulate object compliance [7]. Ayumu et al. developed the Transtiff pen, which alters its stiffness via artificial-muscle contraction at a joint segment, thereby influencing users' perception of material rigidity and improving the interaction experience [8].

Moreover, researchers have explored stylus-based haptics to enhance interaction in virtual reality tasks. Hesham et al.'s VRSketchPen uses pneumatic force feedback to emulate the contact pressure of the pen on virtual surfaces, and vibrotactile feedback to simulate surface textures encountered during pen movement, thereby improving drawing accuracy and reducing error in VR shape creation [9]. Philipp et al. associated stroke texture and color with distinct thermal properties in the ThermalPen for 3D sketching by integrating cooling and heating elements at the pen tip; their experiments demonstrated a significant enhancement in users' virtual sketching experience in 3D VR environments [10].

Previous work has enhanced the stylus-based human–computer interaction experience from various perspectives. However, several limitations remain—for instance, the feedback generated is often static or pre-rendered, lacking variation; it is also frequently uncorrelated with the stylus's dynamic motion state. Moreover, it is worth noting that some approaches require users to maintain fixed or constrained postures during use; in many cases, prototype styluses rely on wired connections, which restrict the movement of the pen and may impose a non-negligible impact on the user's interaction experience.

3 Methods

3.1 Stylus Hardware Design

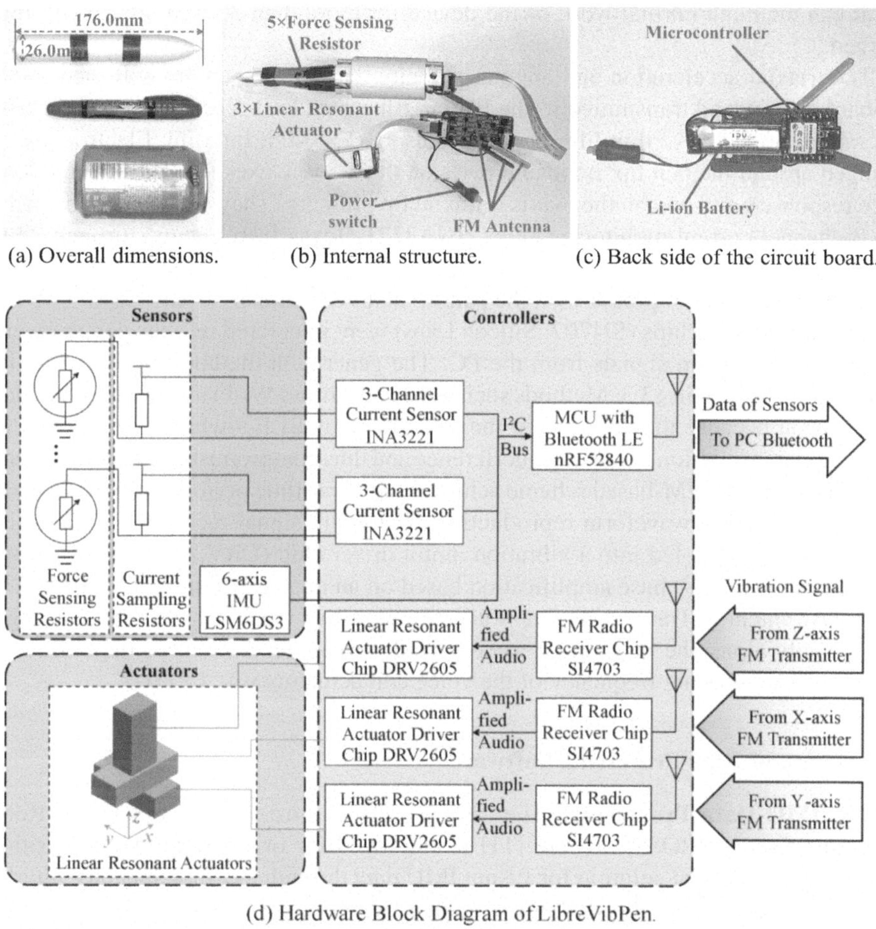

Fig. 1. LibreVibPen hardware.

The structure of LibreVibPen hardware is shown in Fig. 1 (a), and the whole is 3D printed from PLA material, with a total length of 176.0 mm. The main body is cylindrical with a diameter of 26.0 mm, and the overall weight is 70.0 g, comparable to the form factor of a standard whiteboard marker.

A control circuit board, illustrated in Fig. 1 (b) and Fig. 1 (c), is integrated within the stylus housing to acquire pressure, velocity, and acceleration data during writing, and to drive the actuators for vibration generation. The system's hardware block diagram is shown in Fig. 1 (d). A micro development board (XIAO nRF52840 Sense, Seeed Studio) is used as the main controller. The microcontroller is integrated with Bluetooth Low Energy (BLE) 5.0 peripherals, a 6-DOF IMU (LSM6DS3TR-C, STMicroelectronics), and the necessary power management circuit is integrated, while maintaining a small size of 21.0 mm × 17.8 mm × 2.9 mm. The system is powered by a rectangular lithium polymer battery (501235 T, 3.7 V/150 mAh, Zhongshunxin technology) power supply, and it can maintain normal work of the device for more than 30 min after being fully charged.

The triaxial acceleration and angular velocity data of the pen are collected by the onboard sensors and transmitted to the PC via Bluetooth Low Energy (BLE) at a nominal rate of 86 Hz. Five thin-film pressure sensors (FSR400, Interlink Electronics) are arranged around the pen tip: opposing pairs on the x and y axes (providing directional force response), and one on the z-axis for axial tip pressure. They are each connected to two 3-channel current monitoring chips (INA3221, Texas Instruments) through 22 Ω, 0.1% shunt resistors, and then connected to the main control board through the I2C bus to measure the value of pressure on the pen tip in all directions.

Three FM radio chips (Si4702, Silicon Labs) were integrated into the pen to receive vibrotactile waveform signals from the PC. The generation method of these vibration signals is introduced in §3.3. Methods such as Bluetooth and Wi-Fi are not used for audio transmission because they operate in the same band as BLE—which is employed for sensor data transmission—causing interference and thus compromising transmission stability. However, the FM-based scheme achieves high real-time performance while maintaining high-quality waveform reproduction. The audio signal received by each radio chip (~90mV$_{RMS}$) is fed into a vibration motor driver chip (DRV2605L, Texas Instruments) after 11.0x in-phase amplification based on an operational amplifier (LMV321, Texas Instruments). Three miniature voice coil actuators (ELV1411A, AAC) arranged orthogonally along the x, y, and z axes were driven to generate three dimensions of vibration. The resonant frequency of the voice coil actuators was 150 Hz.

3.2 Design of Data Processing Software

6-DOF IMU Data Processing. The `imu_filter_madgwick` package in Robot Operating System (ROS) software [11] is employed for orientation data acquisition. It provides an efficient solution for fusing IMU data through a complementary filtering approach. At its core lies the Madgwick gradient descent complementary filter algorithm [12], which reduces noise and corrects sensor drift by minimizing the error between the measured gravity vector and the orientation estimated from accelerometer data. The fundamental principle involves constructing an error function based on acceleration measurements and iteratively updating the orientation quaternion via gradient descent. The iterative update formula is as follows:

$$q_{t+1} = q_t + \dot{q}_\omega \Delta t - \beta \frac{\nabla F(q_t)}{\|\nabla F(q_t)\|} \tag{1}$$

where $\dot{q}_\omega$ represents the quaternion derivative obtained from the gyroscope integration, ∇F is the gradient of the error function, and β is the filtering gain. For our strong real-time requirement, a higher $\beta = 0.10$ is used to improve the real-time performance.

Processing of Pressure Data. The pressure sensor's current overall is directly proportional to the pressure. The pressure-current curves of the five film pressure transducers are shown in Fig. 2. In the actual conversion, the least square method was used to linearly fit the curve of each sensor. Using the fitted curve to calculate the pressure from the current, the formula is as follows:

$$F_i = k_i I_i + b_i \tag{2}$$

where F_i is the calculated pressure value of the ith sensor, I_i is the current through the ith sensor, and k_i & b_i represent the slope and longitudinal intercept of the fitting curve of the ith sensor, respectively. Each R^2 value of the fitting curve of sensors is not less than 0.96.

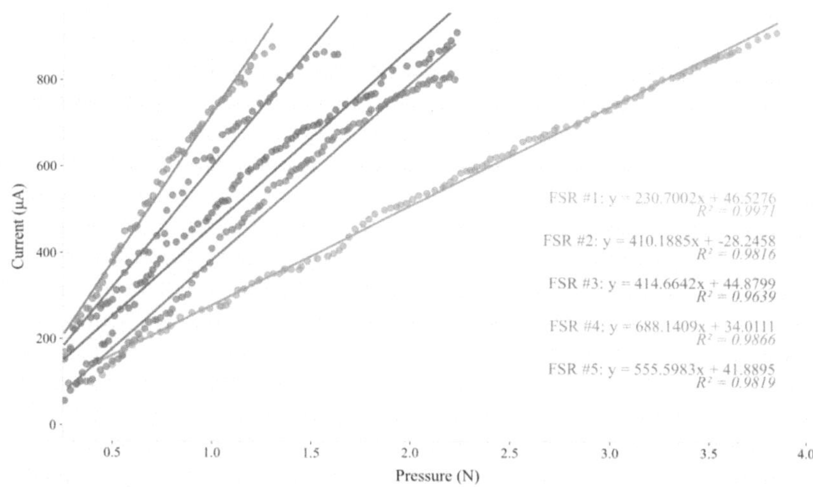

Fig. 2. Scatter plots and linear fitting of pressure–current data for the 5 FSRs.

Using the orientation estimated by the Madgwick filter introduced above, the measured 3D pressure vector is transformed into a global coordinate frame. This decouples the pressure from the pen's instantaneous orientation, enabling its decomposition into grip/posture-invariant tangential and normal components. Consequently, the system achieves attitude-independent pressure interpretation for natural, unconstrained writing akin to a conventional pen.

Generation of Vibrotactile Feedback. The PC uses the haptic vibration rendering model introduced in §3.3 to synthesize the vibration signals from the processed data. The signals are then output to 3 Frequency modulation (FM) transmitting chips (Si4713, Silicon Labs) via the 3 audio output interfaces of the Sound card (Sound Blaster X4, Creative). FM transmission is performed on three non-broadcast frequencies that are widely spaced. The 3 frequencies used in this paper are listed in Table 1.

Table 1. Selected 3 frequencies for FM vibration transmission

Axis	Radio Frequency (MHz)
x	102.3
y	107.5
z	92.3

3.3 Haptic Vibration Rendering Model

To enhance the writing experience for stylus users, we implement a haptic vibration rendering model based on Differentiable Digital Signal Processing (DDSP), a framework pioneered by Engel et al. [6]. This model utilizes real-time sensor inputs—normal pressure, velocity, and acceleration—captured by the pen hardware described in Sect. 2.1. These inputs drive the synthesis of vibration waveforms for Linear Resonant Actuators (LRAs), producing realistic tactile sensations that emulate various writing materials. Crucially, the directional information contained in the velocity and acceleration parameters enables the model to render anisotropic haptic textures, thereby capturing direction-dependent surface characteristics.

Our architecture employs DDSP that uniquely integrates neural network expressivity with the transparency and modularity of classical digital signal processing. By embedding traditional DSP components (e.g., synthesizers, filters) as differentiable modules within the neural network, DDSP has demonstrated remarkable efficacy in audio applications, including sound synthesis [6], voice anonymization [13], and singing voice conversion [14–16]. While neural vocoders like MelGAN [17] and HiFi-GAN [7, 18] have been explored for vibration synthesis, their computational complexity results in significant inference overhead that may challenge system responsiveness requirements. In contrast, DDSP offers an architecturally efficient alternative and provides higher inference efficiency. Nevertheless, its application to vibrotactile waveform generation remains comparatively underexplored, a gap this work addresses through a subtractive synthesis approach [19]. This method synthesizes a harmonically rich source signal (e.g., an ideal impulse train or sawtooth waveform) and dynamically sculpts it into the target vibration profile using a neural network-controlled filter kernel that selectively attenuates spectral components based on the real-time sensor inputs, efficiently generating nuanced tactile signatures necessary for realistic texture simulation.

In this paper, an ideal pulse train is used as the excitation signal of DSP, which can be expressed as a series of equal-interval superpositions of pulses. An ideal pulse train with fundamental frequency f_0 has the following Fourier expansion:

$$s(t) = f_0 \sum_{k=-\infty}^{+\infty} e^{j2\pi k f_0 t} \tag{3}$$

To synthesize the vibration waveform, a time-domain excitation signal is transformed into the frequency domain by the Short Time Fourier Transform (STFT). Then the frequency domain is multiplied element-wise with a filter kernel deduced by the neural network, and the waveform is converted into the time domain by the inverse transform (ISTFT).

The waveform synthesis implementation draws reference from the open-source project DDSP-SVC [20] and has been adjusted and optimized to suit the real-time requirements of vibrotactile rendering.

To enable realistic haptic rendering of the writing surface on a stylus interface, it is essential to utilize authentic tactile texture data for model training. Among the available datasets, HaTT [21] and LMT [22] are widely recognized for their comprehensive coverage of surface textures. Given our requirement for data that includes spatial tracking information, we ultimately adopt the HaTT dataset to evaluate and validate the proposed tactile texture rendering approach. The database contains 100 distinct texture images across 10 categories, along with 10 kHz-sampled recordings of normal force, position, velocity, and vibration acceleration acquired during a 10 s, natural traversal of each surface [21].

In terms of training data preprocessing, the original data with a sampling rate of 10 kHz is upsampled to 44.1 kHz, and the data set is extended in the form of a sliding window by referring to the data processing method in Chen et al. s' work [17], and the time domain data is divided into 44032 (86 $\times$ 512) sampling points with a length of 998.46 ms. On the basis of the sliding window method described in [17], the data is further enhanced by reversing and adding no more than 1% random amplitude white noise to the time domain data, so as to improve the robustness and generalization ability of the model.

The Mean Squared Error (MSE) is used as the loss function. The formula for calculating the MSE between the generated waveform y and the source waveform s is as follows:

$$MSE = \frac{1}{N}\sum_{n=1}^{N}(y[n] - s[n])^2 \tag{4}$$

The network was trained on a PC with an Intel Xeon Gold 6314 U CPU, Nvidia RTX4080 Super GPU with 16GB Video RAM, and 192GB memory. The hyperparameters used for training are shown in Table 2.

Table 2. Haptic vibration waveform rendering model training hyperparameters

Hyperparameters	Value
Initial learning rate	0.0002
Batch size	48
Number of training steps	200,000
Learning rate scheduler	StepLR [23]
Learning rate scheduler decay coefficient γ	0.50

4 Experiments

4.1 Evaluation of Haptic Rendering Algorithm Effectiveness

In this experiment, the model's applicability for synthesizing vibrotactile waveforms is assessed in detail using multiple objective metrics.

For **fidelity evaluation of rendered vibration feedback waveforms,** we specifically selected three representative textures that correspond to large-format writing surfaces commonly encountered in real-world environments, illustrated in Fig. 3. The MSE loss, time domain waveform similarity, and spectral similarity are used to evaluate the fidelity of the synthesized vibration waveform. These indicators collectively provide a comprehensive understanding of the model's ability to reconstruct the essential features of the original waveforms during synthesis.

(a) Book. (b) Whiteboard. (c)Wood.

Fig. 3. Three materials from the 100 in the HaTT dataset commonly used as large-area writing surfaces.

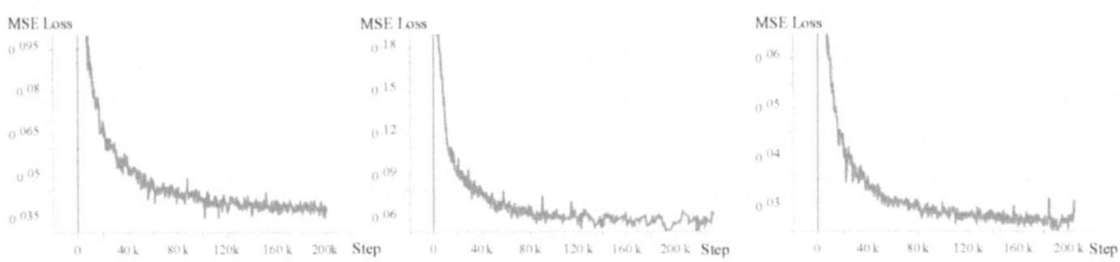

(a)Book. (b)Whiteboard. (c)Wood.

Fig. 4. MSE loss variation during training of the vibration waveform rendering network on the HaTT dataset for different materials.

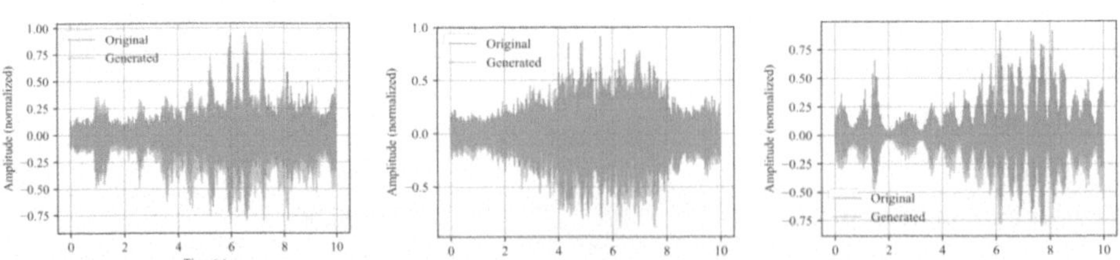

(a)Book. (b)Whiteboard. (c)Wood.

Fig. 5. Time-domain comparisons between the synthesized and original vibration waveforms for different materials using the vibration waveform rendering network.

Figure 4 presents the MSE evolution on the validation set during training. The results show that for all three texture datasets, there exists a certain training step after which the MSE stabilizes at a low level not exceeding 0.06. Furthermore, for each texture, the optimal LOSS weights recorded during training and the final weights after the full 200,000 training steps are used to verify the results on the respective validation sets, and MSEs never exceed 0.08.

Figure 5 compares the source and generated waveforms of three virtual textures in the time domain. Figure 6 compares the source spectra and the generated waveform spectra in the frequency domain for the three virtual textures. It can be seen that both comparisons demonstrate good similarity. In summary, it can be considered that the proposed model demonstrates strong effectiveness in feedback waveform synthesis.

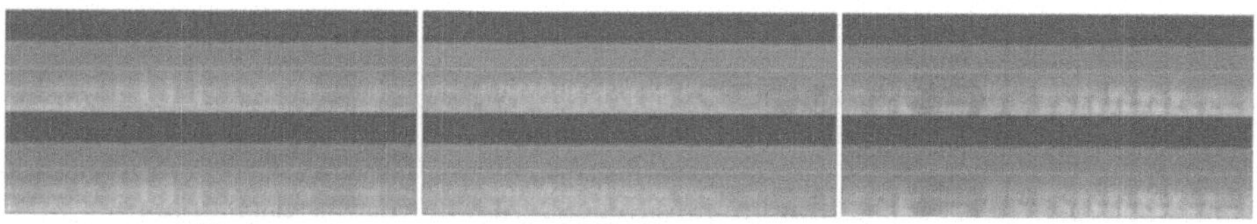

(a)Book. (b)Whiteboard. (c)Wood.

Fig. 6. Frequency-domain comparisons between the synthesized and original vibration waveforms for different materials. The top row shows the spectra of the original waveforms, and the bottom row shows the spectra of the synthesized waveforms.

Figure 7 briefly illustrates the measured end-to-end system delay via an oscilloscope capture. The top trace depicts the synchronization pulse from the pen device, marking the onset of sensor data collection. The lower trace corresponds to the vibration motor output.

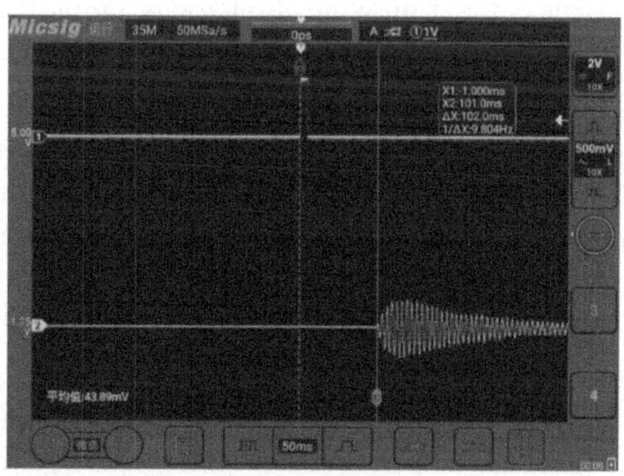

Fig. 7. Illustrative measurement of end-to-end system latency via oscilloscope.

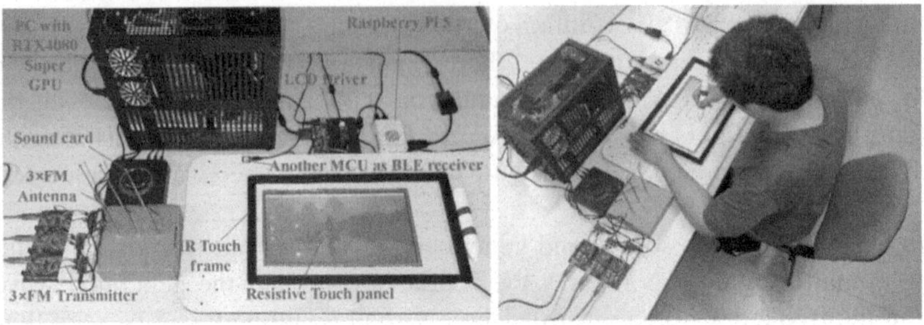

(a)Experimental device setup. (b) Participant performing tasks on the device.

Fig. 8. User experimental setup.

4.2 User Perception Experiment

The purpose of this experiment is to evaluate the ability of the system to enhance the user's interactive experience through the subjective feelings of the participants.

The experimental environment is shown in Fig. 8. A 14.0 in. LCD display (B140XW01, AUO) is used as a writing surface, a resistive touch screen (14.0 in., Greentouch) and an infrared touch frame (18.5 in., Yijing touch) is also used to capture the nib coordinates in the process of writing.

1) Due to the limitations of the individual touch input devices, several challenges must be addressed to ensure accurate detection of the stylus tip:
2) When light pressure is applied, the resistive touch screen may not be triggered. Requiring users to exert additional force to activate it would affect the naturalness and consistency of handwriting during experiments.

To address these issues, the following strategy is employed to ensure reliable estimation of the pen tip position:

1) Primary reliance is placed on the coordinates provided by the resistive touch screen.
2) If no coordinates are detected from the resistive screen, the system queries the infrared touch frame. If valid coordinates are available, the system uses the most recent coordinates from the resistive screen and adds the relative movement reported by the infrared sensor to estimate the current pen position. And if no valid coordinates are available from either device, the pen is considered to have left the screen.

A Raspberry Pi (Model 5, Raspberry Pi Foundation) running the 64-bit Raspberry Pi OS operating system was used to output a video signal containing the test task for the subject to view while collecting the pen tip coordinates from two touch interfaces. Each subject's writing process was recorded as a video for saving.

Table 3. The writing tasks subjects were asked to complete using the stylus. Each set of tasks was performed once without vibration feedback and once with.

Task No.	Task content	Duration (s)
1	Draw rectangles clockwise and counterclockwise, respectively	30
2	Draw circles clockwise and counterclockwise, respectively	30
3	Transcribe English text ("The quick brown fox jumps over the lazy dog")	50
4	Facsimile English text ("The quick brown fox jumps over the lazy dog")	90
5	Transcribe the Chinese character text (Consists of 12 Chinese characters)	70
6	Facsimile single Chinese character "Yong" (shown in Fig. 9, renowned for encapsulating the fundamental brushstroke components found throughout the Chinese writing system)	50

In this paper, six task categories were designed for whiteboard writing scenarios (see Table 3), and eleven participants (6 males and 5 females; mean age = 23, SD = 0.94; all right-handed with unimpaired haptic function) performed experiments on these six tasks. During the experiment, each subject wore a noise-canceling headset playing white noise to eliminate auditory interference. Upon completion of the experiment, each participant received a CNY 30.00 compensation reward.

Fig. 9. The Chinese character "Yong." Each color-coded region corresponds to a distinct stroke component of the character.

After each set of tasks, participants were asked to fill out a one-line seven-point Likert scale to rate their feelings about writing in that task. The title of the scale was: "In the group of tasks just completed, I think the writing experience in the second half of the task was better". Users can choose from a scale of 1 to 7, with 1 representing the least consistent and 7 representing the most consistent. The final average score of each task is shown in Table 4.

Table 4. Subjective rating scale scores for each set of tasks

Task No.	Average score	Standard deviation
1	4.72	1.68
2	5.09	1.51
3	5.55	1.04
4	4.91	1.30
5	5.27	1.10
6	5.64	1.28

5 Discussion

In 4.1, the mean square error (MSE) and the waveform and spectrum similarity between the generated waveform and the source waveform of the model on the HaTT dataset are used to verify the performance of the virtual haptic vibration waveform rendered by the system.

In 4.2, the 7-level Likert scale of consistency, after 11 subjects completed 6 types of writing and drawing tasks, showed that the average score of writing experience under the condition of vibration feedback was increased by 1.20 points compared with that without vibration. Moreover, although structured texture tests were not conducted, participants still spontaneously reported that differences in vibrotactile characteristics were perceptible, and that their sense of localization and tactile realism during writing were significantly enhanced, with immersion notably improved. It can be seen that the proposed system can significantly improve the interaction performance and user satisfaction of the stylus on the large-size touch screen.

Compared with some existing works, our proposed device and method have the following characteristics, which make it superior to previous works:

1) **Untethered operation.** This liberates users from cable constraints during writing.
2) **Multi-axis pressure sensing.** This accommodates natural pen-holding postures without requiring specific device orientations.
3) **On-the-fly haptic synthesis via DDSP.** The algorithm based on the DDSP framework generates dynamic feedback from sensor streams, complementing core functionality with responsive tactile cues.

This study has limitations including: (1) Potential domain gap between training data (HaTT) and our device, affecting novel material generalization; (2) Homogeneous virtual textures in testing; (3) GPU dependency conflicting with miniaturization goals; (4) Validation limited to 14-in. displays; (5) Latency (102 ms) approaching perceptibility thresholds of the perceptible range (60-105 ms) identified for stylus tasks [24–26]. Future work will expand datasets, diversify textures, deploy models on embedded NPUs, verify scalability on larger screens, and reduce latency.

6 Conclusion

In this paper, we propose LibreVibPen, an integrated hardware–software system designed to enhance user interaction on large-area touchscreens. Firstly, a pen-like device with a similar size and weight to the mainstream stylus is designed, and a film pressure sensor and a 6-DOF IMU are integrated into the device to collect feedback on multi-dimensional haptic parameters such as normal pressure, velocity, and acceleration during writing. Secondly, the vibration waveform rendering neural network model based on the differentiable Digital Signal Processing (DDSP) framework and end-to-end learning was combined to render the haptic texture vibration feedback of the virtual writing surface. The method's effectiveness was verified through two avenues: algorithmic performance evaluation and subjective user studies, demonstrating that the system meets its design goal of improving stylus-based interaction on large-format touchscreens.

LibreVibPen remains at the prototype stage. Although we deliberately minimized device volume and optimized its ergonomic form factor during development, there is substantial room for improvement both in hardware miniaturization and in computational efficiency. Future work will focus on refining the device's external and internal design—integrating advanced ergonomic principles to align its size, weight, and battery life with current commercial styluses—to further elevate the user experience in large-scale touchscreen applications.

Acknowledgments. This work was supported by the National Key Research and Development Plan under Grant 2020YFB2104400.

Disclosure of Interests. On behalf of all authors, the corresponding author states that there is no conflict of interest.

References

1. Sun, Z., Zhu, M., Shan, X., Lee, C.: Augmented tactile-perception and haptic-feedback rings as human-machine interfaces aiming for immersive interactions. Nat. Commun. **13**, 5224 (2022)
2. Hoggan, E., Brewster, S.A., Johnston, J.: Investigating the effectiveness of tactile feedback for mobile touchscreens. In: Proceedings of the SIGCHI Conference on Human Factors in Computing Systems, pp. 1573–1582. ACM (2008)
3. Liu, S., He, J., Jiang, S., Zhang, Z., Lv, M.: MatStick: changing the material sensation of objects upon impact. Virtual Reality Intell. Hardware. **6**, 486–501 (2024)
4. Gohlke, K., Sattler, W., Hornecker, E.: AirPinch–an inflatable touch fader with pneumatic tactile feedback. In: Proceedings of the Sixteenth International Conference on Tangible, Embedded, and Embodied Interaction, pp. 1–6. ACM (2022)
5. Zhou, Z., Yang, Y., Liu, J., Zeng, J., Wang, X., Liu, H.: Electrotactile perception properties and its applications: a review. IEEE Trans. Haptics. **15**, 464–478 (2022)
6. Engel, J., Hantrakul, L., Gu, C., Roberts, A.: DDSP: differentiable digital signal processing. arXiv preprint (2020). https://arxiv.org/abs/2001.04643
7. Kodak, B.L., Vardar, Y.: FeelPen: a haptic stylus displaying multimodal texture feels on touchscreens. IEEE/ASME Trans. Mechatron. **28**, 2930–2940 (2023)

8. Ogura, A., Ito, K., Yoshida, S., Tanaka, K., Itoh, Y.: Transtiff: haptic interaction with a stick Interface with various stiffness. In: ACM SIGGRAPH 2023 Emerging Technologies, pp. 1–2. ACM, Los Angeles CA USA (2023)
9. Elsayed, H., et al.: VRSketchPen: unconstrained haptic assistance for sketching in virtual 3D environments. In: In: 26th ACM Symposium on Virtual Reality Software and Technology, pp. 1–11. ACM, Virtual Event Canada (2020)
10. Hoffmann, P.P., Wehbe, R.R., Mühlhäuser, M., Barrera Machuca, M.D.: ThermalPen: investigating the influence of thermal haptic feedback for creativity in 3D sketching. In: Creativity and Cognition, pp. 661–673. ACM, Chicago IL USA (2024)
11. Stanford Artificial Intelligence Laboratory et al.: Robotic Operating System. https://www.ros.org. Accessed 02 Aug 2025
12. Wilson, S., et al.: Formulation of a new gradient descent MARG orientation algorithm: case study on robot teleoperation. Mech. Syst. Signal Process. **130**, 183–200 (2019)
13. Ghosh, S., et al.: Anonymising elderly and pathological speech: voice conversion using DDSP and query-by-example. In: Interspeech 2024, pp. 4438–4442 (2024)
14. Wu, D.-Y., et al.: DDSP-based singing vocoders: a new subtractive-based synthesizer and a comprehensive evaluation (2022). http://arxiv.org/abs/2208.04756
15. Nercessian, S.: End-to-end zero-shot voice conversion using a DDSP vocoder. In: 2021 IEEE Workshop on Applications of Signal Processing to Audio and Acoustics (WASPAA), pp. 1–5. IEEE, New Paltz, NY, USA (2021)
16. Agrawal, P., Koehler, T., Xiu, Z., Serai, P., He, Q.: Ultra-lightweight neural differential DSP vocoder for high quality speech synthesis. In: ICASSP 2024–2024 IEEE International Conference on Acoustics, Speech and Signal Processing (ICASSP), pp. 10066–10070. Seoul, Korea, Republic of, IEEE (2024)
17. Chen, D., Chen, G., Liu, J., Fang, Y., Zhang, Y.: A study on texture haptic reproduction based on texture images and user motion information. J. Instrum. (Yiqi Yibiao Xuebao). **45**, 145–154 (2024)
18. Kong, J., Kim, J., Bae, J.: HiFi-GAN: generative adversarial networks for efficient and high fidelity speech synthesis (2020). http://arxiv.org/abs/2010.05646
19. Hayes, B., Shier, J., Fazekas, G., McPherson, A., Saitis, C.: A review of differentiable digital signal processing for music and speech synthesis. Front. Sig. Process. **3**, 1284100 (2024)
20. Yxlllc: Real-time end-to-end singing voice conversion system based on DDSP (DDSP-SVC). https://github.com/yxlllc/DDSP-SVC. Accessed 02 Aug 2025
21. Culbertson, H., Lopez Delgado, J.J., Kuchenbecker, K.J.: One hundred data-driven haptic texture models and open-source methods for rendering on 3D objects. In: 2014 IEEE Haptics Symposium (HAPTICS), pp. 319–325. IEEE, Houston, TX, USA (2014)
22. Strese, M., Brudermueller, L., Kirsch, J., Steinbach, E.: Haptic material analysis and classification inspired by human exploratory procedures. IEEE Trans. Haptics. **13**, 404–424 (2020)
23. Krizhevsky, A., Sutskever, I., Hinton, G.E.: ImageNet classification with deep convolutional neural networks. Commun. ACM. **60**, 84–90 (2017)
24. Deber, J., Jota, R., Forlines, C., Wigdor, D.: How much faster is fast enough?: user perception of latency & latency improvements in direct and indirect touch. In: Proceedings of the 33rd Annual ACM Conference on Human Factors in Computing Systems, pp. 1827–1836. ACM, Seoul Republic of Korea (2015)

25. Forch, V., Franke, T., Rauh, N., Krems, J.F.: Are 100 ms fast enough? Characterizing latency perception thresholds in mouse-based interaction. In: Harris, D. (ed.) Engineering Psychology and Cognitive Ergonomics: Cognition and Design, pp. 45–56. Springer International Publishing, Cham (2017)
26. Annett, M., Ng, A., Dietz, P., Bischof, W.F., Gupta, A.: How Low Should We Go? Understanding the Perception of Latency While Inking. In: Kry, P.G., Bunt, A. (eds.) Graphics Interface 2014, pp. 167–174. A K Peters/CRC Press (2020)

VR/AR and Natural Human–Computer Interaction

My-Meetings: LLM-Based Multi-agent Conference Scene Designer

Xi Cheng and Guihuan Feng(✉)

Nanjing University, Nanjing, China
fenggh@nju.edu.cn

Abstract. The realization of virtual reality and Meta-verse products relies on 3D virtual scenes with rich function and diverse layouts. Especially in the interior design domain, acquisition threshold of construction tools and tedious manual adjustments of considerable amounts of furniture pieces create a need for simpler and more efficient scene construction methods. Automatic 3D scene generation or reconstruction from images or videos is still experimental, often resulting in models with detail loss. Meanwhile, aligning personal expectations with data-driven training is challenging due to the exclusion of user involvement in the generation process. In this context, we present My-Meetings, an interactive natural-language-driven system to make interior scene generation accessible and controllable. My-Meetings uses a pipeline of large language model agents to identify and extract layout details from user text input, then converts them into structured scene designs using asset retrieval and logical reasoning. Furthermore, interpretable dialogues between agents allow users to recognize and freely adjust generation process. We choose to focus on virtual conference rooms for their salient functional layout features. My-Meetings excels in delivering feasible 3D conference scenes that maintain user conceptual consistency. Extensive user experimentation has showcased its spatial fidelity, diversity and customizability in both quantitative and qualitative measures.

Keywords: LLMs · Text-to-3D · 3D indoor scene synthesis

1 Introduction

Conference and Meeting [1] refer to a series of multi - participant negotiation activities held around a specific theme. Against the backdrop of the increasing prevalence of remote collaboration and communication, an independent meeting room scenario that enables multi - user online interaction has become a crucial requirement. This need is particularly urgent when dealing with time and space constraints, especially in response to emergencies such as natural disasters, public health incidents, and regional conflicts. Existing technical solutions mainly rely on video - based online meeting systems. However, re-search has found that this simple two - dimensional interaction method easily causes users to feel fatigued [2], reducing their concentration and work efficiency.

To address this issue, Virtual Reality (VR) technology offers a solution based on three - dimensional virtual scenarios. The research center of Facebook has revealed

S. Guo et al. (Eds.): HHME 2025, CCIS 2878, pp. 229–256, 2027.
https://doi.org/10.1007/978-981-92-3991-7_16

the divide between video conferencing and natural communication through experiments [3]. Different from traditional video conferencing, participants in a virtual meeting room can perceive the depth and three - dimensionality of the space and interact with other participants in real - time, which is closer to human communication in natural situations. This immersive experience transforms a meeting from merely images and sounds on a screen into a vibrant and interactive three - dimensional space.

3D virtual meeting rooms also break the geographical and time limitations of traditional meetings, enabling team members from around the world to gather in a virtual space via the Internet. Regardless of their locations, participants can enter the same virtual meeting room for real - time communication and collaboration. This borderless communication method not only reduces travel costs but also avoids the troubles caused by time zones, making meetings more flexible and efficient.

To achieve the above effects, virtual meeting rooms require highly customized meeting scenarios to match different meeting themes, such as office meetings, education and training, social gatherings, etc. Existing relatively mature user products overlook this issue. For example, Meta Horizon Workrooms [4] can only offer a limited number of alternative meeting room design schemes.

Currently, the personalized construction of virtual meeting room scenarios remains underexplored, attributable to three major challenges: (1) Vast scene space. Meeting rooms can host from a dozen in a seminar to hundreds in a studio. High user numbers imply larger space and more furniture. Insufficient space restricts interaction, causing discomfort and undermining the scenario's realism. (2) Structured item layout. Items in meeting rooms are regularly arranged with obvious, extractable layout features. (3) Strong layout - functional linkage. Table - chair layouts correspond to meeting functions, with significant differences across function types. Inappropriate layouts hamper user experience and re-duce scenario usability.

Manual scene building with tools like Houdini, Maya, or Blender is traditional. But for virtual meeting rooms, manual modeling has drawbacks. Modeling tools are hard to learn, and adjusting abundant furniture is cumbersome. Repetitive furniture makes manual arrangement tedious and time - consuming. Even professional designers face high costs preparing multiple layouts. Thus, users need a more user - friendly and efficient scene - building approach.

In the field of 3D Indoor Scene Synthesis (3DISS) [5], many methods have been explored to address the virtual meeting room construction problem discussed in this paper. Automatically generating or reconstructing 3D scenes from images or videos is still in the experimental stage and usually results in the loss of model details. Meanwhile, due to the lack of user participation in the generation process, it is challenging to align personal expectations with data - driven training. Such studies attempt to synthesize virtual scenes using various automated algorithms [6, 7]. However, users have their own preferences when choosing and arranging indoor objects, and fully automated generation methods struggle to fully incorporate users' diverse requirements for meeting room scenarios, failing to ensure user satisfaction with the generated results. Incorporating user preferences into the construction process of virtual meeting room scenes poses challenges.

Large Language Models (LLMs), typically referring to AI models with billions or more parameters such as GPT, possess stronger fitting and generalization capabilities compared to traditional machine learning. They can capture complex relationships and patterns in data and handle tasks across different domains without specialized training [8]. More importantly, their language comprehension enables them to handle natural language processing tasks with personalized requirements. Existing research has utilized LLM technology for 3D indoor scene generation [9]. However, due to issues like token limitations and hallucinations that affect output quality, LLMs are only used as design guidance in part of the generation process, not as an end - to - end solution.

In the field of large models, Agent's technology, namely Intelligent Agents or Agents technology, can perceive or parse external inputs, iteratively interact with the environment in multiple rounds, and improve decision - making results through computational reasoning [10]. Some research takes advantage of the highly interactive nature of agent technology to split the task of 3D scene construction into multiple agent - based processes for collaborative completion [11]. However, the design with a single piece of furniture as the scene granularity makes it difficult to ensure generation accuracy in large - scale scenarios, such as virtual meeting rooms with multiple participants.

Therefore, we propose My - Meetings, a user - friendly virtual meeting scene generation system based on LLM multi - agents. The system consists of an LLM - supported multi - agent pipeline. First, it identifies and extracts the details included in the input text, and then transforms them into a structured scene design through asset retrieval and logical reasoning. We have designed unique layout constraints for virtual meeting room scenes, enabling agents to better understand and design complex meeting room scene layouts. In addition, we introduce natural language interaction between agents and users into the iterative generation process. The interpretable additional text provided by agents helps users understand the generation process and control the generation effect.

We conducted user experiments to confirm that My - Meetings is proficient in providing reliable 3D virtual meeting room scenes. Under the premise of maintaining consistency with user concepts, it demonstrated its spatial fidelity, layout diversity, and customizability from both quantitative and qualitative aspects.

Our contributions are summarized as follows:

1. Designing a generation process and scene expression method that converts natural language input into virtual meeting room scenes, offering users a personalized experience of customizing meeting room layouts.
2. Designing and completing a multi-agent-based collaborative system, My - Meetings, and conducting experiments to verify the advantages of this system in terms of the generation efficiency and quality of virtual meeting room scenes.
3. Reflections on interactive design elements in iterative scene generation using natural language and LLMs.

2 Related Work

2.1 Three - Dimensional Indoor Scene Synthesis

The process of a typical 3DISS problem [5] consists of two distinct stages: 3D asset selection and layout synthesis. The latter involves determining the combination of furniture in an indoor space and their spatial arrangements.

In the 3D asset selection stage, mainstream methods rely on dataset - based retrieval. For example, semantic embedding techniques [12] are used to retrieve well - matched models from the asset dataset. Another strategy is to generate the required 3D models from text or image inputs [13, 14], yet generalization ability is usually limited by the size of the training dataset. Given that the fidelity of models in virtual meeting rooms affects users' perception of the overall scene, we adopt a retrieval - based approach, carefully selects, and constructs a 3D asset database to meet specific requirements.

In the layout placement synthesis stage, traditional strategies involve using specific placement rules to restrict furniture placement [15, 16]. Additionally, some research uses conditional grammars to perform procedural or parametric modeling of scenes [17–19]. There are also studies that attempt to utilize users' editing interaction behaviors to assist in generation [20–22].

With the maturity of machine learning technology, some studies have chosen to use prior probability to synthesize indoor scenes. Some works [23, 24] infer the probability distribution of spatial relationships from natural language text and context semantics. Other studies [25] learn the 3D distribution of item placement based on existing spatial scenes. In addition, a study [26] expands the dimensions of prior probability by using scene - related information such as activity types and flow paths, improving the accuracy and practicality of the synthesis results.

Recent research progress has started to adopt generative models to learn prior knowledge from expert - designed layouts. Typical works such as ATISS [6] and SceneFormer [27] use models based on the Transformer architecture to learn the implicit positional relationships between objects and autonomously synthesize indoor environments through an autoregressive process, selecting and placing objects one by one. LEGO - NET [28] learns the regularity criteria of manual layouts through a similar diffusion process and then gradually optimizes the initially given random layout.

The rise of deep learning has prompted the research focus to gradually shift towards neural networks constrained by scene relationship graphs, representing indoor scenes as scene graphs containing hierarchical and positional relationships [29–31]. Recent studies such as Instructscene [32] and Commonscenes [33], based on scene graph representation, utilize the generative capabilities of diffusion models, focusing on room functionality while satisfying various user - defined constraints.

However, the above - mentioned layout placement strategies face challenges such as complex scene representation and high learning costs when dealing with meeting room scenes containing a large number of items. In response, we propose a discrete planar constraint method similar to a scene graph, which improves the representation efficiency while maintaining layout diversity and is suitable for the scene representation of virtual meeting rooms concerned in this paper.

2.2 Scene Generation Based on Diffusion Models

Significant progress has been made in the text - to - shape generation field. Relying on the generalization ability of diffusion models and driven by training data, such methods first generate multi - view continuous image sets or panoramic views according to user - defined categories, and then convert these 2D representations into 3D scenes. Representative works like LucidDreamer [34] and Text2Room [35] use virtual cameras to generate navigation indexes for the space and iteratively generate images and scenes through steps such as monocular depth estimation, 3D lifting, and stitching. Although these methods achieve 2D image generalization with diffusion models and can generate diverse and realistic 3D scenes, they still have difficulties in integrating 3D constraint relationships such as solid walls and floor plans. Also, they usually struggle to generate objects not included in the training dataset.

In addition, MVDiffusion [36] designed a correspondence - aware attention module, which can construct multi - view consistent panoramic image sets in a single generation. The methods used in other works focusing on harmonious new view synthesis [37, 38] are also applicable to the field of indoor scene synthesis. However, the loose semantic coupling across multiple views often causes the generated results to deviate from the constraints of the target semantic of synthesis, reducing authenticity and immersion [39]. The method proposed in this paper is driven by a large model and can meet various context generalization conditions, including meeting room types, overall atmosphere, and item styles, while maintaining reasonable geometric constraints.

2.3 Scene Synthesis Based on Large Language Models

Large Language Models (LLMs) have started to exert a significant impact on the traditional indoor scene synthesis field, although the related applications between LLM technology and scene synthesis have not been fully explored. Some early synthesis methods adopted integrated LLM modules, encoding user textual input into vector representations and leveraging this information during subsequent object placement processes [40].

LayoutGPT [41] made the first attempt to exclusively employ the GPT model in the synthesis process. It placed objects through a retrieval strategy based on absolute coordinates to generate 3D indoor scene representations. AnyHome [9] improved this research by proposing an open - vocabulary, dataset - free method. The challenge commonly faced by such methods is that, at the current stage, GPT models have limited geometric reasoning capabilities, often resulting in object overlap or objects being outside boundaries.

In this paper, for the scene selection of virtual meeting rooms, we introduce a method based on Large Language Models (LLMs), complemented by a constraint - enhanced multi - agent framework. The aim is to improve the scale and complexity of indoor scene layouts while maintaining controllability and fidelity.

3 Method

The virtual meeting room layout design process proposed based on users' natural language input is shown in Fig. 1. The LLM multi - agent pipeline consists of three parts: meeting room information extraction, item retrieval, and layout generation. The information extractor (introduced in Sect. 3.1) first processes the unrestricted text descriptions from users to determine the category of the meeting room and other layout - related information. The item retriever (introduced in Sect. 3.2) retrieves suitable items from the item asset library based on these parameters to form a list of items for use. Then the layout generator (introduced in Sect. 3.3) calculates and designs the meeting room

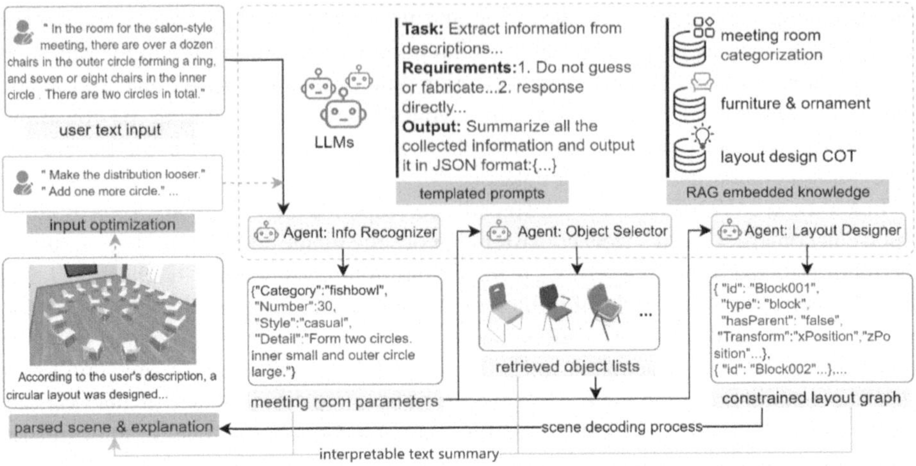

Fig. 1. System process. Given users' natural language descriptions, the LLMs system generates 3D meeting room scenes as follows: (i) identify the meeting room type and extract relevant attributes; (ii) retrieve suitable items based on these attributes; (iii) compute and generate a layout under given constraints, then instantiate the scene; (iv) iteratively optimize the design using 3D scene experience and interpretable text

layout and an explanatory text to help users understand the layout using relevant parameters and the item list. Users can modify the corresponding text description based on the roaming experience of the actual 3D space and the scene explanation to optimize the scene layout.

The scene construction pipeline involves multiple agent - based proxies, each of which plays a different role in the overall construction process. We use template prompt engineering to help agent - based proxies define their responsibilities and functions and guide them to generate interpretable structured outputs as required. The final output of the pipeline is an ensemble that includes the source file of the meeting room scene, a 3D rendered view supporting multi-view browsing, and interpretive explanations (such as communication logs among multi-agent-based proxies). This ensemble serves multiple purposes, such as checking each stage of the multi - agent pipeline and making modifications or reconstructions when necessary.

Simultaneously, we adopted the Retrieval-Augmented Generation (RAG) technique [48]. By integrating RAG with an embedded vector knowledge base [49], our agent can acquire detailed knowledge required for classification, retrieval, and design reference tasks. This approach not only reduces the probability of the Large Language Model generating inaccurate and hallucinatory responses, enhancing output stability and rationality, but also cuts down the cost of fine - tuning the model when expanding relevant knowledge, improving development efficiency. In terms of the retrieval method, we chose a hybrid retrieval mode, combining vector - based retrieval and keyword - based retrieval to balance the retrieval needs of semantic understanding and precise search. Meanwhile, we re-ranked the search results [50], and recalled the three most relevant slices. This improves the accuracy and relevance of RAG results while meeting the token - volume limit of the model input.

The LLMs pipeline used in this paper is built upon the ChatGLM - 4B - Plus [51] and ChatGLM - Embedding3 models. The following are more detailed information about the multi - agent of the intelligent agent.

3.1 Agent: Information Recognizer

The information recognizer, the first LLM agent in the multi - agent pipeline, receives users' natural language input, analyzes and extracts parameter information. It then passes these parameters to the next agent in a prescribed interface format. Parameters to be extracted include: basic meeting room category, number of participants, meeting room style, and layout feature description. The basic meeting room category is inferred by classifying users' natural language input. The temperature and top_p parameters of the agent are set to 0.1 and 0.3 respectively to enhance the output stability and accuracy.

Basic Meeting Room Types

Facing the characteristics of large spaces and numerous objects in virtual meeting rooms, directly extracting or predicting the coordinates of objects from natural language descriptions requires complex algorithm implementation. The unstructured and grammar - unconstrained nature of natural language also leads to a decline in the accuracy and effectiveness of the extracted information.

To understand the characteristics of users' natural language descriptions of meeting room layouts, we conducted preliminary user interviews (6 participants, with a 50–50 gender ratio and an average age of 25). They were asked to describe the scenes of real - world meeting rooms in words. The results show that users' layout requirements for virtu-al meeting rooms have strong categorical and functional characteristics, such as "This is a classroom for teaching" and "This meeting room is suitable for scenarios like academic re-ports and product launches". Therefore, if the functional type of the required meeting room is first determined based on users' functional or detailed descriptions, and then corresponding layout cases are matched according to the layout characteristics of different types of meeting rooms, the information extracted from natural language can be utilized more efficiently, making coordinate and layout generation easier.

After researching conference room types [52, 53], we've summarized six basic layout types covering most needs (see Fig. 2). Their layout cases and features are:

Fishbowl. Composed of multiple circular structures with a centripetal topology. Suited for salons and discussions, as the short distance between participants, per social space theory, fosters close interaction.

Classroom. Features strict row - column alignment, ideal for knowledge - transfer events. All seats face a podium, and paired desks aid note - taking.

Auditorium/Theater. Resembles the classroom type but without tables. From a space - planning view, it's fit for large - scale formal meetings like performances and product launches. Seats face the stage, ensuring good views by visual perception, with low interactivity matching the event nature.

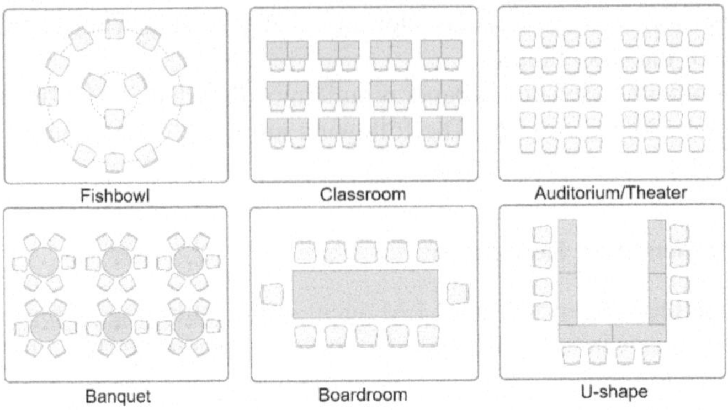

Fig. 2. Six basic types of meeting rooms' layout

Banquet. A distributed layout of round tables like the fishbowl type. Mainly for large - scale events such as parties and annual meetings. Each table is an independent communication unit, and close - range seating gives strong group cohesion.

Boardroom. Characterized by a long - strip table with evenly spaced seats. Meeting small - scale or decision - making needs in space organization, its short user distance aids face - to - face communication following interpersonal - communication principles.

U - Shape Type/Horseshoe. Similar to the boardroom type, but with a U - shaped table. Functionally suitable for group meetings and seminars. The U - shape center is a visual focus for projection, etc. In terms of interactivity, it promotes team communication, being more space - inclusive than the boardroom type for more participants.

Knowledge Base of Conference Room Categories

After identifying basic conference room categories, we built a reference knowledge base for the information recognizer agent. We surveyed 52 users (average age 20) via questionnaires, asking them to describe real - world pictures of specific - category conference rooms. After processing these natural - language descriptions— filtering, splitting, and data augmentation—we converted them into key - value pairs (category and description). This yielded 1.8 k valid records for the conference room type description knowledge base.

Furthermore, when analyzing the slices in the knowledge base, we found that users' descriptions sometimes leaned towards information unrelated to the layout, such as the appearance of specific furniture and style decorations in the conference room, like unexpectedly present flower pots, fans, and floor - to - ceiling windows. To avoid such information from causing hallucinatory interference in subsequent layout generation, in the prompt - engineering process, we specifically required the information recognizer agent to extract only the key layout - related descriptions from the input text and summarize the style into simple categories, thereby simplifying the task difficulty of subsequent layout generation.

3.2 Agent: Object Selector

The object selector agent receives the conference room attribute parameters provided by the information extractor and, based on these parameters, retrieves suitable items from the model asset library to form a group of candidate items for the layout generator to select from. To meet the model requirements of various types and styles of conference rooms, we collected over 60 sets of table and chair models for virtual 3D conference rooms, including common tables and chairs in six basic types of conference rooms, thus forming our 3D asset library. Each model has been normalized to unify the unit of its bounding - box measurement, simplifying the computational difficulty in the layout generation step. Similarly, the temperature and top_p parameters of the agent are set to 0.1 and 0.3 respectively to re-duce the probability of hallucinations during the retrieval process.

Knowledge Base of Item Attributes
In the process of normalizing the model asset library, a tabular representation was adopted to record diverse model attributes, which were then segmented to construct an item - model attribute knowledge base. Model attributes encompassed three - dimensional bounding - box attributes, applicable meeting rooms' category, and item style. Within the prompt - engineering framework, it was explicitly stipulated that precedence be given to the matching of category attributes. This approach was designed to enhance the credibility and realism of generated scenes.

3.3 Agent: Layout Designer

The layout designer agent, a key component in the entire LLM multi - agent pipeline, generates conference room layouts based on the conference room parameters and candidate item groups provided by preceding agents, following the scene - graph constraint form we designed. To enhance generalization ability for diverse user needs, the agent's temperature and top_p parameters are set to 0.3 and 0.5 respectively, making the layout generation more diverse and flexible. The generation results will be output in a strictly prescribed format to ensure correct decoding.

Hierarchical Constraint Method of Scene Expressions
The understanding and generation of 3D scenes by large models essentially rely on converting objects within a scene into a computable set of layout parameters, namely a digital representation system of the scene. To effectively save token consumption and reduce the computational complexity for large models, this paper designs a scene representation method based on a constrained discretized hierarchical structure: a hierarchical layout rule constraint system is constructed by constraining object groups with similar layout features. To ensure that the constraint rules can meet the layout requirements of the six basic conference room categories defined earlier, the representation method designed in this paper includes three types of constraints. Agents will construct a hierarchical scene graph model based on these three constraints, enabling large language models (LLMs) to process layout details more efficiently and reliably (see Fig. 3).

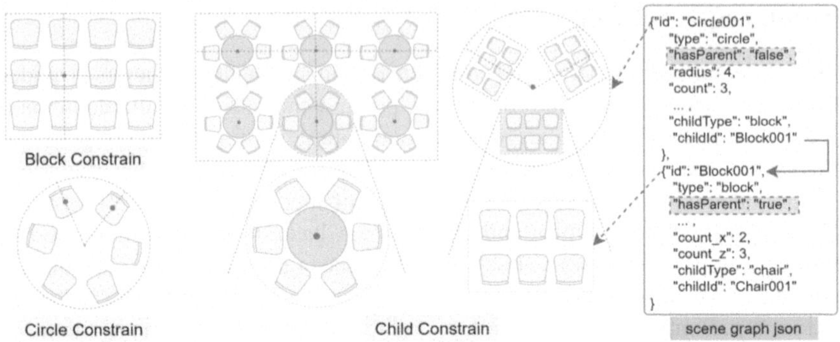

Fig. 3. Three basic layout constraint models. An example json file demonstrates how to determine the reference relationship between parent and child nodes.

Block Constraint. For arranging numerous identical objects regularly. Key params: block coords, rotation angle, row/col. numbers. Objects are arranged in a rectangular area.

Circle Constraint. Fit for circular/ring - shaped object arrangements in conference rooms. Main params: center pos, radius, object capacity. Objects surround a central point.

Child Constraint. Applies when the layout has multiple similar sub - parts with local regular arrangements. Main param is the parent - child relation, indicating block's node type. Sub - block names reference parent block's child nodes, aiding iterative decoding in scene instantiation. Nested parent - child constraints enable complex hierarchical layouts.

By using the above layout constraint rules, a conference room scene layout can be represented as follows: Given unstructured user input T_{user}, the goal is to build a 3D scene G_{scene} that meets the user's layout needs for a virtual conference room, ensuring functionality, design harmony, and consistency. Layout generation aims to construct a set of block-constraint tuples. We define the scene $G_{scene} = \{t_i | \, i = 1, 2, 3, \ldots, n\}$, with an extra tuple $t^{(r)}$ for room node info like dimensions and style. Each tuple t_i shows the boundary layout of a block constraint $t_i = \{a_i, c_i, p_i, s_i, r_i, sub_i\}$, where a_i and c_i are the block's name and category, $p_i \in R^2$ is its position, s_iis its internal structure (e.g., rows/columns, circles, or item dimensions, depending on the block type), and r_i is its rotation angle around the vertical z-axis. The sub-block reference $sub_i = \{a_j, c_j, p_j, s_j, r_j, sub_j\}$ gives the sub-block's boundary layout. Experiments show that for complex scenes like banquet or U-shaped conference rooms, our layout constraints prevent output tokens from exceeding the 8192-token limit, speeding up agent thinking and generation. This advantage is more obvious in scenes with more seats.

Figure 4 shows a comparison between the text scene representation method and traditional methods: the high-dimensional parameter space of digital layouts and the complex relational networks of dense scene graphs lead to computational complexity increasing exponentially with the number of objects. This paper conducts simulated

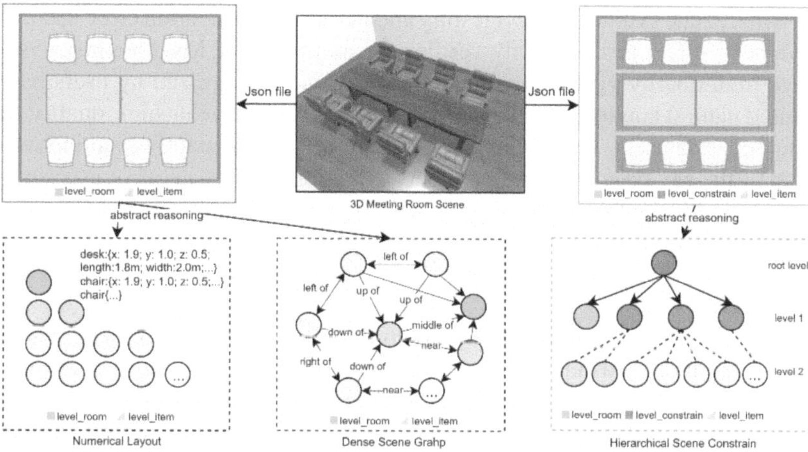

Fig. 4. Comparison of scene expressions based on adjacency graph and hierarchical constraint method

scene representation tests, where the hierarchical constraint representation method significantly outperforms traditional digital layout methods in scene encoding efficiency. Across the overall sample set, average token consumption is only 24.9% of traditional methods, effectively avoiding issues in traditional methods such as token limits being exceeded due to sharp increases in object numbers, large model inference failures, or output interruptions, and ensuring the stability of large model inference processes.

Knowledge Base of Layout Cases

Synthesizing meeting room layouts is a complex process involving the calculation of multiple parameter attributes. We prepared a collection of layout cases for each conference room type and sliced them by case to create a knowledge base for the layout generator. Each case includes input (conference room attributes and candidate item sets), output (scene graph json file), and the corresponding thinking and calculation processes. The thinking process of each case is manually annotated based on the COT (Chain - of - Thought) template [54], including demand analysis, item selection, block division, and parameter calculation parts, aiming to improve the understanding efficiency of slice samples and enhance the output performance of the agent.

In the prompt - engineering process, we specifically require the layout designer agent to generate an additional interpretable text that is easy to understand after completing the task. These texts can help users understand the agent's thinking process and the layout structure of the meeting room scene. Moreover, during the iterative generation process, this text can also serve as a prompt to optimize user descriptions.

4 Experiment

To verify the effectiveness of the multi-agent chain synthesis method and iterative optimization interaction method in the My-Meetings system, this paper designs relevant experiments to evaluate the My-Meetings prototype system. The experiments are divided into two parts: scene synthesis effect testing and iterative optimization effect testing. The scene synthesis effect test primarily verifies the ability of the My-Meetings system to synthesize high-quality virtual conference room scenes recognized by users based on unstructured natural language input, as well as its potential to create high-quality conference room scene datasets. The iterative optimization effect test mainly examines whether the design of the My-Meetings system meets user needs during iterative user optimization, enhancing the usability of user synthesis and modification of virtual conference room scenes.

Baseline Method

The baseline method used in this paper is derived from LayoutGPT [41], which first introduces large models as layout calculation modules into 3D scene generation tasks. The characteristic of this method lies in leveraging the nested features of bounding boxes from a top-down perspective and integrating the expression habits of webpage code CSS styles into scene representation. By supplementing with normalized units and simple prompt descriptions, it achieves indoor scene generation with certain output quality.

Interface and Apparatus

The My - Meetings interface (see Fig. 5) is implemented on the client - side platform using JavaScript technology in the Unity 3D engine. The operations of LLMs for scene generation are implemented on the backend server. The REST API based on Flask is used to connect the frontend and backend subsystems. The PC used in the experiment is equipped with an Intel 14700 k CPU and an NVIDIA GeForce 4070 graphics card, ensuring that users can smoothly observe the decoded and rendered virtual meeting room scenes.

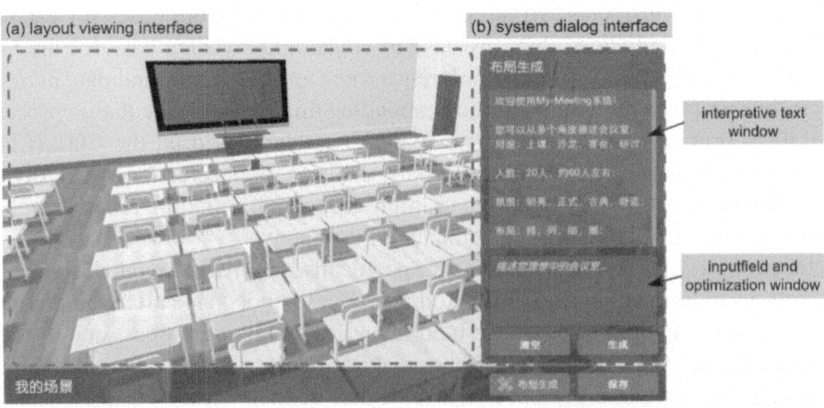

Fig. 5. System Interface. It includes (a) the layout viewing interface, which supports free movement and perspective transformation; (b) the system dialog interface, where interpretable texts can be viewed, and text descriptions can be input and optimized.

4.1 Study 1: Scene Synthesis Quality

The scene synthesis effect test focuses on verifying the quality of scene synthesis, so this experiment is dedicated to the quality verification of single synthesis.

Procedure

Due to the lack of a standard use-case dataset for virtual conference room scenes, this paper screened 1,040 natural language text descriptions of real conference rooms from 52 users through the questionnaire interviews conducted when building the conference room category knowledge base in Chapter 3, and constructed a dedicated test set. Starting from six basic conference room categories, 8 natural language text descriptions were selected for each category to form a 48-input test set. Since only single input is considered without iterative optimization, the test set was screened based on the principle of ensuring information completeness (functions, number of people, and layout). Finally, the layout design of the conference room scene was manually annotated for each text description as a layout distribution validation set.

This paper adopts the objective evaluation indicators used in the baseline method: (1) Overlap Rate (Overlap): Represents the probability of overlap between items, measuring the generation stability of individual layout items; (2) Out-of-Boundary Rate (OOB): Represents the probability of items exceeding the room boundary, measuring the generation stability of the overall layout; (3) KL Divergence (kl_div): Also known as relative entropy, it is used to measure the gap between the item distribution in the generated scene layout and the item distribution probability in the validation set.

In terms of subjective evaluation indicators, based on the indoor digital 3D scene evaluation method proposed in relevant research, this paper summarizes three evaluation indicators: (1) Description Accuracy (ACC): Represents the similarity between the generated result and the text input description; (2) Layout Reasonableness (REA): Includes balance of layout distribution, rationality of traffic flow, activity comfort, etc.; (3) Aesthetic Degree (AD): Includes tidiness, harmony, aesthetic appeal, etc.

The experimental procedure consists of two parts: scene synthesis and result evaluation. In the scene synthesis stage, the prepared test text cases are input, and the output results are decoded into instantiated 3D scenes. In the result evaluation stage, this paper first statistically analyzes objective evaluation indicators based on the instantiated scenes. Additionally, six users (all students with an average age of 22) were recruited. They were first shown the meanings and examples of the selected subjective evaluation indicators, and then evaluated cropped images of 3D conference room scenes based on these criteria (using a 5-point Likert scale).

Considering the impact of conference rooms with different complexity levels on computational reasoning difficulty, the conference rooms were divided into simple (fishbowl and auditorium), medium (classroom and banquet), and complex (boardroom and U-shaped) according to layout complexity during result statistics, making the results clearer and more understandable.

Results

The baseline method uses context learning based on few-shot cases to infer numerical layouts from given examples (see Fig. 6), resulting in incorrect positions and orientations for many objects in the generated layouts. Due to the lack of explicit constraints between objects, overlaps and out-of-boundary issues easily occur (indicated by red and green wireframes). Output interruptions (indicated by blue wireframes) also affect scene integrity. In contrast, the method in this paper does not rigidly imitate sample cases. The design of retrieval enhancement and chain-of-thought enables agents to learn reasoning experiences best matched to requirements and apply them to layout design and calculation, generating more reasonable and feasible scene layouts with more complete output scenes.

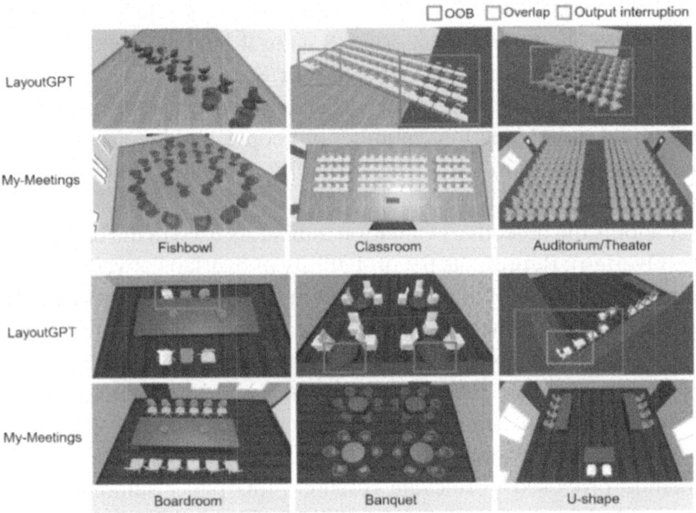

Fig. 6. Synthesis quality results of six basic meeting room types

Table 1. objective result of synthetic quality test. shows the comparison results of objective indicators. In all conference room scene categories, the method in this paper outperforms the baseline method in two aspects: physical feasibility (overlap and out-of-boundary cases) and reasonable relative position placement (KL divergence). In terms of item overlap rate, the method in this paper achieves a 47% improvement in stability compared with the baseline method (average overlap rates of 11.1% and 19.2%, respectively). The baseline method has a higher item out-of-boundary rate, while the independent design of room nodes in the hierarchical constraint representation of this method avoids out-of-boundary issues.

Additionally, in all scenarios, the output process using the baseline method had a failure rate exceeding 10% due to output interruptions (with an average generation time of 72 s), indicating that the inference time or token consumption for most outputs approached or exceeded the upper limit. In contrast, the method in this paper achieved a consistently higher success rate in output results (with an average generation time of 30 s).

Table 2. subjective result of synthetic quality test. shows the comparison results of subjective indicators, where the results of this paper achieved higher scores in all scene categories. The scene accuracy score was relatively higher (average accuracy 4.03,

Table 1. Objective result of synthetic quality test

complexity	Baseline			My-Meetings		
	Overlap(%)	OOB(%)	KL-div	Overlap(%)	OOB(%)	KL-div
simple	11.1	44.4	0.818	5.6	0	0.050
medium	18.7	55.6	0.471	11.1	0	0.120
complex	27.8	77.8	0.119	16.7	0	0.016

Table 2. Subjective result of synthetic quality test

complexity	Baseline			My-Meetings		
	ACC	REA	AD	ACC	REA	AD
simple	1.89	2.11	2.21	4.15	3.78	3.98
medium	2.63	2.40	2.42	4.33	4.23	4.34
complex	2.38	1.81	1.88	3.63	3.33	3.64

$p < 0.05$), indicating that the method in this paper can accurately extract and apply factors such as functional classification, number of people, style, and layout details from natural language descriptions. The layout rationality (average reasonableness 3.78, $p < 0.05$) and scene harmony (average aesthetics 3.98, $p < 0.05$) were also higher, demonstrating that agents can effectively learn layout features from scene examples to generate virtual conference room scenes with higher fidelity.

This paper further analyzes the impact of layout complexity on output results. As layout complexity increases, the system needs to use more blocks to design scene layouts, leading to a higher probability of overlap between blocks. Meanwhile, this paper analyzes users' preferences for subjective evaluation of scenes. When evaluating the quality of generated scenes, users are often stricter in considering layout rationality than description accuracy and scene harmony (with lower comprehensive scores), indicating that improving layout physical feasibility is more important for generating user-satisfactory virtual 3D scenes.

4.2 Study 2: Iterative Optimization Effect

In the scene synthesis result test experiment, this paper found that nearly 20% of the output results failed to meet user satisfaction standards (4 points or above on the 5-point Likert scale) when using the My-Meetings system for single-time scene synthesis. Based on this, an iterative optimization effect test experiment was designed. It is expected to extract practical experience and recommendations for iterative interaction between users and AI systems in the field of 3D scene generation through the experimental results.

Participants

This paper recruited 12 participants (4 females and 8 males, all students with an average age of 21) through campus communities. Before the experiment, each participant submitted a pre-survey on their personal background. Participants were divided into two levels: novices and advanced, based on their experience in conference room layout and 3D engine usage. Participants who rarely attended offline multi-person meetings or lacked experience in conference room layout were classified as novices, while advanced users often undertook conference room layout tasks and were familiar with using 3D engines (such as Unity, UE, etc.).

Procedure

The experiment was carried out in an offline, noise-free environment. First, the re-search background and general situation were introduced to the participants (10 min), and their possible questions were answered. In the tutorial, we explained the operation methods of the user interface and a brief guide for describing conference room layouts.

After the tutorial, we asked the participants to complete two tasks using My - Meeting. In the first task, the participants observed images of real - world conference rooms and used the system to restore the scenes until they considered the generated scenes to match the layout details of the original images (15 min). Each participant was randomly assigned three conference-room scenes for restoration, following an ascending order of complexity: simple, medium, and complex. When judging the success of the task, the participants were required to consider layout conflict types such as out of boundary and overlapped issues [55, 56], so these conflicts were not quantitatively analyzed separately.

In the second task, we only provided a broad functional scenario of a conference room, and the participants were required to describe their ideal conference room layout and conduct free - form design (5 min). The first task corresponded to scenarios with clear layout requirements, aiming to examine the performance of the LLMs system in scenarios of different complexities. The second task, however, enabled us to observe the optimization process of iterative generation.

During the two tasks, we continuously observed the participants' use of the interface. We also asked the participants to think aloud while using My - Meeting to understand their reasons for their reactions.

Finally, we guided the participants to complete the System Usability Scale [57] and the NASA-Task Load Index [58], and conducted a brief interview. We asked about their experiences with My - Meeting, such as how they used the scene generation function, how they iteratively optimized the meeting room description text, and how they would apply My-Meetings to their own work (15 min).

Results

There was a significant difference in task success rate between the baseline method and the method in this paper. The baseline method achieved success rates of only 16.7% and 8.3% for simple and medium layout difficulties, respectively, and all scene syntheses failed for difficult layout difficulties. Notably, 45% (18 out of 40 failed tasks) of all failed tasks ended with users voluntarily giving up and terminating the task during iteration. In contrast, the method in this paper achieved an average success rate of 80% in iterative optimization tests, with the success rate for medium layout difficulty tasks reaching 91.7%, demonstrating stable iterative optimization performance.

Due to the extremely low task success rate of the baseline method and data gaps caused by users' voluntary abandonment of iteration, this paper will focus on the performance of My-Meetings system among users with different proficiency levels in subsequent experimental result analysis, rather than including the baseline method in the analysis scope.

Table 3. Time consumption and iteration count of optimization test

complexity	novices			advanced		
	Average(s)	Total(s)	Iterations	Average(s)	Total(s)	Iterations
simple	68.5	168.5	2.5	65	181.2	2.63
medium	69	110	1.5	63.4	122.6	1.8
complex	66.6	199.8	3	67.4	206.3	3.13
free-design	70.4	147.5	2.25	61	140.4	2.13

In terms of task time and iteration count, this paper excludes system response and generation time, only recording user thinking and input duration (see Table 3). Overall, novices spent more time per iteration (m = 68 s) but used fewer iterations (m = 2.31) compared to advanced users. This indicates novices tended to construct more detailed input texts, allowing the system to synthesize scenes closer to expectations with richer conference room information, requiring fewer iterations. Advanced users preferred more frequent (m = 2.45) and shorter (m = 64 s) iterations, hoping to gain optimization cues from scene feedback and thus needing more attempts. Regarding scene complexity, higher complexity led to more iterations and shorter average optimization time, suggesting users lost patience faster with unsatisfactory results and expected quicker iterative feedback.

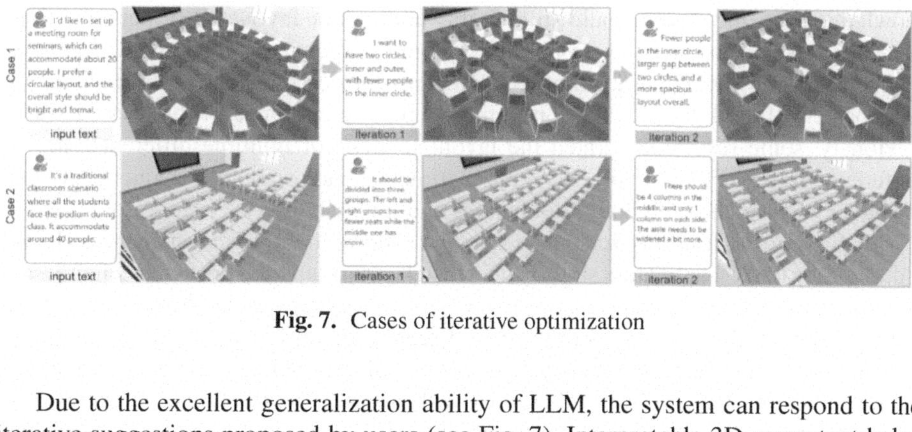

Fig. 7. Cases of iterative optimization

Due to the excellent generalization ability of LLM, the system can respond to the iterative suggestions proposed by users (see Fig. 7). Interpretable 3D scene text helps users understand the agent's thinking preferences, facilitating targeted iterative refinement of descriptions. Figure 7 shows two examples of user - iterative generation results. Whether it is a clear and specific requirement, such as "divided into two circles, inner and outer" in Case 1 and "divided into three groups, left, middle and right" in Case 2; or an abstract adjustment, such as "make the overall layout looser" in Case 1 and "widen the aisles between each group" in Case 2, within the scope of the constraint layout, the system can provide timely feedback. Statistically, 83.3% of single - time iterations can meet the users' optimization requirements for iteration. We also analyzed the 16.7% unsuccessful cases and identified two main causes: First, LLMs occasionally hallucinate in layout design (e.g., irrational components or inconsistent explanatory text), mitigable via prompt engineering or parameter tuning but ineliminable due to inherent generative traits. Second, users may express ambiguous requirements or lack articulation ability—more common initially, but 3D scene explanatory texts later help refine their needs, reducing such failures.

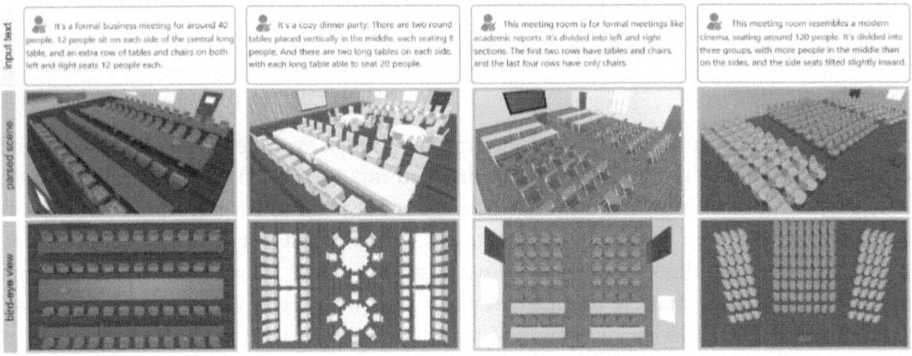

Fig. 8. Cases of participants' successful free-design

Participants demonstrated rich imagination and creativity during the free - design stage. Even when faced with layout requirements with low matching degrees in the knowledge base, the system could still flexibly apply three layout constraint conditions to meet users' needs as much as possible. Figure 8 shows the successful generation results of the free - design task, all of which underwent a certain number of optimization iterations. We found that, in addition to the six basic conference - room types defined previously, some results integrated the layout features of multiple different types of conference rooms. For example, the combination of boardroom and banquet generated a banquet - hall scene with both round tables and long tables.

Analysis of the usability scale (see Fig. 9. a) shows that the reasonableness (REA) and accuracy (ACC) indicators slightly decreased as participants' proficiency increased. This suggests that advanced users, due to their own experience and expertise, were more likely to identify detailed issues in generated scenes, thereby reducing their evaluation of scene credibility and consistency. The emotional experience (EX) and learnability (LNB) indicators had high overall scores with average distributions, indicating that the system performed well in overall user experience and could provide a smooth and

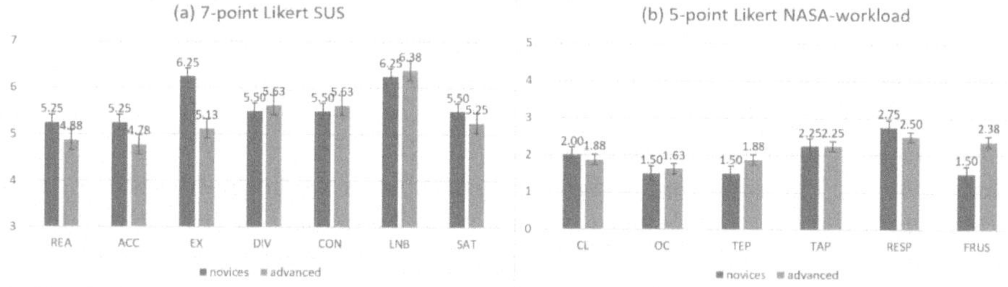

Fig. 9. Results of usability analysis. From left to right are (a) the System Usability Scale and (b) the NASA - Task Load Index. The System Usability Scale is divided into seven score levels, with a higher score indicating a better participant experience on this metric. The NASA - Task Load Index is divided into five score levels, with a lower score indicating a lighter workload for participants on this metric

easy-to-use interaction process for users at different levels. The diversity (DIV) and convenience (CON) indicators increased with users' experience, suggesting that the system can offer more abundant layout options for advanced users and improve the efficiency of completing virtual conference room 3D scene synthesis tasks. Additionally, these two indicators were most closely correlated with the overall satisfaction (SAT) indicator.

Regarding the workload scale (see Fig. 9. b), novice users scored lower on frustration (FRUS) and operational complexity (OC) but invested more effort in responsiveness (RESP) and cognitive load (CL). This indicates that novice users prefer convenient and novel usage experiences, leading to higher tolerance for the system, but the lack of clear psychological expectations or guidance can trap them in decision-making dilemmas. Relatively experienced advanced users performed better than novices in cognitive load required to complete tasks, but higher temporal pressure (TEP) suggests they have higher demands for the system's response performance and are more likely to feel confused and frustrated by the system's hallucinatory outputs.

5 Discussion

Although My-Meetings is currently focused on the scene layout generation of virtual conference rooms, we have summarized experiences and suggestions for the natural-language-based iterative scene generation task, incorporating insights drawn from unstructured interview results. It should be noted that user interview results with the same meaning have been filtered and summarized.

5.1 Generalizing Interaction Based on Natural Language Text

We interacted with LLMs through the medium of natural language and used key-board input to eliminate the impact of repetitive and meaningless colloquial expressions on recognition accuracy. However, using text to describe operations that require layout fi-ne - tuning is a challenge for most users. Participant P3 noted, "For some very precise requirements, if we always rely on verbal descriptions, the process will be extremely cumbersome. In such cases, direct manual dragging is more convenient." We suggest that the design of the scene generation system incorporate some interaction methods for precise regulation to bridge the gap between "almost meeting" and "fully meeting" and enhance the user experience for expert users.

Moreover, the end - to - end design that encapsulates the generation process may affect the sense of control and freedom of some users. Participant P7 provided feedback, "I find it cumbersome and boring to add background and atmosphere information to the conference room. I hope to skip these parts and directly design the meeting room layout." Therefore, for systems that use a classification approach for scene generation, separating individual key attributes from text descriptions and providing users with optional suggestions is a good design idea, enhancing the generalization ability for other types of scenes with diverse attributes.

5.2 Iterative Collaboration Between Human and AI

The iterative generation process based on a dialogue format similar to that with regular LLM can assist users in gradually establishing goal awareness, reducing trial - and - error costs and psychological stress. Participant P6 stated, "Sometimes, I'm not sure about the specific modification direction or how to precisely describe my needs. After multiple modifications, I think it's largely due to my unclear expression of requirements."

In the dialogue format we designed, users can either directly modify the previous descriptive text or directly propose modification suggestions. This format has caused confusion for some users. As Participant P10 said, "I may be uncertain whether to modify the input content or start entering new content. Due to the thinking inertia from previous use of LLM, when I see a dialog box, I naturally expect to conduct continuous and multi - round conversations." Therefore, when designing the dialogue interaction method based on LLMs, it is necessary to pay attention to users' existing dialogue experience and operational inertia to improve the understanding effect of multi - round conversations.

5.3 Limitation and Future Work

In this study, we designed a special expression method for conference-like scenes and conducted quantitative and qualitative investigations into how users generate scenes using My-Meetings. During the experiments, we found that although specific layout constraints can enhance generation efficiency and quality, they struggle to output scenes that deviate significantly from the defined categories, thus limiting the diversity of generation results. Therefore, to generalize such scene expression methods to other categories of scenes, more diverse constraints are required, such as fan-shaped, trapezoidal, or height-difference constraints.

Additionally, the scope of experimental participants is constrained by the recruitment platform, resulting in a homogeneous group (primarily 20-year-old students). While a classification mechanism based on "LLM usage experience" and "3D modeling experience" ensured some user differentiation, the lack of demographics like teachers and designers limits the generalizability of subjective evaluation results—expanding to more professional groups will improve assessment credibility.

Moreover, as our focus was on table and chair layout design, the system still falls short in meeting the granularity of users' target scenes. Key items like monitors, projectors, and podiums (which critically impact conference room functions) require follow-up research. Another limitation is that experiments are limited to conference rooms; our hierarchical scene representation cannot be directly applied to discrete scenes (e.g., bedrooms, living rooms). Notably, existing scene graph-based methods perform well for discrete scenes, and future research will combine our method with these to extend to semi-structured/unstructured scenes, enhancing scalability.

Finally, the temporary asset library used also restricts the embedding dimensionality of the knowledge base. In the future, we plan to explore introducing AIGC technology to integrate item modeling generation and scene synthesis, further enhancing users' sense of control and experience.

6 Conclusions

We introduce My - Meetings, an innovative solution dedicated to solving the challenges of indoor scene synthesis in the fields of virtual reality and the metaverse. Based on interactive natural language and a multi - agent pipeline, the system can accurately identify and extract layout details from users' text inputs. Subsequently, through asset retrieval and logical reasoning, these details are ingeniously transformed into structured scene design schemes. Notably, interpretable texts given by agents endow users with the ability to freely identify and iteratively optimize generation results. Verified by numerous user experiments from both quantitative and qualitative dimensions, My - Meetings system has achieved notable results in generating feasible 3D meeting room scenes, ensuring a high degree of consistency with users' concepts. In the future, we expect to further enhance the system's usability and intelligence by expanding the depth and breadth of natural language interaction, such as integrating multi - modal interaction methods, and contribute more innovative ideas and practical experiences to relevant research domains.

Appendix

Prompt for Information Recognizer Agent

<Role> You are an empathetic meeting room layout requirements consultant. </Role>

<Task> Read the text description provided by the user, analyze the key information with meeting room attributes therein, and output accurate meeting room requirement parameters. The parameters include: meeting room category Category, number of participants Number, meeting room style Style, and layout detail description Detail. </Task>

<Background> A meeting room is an indoor scenario where people conduct work, so-cialize, study, and gather. Different meeting rooms have different categories and functions, and the differences in people's descriptions of meeting rooms determine the different categories and functions of meeting rooms. </Background>

<Task Process>

1. Extract the layout detail description in {{User Input/Conversation}}, focusing on the following keywords, such as: row, column, circle, surround, enclose, face, around, side, etc.

**Note: Do not guess or fabricate layout details not included in {{User Input/Conversation}}. If no obvious layout information is extracted, the value of "Detail" is output as "null". For example, when the input is "a lecture hall that can seat many people", since no obvious layout information appears, the value of "Detail" should be output as "null".

2. Based on {{User Input/Conversation}}, query the data.xlsx file named in the knowledge base. After matching {{Knowledge}} with {{User Input/Conversation}}, extract the most corresponding meeting room type. There are 6 types of meeting rooms, namely: classroom, fishbowl, U-shape, auditorium, huddleBoard, and banquet.

**Note: In the data.xlsx file, the first column "input" represents the user's input description, and the second column "category" represents the corresponding meeting room category. Each row represents the result of a user description corresponding to a meeting room category. Only the information within one row (one "input" corresponding to one "category") is referenced during retrieval.

3. Based on {{User Input/Conversation}}, extract the number of participants corresponding to the meeting room, expressed in Arabic numerals.

**Note: If the input text does not contain the target number of people, start from the possible scale of the meeting room and infer the number of participants. For small - scale meetings, 3–15 people are recommended; for medium - scale meetings, 15–40 people are recommended; for large - scale meetings, 40–150 people are recommended. Generally, U-shape and huddleBoard - type meeting rooms are small - scale; classroom and fishbowl - type meeting rooms are medium - scale; auditorium and banquet - type meeting rooms are large - scale.

4. Based on {{User Input/Conversation}}, extract the style of the meeting room that best matches the description. There are 4 types of meeting room styles, namely: cozy (soft and comfortable), classic (classical and elegant), official (formal and business - like), bright (re-laxed and lively).
5. Summarize all the collected information, output it in json format, and provide an easy - to - understand explanation (excluding specific nouns) for the file content. The output result only needs to include the json file and the corresponding explanation (no more than 100 words), and do not output other irrelevant content. </Task Process>

<Execution Requirements>

1. Do not guess, fabricate, or supplement layout details that do not exist in {{User In-put/Conversation}}.
2. Do not repeat the question. Start answering directly. </Execution Requirements>

<Output Requirements> The json file should contain the following content:

1. "Category" (string type, representing the meeting room type).

2. "Number" (int type, representing the number of participants).
3. "Style" (string type, representing the meeting room style).
4. "Detail" (string type, representing the layout detail description of the meeting room). Here is an example of a json file: {json_schema} </Output Requirements>

Prompt for Object Selector Agent

<Role> You are a professional retrieval agent for meeting room object parameters, proficient in table retrieval. </Role>

<Task>According to a series of input meeting room parameters, match the meeting room item groups corresponding to the parameters from the item database and output the relevant parameters of the items in the required format. </Task>

<Background> Different virtual meeting room scenarios contain items in various styles, and these items with diverse styles jointly constitute the overall style of the meeting room. </Background>

<Task Process>

1. Based on the json - formatted file input {{User Input/Conversation}}, parse the meeting room parameters in the json file, including the meeting room category Category and the meeting room style Style.
2. Based on the parsed meeting room parameters, query the objData.xlsx file in the knowledge base and identify the items {{Knowledge}} that match all the meeting room parameters to form a meeting room item group. The item group may include multiple items, and each item includes the following parameters: item number Id, item type Type, and item dimensions (X - axis dimension X_size, Y - axis dimension Y_size, Z - axis dimension Z_size).
3. Check the found item group and eliminate all items whose Category parameter does not match {{User Input/Conversation}}.
4. Summarize all the collected information and output according to the output requirements. Do not output other irrelevant content.</Task Process>

<Execution Requirements>

1. Do not guess, fabricate, or supplement layout details that do not exist in {{User In-put/Conversation}}.
2. Do not repeat the question. Start answering directly.
3. When Category is Classroom, Auditorium, or Fishbowl, recommend no more than 3 items of the chair type. When Category is U-shape, HuddleBoard, or Banquet, recommend both chair and desk types of items, with no more than 3 items of each type. </Execution Requirements>

<Output Requirements>The output consists of two parts: the thinking process (how to think in each step of the task process), the final output file in json format, and the corre-sponding explanation.

The json file should contain the following content:

1. "Id" (string type, representing the item name);
2. "Type" (string type, representing the item type);

3. "length" (float type, representing the item's X - axis dimension, corresponding to the queried X_size parameter);
4. "width" (float type, representing the item's Z - axis dimension, corresponding to the queried Z_size parameter);

**Here is an example of a json file that conforms to the output for-mat: {json_schema}</Output Requirements>

Prompt for Layout Designer Agent
<Role> You are a meeting room layout designer, proficient in the computational and planning capabilities required for 2D graphic design, and able to design appropriate graphic layouts according to users' layout requirements. </Role>

<Task>Parse the meeting room parameters and item data provided by the user, and then, based on the layout requirements and in combination with cases in the knowledge base, perform fine calculations and design the graphic layout of the meeting room. </Task>

<Background> A meeting room is an indoor scenario where people conduct work, socialize, study, and gather. Meeting rooms of different categories and functions have different arrangements of tables and chairs.

Background knowledge:

1. The meeting room layout consists of individual blocks. There are two basic types of blocks: block and circle. The block type is suitable for square - shaped layout requirements characterized by arrangements, and the circle type is suitable for circular - shaped layout requirements characterized by rings.
2. Parent - child relationships between different blocks can be specified using hasParent. Sub - blocks will participate in the layout rules of the parent module as a whole. </Background>

<Task Process>Judge the user's intention. If the user inputs a piece of data in json format, it is for layout generation; if the user only inputs a piece of text, it is for layout modification.

Task process for layout generation:

1. Extract the meeting room parameters and item data contained in {{User Input/Conversation}}, including the meeting room category Category (string type), the number of participants Number (int type), the meeting room style Style (string type), the layout detail description Detail (string type), and an optional item group ItemGroups. The ItemGroups contains multiple items, and each item has 4 parameters: "Id" (string type, representing the item name), "Type" (string type, representing the item type), "length" (float type, representing the item's size on the X - axis), and "width" (float type, representing the item's size on the Z - axis).
2. When reaching this step, don't rush. Think slowly and systematically. Summarize and learn layout calculation experience rules from {{Knowledge}}. Apply the meeting room parameter Number, layout detail description Detail, and item group ItemGroups parsed in the previous step to these experience rules to design and calculate the meeting room lay-out.

3. Output according to the output requirements and do not output other irrelevant content. </Task Process>

<Execution Requirements>

1. Do not guess, fabricate, or supplement layout details that do not exist in {{User In-put/Conversation}}.
2. Do not repeat the question. Start answering directly.
3. When calculating the layout, don't rush. Think slowly. </Execution Requirements>

<Output Requirements>The output content includes three parts: the thinking process (not less than 500 words), a json file in the correct format, and the corresponding explanation.

The json file should contain the following content:

1. "ItemGroups" (representing an item group).
2. "LayoutGraph" (layout table, representing the specific parameter details of the module).

Here is an example of a json file: {json_schema}
Explanation part requirements:

1. The number of words should not exceed 100.
2. Do not include nouns, internal ids, numbers, or English symbols that ordinary users cannot understand.
3. The content should be consistent with the content of the output json file (do not fab-ricate corridor descriptions when there is no corridor).

**Here are several examples of compliant explanations: {json_schema} </Output Requirements>

References

1. Chen, H, Perich, F, Chakraborty, D, et al.: Intelligent agents meet semantic web in a smart meeting room. In: Proceedings of the Third International Joint Conference on Autonomous Agents & Multi Agent Systems (AAMAS 2004) (2004). Author, F., Author, S.: Title of a proceedings paper. In: Editor, F., Editor, S. (eds.) Conference 2016, LNCS, vol. 9999, pp. 1–13. Springer, Heidelberg (2016)
2. Overload, N.A.: Theoretical Argument for the Causes of Zoom Fatigue. Technology, Mind, and Behavior. (2021) URL: https://tmb.apaopen.org/pub/nonverbal-overload/release/2
3. Abdullah, A., Kolkmeier, J., Lo, V., et al.: Videoconference and embodied VR: communication patterns across task and medium. In: Proceedings of the ACM on Human-Computer Interaction, vol. 5, pp. 1–29. CSCW2 (2021)
4. Abramczuk, K., Bohdanowicz, Z., Muczyński, B., et al.: Meet me in VR! Can VR space help remote teams connect: a seven-week study with horizon workrooms. Int. J. Hum.-Comput. Stud. **179**, 103104 (2023)
5. Zhang, S.H., Zhang, S.K., Liang, Y., et al.: A survey of 3d indoor scene synthesis. J. Comput. Sci. Technol. **34**, 594–608 (2019)
6. Paschalidou, D., Kar, A., Shugrina, M., et al.: Atiss: autoregressive transformers for indoor scene synthesis. Adv. Neural Inf. Proces. Syst. **34**, 12013–12026 (2021)

7. Tang, J., Nie, Y., Markhasin, L., et al.: Diffuscene: Denoising diffusion models for generative indoor scene synthesis. In: Proceedings of the IEEE/CVF Conference on Computer Vision and Pattern Recognition, pp. 20507–20518 (2024)
8. Ma, Y., Yang, Q., Cao, R., et al.: How to understand whole software repository?. arXiv preprint (2024). https://arxiv.org/abs/2406.01422
9. Fu, R., Wen, Z., Liu, Z., et al.: Anyhome: open-vocabulary generation of structured and textured 3d homes. In: European Conference on Computer Vision, pp. 52–70. Springer Nature Switzerland, Cham (2024)
10. Wang, J, Xu, H, Jia, H, et al.: Mobile-agent-v2: Mobile device operation assistant with effective navigation via multi-agent collaboration. arXiv preprint (2024). https://arxiv.org/abs/2406.01014
11. Çelen, A., Han, G., Schindler, K., et al.: I-design: Personalized llm interior designer. arXiv preprint (2024). https://arxiv.org/abs/2404.02838
12. Liu, M., Shi, R., Kuang, K., et al.: Openshape: scaling up 3d shape representation towards open-world understanding. Adv. Neural Inf. Proces. Syst. **36**, 44860–44879 (2023)
13. Liu, M., Xu, C., Jin, H., et al.: One-2-3-45: any single image to 3d mesh in 45 s without per-shape optimization. Adv. Neural Inf. Proces. Syst. **36**, 22226–22246 (2023)
14. Roberts, M., Ramapuram, J., Ranjan, A., et al.: Hypersim: a photorealistic synthetic dataset for holistic indoor scene understanding. In: Proceedings of the IEEE/CVF International Conference on Computer Vision, pp. 10912–10922 (2021)
15. Xu, K., Stewart, J., Fiume, E.: Constraint-based automatic placement for scene composition. Graph. Interface. **2**, 25–34 (2002)
16. Weiss, T., Litteneker, A., Duncan, N., et al.: Fast and scalable position-based layout synthesis. IEEE Trans. Vis. Comput. Graph. **25**(12), 3231–3243 (2018)
17. Müller, P., Wonka, P., Haegler, S., et al.: Procedural modeling of buildings. In: ACM SIGGRAPH 2006 Papers, pp. 614–623 (2006)
18. Deitke, M., VanderBilt, E., Herrasti, A., et al.: ProcTHOR: large-scale embodied ai using procedural generation. Adv. Neural Inf. Proces. Syst. **35**, 5982–5994 (2022)
19. Mamajonova, N., Oydin, M., Usmonali, T., et al.: Parametric design: enhancing architectural environments through computational Innovation. Holders Reason. **2**(1), 334 (2024)
20. Xu, K., Chen, K., Fu, H., et al.: Sketch2Scene: sketch-based co-retrieval and co-placement of 3D models. ACM Trans. Graph. (TOG). **32**(4), 1–15 (2013)
21. Savva, M., Chang, A.X., Agrawala, M.: Scenesuggest: context-driven 3d scene design. arXiv preprint (2017). https://arxiv.org/abs/1703.00061
22. Zhang, S.K., Li, Y.X., He, Y., et al.: Mageadd: real-time interaction simulation for scene synthesis. In : Proceedings of the 29th ACM International Conference on Multimedia, pp. 965–973 (2021)
23. Chang, A., Savva, M., Manning, C.D.. Learning spatial knowledge for text to 3D scene generation. In: Proceedings of the 2014 conference on empirical methods in natural language processing (EMNLP), pp. 2028-2038 (2014)
24. Liang, H., Bao, F., Sun, Y., et al.: Virtual Scenes Construction Promotes Traditional Chinese Art Preservation. In: Advances in Computer Graphics: 38th Computer Graphics International Conference, CGI 2021, pp. 621–632. Proceedings 38. Springer Ienternational Publishing, Virtual Event, September 6–10, 2021 (2021)
25. Fisher, M., Ritchie, D., Savva, M., et al.: Example-based synthesis of 3D object arrangements. ACM Trans. Graph. (TOG). **31**(6), 1–11 (2012)
26. Qi, S., Zhu, Y., Huang, S., et al. Human-centric indoor scene synthesis using stochastic grammar. In: Proceedings of the IEEE Conference on Computer Vision and Pattern Recognition, pp. 5899–5908 (2018)

27. Wang, X., Yeshwanth, C., Nießner, M.: Sceneformer: Indoor scene generation with transformers. In: 2021 International Conference on 3D Vision (3DV). IEEE, pp. 106–115 (2021)
28. Wei, Q.A., Ding, S., Park, J.J., et al.: Lego-net: learning regular rearrangements of objects in rooms. In: Proceedings of the IEEE/CVF Conference on Computer Vision and Pattern Recognition. pp. 19037–19047 (2023)
29. Fu, Q., Chen, X., Wang, X., et al.: Adaptive synthesis of indoor scenes via activity-associated object relation graphs. ACM Trans. Graph. (TOG). **36**(6), 1–13 (2017)
30. Chang, A.X., Eric, M., Savva, M, et al.: SceneSeer: 3D scene design with natural language. arXiv preprint (2017). https://arxiv.org/abs/1703.00050
31. Li, M., Patil, A.G., Xu, K., et al.: Grains: generative recursive autoencoders for indoor scenes. ACM Trans. Graph. (TOG). **38**(2), 1–16 (2019)
32. Lin, C., Mu, Y.: Instructscene: instruction-driven 3d indoor scene synthesis with semantic graph prior. arXiv preprint (2024). https://arxiv.org/abs/2402.04717
33. Zhai, G., Örnek, E.P., Wu, S.C., et al.: Commonscenes: generating commonsense 3d indoor scenes with scene graph diffusion. Adv. Neural Inf. Proces. Syst. **36**, 30026–30038 (2023)
34. Chung, J., Lee, S., Nam, H., et al.: Luciddreamer: domain-free generation of 3d gaussian splatting scenes. arXiv preprint (2023). https://arxiv.org/abs/2311.13384
35. Höllein, L., Cao, A., Owens, A., et al.: Text2room: extracting textured 3d meshes from 2d text-to-image models. In: Proceedings of the IEEE/CVF International Conference on Computer Vision, pp. 7909–7920 (2023)
36. Deng, Z., He, X., Peng, Y., et al.: MV-diffusion: motion-aware video diffusion model. In: Proceedings of the 31st ACM International Conference on Multimedia, pp. 7255–7263 (2023)
37. Fridman, R., Abecasis, A., Kasten, Y., et al.: Scenescape: Text-driven consistent scene generation. Adv. Neural Inf. Proces. Syst. **36**, 39897–39914 (2023)
38. Cai, S., Chan, E.R., Peng, S., et al.: Diffdreamer: towards consistent unsupervised single-view scene extrapolation with conditional diffusion models. In: Proceedings of the IEEE/CVF International Conference on Computer Vision, pp. 2139–2150 (2023)
39. Fang, C., Dong, Y., Luo, K., et al.: Ctrl-room: controllable text-to-3D room meshes generation with layout constraints. arXiv preprint (2023). https://arxiv.org/abs/2310.03602
40. Liu, J., Xiong, W., Jones, I., et al.: Clip-layout: style-consistent indoor scene synthesis with semantic furniture embedding. arXiv preprint (2023). https://arxiv.org/abs/2303.03565
41. Feng, W., Zhu, W., Fu, T., et al.: Layoutgpt: compositional visual planning and generation with large language models. Adv. Neural Inf. Proces. Syst. **36**, 18225–18250 (2023)
42. Yang, H., Yue, S., He, Y.: Auto-GPT for online decision making: Benchmarks and additional opinions. arXiv preprint (2023). https://arxiv.org/abs/2306.02224
43. Jin, Q., Yang, Y., Chen, Q., et al.: Genegpt: augmenting large language models with domain tools for improved access to biomedical information. Bioinformatics. **40**(2), btae075 (2024)
44. Lin, B.Y., Fu, Y., Yang, K., et al.: Swiftsage: a generative agent with fast and slow thinking for complex interactive tasks. Adv. Neural Inf. Proces. Syst. **36**, 23813–23825 (2023)
45. Wang, Z., Cai, S., Liu, A., et al.: Jarvis-1: open-world multi-task agents with memory-augmented multimodal language models. IEEE Trans. Pattern Anal. Mach. Intell. (2024)
46. Shen, Y., Song, K., Tan, X., et al.: Hugginggpt: solving ai tasks with chatgpt and its friends in hugging face. Adv. Neural Inf. Proces. Syst. **36**, 38154–38180 (2023)
47. Song, C.H., Wu, J., Washington, C., et al.: LLM-planner: few-shot grounded planning for embodied agents with large language models. In: Proceedings of the IEEE/CVF International Conference on Computer Vision, pp. 2998–3009 (2023)
48. Lewis, P., Perez, E., Piktus, A., et al.: Retrieval-augmented generation for knowledge-intensive NLP tasks. Adv. Neural Inf. Proces. Syst. **33**, 9459–9474 (2020)

49. Fan, W., Ding, Y., Ning, L., et al.: A survey on rag meeting llms: towards retrieval-augmented large language models. In: Proceedings of the 30th ACM SIGKDD Conference on Knowledge Discovery and Data Mining, pp. 6491–6501 (2024)
50. Wang, Z., Ng, P., Nallapati, R., et al.: Retrieval, re-ranking and multi-task learning for knowledge-base question answering. In: Proceedings of the 16th Conference of the European Chapter of the Association for Computational Linguistics: Main Volume, pp. 347–357 (2021)
51. GLM, T., Zeng, A., Xu, B., et al.: Chatglm: a family of large language models from glm-130b to glm-4 all tools. arXiv preprint (2024). https://arxiv.org/abs/2406.12793
52. 6 Ideas To Choose the Best Meeting Room Styles & Tips of Meeting Room Design. Available online: https://www.dious-furniture.com/spaces/6-ideas-best-meeting-room-design-styles.
53. 7 Types of Meeting Room Layouts. Available online: https://robinpowered.com/blog/7-types-of-meeting-room-layouts.
54. Sprague, Z., Yin, F., Rodriguez, J. D., et al.: To cot or not to cot? chain-of-thought helps mainly on math and symbolic reasoning. arXiv preprint (2024). https://arxiv.org/abs/2409.12183
55. Hua, Y., Loftness, V., Kraut, R., et al.: Workplace collaborative space layout typology and occupant perception of collaboration environment. Environ. Plann. B. Plann. Des. **37**(3), 429–448 (2010)
56. Addor, M.R.A., Santos, E.T.: BIM coordination room layout: assessment criteria and metrics. In: Proceedings of the 32nd CIB W78 Conference (2015)
57. Brooke, J.: SUS: a retrospective. J. Usability Stud. **8**(2) (2013)
58. Hart, S.G., Staveland, L.E.: Development of NASA-TLX (task load index): results of empirical and theoretical research. In: Advances in Psychology, vol. 52, pp. 139–183, North-Holland (1988)

Applicability Analysis and Interaction Optimization of Pen Pressure Input for Fitts and Steering's Tasks

Yizhong Xin[1](✉), Liang Sun[1], and Lijun Zhang[2]

[1] Shenyang University of Technology, Shenyang, China
xyz@sut.edu.cn, smusudl@smail.sut.edu.cn
[2] Liaoyang Hongyu Crystal Co., Ltd., Liaoyang, China

Abstract. Due to the low pen input capability, the performance of the pen pressure input mode is studied in detail in order to increase the input capability of pen interaction. The clicking and sliding experiments were conducted to verify whether the clicking and sliding behaviours of the pen pressure input mode comply with Fitts' Law and Steering's Law, so as to derive the feasibility of using the pen pressure input mode to increase the input capability of the pen, as well as the feasibility of expanding the findings of the Fitts' Law and Steering's Law to the field of the pen input mode. The data collected from the clicking experiment was then analysed to derive a range of parameters for which the pen pressure input mode is suitable for user operation. The data collected from the sliding experiments were analysed to determine which parameter ranges of the pen pressure input mode are more suitable for performing the sliding task. The results of the experiments show that pen pressure complies with Fitts' Law for the clicking task and Steering's Law for the sliding task. Finally, principles and recommendations for the use of pen pressure input are given, which are instructive for pen pressure interaction in pen interface.

Keywords: pen-based interaction · pencil pressure · Fitts' Law · the Steering's Law

1 Introduction

Proceedings without editors [1], Pen-based interaction has become increasingly popular due to its advantages such as convenient writing, short learning time, support for direct manipulation, and user-friendly portability. However, compared to traditional input devices, the pen's input capability is limited, supporting only the two-dimensional coordinate information of the pen tip, and it cannot continuously complete the two tasks of clicking and command selection. The mouse, on the other hand, has a much higher input capability than the pen due to its two left and right buttons. After further examination and study of pen interaction, proceedings without editors [2], researchers have found that the pen can also be used through input modes such as nib pressure, tilt angle, azimuth, etc., which increase the input bandwidth and input capability of the pen. Journal articles

S. Guo et al. (Eds.): HHME 2025, CCIS 2878, pp. 257–269, 2027.
https://doi.org/10.1007/978-981-92-3991-7_17

[3], It was shown that pen pressure operation gave the best performance with the lowest error rate. Therefore, the performance related to pen pressure based on different tasks was systematically examined to see whether people would comply with Fitts' Law for clicking behaviour using pen pressure and Steering's Law for sliding tasks using pressure. Finally, based on the accuracy performance index and speed performance index, the reasons why different directions affect pen pressure performance are explored, and future work is prospected.

2 Related Work

Clicking tasks are common tasks in human-computer interaction, such as selecting a menu item, clicking an icon or button, etc. Journal articles [4], Fitts' Law is a robust model for evaluating click operation tasks. Therefore, in click task operations, many previous studies have examined the performance of the pen input channel based on Fitts' Law. Journal articles [5], Fitts' Law describes the linear relationship between the operation time (MT) to complete the task and the difficulty index (ID). Among them, the difficulty index is formula (1):

$$ID = \log_2(A/W + 1) \tag{1}$$

where A represents the moving distance, W represents the width of the target, and the linear relationship between MT and ID is formula (2):

$$MT = a + b^{*}ID \tag{2}$$

Literature on pen pressure only began to emerge after the turn of the century, and most of the literature focuses on the design of novel interactive applications. Proceedings without editors [6], Mizuno et al. invented a user interaction system for virtual engraving, which changes the depth and angle of engraving by controlling the pressure of the pen, and performs engraving by simulating real objects. Proceedings without editors [7], Ramos and Balakrishnan proposed pressure markers, which enable users to draw and select commands simultaneously by controlling the pressure when drawing with a pen. Some other studies focus on increasing the freedom of the pen by using pen pressure channels. Proceedings without editors [8], Ren et al. proposed an adaptive hybrid cursor, which automatically adjusts the cursor size by pen pressure to improve the ability to select targets. Proceedings without editors [9], Brewster and Hughes proposed a pressure-based text input on mobile devices, which switches the case of letters by the size of the pressure, thereby shortening the input time and increasing the input throughput. Proceedings without editors [10], Hasan et al. proposed A-Coord Input, which studied the control ability and channel usage performance of users when using two input channels of the pen to operate in coordination, and found that users can well control at least two channels to operate in coordination. Other studies have focused on the ability of humans to control pen pressure. Proceedings without editors [11], Ramos et al. studied the ability of humans to complete selection tasks by controlling pen pressure and found that the pressure space can be divided equally into 6 levels to achieve optimal control. On this basis, proceedings without editors [1], Xin et al. found that based on the pressure distribution map of individual users when they naturally use the pen, the pressure space can be unevenly divided into 8 levels to achieve optimal control. Proceedings without editors [12], Zhou et al. examined the impact of four different starting operation positions on user control ability in a sliding task. In addition, journal articles [13], Dillen et al. found that direction affects the duration of cursor movement.

The findings above demonstrate the efficacy of pen pressure as an input modality in human-computer interaction. However, several aspects remain under-researched: few studies have examined pen pressure performance in Fitts' and Steering's tasks, nor have definitive conclusions been reached regarding parameter range optimisation or discretisation strategies for pen pressure input. This limits the practical application of pen pressure input in interaction design, necessitating systematic investigation into its suitability and optimisation for Fitts' and Steering's tasks. This paper employs empirical research methods, utilising statistical analysis to quantify experimental data. It examines pen pressure performance in click and slide tasks respectively, offering interaction design recommendations for pen pressure input to provide a reference framework for stylus-based interaction. In summary, the primary research contributions of this paper are as follows:

1. It is the first study to validate that pen pressure input complies with Fitts' Law in click tasks and with the Steering's Law in slide tasks, providing a theoretical basis for interaction optimization;
2. It clarifies the parameter optimisation ranges and interaction design principles for pen pressure input in both click and slide tasks, offering reference for pressure interaction design in pen-based interfaces;
3. It advances the research framework for stylus interaction input channels, laying foundations for future multi-channel interaction optimization.

3 Experiment

3.1 Study on Pressure Performance under Click Task

Purpose of the study examine the performance of pen pressure in a clicking task. If using pen pressure for clicking tasks to augment input capabilities is feasible, what is the feasibility of this technique? If feasible, which pen pressure spaces are most suitable for use? If the continuous pen pressure space is discretized, what is the maximum number of discretization levels? In the experiment, first, a clicking experiment will be conducted to verify whether the clicking behavior of pen pressure conforms to Fitts' Law. Next, a detailed analysis will be conducted on human control over pen pressure.

Experimenters and experimental equipment the experiment involved 12 volunteers, including four women and eight men, aged between 20 and 35. All participants had been using computers for at least three years. To maintain consistency, all participants were right-handed. The equipment used in the experiment consisted of a Wacom Cintiq 21UX LCD flat-panel display and a wireless electronic stylus that could recognize pen movements. The program used was designed in the Java programming environment and ran on a computer running Windows 10. The pressure applied by the experimenter to the stylus tip was detected by the display, which evenly divided the pressure from 0 to 4 N into a range of 0 to 1023. Pressure exceeding 1023 was also recognized by the computer as 1023.

Experimental design and procedure the subjects were first asked to perform simple click and drag operations with the pen to familiarize themselves with the pen device's functionality. They were then given a 5–10 min warm-up exercise to familiarize themselves with the experimental requirements and procedures. The subjects were asked to sit in front of a Wacom Cintiq 21UX interactive pen display, positioned horizontally at a comfortable height for operation. Upon entering the program, a 400-pixel rectangle appeared on the display. This 400-pixel length was mapped to 1024 pressure levels, with four different orientations for the rectangle: north-south, west-east, northeast-southwest, and northwest-southeast. In Fig. 1, Two rectangular targets were placed on the rectangle, initially pink and red. Each target had three different widths: 22, 30, and 40 pixels, and the distance between the two targets was 100, 200, and 300 pixels. At the initial position of the rectangle, a pointer changes position depending on the amount of pressure applied. The subject's task is to acquire and select the target. First, the subject must apply appropriate pressure to acquire and select the pink target. When the pointer reaches the target area with appropriate pressure, the target turns green. When the target turns green, the subject uses their other hand to press the spacebar to indicate that the target has been selected. If the target has been selected, the target's color turns blue; if it has not been selected, the result area displays "Error." After the first selection, the first target turns gray and the second turns pink. Then, without removing the pen tip from the screen, continue to increase pressure to acquire and select the pink target. Finally, in Fig. 2, the subject reduces pressure to return to acquiring and selecting the pink target. During this process, the user is reminded to click the target as quickly and accurately as possible. To eliminate the influence of trial order on the results, this experiment uses the Latin square method to determine the order in which each subject selects the four rectangle directions. To test the learning effect of the subjects, each subject performed five trials. Each completion of an experimental task with a different combination of factors is called a trial. The total number of trials is 12 people × 4 different directions × 3 target distances × 3 target widths × 5 groups × 2 repetitions = 4320 trials.

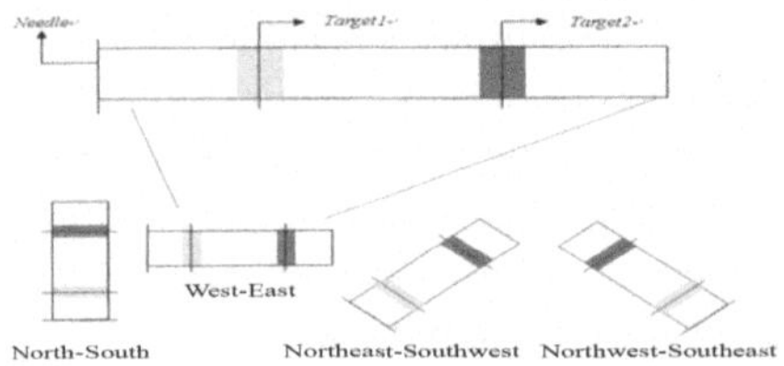

Fig. 1. Four different directions of the experiment

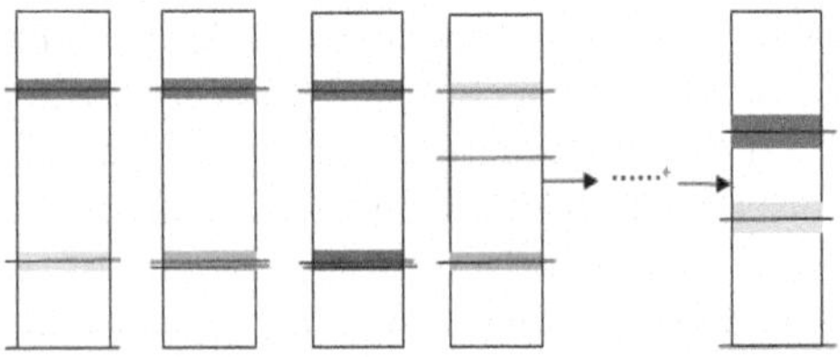

Fig. 2. The whole process of a test

3.2 Study of Pen Pressure Performance under Sliding Task

Purpose of the study sliding is a fundamental computer operation, such as using a slider to navigate an interface. However, utilizing pen pressure for sliding tasks remains an unresolved issue. To address these issues, we first conducted sliding experiments to verify whether the sliding behavior of pen pressure conforms to the Steering's Law. We then investigated the ability of humans to control pen pressure during sliding tasks.

Experimenters and experimental equipment the experiment involved nine volunteers, four women and five men, aged between 20 and 35. All had been using computers for at least three years. To maintain consistency, all participants were right-handed. The experiment used a Wacom Cintiq 21UX LCD flat-panel display and a wireless electronic stylus that could detect pen movements. The program was designed in the Java programming environment and ran on a computer running Windows XP. The display detected the pressure applied by the experimenter to the stylus tip, evenly dividing the pressure from 0 to 4 N into a scale of 0 to 1023. If the pressure exceeded 1023, the computer would also register it as 1023.

Implementation Procedure the subjects were asked to sit in front of a Wacom Cintiq 21UX interactive pen display positioned horizontally at a comfortable height for operation. When the program entered the main screen, a bar or circular track appeared in the center of the screen, depending on the selected track type. Both the bar and circular tracks had three widths: 40 px, 28 px, and 18 px, and three lengths: R, 37.5 px, 62.5 px, and 100 px. When the subject placed the pen tip into the input area, a triangle indicated the pressure level. If the pressure applied was within a specified range, in Fig. 3, the triangle turned green. When the subject crossed the start line while maintaining the specified pressure, a trial began. The subject then manipulated the pen tip across the track while maintaining the same pressure range. When the subject crossed the end line, the trial ended, and the next trial appeared on the screen. Two errors can occur while navigating the track: one is the pen tip moving outside either side of the track, in which case the system emits a beep to alert the user; the other is the pressure not being within the specified range, in which case the triangle indicating the pressure level turns red. To eliminate the influence of experimental order on the results, this experiment used a Latin square method to determine the order of the six pressure ranges each experimenter performed. Within each pressure range, experiments with different track widths and lengths were repeated once, but the order of each experiment was randomized. To test the learning effect of the experimenters, all possible experiments were grouped together, and each experimenter repeated the experiment five times. Each completion of the experimental task with different factor combinations was called a trial. The total number of trials was 9 participants $\times$ 2 track types $\times$ 3 track widths $\times$ 3 track lengths $\times$ 5 groups $\times$ 2 repetitions = 1620 trials.

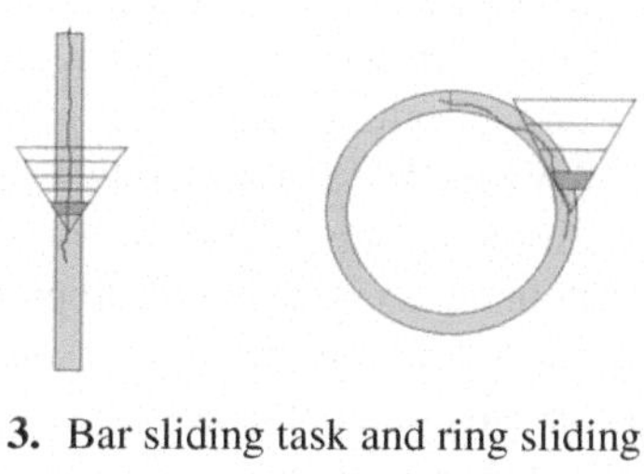

Fig. 3. Bar sliding task and ring sliding task

4 Results

4.1 Clicking Tasks

Select time in Fig. 4, selection time within a low pressure range refers to the time from when the pen tip touches the display to when the spacebar is pressed to select target 1. The figure shows that the selection time is the shortest when target 1 is 150 pixels from the starting position; the time taken is longer when target 1 is 100 pixels from the starting position than when it is 150 pixels from the starting position; and the time taken is the longest when target 1 is 50 pixels from the starting position. The same results are observed for target width: when the target width is 20 pixels, the time taken to select the target is significantly longer than when the target widths are 30 and 40 pixels. These results indicate that: 1) the wider the target width, the shorter the target selection time. 2) within a low pressure range, the greater the distance from the starting position, the shorter the target selection time. The experiment also found that selecting a target at a distance of 50 pixels was difficult, and even selecting a target at a width of 40 pixels still took a long time. This effect may be due to the pen's inherent weight. When the subject applies minimal force, a high pressure is applied, causing the pointer to overshoot the target and requiring it to return to the selected target, thus wasting time. Based on the above results, it is extremely difficult to select a target within a small pressure range. Only by enlarging the target or moving it further away from the starting point can the selection time be reduced. What are the consequences of clicking a target across the entire pressure range? In Fig. 5, The following shows the relationship between selection time, target width, and distance across the entire pressure range. The experimental results show that wider targets require less time, and shorter distances between targets also require less time. Furthermore, the effect of target widths of 30 pixels and 20 pixels on selection time differs significantly, suggesting that target widths greater than 30 pixels are more suitable for experimenters. These results are consistent with Fitts' Law. In Fig. 6, Linear regression of experimental data between MT (mean selection time) and ID (difficulty coefficient) also confirms that clicking behavior across the entire pressure range conforms to Fitts' Law.

Selection error rate in Fig. 7, the selectin error rate is the ratio of the number of trials in which the experimenter incorrectly selected target 1 to the total number of trials, the error rate at a distance of 50 pixels is significantly greater than the error rates at distances of 100 and 150 pixels. The above results indicate that the target selection error rate is very high within a small pressure range. However, in Fig. 8, the effects of target width and distance on the selection error rate across the entire pressure range differ. The experimental results show that the narrower the target width, the higher the selection error rate. The error rate for a target width of 20 pixels is significantly higher than for targets with widths of 30 and 40 pixels. We also found that the target selection error rate is highest when the distance between targets is 200 pixels. The error rate for a distance of 300 pixels is actually lower than for a distance of 200 pixels. This result may be due to the natural slowdown of the speed as pressure increases to a larger pressure range, allowing users ample time to correctly select the target.

Number of passes when the subject attempts to approach a target, they sometimes pass through it. The number of passes refers to the number of times the subject controls pressure across the centerline of target 1 before selecting it. In Fig. 9, it shows that the number of passes decreases with increasing width and distance, indicating that within a small pressure range, wide targets and targets farther from the starting point are more likely to be selected. Regarding the distance between targets, the number of passes decreases as the distance between them increases.

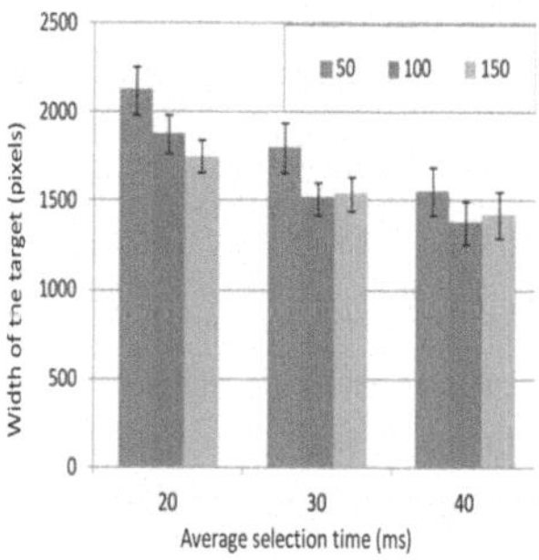

Fig. 4. Effect of target broadband and distance on selection time

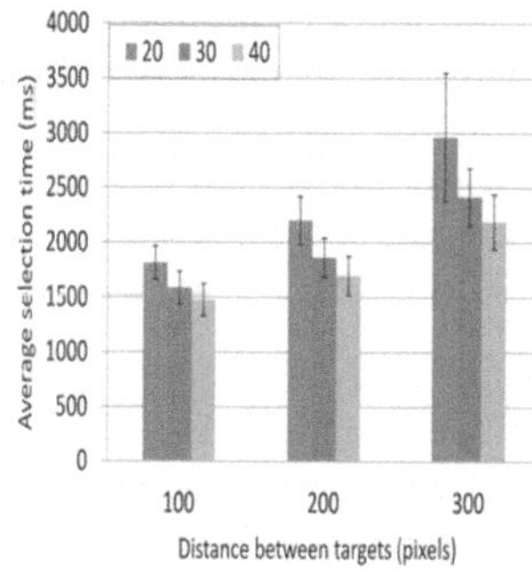

Fig. 5. Selection time for different target widths and distances

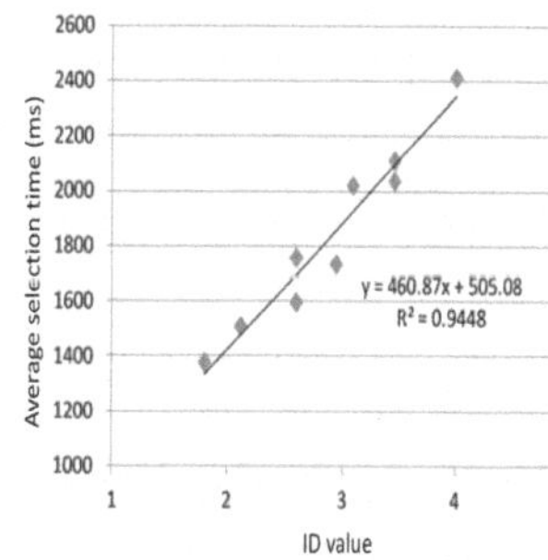

Fig. 6. Linear regression of MT vs. ID for pressure inter-target clicking experiments

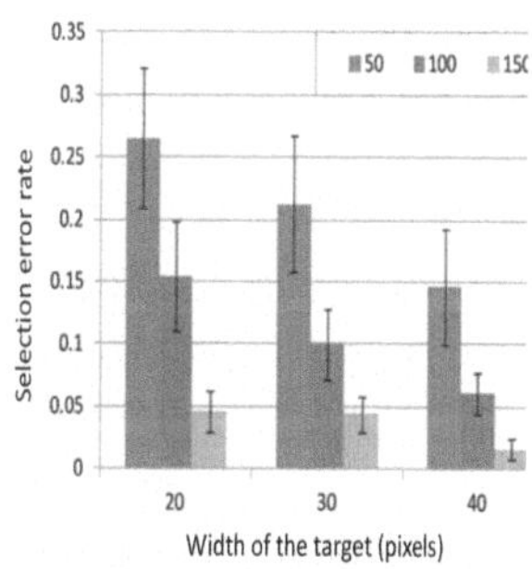

Fig. 7. Selection error rate at different target widths and distances

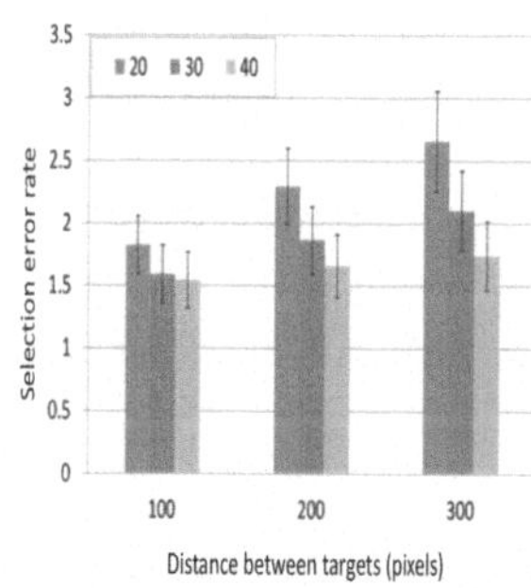

Fig. 8. Selection error rate at different target widths and distances

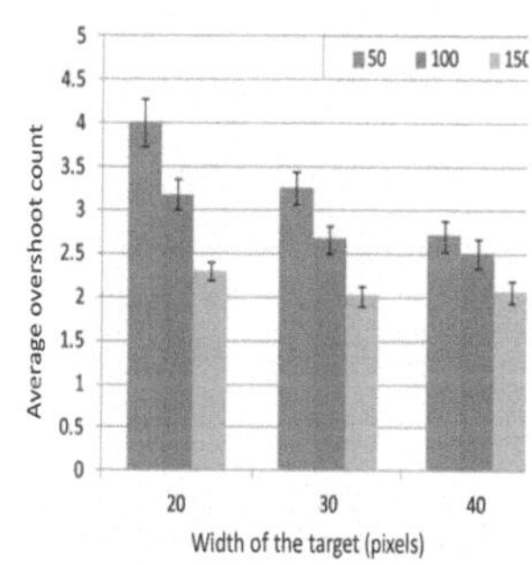

Fig. 9. Number of penetrations at different target widths and distances

4.2 Sliding Tasks

Select time Selection time refers to the time it takes for the pen tip to slide from the starting point to the end point of the track. A detailed analysis of the effect of track shape on selection time revealed a significant effect of track shape ($F_{1,8} = 1.891$, $p < .001$), in Fig. 10. Regardless of the pressure range, the time it takes to navigate the circular track is significantly longer than the time it takes to navigate the bar track. Analyzing the effect of pressure range on selection time, we found that the pressure range of [850, 1023] for both the bar track and the circular track resulted in the least amount of time for traversing the track. Beyond this pressure range, the pressure ranges of [170, 340], [340, 510], [510, 680], and [680, 850] also resulted in shorter traversal times. In Fig. 11, in the case of linear tracks, we also analyzed the effect of track width on choice time. A repeated measures ANOVA revealed a significant effect of track width ($F_{2,16} = 1.891, p < .001$). The effect on choice time was particularly pronounced when the track width ranged from 18 pixels to 28 pixels. Therefore, it is concluded that a track width greater than 28 pixels is optimal for the sliding task. According to the Steering's Law, the difficulty coefficient of the sliding task is formula (3):

$$ID = A/W \tag{3}$$

where A represents the movement distance and W represents the width of the target. This law shows that the average selection time is linearly related to ID. Through linear regression of MT and ID, in Fig. 12, it can be shown that pressure-based manipulation behavior conforms to the Steering's Law.

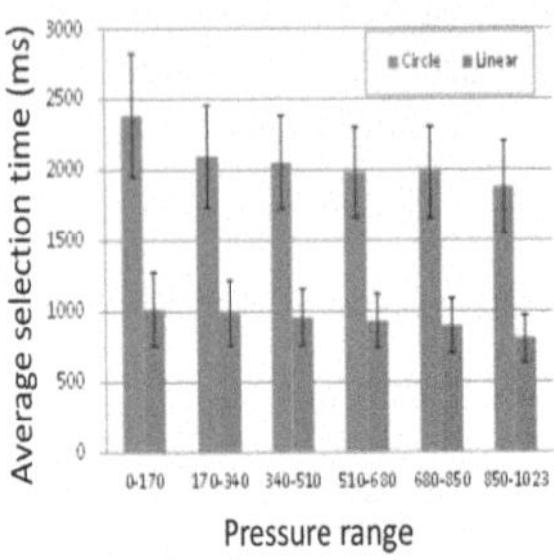

Fig. 10. Selection time for track shape and pressure range

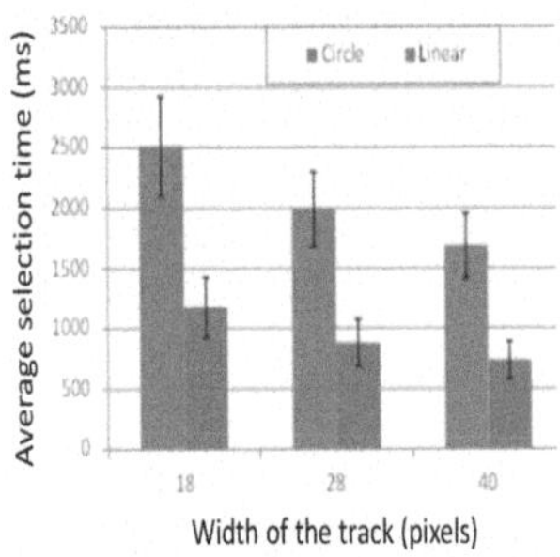

Fig. 11. Selection time for different widths of linear tracks

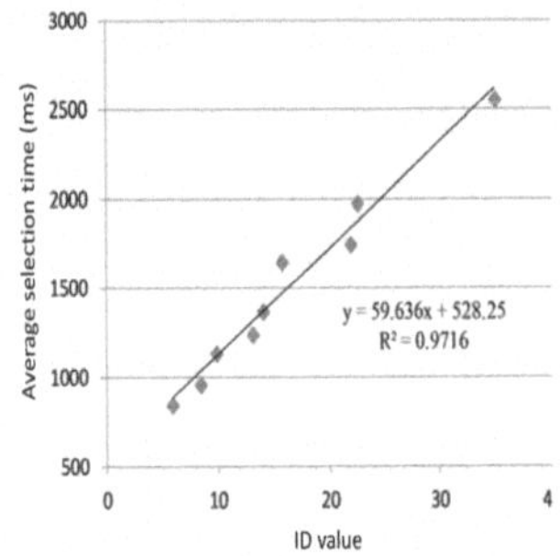

Fig. 12. Linear regression of MT vs. ID for pressure manipulation experiments

Trajectory error rate the trajectory error rate is the ratio of the number of times the pen tip's trajectory was outside the track to the total number of acquisitions in a single experiment. In Fig. 13, A detailed analysis of the effect of track shape on the trajectory error rate, reveals that track shape ($F_{1,8} = 10.551, p < .001$) has a significant effect on the trajectory error rate. Regardless of the pressure range, the trajectory error rate for the sliding task using pressure on the circular track is significantly higher than that for the sliding task using pressure on the bar track. Analyzing the effect of pressure range on the trajectory error rate reveals different results for different track shapes. For the linear track, the trajectory error rate for the pressure ranges [340, 510], [510, 680], and [680, 850] is lower than for the other pressure ranges. For the circular track, the trajectory error rate for manipulating the pen tip through the track while maintaining pressure within the range [510, 680] is significantly lower than for the other pressure ranges. In Fig. 14, In the case of linear tracks, we also analyzed the effect of track width on track error rates. The results show that track width has a significant effect on track error rates ($F_{2,16} =$

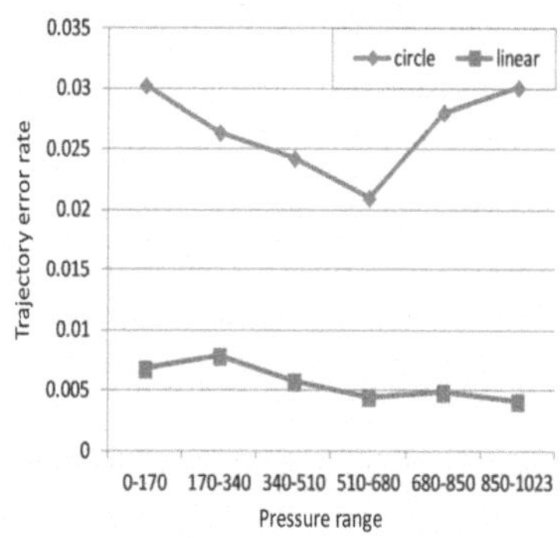

Fig. 13. Track error rates under different track shapes and pressure ranges

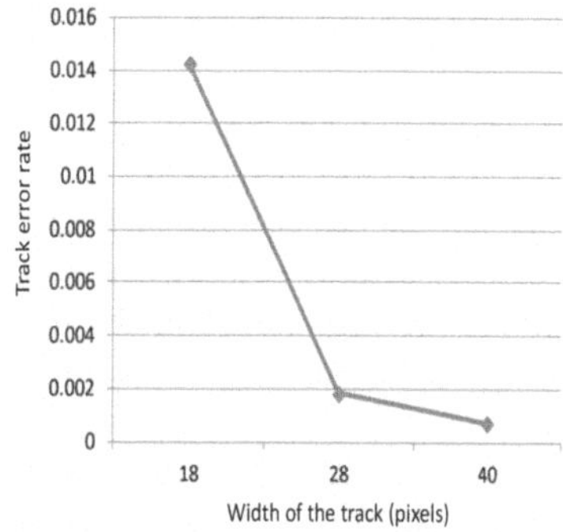

Fig. 14. Track error rate under different linear track widths

1.158, p < .001). In particular, the effect on track error rates differs significantly when the track width ranges from 18 pixels to 28 pixels. Therefore, we can conclude that in the sliding task, if the track width is too thin, the error rate of this technique increases, thus affecting its performance.

Pressure error rate the pressure error rate is the ratio of the number of times the pen tip pressure falls outside the specified pressure range to the total number of acquisitions during an experiment. In Fig. 15, Data analysis shows that the pressure error rate for circular tracks is significantly higher than that for bar tracks, and the pressure error rate decreases with increasing pressure range. In particular, the pressure error rate is almost zero when the pressure range is [850, 1023]. However, the pressure range [850, 1023] is not suitable for user operation. Therefore, in terms of pressure error rate, the pressure ranges [510, 680] and [680, 850] are most suitable for users to perform sliding tasks. For linear tracks, we also analyze the impact of track width on the pressure error rate (as shown in Fig. 16). The results show that the impact on the pressure error rate varies significantly when the track width is between 18 pixels and 28 pixels.

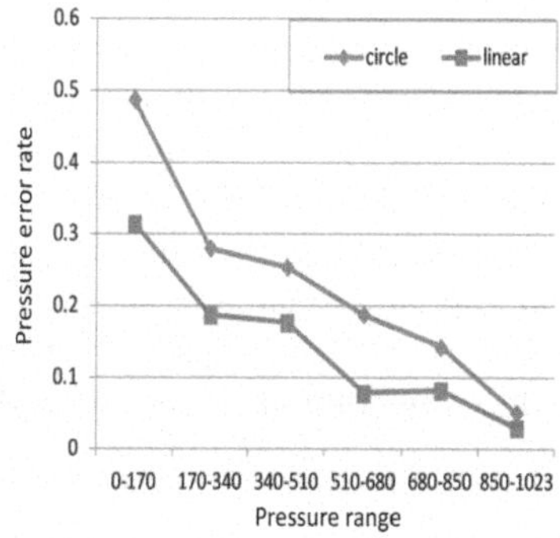

Fig. 15. Pressure error rate under different track shapes and pressure ranges

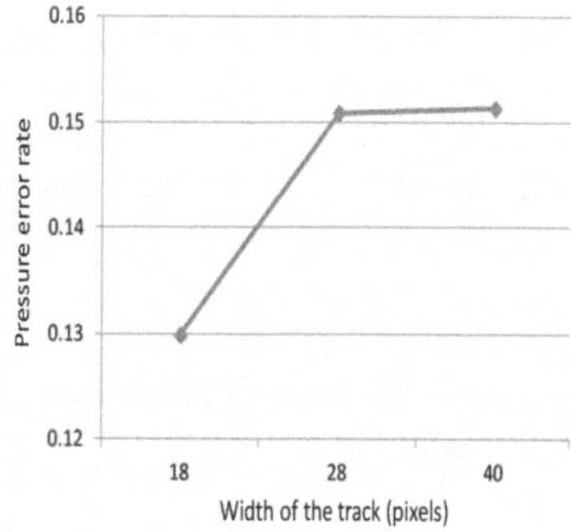

Fig. 16. Pressure error rate under different linear track widths

5 Discussion

5.1 The Impact of Pen Pressure Performance on Different Task Types

When selecting a target within a small pressure range, the wider the target or the farther it is from the starting point, the easier it is for the subject to select it. When the target is 50 pixels from the starting point, the time to select the target, the error rate, and the number of passes are all the highest. Therefore, a target distance greater than 50 pixels from the starting point improves performance. When selecting a target across the entire pressure range, the wider the target, the easier it is for the subject to select it. Furthermore, we found that the performance difference between target widths of 30 and 40 pixels is not significant, suggesting that a target width greater than 30 pixels is more effective for the pressure-clicking task. Selection time increases with increasing target distance. Selection error rate and pass count decrease for targets with a large pressure range. The above experimental results show that linear tracks have lower values for selection time, track error rate, and pressure error rate than circular tracks. For linear tracks, a comprehensive analysis of selection time, track error rate, and pressure error rate indicates that the pressure error rate is almost zero within the pressure range [850, 1023]. Therefore, the pressure ranges of [510, 680] and [680, 850] are more suitable for the sliding task. For the circular track, these three observations indicate that the pressure range of [510, 680] is more suitable for the sliding task. In the linear case, both selection time and track error rate decrease with increasing track width, but the reduction slows down when the track width is greater than 28 pixels. Therefore, tracks wider than 28 pixels are more suitable for the sliding task. As for the pressure error rate, we found that pressure error increases with increasing track width. This may be because when the track is narrow, users slow down to ensure that the pressure is within the specified range.

Within a small pressure range, ensuring the target button is wide and farther from the starting point allows pressure to be used to adjust the transparency, thickness, and eraser function of the brush in digital painting software such as Photoshop and Procreate; in the mobile office application Notion, pressure can be used to switch between different tasks, such as scrolling, word selection, and pop-up menus, effectively reducing misoperations and significantly improving operational performance. Within a large pressure range, due to the large target width, pen pressure input is more suitable for implementing advanced functions such as layer switching and tool parameter adjustment in digital painting software, as well as high-precision text editing and drawing operations through heavy pressure operations on mobile devices such as iPadOS and Android. In the XR/spatial computing scenario Vision Pro, the 3D color palette implements pressure to control hue, saturation, and confirmation operations, and appropriately increases the width of the virtual slider to improve operational stability and accuracy. This helps users interact more accurately in three-dimensional space and reduces operational errors caused by insufficient track width.

5.2 Degree of Fit

The above research results show that pressure-clicking behavior across the entire pressure range conforms to Fitts' Law. Therefore, we can apply some of the theories in Fitts' Law to pressure-clicking tasks. The linear regression results of experimental data (MT) and ID (Difficulty Index) show that the dual-target click experiment has a high fit to the Fitts' Law data model ($R^2 \geq 0.94$). This indicates a very high degree of fit with Fitts' Law. Therefore, pen pressure also conforms to Fitts' Law in the click task. The above research results also show that the linear regression results of experimental data (MT) and ID (Difficulty Index) show that the sliding task has a high fit to the Steering's Law data model ($R^2 \geq 0.97$). Pen pressure-based sliding tasks conform to the Steering's Law. Therefore, designers can apply some of the research findings of the Steering's Law to pen pressure-based interaction design.

At the system level, Windows Ink and the "Pressure Normalization Service" in Win11 24H2 include improvements related to pressure sensing, enabling unified processing of pressure sensing data from different devices, thereby improving consistency and compatibility across devices. For example, some users have experienced pressure sensing failure or inaccuracy when using Wacom tablets. In XR/spatial computing scenarios, Vision Pro's pen XR interaction framework maps linear track results to 3D space, optimizing the virtual slide width and pressure range, and improving user success rate; circular tracks use a specific pressure range and increase dead zone, using the Steering's Law to predict completion time and reduce error rates.

5.3 Discretization of Pressure

Discretizing a continuous range of pen pressure values is a common practice. For example, the range is divided into several subranges, each representing a command. Users can trigger different commands by controlling the pen pressure within different subranges. However, discretizing the range of pen pressure has always been a thorny issue. During the discretization process, if the range is divided too finely, user operation becomes difficult and prone to errors; if the range is divided too widely, the range cannot be used efficiently.

When selecting a target within a small pressure range, the wider the target or the farther it is from the starting point, the easier it is for the subject to select it. When the target is 50 pixels away from the starting point, the time, error rate, and number of clicks are all the greatest. Therefore, the distance between the target and the starting point must be greater than 50 pixels to improve the performance of the operation. When selecting a target within the entire pressure range, the wider the target, the easier it is for the subject to select it. We also found that the performance difference between target widths of 30 pixels and 40 pixels is not very large, so a target width greater than 30 pixels can more effectively perform the pressure clicking task. In terms of selection time, selection time increases with increasing distance from the target. In terms of selection error rate and number of clicks, the error rate and number of clicks are reduced for targets with a large pressure range.

To effectively apply pen pressure input to practical interaction design, this paper proposes a series of specific application strategies for pressure discretization. Building on the existing functionality of iPadOS's Pencil Kit, this paper further expands the pressure template feature, allowing developers to import multiple layers of pressure nodes and dynamically adjust the number of exposed layers based on user needs. Micro-vibration technology also provides instant feedback, significantly reducing false touches. At the user level, a user guidance mechanism is implemented to allow users to perform a series of pen pressure input operations. The device system then generates a personalized pressure mapping based on the user's actual actions. Using a Bayesian update algorithm, the system optimizes the pressure ranges in real time to adapt to the operating habits of different user groups, thereby improving the user interaction experience. Regarding the developer toolchain, the Unity Input System is extended to support pressure input devices, enabling it to receive and process pressure data. This provides developers with an interface for inputting pressure discretization parameters, generating and adjusting pressure discretization curves based on these parameters, and providing real-time previews to ensure design accuracy and efficiency.

6 Conclusion

Based on the above research results on pen pressure performance in click and slide tasks, we can draw the following conclusions. In the click task, the click behavior of pen pressure conforms to Fitts' Law. Therefore, using pen pressure for click tasks to increase the bandwidth of pen-based interaction is feasible. For users to select the target more effectively, the target must be greater than 50 px from the starting point (relative to a 400-px rectangle). This means that users cannot select the target using a pressure range of 0–0.5 N, so the available pressure range is 0.5–4 N. For more effective pressure-based target selection, the target width must be greater than 30 px (relative to a 400-px rectangle). This means that the available space can be divided into up to 11 layers. Furthermore, while target selection within a large pressure range takes longer, the error rate and number of passes are lower. In the slide task, the sliding behavior of pen pressure conforms to the Steering's law. Therefore, using pen pressure for slide tasks to increase the bandwidth of pen-based interaction is feasible. When using pen pressure for slide tasks, linear tracks perform better than circular tracks. For linear tracks, the pressure ranges of [510, 680] and [680, 850] are more suitable for sliding tasks. For circular tracks, the pressure range of [510, 680] is more suitable for sliding tasks. Therefore, these pressure ranges can be selected as sliding tasks in interaction design. In summary, we can rationally use pen pressure to increase the pen's input bandwidth and achieve high efficiency in pen-based interaction technology.

Because this study focused on right-handed subjects, in the next phase of our work, we will examine the performance of pen pressure tasks for subjects with different handednesses. We will also further investigate the impact of screen tilt on pen pressure input performance. Furthermore, building on the results of this study, we will examine the performance of other pen input channels in tapping and sliding tasks, explore the feasibility of integrating two or more channels, and develop more user-friendly strategies for pen channel usage.

Acknowledgments. This work was partially supported by the Liaoning Provincial Department of Science and Technology's "Unveiled and Leading" Science and Technology Project (2023JH1/10400081), the "Transplantation with Soil" Innovation Team Project of the "Liaoyang Talent Plan" (LYYC220501), the National Natural Science Foundation of China (No. 61100091), the Program for Liaoning Excellent Talents in University (LJQ2012007), and the SRF for ROCS, SEM ([2013]693).

Disclosure of Interests. The authors declare that they have no competing interests relevant to the content of this article.

References

1. Xin, Y.Z., Bi, X.J., Ren, X.S.: Acquiring and pointing: an empirical study of pen-tilt-based interaction. In: Proceedings of the SIGCHI Conference on Human Factors in Computing Systems, pp. 849–858. ACM Press, New York (2011)
2. Xin, Y.Z., Bi, X.J., Ren, X.S.: Natural use profiles for the pen: an empirical exploration of pressure. In: Proceedings of the SIGCHI Conference on Human Factors in Computing Systems, pp. 801–804. ACM Press, New York (2012)
3. Xin, Y.Z., Ren, X.S.: A study of inherent pen input modalities for precision parameter manipulations during trajectory tasks. IEICE Trans. Inf. Syst. **E92D**(12), 2454–2461 (2009)
4. MacKenzie, I.S.: Fitts' law as a research and design tool in human-computer interaction. Hum. Comput. Interact. **7**(1), 91–139 (1992)
5. Fitts, P.M.: The information capacity of the human motor system in controlling the amplitude of movement. J. Exp. Psychol. **47**(6), 381–391 (1954)
6. Mizuno, S., Kobayashi, D., Okada, M., et al.: Virtual sculpting with a pressure sensitive pen. In: Computer Graphics Proceedings, pp. 1–1. ACM Press, New York (2003)
7. Ramos, G., Balakrishnan, R.: Pressure marks. In: Proceedings of the SIGCHI Conference on Human Factors in Computing Systems, pp. 1375–1384. ACM Press, New York (2007)
8. Ren, X., Yin, J., Zhao, S.D., et al.: The adaptive hybrid cursor: a pressure-based target selection technique for pen-based user interfaces. In: Human-Computer Interaction – INTERACT 2007, pp. 310–323. Springer, Ber Lin (2007)
9. Brewster, S.A., Hughes, M.: Pressure-based text entry for mobile devices. In: Proceedings of the 11th International Conference on Human-Computer Interaction with Mobile Devices and Services, pp. 1–4. DBLP, Germany (2011)
10. Hasan, K., Yang, X.D., Bunt, A., et al.: A-coord input: coordinating auxiliary input streams for augmenting contextual pen-based interactions. In: Proceedings of the SIGCHI Conference on Human Factors in Computing Systems, pp. 805–814. ACM Press, New York (2012)
11. Ramos, G., Boulos, M., Balakrishnan, R.: Pressure widgets. In: Proceedings of the SIGCHI Conference on Human Factors in Computing Systems, pp. 487–494. ACM Press, New York (2004)
12. Zhou, X.L., Ren, X.S., Hui, Y.: Effect of Start Position on Human Performance in Steering's Tasks. In: Proceedings of the 2008 International Conference on Computer Science and Software Engineering, pp. 1098–1101. IEEE, New York (2008)
13. Dillen, H., Phillips, J.G., Meehan, J.W.: Kinematic analysis of cursor trajectories controlled with a touchpad. Int. J. Hum. Comput. Interact. **19**(2), 223–239 (2005)

Gesture Recognition Based on Improved VanillaNet for sEMG-Driven Prosthetic Hand Control

Yazhou Li and Kairu Li(✉)

School of Electrical Engineering, Shenyang University of Technology, No. 111 Shenliao Road (West), Economic and Technological Development Area, Shenyang, Liaoning 110870, China
Kairu.li@sut.edu.cn

Abstract. In the application of surface electromyography (sEMG)-driven prosthetic hands, deep learning models face the challenge of relying heavily on large-scale data and computational resources. This paper proposes an improved VanillaNet-based algorithm for sEMG gesture recognition. The model includes raw signal preprocessing through filtering, rectification, and data format reshaping. It simplifies convolutional layers by introducing point-wise convolution and linking dual-convolution activation. To address overfitting and class imbalance, the model incorporates Dropout and stratified K-fold cross-validation for optimization. Experiments show that the model with 1.43 M parameters achieves accuracies of 88.78% and 91.67%, with inference times of 6.83 ms and 7.53 ms on the NinaPro DB3 and DB7 datasets, respectively, enabling efficient gesture decoding on edge platforms and providing a lightweight, high-performance solution for practical sEMG-driven prosthetic hand applications.

Keywords: Surface electromyography (sEMG) · Prosthetic hands · Improved VanillaNet · Edge platforms

1 Introduction

The human hand, as a vital and indispensable organ, serves as a key pathway for proprioceptive sensation. However, hand amputation in reality not only has a significant impact on an individual's daily life but also poses substantial obstacles to their career development and life trajectory. Surface electromyography (sEMG), a physiological electrical signal generated by muscle activity, has found extensive application in prosthetic control owing to its non-invasive and easily accessible advantages [7]. This has opened up new possibilities for rehabilitation assistive technologies and human-computer interaction scenarios. Currently, numerous studies have applied sEMG signals to gesture recognition, demonstrating the potential of sEMG-based approaches in this field [5,6].

S. Guo et al. (Eds.): HHME 2025, CCIS 2878, pp. 270–282, 2027.
https://doi.org/10.1007/978-981-92-3991-7_18

In recent years, deep learning has made remarkable progress in sEMG-based gesture recognition tasks. By autonomously learning complex features from input signals, deep learning models have demonstrated superior performance, leveraging their strong representation learning capability to address the challenges of sEMG signal analysis [11]. Hu et al. [9] implemented a combination of recurrent neural network (RNN) and convolutional neural network (CNN) for sEMG signals from NinaPro DB1, achieving an accuracy of 87%. Cheng et al. [4] utilized the NinaPro DB1 to apply CNN on sEMG feature images extracted from raw signals, yielding a classification accuracy of 82.54%. Xu et al. [19] proposed a connection feature fusion recurrent convolutional neural network (CFF-RCNN) with a CFF strategy, achieving remarkable accuracy. The model outperformed previous results, reaching 88.87% on DB1, 99.51% on DB2, and 99.29% on DB4 for over 50 gesture classes. Qureshi et al. [14] proposed the efficient cascade convolutional network (E2CNN) for real-time sEMG classification. By converting raw signals to log-mel spectrograms (LMS) and using connection layers, E2CNN achieved high accuracy and low latency for both non-disabled and amputee users, making it suitable for real-world prosthetic control. Wang et al. [17] proposed a temporal deep convolutional network achieving 80.68% accuracy on NinaPro DB2. Zhang et al. [20] designed the LST-EMG-Net, a long-short-term feature fusion network, attaining 81.47% accuracy for 12 gestures in DB2. Despite the excellent performance of deep learning algorithms, their complex network architectures pose challenges for deployment on devices with limited computational resources. Chen et al. [2] proposed VanillaNet, which demonstrates strong lightweight characteristics via minimalist blocks in computer vision, balancing recognition accuracy and computational cost. However, due to inherent differences in data dimensions and feature complexity between images and sEMG signals, this network cannot be directly applied to the sEMG field.

To balance recognition performance and computational efficiency, we propose an improved VanillaNet algorithm for sEMG-based upper-limb prosthetic gesture recognition. Considering the fundamental differences between sEMG signals and image data in terms of multi-channel characteristics, temporal properties, etc., we have undertaken a series of efforts to address these challenges, organized as follows: Sect. 2 introduces sEMG datasets and preprocessing techniques; Sect. 3 presents the proposed improved model; Sect. 4 discusses the experimental results and statistical analysis; and Sect. 5 concludes the work.

2 sEMG Datasets and Preprocessing

Data preprocessing serves as the foundation for efficient model learning, significantly enhancing model performance and robustness. This section first introduces the datasets selected for the experiments, then presents the preprocessing procedures, including signal denoising, segmentation, and mitigation of class imbalance.

2.1 Introduction of sEMG Datasets

To comprehensively evaluate the generalization ability of the proposed model under different conditions, two public datasets are selected: NinaPro DB3 (50 gestures) and NinaPro DB7 (41 gestures).

NinaPro DB3 Dataset. [1] The dataset comprises data from 11 transradial amputees, consisting of 3 left-hand and 8 right-hand amputees. The classified movements cover 49 actions plus rest, totaling 50 categories (exercises B, C, D, and rest gestures), as shown in Fig. 1. The dataset uses a Delsys Trigno wireless system to sample 12-channel sEMG signals at a rate of 2 kHz. During data collection, subjects were instructed to use their amputated limb. Each action was repeated for 5 s, followed by a 3-second rest.

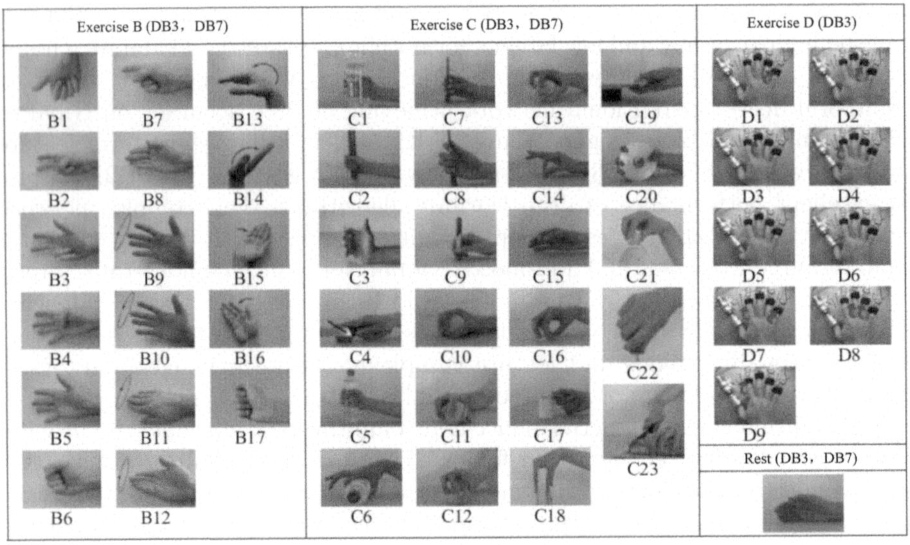

Fig. 1. Gesture types in NinaPro DB3 (Exercise B, C, D and Rest Gesture) and NinaPro DB7 (Exercise B, C and Rest Gesture)

NinaPro DB7 Dataset. [10] The dataset includes 22 subjects, comprising 20 healthy individuals and 2 right-hand amputees. The classified movements cover 40 actions plus rest, totaling 41 categories (Exercises B, C, and rest gestures), where one amputee subject (Subject 21) did not complete the last two (functional) actions of Exercise 2, as shown in Fig. 1. The dataset employs a Delsys Trigno wireless system to sample 12-channel sEMG signals at 2 kHz. During data collection, subjects were instructed to repeat movements with their right hands six times. Each action lasted 5 s, followed by a 3-second rest. This study uses data from the first 11 healthy subjects for experimental validation.

2.2 sEMG Signal Denoising.

The sEMG signals are extremely weak, with studies showing that the effective sEMG spectrum ranges from 20 to 500 Hz, with most energy concentrated in 50–150 Hz [16]. Raw sEMG signals are often contaminated with various interferences, requiring denoising to obtain valid signals. The data processed through high-frequency noise filtering, full-wave rectification, data smoothing, and low-frequency noise suppression are shown in Fig. 2.

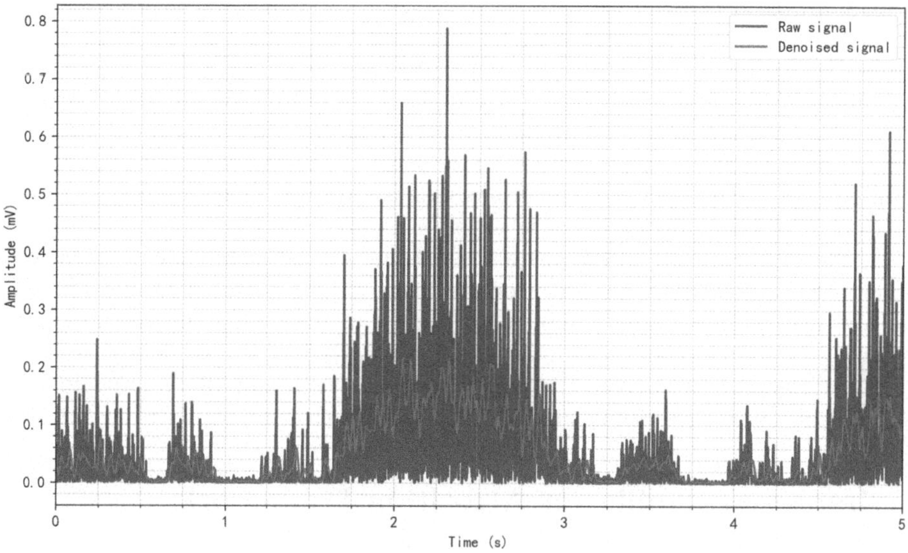

Fig. 2. sEMG signals denoising performance of one channel (Raw vs Denoised)

2.3 sEMG Signal Segmentation of Effective Hand Movements

Since the sEMG signal data in the NinaPro database are stored in multiple files per subject, data segmentation and recombination are required for processing. Actions corresponding to the same label are merged into a single matrix for storage. Taking DB7 as an example, the comparison diagram of sEMG signals before and after segmentation of 6 repeated action data is shown in Fig. 3.

2.4 Mitigating Class Imbalance and Constructing Input Signals

To tackle the notable imbalance in data volume among gesture categories in the NinaPro DB3 and DB7 datasets, this study adopts stratified K-fold cross-validation ($K = 5$). This method is designed to mitigate evaluation bias caused

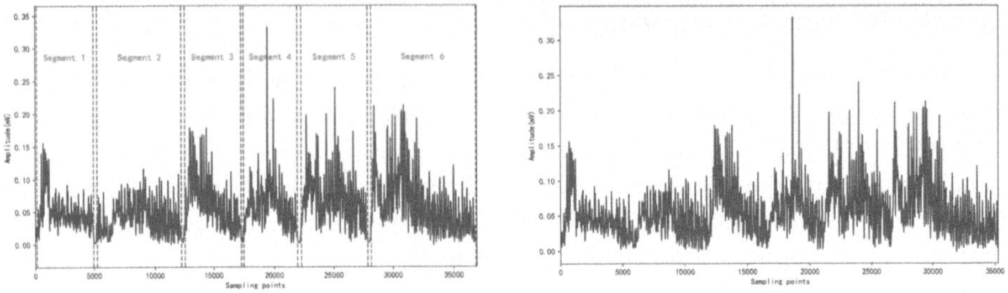

Fig. 3. Segmentation and reconstruction of raw sEMG signals for NinaPro dataset

by sample distribution imbalance in standard K-fold cross-validation. Specifically, it maintains the class sample proportion in each fold consistent with the original dataset, uses each fold alternately as the validation set (with the rest as training sets), and aggregates results across iterations—thus enabling a robust assessment of the multi-class model's performance.

In the gesture recognition process, this study constructs time-domain data as network input. First, the preprocessed signals are normalized and fed into the network as time-domain signals, as shown in Fig. 4. To ensure the sliding window has sufficient data volume, the sliding window length is set to 96 ms with a stride of 25 ms, given the 2 kHz sampling rate and 12 channels in DB3 and DB7 datasets. The input size is (192, 12), which is reshaped to (1, 48, 48).

3 Improved VanillaNet Algorithm Framework

This section first introduces the lightweight principle of the VanillaNet Block, followed by the improved VanillaNet gesture recognition algorithm adapted to sEMG signals.

3.1 VanillaNet Block

The principal merit of the VanillaNet block is its reduced network complexity, which significantly enhances real-time detection performance and makes it well-suited for deployment in resource-constrained environments. The fundamental divergence from conventional convolutional modules lies in its novel training paradigm and method to enhance the nonlinearity of the neural network.

(1) Training Method: The model's performance is enhanced by incorporating stronger nonlinear capabilities during the training phase [3]. Specifically, an activation function is used to jointly train two convolutional layers. As training progresses and an identity mapping is achieved, the outputs of these layers become identical. The fusion of these layers not only improves computational efficiency but also accelerates inference speed. The relationship between the activation function and identity mapping is mathematically expressed by equation (1):

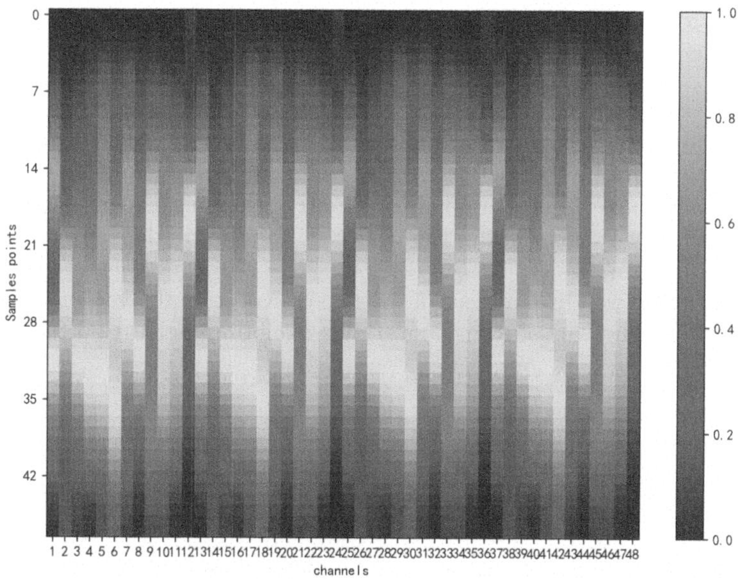

Fig. 4. Time-domain signal normalization

$$A'(x) = (1 - \lambda)A(x) + \lambda x \tag{1}$$

where λ is a hyperparameter used to balance and adjust the nonlinearity of the activation function A'. e and E represent the current epoch and the total number of training epochs, respectively, with $\lambda = \frac{e}{E}$. At the start of training, $e = 0$ and $A'(x) = A(x)$, resulting in strong nonlinearity in the network. As training progresses and converges, $A'(x) = x$, effectively removing the activation function between the two convolutional layers and resulting in a linear mapping.

In the convergence phase, the first step is to convert each batch normalization layer into a single convolution. Let $W \in \mathbb{R}^{C_{out} \times (C_{in} \times k \times k)}$ and $B \in \mathbb{R}^{C_{out}}$ represent the weight matrix and bias matrix, respectively, where C_{in} is the number of input channels, C_{out} is the number of output channels and k is the kernel size. The scale, offset, mean and variance in batch normalization are denoted as γ, β,μ and $\sigma \in \mathbb{R}^{C_{out}}$, respectively. The combined weight and bias matrices are defined by Eq. (2):

$$W_i' = \frac{\gamma_i}{\sigma_i} W_i, \quad B_i' = \frac{(B_i - \mu_i)\gamma_i}{\sigma_i} + \beta_i \tag{2}$$

where the subscript $i \in \{1, 2 \ldots, C_{out}\}$ denotes the value in the i-th output channel.

Next, proceed to merge the two 1×1 convolutions. Let $x \in \mathbb{R}^{C_{in} \times H \times W}$ and $y \in \mathbb{R}^{C_{out} \times H' \times W'}$ represent the input and output features, respectively. The convolution formula is defined by equation (3):

$$y = W * x = W \cdot im2col(x) = W \cdot X \tag{3}$$

where $*$ denotes the convolution operation, $X \in \mathbb{R}^{(C_{in}\times 1\times 1)\times(H'\times W')}$ denotes matrix multiplication, derived from the $im2col(x)$ operation (from image to matrix), which converts the input into a matrix that matches the shape of the kernel. For the 1×1 convolution, the $im2col(x)$ operation does not require overlapping sliding kernels.

Finally, let the weight matrices of the two convolutional layers be represented as W^1 and W^2. The convolution operations, excluding activation functions, are defined by equation (4):

$$\begin{aligned} y &= W^1 * (W^2 * x) \\ &= W^1 \cdot W^2 \cdot \mathrm{im2col}(x) \\ &= (W^1 \cdot W^2) * X \end{aligned} \tag{4}$$

Therefore, the 1×1 convolution can be merged without increasing inference time.

(2) Improving Inference Speed by Enhancing the Nonlinearity of Activation Functions: This module increases the nonlinearity of each activation layer by stacking multiple activation functions. Let x denote the input and $A(x)$ represent a single activation function. The stacked activation functions can be defined by equation (5):

$$A_s(x) = \sum_{i=1}^{n} a_i A(x + b_i) \tag{5}$$

where n represents the number of activation functions, and a_i and b_i are the scale and bias for each activation, respectively. This method prevents excessive nonlinearity that could arise from simply stacking activation functions, which might make the network difficult to converge. Instead, it learns global information by varying adjacent inputs. Given an input feature tensor $x \in \mathbb{R}^{H\times W\times C}$, where H, W and C denote its height, width and number of channels, respectively, the activation function can be defined by equation (6):

$$A_s(x_{h,w,c}) = \sum_{i,j\in\{-n,n\}} a_{i,j,c} A(x_{i+h,j+w,c} + b_c) \tag{6}$$

where $h \in \{1, 2, \dots, H\}$,$w \in \{1, 2, \dots, W\}$, and $c \in \{1, 2, \dots, C\}$. It can be observed that when $n = 0$, the activation function $A_s(x)$ degenerates into a pure activation function $A(x)$, resulting in a computational cost significantly lower than that of conventional convolutional layers using multiple stacked nonlinear activation layers.

3.2 Improved VanillaNet

Reducing the number of model parameters is the primary means of minimizing inference time. Beyond using lightweight VanillaNet Blocks for feature extraction, appropriate network input design and optimal layer depth are critical, as sEMG signals require less complex feature extraction than images. The depth of the feature extraction network directly impacts both recognition accuracy and computational complexity. As shown in Fig. 5 (using DB7 as an example), the normalized time-domain input $1 \times 192 \times 12$ is reshaped into a $1 \times 48 \times 48$ input. The 6-layer architecture includes a point-wise convolution layer (kernel=1, stride=1, padding=0, out_channels=64, output $64 \times 48 \times 48$), followed by four VanillaNet modules with outputs of $128 \times 24 \times 24$, $256 \times 12 \times 12$, $512 \times 6 \times 6$, and $1024 \times 3 \times 3$, respectively, and a global max pooling layer (output 1024×1). Leveraging VanillaNet's lightweight design, minimal structure, and compact input size significantly reduces parameters and inference time. During training, dropout (rate 0.5), data augmentation, and stratified K-fold cross-validation ($K = 5$) mitigate overfitting. The model uses cross-entropy loss with SGD optimizer (learning rate 0.001, batch size 64, 100 epochs).

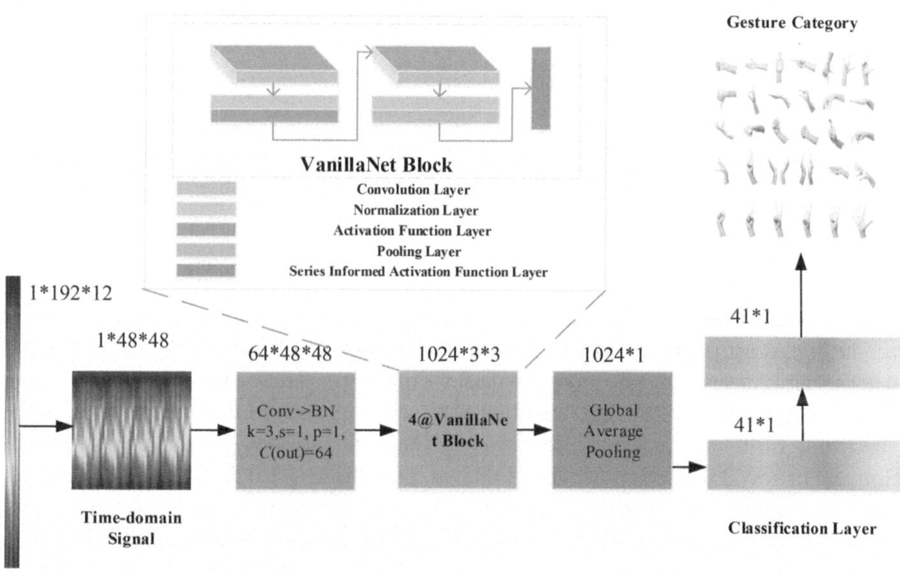

Fig. 5. Improved VanillaNet algorithm framework

4 Evaluation Metrics and Confusion Matrix

To evaluate the performance of the proposed model, we report multiple evaluation metrics, confusion matrices, and comparisons with prior work on public datasets.

As shown in Fig. 6, the test curves for gesture recognition of transradial amputees (DB3 dataset, 50 gesture classes) and able-bodied subjects (DB7 dataset, 41 gesture classes), with one subject selected from each dataset for visualization, show a convergence trend with decreasing test loss and increasing Top-1 accuracy. The model rapidly learns basic features in the early stage, followed by a convergence plateau in the later stage. However, the DB3 task is significantly more challenging due to its larger number of gesture classes and variability in amputee data (including amputation types and wearable devices), resulting in a loss curve with substantial fluctuations and a final accuracy of approximately 88% (with variations). In contrast, DB7 features more regular data distribution and fewer classes, demonstrating a smooth loss decline and accuracy stably exceeding 90%.

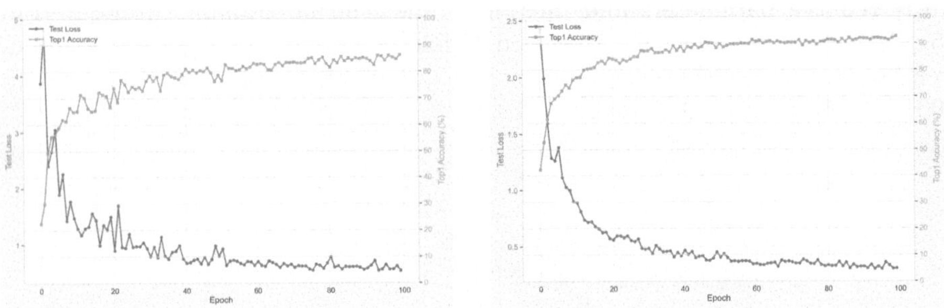

(a) Top-1 accuracy of one subject in DB3 (b) Top-1 accuracy of one subject in DB7

Fig. 6. Training metrics evolution of test loss and Top-1 accuracy across epochs

As shown in Table 1, the classification performance analysis of NinaPro DB3 (transhumeral amputee gestures, 50 classes, 11 subjects) and DB7 (able-bodied gestures, 41 classes, 11 subjects) datasets indicates that DB3 presents higher task difficulty due to its larger number of gesture classes, data variability caused by residual limb conditions, and inter-subject variability. In terms of classification accuracy, DB7 outperforms DB3 in precision (91.02%), recall (90.65%), and F1 score (90.08%) owing to its smaller number of gesture classes and more consistent data distribution. In contrast, DB3 compensates with an efficiency advantage, showing 6.83 ms inference time. This overall suggests that amputee gesture recognition faces greater challenges due to task complexity.

Table 1. Performance metrics of the model on NinaPro DB3 and DB7

Dataset	Classes	Subjects	Prec. (%)	Rec. (%)	F1 (%)	Inference time (ms)
DB3	50	11	88.85	88.89	88.57	6.83
DB7	41	11	91.02	90.65	90.08	7.53

As shown in Fig. 7, the normalized confusion matrix analysis for DB3 (amputee gestures, 50 classes) and DB7 (able-bodied gestures, 41 classes) reveals dark diagonal blocks in both matrices, indicating the model effectively classifies most categories. However, DB3 exhibits more light-colored off-diagonal spots due to diverse residual limb morphologies, high overlap of gesture features, and highly similar features among some classes, which collectively lead to class confusion, especially for edge classes affected by long-tail distribution. In contrast, DB7 features purer dark diagonal blocks, clear classification boundaries, and better class balance, attributed to the consistent gesture features and regular data distribution of able-bodied subjects. This visually demonstrates that amputee gesture recognition faces higher inter-class confusion risks due to data complexity.

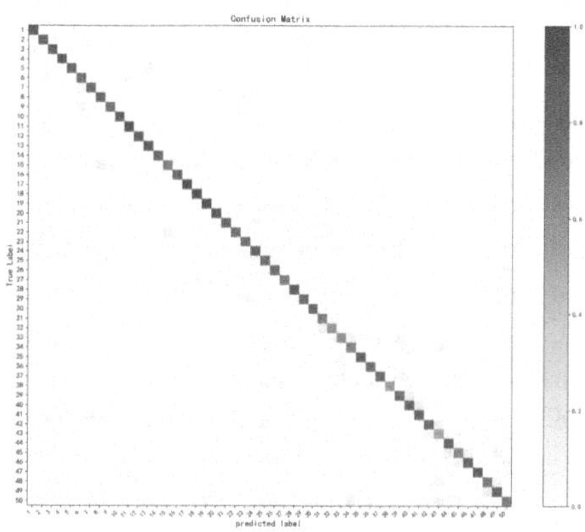

(a) Confusion matrix from DB3

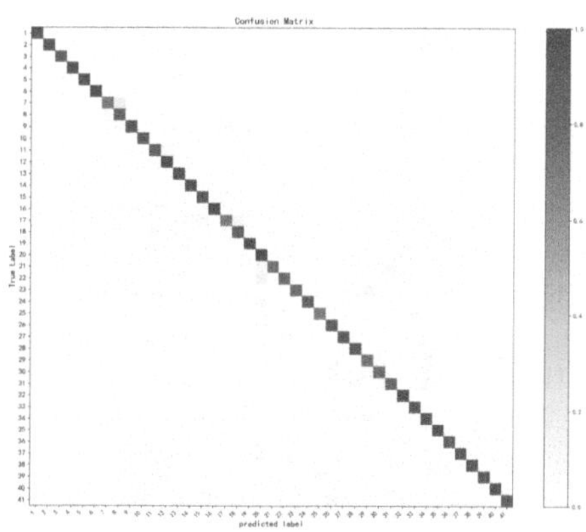

(b) Confusion matrix from DB7

Fig. 7. Normalized confusion matrices of Top-1 accuracy

In this study, we evaluated the performance of the Improved VanillaNet model on the publicly available NinaPro datasets. To validate the effectiveness of this approach, we compared the results with previous studies that employed deep learning techniques on the same datasets. The proposed Improved VanillaNet model was compared with earlier research on two databases: DB3 and DB7. As shown in Table 2, the Improved VanillaNet model achieved an accuracy of 88.78% on DB3, outperforming the previous research range of 64.30% to 85.36%. Meanwhile, on DB7, the model attained an accuracy of 91.67%, surpassing the prior accuracy range of 88.30% to 89.72%. These results demonstrate that the proposed Improved VanillaNet model successfully enables gesture classification across the two datasets, with accuracy superior to that of previous studies.

Table 2. Comparison across models on NinaPro DB3 and DB7

Reference	Dataset	Year	Model	Accuracy (%)
Pancholi et al. [12]	DB3	2021	DLPR	81.67
Sandoval–Espino et al. [15]	DB3	2022	CNN	74.24
Qamar et al. [13]	DB3	2024	DP-CNN	85.36
This Work	**DB3**	**2025**	**Improved VanillaNet**	**88.78**
Fatayer et al. [8]	DB7	2022	ALR-CNN	88.50
Xie et al. [18]	DB7	2022	Bi-ConvGRU	89.72
This Work	**DB7**	**2025**	**Improved VanillaNet**	**91.67**

5 Conclusion

To address the challenges of deep learning model performance degradation and resource constraints in sEMG-driven prosthetic hand applications, specifically when facing increased class counts and inter-subject variability, this paper proposes the improved VanillaNet algorithm tailored for diverse datasets comprising both able-bodied and amputee subjects. Validated on NinaPro DB3 and DB7, the model is benchmarked against other CNN implementations on the same datasets, demonstrating superior performance: improved VanillaNet achieves 88.78% mean classification accuracy on DB3 (a 3.42%-point improvement over the previous best) and 91.67% on DB7 (a 1.95%-point improvement over the previous best), highlighting its stable and robust performance across diverse datasets.

Acknowledgments. This work is supported in part by the LiaoNing Revitalization Talents Program (Grant No. XLYC2203104), Research Fund of Liaoning Provincial Department of Education (Grant No. LJ222410142058) and the National Natural Science Foundation of China (Grant No. 62003222).

Disclosure of Interests. The authors have no competing interests to declare that are relevant to the content of this article.

References

1. Atzori, M., et al.: Electromyography data for non-invasive naturally-controlled robotic hand prostheses. Sci. Data **1**, 140053 (2014). https://doi.org/10.1038/sdata.2014.53
2. Chen, H., Wang, Y., Guo, J., Tao, D.: VanillaNet: the power of minimalism in deep learning. arXiv preprint https://doi.org/10.48550/arXiv.2305.12972 (2023)
3. Chen, H., Wang, Y., Xu, C., et al.: Universal adder neural networks. arXiv preprint https://doi.org/10.48550/arXiv.2105.14202 (2021)
4. Cheng, Y., Li, G., Yu, M., Jiang, D., Yun, J., Liu, Y., Liu, Y., Chen, D.: Gesture recognition based on surface electromyography—feature image. Concurrency Comput. Pract. Experience **33**, e6051 (2021). https://doi.org/10.1002/cpe.6051

5. Duan, F., Ren, X., Yang, Y.: A gesture recognition system based on time domain features and linear discriminant analysis. IEEE Trans. Cogn. Dev. Syst. **13**(1), 200–208 (2021). https://doi.org/10.1109/TCDS.2018.2884942
6. Duan, F., Yang, Y.: Recognizing missing electromyography signal by data split reorganization strategy and weight-based multiple neural network voting method. IEEE Trans. Neural Netw. Learn. Syst. **33**(5), 2070–2079 (2022). https://doi.org/10.1109/TNNLS.2021.3105595
7. Fang, B., et al.: Simultaneous sEMG recognition of gestures and force levels for interaction with prosthetic hand. IEEE Trans. Neural Syst. Rehabil. Eng. **30**, 2426–2436 (2022). https://doi.org/10.1109/TNSRE.2022.3199809
8. Fatayer, A., Gao, W., Fu, Y.: sEMG-based gesture recognition using deep learning from noisy labels. IEEE J. Biomed. Health Inform. **26**(9), 4462–4473 (2022). https://doi.org/10.1109/JBHI.2022.3179630
9. Hu, Y., Wong, Y., Wei, W., Du, Y., Kankanhalli, M., Geng, W.: A novel attention-based hybrid CNN–RNN architecture for sEMG-based gesture recognition. PLoS ONE **13**(10), e0206049 (2018). https://doi.org/10.1371/journal.pone.0206049
10. Krasoulis, A., Kyranou, I., Erden, M.S., Nazarpour, K., Vijayakumar, S.: Improved prosthetic hand control with concurrent use of myoelectric and inertial measurements. J. Neuroeng. Rehabil. **14**(1), 71 (2017). https://doi.org/10.1186/s12984-017-0284-4
11. Liu, H., Zhang, Z., Qian, J., Wang, W., Kang, K.: Hand gesture recognition based on deep neural network and sEMG signal. In: 2019 IEEE International Conference on Robotics and Biomimetics (ROBIO), pp. 3001–3006 (2019). https://doi.org/10.1109/ROBIO49542.2019.8961445
12. Pancholi, S., Joshi, A.M., Joshi, D.: A robust and accurate deep learning based pattern recognition framework for upper limb prosthesis using sEMG. arXiv preprint (2021). https://doi.org/10.48550/arXiv.2106.02463
13. Qamar, H.G.M., et al.: EMG gesture signal analysis towards diagnosis of upper limb using dual-pathway convolutional neural network. Math. Biosci. Eng. **21**(4), 5712–5734 (2024). https://doi.org/10.3934/mbe.2024252
14. Qureshi, M.F., Mushtaq, Z., Rehman, M.Z.U., Kamavuako, E.N.: E2CNN: an efficient concatenated CNN for classification of surface EMG extracted from upper limb. IEEE Sens. J. **23**(8), 8989–8996 (2023). https://doi.org/10.1109/JSEN.2023.3255408
15. Sandoval-Espino, J.A., Zamudio-Lara, A., Marbán-Salgado, J.A., Escobedo-Alatorre, J.J., Palillero-Sandoval, O., Velásquez-Aguilar, J.G.: Selection of the best set of features for sEMG-based hand gesture recognition applying a CNN architecture. Sensors **22**(13), 4972 (2022). https://doi.org/10.3390/s22134972
16. Sbrollini, A., et al.: Evaluation of the low-frequency components in surface electromyography. In: 2016 38th Annual International Conference of the IEEE Engineering in Medicine and Biology Society (EMBC), pp. 3622–3625 (2016). https://doi.org/10.1109/EMBC.2016.7591512
17. Wang, Z., Yao, J., Xu, M., Jiang, M., Su, J.: Transformer-based network with temporal depthwise convolutions for sEMG recognition. Pattern Recogn. **145**, 109967 (2024). https://doi.org/10.1016/j.patcog.2023.109967
18. Xie, B., Meng, J., Li, B., Harland, A.: Biosignal-based transferable attention Bi- ConvGRU deep network for hand-gesture recognition towards online upper-limb prosthesis control. Comput. Methods Programs Biomed. **224**, 106999 (2022). https://doi.org/10.1016/j.cmpb.2022.106999

19. Xu, P., Li, F., Wang, H.: A novel concatenate feature fusion RCNN architecture for sEMG-based hand gesture recognition. PLoS ONE **17**(1), e0262810 (2022). https://doi.org/10.1371/journal.pone.0262810
20. Zhang, W., Zhao, T., Zhang, J., Wang, Y.: Lst-EMG-net: long short-term transformer feature fusion network for sEMG gesture recognition. Front. Neurorobot. **17**, 1127338 (2023). https://doi.org/10.3389/fnbot.2023.1127338

NanyinVR: Gesture-Based Immersive Virtual Reality Game for Enhancing Learning of Ancient Chinese Music and Instruments

Yiping Wu[1,3,4,5], Kai Chen[2], and Yue Li[2,3,4,5](✉)

[1] School of Mathematics and Computer Science, Quanzhou Normal University, Quanzhou, Fujian, China

[2] School of Advanced Technology, Xi'an Jiaotong-Liverpool University, Suzhou, Jiangsu, China

[3] Fujian Provincial Key Laboratory of Data-Intensive Computing, Quanzhou, Fujian, China

[4] Fujian Higher Education Key Laboratory of Intelligent Computing and Information Processing, Quanzhou, Fujian, China

[5] Fujian Provincial Big Data Research Institute of Intelligent Manufacturing, Quanzhou, Fujian, China

yue.li@xjtlu.edu.cn

Abstract. *Nanyin* is a traditional genre of Chinese music originating from Quanzhou, Fujian, characterized by its distinctive melodies, use of traditional instruments, and rich cultural heritage. Virtual reality has made it more accessible for people to experience, learn, and transmit intangible cultural heritage, contributing to its presentation, preservation, and dissemination. In this paper, we present the design and implementation of NanyinVR, a gesture-based immersive virtual reality game. It consists of two parts: Nanyin learning and instrument playing. We systematically evaluated the usability, user experience, and game experience of NanyinVR with both children and young adults. The results showed that children found it more challenging and showed less competence and flow of game experience; adults reported greater ease of use and ease of learning, and rated higher on usability, pragmatic quality, and overall user experience than children. Our research revealed design implication of demographic difference between age groups in music learning and instrument playing in gesture-based virtual reality.

Keywords: Virtual Reality · Gesture Interaction · Cultural Heritage · Music Education · Nanyin

Y. Wu and K. Chen—The two authors contributed equally to this work.

S. Guo et al. (Eds.): HHME 2025, CCIS 2878, pp. 283–301, 2027.
https://doi.org/10.1007/978-981-92-3991-7_19

1 Introduction

Nanyin (南音), also known as Nanguan or Nanqu, was recognized as an intangible culture heritage of UNESCO in 2009 [28]. It is a traditional Chinese music genre originating from Tang Dynasty [29] and has been passed down through mentorship and oral instruction. Nanyin consists of three types of music "zhi" (指), "pu" (谱) and "qu" (曲) [16]. The first type is purely instrumental, the second includes vocals, and the third consists of ballads accompanied by the ensemble and sung in the Quanzhou dialect [16]. There are over ten different types of instruments used in Nanyin. This genre has spread to regions such as Taiwan, Hong Kong, Macao, Singapore, Malaysia, Indonesia, and Philippines, as Minnan people explore new opportunities in other countries [28].

The recent advancements in digitization [13], virtual reality [22,30], augmented reality [4,5,22], mixed reality [32,33], artificial intelligence [9,19], and metaverse [27] have created new opportunities for the presentation, preservation, and dissemination of intangible cultural heritage. These versatile techniques and resources have made intangible cultural heritage more accessible to the public around the world [13]. By facilitating immersive experiences through virtual reality (VR), augmented reality (AR), and gamified interactions, the knowledge of intangible heritage can be effectively communicated to users.

Immersive experiences in VR and AR not only communicate knowledge and skills of intangible heritage [30], but also enhance cultural understanding and emotional connections [33]. For example, Wang et al. [30] designed the FloraJing VR system for traditional Chinese flower arrangement, which promoted progressive reflection, and continuous technical improvement. Similarly, the KiteMR system [33] greatly enhanced participants' cultural understanding and emotional connections of Beijing swallow kites.

Furthermore, immersive technologies have made intangible cultural heritage more accessible to various people [7,8,13,32]. For example, the VirGuqin and MRGuqin systems [32] have made Guqin more accessible to the general public. Additionally, virtual reality has provided immersive musical experiences and music performances that are accessible to individuals who are blind or have low-vision [7,8].

However, learning music or playing music instrument in immersive technologies are still facing many challenges [21], and research on music-related application remains limited [2]. Musical instrument performance involves not only the consideration of melody but also complex expressive techniques [18], necessitating high precision and low latency. Immersive technologies have yet to effectively simulate playing techniques, such as breath control and strength control. Issues like latency in visual and auditory feedback [26], as well as haptic and strength aspects, continue to pose significant challenges.

In this paper, we aim to expand the learning approach for Nanyin beyond traditional methods. We aim to design and develop a gesture-based immersive VR game that can be used for not only adults, but also children in primary schools. We developed and implemented NanyinVR for learning Nanyin music and for playing the pipa (琵琶) and dongxiao (洞箫), the two most typical music instruments in Nanyin. We conducted empirical research to assess differences in usability, user experience, and core game experience between young adults and children. The evaluation revealed that children found it more challenging to learn and play the instrument compared to adults, while adults reported a higher pragmatic quality of user experience, competence, and flow during gameplay than children.

Our research makes the following contributions: First, we present one of the first studies that explores gesture control and immersive VR gaming as a means for the public to learn about Nanyin. We designed and implemented the NanyinVR system utilizing hand-tracking technology for playing the pipa and dongxiao. Additionally, we conducted an evaluation of the NanyinVR system, comparing adults and children in terms of usability, user experience, and game experience, which resulted in overall positive feedback. We also identify the challenges that children face when learning to use VR systems for playing musical instruments, highlighting several key areas that require further research.

2 Background

2.1 Nanyin Music and Instruments

As an ancient form of music, the Nanyin Gongche notation (工乂谱) has been preserved through handwritten manuscripts, as shown in Fig. 1. In a traditional Nanyin performance, the sequence begins with zhi (fingerings), followed by qu (melodic pieces), and concludes with pu (instrumental arrangements). There are over ten types of instruments used, including the Chinese lute (Nanyin pipa), two-stringed fiddle (Erxian), three-stringed fiddle (Sanxian), Chinese vertical

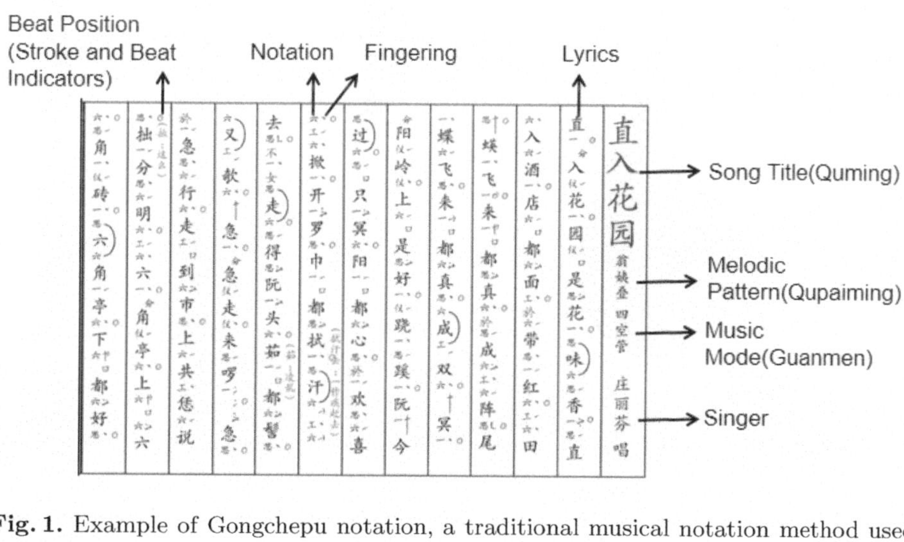

Fig. 1. Example of Gongchepu notation, a traditional musical notation method used in Nanyin.

flute (Dongxiao), clappers (Paiban), small gong (Xiangzhan), four bamboo clappers (Sibao), bronze bells (Shuangling), wooden fish (Muyu), flat drum (Biangu), and alto suona (Nan'ai) [31].

Notably, pipa is a traditional Chinese lute with a pear-shaped body and four strings, while Nanyin pipa is one sort of them (see Fig. 2, left). It has four strings, one tuning peg and one sound bridge. Nanyin pipa players perform on the pipa by following the fingering techniques and musical notes indicated in the notation. The performance of pipa is accomplished through the coordination of fingering and strength. During the performance, the combination of fingering techniques and varying degrees of strength is used to express the charm and emotion of the music.

Dongxiao is a traditional Chinese bamboo flute. It has a mouthpiece, five holes and one brass joint for music creation, as shown in Fig. 2 (right). Dongxiao has a wide range of playing techniques, which involve fingering, breath control, and posture [6]. Fingering techniques include covering holes, glissando (sliding between notes), and vibrato (a rapid, slight variation in pitch). Breath control refers to the player's ability to manipulate the tone and volume through the strength of their breath. The player blows into the mouthpiece while using their right hand to hold the dongxiao and their left hand to cover the holes to express the music [6].

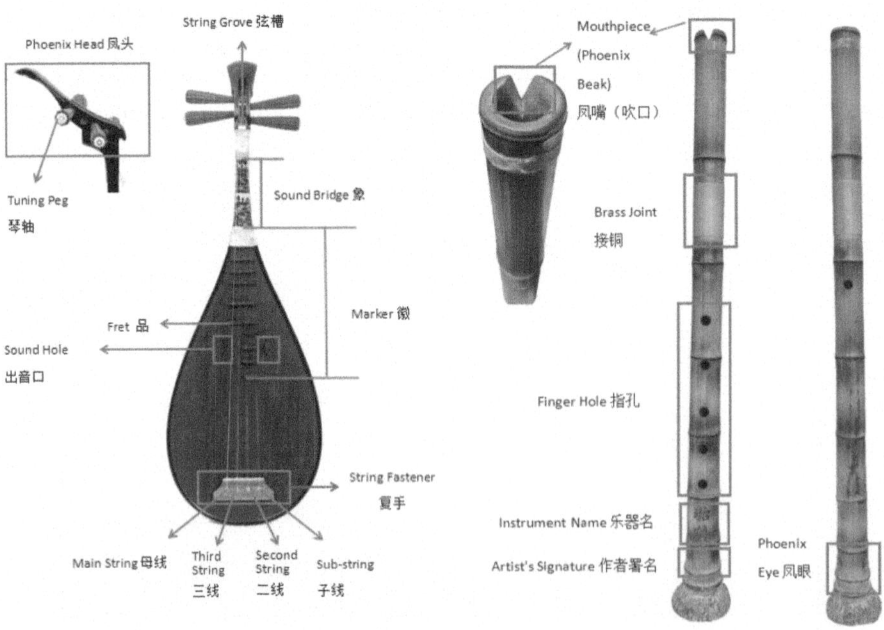

Fig. 2. Illustration of the two key music instruments used in Nanyin: Pipa (left) and Dongxiao (right).

2.2 Immersive Technologies for Music Learning and Instrument Playing

In music education, immersive technologies have introduced innovative applications for educators and students [15,25]. For example, HoloKeys [25], using augmented reality headset and wifi-based microcontrollers, allows instructors to play remotely located pianos while remote students could observe live instructional demonstration on a physical keyboard in their traditional settings. Additionally, mobile virtual reality has been employed to teach music genre in elementary schools [15]. Patrick et al. [23] proposed a method for basic music theory education in virtual reality that leverages sound-color cross-modal associations.

Despite the benefits of learning music instrument, the associated costs and the frustrations experienced by children have led many students to drop out [1]. However, immersive technologies in music instrument learning have been shown to enhance learners' engagement and confidence [17]. They also provide the general public with opportunities to learn about the endangered musical instrument, such as Guqin [32]. Researchers also studied ways to augment instrument learning of the popular ones, such as piano. For instance, the PianoSyncAR system [20] superimposes hand postures of a teacher over the hand of a learner, facilitating piano instruction. In addition, by simulating ambient light and audience distance in a virtual auditorium, performance anxiety for musicians can be significantly reduced [11].

Nonetheless, challenges in virtual instrument performance remain underexplored in immersive technologies [12,18]. Limitations in immersive technologies [12], such as input technologies, have hindered the ability to simulate the play of instruments based on breath control in VR, such as the dongxiao and flute. In addition, The timing requirements for playing instruments in virtual reality present challenges related to high precision and low latency [2]. Moreover, latency in visual, audio, and haptic [10], may affect user experience in virtual music instrument learning and playing [2]. For example, timing asynchrony and variance among different input techniques can yield distinct outcomes [2]. In addition, the differing playing techniques required for various musical instruments necessitate appropriate input technologies in virtual reality, such as simulating guitar plucking [10], or tapping in music-related applications [2]. In these cases, using VR hand-held controllers can feel very unnatural, as they differ greatly from the gripping gestures and fingering techniques needed for playing the instrument. Therefore, there is a need to explore natural input techniques that are suitable for playing musical instruments in virtual reality, such as free-hand gesture control.

Overall, our review highlights the benefits of immersive technologies in music education and instrument performance, as well as the challenges encountered in this context. Specifically, there is a need for empirical research examining the use of gesture-based virtual reality applications across different age groups for learning intangible cultural heritage and playing instruments.

2.3 Research Aims

Based on the review of related work, we aim to create a gesture-based immersive VR game for Nanyin learning and instrument playing, providing an interactive experience of local music culture for different age groups. Specifically, we formulate two research questions with hypotheses:

RQ1 Can NanyinVR effectively enhance Nanyin learning and instrument playing?
RQ2 Do the usability, user experience, and game experience of NanyinVR differ between adults and children?

H1 NanyinVR can effectively enhance Nanyin learning and instrument playing.
H2 There is no difference between adults and children in the usability, user experience, or game experience of NanyinVR.

3 System Design and Implementation

3.1 System Design

The NanyinVR system consisted of two parts: (1) Nanyin learning stage and (2) instrument playing stage. Figure 3 illustrates the system features.

Nanyin Learning Stage. At this stage, we present a virtual auditorium, where a virtual 3D pipa was placed on a table accompanied with a knowledge panel (see Fig. 3a). The knowledge panel presents information about Nanyin through text, audio, and video. Additionally, it displays the structure and playing techniques for both the pipa and dongxiao, as shown in Fig. 3b. In addition to the fundamental theory of Nanyin and its instruments, the visual 3D representations of the pipa and dongxiao provide a realistic and immersive experience for learning about musical instruments, particularly since most audiences have limited or no access to these instruments in real life.

Players can grasp the instrument with their hands to examine its structure. Instead of presenting large chunks of texts, we mark certain parts of the instrument with highlighted dots (i.e., hotkeys). When players touch these dots, a knowledge panel related to that specific part appears in front of them, allowing for deeper understanding of the instrument's history, structure, and playing methods. Players can also open the video instruction panel and interact with it using raycasting control or proximity touch. They have the freedom to adjust the volume, control playback progress, and pause or play the video.

Instrument Playing Stage. The instrument playing adopts a rhythmic music game approach, where the notes flow from the strings of pipa and pass through the holes of dongxiao. Players use hand triggers at the appropriate timing to simulate the play of the instruments. This approach allows participants to engage with and appreciate the art form of Nanyin in an immersive manner.

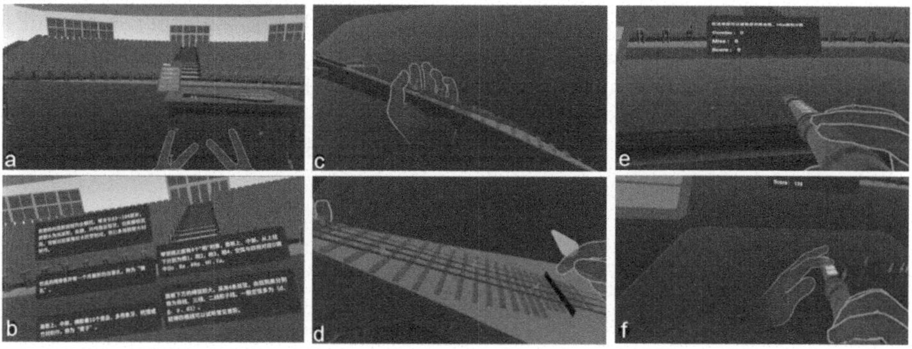

Fig. 3. System illustrations of NanyinVR. (a) The virtual auditorium environment for NanyinVR system, simulating a stage with music instruments and audience seats, (b) knowledge panels used to introduce Nanyin and the instruments, (c-d) gesture control for grabbing and playing the *pipa*, (e-f) gesture control for grabbing and playing the dongxiao.

Additionally, combo, miss, and scoring panels are displayed to motivate players through gamification. Points serve as feedback, indicating the player's real-time status in the game and their performance in real time, thus providing a way to track game progress. This point system encourages players to strive for higher levels of achievement.

Players hold the pipa with their left hand, as illustrated in Fig. 3c-d. As the notes flow across the strings, the player uses the right hand to pluck the strings at the right moments when a note arrives and align with the rhythm of the music being played. The playing action was based on collision detection between the fingertips and the notes. For the dongxiao, player hold the instrument with their right hands, as shown in Fig. 3e-f. As the notes flow horizontally through the holes of the dongxiao, the player presses the holes with their left hand when it is triggered. The pressing action was executed using button presses in Unity, while the playing action relied on collision detection between the button presses and the notes. These two triggering methods enable users to simulate the postures, gestures, and movements involved in playing the two instruments in real life, creating a truly immersive experience.

3.2 System Implementation

We used Unity (version 2021.3.34.f1c1) and a laptop with an 12th Gen Intel(R) Core (TM) i9-12900H @ 2.50GHz CPU and an NVIDIA GeForce RTX 3060 graphics card for the system development. The rhythm is set using the Koreographer toolkit[1]. We used the Meta XR SDK for the development of hand-tracking in Unity. For the system deployment, we used Meta Quest 3, an all-in-one head-mounted display (HMD) featuring a Snapdragon® XR2 processor. It

[1] https://assetstore.unity.com/packages/tools/audio/koreographer-54639.

has a binocular resolution of 3600 × 1920 pixels (2064 × 2208 per eye) and a field of view of 110° horizontally and 96° vertically. The headset provides hand gesture tracking through four integrated cameras, with 21 tracking anchor points per hand. It allows the recognition of distances between the hand and the HMD ranging from 20 to 50 cm, with a gesture tracking field of view of 110° × 96° and a recognition accuracy of approximately 10 mm.

4 Evaluation

4.1 Study Design and Procedure

We designed a between-group study with two age groups: young adults and children. Participants first filled in a consent form after been briefed about the experiment. The experiment includes two sessions: (1) Nanyin introduction and (2) instrument playing. After participants have completed both sessions, they are invited to fill out a post-experiment questionnaire. Figure 4 shows the experimental setup with adults and children participants. The data collection took place at a university laboratory for adults, and a primary school classroom for children. Specifically for children participants, their parental consent was obtained. In addition, the experiments were conducted under the supervision of a teacher of the primary school. The study received ethics approval prior to the data collection.

Fig. 4. Experimental setup: adult participants at a university laboratory (left) and children participants at a primary school classroom (right).

4.2 Measurements

The post-experiment questionnaire consisted of three sections: (1) demographic information of participants, (2) subjective questions measuring usability, user experience, and game experience, and (3) open-ended questions eliciting learning outcomes and subjective feedback.

The demographic information includes age, gender, occupation, knowledge of Nanyin, familiarity of virtual reality application, familiarity of hand-tracking in virtual reality, and familiarity of electronic games.

Usability [3], user experience [24], and game experience [14] questions were derived from validation questionnaires. Consistent with the original questionnaires, usability and game experience were rated on a 5-point Likert scale (5 = strongly agree), and the user experience was rated on a 7-point scale. Detailed questionnaire items are shown in Appendix A.

Open-ended questions were used to collect players' knowledge and experience of our system. Specifically, four questions were asked:

Q1 What have you learned at the *Nanyin Learning* stage?
Q2 Please list two aspects you like about *Nanyin Learning.*
Q3 What have you learned at the *Instrument Playing* stage?
Q4 Please list two aspects you like about *Instrument Playing.*

4.3 Participants

Forty-one participants (19 males and 21 females) joined in our experiment, including 19 young adults (age $M = 22.95, SD = 2.59$) and 22 children (age $M = 10.63, SD = 0.79$). For young adults, most of them (14 out of 19) were unfamiliar with Nanyin, while a smaller pool of children (9 out of 21) also did not know about it. This can be attributed to the fact that all children attend the same primary school in Quanzhou, a key area within the Minnan region where Nanyin is included in their education syllabus. The data collected showed that young adults were less familiar with virtual reality applications ($M = 1.89, SD = 0.79$) compared to children ($M = 2.50, SD = 1.01$). Additionally, young adults were less familiar with hand-tracking in virtual reality ($M = 1.37, SD = 0.76$) than children ($M = 2.32, SD = 0.84$). In contrast, young adults reported a higher familiarity with electronic games ($M = 3.32, SD = 1.33$) compared to children ($M = 2.91, SD = 1.27$).

5 Results and Analysis

Data analysis was performed using IBM SPSS Statistics. We examined the Shapiro-Wilk test results to see whether the distribution meet the parametric test assumptions. For data that meet normal distribution, we conducted independent-samples t-tests for the comparisons between children and adults. Otherwise, we performed the Mann-Whitney U tests for between-group comparisons. Table 1 includes the detailed descriptive statistics of the questionnaire analysis.

5.1 Usability

According to the Shapiro-Wilk test, the usability data conformed to a normal distribution, $p = 0.238$. An independent samples t-test showed a significant

Table 1. Detailed descriptive statistics of the questionnaire analysis.

Measurements	Group	Min	Max	Mean	SD	Median
Usability	Adults	2.80	4.40	3.84	0.53	4.00
	Children	2.30	4.30	3.40	0.45	3.45
Ease of Use	Adults	2.75	4.50	3.99	0.54	4.25
	Children	2.38	4.63	3.61	0.51	3.69
Ease of Learning	Adults	2.00	4.00	3.24	0.69	3.50
	Children	1.50	4.00	2.55	0.65	2.50
User Experience	Adults	4.88	7.00	6.30	0.70	6.63
	Children	3.88	7.00	5.68	0.97	5.81
Pragmatic Quality	Adults	4.75	7.00	6.30	0.66	6.50
	Children	3.75	7.00	5.42	0.93	5.50
Hedonic Quality	Adults	4.25	7.00	6.30	0.86	6.75
	Children	2.50	7.00	5.94	1.20	6.00
Competence	Adults	2.60	5.00	4.04	0.65	4.20
	Children	2.00	5.00	3.41	0.74	3.40
Immersion	Adults	2.50	5.00	4.27	0.62	4.67
	Children	2.33	5.00	4.21	0.71	4.25
Flow	Adults	3.00	5.00	3.93	0.61	3.60
	Children	2.40	5.00	3.46	0.77	3.20
Tension	Adults	1.00	2.67	1.30	0.53	1.00
	Children	1.00	3.33	1.52	0.71	1.17
Challenge	Adults	1.40	2.80	1.93	0.41	1.80
	Children	1.40	3.80	2.43	0.53	2.40
Negative Affect	Adults	1.00	2.50	1.49	0.46	1.25
	Children	1.00	3.50	1.76	0.69	1.50
Positive Affect	Adults	3.20	5.00	4.35	0.53	4.40
	Children	2.80	5.00	4.27	0.69	4.40

difference between young adults ($M = 3.84, SD = 0.53$) and children ($M = 3.40, SD = 0.45$) in the system usability, $t(39) = 2.884, p = .006, d = .903$. Specifically, adults rated significantly higher on the ease of use ($M = 3.99, SD = 0.54$) than children ($M = 3.61, SD = 0.51$), $t(39) = 2.347, p = .024, d = .735$. The system was also found easier to learn for adults ($M = 3.24, SD = 0.69$) than children ($M = 2.55, SD = 0.65$), $z = -2.903, p = .004$. The overall usability scores were 83.55 and 72.50 for adults and children, respectively, surpassing the threshold value of 68 [3]. Overall, adults found the NanyinVR system easier to use and easier to learn than children (Fig. 5).

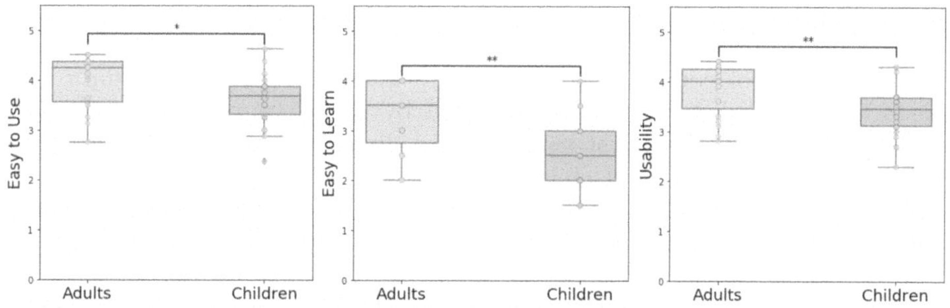

Fig. 5. Results showing the system usability of NanyinVR, measured in two dimensions: ease of use and ease of learning.

5.2 User Experience

Shapiro-Wilk test indicated that the pragmatic quality ($p = 0.011$), hedonic quality ($p < 0.001$), and overall user experience ($p = 0.001$) did not conform to normal distribution. Results of the Mann-Whitney U test show a significant difference between adults ($M = 6.30, SD = 0.66$) and children ($M = 5.42, SD = 0.93$) in the pragmatic quality, $z = -2.958, p = .003$. No significant difference was found in hedonic quality between adults ($M = 6.75, SD = 0.86$) and children ($M = 5.94, SD = 1.20$), $z = -0.562, p = .574$. The overall user experience was rated significantly higher for adults ($M = 6.30, SD = 0.70$) than children ($M = 5.68, SD = 0.97$), $z = -2.293, p = .022$. Comparing against the benchmark dataset [24], the pragmatic quality, hedonic quality, and the overall user experience all fell in the *excellent* category. Overall, adults and children perceived a similar level of hedonic quality in the user experience, but the pragmatic quality was perceived higher by adults, leading an overall heightened user experience than children (Fig. 6).

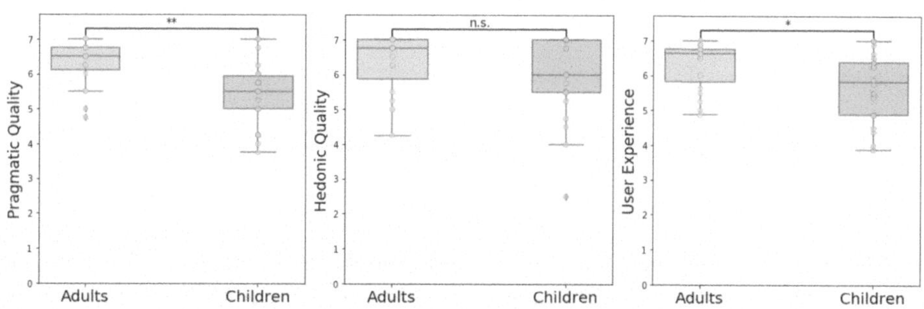

Fig. 6. Results showing the user experience of NanyinVR, measured in two dimensions: pragmatic quality and hedonic quality.

5.3 Game Experience

The distribution of competence ($p = 0.310$) and flow ($p = 0.204$) data conformed to normal distribution, as indicated by the Shapiro-Wilk test results. An independent samples t-test showed a significant difference between adults ($M = 4.04, SD = 0.65$) and children ($M = 3.41, SD = 0.74$) in their competence, $t(39) = 2.880, p = .006, d = .902$. Similarly, adults reported significantly greater flow experience ($M = 3.93, SD = 0.61$) than children ($M = 3.46, SD = 0.77$), $t(39) = 2.150, p = .038, d = .673$. Sensory and imaginative immersion ($p = .001$), positive affect ($p = .002$), tension ($p < 0.001$), challenge ($p = .009$) and negative affect ($p < .001$) do not conformed to normal distribution. The Mann-Whitney U test showed a significant difference between adults ($M = 1.93, SD = 0.41$) and children ($M = 2.43, SD = 0.53$) in the perceived challenge, $z = -3.182, p = .001$. However, there are no significant difference between adults and children in their sensory and imaginative immersion ($z = -0.158, p = .874$), positive affect ($z = -0.066, p = .947$), tension ($z = -1.143, p = .253$), and negative affect ($z = -1.287, p = .198$). Overall, there were significant differences between adults and children in three dimensions of game experience: competence, flow, and challenge. Specifically, children reported less competence and flow, but more challenge than adults in the game experience. No significant difference was found in sensory and imaginative immersion, positive affect, tension, or negative affect between groups (Fig. 7).

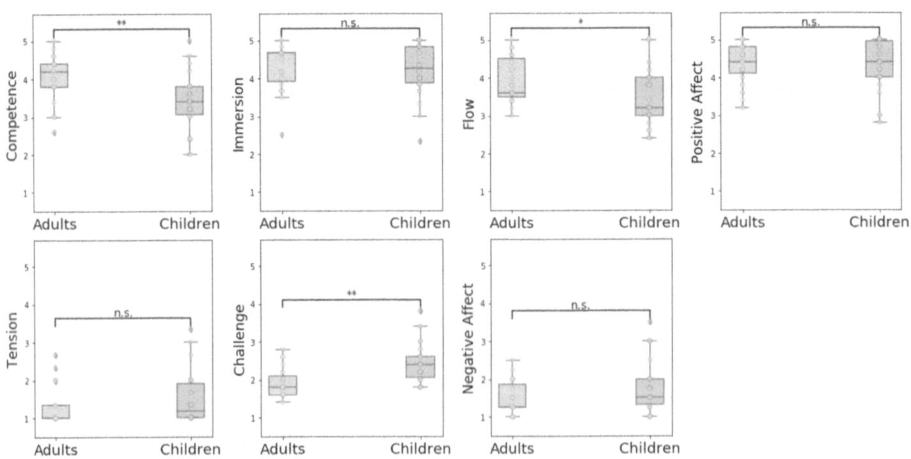

Fig. 7. Results showing the game experience of NanyinVR, measured in seven dimensions: competence, sensory and imaginative immersion, flow, positive affect, tension, challenge, and negative affect.

5.4 Open-Ended Questions

Nanyin Learning Stage. Many participants (28/41, 14 adults, 14 children) reported Nanyin related knowledge about color, shape, and structure of the Nanyin pipa and dongxiao. In addition, some mentioned they learned about the VR technology, such as the gesture control. For example, P18 (adult) reported that they have learned about Nanyin instrument and VR gesture. In addition, two participants (P21, P40) (children) reported that they learned about the use of virtual reality technology in learning music. Regarding the two aspects that participants like about the Nanyin learning stage, about half participants (20/41, 9 adults, 11 children) reported that they like the novelty, interest and fun in listening to music, learning about Nanyin and playing instruments. Eleven participants (5 adults, 6 children) reported on virtual reality related features, such as visual and audio immersion, hand-tracking, instruction video in VR, and the introduction text panels. Ten reported none for both two questions.

Instrument Playing Stage. In Nanyin instrument playing stage, over half participants (22/41, 14 adults, 8 children) reported that they have learned how to playing pipa and dongxiao. Notably, the number of adults acknowledging knowledge learned is greater than children, which indicated that adults perceived higher performance in the instrument playing stage. Eight participants (2 adults, 6 children) reported on shape and knowledge of pipa and dongxiao, and knowledge of Nanyin. One reported the power of technology. Regarding the two aspects that participants like about the instrument playing stage, twenty-seven participants (14 adults, 13 children) reported immersion, presence, realism and fun in playing pipa and dongxiao in VR. Five participants (0 adults, 5 children) reported on structure, knowledge and shape of pipa and dongxiao. In summary, the four open-ended questions revealed that both adults and children learned basic theory of Nanyin, as well as the structure, knowledge and shape of the music instruments, pipa and dongxiao. In addition, gesture-based immersive VR are well accepted by both groups in learning music and playing music instruments. In addition, adults showed greater performance on instrument playing in NanyinVR.

6 Discussion

6.1 Hypotheses Testing Results

In this study, we investigated the usability, user experience and game experience between young adults and children in learning Nanying and playing music instruments in a gesture-based immersive virtual reality game.

H1 is supported - overall positive results were observed for the usability, user experience and game experience evaluations for both groups. Both adults and children found the NanyinVR system effective for in learning Nanyin and playing instrument with hand-tracking gestures. Specifically, the open-ended questions showed that adults reported more knowledge learned and performed better in instrument playing than children. This is likely associated with the higher cognitive level of adults than children. Additionally, our informal conversations with participants indicated that some adult participants possess advanced instrument playing skills, which may contribute to the differences observed between adults and children. However, since we did not collect this demographic information, we cannot draw definitive conclusions about its impact.

H2 is partially supported - no significant difference was found between the two age groups in the perceived hedonic quality of user experience, sensory and imaginative immersion, positive affect, tension, or negative affect of game experience. However, we found significant differences between adults and children in their evaluations of usability and user experience, notably the pragmatic quality. The competence, flow, as well as challenge dimensions of game experience also differed significantly. The results revealed that children encountered more difficulties in using and learning NanyinVR, and found it more challenging than adults. This was associated with the less perceived pragmatic quality, competence and flow. These results are also consistent with open-ended questions in instrument playing stage that more adults reported positively on the instrument playing in NanyinVR.

6.2 Research Contributions

We present one of the first studies exploring gesture control and immersive VR gaming as a means for the public to learn about Nanyin, a UNESCO-recognized intangible cultural heritage. The NanyinVR system was designed and implemented with hand-tracking technology for playing the pipa and dongxiao. In addition, we conducted an evaluation of the NanyinVR system comparing adults and children in terms of usability, user experience, and game experience, which yielded overall positive feedback. We identify the perceived challenges faced by children when learning to use VR systems for playing musical instruments, highlighting several key areas that require further attention and research.

6.3 Limitations and Future Work

Our study has some limitations and indicates the need for future work. First, we found differences in perceived ease of use and learnability between adults and children, which have prompted us to further investigate demographic variations in instrument learning and playing experiences. The significant disparities observed between the two groups in our findings suggest that the demographic differences (e.g., cognitive capability, motor skills, instrument proficiency, etc.) may influence the effectiveness of instrument education. Data related these sample characteristics should be more comprehensively collected in future studies to obtain in-depth understanding of the differences. Additionally, the stability of tracking while playing the pipa and dongxiao presents another limitation, highlighting the need for system improvements as VR technology continues to evolve. One area of improvement is to combine VR simulations with tangible interactions to provide more realistic haptic feedback. In future work, it is also essential to focus more on children's understanding of music and instrument playing to enhance their music learning effectiveness and experience in VR.

7 Conclusion

In this paper, we present NanyinVR, a gesture-based immersive virtual reality game designed to help the public learn about Nanyin and instrument playing. We conducted a between-group study to evaluate usability, user experience, and game experience among adults and children, showing significant differences in usability, user experience, competence, flow, and the challenges faced during gameplay. Children reported experiencing more challenges and lower levels of usability, user experience, competence, and flow in NanyinVR compared to adults. Despite these differences, both groups effectively learned Nanyin and instrument playing through our system. Moving forward, we aim to improve the user-friendliness of our system specifically for children.

Acknowledgements. This work is supported by the National Natural Science Foundation of China (62207022) and the Fujian Provincial Key Laboratory of Data-Intensive Computing, Quanzhou Normal University (SJXY202402). We would like to express our gratitude to Zhenmei Chen, Longtao Zhang, Shihao Fan, and Zhenni Cai for their valuable guidance on Nanyin performance throughout this project. Additionally, we thank our participants for their time, efforts, and valuable suggestion in the evaluation studies.

Appendix A: Post-experiment questionnaires

Usability - Ease of Use	
U1	I think that I would like to use this system frequently.
U2	I found the system *unnecessarily complex.*
U3	I thought the system was easy to use.
U5	I found the various functions in this system were well integrated.
U6	I thought there was *too much inconsistency in this system.*
U7	I would imagine that most people would learn to use this system very quickly.
U8	I found the system *very cumbersome to use.*
U9	I felt very confident using the system.
Usability - Ease of Learning	
U4	I think that I would *need the support of a technical person to be able to use this system.*
U10	I needed to *learn a lot of things before I could get going with this system.*
User Experience - Pragmatic Quality	
Q1	Obstructive/Supportive
Q2	Complicated/Easy

Q3	Inefficient/Efficient
Q4	Confusing/Clear
User Experience - Hedonic Quality	
Q5	Boring/Exciting
Q6	Not interesting/Interesting
Q7	Conventional/Inventive
Q8	Usual/Leading-edge
Game Experience - Competence	
G2	I felt skillful.
G10	I felt competent.
G15	I was good at it.
G17	I felt successful.
G21	I was fast at reaching the game's targets.
Game Experience - Sensory and Imaginative Immersion	
G3	I thought it was fun.
G12	It was aesthetically pleasing.
G18	I felt imaginative.
G19	I felt that I could explore things.
G27	I found it impressive.
G30	It felt like a rich experience.
Game Experience - Flow	
G5	I was fully occupied with the game.
G13	I forgot everything around me.
G25	I lost track of time.
G28	I was deeply concentrated in the game.
G31	I lost connection with the outside world.
Game Experience - Tension	
G22	I felt *annoyed.*
G24	I felt *irritable.*
G29	I felt *frustrated.*
Game Experience - Challenge	
G11	I thought it was *hard.*
G23	I felt *pressured.*
G26	I felt *challenged.*
G32	I felt *time pressure.*
G33	I had to *put a lot of effort into it.*
Game Experience - Negative Affect	
G7	It gave me a *bad mood.*
G8	I *thought about other things.*
G9	I found it *tiresome.*
G16	I felt *bored.*
Game Experience - Positive Affect	

G1	I felt content.
G4	I was interested in the game
G6	I felt happy.
G14	I felt good.
G20	I enjoyed it.

References

1. Blewett, D.J., Gerhard, D.: Brass haptics: comparing virtual and physical trumpets in extended realities. Arts **12**(4), 145 (2023). https://doi.org/10.3390/arts12040145
2. Boem, A., Turchet, L.: Selection as tapping: an evaluation of 3d input techniques for timing tasks in musical virtual reality. Int. J. Hum Comput Stud. **185**, 103231 (2024). https://doi.org/10.1016/j.ijhcs.2024.103231
3. Brooke, J.: SUS - A quick and dirty usability scale. In: Jordan, P.W., Thomas, B., McClelland, I.L., Weerdmeester, B. (eds.) Usability Evaluation in Industry, pp. 189–194. CRC Press, Boca Raton, FL (1996). https://doi.org/10.1201/9781498710411
4. Chen, M., Liang, S., Smith, G.: Stackable music: a marker-based augmented reality music synthesis game. In: Companion Proceedings of the Annual Symposium on Computer-Human Interaction in Play (CHI PLAY Companion '23), pp. 22–28. Association for Computing Machinery, New York, NY, USA (2023). https://doi.org/10.1145/3573382.3616071
5. Chen, Y., Mao, Q., Huang, X., Xu, N.: LanternOperAR: a hybrid cultural gift for quality education and family well-being. In: Extended Abstracts of the CHI Conference on Human Factors in Computing Systems (CHI EA '24). Association for Computing Machinery, New York, NY, USA (2024). https://doi.org/10.1145/3613905.3647972
6. Chi, Y.: A preliminary study on the nanyin flute and its artistic characteristics. Chin. Music. **4**, 97–100 (2006)
7. Dang, K., Burke, G., Korreshi, H., Lee, S.: Towards accessible musical performances in virtual reality: designing a conceptual framework for omnidirectional audio descriptions. In: Proceedings of the 26th International ACM SIGACCESS Conference on Computers and Accessibility (ASSETS '24). Association for Computing Machinery, New York, NY, USA (2024). https://doi.org/10.1145/3663548.3675618
8. Dang, K., Korreshi, H., Iqbal, Y., Lee, S.: Opportunities for accessible virtual reality design for immersive musical performances for blind and low-vision people. In: Proceedings of the 2023 ACM Symposium on Spatial User Interaction (SUI '23). Association for Computing Machinery, New York, NY, USA (2023). https://doi.org/10.1145/3607822.3614540
9. Flanagan, P.J., Fraietta, A.: Tracing the intangible: the curious gestures of crafts' cultural heritage. In: Adjunct Proceedings of the 2019 ACM International Joint Conference on Pervasive and Ubiquitous Computing and Proceedings of the 2019 ACM International Symposium on Wearable Computers, pp. 49–52. ACM, London, United Kingdom (2019). https://doi.org/10.1145/3341162.3343799
10. Fontana, F., Paisa, R., Ranon, R., Serafin, S.: Multisensory plucked instrument modeling in unity3D: from keytar to accurate string prototyping. Appl. Sci.-Basel **10**(4), 1452 (2020). https://doi.org/10.3390/app10041452

11. Gomez-Sirvent, J.L., Fernandez-Sotos, A., Fernandez-Caballero, A., Fernandez-Sotos, D.: Assessment of music performance anxiety in a virtual auditorium through the study of ambient lighting and audience distance. Virtual Reality **28**(2), 947–961 (2024). https://doi.org/10.1007/s10055-024-00947-8
12. Gomez-Sirvent, J.L., Lopez de la Rosa, F., Sanchez-Reolid, R., Morales Herrera, R., Fernandez-Caballero, A.: Musical instruments in extended reality: a systematic review. Int. J. Hum.-Comput. Interact. (2024). https://doi.org/10.1080/10447318.2024.2431352
13. Hou, Y., Kenderdine, S., Picca, D., Egloff, M., Adamou, A.: Digitizing intangible cultural heritage embodied: state of the art. J. Comput. Cultural Heritage **15**(3), 1–20 (2022). https://doi.org/10.1145/3494837
14. IJsselsteijn, W., de Kort, Y., Poels, K.: The Game Experience Questionnaire. Technische Universiteit Eindhoven (2013). https://pure.tue.nl/ws/files/21666907/Game_Experience_Questionnaire_English.pdf
15. Innocenti, E.D., et al.: Mobile virtual reality for musical genre learning in primary education. Comput. Educ. **139**, 102–117 (2019). https://doi.org/10.1016/j.compedu.2019.04.010
16. Jing, Z.: Unesco intangible cultural heritage: Nanyin. http://www.china.org.cn/arts/2024-04/15/content_117125444.htm (2024). Retrieved 5 Jun 2024
17. Johnson, D., Damian, D., Tzanetakis, G.: Evaluating the effectiveness of mixed reality music instrument learning with the theremin. Virtual Reality **24**(2), 303–317 (2019). https://doi.org/10.1007/s10055-019-00388-8
18. Kyriakou, T., de la Campa Crespo, M.A., Panayiotou, A., Chrysanthou, Y., Charalambous, P., Aristidou, A.: Virtual instrument performances (VIP): a comprehensive review. Comput. Graph. Forum **43**(2) (2024). https://doi.org/10.1111/cgf.15065
19. LC, R.: The present is in the future: participatory generative AI co-created visions as intangible cultural heritage. In: Proceedings of the 17th International Symposium on Visual Information Communication and Interaction (VINCI '24), pp. 1–2. Association for Computing Machinery, New York, NY, USA (2024). https://doi.org/10.1145/3678698.3687200
20. Liu, R., Wu, E., Liao, C.C., Nishioka, H., Furuya, S., Koike, H.: PianoSyncAR: enhancing piano learning through visualizing synchronized hand pose discrepancies in augmented reality. In: 2023 IEEE International Symposium on Mixed and Augmented Reality (ISMAR), pp. 859–868. IEEE (2023). https://doi.org/10.1109/ISMAR59233.2023.00101
21. Liu, Y.: Research on immersive music education model based on virtual reality. In: Ghani, M.F.A., Ang, L.H., Othman, M.S., Rahman, M.N.B.A. (eds.) Proceedings of the 2024 4th International Conference on Education, Language and Art (ICELA 2024), pp. 268–272. Atlantis Press SARL, Paris (2025). https://doi.org/10.2991/978-2-38476-364-1_34
22. Lu, Y., Liu, Z., Yan, X., Yan, S.: Flower and the youth: virtual narrative and creative methods of oral performance in China intangible cultural heritage. In: SIGGRAPH Asia 2021 XR (SA '21 XR), pp. 1–2. Association for Computing Machinery, New York, NY, USA (2021). https://doi.org/10.1145/3478514.3487623
23. O'Toole, P., Mancini, M., Pitt, I., Maye, L.: Chromaesthetica: a virtual reality app for learning musical theory using sound-colour cross-modal associations. In: Proceedings of the 23rd the International Conference on Mobile and Ubiquitous Multimediam, pp. 513–515. MUM '24, Association for Computing Machinery, New York, NY, USA (2024). https://doi.org/10.1145/3701571.3703369

24. Schrepp, M., Hinderks, A., Thomaschewski, J.: Design and evaluation of a short version of the user experience questionnaire (UEQ-S). Int. J. Interact. Multimedia Artif. Intell. **4**(6), 103–108 (2017). https://www.ijimai.org/journal/sites/default/files/files/2017/09/ijimai20174_6_14_pdf_20309.pdf
25. Stanbury, A.J., Said, I., Kang, H.J.: Holokeys: interactive piano education using augmented reality and IoT. In: Proceedings of the 27th ACM Symposium on Virtual Reality Software and Technology (VRST '21). Association for Computing Machinery, New York, NY, USA (2021). https://doi.org/10.1145/3489849.3489921
26. Syukur, A., Andono, P.N., Syarif, A.M.: Gamelan land: a multiplayer virtual reality game based on a social presence approach. J. Metaverse **4**(1) (2024). https://doi.org/10.57019/jmv.1334412
27. Tan, Q., Kamarudin, K.M., Herman, S.S.: Systematic review of empowering intangible cultural heritage with metaverse technology. J. Comput. Cultural Heritage **18**(2), 1–18 (2025). https://doi.org/10.1145/3723169
28. UNESCO: Nanyin. https://www.unesco.org/archives/multimedia/document-353 (2008). Retrieved 5 Jun 2024
29. Wang, S.: Extending attention beyond the "heritage application"—taking the ten-year plan for the protection and revitalization of Quanzhou Nanyin as an example. Musicology in China (04), 50–52 (2004). https://doi.org/10.14113/j.cnki.cn11-1316/j.2004.04.005
30. Wang, Y., Liu, Q., Wei, X., Fan, M.: Facilitating daily practice in intangible cultural heritage through virtual reality: a case study of traditional Chinese flower arrangement. In: Proceedings of the 2025 CHI Conference on Human Factors in Computing Systems (CHI '25), pp. 1–17. Association for Computing Machinery, New York, NY, USA (2025). https://doi.org/10.1145/3706598.3713409
31. Web, F.N.: Nanyin theory. http://www.fjnanyin.com/index.do?method=musicTheoryLink&id=403 (2009). Retrieved 9 Jun 2025
32. Yu, M., Zhang, M., Yu, C., Ma, X., Yang, X.D., Zhang, J.: We can do more to save Quqin: design and evaluate interactive systems to make Guqin more accessible to the general public. In: Proceedings of the 2021 CHI Conference on Human Factors in Computing Systems, pp. 1–12. ACM, Yokohama, Japan (2021). https://doi.org/10.1145/3411764.3445175
33. Zhang, S., Xie, X., Lyu, D., Shu, Y.: KiteMR: an interactive mixed reality system for preserving and experiencing traditional Chinese kite craftsmanship. Int. J. Hum.-Comput. Interact., 1–22 (2025). https://doi.org/10.1080/10447318.2025.2482746

StringWave VR—An Immersive Interactive System for Traditional Music Intangible Cultural Heritage

Wei Hui, Huancheng Jiang, and Zichun Guo(✉)

Department of Art and Design, Beijing University of Chemical Technology, Beijing 102202, China
guozichun@buct.edu.cn

Abstract. Virtual reality (VR) technology can enhance human-computer interaction experiences. However, the current application fields of VR technology are often limited to exhibitions, education, medical surgeries, etc., with few applications in the protection of intangible cultural heritage (ICH). In this paper, we explore VR technology as a new way of digitizing ICH. Taking Guqin music as an example, we have built an interactive system called StringWave VR based on the head-mounted TGAM module. This system combines brainwave data with digital art to create a VR space. We recruited 102 volunteers to test our system and collect feedback on the impact of ethnic music combined with a visualized space on their psychological states. 75% of the participants believed that StringWave VR could guide their emotions to a certain extent, and 80% of the participants hoped to further utilize the system for cultural experiences. In conclusion, this study developed a VR system based on brainwave detection, taking Chinese traditional musics as a specific case, it has enhanced the motivation of most people to further understand ICH, demonstrating the potential of this system in the inheritance of traditional music culture.

Keywords: Virtual reality technology · Traditional music · Intangible cultural heritage · Digitalization

1 Introduction

Since the beginning of the Industrial Revolution, urbanization has developed rapidly in various countries, and the speed of cultural change has been unprecedented. Intangible Cultural Heritage (ICH) is threatened with discontinuation due to its mode of transmission and the unrecordable nature of its skills [1]. Most ICH is passed down through family and master-apprentice relationships, and the social environment it relies on has been encroached upon by modern civilization. Moreover, the majority of the inheritors are relatively old, and the younger generation, influenced by modern culture, lacks the interest and energy to carry on the tradition. In response to this, the United Nations is committed to transforming ICH into a digital information-based cultural form [2], and China has also responded positively to the UN's call by incorporating the protection of ICH into relevant plans for economic and social development [3].

S. Guo et al. (Eds.): HHME 2025, CCIS 2878, pp. 302–312, 2027.
https://doi.org/10.1007/978-981-92-3991-7_20

Traditional Chinese music refers to music created by the Chinese people using their own methods and forms, with distinct characteristics of their own [4]. According to the Convention for the Safeguarding of Intangible Cultural Heritage, it belongs to the performing arts and is part of ICH, which can be called traditional music intangible cultural heritage (TMICH).

Guqin music is a typical form of TMICH. The guqin is the most prestigious musical instrument in ancient China, ranking first among the four arts of "qin, qi, shu, and hua". In 2003, the art of the guqin was officially recognized by UNESCO as an ICH [3], making it the only intangible cultural heritage project in the world to be nominated based on an instrument. The guqin is a seven-stringed instrument. Its tuning system combines the Pythagorean tuning and just intonation [5, 6]. The open strings of the guqin are tuned according to the Pythagorean tuning, while the harmonics are tuned according to the just intonation. When making a guqin, 13 frets are marked on the surface of the instrument. These frets are based on the total length from the nut to the bridge of the strings. Analyzed by the inverse proportion of string length and frequency, the placement of the 13 frets conforms to the rules of just intonation. Despite its significant position in Chinese intangible culture, the current protection of the guqin is often limited to performances in specific tourist areas and preservation on some digital online music platforms. However, the current protection of Guqin music is often limited to performances in specific tourist areas and preservation on some digital online music platforms.

Virtual Reality (VR) technology, as a digital means, builds three-dimensional dynamic virtual scenes with computer technology. Participants use devices to interact with objects in the virtual world and immerse themselves in it through interaction. VR technology has been applied in multiple fields such as exhibitions, healthcare, and education, but its application in the protection of intangible cultural heritage is still lacking [7]. In the digital protection of ICH, traditional recording methods are often limited to the one-way collection of audio-visual information. This passive preservation approach is difficult to capture the cognitive feedback of the audience and cannot establish a deep connection between cultural symbols and neural cognition [8]. The biofeedback mechanism based on EEG provides a new path to solve this dilemma: dynamically coupling neural representations with VR scenes can build a culturally immersive system with neural adaptability, enabling the dissemination of intangible cultural heritage to break through superficial sensory stimulation and achieve cultural resonance at the neural cognitive level.

Electrophysiological signals are common signals in biological activity processes. The human body generates many types of electrophysiological signals, such as electromyography from muscle activity, electrocardiogram from heartbeats, and electroencephalogram (EEG) from brain activity [9]. EEG is generated by the activity of neurons in the brain, caused by the postsynaptic potential resulting from the release of neurotransmitters from the axon terminals of presynaptic neurons into the synaptic cleft. The collective activity of numerous synapses forms EEG. EEG is a non-stationary and nonlinear signal related to brain activity. Classified by frequency bands, it can be divided into several different waves: delta (δ) waves, theta (θ) waves, alpha (α) waves, beta (β) waves, and gamma (γ) waves [10]. δ waves are generally produced during deep sleep or deep anesthesia when brain activity is very low; θ waves are typically generated when brain activity is low, such as during sleep or just before sleep; α waves dominate when a person is awake or relaxed and can be received at any part of the head, characterized by high amplitude, good rhythm, and regular waveforms; β waves occur during rapid thinking or when brain activity is relatively active; γ waves are produced by different groups of neurons in neural networks with specific motor or cognitive functions. Additionally, waves with frequencies lower than α waves are generally called slow waves, and those higher are called fast waves. The application of EEG is usually related to medical diagnosis, although there have been studies on the classification of EEG and fatigue or emotions, the related application outlets are still limited.

In this study, we take Chinese Guqi music as a specific case and design an immersive interactive system called StringWave VR based on the Tao Glass Application Module (TGAM). The aim is to enhance the public's interest in the experience and protection of intangible cultural heritage through digital interaction with TMICH. Through this approach, the research hopes to increase public awareness and interest in cultural heritage such as ethnic music by enhancing the immersion and interactivity of the experience.

2 Construction of StringWave VR System

To construct the StringWave VR system, three primary steps are essential: information extraction, interactive model construction, and projection into the VR space, as depicted in Fig. 1. The objective is to transform EEG signals and selected guqin music into a visual VR environment.

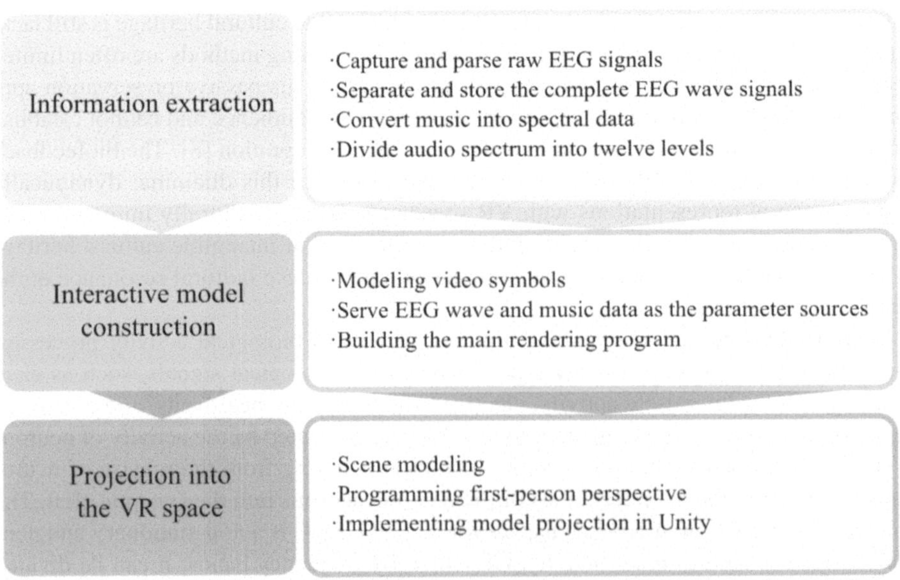

Fig. 1. Schematic diagram of the StringWave VR system

2.1 EEG Information Extraction

For EEG extraction, the TGAM EEG sensor is employed to capture the user's raw EEG signals (Fig. 2). The raw files output by the sensor are parsed in HEX format, and the complete δ, θ, α, β, and γ EEG wave signals are separated and stored as time-series data (Fig. 3). To convert the selected music into time-series spectral data, the audio spectrum is divided into twelve levels from low to high frequency, and the data are classified and stored according to the time series.

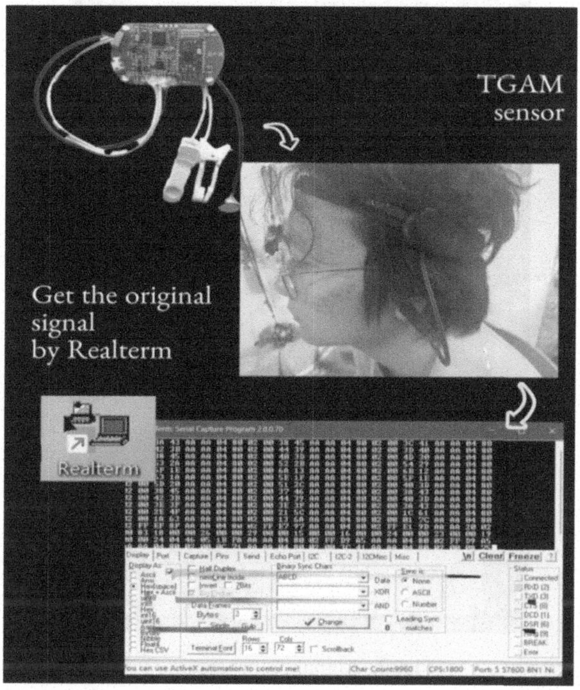

Fig. 2. Equipment and signal extraction of EEG

2.2 Model Construction

For the construction of the interactive model, the pre-built model in TouchDesigner is utilized, with the EEG wave signal data and music data serving as the parameter sources for the image rendering program (Fig. 4). The EEG data control the hue of the image, with δ representing blue, θ representing cyan, α representing green, β representing yellow, and γ representing red. Different EEG waves exist within distinct frequency ranges, and the image displays the color corresponding to the dominant EEG frequency The music data control the rhythm and movement of the model. As the music level decreases or increases, the particle movement in the image becomes more ordered or disordered, and the symbol levels representing the particles also decrease or increase (Fig. 5).

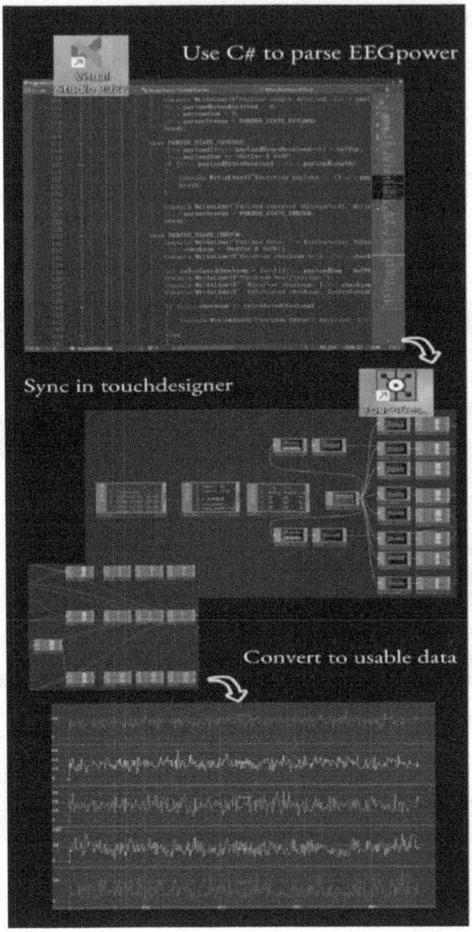

Fig. 3. Signal preprocessing

2.3 Construction of VR Space

To project the constructed model into the VR space, scene modeling is conducted in Unity (Fig. 6), and a first-person perspective main object is developed to provide the VR main viewing angle. The image is synchronously projected into the scene to form a VR interactive experience.

3 StringWave VR System Usage Test

To test the application potential of the StringWave VR system in ICH protection, we recruited 102 volunteers from Beijing University of Chemical Technology to experience our system and evaluate its usage effect. All participants had no obvious psychological problems. The experiment was conducted in January 2025. Before participation, basic

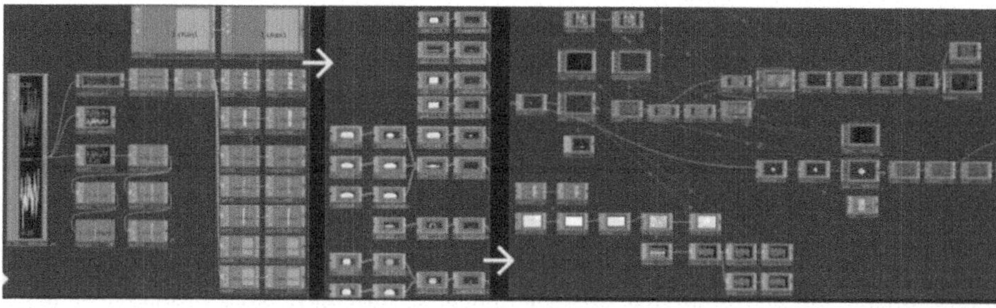

Fig. 4. Process of model construction

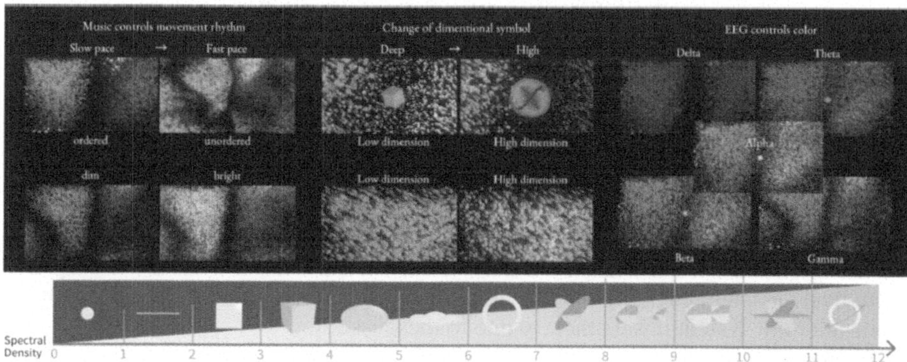

Fig. 5. Schematic diagram of the StringWave VR system

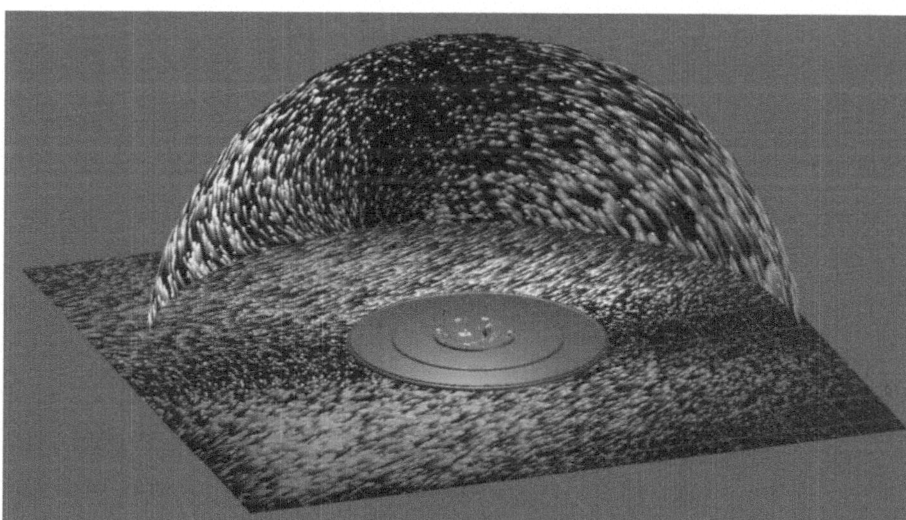

Fig. 6. VR panoramic schematic diagram

information of the participants was collected, as shown in Table 1. Among them, the gender distribution was relatively balanced, with slightly more females than males. The majority of participants were aged 18 to 24, mainly undergraduate students pursuing a bachelor's degree. Those aged 25 to 34 were the second largest group, mainly postgraduate students pursuing a master's or doctoral degree. Participants aged 35 to 44 were young teachers, and those over 45 were all teachers within the university.

To assess the system usage experience, all participants were asked to fill out a system usage experience questionnaire, as shown in Table 2. The results indicated that 82% of the participants felt an immersive VR experience. Surprisingly, 80% of the participants who used the StringWave VR system were willing to continue using this technology for cultural experiences. The StringWave VR system also demonstrated a certain role in emotion guidance, with 75% of the participants stating that the system could guide emotions, and the most frequently expressed emotion was curiosity. However, 18% of the participants could not achieve a relatively immersive VR experience, and 5% experienced psychological discomfort. Additionally, 13% of the participants felt that their psychological activities were not accurately reflected.

To understand the reasons for the current usage limitations of the system, we distributed a system feedback questionnaire to the participants online after the experience, as shown in Table 3. Although only 8% of the participants were dissatisfied with our system, several issues were highlighted, such as discomfort with the equipment, delayed system response, and unclear visualization effects. However, at least some of them did not consider the system unsatisfactory due to these issues.

Table 1. Basic information of respondents

Item	Category	Frequency	Percentage (%)
Gender	Male	48	47
	Female	54	53
Age	18–24 years old	59	58
	25–34 years old	30	29
	35–44 years old	8	8
	45 years and above	5	5
Exposure to Guqin Music	Yes	63	62
	No	39	38

4 Discussion

Our system is attractive in the protection of ICH. 93% of the participants showed strong curiosity, and about 80% of the participants were full of expectations for the application of this interactive VR image in cultural experience. In the image setting with Guqin music as the data source, 70% of the participants were willing to further understand Guqin culture, which is in line with our initial idea of spreading and protecting ICH.

Our equipment also demonstrated a strong potential in guiding emotions, which may be due to the rhythm of the music [11]. After being visualized by the VR system, it can stimulate the mobilization of emotions under the dual guidance of vision and hearing. At the same time, it will adjust the image space according to the participant's own brain electrical signals. If further optimized in the future, it can be designed for visual space to enhance its ability in this aspect [12].

Table 2. System using experience

Item	Category	Frequency	Percentage (%)
Experience of Immersion	Fully immersed	33	32
	Highly immersed	51	50
	Average	12	12
	Slightly immersed	2	2
	Not immersed at all	5	4
System Reflection of Psychological State	Very accurate	30	29
	Relatively accurate	48	47
	Average	11	11
	Slightly inaccurate	9	9
	Completely inaccurate	4	4
Guqin Music Visualization Expectations	Exceeded expectations	9	9
	Fully met expectations	17	17
	Generally met expectations	58	57
	Slightly deviated	12	12
	Completely unmet	5	5
Psychological State Perception Change	Curious	95	93
(Multiple choices)	Excited	33	32
	Relaxed	80	78
	Confused	9	9
	Uncomfortable	5	5
Emotional Guidance Influence	Highly influential	19	19
	Somewhat influential	58	56
	Not very influential	18	18
	Not influential at all	7	7

(*continued*)

Table 2. *(continued)*

Item	Category	Frequency	Percentage (%)
Change in View on Intangible Cultural Heritage	Highly changed	19	19
	Somewhat changed	47	46
	Not very changed	29	28
	No change	7	7
Increased Interest in Guqin Music	Significantly increased	21	21
	Slightly increased	50	49
	No change	9	9
	Decreased	0	0
	Uncertain	21	21
Future Willingness to Use	Very willing	36	35
	Quite willing	46	45
	Uncertain	15	15
	Not very willing	5	5
	Not willing at all	0	0

However, in our test, some people's psychological state perception showed discomfort, which may be due to a symptom called 3D vertigo, which can cause severe dizziness when watching VR images [13]. Based on our system, in future tests, we also need to pay attention to patients with photosensitive epilepsy. The rapid changes in color and image may cause the onset of this type of patient [14]. To prevent the occurrence of such sudden diseases, our system still needs to be equipped with an alarm system to protect users.

It is worth noting that in the software and hardware of EGG signal analysis, noise reduction has always been a topic of concern. The mixture of electromyographic signals and electroencephalographic signals will interfere with the sampling results [15]. Medical EGG acquisition devices are accurate but cumbersome, and the wet medium leads to an unpleasant experience. Our EGG acquisition device is a dry sensor for portability and comfort, but the electromyographic signal has a significant impact [16]. Even though our module has built-in noise reduction processing, participants still need to minimize their activities during the test. In our test, some participants observed rapid changes in the image due to large head movements or blinking, suggesting that the system is still significantly affected by electromyographic signals. If better sensors or improved noise algorithms are used, the stability of the system may be enhanced [17].

We also noticed that some people were not satisfied with the comfort of the equipment because our system is currently bulky, and wearing it for a long time may cause neck

Table 3. System feedback and suggestions

Item	Category	Frequency	Percentage (%)
Overall Experience	Very satisfied	23	23
	Satisfied	58	56
	Average	13	13
	Dissatisfied	6	6
	Very dissatisfied	2	2
Liked Feature	Visualization of Guqin music	61	60
(Multiple choices)	System's emotional guidance	77	75
	Immersive virtual space experience	72	71
	Other	5	4
Problems Encountered	None	63	62
(Multiple choices)	Equipment discomfort	38	37
	System response delay	16	16
	Unclear visualization effects	20	20
	Screen discomfort	5	5

discomfort. In addition, our processing system can be integrated in the future and use higher-definition display devices to obtain more real-time and realistic images.

5 Conclusion

Our research is based on the TGAM module combined with Guqin music, and we have developed the StringWave VR system. This system demonstrated strong emotional guidance capabilities and, in our tests, sparked the interest of most participants in understanding ICH. However, the system still has significant room for improvement, with stability, accuracy, and comfort being the core optimization directions for its future application. In conclusion, our research has exhibited the powerful potential of the StringWave VR system in ICH preservation and its promise as a valuable tool for digital cultural heritage protection.

References

1. Wang, X., Zhuo, J.: Research on the Current Status of Digital Preservation of Intangible Cultural Heritage: A Case Study of Han Opera Culture. In: ADDT 2024. EAI/Springer Innovations in Communication and Computing (2024)

2. Blake, J.: Convention for the safeguarding of intangible cultural heritage (2003). In: Smith, C. (ed.) Encyclopedia of Global Archaeology, pp. 1706–1711. Springer, New York (2014)
3. Tan, N., Anwar, S., Jiang, W.: Intangible cultural heritage listing and tourism growth in China. J. Tour. Cult. Chang. **21**(2), 188–206 (2023)
4. Jin, J.: Chinese Music. Cambridge University Press, Cambridge (2011)
5. Xu, J.: Exploring the art of Guqin. In: SHS Web of Conferences, vol. 183, p. 03014. EDP Sciences (2024)
6. Yu, M., Zhang, M., Yu, C., Ma, X., Yang, X.D., Zhang, J.: We can do more to save guqin: Design and evaluate interactive systems to make guqin more accessible to the general public. In: Proceedings of the 2021 CHI Conference on Human Factors in Computing Systems, pp. 1–12 (2021)
7. Bekteshi, L.: Education in the era of AI and immersive technologies—a systematic review. J. Res. Eng. Comput. Sci. **3**(1), 1–14 (2025)
8. Lai, S., Tian, Y., Zhang, Q.: The impact of AI-generated technologies-driven digital cultural heritage platforms on users' offline cultural participation intentions. NPJ Heritage Sci. **13**, 574 (2025)
9. Kamarajan, C., Porjesz, B.: Advances in electrophysiological research. Alcohol Res. **37**(1), 53–87 (2015)
10. Klimesch, W.: An algorithm for the EEG frequency architecture of consciousness and brain body coupling. Front. Hum. Neurosci. **7**, 766 (2013)
11. Moore, J.: The impact of visual-music interaction on music perception: the influence of agreement and disagreement. Doctoral dissertation, Baylor University (2010).
12. Naef, A.C., Jeitziner, M.-M., Knobel, S.E., Exl, M.T., Müri, R.M., Jakob, S.M.: Investigating the role of auditory and visual sensory inputs for inducing relaxation during virtual reality stimulation. Sci. Rep. **12**, 17073 (2022)
13. Benzeroual, K., Allison, R.S.: Cyber (motion) sickness in active stereoscopic 3D gaming. In: 2013 International Conference on 3D Imaging, pp. 1–7. IEEE (2013)
14. Da Silva, A.M., Leal, B.: Photosensitivity and epilepsy: current concepts and perspectives—a narrative review. Seizure **50**, 209–218 (2017)
15. Al-Fahoum, A.S., Al-Fraihat, A.A.: Methods of EEG signal features extraction using linear analysis in frequency and time—frequency domains. Int. Scholarly Res. Not. 730218 (2014)
16. Hinrichs, H., Scholz, M., Baum, A.K., Kam, J.W., Knight, R.T., Heinze, H.-J.: Comparison between a wireless dry electrode EEG system and a conventional wired wet electrode EEG system for clinical applications. Sci. Rep. **10**, 5218 (2020)
17. Mathewson, K.E., Harrison, T.J., Kizuk, S.A.: High and dry? Comparing active dry EEG electrodes to active and passive wet electrodes. Psychophysiology **54**(1), 74–82 (2017)

A Study on Construction and Classification of Multi-condition EEG Datasets for Chinese Mandarin Speech Decoding

Haoming Wang[1,2,3], Gaoyuan Zhang[2], Xurong Xie[2(✉)], Ying Qin[1,3(✉)], Chao Zhou[2], Hui Chen[2], and Feng Tian[2]

[1] Institute of Information Science, Beijing Jiaotong University, Beijing, China
haomingwangbjtu@163.com, yingqin@bjtu.edu.cn
[2] Institute of Software, Chinese Academy of Sciences, Beijing, China
{zhanggaoyuan2023,xurong,zhouchao,chenhui,tianfeng}@iscas.ac.cn
[3] Visual Intelligence +X International Cooperation Joint Laboratory of MOE, Beijing, China

Abstract. Brain-computer interface (BCI) has become a highly promising research field in human-computer interaction due to its potential to help patients who have lost the ability to speak due to central nervous system diseases or injuries restore normal communication. Electroencephalogram (EEG) is an important neuroimaging method in the field of language disorder treatment, distinguished by its noninvasiveness, cost-effectiveness, and versatility [12]. Therefore, BCI based on EEG signals offers a novel approach to assist in rehabilitation by directly capturing the patient's speech intentions without relying on verbal output. Currently, most EEG datasets are developed based on Western languages. In contrast, Chinese is a kind of tonal language. Tones are used to distinguish different meanings in Chinese, which differs greatly from Western languages. Consequently, these EEG datasets often do not adequately support research into assistive communication techniques for patients with Chinese communication disorders. This study investigates the methods of EEG data construction and classification for Chinese Mandarin speech decoding, via simulating patients with various types of communication disorders by multiple experimental conditions: overt, overt-noisy, intend, and imagine speech. The goal is to construct a high-quality and standardized Chinese EEG dataset that encompasses vowel tone combinations and vocabulary relevant to the Chinese Mandarin. Based on this dataset, Support Vector Machine (SVM) and Shallow ConvNet (ShallowCNN) have been used to perform classification research on EEG signals. The classification results indicate that when using a deep convolutional neural network as the classifier, the accuracy for vocabulary classification in different conditions is all significantly better than random, with the best accuracy up to 75.6%.

H. Wang and G. Zhang—The two authors contributed equally to this work.

S. Guo et al. (Eds.): HHME 2025, CCIS 2878, pp. 313–324, 2027.
https://doi.org/10.1007/978-981-92-3991-7_21

Keywords: brain computer interfaces (BCI) · electroencephalogram (EEG) · Chinese EEG dataset · deep learning (DL)

1 Introduction

Language, as the fundamental medium of human social interaction, serves critical roles in information transmission and emotional expression. Verbal communication is an important way of natural interaction. However, due to various neurological disorders such as amyotrophic lateral sclerosis and aphasia, some individuals have lost their ability to engage in normal linguistic communication, leading to numerous challenges and inconveniences in daily life. Currently, speech recognition technology has been employed to predict and interpret patients' pronunciation. Nevertheless, its effectiveness is constrained by the high noise levels inherent in speech signals and the reliance on intact vocal organs. Consequently, this approach is only applicable to individuals with residual speaking abilities. To address these limitations, the direct-speech brain-computer interface (DS-BCI) has emerged as a promising alternative, establishing a nonmuscular channel between the human brain and external devices [18]. In DS-BCI applications, electroencephalogram (EEG) has become a popular neuroimaging method, characterized by non-invasiveness, high temporal resolution, portability and multi-functionality [23]. The DS-BCI captures and decodes EEG signals associated with speech production, facilitating a more natural and intuitive mode of communication [13].

The current studies of DS-BCI cover a variety of speech-related EEG signals, including overt speech [4], intended speech [11] and imagined speech [10], which are different in generation mechanisms. Overt speech produces audible acoustic output that is perceptible both to the speaker and to nearby listeners. Intended speech refers to a situation where a person attempts to speak but is unable to produce audible output, or has a confused pronunciation that cannot be understood, even unable to make a sound. Imagined speech means the internal pronunciation of words without any audible output or associated movement.

In order to support the research of the DS-BCI system, it's necessary to construct high-quality and effective datasets to provide a basis for the modeling of EEG signals. Currently, most of the publicly available EEG datasets are in English [24] [19], and researchers are more committed to the development of imagined speech.

Dasalla et al. [9] developed the dataset contains recordings from three subjects (aged 26 to 29, 2 males) who discriminated imagined speech of the English vowels /a/ and /u/. Arizona State University (ASU) [17] discriminated three different types of tasks, including short words ("in" "out" and "up"), vowels (/a/, /i/, /u/) and long words ("cooperate" and "independent"), which based on imagined speech from recordings from 15 subjects (aged from 22 to 32, 11 males). The speech imaging of two tasks, including vowels (/a/,/e/, /i/,/o/, and/u/) and English words (up, down, right, left, forward, and backward) were classified in the study of Coretto et al. [7], resulting in accuracies from 17.26% to 23.68%.

Meanwhile, for the Chinese EEG dataset, Mou et al. constructed a Chinese linguistic corpora EEG dataset for semantic alignment and neural decoding (ChineseEEG) [16], which based on overt speech. This dataset contains high-density EEG data and simultaneous eye-tracking data recorded from 10 participants, which can serve as a valuable resource in neuroscience, linguistics, and other related fields.

The above-mentioned public datasets collected high-quality EEG signal data. However, few datasets combine different speech types for comparative trials, and for patients with communication disorders in different situations, more practical scenarios need to be taken into consideration. For instance, some patients can attempt articulation, while lacking auditory feedback. Existing datasets do not account for this condition. Meanwhile, Chinese has an essential difference from English in pronunciation patterns [14], so it is particularly important to construct a Chinese EEG dataset under multiple conditions. To address these gaps, we have developed a Multi-Condition EEG dataset for Chinese Mandarin Speech including Chinese vowels and vocabulary. Our methodological framework employs two distinct classification approaches: Support Vector Machines (SVM) [8] and Shallow Convolutional Neural Networks (ShallowCNN) [22]. Figure 1 shows the overall flowchart of this study. Our contributions are as follows: 1. To the best of our knowledge, we are the first to develop multi-condition Chinese Mandarin dataset under four conditions, including overt, overt-noisy, intend and imagine; 2. We took into the patients who could speak normally but had no auditory feedback, and thus designed the experimental scenario called overt-noisy; 3. We are the first to combine all Chinese vowels with four tones in the Chinese EEG dataset. Meanwhile, in the vocabulary classification task, the dataset exhibited an accuracy ranging from 28.16% to 75.6% when employing deep learning (DL) methods, comparable to the researches on the English dataset [20] [2].

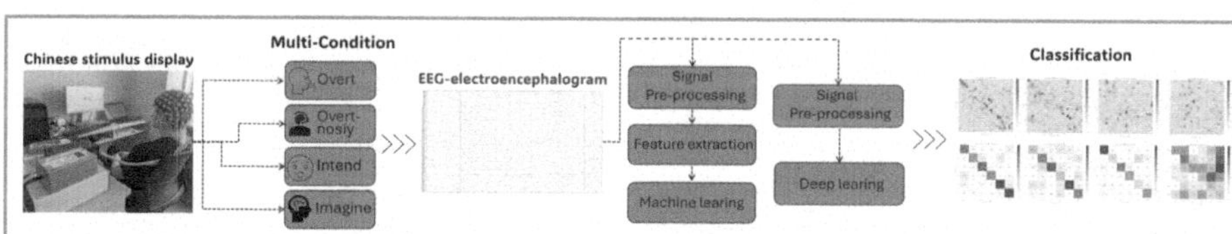

Fig. 1. The experimental procedure of this study, including multi-condition EEG signal acquisition, EEG signal preprocessing and EEG signal modeling and classification.

2 Materials and Methods

2.1 Participants

In the study we collected data from a single participant (aged 22, male) to eliminate the influence of individual specificity on the experiment. The participant had no history of neurological or psychological disorders and exhibited normal hearing. His native language is Mandarin Chinese. The participant is right-handed and possessed normal vision. Prior to the formal experiment, the participant engaged in a pre-experimental test to ensure the validity of the experimental procedure and the stability of the equipment. The participant voluntarily enrolled in the study, signed an informed consent form before the experiment.

2.2 Experimental Materials

The experimental materials comprise two sections: vowels and vocabulary. The vowel stimuli consist of 6 Chinese vowel phonemes combined with 4 lexical tones, yielding 24 unique stimuli (6 vowels × 4 tones). Each stimulus was repeated over 30 trials, resulting in 720 trials total. This section generated 6.35 h of valid experimental data. The vocabulary stimuli include 6 Chinese words selected for their relevance to patients' activities of daily living. Each word was presented over 80 trials, totaling 480 trials. This section yielded 4.29 h of valid data. Schematic diagrams of the experimental materials are presented in Tables 1 and 2.

Table 1. The list of word stimuli.

Vowel	Tone 1	Tone 2	Tone 3	Tone 4
a	ā	á	ǎ	à
o	ō	ó	ǒ	ò
e	ē	é	ě	è
i	ī	í	ǐ	ì
u	ū	ú	ǔ	ù
ü	ǖ	ǘ	ǚ	ǜ

Note:The text stimulus of the vowel task are from 6 Chinese vowel phonemes combined with 4 tones.

Table 2. The list of word stimuli.

Scene	Word
Daily life scenes	吃饭(Have meal), 喝水(Drink), 睡觉(Sleep)
Hospital scene	厕所(Toilet),头疼(Headache), 换药(Change dressing)

Note: The text stimulus of the word task come from 6 Chinese words commonly used in life scenarios and hospital scenarios.

2.3 Multi-condition Settings

Four conditions are designed to simulate patients with various types of communication disorders. The structure of the dataset is shown in Table 3.

- Overt: The participant was required to speak normally with correct and clear pronunciation. This condition establishes baseline EEG signals for subsequent patient comparisons.
- Overt-noisy: The participant was required to speak normally and pronounce correctly. In order to simulate those patients who can't obtain clear auditory feedback or even can't hear themselves completely, we put headphones on the participant and played white noise to deprive them of auditory feedback, thereby eliminating the participation of audience-related brain regions in the generation of EEG signals.
- Intend: The participant was required to move the corresponding laryngeal muscles to attempt pronunciation, but his pronunciation was disordered or failed. The aim is to simulate those patients with pronunciation difficulties. Compared with the patients that they can only imagine, they can attempt to pronounce, but it is difficult and chaotic.
- Imagine: The participant was required to imagine the pronunciation of the corresponding text stimulus in their minds throughout the process. It is used to simulate those patients who have completely lost the ability to communicate and can only imagine in their minds.

Table 3. The structure of collected data.

Dataset structure	Healthy population	Patient
vowel with tone	Overt(1.64h)	Overt-noisy(2.1h), Intend(1.87h), Imagine(1.67h)
word	Overt(1.15h)	Overt-noisy(1.15h), Intend(1.17h), Imagine(1.23h)

Note: The data was collected using Netstation, totaling a duration of 11.98 h, the valid time is 10.64 h.

2.4 Experimental Paradigm and Procedure

The paradigm of this experiment is based on the BCI Competition V-3 [1], ensuring the rationality of the overall process design and a reasonable time allocation among each module. The experimental paradigm consists of stimulus display, attention focus, task execution, and rest periods. Figure 2 illustrates the schematic diagram of one trial within the experimental paradigm, with descriptions as follows:

- Stimulus: In this module, Chinese text stimuli were presented on the screen for a duration of 2 s, including the vowels with tones or words.

- Cross: A black "+" symbol appeared on the screen for 1 s to prompt participants to concentrate and prepare for the subsequent task.
- Task: Participants were instructed to perform vowel or word speech tasks under four conditions—overt, overt-noisy, intend, and imagine—each lasting 2 s. Among them, in the overt-noisy condition, the white noise volume in the headphones worn by the participant was adjusted so that he couldn't hear his own voice.
- Rest: This phase lasted for 3 s and was intended for relaxation. During this period, participants were advised to minimize movement and clear their thoughts.

An EGI (NetAmps 400) 128-channel electrode cap was employed to record scalp EEG signals. Scalp electrodes were positioned according to extended EGI usage regulations. The reference point for electrode placement included intersection points formed by lines connecting the centers of both ears with those connecting from brow center to back-of-brain center. Throughout the entire experiment, all electrode impedances remained below 50 kΩ. The experimental paradigm was constructed using E-Prime 2.0 (Psychology software), while EEG data were displayed in real-time and collected via Netstation.

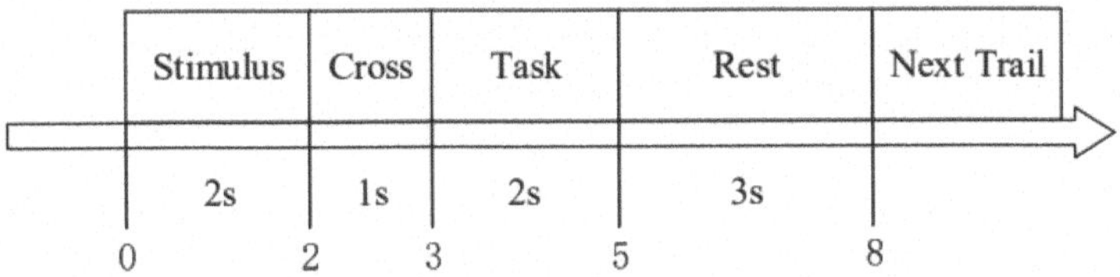

Fig. 2. Experimental paradigm, the participant completed vowel and word tasks in four conditions in the task module. The vowel task was 720 times in total, and the word task was 480 times in total.

The entire experiment is divided into three phases, which includes the initial equipment calibration, the formal experiment and the subsequent data preprocessing.

Phase 1: Equipment Calibration. Initially, the capacitive solution was prepared by mixing distilled water with potassium chloride, then adding baby shampoo. After soaking the electrode cap for 8 min, it was placed on the subject according to standard procedures and adjusted the resistance of each electrode accordingly. The participant seated comfortably in an adjustable chair, with their eyes positioned approximately 72 cm away from the screen.

Phase 2: Formal Experiment. During the experimental procedure, several factors can influence the quality of EEG data, such as eye and head movements. Therefore, participant was instructed to refrain from doing unnecessary activities during the experiment and was encouraged to minimize blinking as much as possible within the Task module. Following every 100 trials executed in accordance with paradigm requirements, there will be a scheduled interruption for participants to take a prolonged rest and make necessary adjustments. This is intended to prevent fatigue and boredom among subjects throughout the experimental process. In data collection, data from the vowel task conducted in the Overt-noisy were excluded and re-collected due to multiple instances of incorrect participant pronunciations. Additionally, during the vocabulary task in the Imagine scenario, the participant reported headaches and discomfort, leading to an interruption of the experiment. Data collection for this task was subsequently resumed and completed at a later time.

Phase 3: Data preprocessing. First of all, the EEG data was collected with sampling rate of 1000 Hz originally, and down-sampled to 250 Hz for the following processing, effectively reducing the computational complexity. This helps to accelerate subsequent processing such as filtering, feature extraction, and DL modeling. Then, bad channel interpolation and notch filtering operations were employed to replace abnormal electrodes and remove power frequency interference. Finally, the ICA component analysis was employed to remove potential interfering signals [3].

3 Classification Model Settings

In order to investigate the performance on the proposed dataset across different methodologies. This study employed a traditional machine learning (ML) model, utilizing short-time Fourier Transform (STFT) for feature extraction and SVM for classification. Table 4 presents the experimental parameters associated with STFT and SVM. Subsequently, the DL model ShallowCNN was also applied for classification purposes. Table 5 presents the experimental parameters.

Fourier transform (FT) converts time-domain signals into frequency-domain amplitude and phase representations [5], but discards temporal information. To resolve this limitation, short-time Fourier transform (STFT) decomposes the signal into fixed-length stationary segments. Applying FT to these segments enables time-localized spectral analysis of EEG signals, revealing frequency-band characteristics while preserving timing information [15]. Following this decomposition, Fourier transform is applied to these segments, thereby transforming long time series EEG signals from the time domain into frequency-domain representations that allow for an analysis of EEG characteristics across different frequency bands.

SVM [8]represents a well-established supervised ML technique capable of managing high-dimensional data effectively. By identifying the optimal classification hyperplane that accurately separates different types of samples within the original data space, SVM ensures stable classification performance even in scenarios where training samples are limited.

We utilize a sliding window of 100 time samples to traverse between task intervals [125, 425], employing a step size of 50. This approach yields five distinct windows within which Short-Time Fourier Transform (STFT) is applied. Each of these five windows is assigned the same event ID and will be trained independently during the training phase. At the conclusion of this process, an internal voting mechanism is implemented to aggregate model results, which

Table 4. Summary of the ML parameters.

	Parameter	Values
STFT	Sampling rate	250 Hz
	Window size	100 Samples
	Step	50 Samples
	Start	125th Sample
	End	425th Sample
	Frequency band	Delta:[1,4] Hz, Theta:[4,8] Hz, Alpha:[8,12] Hz, Beta:[12,30] Hz
SVM	Kernel	RBF
	Gamma	0.01
	C	10

Note: We took into account the reaction time of the participant in the task and the spare time after the task was completed. After multiple combination attempts, we set the start time point of feature extraction as the 125 time point and the end time point as the 425 time point to help STFT better focus on the main body of the task.

are then presented as a unified output. In view of the different characteristics of patients with different language disorders on different EEG frequency bands, the average value of the four frequency bands and the total maximum value were selected as the final features.

ShallowCNN [22] is a shallow architecture that refers to Shallow ConvNet, specifically tailored to decode band power features. The first two layers of the ShallowCNN perform a temporal convolution and a spatial filter. Then, the Pooling layer and Logarithmic Activation layer are executed, and finally classification is carried out. ShallowCNN embeds all the computational steps in a single network, allowing for simultaneous optimization across all stages.

4 Results and Discussion

We evaluated classification performance using 10-fold cross-validation, measuring accuracy, precision, recall, and F1-score. Meanwhile, we calculated the classification accuracy of the model for vowels and tones in the vowel task. The classification results for SVM and ShallowCNN are summarized in Tables 6 and 7 respectively.

The experimental results demonstrate classification accuracy rates were consistently above chance level across all tasks, which confirms the dataset's validity. Notably, the word classification task using ShallowCNN achieved the highest accuracy up to 75.6%, while comparative results from Coretto et al. [7] using similar methods on English stimuli showed comparable performance levels (21.9% for vowels, 18.2% for vocabulary). These findings validate the successful development of an effective Mandarin Chinese EEG dataset under our multi-condition experimental paradigm.

Table 5. Summary of the DL parameters.

	Parameters	Values
Input layer	Signal dimension	(128,500)
Temporal Convolution	Kernel	(25,1)
	No. of filters	25
Spatial Filtering	Kernel	(1,128)
	No. of filters	25
Squaring Nonlinearity	Function	Square
Pooling layer	Stride	15
	Window size	(75,1)
	Pooling	Mean-pooling
Logarithmic Activation	Activation	Logarithmic
	Dropout	0.2
Classification	Loss function	Cross entropy
	Activation	Softmax
Training	Optimizer	Adam
	Learning rate	0.0625
	Epochs	300
	Batch size	64

It can be inferred from the information presented in Tables 6 and 7 that the accuracy rate of the word classification task was significantly higher than that of the vowel classification task. This discrepancy arises due to the substantially larger number of classification categories in the vowel task, as well as the inherent semantics of Chinese vocabulary that is absent in isolated vowels. In the experiment, the participant progressively adapt to and comprehend the semantic distinctions among the six types of vocabulary. In contrast, the vowel combinations either lack clear semantics or possess ambiguous meanings, and with feature similarity due to overlapping articulatory components. These characteristics may reduced the model's ability to discriminate between vowel categories, as evidenced by the lower classification accuracy.

Besides, DL has demonstrated superior performance compared to traditional ML methods, particularly in handling complex and high-dimensional input data while maintaining robust classification accuracy [6]. The accuracy rate varies generally according to different scenarios:overt>overt-noisy>intend>imagine. This performance gradient is in line with the severity of the patients. Notably, the imagined speech condition yields the lowest accuracy rates, may since the fewest brain regions of the participant are involved in the trials [21] and whether the participant has correctly imagined every text stimulus cannot be guaranteed.

The limitation of this study lies in the fact that the scale of the vowel data is not large enough, with only 30 trials allocated to each category. This makes

Table 6. Classification results of the SVM.

Task type	Accuracy	Precision	Recall	F1	Accuracy-Tone	Accuracy-Vowel
Vowel-Overt	11.8%	10.6%	11.5%	11%	30.9%	35.6%
Vowel-Overt-noisy	8.3%	8.1%	8.3%	8.2%	27.1%	31.9%
Vowel-intend	4.4%	3.4%	3.9%	3.6%	28%	18.8%
Vowel-imagine	4.3%	4.1%	4.2%	4.1%	27.6%	17.5%
Word-Overt	32.1%	33.1%	32.1%	32.6%		
Word-Overt-noisy	29.3%	28.4%	29.4%	28.9%		
Word-intend	21.3%	21.9%	21.3%	21.6%		
Word-imagine	16%	16.3%	16%	16.15%		

Table 7. Classification results of the ShallowCNN.

Task type	Accuracy	Precision	Recall	F1	Accuracy-Tone	Accuracy-Vowel
Vowel-Overt	24.3%	30.7%	24.3%	27%	53.7%	45.1%
Vowel-Overt-noisy	13.2%	18%	13.2%	15.4%	50.1%	40.9%
Vowel-intend	9%	10.5%	9%	9.7%	31%	37.7%
Vowel-imagine	6%	8.9%	6.9%	7.7%	22.3%	16.4%
Word-Overt	75.6%	71.2%	69.3%	70.24%		
Word-Overt-noisy	60.6%	58.7%	56.2%	57.4%		
Word-intend	69.5%	66.5%	65.6%	66%		
Word-imagine	28.1%	29.3%	26.6%	27.9%		

the model unable to learn the features well, directly affecting the classification performance. At the same time, the number of participants is insufficient, so the reliability of the data still needs to be improved. Subsequently, we will gather more participants, collect larger-scale data, and expand the dataset to the Chinese sentences.

5 Conclusion

In this study, we develop a novel multi-condition Chinese EEG dataset, acquired through experimentally controlled simulations of patient pronunciation scenarios. The dataset comprehensively incorporates pronunciation and linguistic characteristics of Mandarin Chinese, including vowels, unique tones and commonly used words. We also perform classification on the proposed dataset and demonstrate the superior performance of ShallowCNN compared to traditional SVM method. The experimental results not only validate the research utility of our multi-condition dataset but also highlight the significant potential of deep learning in advancing EEG-based speech decoding. In the future, we will gather more participants, collect larger-scale data, and expand the dataset to the Chinese sentences.

Acknowledgment. We acknowledge the support of National Science and Technology Major Project 2022ZD0118002, the Research Project of Institute of Software, Chinese Academy of Sciences (ISCAS-ZD-202401, ISCAS-JCMS-202306), the project of China Disabled Persons Federation CDPF2023KF00002 and the China Postdoctoral Science Foundation 2024M763393, National Key R&D Program of China (No. 2024YFB3909900), the Fundamental Research Funds for the Central Universities 2025JBZX018.

References

1. 2020 international BCI competition. OSF (2020). https://osf.io/pq7vb/. Accessed Apr 2020
2. Agarwal, P., Kumar, S.: Electroencephalography-based imagined speech recognition using deep long short-term memory network. ETRI J. **44**(4), 672–685 (2022)
3. Albera, L., et al.: ICA-based EEG denoising: a comparative analysis of fifteen methods. Bull. Polish Acad. Sci. Tech. Sci. **60**(3), 407–418 (2012). Special issue on Data Mining in Bioengineering
4. Blakely, T., Miller, K.J., Rao, R.P., Holmes, M.D., Ojemann, J.G.: Localization and classification of phonemes using high spatial resolution electrocorticography (ECoG) grids. In: 30th Annual International Conference of the IEEE Engineering in Medicine and Biology Society, pp. 4964–4967. IEEE (2008)
5. Bracewell, R.N.: The fourier transform. Sci. Am. **260**(6), 86–95 (1989)
6. Cooney, C., Folli, R., Coyle, D.: Optimizing layers improves CNN generalization and transfer learning for imagined speech decoding from EEG. In: 2019 IEEE International Conference on Systems, Man and Cybernetics (SMC), pp. 1311–1316. IEEE (2019)
7. Coretto, G.A.P., Gareis, I.E., Rufiner, H.L.: Open access database of EEG signals recorded during imagined speech. In: 12th International Symposium on Medical Information Processing and Analysis, vol. 10160, p. 1016002. SPIE (2017)
8. Cortes, C., Vapnik, V.: Support-vector networks. Mach. Learn. **20**, 273–297 (1995)
9. DaSalla, C.S., Kambara, H., Sato, M., Koike, Y.: Single-trial classification of vowel speech imagery using common spatial patterns. Neural Netw. **22**(9), 1334–1339 (2009)
10. D'Zmura, M., Deng, S., Lappas, T., Thorpe, S., Srinivasan, R.: Toward EEG sensing of imagined speech. In: Jacko, J.A. (ed.) HCI 2009. LNCS, vol. 5610, pp. 40–48. Springer, Heidelberg (2009). https://doi.org/10.1007/978-3-642-02574-7_5
11. Guenther, F.H., et al.: A wireless brain-machine interface for real-time speech synthesis. PLoS ONE **4**(12), e8218 (2009)
12. Hochberg, L.R., et al.: Reach and grasp by people with tetraplegia using a neurally controlled robotic arm. Nature **485**(7398), 372–375 (2012)
13. Iljina, O., et al.: Neurolinguistic and machine-learning perspectives on direct speech BCIs for restoration of naturalistic communication. Brain-Comput. Interfaces **4**(3), 186–199 (2017)
14. Liu, Y., Fung, P.: Pronunciation modeling for spontaneous mandarin speech recognition. Int. J. Speech Technol. **7**, 155–172 (2004)
15. Mateo, C., Talavera, J.A.: Short-time fourier transform with the window size fixed in the frequency domain. Digit. Signal Process. **77**, 13–21 (2018)
16. Mou, X., et al.: Chinese EEG: a Chinese linguistic corpora EEG dataset for semantic alignment and neural decoding. Sci. Data **11**(1), 550 (2024)

17. Nguyen, C.H., Karavas, G.K., Artemiadis, P.: Inferring imagined speech using EEG signals: a new approach using Riemannian manifold features. J. Neural Eng. **15**(1), 016002 (2017)
18. Nicolas-Alonso, L.F., Gomez-Gil, J.: Brain computer interfaces, a review. Sensors **12**(2), 1211–1279 (2012)
19. Nieto, N., Peterson, V., Rufiner, H.L., Kamienkowski, J.E., Spies, R.: Thinking out loud, an open-access EEG-based BCI dataset for inner speech recognition. Sci. Data **9**(1), 52 (2022)
20. Panachakel, J.T., Ramakrishnan, A., Ananthapadmanabha, T.: A novel deep learning architecture for decoding imagined speech from EEG. arXiv preprint arXiv:2003.09374 (2020)
21. Poldrack, R.A., Wagner, A.D., Prull, M.W., Desmond, J.E., Glover, G.H., Gabrieli, J.D.: Functional specialization for semantic and phonological processing in the left inferior prefrontal cortex. Neuroimage **10**(1), 15–35 (1999)
22. Schirrmeister, R.T., et al.: Deep learning with convolutional neural networks for EEG decoding and visualization. Hum. Brain Mapp. **38**(11), 5391–5420 (2017)
23. Zhang, Y.J., Yu, Z.F., Liu, J.K., Huang, T.J.: Neural decoding of visual information across different neural recording modalities and approaches. Mach. Intell. Res. **19**(5), 350–365 (2022)
24. Zhao, S., Rudzicz, F.: Classifying phonological categories in imagined and articulated speech. In: IEEE International Conference on Acoustics, Speech and Signal Processing (ICASSP), pp. 992–996. IEEE (2015)

Roughness Rendering in XR Via Pseudo-Haptics and Auditory Feedback

Ming Ye, Yang Tian(✉), Zhao Su, and Zhenrong Zhang

Guangxi university, Nanning, China
ytian@gxu.edu.cn

Abstract. With the increasing adoption of hand tracking in XR devices,the lack of tactile feedback in bare-hand interaction has become a critical bottleneck for enhancing immersive experiences. Traditional vibration/force feedback solutions face challenges in widespread adoption due to cost and hardware limitations, while the pseudo-haptic method that induces tactile illusions through audio-visual multimodal stimulation has gained attention. The "kinesthetic appendage" represents a newly-proposed pseudo-haptic technique, which is a virtual tool attached to the user's body that deforms when contacting virtual objects to evoke tactile illusions. This study focuses on roughness, a core dimension of tactile perception. We innovatively designed three pseudo-haptic techniques for inducing the roughness illusion based on existing kinesthetic appendage theory: appendage vibration during sliding on surfaces, brush texture sound effects during sliding , and their multimodal combination. Experimental comparisons revealed that single-channel audio/visual techniques can significantly enhance virtual surface roughness perception, while the audio-visual fusion scheme outperforms single-channel techniques in subjective metrics like immersion and pleasure. The research validates the feasibility of low-cost multisensory synesthesia as an alternative haptic feedback mechanism, offering new pathways for natural interaction design in consumer-grade XR devices.

Keywords: Extended Reality · Virtual Appendage · Freehand Interaction · Pseudo-haptic

1 Introduction

With mainstream spatial computing devices (e.g., Pico, Meta Quest, etc.) widely supporting the hand-tracking functionality, users can now perform rich interactions in XR environments using only their hands, such as directly touching virtual surfaces. However, the absence of tactile feedback remains a core challenge hindering immersive experiences. Traditional solutions often rely on vibration motors or force feedback devices, which are costly and cumbersome, limiting their adoption in consumer-grade products. Consequently, researchers have proposed the concept of "pseudo-haptics," which attempts to simulate realistic tactile sensations through non-tactile channels such as vision or hearing, thereby eliciting tactile illusions in users. Among these, "roughness"

S. Guo et al. (Eds.): HHME 2025, CCIS 2878, pp. 325–339, 2027.
https://doi.org/10.1007/978-981-92-3991-7_22

is a crucial aspect of tactile perception and a key element for XR systems to deliver natural and intuitive bare-hand interaction experiences. Nevertheless, current XR systems lack cost-effective techniques for rendering roughness.

Existing studies have shown that audio-visual stimuli can modulate users' tactile perception. Costes et al. (Costes et al. 2019) discovered that dynamic visual deformations can induce illusions of surface roughness, while the Fleureau team further demonstrated that combining audio with tactile feedback enhances users' perception of surface textures (Fleureau et al. 2016). Although these findings have not yet been validated in XR environments, they lay a theoretical foundation for developing tactile feedback systems that do not rely on additional hardware. Despite substantial research on auditory aspects, there remains considerable room for exploration in visually induced roughness perception illusions.

Tian et al. introduced the concept of "kinesthetic appendages": in mixed reality (MR) environments, virtual appendages grow from users' body parts, such as fingertips (Tian et al. 2022). When these appendages come into contact with virtual objects, they deform according to real-world physical laws (e.g., "shattering," "bending," "breaking"), thereby evoking kinesthetic feedback illusions—the sensation of the hand being constrained or hindered by virtual objects. When the appendages disengage from the virtual objects, they revert to their original appearance. Additionally, vibrotactile stimuli have been proven to significantly enhance users' perception of virtual texture surface properties. When such tactile feedback aligns with visual information, users' perception of the surface's "authenticity" is notably enhanced (Culbertson and Kuchenbecker 2016).

Building on this research, this paper designs three types of pseudo-haptic stimuli. The visual stimulus involves introducing a controlled range of jitter to the kinesthetic appendages as they slide across a surface. The auditory stimulus entails playing the sound of a brush sliding over a physical surface while the kinesthetic appendages slide. Both visual and auditory stimuli persist until the interaction concludes. This study compares three feedback conditions (visual, auditory, and combined audio-visual) and guides participants to slide their fingers across virtual surfaces of three different materials in an XR environment. Experimental results indicate that either visual or auditory stimulus alone can elicit significant roughness perception, while the multi-channel feedback combining audio and visual inputs is significantly more effective than single-channel feedback. Compared to the no-feedback condition, audio-visual feedback demonstrates notable improvements in subjective experience metrics such as immersion and pleasure.

2 Related Work

Pseudo-haptic feedback is a technique that relies on cross-sensory channel information rather than tactile stimuli to convey tactile perception (Lécuyer et al. 2000), serving as an augmentation of tactile experience through other sensory channels. Psychological science has long studied both unimodal tactile perception and visual-tactile cross-modal interactions, demonstrating that multimodal integration significantly enhances neurocognitive functions compared to tactile-only modalities. The goal of pseudo-haptic feedback is to generate tactile illusions—tactile perceptions evoked under the influence of other senses. Pseudo-haptic feedback based on multisensory illusions has been used to simulate various tactile properties, such as the stiffness of virtual springs, object textures, or mass. In interface displays and virtual environments, pseudo-haptic feedback techniques can flexibly alter the visual representation of virtual objects to simulate multimodal tactile attributes. This approach borrows from the tactile perceptual characteristics of other senses, and in complex intelligent system design, it can be combined with appropriate synesthetic stimuli of other sensory modalities to improve the tactile experience.

2.1 Vision-Based Pseudo-Haptics

Visually induced pseudo-haptic feedback mechanisms have become a key research focus in recent years. When human body movements conflict with observed visual behavior, the perceptual system generates contradictory illusions (Lécuyer et al. 2000), thereby triggering pseudo-haptic effects. These effects are achieved through dynamic control/display (C/D) ratios for tactile simulation. The C/D ratio, as a core parameter, maps the physical displacement of a pointing device to the movement trajectory of the on-screen cursor (Blanch et al. 2004). Notably, pseudo-haptic feedback on touchscreens has been proven to significantly influence users' memory encoding processes of graphical information (Hashimoto et al. 2018). Lécuyer et al. (Lécuyer 2009). proposed leveraging users' visual dominance to induce kinesthetic feedback illusions in XR through visual cues. Typical pseudo-haptic techniques induce kinesthetic feedback illusions by creating discrepancies between users' vision and proprioception. Rietzler et al. (Rietzler et al. 2018).introduced positional offsets between the virtual hand lifting a virtual object and the corresponding real hand to convey the virtual object's weight. Samad et al. (Samad et al. 2019). provided experimental research defining the range of control-display ratios for adjusting such offsets. By slowing down the movement speed of users' virtual limbs or head, an illusion of being submerged in water can be created (Kang et al. 2019; Lee et al. 2019). Bouzbib et al. (Bouzbib et al. 2023) evaluated the range of compliance and stiffness that can be induced on non-compressible physical objects when users observe deformations of their virtual counterparts.

A breakthrough study by Ota and Ujitoko (Ota et al. 2020) demonstrated that visual oscillation stimuli not only induce friction illusions but can also modify users' judgments of real texture roughness through a finger-surface interaction paradigm. Similarly, visualizing the contact deformation between virtual fingers and objects can effectively modulate users' perception of attributes such as object stiffness (Morimoto et al. 2023), providing empirical support for tactile rendering without haptic devices. Furthermore, existing pseudo-haptic studies indicate that combining visual and haptic sensory information can not only alter users' actual tactile perception but also influence their proprioception of object shape, angle, and size (Ban et al. 2012a, b; Ban et al. 2013). However, research on vision-only friction simulation in purely virtual reality environments remains underexplored.

2.2 Research on Visual Information's Impact on Roughness

Multiple studies have shown that the visual representation of tactile feedback can induce tactile illusions without physical stimulation (Biocca et al. 2002). Compared to unimodal tactile channels, visually coordinated feedback exerts more significant regulatory effects on perception formation (Gibbs et al. 2022). Particularly noteworthy is that visual stimuli alone can effectively modify users' subjective judgments of interface friction, confirming the feasibility of visually induced pseudo-haptic effects. The haptic simulation method developed by Antoine Costes et al. (Costes et al. 2019) enables roughness perception on touchscreens without physical actuators by altering the movement trajectory or morphological features of a cursor co-located with the user's finger. The synergistic effect of cursor displacement deviation and visual expansion can induce fine-grained texture sensations. Argelaguet et al. (Argelaguet et al. 2013) developed a similar cursor control technique for desktop systems, using press duration Dt (rather than physical force measurement) as an input parameter to establish a mapping between Dt and image deformation d, successfully achieving visual characterization of material compliance. The Fleureau team (Fleureau et al. 2016) further extended this technique to digital tablets, augmenting it with audio feedback to enhance roughness simulation. After introducing vibration feedback devices, studies found that users could not only perceive gradient changes in surface roughness but also develop illusions of other material physical properties. These stimulus differences manifest not only in particle size dimensions but also involve multiple physical parameters affecting roughness perception. By controlling pressure application patterns via wearable devices, the apparent compliance of tangible objects can be enhanced. Combining real-time pressure and skin-stretch feedback enables systems to simulate tactile perception of surface concave-convex features. Experimental data show that haptic recognition accuracy based on friction modulation is significantly higher than random probability levels (Salazar et al. 2020). In the field of physical haptic enhancement, when vibration feedback is superimposed as users touch a static surface, the perceived intensity of surface roughness correlates positively with vibration amplitude (Asano et al. 2012).

2.3 Audio-Based Pseudo-Haptics

Bosman et al. (de Villiers Bosman et al. 2021) primarily explored cross-modal illusions, where experimental results using auditory cues to induce haptic feedback indicated that sound feedback resembling real-world interactions is necessary for inducing pseudo-haptics in XR environments. The Kaneko team (Kaneko et al. 2022) proposed a method to alter the perceived heaviness of objects by modifying users' auditory feedback, suggesting that the heaviness traditionally induced by adjusting visual feedback can also be generated through auditory modulation. Zhexuan and Zhong (Zhexuan and Zhong 2022) investigated relationships between various sound parameters—such as pitch, waveform shape, and decay duration—and found through experiments that the influence of square and sine waves on roughness perception decreases with increasing pitch, while the effect of triangle waves is independent of pitch. Their work also revealed correlations between decay duration, pitch, and the perception of wetness: lower frequencies combined with shorter decay durations enhance the perception of wetness. Malpica et al. (Malpica et al. 2020) focused on the impact of sound on visual cues in head-mounted displays, particularly material perception in virtual reality. They explored how sound affects the perception of virtual material textures (softness/hardness, glossiness, roughness) and high-level descriptors (e.g., fabric, plastic), showing that sound can influence users' perception of virtual material textures.

In the field of audio-haptic interaction, Collins and Kapralos noted (Collins and Kapralos 2019) that auditory cues can effectively convey information about object size, properties, and texture, especially sounds generated by material interactions. Prior to the pandemic, Collins and Kapralos (Collins and Kapralos 2019) focused on multimodal interaction, conducting a series of experiments to explore the interplay between sound and vision in virtual environments, revealing significant subjective effects of sound on visual fidelity perception and task performance (Kapralos et al. 2017). This research was extended to audio-tactile interaction, particularly in virtual drilling tasks, examining the impact of sound on the perception of haptic fidelity when using a virtual drill (Melaisi et al. 2018) to reach a predetermined depth within a virtual wood block. Chan et al. (Chan et al. 2021) argued that physical interactions with objects in the real world produce not only tactile feedback but also vibrations and sounds. They proposed a method to synthesize realistic auditory and vibrotactile stimuli in virtual environments based on geometric features and material properties at macro, meso, and micro scales. The authors believe that synthesizing realistic feedback for virtual objects through the interaction of vision, hearing, and touch can enhance the virtual environment experience.

Given the limitations visually impaired individuals face in perceiving graphical information and their need to substitute vision with other senses, Maćkowski et al. introduced a tablet-based method (Maćkowski et al. 2023) to present visual information as "tactile images", combining tactile and audio cues to provide contextual selection information. Tactile images contain raised lines and elevated surfaces detectable by fingers. Despite guidelines for line/surface dimensions, shapes, and spacing, the method had shortcomings. To address these, Maćkowski et al. (Maćkowski et al. 2023) incorporated speech-based descriptions of tactile images (implemented via a Braille printer placed on the tablet screen) to supplement tactile cues. User studies found that accompanying auditory descriptions improved the understanding and interpretation of tactile image information. Results indicated that description durations should be 5 to 10 s; beyond this, information becomes difficult to comprehend. Although it is foreseeable that integrating auditory information will greatly benefit traditional vision-based pseudo-haptic feedback techniques in virtual reality, its effectiveness and usability in simulating tactile perception still require in-depth investigation.

3 Implementation of the Visual Jitter Effect

This study builds upon the concept of kinesthetic appendages by introducing a jitter effect. Tian et al. (Tian et al. 2025) designed and utilized a virtual brush in their research to enhance users' touch interactions in virtual space. The implementation principle is as follows:

First, a brush is rendered using 50 connected cylindrical segments of equal height. The brush is attached to the user's right fingertip, denoted as P0. The brush length L is predefined. A ray is cast from P0 along the fingertip direction, and using ray detection, the intersection point between the ray and the virtual plane is calculated and denoted as P2. The distance from the fingertip to the plane is compared with the brush length L. If the distance is greater than L, the brush is considered not in contact with the plane. In this case, the virtual brush appears as a straight vertical cylinder of length L, with its axis aligned along the direction of P0P1. If the distance is less than L, the brush is considered in contact with the plane. The cylindrical segments' axes then align along a Bézier curve connecting the fingertip (P0) and the point where the virtual brush tip touches the user interface, denoted as Ptip.

The line segment P1P2 is projected onto the plane to obtain the projected line P2P′1. The point Ptip lies on the extension of this projected line beyond P2. A point P3 is defined along this extension at a sufficient distance from P2. Thus, Ptip is located somewhere on the segment P2P3. A binary search strategy is employed to precisely determine the position of Ptip. In each iteration, the midpoint between Pmax (initialized as P3) and Pmin (initialized as P2) is calculated. Using P0, P2, and Pmin as control points, the length of the corresponding Bézier curve is computed. If the curve length exceeds L, Pmax is updated to the current midpoint; otherwise, Pmin is updated. The specific implementation principle is illustrated in Fig. 1 (Tian et al. 2025), reproduced from the work of Tian et al. (Tian et al. 2025).

In this study, the kinesthetic appendage is a cylinder with a height of 15 mm and a diameter of 2 mm. Once attached to the fingertip, it can bend and rotate. Our work introduces a transparent sphere as an "intermediate joint" between the fingertip and the kinesthetic appendage. By controlling the rotation of this sphere, the direction of the ray emitted from the fingertip is altered, consequently changing the ray-plane intersection point and the shape of the Bézier curve. The sphere rotates randomly within a certain range in all directions (left, right, up, down), achieved by adding random values to the sphere's rotation parameters.

The oscillation is controlled by a sine wave. The perturbation frequency along the Z-axis is 15 complete sine wave cycles per second, with a base perturbation range of ± 4 mm. On top of this base range, an additional minor noise perturbation with a random small amplitude is superimposed. This is intended to make the jitter appear less perfectly periodic and incorporate subtle, natural variations, avoiding an overly rigid appearance. This additional perturbation range is set to ± 1 mm.

Rotation around the Y-axis has an intended rotation rate of 100°/s. Each frame, a random number between -10 and $+ 10$ is generated. This random number is multiplied by the intended rotation rate to determine the rotation speed for that frame, which is then multiplied by the frame time to yield the rotation angle for the frame.

Based on the above design, the visual jitter effect appears more natural. The implementation result is shown in Fig. 2.

4 Implementation of Auditory Feedback

In this work, we aim to provide users with an authentic "drawing/writing" experience in XR scenarios, moving beyond mere visual line feedback by incorporating an auditory element. To achieve this, we refrained from using ordinary synthetic sound effects and instead utilized recorded sounds of a real brush sliding across physical surfaces (such as paper, wood, canvas, etc.). The nuanced details captured in these authentic recordings—such as variations in pressure, frictional noise, and the acoustic characteristics of material granularity—help users more naturally associate their actions in the virtual environment with contacting and writing on a specific material. This design draws inspiration from

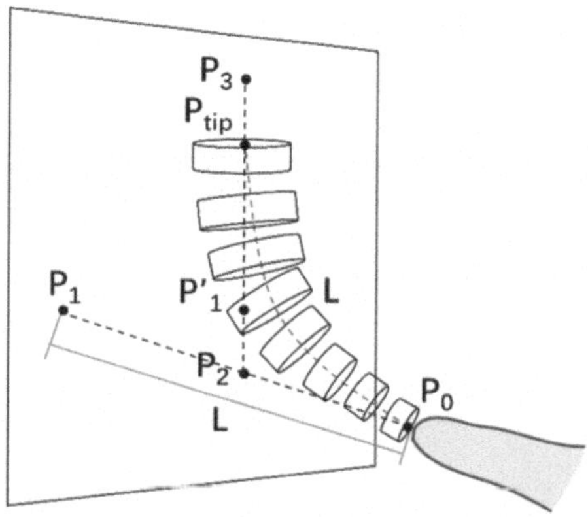

Fig. 1. Implementation principle of kinesthetic appendages (adapted from the related work of Tian et al. (Tian et al. 2025))

the research of Klatzky and Lederman (Klatzky and Lederman 2010), who highlighted the significant value of auditory cues in enhancing tactile experiences, particularly in perceiving surface properties or operational states.

On the technical implementation side, we equipped each virtual plane potentially contacted by the user's finger or virtual brush with an audio component, controlled precisely via scripting. Sound playback is triggered only when the system detects a sliding contact between the user's finger/virtual brush and the plane. This approach prevents accidental sound activation and enhances the naturalness of the interaction. To accomplish this, the audio component is initially disabled at program start to prevent automatic playback. Looping is enabled, allowing the sound to play continuously during the sliding interaction rather than stopping after a single playback cycle.

Spatial sound positioning is also crucial. We configured the sound to be nearly fully 3D, enabling users to clearly perceive the sound emanating from the specific location where the line is being drawn, thereby improving their ability to localize their sliding actions. The volume is set to a dynamic range between 0.5 and 1.4, allowing it to adjust based on sliding speed or pressure, simulating the real-world phenomenon where faster sliding produces louder sounds and slower sliding produces quieter ones. The sound priority is set to a medium level, ensuring it is audible without being prematurely discarded when the system processes multiple sound effects simultaneously. The speed parameter is set to 205 m, defining the spatial range over which the sound propagates. This prevents the sound from fading too abruptly and instead allows it to attenuate gradually with distance, aligning more closely with real-world auditory behavior.

For Volume Rolloff, the Linear model was selected, meaning the sound attenuates uniformly with distance, simulating the natural human perception of sound fading with increasing distance. To avoid the Doppler effect (i.e., pitch distortion) caused by rapid finger movement, the Doppler Level was set to 0, ensuring stable pitch.

Through these configurations, the simulated drawing/writing sound in XR possesses positional awareness, directional characteristics, and dynamic variation, closely resembling the acoustic features of real handwriting. This enhances the user's sense of immersion and action feedback, effectively making sound a form of meaningful "tactile cue."

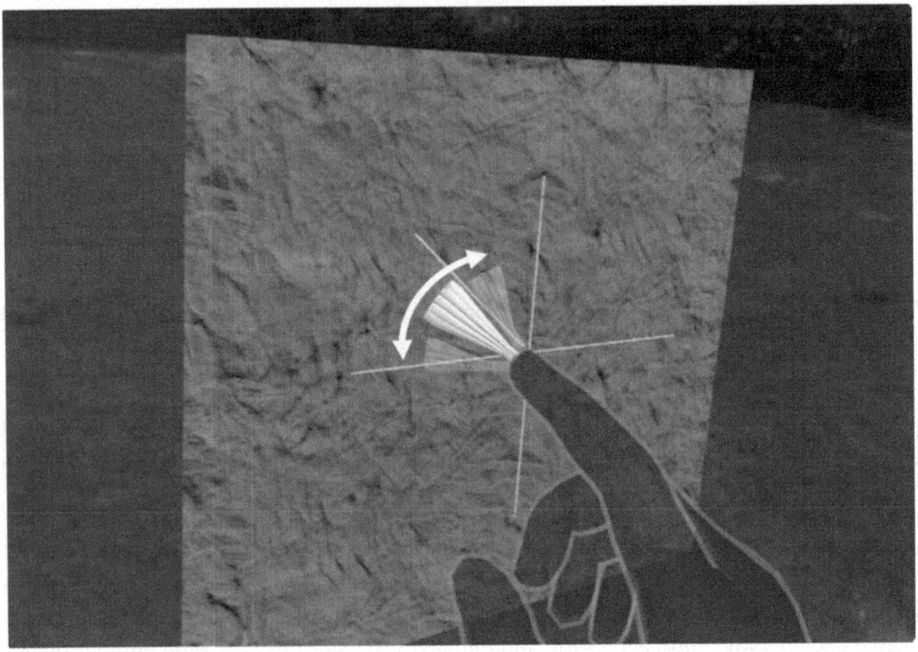

Fig. 2. This figure illustrates the implementation process of the jitter effect. A brush-like appendage is attached to the fingertip, which exhibits jittering motions during the participant's sliding movement. In this figure, the semi-transparent brush depicts the left-right swinging motion of the appendage as the participant slides along a 45° diagonal line

5 Experiment

We compared three forms of feedback and introduced a no-feedback condition as a control group to evaluate the impact of different feedback methods on user perception. This study designed and conducted experiments based on the concept of kinesthetic appendages. Tian et al. (Tian et al. 2025) designed and utilized a virtual brush in their research to enhance users' touch interactions in virtual space. The virtual brush bends upon contact with a surface, with the degree of bending positively correlated with the applied pressure—the harder the press, the more the brush bends. In this study, a cylinder with a height of 15 mm and a diameter of 2 mm was selected as the kinesthetic appendage, attached to the tip of the user's right index finger. This appendage bends when it contacts a virtual surface. The detailed conditions are as follows:

- **NB (No Brush):** This condition provides no feedback and does not display the brush effect, serving as the baseline control group.

- **SO (Sound Only):** Feedback is provided only through auditory cues. When the user's finger or brush slides on the virtual plane, the system plays a sound simulating a physical brush sliding on a physical surface.
- **VO (Vibrate Only):** Feedback is provided only through visual cues. During user interaction with the virtual plane, a jitter effect is visually added to the brush, causing it to shake due to friction, with the jitter intensity proportional to the material's roughness.
- **VS (Vibrate and Sound):** Combines both auditory and visual feedback, exploring the synergistic effects of sound and visual vibration.

In the formal experiment, we further investigated whether different feedback mechanisms could enhance users' sense of touch, friction, overall experience, and immersion in the XR virtual environment.

Participants and Equipment

The formal experiment recruited 24 participants in total, including both males and females, aged between 22 and 30 years, with an average age of 25. All participants were right-handed and had no tactile perception impairments. Some participants had prior experience with XR devices, while others were encountering an XR environment for the first time. The experiment was conducted using the Oculus Quest 2 all-in-one XR headset. The experimental application was developed based on the Unity engine and utilized the Oculus Quest 2's hand-tracking technology to map the virtual hand to the user's real hand.

Experimental Task

Participants were required to use the brush or their finger to draw lines on virtual planes and then rate the realism and experience of the drawing. The experimental task procedure was as follows: Participants put on the XR headset and entered the experimental environment. The system prompted the start of the current task. Participants completed the specified line-drawing task (using the brush or finger) according to the prompts. After drawing the line, participants filled out a questionnaire to rate the feedback mechanisms. Following the questionnaire, the experimenter conducted an interview to gather participants' subjective impressions.

Experimental Environment Design and Implementation

Three 20 cm x 20 cm planes with different textures were placed horizontally 30 cm in front of the user, at eye level. The planes were spaced 2 cm apart, and each surface was marked with sliding directions, as well as start and end points. The materials of the three planes differed: from left to right, they were a relatively smooth fine-grained surface, a medium-roughness surface with irregular undulations, and a highly rough surface with a wrinkled or fibrous texture. The material qualities were rendered using different normal maps and texture processing.

A white 7 cm line forming a cross mark and diagonal lines were drawn at the center of each plane, presenting six line segments in total. These lines indicated the sliding direction and distance for the user. Vertical, horizontal, and diagonal (approximately 45°) lines radiated from the center point, clearly marking the directional requirements for the tactile sliding experiment. These lines also indicated the start and end points of the sliding operation to standardize the user's movement path.

The ground was displayed using Unity's built-in coordinate grid guide lines, ensuring that the planes were placed strictly perpendicular to the ground and precisely aligned with the user's eye level to guarantee a standardized visual perspective input. The virtual planes were positioned perpendicular to the ground. The experimental layout is shown in Fig. 3.

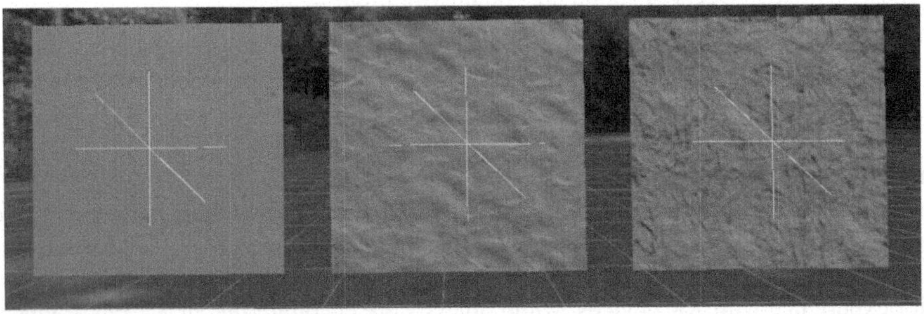

Fig. 3. Experimental Scene Layout. The figure shows three planes with different levels of surface roughness, increasing sequentially from left to right. Each plane features three white line segments of equal length but different slopes at its center, indicating the sliding directions and start/end points

This experiment is based on the concept of kinesthetic appendages proposed by Tian et al. (Tian et al. 2022). When the kinesthetic appendage undergoes visual bending deformation, a visual jitter effect is applied and combined with corresponding audio feedback to study the impact of different feedback mechanisms on users' tactile experience. In the experiment, the kinesthetic appendage is a cylinder with a height of 15 mm and a diameter of 2 mm, attached to the tip of the user's right index finger. Each interaction by the user triggers one feedback form, which persists until the interaction ends.

Each participant completed the planar interaction task using all four techniques, with the order balanced using a Latin Square design. The experiment incorporated four feedback mechanisms. To enhance diversity, we included 3 different plane materials, 3 sliding directions, and 2 repetitions, resulting in a total of 36 trials per participant. Before the main experiment, participants had a one-minute rest period and a one-minute practice session to familiarize themselves with the procedure.

Experimental Data Collection

After completing the experiment, all participants were required to fill out the NASA-TLX scale and a survey questionnaire to collect relevant rating data. The questionnaire was designed using the E^2I questionnaire (Klatzky and Lederman 2010) and relevant questions adapted from the experiment by Rietzler et al. (Lin et al. 2002). The questionnaire employed a 7-point Likert scale (1: Strongly Disagree, 7: Strongly Agree) and collected the following qualitative data: (1) Workload, (2) Immersion, (3) Enjoyment, (4) Sensation of Touch, (5) Sensation of Friction, (6) Realism, (7) Effectiveness, (8) Preference, (9) Level of Distraction, (10) Overall Evaluation. The content of the survey questionnaire is shown in Table 1. At the end of the experiment, the experimenter asked about and recorded the participants' subjective impressions of all the techniques.

Table 1. Questionnaire items

Q1	I had the sensation of touching the plane	Sensation of Touch
Q2	I could feel friction while drawing lines on the plane	Sensation of Friction
Q3	This feedback mechanism appears realistic	Realism
Q4	I consider this feedback mechanism sufficiently refined	Effectiveness
Q5	I like this feedback mechanism	Preference
Q6	The feedback mechanism interfered with the completion of my line-drawing task	Level of Distraction
Q7	I enjoyed using this feedback mechanism to draw lines on the plane	Enjoyment
Q8	My overall evaluation of this feedback mechanism is	Overall Evaluation

The immersion score was calculated as the mean of the results from questions Q1, Q2, Q3, and Q6. Each question in the questionnaire used a 7-point Likert scale, with scores for each question ranging from 1 to 7 (1: Strongly Agree, 7: Strongly Disagree).

Experimental Results

After the formal experiment, the researchers analyzed the participants' subjective ratings. The results showed that the No Brush (NB) condition provided the poorest experience, with participants reporting a lack of realism and tactile feedback. The Sound Only (SO) and Vibrate Only (VO) conditions received similar subjective scores; both provided a certain level of feedback but failed to fully enhance immersion. The Vibrate and Sound (VS) condition received the highest ratings. Participants found this feedback mechanism to be the most realistic, providing the best sensation of touch and friction, while also performing best in terms of enjoyment and immersion.

After collecting the participants' questionnaires, we performed statistical analysis on the data. The experimental results are shown in Table 2. After verifying the normality and homogeneity of variances, a non-parametric Friedman test followed by post-hoc Wilcoxon Signed-Rank analyses was conducted for all dependent variables. The ratings for all metrics showed significant differences ($p < 0.001$). The workload scores for all four methods were low (NB: 2.39, SO: 2.36, VO: 2.43, VS: 2.28) and the differences were not statistically significant ($p > 0.05$).

These experimental results indicate that the feedback mechanism combining sound and visual jitter effectively enhances the user's tactile experience and increases their sense of immersion and satisfaction in the XR environment.

Table 2. Experimental results

Experimental data	1 NB	2 SO	3 VO	4 VS	Friedman test	Post-hoc Wilcoxon rank-sum test
Sensation of Touch	2.08 (1.42)	2.33 (1.69)	4.20 (2.94)	6.37 (3.96)	χ^2 (2) = 67.36, P < 0.001	1–2,1-3,1-4,2–4, 3–4
Sensation of Friction	1.66 (1.06)	4.37 (2.75)	3.75 (2.23)	6.00 (3.96)	χ^2 (2) = 66.49, P < 0.001	1–2,1-3,1-4,2-4,3–4
Realism	2.20 (1.13)	4.33 (2.54)	4.25 (2.48)	6.12 (3.85)	χ^2 (2) = 63.44, P < 0.001	1–2,1-3,1-4,2-4,3–4
Effectiveness	2.12 (1.13)	4.04 (2.31)	4.33 (2.63)	5.91 (3.94)	χ^2 (2) = 63.24, P < 0.001	1–2,1-3,1-4,2-4,3–4
Preference	1.91 (1.00)	4.20 (2.58)	4.12 (2.48)	6.12 (3.94)	χ^2 (2) = 68.54, P < 0.001	1–2,1-3,1-4,2-4,3–4
Level of Distraction	3.375 (1.31)	4.75 (2.65)	4.33 (2.19)	5.91 (3.85)	χ^2 (2) = 54.82, P < 0.001	1–2,1-3,1-4,2-4,3–4
Enjoyment	1.91 (1.00)	4.33 (2.58)	4.33 (2.56)	5.70 (3.85)	χ^2 (2) = 67.83, P < 0.001	1–2,1-3,1-4,2-4,3–4
Overall Evaluation	2.37 (1.06)	4.12 (2.52)	4.20 (2.56)	5.83 (3.85)	χ^2 (2) = 65.25, P < 0.001	1–2,1-3,1-4,2-4,3–4
immersion	2.33 (1.04)	3.94 (2.19)	4.13 (2.79)	6.10 (3.98)	χ^2 (2) = 65.58, P < 0.001	1–2,1-3,1-4,2-4,3–4

6 Discussion

The formal experimental data validated the preliminary findings: the unimodal auditory feedback (SO) and unimodal visual jitter feedback (VO) showed high consistency in core metrics such as task completion efficiency and accuracy, whereas the multimodal combined audiovisual feedback (VS) was significantly superior in overall performance, and the no-haptic feedback group (NB) consistently ranked the lowest. The study revealed that while the four pseudo-haptic feedback conditions (NB/SO/VO/VS) showed no statistically significant difference in cognitive workload ($p > 0.05$), analysis at the proprioceptive level indicated that SO and VO were equivalent in dimensions such as realism, touch sensation, immersion, and friction sensation. This suggests that single-sensory-channel stimulation may struggle to surpass the perceptual gain threshold achieved by multimodal integration.

Notably, in scenarios involving high-frequency hand-plane interactions, the VS group significantly outperformed the other groups ($p < 0.05$) across nine subjective metrics, including immersion ($d = 1.32$), touch sensation ($d = 1.28$), and preference ($d = 1.15$). This phenomenon may stem from the spatiotemporal coupling mechanism of auditory and visual signals within the action-perception loop. Their dual-channel redundant encoding effectively compensates for the perceptual uncertainty caused by the lack of haptic feedback, thereby constructing a more complete cognitive schema of material interaction at the neural representation level. The mechanism underlying the illusion induced by the transformation phenomenon of the kinesthetic appendage requires further investigation.

In the work of Tian et al., several questions were raised. Their study suggested that visual changes during limb interaction with the virtual environment can induce corresponding illusions in participants. Tian et al. proposed a psychological hypothesis that, with the involvement of kinesthetic appendages, participants might come to perceive the appendage as part of their own body after becoming proficient with it. Consequently, a discrepancy between vision and proprioception could generate corresponding illusions, guiding participants to experience sensations such as "friction." Our proposed feedback method innovatively employs a randomized visual oscillation modulation strategy with limited amplitude. Although this algorithm does not yet fully replicate the dynamic characteristics of real bristles (such as nonlinear damping effects and material-dependent frequency response characteristics), it preliminarily verifies the feasibility of cross-modal perceptual compensation. Future research will introduce physics-based bristle motion models (including calculations of bending stiffness matrices and contact force field mapping algorithms) to enhance multidimensional perceptual metrics (e.g., immersion, preference, touch sensation).

7 Conclusion

Addressing the lack of tactile feedback in surface interactions within virtual reality environments, this study innovatively developed a multimodal tactile enhancement strategy. Based on cognitive neuroscience principles, we designed and compared several feedback modalities, including combined audiovisual feedback (VS), dynamic visual deformation (VO), audio-tactile mapping (SO), and no feedback (NB). Experimental data indicate that during two-dimensional interface operation tasks, different feedback modalities demonstrated significant behavioral differences and perceptual gain differentiation (Kruskal-Wallis $H = 23.7$, $p < 0.001$). Notably, the VS group achieved breakthrough improvements in core metrics such as immersion, friction sensation, and enjoyment compared to the NB group.

References

Argelaguet, F., Jáuregui, D.A.G., Marchal, M., Lécuyer, A.: Elastic images: perceiving local elasticity of images through a novel pseudo-haptic deformation effect. ACM Trans. Appl. Percept. (TAP). **10**, 1–14 (2013)

Asano, S., Okamoto, S., Matsuura, Y., Nagano, H., Yamada, Y.: Vibrotactile display approach that modifies roughness sensations of real textures. In: 2012 ieee ro-man: The 21st ieee international symposium on robot and human interactive communication. IEEE, pp. 1001–1006 (2012)

Ban, Y., Kajinami, T., Narumi, T., Tanikawa, T., Hirose, M.: Modifying an identified angle of edged shapes using pseudo-haptic effects. In: International Conference on Human Haptic Sensing and Touch Enabled Computer Applications, pp. 25–36. Springer (2012a)

Ban, Y., Kajinami, T., Narumi, T., Tanikawa, T., Hirose, M.: Modifying an identified curved surface shape using pseudo-haptic effect. In 2012 IEEE Haptics Symposium (HAPTICS), pp. 211–216. IEEE (2012b)

Ban, Y., Narumi, T., Tanikawa, T., Hirose, M.: Modifying perceived size of a handled object through hand image deformation. Presence Teleop. Virt. **22**, 255–270 (2013)

Biocca, F., Inoue, Y., Lee, A., Polinsky, H., Tang, A.: Visual cues and virtual touch: role of visual stimuli and intersensory integration in cross-modal haptic illusions and the sense of presence. Proc. Presence **19** (2002)

Blanch, R., Guiard, Y., Beaudouin-Lafon, M.: Semantic pointing: improving target acquisition with control-display ratio adaptation. In Proceedings of the SIGCHI conference on Human factors in computing systems, pp. 519–526 (2004)

Bouzbib, E., Pacchierotti, C., Lécuyer, A.: When tangibles become deformable: studying pseudo-stiffness perceptual thresholds in a vr grasping task. IEEE Trans. Vis. Comput. Graph. **29**, 2743–2752 (2023)

Chan, S., Tymms, C., Colonnese, N.: Hasti: haptic and audio synthesis for texture interactions. In: 2021 IEEE World Haptics Conference (WHC), pp. 733–738. IEEE (2021)

Collins, K., Kapralos, B.: Pseudo-haptics: leveraging cross-modal perception in virtual environments. Senses Soc. **14**, 313–329 (2019)

Costes, A., Argelaguet, F., Danieau, F., Guillotel, P., Lécuyer, A.: Touchy: a visual approach for simulating haptic effects on touchscreens. Front. ICT. **6**, 1 (2019)

Culbertson, H., Kuchenbecker, K.J.: Importance of matching physical friction, hardness, and texture in creating realistic haptic virtual surfaces. IEEE Trans. Haptics **10**, 63–74 (2016)

de Villiers Bosman, I., De Beer, K., Bothma, T.J.: Creating pseudo-tactile feedback in virtual reality using shared crossmodal properties of audio and tactile feedback. S. Afr. Comput. J. **33**, 1–21 (2021)

Fleureau, J., Lefevre, Y., Danieau, F., Guillotel, P., Costes, A.: Texture rendering on a tactile surface using extended elastic images and example-based audio cues. In: International Conference on Human Haptic Sensing and Touch Enabled Computer Applications, pp. 350–359. Springer (2016)

Gibbs, J.K., Gillies, M., Pan, X.: A comparison of the effects of haptic and visual feedback on presence in virtual reality. Int. J. Hum.-Comput. Stud. **157**, 102717 (2022)

Hashimoto, T., Narumi, T., Nagao, R., Tanikawa, T., Hirose, M.: Effect of pseudo-haptic feedback on touchscreens on visual memory during image browsing. In: International Conference on Human Haptic Sensing and Touch Enabled Computer Applications, pp. 551–563. Springer (2018)

Kaneko, S., Yokosaka, T., Kajimoto, H., Kawabe, T.: A pseudo-haptic method using auditory feedback: the role of delay, frequency, and loudness of auditory feedback in response to a user's button click in causing a sensation of heaviness. IEEE Access **10**, 50008–50022 (2022)

Kang, H., Lee, G., Han, J.: Visual manipulation for underwater drag force perception in immersive virtual environments. In: 2019 IEEE Conference on Virtual Reality and 3D User Interfaces (VR), pp. 38–46. IEEE (2019)

Kapralos, B., Moussa, F., Collins, K., Dubrowski, A.: Fidelity and multimodal interactions. In: Wouters, P., van Oostendorp, H. (eds.) Instructional Techniques to Facilitate Learning and Motivation of Serious Games, pp. 79–101. Springer International Publishing, Cham (2017)

Klatzky, R.L., Lederman, S.J.: Multisensory texture perception. In: Multisensory Object Perception in the Primate Brain, pp. 211–230. Springer (2010)

Lécuyer, A.: Simulating haptic feedback using vision: a survey of research and applications of pseudo-haptic feedback. Presence Teleop. Virt. **18**, 39–53 (2009)

Lécuyer, A., Coquillart, S., Kheddar, A., Richard, P., Coiffet, P.: Pseudo-haptic feedback: can isometric input devices simulate force feedback? In: Proceedings IEEE Virtual Reality 2000. (Cat No 00CB37048), pp. 83–90. IEEE (2000)

Lee, E.-C., Cho, Y.-H., Lee, I.-K.: Simulating water resistance in a virtual underwater experience using a visual motion delay effect. In: 2019 IEEE Conference on Virtual Reality and 3D User Interfaces (VR), pp. 259–266. IEEE (2019)

Lin, J-W, Duh, HB-L, Parker, DE, Abi-Rached, H, Furness, TA: (2002) Effects of field of view on presence, enjoyment, memory, and simulator sickness in a virtual environment. In: Proceedings IEEE virtual reality 2002. IEEE, pp. 164–171

Maćkowski, M., Brzoza, P., Spinczyk, D.: An alternative method of audio-tactile presentation of graphical information in mathematics adapted to the needs of blind. Int. J. Hum.-Comput. Stud. **179**, 103122 (2023)

Malpica, S., Serrano, A., Allue, M., Bedia, M.G., Masia, B.: Crossmodal perception in virtual reality. Multimed. Tools Appl. **79**, 3311–3331 (2020)

Melaisi, M., Rojas, D., Kapralos, B., Uribe-Quevedo, A., Collins, K.: Multimodal interaction of contextual and non-contextual sound and haptics in virtual simulations. In: Informatics. MDPI, p. 43 (2018)

Morimoto, K., Hashiura, K., Watanabe, K.: Effect of Virtual Hand's Fingertip Deformation on the Stiffness Perceived Using Pseudo-Haptics. In: Proceedings of the 29th ACM Symposium on Virtual Reality Software and Technology. pp. 1–10 (2023)

Ota, Y., Ujitoko, Y., Ban, Y., Sakurai, S., Hirota, K.: Surface roughness judgment during finger exploration is changeable by visual oscillations. In: International Conference on Human Haptic Sensing and Touch Enabled Computer Applications, pp. 33–41. Springer (2020)

Rietzler, M., Geiselhart, F., Gugenheimer, J., Rukzio, E.: Breaking the tracking: Enabling weight perception using perceivable tracking offsets. In: Proceedings of the 2018 CHI Conference on Human Factors in Computing Systems, pp. 1–12 (2018)

Salazar, S.V., Pacchierotti, C., De Tinguy, X., Maciel, A., Marchal, M.: Altering the stiffness, friction, and shape perception of tangible objects in virtual reality using wearable haptics. IEEE Trans. Haptics **13**, 167–174 (2020)

Samad, M, Gatti, E, Hermes, A, Benko, H, Parise, C: (2019) Pseudo-haptic weight: Changing the perceived weight of virtual objects by manipulating control-display ratio. In Proceedings of the 2019 CHI Conference on Human Factors in Computing Systems, pp. 1–13

Tian, Y., et al.: Kine-appendage: enhancing freehand vr interaction through transformations of virtual appendages. IEEE Trans. Vis. Comput. Graph. **30**, 3298–3313 (2022)

Tian, Y., et al.: SummonBrush: enhancing touch interaction on large XR user interfaces by augmenting users' hands with virtual brushes. IEEE Trans. Vis. Comput. Graph. (2025)

Zhexuan, W., Zhong, W.: Research on a method of conveying material sensations through sound effects. J. New Music Res. **51**, 121–141 (2022)

Transcendent Vehicles: Augmented Reality-Based Transportation Experiences for Cultural Heritage

Ji Yaru, Shen Ruohan, Sun Xueyang, Chen Ziyi, Ren Yuetong, and Yao Yuan(✉)

School of Architecture and Design, Beijing Jiaotong University, Beijing 100044, China
yuanyao@bjtu.edu.cn

Abstract. This study uses the World Heritage site of Beijing's Central Axis as a case study to explore innovative methods for transmitting urban cultural memories in the digital age. By integrating augmented reality (AR) with various modes of transportation, including bicycles, buses, and private cars, within iconic locations such as Tiananmen Square, the Drum Tower, and the Qianmen commercial district, the aim is to create an immersive cultural experience that bridges different historical periods. The research incorporates elements such as speed, viewpoint, and soundscapes to enhance the emotional and symbolic connection of these transport modes with the landmarks. Based on a survey and interviews, the study demonstrates the effectiveness of AR-driven experiences in evoking urban memories across diverse demographic groups, fostering profound emotional resonance among users from various backgrounds. Our research introduces a novel perspective on the use of AR in cultural heritage, offering fresh insights into the digital preservation of urban memories. It highlights the role of AR in fostering intergenerational connections and strengthening cultural identity, thus paving the way for new approaches to cultural heritage conservation and dissemination.

Keywords: Augmented Reality · Cultural Heritage · Urban Memory · Interaction Design

1 Introduction

With the widespread adoption of AR technology in cultural heritage presentation [2,14,28], enhancing users' emotional connection with cultural heritage through AR has become a critical challenge. While existing research demonstrates significant progress in visual reconstruction, there remains room for improvement in user emotional experience and deep cultural reflection [1,20,25].

Meanwhile, urban memory studies indicate that transportation, as an essential component of urban life, often carries collective memories of specific historical periods [19,26]. However, current AR cultural heritage exhibitions rarely

S. Guo et al. (Eds.): HHME 2025, CCIS 2878, pp. 340–351, 2027.
https://doi.org/10.1007/978-981-92-3991-7_23

explore the unique value of viewing urban memories through the lens of transportation vehicles.

This research takes the UNESCO World Heritage site—the Beijing Central Axis[1] a case study to investigate how AR technology can evoke emotional connections to urban cultural heritage through simulated transportation perspectives. We designed an AR interactive system featuring three vehicle experiences—bicycle, bus, and private car—corresponding to three historical sites along the axis: Tiananmen Square, Drum Tower, and Qianmen Commercial District. This design creates an immersive time-travel experience by considering historical connections between vehicles and sites, while incorporating vehicle speed, viewpoint, and soundscape design.

Through questionnaire surveys (N=122) and in-depth interviews (N=15), our research reveals that AR vehicle experiences effectively evoke urban memories across different demographic groups: the bicycle perspective embodies the democratization of public spaces, the bus perspective consolidates collective memories of neighborhood life, and the private car perspective prompts reflection on modern urban rhythms. The innovative contributions of this research include:

- 1) Introducing transportation vehicles into AR cultural heritage presentation, proposing a novel form of cultural tourism experience.
- 2) Providing new approaches for the digital preservation of urban memories.

2 Background and Related Work

2.1 Gamification Experience in AR Cultural Heritage

AR technology enhances cultural heritage preservation through virtual experiences. "Footprints of Travel" combines AR and AIoT to offer real-time virtual overlays at heritage sites. The system uses AIoT for crowd tracking, positioning, and environmental monitoring, while creating personalized tours and digital twin models of historical sites [11]. While AR games incorporate various elements, soundscape design remains underexplored. Our goal is to integrate acoustic environments into AR scenes to bridge present and past experiences.

Participants in cultural heritage narratives often lack appropriate tools for effective expression, a limitation that has been partially addressed by the development of AR technology combined with physical props. AR interaction incorporates various gameplay elements including prop interaction and gesture interaction, as demonstrated in an AR project about Cave 220 of the Mogao Grottoes in Dunhuang, where designers combined wireframe designs on stone tablet props with virtual displays on tablets to bridge physical space and digital content. Creating an illusion that "the virtual cave manifests directly on the physical wall" [9]. Nevertheless, most AR design work uses "props" merely as visual display

[1] Beijing Central Axis: A Building Ensemble Exhibiting the Ideal Order of the Chinese Capital https://whc.unesco.org/zh/list/1714—as.

mediums, failing to achieve multidimensional sensory integration for users. To enhance user experience, we designed narrative devices with planar displays and planned to create interactive props based on transportation vehicles as interaction media.

2.2 Affective Design in AR Cultural Heritage

Recent research has explored affective design in AR cultural heritage applications through three key approaches. First, narrative-based interactions have proven effective in fostering emotional connections. For instance, the Museum of Memory in Colombia employed "memory layers" through AR to evoke empathy in historical narratives [4], while Liu et al. leveraged embodied storytelling to enhance users' cultural identity with intangible heritage [15]. These designs not only present historical content but guide viewers to reflect on its contemporary relevance. And the multisensory interactions have been shown to enhance experiential authenticity. Petrelli et al. demonstrated that physical props generate stronger emotional engagement compared to purely digital interfaces [23]. Similarly, Ryding's research highlighted how soundscape design significantly contributes to creating immersive experiences [24]. These multisensory approaches help users form deeper connections with cultural artifacts. Finally, social interaction features have transformed cultural transmission into a participatory experience. Koleva explored mechanisms for visitors to share experiences [10], while Muntean integrated cultural values into interactive design [20]. These examples illustrate how affective design is shifting AR heritage experiences from unidirectional presentation to multi-way engagement by enriching experiential channels for authentic cultural experiences.

AR technology enhances users' experience of historical memory, guiding them toward deeper reflections. In this context, the research team designed an AR exhibition titled "Memory Layers," where visitors trigger virtual content by scanning AR markers on the exhibits, presenting a full narrative alongside the real artifacts. This design aims to inspire viewers to reflect on and respect history [4], understand the significance of identity [5,21] and narrative [15], and incorporate values into interactive AR tools within cultural tourism [6,20]. For example, in Koleva's study[10], they explored methods for on-site visitors to share their experiences with family and friends, allowing them to engage with artifacts by giving gifts through the museum. Additionally, immersive audio walks can be used to offer emotional experiences and visual wonders during cultural village activities [24].

3 Game Concept Design

3.1 Overall Design Overview

The Central Axis of Beijing is a representative of world cultural heritage. Stretching from north to south, it spans significant historical landmarks such as the Bell and Drum Towers, Tiananmen, the Forbidden City, and the Temple of Heaven.

It serves as an important symbol of traditional Chinese culture, connecting the cultural links between the past and the present. As a daily means of transportation for urban residents, transit vehicles profoundly influence people's perception of space [17].

From bicycles to cars, specific vehicles from different eras bring unique historical memory experiences to the Central Axis. The three types of vehicle experiences we selected demonstrate a progressive relationship: the bicycle represents the populism of transportation experiences, the bus embodies the collectivism of vehicle development, and the private car symbolizes the modernity of lifestyle. These three vehicles connect the past and the present, outlining the trajectory of Beijing's urban development. This design goes beyond mere scene restoration, allowing users to reconsider the relationship between tradition and modernity, efficiency and quality, and the individual and the collective through the everyday experience of transportation. We aim to use AR to transport visitors from the real urban landscape into spaces of historical culture, creating an interactive experience of "traveling through time and space" through the use of vehicles.

3.2 Core Concept Design of "Central Axis Tour Chronicle" Three Scene Designs and Corresponding Vehicle Experiences

Tiananmen Square, Bicycle Experience: Historical Background: The connection between Tiananmen Square and bicycles reflects the "populist" transformation in China's modernization process. In the early years of the founding of the People's Republic of China, bicycles, as the most common means of transportation, allowed ordinary people to closely experience the historical shift of this once imperial and aristocratic space. The gentle speed of bicycles contrasts with the grand scale of the square, enhancing the solemn atmosphere of the site. Furthermore, travelers using bicycles in surveys reported greater enjoyment than those using other vehicles [18], with this sense of joy closely related to the users' perception of their surroundings [3].

Interaction Design: Through AR, different historical landscapes of Tiananmen Square will be restored, allowing users to witness the transformation of the space from the enclosed imperial palace to the People's Square from a bicycle perspective. The experience will be complemented by sound effects from significant historical events, such as the founding ceremony, offering an emotional interpretation of the theme "belonging to the people".

Drum Tower, Bus Experience: Historical Background: The combination of the Bell Tower and buses encapsulates the collective characteristics of Beijing's urban memory. As an early representative of public transportation, buses witnessed the transformation of Old Beijing from traditional living spaces to a modern metropolis. The bus window, as a moving frame, also provides passengers with a dynamic perspective on the city's changes [27].

Interaction Design: AR technology offers users the perspective of a bus window, restoring the appearance of neighborhoods from different periods and allowing users to experience the spatial shift from the ancient city's charm to the modern urban landscape. The soundscape design, ranging from the noise inside the modern bus to the street vendors' calls in historical scenes, enhances the immersive experience of time travel. This design offers new ways for different generations to understand the city's history, while also fostering intergenerational connections through this digital tool [13].

Central axis city section, private car experience: Historical Background: The private car experience from Qianmen to the Bell Tower reflects a reflection on the rhythm of modern urban life. The number of private cars is, to some extent, a reflection of the urbanization process [12]. This segment has undergone a transformation from an ancient commercial district to a modern business area, and the fast movement of private cars mirrors the shift in the urban lifestyle brought about by modernization.

Interaction Design: In the AR-constructed perspective, users virtually drive through the car window, experiencing the evolution of neighborhood spaces from traditional dense textures to the open scales of modernity. The dynamic relationship between car speed and urban space prompts users to reflect: in the pursuit of efficiency in modern life, have we overlooked the opportunity to observe and experience the finer details of the city?

3.3 Technical Implementation and Visual Designn

At the basic medium level, books are a common physical carrier in AR games, and their linear narrative aligns with the spatial relationship of the Central Axis. Therefore, we chose folded books as the carrier. We selected common vehicle perspectives for the book's visual content, with the image sequence in the book corresponding to the north-to-south order of the Central Axis. The design of the book simulates a depth effect with foreground, middle ground, and background perspectives.

In game development, the content script guides users through historical scenes via tasks. Users can experience other game elements in spatial sequence, unlocking new scenes after completing specific tasks. The physical interactive devices are arranged in this sequence as well. The game system also features a point-based reward mechanism to encourage users to explore and switch between scenes. Upon completing historical tasks or switching scenes, users receive points based on task completion and exploration depth. These points allow users to unlock additional historical events, virtual items, or special historical scenes, further motivating them to explore the cultural significance of different historical points along the Central Axis. The technical implementation uses Unity and Vuforia SDK to develop AR features, with interaction enabled through virtual buttons and recognition tracking (Figs. 1, 2 and 3).

For visual design, we created hand-drawn sketches and used generative AI for style transfer to simulate historical architectural styles. We integrated these with historical Central Axis images in a flattened artistic style in Unity, while incorporating distinct vehicular perspectives into the visual design.

Fig. 1. (a)Book closed state. (b)Book opens side view. (c)The book opens to the front view. (d)Enter the operation. (e)Interactive interface.

Fig. 2. (a)Central Axis urban art style references. (b)Gulou art style references. (c)Tian'anmen Square art style references. (d)AR scenes of the Central Axis urban. (e)AR scenes of Gulou. (f)AR scenes of Tian'anmen Square.

In the future, we can add physical sensing props to provide a richer immersive experience through various sensors. The steering wheel device could be embedded with a gyroscope to detect steering changes and feedback to the AR system via Unity, dynamically adjusting the Central Axis landscape. The bicycle device could incorporate a gyroscope sensor to simulate forward motion while cycling. For the bus component, an accelerometer sensor could be introduced to control changes in the outdoor scenery based on users' hand movements, such as swiping or tapping.

4 User Research and Analysis

4.1 Research Methodology and Data Collection

To investigate the potential of AR technology in the transmission of urban memory, we collected 122 responses through an online survey, the majority of participants being students and employees aged 18 to 30 years. The survey addressed the perceptions of the participants, their emotional connections to the Central Axis of Beijing, their awareness of AR technology, and its influence on cultural experiences. The results revealed that while most of the users had a limited emotional attachment to the Central Axis of Beijing, they demonstrated a strong interest in history and culture, suggesting that AR technology can enhance cultural immersion and foster social connections.

Based on the survey results, we conducted offline user testing by recruiting people connected to the research and asking them to recommend other eligible participants, while also expanding the recruitment scope through social media to ensure a diverse user group was covered. In the end, we selected 15 users from different backgrounds, including non-Beijing residents, young migrants to Beijing, and elderly Beijing natives. The various memory differences promoted

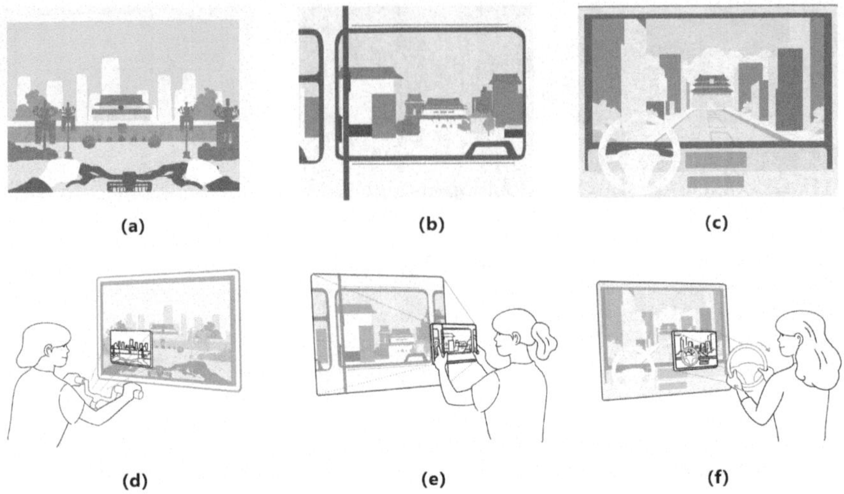

Fig. 3. (a)Bicycle perspective. (b)Bus perspective. (c)Private car perspective. (d)Bicycle physical interaction. (e)Bus physical interaction. (f)Private car physical interaction.

intergenerational transmission of urban memory, helping to create a comprehensive memory space. In order to further explore the participants' subjective experiences, we employed a phenomenological analysis method. Collected data through interviews and observations, with audio and video recordings made with the participants' consent [16]. The interviews were conducted using think-aloud and semistructured approaches, and after transcription, thematic analysis was performed to present the research findings in a narrative form.

4.2 Vehicle Experience and Memory Resonance

Different vehicles trigger varying levels of memory resonance. The bicycle perspective is the most likely to evoke emotional resonance, especially for elderly Beijing natives, whose memories are closely tied to personal experiences. For instance, a retired woman expressed before the experience: *"I feel that the Beijing I know is drifting further away from me."* After the experience, she shared her joy: *"Riding along Chang'an Street, I felt like I was back in the slow-paced days of the past."*

The bus perspective triggers collective memories, with older people often reminiscing about the city's past landscapes, while younger people tend to focus more on the modernization of the city. The private car perspective sparks participants' reflections on the pace of urban life, particularly among the migrant population in Beijing. One participant remarked: *"When I recall my memory of the central axis, my first thought is which roads are more likely to be congested during the morning and evening rush hours."* The immersive experience we provided made participants feel that the city is no longer a cold, abstract concept, but rather a living scene that can be re-experienced and personally perceived.

4.3 Transmission of Culture and Emotional Connection Across Generations

In intergenerational dialogue, AR devices serve not only as tools for historical reproduction but also as bridges for emotional connections. In particular, when elders share memories with the younger generation, both sides can gain a sense of happiness by establishing emotional ties [22]. In the experiment, elderly participants shared personal historical stories, such as their childhood experiences in Beijing's alleys and the urban transformations, helping the younger generation understand the city's history. In addition, many young respondents mentioned that elders would unconsciously share past experiences after the activity. These impromptu stories enhanced the participants' understanding of the city's history and strengthened the emotional ties between generations.

4.4 Formation of Emotional Identity Mechanisms

The vehicle experience lowers the threshold for historical perception and helps users establish emotional identification through the design of the AR vehicle perspective, especially for the younger generation and new urban residents. Through the immersive experience of "Central Axis Tour Chronicle", they reconnected with the city's history, strengthening their emotional connection to the central axis. One participant stated: *"I always took the subway through Gulou Street for work, but today, for the first time, I 'sat' on a bus and saw the view outside the window, experiencing the vibrant city life."* This design offered them an opportunity to create an emotional connection with the city.

Meanwhile, the design of time-space conversion allows users to feel like 'witnesses' rather than observers. By switching between different historical periods and real-world scenarios, users can personally experience historical changes from multiple perspectives.

4.5 Soundscape Design Enhances Memory Immersion

The soundscape design enhances the immersion of memory by combining sound with historical scenes, providing a powerful medium for cultural transmission. Elderly users recall historical scenes associated with sound, especially in the bus perspective design, where the sound effects of the windows and time-space transitions create an immersive experience across time and space. One participant stated: *"The conductor's station announcements and the street vendors' calls outside the window instantly took me back to the past."*

4.6 Conclusion

Our study confirms the role of AR devices in the transmission of urban memory, with different vehicles triggering varying levels of memory resonance. The bicycle perspective evokes personal emotional recollections, the bus perspective triggers collective memories of urban changes, and the private car perspective encourages reflection on the pace of modern life. In intergenerational dialogue, AR technology serves as a bridge for emotional connection, enabling elders and the younger generation to strengthen their emotional ties through shared memories. Furthermore, AR design aids users in building emotional identification through familiar transportation perspectives and enhances memory immersion through soundscape design, thereby amplifying emotional resonance with history and fostering cultural identity.

5 Discussion

As our research results indicate, the experience of the AR vehicle with three different perspectives on transportation can evoke multilayered memory resonance in users, strengthening their emotional identification with the history of the city. The bicycle perspective, with its "people-centered" nature, triggers emotional resonance, beloved by older Beijingers, while providing young tourists with a "localized" viewpoint. The "collectivity" of the bus perspective stimulates collective memory and promotes intergenerational communication. In contrast, the "modernity" of the private car perspective leads to reflections on the pace of life, allowing users to experience the layered changes in urban space as they move quickly through it. Furthermore, the addition of soundscape design significantly enhances the authenticity of historical memories, transforming users from observers to participants, immersing them more deeply in historical settings.

5.1 Limitation

Offline experiments have shown that hardware limitations can affect the effectiveness of AR experiences. Existing devices lack recognition accuracy in complex scenes, and when lighting is complicated or the scene contains dense details, the integration between virtual and real elements becomes unstable, disrupting user immersion. In addition, there is still room for improvement in the integration of vehicle design with cultural content. Current designs focus more on interactivity, but insufficiently incorporate historical events and cultural contexts. Moreover, current AR cultural communication designs focus primarily on single-user experiences, while the potential for multi-user collaboration remains largely untapped [8]. Improving design to improve user experience and cultural dissemination remains a crucial challenge to address in the future.

5.2 Future Design Direction

First, by enhancing sensor accuracy and computational power, the performance of devices in complex scenes can be improved, ensuring a more stable and natural integration of the virtual and real worlds. Second, the multi-vehicle experience can be extended to other urban cultural heritage scenes, designing engaging levels to connect historical timelines, selecting vehicles that adapt to local characteristics and interact with historical settings, thereby strengthening users' recognition and emotional connection with more urban cultures [7]. Third, deepening multi-user collaboration and social design by building social platforms where users can share cultural memories through interaction will not only enhance the fun of cultural dissemination, but also enable cross-group communication and the continuation of cultural transmission.

In conclusion, this study introduces a new approach to integrating vehicle experiences into AR cultural dissemination, and through the design and practice of the "Central Axis Tour Chronicle" explores its potential in enhancing historical memory and emotional resonance. Despite some limitations, with further improvements in hardware and interaction design and a stronger integration of historical scenes with cultural contexts, AR technology will open up more possibilities for the dissemination and preservation of digital heritage.

6 Conclusion

The game experience of AR transportation vehicles strengthens users' emotional connection with the city and evokes their urban memories to different extents. Our research findings reveal the potential of AR technology in evoking urban cultural memories and highlight the importance of memory for cultural identity and intergenerational cultural transmission. In addition, the multi-vehicle interactive design provides an innovative practical case for the dissemination of cultural heritage. Future work related to urban historical memory could also develop communication experiences that span time and cultural dimensions, while considering the differing cultural memories and perceptions of intergenerational users.

References

1. Agenda, I.: New vision for education: Fostering social and emotional learning through technology. World Economic Forum **36** (2016)
2. Bekele, M.K., Pierdicca, R., Frontoni, E., Malinverni, E.S., Gain, J.: A survey of augmented, virtual, and mixed reality for cultural heritage. J. Comput. Cultural Heritage **11**(2), 7 (2018). https://doi.org/10.1145/3145534
3. Böcker, L., Dijst, M., Faber, J.: Weather, transport mode choices and emotional travel experiences. Transp. Res. Part A: Policy Pract. **94**, 360–373 (2016). https://doi.org/10.1016/j.tra.2016.09.021

4. Cárdenas Gasca, A.M., Jacobs, J.M., Monroy-Hernández, A., Nebeling, M.: Ar exhibitions for sensitive narratives: designing an immersive exhibition for the museum of memory in Colombia. In: Proceedings of the 2022 ACM Designing Interactive Systems Conference, pp. 1698–1714. ACM (2022). https://doi.org/10.1145/3532106.3533549
5. Falk, J.H.: Identity and the Museum Visitor Experience. Routledge, 1 edn. (2009). https://doi.org/10.4324/9781315427058
6. Fu, X., Zhu, Y., Xiao, Z., Xu, Y., Ma, X.: RestoreVR: generating embodied knowledge and situated experience of dunhuang mural conservation via interactive virtual reality. In: Proceedings of the 2020 CHI Conference on Human Factors in Computing Systems, pp. 1–13. ACM (2020). https://doi.org/10.1145/3313831.3376673
7. Haahr, M.: Creating location-based augmented-reality games for cultural heritage. In: Alcañiz, M., Göbel, S., Ma, M., Fradinho Oliveira, M., Baalsrud Hauge, J., Marsh, T. (eds.) JCSG 2017. LNCS, vol. 10622, pp. 313–318. Springer, Cham (2017). https://doi.org/10.1007/978-3-319-70111-0_29
8. Ismail, A.W., Sunar, M.S.: Collaborative augmented reality: multi-user interaction in urban simulation. In: Badioze Zaman, H., Robinson, P., Petrou, M., Olivier, P., Schröder, H., Shih, T.K. (eds.) IVIC 2009. LNCS, vol. 5857, pp. 382–391. Springer, Heidelberg (2009). https://doi.org/10.1007/978-3-642-05036-7_36
9. Kenderdine, S., Chan, L.K.Y., Shaw, J.: Pure land: futures for embodied museography. J. Comput. Cult. Heritage **7**(2), 8 (2014). https://doi.org/10.1145/2614567
10. Koleva, B., et al.: Designing hybrid gifts. ACM Trans. Comput.-Hum. Interact. **27**(5), 37 (2020). https://doi.org/10.1145/3398193
11. Lai, S.Y., et al.: Footprints of travel: AIoT and AR enhanced tourist gaming experience in unmanned cultural sites. In: Extended Abstracts of the CHI Conference on Human Factors in Computing Systems (202)
12. Li, Q., Yu, J., Jiang, H.: The study of the impacts of urbanization to private car holding quantity in China. J. Yunnan Agric. Univ. (Soc. Sci.) **9**(4), 1–5 (2015). https://doi.org/10.3969/j.issn.1004-390X(s).2015.04.001
13. Liaqat, A., Axtell, B., Munteanu, C.: "with a hint she will remember": collaborative storytelling and culture sharing between immigrant grandparents and grandchildren via magic thing designs. In: Proceedings of the ACM on Human-Computer Interaction, vol. 6, p. 268. ACM (2022). https://doi.org/10.1145/3555158
14. Liu, Y.: Evaluating visitor experience of digital interpretation and presentation technologies at cultural heritage sites: a case study of the old town, Zuoying. Built Heritage **4**(1), 14 (2020)
15. Liu, Z., Yan, S., Lu, Y., Zhao, Y.: Generating embodied storytelling and interactive experience of China intangible cultural heritage "hua'er" in virtual reality. In: Extended Abstracts of the 2022 CHI Conference on Human Factors in Computing Systems. ACM (2022). https://doi.org/10.1145/3491101.3519761
16. Mallon, B., Webb, B.: Applying a phenomenological approach to games analysis: a case study. Simul. Gaming **37**(2), 209–225 (2006)
17. Mondschein, A., Blumenberg, E., Taylor, B.D.: Accessibility and cognition: the effect of transportation mode on spatial knowledge. Tech. rep., UC Berkeley: University of California Transportation Center (2008). https://escholarship.org/uc/item/8kz7722k
18. Morris, E.A., Guerra, E.: Mood and mode: does how we travel affect how we feel? Transportation **42**(1), 25–43 (2014). https://doi.org/10.1007/s11116-014-9521-x
19. Mumford, L.: The city in history: its origins, its transformations, and its prospects, vol. 67, Houghton Mifflin Harcourt (1961)

20. Muntean, R., Antle, A.N., Matkin, B., Hennessy, K., Rowley, S., Wilson, J.: Designing cultural values into interaction. In: Proceedings of the 2017 CHI Conference on Human Factors in Computing Systems, pp. 6062–6074 (2017)
21. Neale, S., Chinthammit, W., Lueg, C., Nixon, P.: Facilitating learning through hands-on engagement with virtual museum artefacts. In: Proceedings of the 28th International BCS Human Computer Interaction Conference on HCI 2014, pp. 222–227. BCS Learning & Development Ltd (2014). https://doi.org/10.14236/ewic/hci2014.27
22. Pecorini, B., Duplaa, E.: Narrative gerontology and digital storytelling: what benefits for elders. MOJ Public Health **6**(6), 00192 (2017)
23. Petrelli, D., O'Brien, S.: Phone vs. tangible in museums: a comparative study. In: Proceedings of the 2018 CHI Conference on Human Factors in Computing Systems, pp. 1–12. ACM (2018). https://doi.org/10.1145/3173574.3173686
24. Ryding, K.: The silent conversation: designing for introspection and social play in art museums. In: Proceedings of the 2020 CHI Conference on Human Factors in Computing Systems, pp. 1–10. ACM (2020). https://doi.org/10.1145/3313831.3376357
25. Schaper, M.M., Pares, N.: Enhancing students' social and emotional learning in educational virtual heritage through projective augmented reality. In: Extended Abstracts of the 2022 CHI Conference on Human Factors in Computing Systems. ACM (2022). https://doi.org/10.1145/3491101.3503551
26. Smith, L.: Intangible heritage: a challenge to the authorised heritage discourse? Revista d'etnologia de Catalunya **40**, 133–142 (2015)
27. Stradling, S., Carreno, M., Rye, T., Noble, A.: Passenger perceptions and the ideal urban bus journey experience. Transp. Policy **14**(4), 283–292 (2007). https://doi.org/10.1016/j.tranpol.2007.02.003
28. Xu, N., Liang, J., Shuai, K., Li, Y., Yan, J.: Heritagesite AR: an exploration game for quality education and sustainable cultural heritage. In: Extended Abstracts of the 2023 CHI Conference on Human Factors in Computing Systems. ACM (2023). https://doi.org/10.1145/3544549.3583837

Assisted Driver System Based on Augmented Reality

Peifeng Zhang[1](✉), Pan Jiang[1], Kaifan Sun[1], Xiaoxu Sun[1], Hao Wen[1], Dejian Zhang[2], and Hao Zhang[3]

[1] University of Chinese Academy of Sciences, Beijing 100049, China
zhangpeifeng22@mails.ucas.ac.cn
[2] Department of Information Technology, Changsha Preschool Education College, Changsha 410116, China
[3] Institute of Software, Chinese Academy of Sciences, Beijing 100190, China

Abstract. Augmented Reality, which involves the real-time integration of digital information with our physical environment, has been steadily growing over the past few years, entering several areas of our lives. Augmented reality in automobiles can effectively enhance the driver's ability to be informed while driving. According to a survey, 45% of road traffic accidents are caused by drivers' lack of vision and improper operation, resulting in collisions between vehicles and objects in front of them. Therefore, some car manufacturers have applied Head-Up Display technology to their vehicles to display some important driving information in the form of AR in the focused area of the driving field of view, but this may also distract the driver occasionally. Therefore, this system plans to combine AR to design a variable intensity road target detection and alert system, which can improve the driver's emergency obstacle avoidance ability by providing early warning of obstacles according to different driving habits and driving scenarios.

Keywords: Augmented Reality · Drive · Heads-up Display · Object Detection · Human-Computer Interaction

1 Introduction

As one of the most common modes of transportation globally, automobiles play a crucial role in daily travel. Despite the continuous development of the automotive industry and technological advancements, traffic safety remains a severe issue. When driving at high speeds, particularly in special scenarios such as night driving, if a driver lowers their head to view the dashboard or navigation display, they may fail to react in time to sudden emergencies ahead, potentially leading to traffic accidents. According to an international statistical survey, 45% of road traffic accidents result from collisions caused by the driver's insufficient field of view or improper operation.

Research reports indicate that warning the driver 0.5 s before an accident, thereby allowing them to react earlier, can reduce accidents by 60%. If the warning is issued 1 s in advance, accidents can be reduced by 90%. Therefore, utilizing equipment such as

S. Guo et al. (Eds.): HHME 2025, CCIS 2878, pp. 352–370, 2027.
https://doi.org/10.1007/978-981-92-3991-7_24

object detection or sensors to identify information easily overlooked in the driver's field of view and providing timely warnings can prevent many traffic accidents.

In recent years, with the rapid development of information technology, increasingly powerful driver assistance systems have emerged, capable of perceiving the environment in real-time and providing diverse auxiliary information [1]. Against this background, Augmented Reality (AR) technology for intelligent assisted driving has also gradually entered the public view [3].

AR involves the real-time integration of digital information with our physical environment, bringing computers into the user's real world. By enhancing the perception of reality through hearing, seeing, touching, and smelling virtual information, AR achieves a shift from "humans adapting to machines" to "human-centric" technology compared to VR.

Automotive AR helps revolutionize how passengers and drivers acquire information and knowledge, as well as how they integrate into the physical spaces they visit. It adds extra information to the driving environment in real-time to help drivers better perceive road conditions. Since drivers must continuously control the vehicle, their interaction capabilities are somewhat reduced. Previous studies have seen car manufacturers apply Head-Up Display (HUD) technology to vehicles to minimize driver distraction caused by secondary in-car systems [2, 4]. Additionally, AR glasses developed by BMW in collaboration with ODG can display various driving information on a standalone screen.

2 Related Work

2.1 Driver Assistance System Technologies

Currently, many companies have launched unique driver assistance systems, widely applied in the development of intelligent transportation and autonomous driving [6].

First, Israel's Mobileye pioneered a purely vision-based driving assistance solution. This system primarily uses a low-cost camera installed inside the vehicle combined with advanced computer vision algorithms. It achieves various practical functions, including Lane Departure Warning, Forward Collision Warning, headway monitoring and warning, pedestrian recognition and collision prevention, and intelligent high-beam control. A significant advantage of this solution is that it does not directly intervene in vehicle control, effectively ensuring the vehicle's original safety structure remains intact.

Second, the driver assistance system introduced by Germany's Bosch Group integrates multiple sensors, such as stereo cameras and medium-to-long-range radar. Through multi-source information fusion, the system achieves functions like Traffic Jam Assist, Adaptive Cruise Control, intelligent lighting control, traffic sign recognition, automatic parking, lateral blind spot monitoring, and reversing image assistance, further enhancing driving intelligence and safety.

Furthermore, Tesla has launched its representative driver assistance system, primarily using radar as the core sensor combined with optimized algorithms for environmental perception. The system converts environmental information around the vehicle into 3D visual effects and displays them in real-time on the onboard LCD instrument panel, improving the driver's understanding and judgment of the surrounding environment [8].

Google's autonomous vehicles employ a collaborative approach using multiple sensing technologies. The vehicles are equipped with cameras for image acquisition and a rotating LiDAR on the roof capable of high-precision 3D reconstruction of the surrounding environment. This generates real-time 3D maps, providing reliable environmental perception and path-planning support for autonomous driving.

2.2 Augmented Reality Display Technologies

In 1988, Vallino classified AR image presentation methods into three categories: standard monitors, head-mounted video displays, and head-mounted optical see-through displays. Traditional vehicle dashboards and central navigation consoles are located below the driving line of sight. When drivers look down to check or operate them, their gaze shifts inside the vehicle, causing brief "blind driving" behavior that poses a serious threat to road traffic safety. However, automotive Head-Up Display technology can project information regarding the vehicle, road, and entertainment onto the windshield. This allows drivers to acquire information and interact without taking their eyes off the road ahead, effectively resolving the conflict between safe driving and information interaction.

Therefore, domestic and international researchers have investigated various display methods based on driving scenarios:

1. Head-Up Display (HUD) Technology: This technology uses photoelectric projection devices to display key information, such as current speed and navigation paths, directly on the windshield. It forms a transparent image in front of the driver, helping them read information without shifting their gaze. It has become a relatively common form of AR application in modern automobiles.
2. AR Glasses Technology based on Binocular Parallax: This technology simulates the imaging difference between the left and right retinas of the human eye, forming stereoscopic vision through image fusion to enhance spatial perception. However, due to potential visual fatigue from long-term use, it is currently mainly used for short-term driving assistance or specific application scenarios.
3. AR Display Technology based on Non-Binocular Parallax: This includes methods such as holographic displays, integral imaging stereoscopic displays, and volumetric 3D displays. These technologies do not rely on the principle of binocular parallax and offer higher visual comfort and immersion. In recent years, they have gradually become an important research direction in AR display, suitable for overlaying multiple types of information in complex driving environments.

3 System Design Scheme

Previous research indicates that drivers often fail to identify obstacles on the road in time due to various reasons, such as lack of concentration, low environmental visibility, and cognitive decline caused by aging. Therefore, this system is designed to combine AR to create a driver assistance system that improves obstacle avoidance and emergency evasion capabilities across different scenarios.

The system is divided into four modules: the function setting module, the object detection module, the attention determination module, and the interaction module. The overall architecture is shown in Fig. 1.

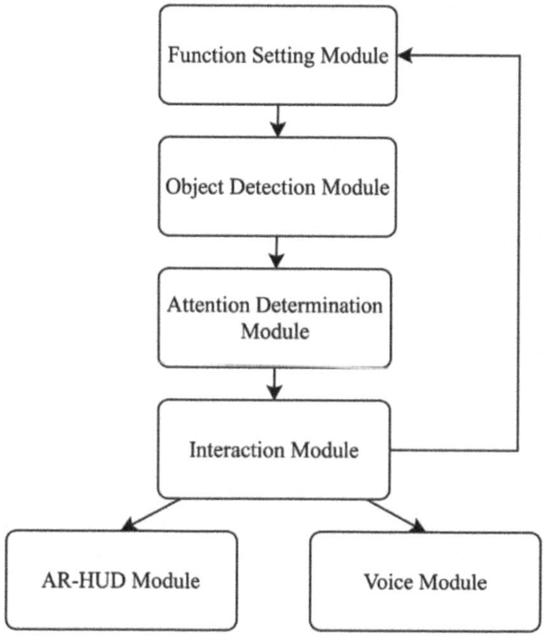

Fig. 1. Overall architecture diagram

The operation flow of the system is shown in Fig. 2, which includes the following steps:

1. The driver starts the assistance system and sets the intensity and mode of alerts (e.g., voice, visual prompts) based on personal preference.
2. Based on the preset field of view, the system detects potential risks in advance and issues warning messages at appropriate times.
3. Upon receiving the system prompt, the driver makes timely driving decisions or operations.
4. When external conditions such as weather or road status change, the driver can dynamically adjust the alert intensity via voice commands to adapt to new driving requirements.

3.1 Object Detection Module

With the development of 3D imaging technology, techniques such as structured light measurement, laser scanning, and Time-of-Flight (ToF) are maturing. These technologies allow for the precise and rapid acquisition of 3D coordinates on object surfaces, generating 3D data of the scene to better perceive and understand the surrounding environment. 3D data contains depth information and can represent the surface shape of objects, offering broad application prospects in robotics, AR/VR, human-computer interaction, remote sensing, and mapping. 3D scene recognition is widely used in autonomous

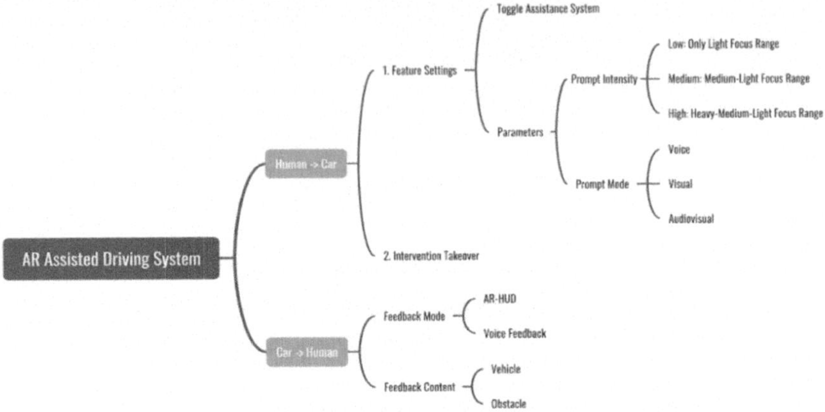

Fig. 2. System operation flow

driving, including road object detection, drivable area prediction, and domain adaptation for semantic segmentation.

To achieve 3D scene semantic segmentation in the autonomous driving domain, this work utilizes the SemanticKITTI dataset. Semantic scene understanding is essential for many applications and is an integral part of autonomous vehicles. In particular, the fine-grained understanding provided by semantic segmentation is necessary to distinguish between drivable and non-drivable surfaces and to reason about functional attributes such as parking areas and sidewalks. Currently, this understanding is primarily represented by High-Definition (HD) maps generated in advance by survey vehicles. However, if the environment changes, autonomous vehicles must be able to drive in unmapped areas and adjust their behavior accordingly.

Currently, most autonomous vehicles use multiple different sensors to perceive the environment. Complementary sensor modes can address the defects or failures of specific sensors. In addition to cameras, LiDAR (Light Detection and Ranging) sensors are frequently used because they provide precise distance measurements unaffected by lighting conditions. Publicly available datasets and benchmarks are crucial for empirical evaluation of research. They serve three main purposes: providing a basis for measuring progress by allowing for replicable and comparable results; revealing deficiencies in the current state of the art, thereby paving the way for new methods and research directions; and enabling the development of methods without the laborious task of collecting and labeling data first. SemanticKITTI is a large dataset showing unprecedented detail in point annotations, containing 28 classes suitable for various tasks. It is primarily used for research on laser-based semantic segmentation and semantic scene completion. This dataset differs from other laser datasets as it provides precise sequential scan annotations.

The dataset consists of 22 sequences. Sequences 00 to 10 are split into the training set, and sequences 11 to 21 are split into the test set. To maintain consistency with the original benchmark, the same split is adopted for training and testing.

To implement the object detection algorithm, we use the RandLA-Net model to perform 3D point cloud semantic segmentation on the SemanticKITTI dataset, thereby identifying target areas. The RandLA-Net model uses random sampling to extract points. Random sampling may accidentally discard features; if the lost features are critical, the semantic segmentation results will be affected. RandLA-Net uses a unique local feature aggregation module to gradually increase the receptive field of each 3D point to reduce model error, ensuring that key features are effectively retained. The local feature aggregation module used by the RandLA-Net model is shown in Fig. 3.

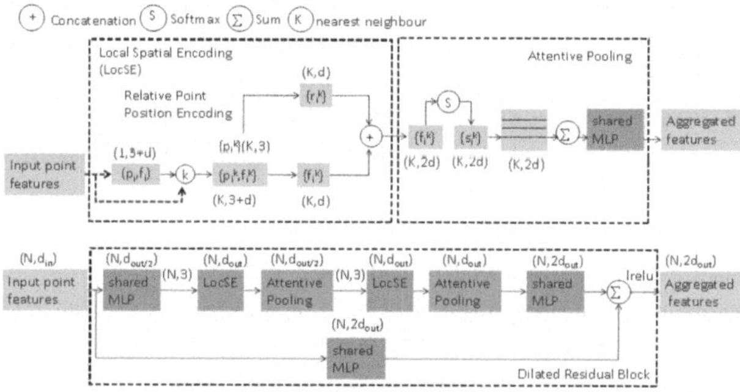

Fig. 3. RandLA-Net model local feature aggregation module

The upper part of Fig. 3 shows the location spatial encoding block for extracting features and attentive pooling. Attentive pooling weights the most important neighboring features through local context and geometric structure. The lower part shows how these two parts are connected to increase the size of the receptive field within a residual block. Three units—Local Spatial Encoding (LocSE), Attentive Pooling, and Dilated Residual Block—jointly constitute the local feature aggregation module of RandLA-Net.The point sampling method used by the RandLA-Net model is random sampling. Existing point sampling methods can be divided into two main categories: heuristic sampling and learning-based sampling. Heuristic sampling includes Farthest Point Sampling (FPS), Inverse Density Importance Sampling (IDIS), and Random Sampling (RS). When using semantic segmentation on small point sets, FPS is suitable. FPS can process the entire point cloud, but its computational complexity is $O(n^2)$, meaning FPS cannot be applied to large-scale point cloud sampling. Sampling with IDIS has a computational complexity of $O(n)$; it reorders n points based on density and selects the top k points. The computational complexity of RS is $O(1)$. Compared with FPS and IDIS, RS has the highest computational efficiency. Therefore, for large-scale point cloud datasets, random sampling reduces computational costs. In RandLA-Net, the local feature aggregator shown in Fig. 3 is applied to retain key geometric feature details.

Local Spatial Encoding

The purpose of local spatial encoding is to acquire the neighborhood features of each point. The process is divided into three steps. Finding Neighboring Points: The K-Nearest Neighbor (KNN) algorithm is used to collect the nearest K points. At this time, the neighborhood representation of the point is (K, 3 + d). Relative Position Encoding: For each center point pi, let its surrounding K points be {pi1,pi2,...piK}. The relative point position encoding formula is as follows:

$$r_i^k = MLP\left(p_i(+)p_i^k(+)p_i - p_i^k(+)\left\|p_i - p_i^k\right\|\right) \tag{1}$$

In Formula 1, ${p_i}^K$ represents the k-th point surrounding i. This step re-encodes ${p_i}^k$ by creating a shared Multi-Layer Perceptron (MLP). The input of the MLP includes the coordinates of point p_i, the coordinates of point ${p_i}^k$, the coordinate difference, and the distance between the two points. After MLP encoding, the feature of the relative point is r_k, which has the same dimension d as the point cloud feature attributes. Position encoding is performed once for all K points. Point Feature Enhancement: The final step is to stack the position feature r_k obtained from the encoding with the original attribute feature f_k for the k-th neighbor of i. Ultimately, K enhanced vectors are obtained.

Attentive Pooling

The purpose of attentive pooling is to aggregate neighborhood features. To perform attentive pooling, attention scores must first be calculated. Using the vector f_k obtained after local spatial encoding as input, an MLP network and a Softmax function are used to calculate the weight s_k corresponding to vector f_k. Then, the sum of the weights is calculated, and the K weighted feature vectors are summed to obtain a new feature vector. Attentive pooling is performed for every input point, ensuring that each input point aggregates information from its surrounding neighbors.

Dilated Residual.

BlockThe purpose of using dilated residual blocks is to increase the point cloud receptive field, thereby accelerating learning speed and improving accuracy. Each dilated residual block consists of two rounds of local spatial encoding and attentive pooling. Similar to the residual structure of ResNet, it adds the input features to the enhanced features.

Test Results

Using the SemanticKITTI dataset, sequences 00–07 and 09–10 were used for training, sequence 08 for validation, and sequences 11–21 for testing. An mIoU (Mean Intersection over Union) of 0.774 was achieved. The classification includes road, parking, sidewalk, other-ground classes, and other non-ground classes. Visualizing the results: the road class is dark blue, parking class is red, sidewalk is yellow, other-ground is purple, and other classes are light blue. The visualization results of the SemanticKITTI dataset are shown in the figures below (Figs. 4 and 5).

3.2 Attention Region Determination Module

Although AR-HUD can effectively improve a driver's ability to acquire external information while driving, experiments have proven that it may also lead to "inattentional blindness" [3]. This means the information displayed by AR causes a lack of attention to information in the physical world.

To address this "unconscious blindness," this system designed an Attention Region Determination Module using the open-source dataset DR (eye) VE, which is based on attention tasks. This dataset consists of 74 video sequences, each 5 min long, containing

Fig. 4. SemanticKITTI dataset visualization scene 1

Fig. 5. SemanticKITTI dataset visualization scene 2

the driver's focus points and timestamps, along with related display maps and geographical locations. Based on this dataset, this module analyzes and obtains the driver's concentration levels in different scenarios, dividing the field of view into three zones (High Concentration, Medium Concentration, Low Concentration). Subsequently, obstacles in different fields of view are detected and alerted according to the warning intensity set on the dashboard. Customized prompt intensities are used to reduce instances of "unconscious blindness."

Processing Raw Data in the Dataset

The video sequences in the dataset are filtered and distinguished, and finally classified by time, weather conditions, and location. Subsequent work processes the video data for each category separately. For example, selecting a video sequence from a specific category: the video is 5 min long and contains 18,000 frames of data. Each frame contains the U and V coordinates of the driver's focus point in the image coordinate system. The selected video clips were recorded by a 720p camera. Invalid U and V coordinates are removed based on image size constraints. Representing one coordinate point as 5 pixel colors, MATLAB is used to overlay these data points onto a 720p image to generate a pixel map, i.e., the Attention Distribution Map (as shown in Fig. 6).

Determining Attention Regions in the Driving Field of View

The attention distribution map is converted into a heat map via MATLAB, and the heat map is fused with the image of the driving field of view. Finally, we obtain a rough graphic

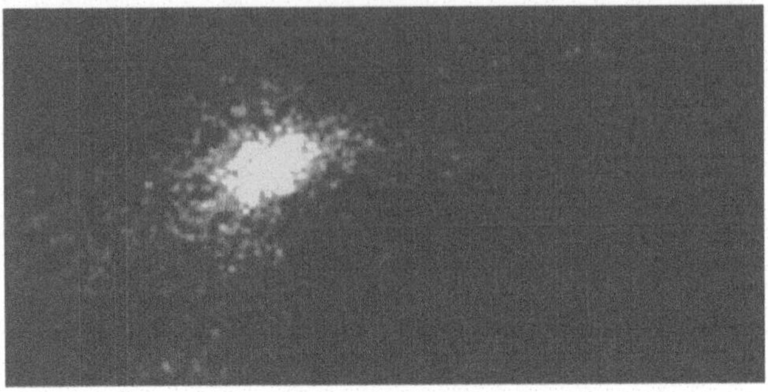

Fig. 6. Attention distribution map.

regarding attention division (as shown in the figures below). Based on this graphic, we can design a reasonable distribution of prompt intensities within the driving field of view in a targeted manner.

- Redder areas: Indicate high concentration areas.

Fig. 7. Attention distribution map in driving field of view - daytime cloudy scenario

Fig. 8. Attention distribution map in driving field of view - nighttime rainy scenario.

- Blue-green point cluster areas: Indicate medium concentration areas.
- Sparse edge positions: Indicate low concentration areas (Figs. 7 and 8).

4 Experimental Testing

This study recruited a diverse range of participants to perform simulated driving using first-person driving videos displayed on a screen. The objective was to select the most efficient method for prompt feedback. We tested four conditions—no prompt, visual prompt, auditory prompt, and audiovisual prompt—to determine whether they can enhance the driver's ability to identify key road targets and to observe any differences in the level of enhancement.

4.1 Experimental Design

This experiment selected 30 participants to perform simulated driving while facing a screen displaying first-person driving footage. We recorded the reaction time for successfully identifying traffic lights, pedestrians, and vehicles, as well as the action time for completing turning maneuvers, for each subject under four conditions: no prompt, auditory prompt, visual prompt, and audiovisual prompt. The recorded data was analyzed to evaluate whether visual and auditory prompts could enhance the driver's recognition capabilities in various scenarios and to determine if there were differences in effectiveness.

- Visual Prompts: The video data was processed to include specific markers to alert the driver.
- Auditory Prompts: Mechanical sounds were used to indicate different obstacles.
- Measurement: User reaction time was recorded using a stopwatch. This was measured as the difference between the start time when the object detection module identified the obstacle and the time the simulated driver responded.

4.2 Experimental Process and Results

The test scenes for the different scenarios are shown below (Figs. 9, 10,11, 12 and 13):

The test data records are shown in the following tables:

Scatter plots were drawn based on Tables 1 through 4 as follows (Figs. 14, 15 16 and 17):

Fig. 9. Traffic light recognition scene

Fig. 10. Turning navigation scene

Fig. 11. Pedestrian recognition scene

Fig. 12. Vehicle recognition scene

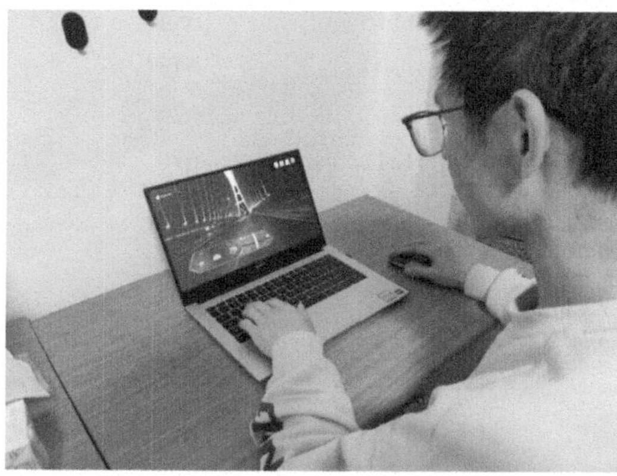

Fig. 13. Test screen interface

After analyzing the data from Tables 1, 2,3 and 4, the following mean statistics table was obtained:

Mean Reaction Time	No Prompt	Visual Prompt	Auditory Prompt	Audiovisual Prompt
Traffic Light (ms)	2094	1220	665	696
Turning (ms)	9065	7419	8173	7309
Pedestrian (ms)	1843	1311	637	647
Vehicle (ms)	1910	1185	679	702

4.3 Test Result Analysis

- Recognition Scenarios: In the cases of traffic light recognition, pedestrian recognition, and vehicle recognition, the presence of prompts significantly enhanced the driver's

Table 1. Traffic light recognition test data

	Traffic light recognition(ms)			
Sequence No.	No Prompt (ms)	Visual Prompt (ms)	Auditory Prompt (ms)	Audiovisual Prompt (ms)
1	1816	1276	682	712
2	1930	1245	642	685
3	1986	1169	672	719
4	2037	1146	675	675
5	1920	1138	647	737
6	2093	1204	683	626
7	2169	1345	658	724
8	2173	1123	667	704
9	2214	1116	684	695
10	2205	1304	648	707
11	2077	1267	626	683
12	2107	1212	670	688
13	2247	1176	644	682
14	2132	1220	689	693
15	2169	1273	632	659
16	2382	1194	675	733
17	2158	1215	676	713
18	2046	1254	675	687
19	1982	1260	690	675
20	2085	1179	656	685
21	2146	1254	677	682
22	1932	1265	636	707
23	2149	1193	682	665
24	2152	1210	639	722
25	2094	1212	674	726
26	2008	1256	676	682
27	2073	1169	658	700
28	2020	1272	687	724
29	2230	1184	658	681
30	2096	1255	678	714
Mean	2094	1220	665	696

Table 2. Turning test data

	Turning(ms)			
Sequence No.	No Prompt (ms)	Visual Prompt (ms)	Auditory Prompt (ms)	Audiovisual Prompt (ms)
1	9856	7235	8332	7147
2	9166	6958	7682	7629
3	9475	8007	8573	6929
4	7667	7660	9020	7315
5	8125	7962	8254	8117
6	9745	7645	8327	7160
7	9514	7602	7804	7104
8	8800	6956	7749	7957
9	9318	7062	8406	7644
10	9552	7205	8516	6871
11	8352	7534	7600	7889
12	9430	7510	8247	7096
13	9541	7065	7610	6512
14	8679	7900	8515	7328
15	9218	7567	8074	7208
16	8466	7176	8932	7278
17	8926	7115	7943	7244
18	9406	7871	7751	6964
19	9477	7601	7354	7295
20	8923	7272	8065	7468
21	8715	7447	8339	7691
22	9430	7408	8074	7280
23	8615	7039	7821	6878
24	8920	6904	7891	7243
25	8245	7313	7069	7320
26	9169	7321	9155	7256
27	9225	7732	7974	7548
28	8809	7357	8550	7273
29	9955	7217	8204	7790
30	9231	7934	9355	6849
Mean	9065	7419	8173	7309

Table 3. Pedestrian recognition test data

	Pedestrian recognition(ms)			
Sequence No.	No Prompt (ms)	Visual Prompt (ms)	Auditory Prompt (ms)	Audiovisual Prompt (ms)
1	1683	1155	633	648
2	1877	1443	646	681
3	1800	1396	618	635
4	1788	1197	642	659
5	1874	1043	640	657
6	1654	1327	635	618
7	1871	1376	635	650
8	1999	1418	646	639
9	2016	1281	645	655
10	1540	1177	642	668
11	1872	1312	631	636
12	1902	1189	634	668
13	1879	1409	628	653
14	1850	1334	625	667
15	1716	1492	645	633
16	1754	1332	646	623
17	1713	1328	647	645
18	1563	1140	637	632
19	1777	1426	647	657
20	1887	1442	630	636
21	2014	1315	634	649
22	2032	1426	645	656
23	2051	1321	637	632
24	2285	1313	617	626
25	1862	1224	635	627
26	1910	1453	636	638
27	1570	1269	639	640
28	1476	1262	644	669
29	2165	1206	637	637
30	1909	1318	638	673
Mean	1843	1311	637	647

Table 4. Vehicle recognition test data

	Vehicle recognition(ms)			
Sequence No.	No Prompt (ms)	Visual Prompt (ms)	Auditory Prompt (ms)	Audiovisual Prompt (ms)
1	1968	1297	701	658
2	1977	1214	676	763
3	1994	1204	667	688
4	2074	1278	702	731
5	2076	1144	645	746
6	1682	1054	664	720
7	1745	1217	697	668
8	2008	1177	671	753
9	2007	945	687	658
10	1865	1200	664	738
11	1905	1171	634	653
12	1725	1224	656	672
13	1672	1306	666	660
14	2132	1074	687	739
15	2237	1303	690	700
16	1811	1231	667	745
17	1761	1066	665	708
18	1899	1227	689	748
19	1741	1151	692	681
20	2158	1229	703	719
21	1982	1157	703	643
22	1736	1292	698	705
23	1988	1185	689	695
24	1911	1121	685	725
25	2096	1197	664	666
26	1811	1049	709	743
27	1734	1299	663	656
28	1654	1259	653	713
29	2022	1104	698	632
30	1930	1164	697	727
Mean	1910	1185	679	702

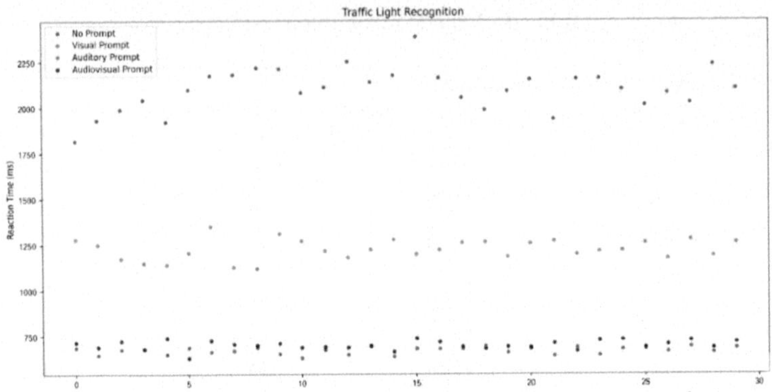

Fig. 14. Traffic light recognition test scatter plot

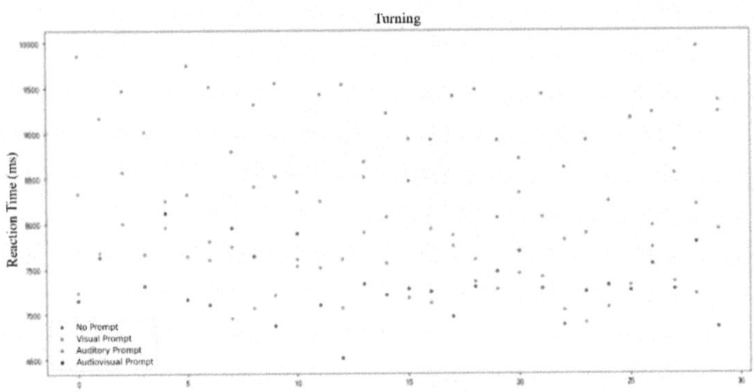

Fig. 15. Turning test scatter plot

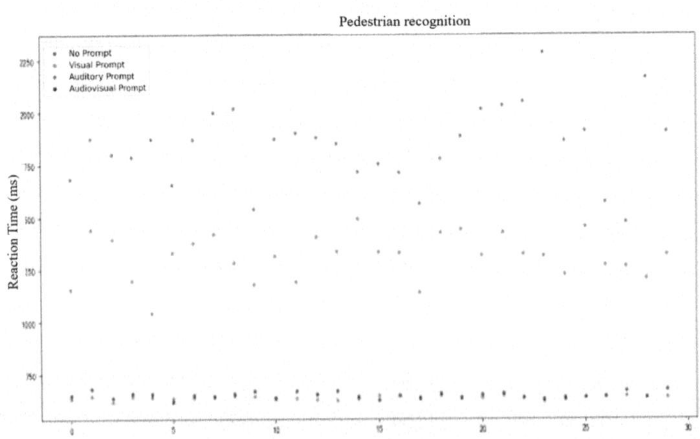

Fig. 16. Pedestrian recognition test scatter plot

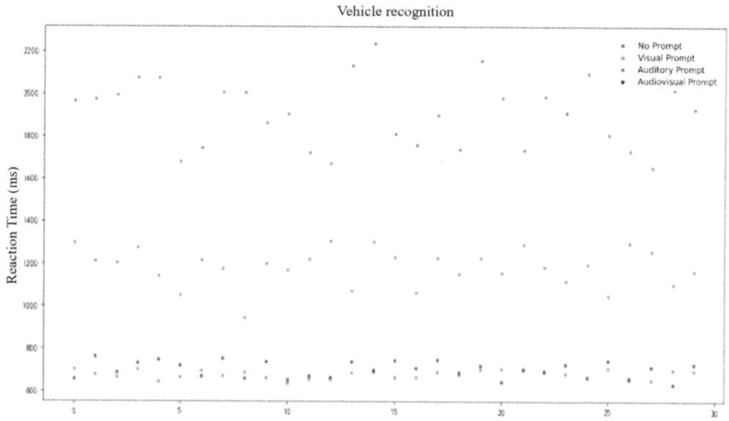

Fig. 17. Vehicle recognition test scatter plot

recognition ability. Furthermore, auditory and audiovisual prompts were significantly more effective than visual prompts alone.

- Turning Scenario: In the turning scenario, prompts also clearly enhanced the driver's recognition ability. However, visual and audiovisual prompts were significantly more effective than auditory prompts alone.

The reason for this difference is that the first three scenarios (lights, pedestrians, vehicles) require instantaneous warnings to trigger braking or deceleration, where audio provides a faster stimulus. Conversely, turning requires continuous operational assistance for lane changing, where visual cues are more helpful.

5 Conclusion and Outlook

This system primarily combines AR and object detection technologies to achieve detection and early warning of traffic conditions within the driver's field of view. Experiments have proven that it can effectively strengthen the driver's information acquisition capabilities during driving and improve their reaction speed to emergencies. Additionally, through the differentiation of attention concentration areas, the system can adjust prompt intensity based on different drivers and driving scenarios, mitigating "blindness" caused by shifts in attention.

However, limited by experimental equipment and real-world experimental data, there are certain deficiencies in accuracy, and high-precision recognition and feedback have not yet been achieved. Furthermore, the division of attention regions and the specific AR-HUD prompt schemes are not yet sufficiently scientific or accurate and still require further improvement.

Acknowledgments. This study was funded by National Natural Science Foundation of China Project (No.62402486).

Disclosure of Interests. The authors have no competing interests to declare that are relevant to the content of this article.

References

1. Winner, H., Hakuli, S., Lotz, F., et al.: Handbook of Driver Assistance Systems. Springer International Publishing, Amsterdam (2014)
2. Betancur, J.A., Villa-Espinal, J., Osorio-Gómez, G., et al.: Research topics and implementation trends on automotive head-up display systems. Int. J. Interact. Des. Manuf. (IJIDeM) **12**(1), 199–214 (2018)
3. Rusch, M.L., Schall Jr., M.C., Lee, J.D., et al.: Augmented reality cues to assist older drivers with gap estimation for left-turns. Accid. Anal. Prev. **71**, 210–221 (2014)
4. Wang, Y., Wu, Y., Chen, C., et al.: Inattentional blindness in augmented reality head-up display-assisted driving. Int. J. Hum.–Comput. Interact. **38**(9), 837–850 (2022)
5. Malawski, F.: Driver assistance system using augmented reality headset. In: 2018 41st International Conference on Telecommunications and Signal Processing (TSP), pp. 1–4 (2018)
6. Murugan, S., Sampathkumar, A., Kanaga Suba Raja, S., et al.: Autonomous vehicle assisted by heads up display (HUD) with augmented reality based on machine learning techniques. In: Virtual and Augmented Reality for Automobile Industry: Innovation Vision and Applications, pp. 45–64. Springer (2022)
7. Liang, Y., Zheng, P., Xia, L.: A visual reasoning-based approach for driving experience improvement in the AR-assisted head-up displays. Adv. Eng. Inform. **55**, 101888 (2023)
8. Dikmen, M.: Investigating Driver Experience and Augmented Reality Head-up Displays in Autonomous Vehicles. University of Waterloo (2017)
9. Kadav, P., Sharma, S., Fanas Rojas, J., et al.: Automated lane centering: an off-the-shelf computer vision product vs. infrastructure-based chip-enabled raised pavement markers. Sensors **24**(7), 2327 (2024)
10. Langlois, S., Soualmi, B.: Augmented reality versus classical HUD to take over from automated driving: an aid to smooth reactions and to anticipate maneuvers. In: 2016 IEEE 19th International Conference on Intelligent Transportation Systems (ITSC), pp. 1571–1578. IEEE (2016)

Author Index

C
Cao, Jiacheng 54
Cao, Rongqi 210
Chen, Hui 313
Chen, Kai 283
Chen, Yulu 54
Cheng, Xi 229
Chunhao, Cen 128

D
Deng, Wenjing 113
Dong, Shiyu 13
Dong, Tianshu 54
Duan, Yishan 113

F
Fawzy, Ziyad 81
Feng, Guihuan 229

G
Gang, Liu 128
Gao, Yan 169
Guo, Yijie 3, 113
Guo, Zichun 302

H
Han, Hui-Zhu 98
Hansen, Preben 54
He, Jian 210
Hou, Shuo 13
Hui, Wei 302

J
Jiang, Huancheng 302
Jiang, Lijun 13
Jiang, Pan 352
Jiang, Shengsheng 210
Jiang, Yanli 188
Jiao, Yang 139
Jin, Xuzhu 25

L
Lee, Chih-Hung 68
Li, Dongliang 25
Li, Jiaji 54
Li, Juan 40
Li, Kairu 270
Li, Xueqing 113
Li, Xuri 40
Li, Yazhou 270
Li, Yu-Chen 98
Li, Yue 188, 283
Li, Zhelin 13
Li, Zhiyu 113
Liang, Jiachen 188
Liu, Beituo 3
Liu, Fang 156
Liu, Guanhong 3, 113
Liu, Runjun 54
Liu, Ziqi 3
Lu, Qi 68
Lu, Yao 3, 113

M
Ma, Cuixia 156
Ma, Xiao-Na 98
Mi, Haipeng 3, 113

N
Ni, Jialu 113

P
Pan, Yiheng 210

Q
Qiao, Yu 169
Qin, Ying 313

R
Ruohan, Shen 340

S. Guo et al. (Eds.): HHME 2025, CCIS 2878, pp. 371–372, 2027.
https://doi.org/10.1007/978-981-92-3991-7

S
Shao, Hongming 40
Sheng, Lily 81
Su, Zhao 325
Sun, Kaifan 352
Sun, Liang 257
Sun, Xiaoxu 352
Sun, Yuchi 68

T
Tian, Feng 313
Tian, Yang 325

W
Wang, Guanyun 54
Wang, Haoming 313
Wang, Qin 13
Wang, Wenyu 13
Wang, Xiaoyi 40
Wang, Xin-Yu 98
Wang, Xuezhu 3, 113
Wang, Yicheng 54
Wang, Yuntao 81
Wei, Suhang 68
Wen, Hao 352
Wu, Huang-Yi-Ming 98
Wu, Yiping 283

X
Xie, Mingzhen 3
Xie, Xurong 313
Xin, Yizhong 25, 257
Xinyue, Lin 128
Xueyang, Sun 340

Y
Yan, Hanlin 156
Yang, Zhaojia 54
Yao, Xiwen 3, 113
Yao, Yuan 113
Yao, Zhihao 3
Yaru, Ji 340
Ye, Dong 98
Ye, Ming 325
Yi, Grace 81
Yu, Kejin 113
Yu, Tianyu 3, 113
Yuan, Yao 340
Yuetong, Ren 340

Z
Zhang, Dejian 352
Zhang, Gaoyuan 313
Zhang, Hao 352
Zhang, Jiarong 54
Zhang, Lijun 25, 257
Zhang, Peifeng 352
Zhang, Rui 68, 139
Zhang, Yingpin 188
Zhang, Yiyi 169
Zhang, Zhenrong 325
Zhang, Ziyao 139
Zhao, Yijun 54
Zhen, Yifan 210
Zhou, Chao 313
Zhou, Hanyu 81
Ziyi, Chen 340
Zou, Shuyuan 169

The manufacturer's authorised representative in the EU is Springer Nature Customer Service Centre GmbH, Europaplatz 3, 69115 Heidelberg, Germany. If you have any concerns regarding our products, please contact ProductSafety@springernature.com

Printed and bound by CPI Group (UK) Ltd, Croydon, CR0 4YY
21/09/2026
02219987-0009